1

Grammar in Context

Teacher's Annotated Edition

4TH EDITION

SANDRA N. ELBAUM

HILARY GRANT

THOMSON

™

HEINLE

Australia • Canada • Mexico • Singapore • Spain • United Kingdom • United States

P9-DYA-034

Grammar in Context 1, Fourth Edition
Teacher's Annotated Edition
ELBAUM/GRANT

Publisher, Adult & Academic: *James W. Brown*
Senior Acquisitions Editor, Adult & Academic:
 Sherrise Roehr
Director of Product Development: *Anita Raducanu*
Development Editor: *Yeny Kim*
Associate Development Editor: *Tom Jeffries*
Production Manager: *Sally Giangrande*
Director of Marketing: *Amy Mabley*
Senior Field Marketing Manager:
 Donna Lee Kennedy

Marketing Manager: *Laura Needham*
Senior Print Buyer: *Mary Beth Hennebury*
Compositor: *Nesbitt Graphics, Inc.*
Project Manager: *Lois Lombardo*
Photo Researcher: *Connie Gardner*
Illustrators: *Ralph Canaday, James Edwards,*
 Larry Frederick, and Brock Nichol
Interior Designer: *Jerilyn Bockorick*
Cover Designer: *Joseph Sherman*
Printer: *West Group*

Cover Image: Brooklyn Bridge, New York by Julian
Barrow/Private Collection/Bridgeman Art Library

Copyright © 2006 by Sandra N. Elbaum

All rights reserved. No part of this work covered by
the copyright hereon may be reproduced or used in
any form or by any means—graphic, electronic,
or mechanical, including photocopying, recording,
taping, Web distribution or information storage and
retrieval systems—without the written permission
of the publisher.

For permission to use material from this text or product,
submit a request online at http://www.thomsonrights.com

Any additional questions about permissions can be
submitted by email to thomsonrights@thomson.com

ISBN: 1-4130-0741-4

Printed in the United States of America.
1 2 3 4 5 6 7 8 9 10   09 08 07 06 05

For more information contact Thomson Heinle,
25 Thomson Place, Boston, Massachusetts 02210
USA, or you can visit our Internet site at
elt.thomson.com

Photo credits appear on the inside back cover, which
constitutes a continuation of this copyright page.

Contents

Lesson 14   401

Appendices

In memory of

Herman and Ethel Elbaum

Acknowledgments

Many thanks to Dennis Hogan, Jim Brown, Sherrise Roehr, Yeny Kim, and Sally Giangrande from Thomson Heinle for their ongoing support of the *Grammar in Context* series. I would especially like to thank my editor, Charlotte Sturdy, for her keen eye to detail and invaluable suggestions.

And many thanks to my students at Truman College, who have increased my understanding of my own language and taught me to see life from another point of view. By sharing their observations, questions, and life stories, they have enriched my life enormously—*Sandra N. Elbaum*

Heinle would like to thank the following people for their contributions:

Marki Alexander
Oklahoma State
  University
Stillwater, OK

Joan M. Amore
Triton College
River Grove, IL

**Edina Pingleton
Bagley**
Nassau Community
  College
Garden City, NY

Judith A. G. Benka
Normandale Community
  College
Bloomington, MN

**Judith Book-
Ehrlichman**
Bergen Community
  College
Paramus, NJ

Lyn Buchheit
Community College of
  Philadelphia
Philadelphia, PA

Charlotte M. Calobrisi
Northern Virginia
  Community College
Annandale, VA

Sarah A. Carpenter
Normandale Community
  College
Bloomington, MN

Jeanette Clement
Duquesne University
Pittsburgh, PA

Allis Cole
Shoreline Community
  College
Shoreline, WA

**Jacqueline M.
Cunningham**
Triton College
River Grove, IL

Lisa DePaoli
Sierra College
Rocklin, CA

Maha Edlbi
Sierra College
Rocklin, CA

Rhonda J. Farley
Cosumnes River College
Sacramento, CA

Jennifer Farnell
University of Connecticut
American Language
  Program
Stamford, CT

**Abigail-Marie
Fiattarone**
Mesa Community College
Mesa, AZ

Marcia Gethin-Jones
University of Connecticut
American Language
  Program
Storrs, CT

Linda Harlow
Santa Rosa Junior
  College
Santa Rosa, CA

Suha R. Hattab
Triton College
River Grove, IL

Bill Keniston
Normandale Community
  College
Bloomington, MN

Walton King
Arkansas State
  University
Jonesboro, AR

Kathleen Krokar
Truman College
Chicago, IL

John Larkin
NVCC-Community and
  Workforce
  Development
Annandale, VA

Michael Larsen
American River College
Sacramento, CA

Bea C. Lawn
Gavilan College
Gilroy, CA

Rob Lee
Pasadena City College
Pasadena, CA

**Oranit
Limmaneeprasert**
American River College
Sacramento, CA

Gennell Lockwood
Shoreline Community
  College
Shoreline, WA

Linda Louie
Highline Community
  College
Des Moines, WA

Melanie A. Majeski
Naugatuck Valley
  Community College
Waterbury, CT

Maria Marin
De Anza College
Cupertino, CA

Karen Miceli
Cosumnes River College
Sacramento, CA

Jeanie Pavichevich
Triton College
River Grove, IL

Herbert Pierson
St. John's University
New York City, NY

Dina Poggi
De Anza College
Cupertino, CA

Mark Rau
American River College
Sacramento, CA

John W. Roberts
Shoreline Community
  College
Shoreline, WA

Azize R. Ruttler
Bergen Community
  College
Paramus, NJ

Ann Salzmann
University of Illinois,
Urbana, IL

Eva Teagarden
Yuba College
Marysville, CA

Susan Wilson
San Jose City College
San Jose, CA

Martha Yeager-Tobar
Cerritos College
Norwalk, CA

A word from the author

It seems that I was born to be an ESL teacher. My parents immigrated to the U.S. from Poland as adults and were confused not only by the English language but by American culture as well. Born in the U.S., I often had the task as a child to explain the intricacies of the language and allay my parents' fears about the culture. It is no wonder to me that I became an ESL teacher, and later, an ESL writer who focuses on explanations of American culture in order to illustrate grammar. My life growing up in an immigrant neighborhood was very similar to the lives of my students, so I have a feel for what confuses them and what they need to know about American life.

ESL teachers often find themselves explaining confusing customs and providing practical information about life in the U.S. Often, teachers are a student's only source of information about American life. With *Grammar in Context, Fourth Edition,* I enjoy sharing my experiences with you.

Grammar in Context, Fourth Edition connects grammar with American cultural context, providing learners of English with a useful and meaningful skill and knowledge base. Students learn the grammar necessary to communicate verbally and in writing, and learn how American culture plays a role in language, beliefs, and everyday situations.

Enjoy the new edition of *Grammar in Context!*

Sandra N. Elbaum

Grammar in Context

Students learn more, remember more, and use language more effectively when they learn grammar in context.

Learning a language through meaningful themes and practicing it in a contextualized setting promote both linguistic and cognitive development. In *Grammar in Context,* grammar is presented in interesting and culturally informative readings, and the language and context are subsequently practiced throughout the chapter.

New to this edition

- **New and updated readings** on current American topics such as Instant Messaging and eBay.
- **Updated grammar charts** that now include essential language notes.
- **Updated exercises and activities** that provide contextualized practice using a variety of exercise types, as well as additional practice for more difficult structures.
- **New lower-level** *Grammar in Context Basic* for beginning level students.
- **New wrap-around Teacher's Annotated Edition** with page-by-page, point-of-use teaching suggestions.
- **Expanded Assessment CD-ROM** with *ExamView® Pro* Test Generator now contains more questions types and assessment options to easily allow teachers to create tests and quizzes.

Distinctive Features of *Grammar in Context*

Students are prepared for academic assignments and everyday language tasks.

Discussions, readings, compositions, and exercises involving higher-level critical thinking skills develop overall language and communication skills.

Students expand their knowledge of American topics and culture.

The readings in *Grammar in Context* help students gain insight into and enrich their knowledge of American culture and history. Students gain ample exposure to the practicalities of American life, such as writing a résumé, dealing with telemarketers, and junk mail, and getting student internships. Their new knowledge helps them adapt to everyday life in the U.S.

Students learn to use their new skills to communicate.

The exercises and Expansion Activities in *Grammar in Context* help students learn English while practicing their writing and speaking skills. Students work together in pairs and groups to find more information about topics, to make presentations, to play games, and to role-play. Their confidence in using English increases, as does their ability to communicate effectively.

Grammar in Context Student Book Supplements

Audio Program
- Audio CDs and Audio Tapes allow students to listen to every reading in the book as well as selected dialogs.

More Grammar Practice Workbooks
- Workbooks can be used with *Grammar in Context* or any skills text to learn and review the essential grammar.
- Great for in-class practice or homework.
- Includes practice on all grammar points in *Grammar in Context*.

Teacher's Annotated Edition
- New component offers page-by-page answers and teaching suggestions.

Assessment CD-ROM with *ExamView®Pro* Test Generator
- Test Generator allows teachers to create tests and quizzes quickly and easily.

Interactive CD-ROM
- CD-ROM allows for supplemental interactive practice on grammar points from *Grammar in Context*.

Split Editions
- Split Editions provide options for short courses.

Instructional Video/DVD
- Video/DVD offers teaching suggestions and advice on how to use *Grammar in Context*.

Web Site
- Web site gives access to additional activities and promotes the use of the Internet.

Welcome to *Grammar in Context, Fourth Edition*

Students learn more, remember more, and use language more effectively when they learn grammar in context.

Grammar in Context, Fourth Edition connects grammar with rich, American cultural context, providing learners of English with a useful and meaningful skill and knowledge base.

An **Audio Program** allows students to hear the readings and dialogs, and provides an opportunity to practice their listening skills.

Readings on American topics such as Instant Messaging, eBay, and The AIDS Ride present and illustrate the grammatical structure in an informative and meaningful context.

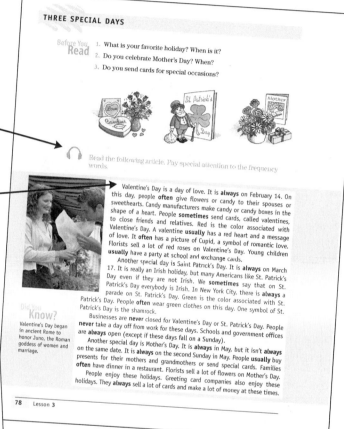

THREE SPECIAL DAYS

Before You Read
1. What is your favorite holiday? When is it?
2. Do you celebrate Mother's Day? When?
3. Do you send cards for special occasions?

Read the following article. Pay special attention to the frequency words.

Valentine's Day is a day of love. It is **always** on February 14. On this day, people **often** give flowers or candy to their sweethearts. Candy manufacturers make candy or candy boxes in the shape of a heart. People **sometimes** send cards, called valentines, to close friends and relatives. Red is the color associated with Valentine's Day. A valentine **usually** has a red heart and a message of love. It **often** has a picture of Cupid, a symbol of romantic love. Florists sell a lot of red roses on Valentine's Day. Young children **usually** have a party at school and exchange cards.

Another special day is Saint Patrick's Day. It is **always** on March 17. It is really an Irish holiday, but many Americans like St. Patrick's Day even if they are not Irish. We **sometimes** say that on St. Patrick's Day everybody is Irish. In New York City, there is **always** a parade on St. Patrick's Day. Green is the color associated with St. Patrick's Day. People **often** wear green clothes on this day. One symbol of St. Patrick's Day is the shamrock.

Did You Know?
Valentine's Day began in ancient Rome to honor Juno, the Roman goddess of women and marriage.

Businesses are **never** closed for Valentine's Day or St. Patrick's Day. People **never** take a day off from work for these days. Schools and government offices are **always** open (except if these days fall on a Sunday).

Another special day is Mother's Day. It is **always** in May, but it isn't **always** on the same date. It is **always** on the second Sunday in May. People **usually** buy presents for their mothers and grandmothers or send special cards. Families **often** have dinner in a restaurant. Florists sell a lot of flowers on Mother's Day. People enjoy these holidays. Greeting card companies also enjoy these holidays. They **always** sell a lot of cards and make a lot of money at these times.

78   Lesson 3

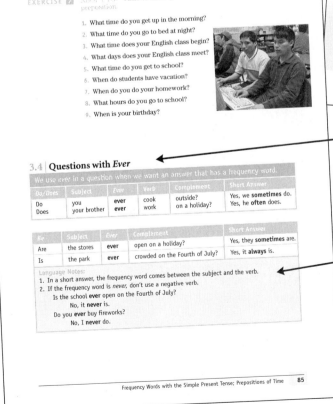

EXERCISE 7   ABOUT YOU Answer these questions. Use the correct preposition.

1. What time do you get up in the morning?
2. What time do you go to bed at night?
3. What time does your English class begin?
4. What days does your English class meet?
5. What time do you get to school?
6. When do students have vacation?
7. When do you do your homework?
8. What hours do you go to school?
9. When is your birthday?

3.4 | Questions with *Ever*

We use *ever* in a question when we want an answer that has a frequency word.

Do/Does	Subject	Ever	Verb	Complement	Short Answer
Do	you	ever	cook	outside?	Yes, we **sometimes** do.
Does	your brother	ever	work	on a holiday?	Yes, he **often** does.

Be	Subject	Ever	Complement	Short Answer
Are	the stores	ever	open on a holiday?	Yes, they **sometimes** are.
Is	the park	ever	crowded on the Fourth of July?	Yes, it **always** is.

Language Notes:
1. In a short answer, the frequency word comes between the subject and the verb.
2. If the frequency word is *never*, don't use a negative verb.
   Is the school **ever** open on the Fourth of July?
     No, it **never** is.
   Do you **ever** buy fireworks?
     No, I **never** do.

Frequency Words with the Simple Present Tense; Prepositions of Time   85

Grammar charts offer clear explanations and provide contextualized examples of the structure.

Language Notes refine students' understanding of the target structure.

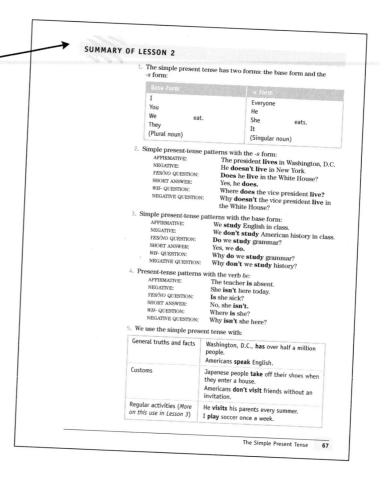

EXERCISE 13 ABOUT YOU Write a few sentences about a member of your family or another person you know. Use frequency words.

EXAMPLE My sister never helps with the housework.
She sometimes leaves dirty dishes in the sink.
She always gets good grades.

_____
_____
_____

EXERCISE 14 Use the words in parentheses ( ) to complete this conversation. Put the words in the correct order. Use the correct form of the verb.

A: Let's go to a movie tonight.

B: I can't. My mother ___always makes___ dinner for me on Fridays.
(example: make/always)

If I don't visit her, she _____.
(1 complain/usually)

And if I don't call her, she worries.

A: _____ her?
(2 how/often/you/call)

B: _____.
(3 I/every day/call her)

A: Why do you call her so often?

B: She's old now, and she _____ lonely.
(4 often/be)

A: Well, invite your mother to go to the movies.

B: Thanks, but she has a favorite TV show on Friday nights.
She _____ it.
(5 watch/always)

A: _____ go out?
(6 ever/she)

B: She _____. She prefers to stay home.
(7 rarely/do)
She likes to cook, knit, and watch TV.

A: Is she a good cook?

B: Not really. She _____ the
(8 usually/cook)
same thing every week: chicken on Friday, fish on Saturday, meatloaf
on Sunday. . . . Her routine _____.
(9 change/never)
Only Mother's Day is different.

90   Lesson 3

A variety of contextualized activities keeps the classroom lively and targets different learning styles.

A **Summary** provides the lesson's essential grammar in an easy-to-reference format.

SUMMARY OF LESSON 2

1. The simple present tense has two forms: the base form and the -s form:

Base Form		-s Form	
I		Everyone	
You		He	
We	eat.	She	eats.
They		It	
(Plural noun)		(Singular noun)	

2. Simple present-tense patterns with the -s form:
   AFFIRMATIVE: The president **lives** in Washington, D.C.
   NEGATIVE: He **doesn't live** in New York.
   YES/NO QUESTION: **Does** he **live** in the White House?
   SHORT ANSWER: Yes, he **does.**
   WH- QUESTION: Where **does** the vice president **live?**
   NEGATIVE QUESTION: Why **doesn't** the vice president **live** in the White House?

3. Simple present-tense patterns with the base form:
   AFFIRMATIVE: We **study** English in class.
   NEGATIVE: We **don't study** American history in class.
   YES/NO QUESTION: **Do** we **study** grammar?
   SHORT ANSWER: Yes, we **do.**
   WH- QUESTION: Why **do** we **study** grammar?
   NEGATIVE QUESTION: Why **don't** we **study** history?

4. Present-tense patterns with the verb be:
   AFFIRMATIVE: The teacher **is** absent.
   NEGATIVE: She **isn't** here today.
   YES/NO QUESTION: **Is** she sick?
   SHORT ANSWER: No, she **isn't.**
   WH- QUESTION: Where **is** she?
   NEGATIVE QUESTION: Why **isn't** she here?

5. We use the simple present tense with:

General truths and facts	Washington, D.C., **has** over half a million people.
	Americans **speak** English.
Customs	Japanese people **take** off their shoes when they enter a house.
	Americans **don't visit** friends without an invitation.
Regular activities (More on this use in Lesson 3)	He **visits** his parents every summer. I **play** soccer once a week.

The Simple Present Tense   67

Editing Advice gives students pre-writing practice by alerting them to common errors.

Test/Review at the end of each lesson provides a chance to review and/or assess the grammar from the lesson.

Expansion Activities provide opportunities for students to interact with one another and further develop their speaking and writing skills.

Internet Activities encourage students to use technology to explore a wealth of online resources.

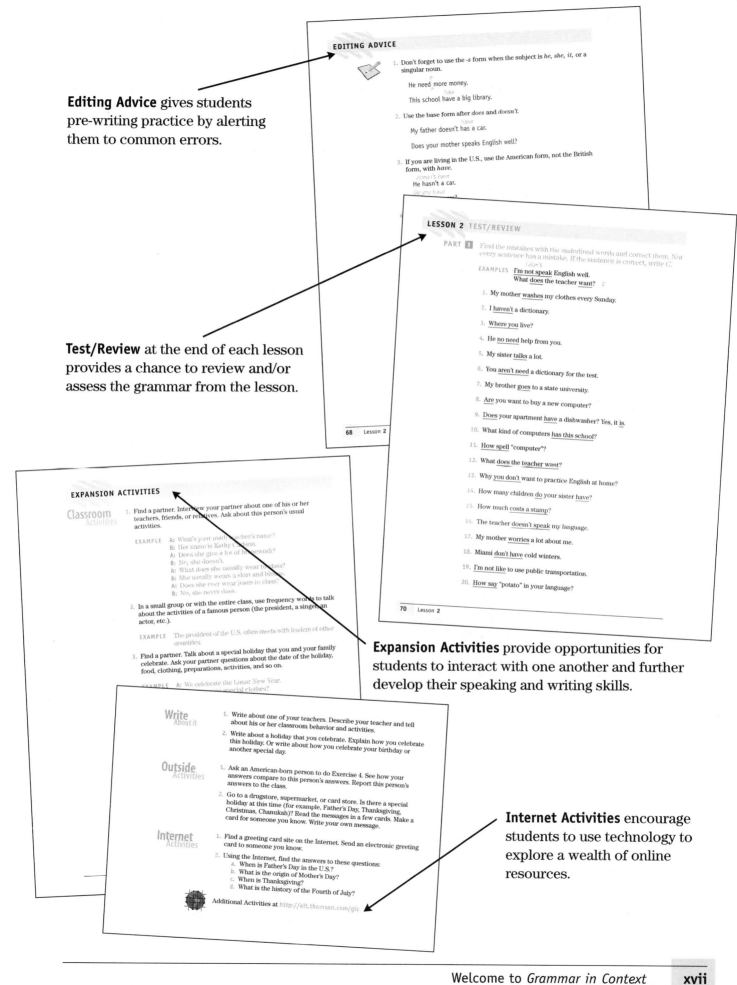

EDITING ADVICE

1. Don't forget to use the -s form when the subject is *he, she, it,* or a singular noun.

   He ~~need~~ more money.

   This school ~~have~~ a big library.

2. Use the base form after *does* and *doesn't*.

   My father doesn't ~~has~~ a car.

   Does your mother ~~speaks~~ English well?

3. If you are living in the U.S., use the American form, not the British form, with *have*.

   He ~~hasn't~~ a car.

   ~~Do you have~~

LESSON 2 TEST/REVIEW

PART 1 Find the mistakes with the underlined words and correct them. Not every sentence has a mistake. If the sentence is correct, write C.

EXAMPLES   ~~I'm not speak~~ English well.
           What <u>does</u> the teacher <u>want</u>?   C

1. My mother <u>washes</u> my clothes every Sunday.
2. I <u>haven't</u> a dictionary.
3. Where <u>you live</u>?
4. He <u>no need</u> help from you.
5. My sister <u>talks</u> a lot.
6. You <u>aren't need</u> a dictionary for the test.
7. My brother <u>goes</u> to a state university.
8. <u>Are</u> you want to buy a new computer?
9. <u>Does</u> your apartment <u>have</u> a dishwasher? Yes, it <u>is</u>.
10. What kind of computers <u>has this school</u>?
11. <u>How spell</u> "computer"?
12. What <u>does</u> the <u>teacher want</u>?
13. Why <u>you don't</u> want to practice English at home?
14. How many children <u>do</u> your sister <u>have</u>?
15. How much <u>costs a stamp</u>?
16. The teacher <u>doesn't speak</u> my language.
17. My mother <u>worries</u> a lot about me.
18. Miami <u>don't have</u> cold winters.
19. I'm <u>not like</u> to use public transportation.
20. <u>How say</u> "potato" in your language?

70   Lesson 2

68   Lesson 2

EXPANSION ACTIVITIES

Classroom Activities

1. Find a partner. Interview your partner about one of his or her teachers, friends, or relatives. Ask about this person's usual activities.

   EXAMPLE   A: What's your math teacher's name?
             B: Her name is Kathy Carlson.
             A: Does she give a lot of homework?
             B: No, she doesn't.
             A: What does she usually wear to class?
             B: She usually wears a skirt and blouse.
             A: Does she ever wear jeans to class?
             B: No, she never does.

2. In a small group or with the entire class, use frequency words to talk about the activities of a famous person (the president, a singer, an actor, etc.).

   EXAMPLE   The president of the U.S. often meets with leaders of other countries.

3. Find a partner. Talk about a special holiday that you and your family celebrate. Ask your partner questions about the date of the holiday, food, clothing, preparations, activities, and so on.

   EXAMPLE   A: We celebrate the Lunar New Year.
             special clothes?

Write About it

1. Write about one of your teachers. Describe your teacher and tell about his or her classroom behavior and activities.

2. Write about a holiday that you celebrate. Explain how you celebrate this holiday. Or write about how you celebrate your birthday or another special day.

Outside Activities

1. Ask an American-born person to do Exercise 4. See how your answers compare to this person's answers. Report this person's answers to the class.

2. Go to a drugstore, supermarket, or card store. Is there a special holiday at this time (for example, Father's Day, Thanksgiving, Christmas, Chanukah)? Read the messages in a few cards. Make a card for someone you know. Write your own message.

Internet Activities

1. Find a greeting card site on the Internet. Send an electronic greeting card to someone you know.

2. Using the Internet, find the answers to these questions:
   a. When is Father's Day in the U.S.?
   b. What is the origin of Mother's Day?
   c. When is Thanksgiving?
   d. What is the history of the Fourth of July?

   Additional Activities at http://elt.thomson.com/gic

Frequently Asked Questions About Teaching with *Grammar in Context*

1. **"What role do the readings play in teaching grammar? How much time do I spend on the readings? Should students read them for homework? Should they be read with the audio? What is most effective for grammar students?"**

The readings are important in introducing the grammar in context. The readings should not be skipped. They can be done as either readings or listening activities. To save class time, the reading/listening can be done at home. The reading level is low enough that classroom instruction on "how to" read should not be necessary. The readings are not meant to challenge and improve one's reading skills; they are meant to illustrate the grammar in a stimulating context. In class, you can ask if there are any questions about the readings or the vocabulary within. There can be a short discussion on the "Before You Read" questions, if time allows. If there is sufficient class time, it is a good idea to have students listen to the audio and answer some comprehension questions as well. But this is not necessary in a grammar class. If there is a speech component in your program, the speech teacher can handle the listening activity.

2. **"There is so much material. Do I have to do all of the exercises? If not, which ones do I cut, and which ones do I focus on?"**

There is a lot of material, but you, as a teacher, are not required or expected to cover everything in a lesson. It would simply be impossible to do so in most ESL programs. If your program focuses on interactive oral communication, do the ABOUT YOU activities. If your students attend another class for speech and conversation, these exercises can be skipped. These exercises are fun to do, and, if you find your students' attention waning, you can insert one of these activities. The other exercises can be split into classroom exercises and homework exercises. The simpler exercises can be done in class, leaving the more challenging combination exercises for home. Or, you can do half of an exercise in class, leaving the other half to be done at home.

One way to find out how much practice your students need is to give them the Test/Review at the beginning of the lesson. If you find that most of your students can do this with relatively few errors, then you can skip the lesson altogether or focus only on the sticking points. It may be enough to only do the editing exercise, as this will reveal typical mistakes students make; they may just need to be reminded of these mistakes rather than being taught the entire lesson. For example, most students in level two and three "know" that they have to use the -s ending for third person singular, but many still leave it out. There's no point in *teaching* the base form and the -s form when a simple reminder may be enough.

In some cases, a section of a lesson can be omitted altogether or assigned for self-study extra credit to save class time. For example, in the lesson on adjective clauses in Book 3, a teacher can skip the part about the nonrestrictive clauses altogether. Or it may be enough to teach contrary-to-fact clauses in the present without getting into the past or mixed tenses. Let your curriculum guide you on what is absolutely necessary. Some lessons can probably be skipped altogether if your program teaches the grammar point in a higher or lower level.

3. **"If my students need more writing practice, what should I do?"**

In addition to the "Write About it" activities any of the "Talk About it" questions can be used as a writing activity if more writing practice is needed in paragraph or essay writing. If students need help at a sentence level of writing, the ABOUT YOU exercises can be assigned for writing. The Internet Activities, which suggest that the students look up some information on a Web site, can be used for summary writing. (Write a summary of the information you found on the Web site.) There are also additional writing activities on the Web site (http://elt.thomson.com/gic).

4. **"I have students from the UAE (or wherever), and they always have trouble with this grammar point. How can I help them specifically?"**

If you know a lot about the student's native language and the grammar mistakes the student is likely to make because of L1 interference, you can focus in on the editing activities that correct for that particular mistake. For example, if you have eastern Europeans (Russians, Poles, etc.) in your class, you will want to do a lot of work with articles. They also have confusion with *that* and *what* in noun clauses: *I know what you like pizza.* If you have students who speak Ethiopian languages, they are likely to make mistakes in past tenses by using the verb *be: He was go* instead of *He went.* Near-native speakers who learned English by ear rather than through grammar classes are likely to leave off endings and leave out words: *I am concern about my health. I been here for two hours.* The focus should be less on grammatical terms and categories for them and more on error correction.

It is not necessary to be a native speaker of your students' languages to know what kind of interference is likely to occur; if you have a large number of students from one language background, over time you will learn the consistent mistakes that are made. When I do the editing activity, I always call on the student who is most likely to make that particular mistake. In some cases, almost all students are likely to make a mistake; subject/verb reversal in dependent clauses is a common mistake for almost all students: *When arrived the teacher, the class began.*

5. **"Any tips for doing the Expansion Activities?"**

The Expansion Activities at the end of lessons are fun, but time is limited. Ideally, there is a speech component in your program that can pick up on the oral activities here. If not, try to choose the activity that seems the most enjoyable. Students are likely to remember the lesson better if there is a fun element.

LESSON

1

GRAMMAR

The Present Tense of the Verb *Be*
Prepositions of Place
This, That, These, Those

CONTEXT: College Life

Community College Life in the U.S.
Letter from College
Instant Message from a Student in the U.S.
In the School Cafeteria

1

Lesson | 1

Lesson Overview

GRAMMAR

Ask: *What tense will we study in this lesson?* (present tense of the verb *be*) *What else will we study?* (prepositions of place and *this, that, these, those*) *Do you know any prepositions of place?* (*on, between, behind*, etc.) Have students give examples. Write the examples on the board.

CONTEXT

1. Activate students' prior knowledge. Ask: *What will we learn about in this lesson?* (college life) If students are college students ask: *What is college life like in the United States?* If students are not in college ask: *What do you think college life is like in the U.S.?*
2. Have students share their knowledge and personal experiences.

Photo

1. Direct students' attention to the photo. Ask: *Who are the people?* (two friends study partners) *What are they doing?* (studying, doing homework, working on a project) *What do they have with them?* (a notebook and a computer)
2. Ask: *Do you like to study with someone or do you like to study alone?*

To save class time, have students do the Test/Review at the end of the lesson, or administer a lesson test generated from the Assessment CD-ROM with *ExamView® Pro*. Skip sections of the lesson that students have already mastered. You may also assign some sections for self-study for extra credit.

Expansion

Theme The topic for this lesson can be enhanced with the following ideas:

1. College catalogues and brochures
2. Posters from colleges
3. Your college yearbook or any college yearbook

Theme Talk about your own college experience. Tell students what you studied, where you studied, what you liked about your college, and anything else that might interest them. Show students your yearbook. Encourage them to ask you questions about your experiences.

Theme Let groups look through college catalogues and brochures you brought along to class. Say: *Compare these programs with colleges and universities in your native countries. What's the same? What's different?*

Community College Life in the U.S. (Reading)

1. Have students look at the photo. Ask: *Who are the people?* (students, a teacher) *What are they doing?* (They're in class. They're having a discussion.)
2. Have students look at the title of the reading. Ask: *What is the reading about? How do you know?* Have students make predictions.
3. Preteach any vocabulary words your students may not know, such as *tuition, attention, convenient, semester,* and *child-care center.*

BEFORE YOU READ

1. Have students discuss the questions in pairs.
2. Ask for a few volunteers to share their answers with the class.

To save class time, skip "Before You Read" or have students prepare answers for homework ahead of time.

Reading 🎧 *CD 1, Track 1*

1. Have students read the text silently. Tell them to pay special attention to the verb *be.* Then play the audio and have students read along silently.
2. Check students' comprehension. Ask questions, such as: *Is a community college usually bigger or smaller than a university?* (smaller) *Why is Truman College so convenient?* (It is near city transportation. It has evening and weekend classes. It has a child-care center) *How long is the summer semester?* (eight weeks)

To save class time, have students do the reading for homework ahead of time.

COMMUNITY COLLEGE LIFE IN THE U.S.

 Before You Read

Circle *T* for True or *F* for False and discuss your answers.

1. Most of the students in my class are immigrants.   T   F
2. My school is in a convenient[1] location.   T   F

🎧 Read the following article. Pay special attention to *is, am, are.*

A community college (or two-year college) **is** a good place to begin your education in the U.S. The tuition **is** usually cheaper than at a university. Because a community college **is** often smaller than a university, foreign students **are** often more comfortable. They **are** closer to their professors and get more attention.

Truman College **is** a typical community college. It **is** one of seven City Colleges of Chicago. It **is** a two-year college on the north side of Chicago. It **is** near public transportation—buses and trains—so it **is** convenient for everyone. For students with a car, parking **is** free. Credit classes **are** $70 per credit hour. Adult education classes **are** free.

Truman College **is** an international school. Many of the students **are** from other countries and **are** in ESL courses. Some of the students **are** immigrants. Some of the students **are** international students. International students **are** in the U.S. only to study. Tuition for international students **is** much higher.

Many of the students have jobs, so evening and weekend classes **are** convenient for these students. Some students have small children, so Truman has a child-care center.

The semester **is** 16 weeks long. Summer semester **is** eight weeks long. Students **are** free to choose their own classes.

[1]Something that is *convenient* is easy for you. A convenient location is near your house or near public transportation. Convenient classes are at a time that is good for you.

---

2   Lesson 1

Reading Variation

To practice listening skills, have students first listen to the audio alone. Ask a few comprehension questions. Repeat the audio if necessary. Then have students open their books and read along as they listen to the audio.

Reading Glossary

attention: work, care
child-care center: school-like place where parents pay to have small children cared for while the parents work
convenient: easy and comfortable to do or get to
semester: half of the school year
tuition: the cost of attending an educational institution

Culture Note

At present, there are 1,075 community colleges in the United States. More than 5.5 million students are enrolled in degree programs at community colleges.

Read the following student composition. Pay special attention to *is, am, are.*

My name **is** Rolando Lopez. I **am** from Guatemala. I **am** a student at Truman College. My major **is** engineering. I **am** married, and I work during the day. My classes **are** at night and on Saturdays. The college **is** a good place for me to start my education in the U.S. because the tuition **is** low and the attention to students **is** very high. My plan **is** to take 60 credit hours here and then go to a four-year college, such as the University of Illinois. I like it here because the teachers **are** friendly and helpful and the students from other countries **are** interesting.

1.1 | Forms of *Be*

Examples			Explanation
Subject	Form of *Be*	Complement	
I	**am**	a college student.	Use *am* with *I.*
My teacher He Truman It My wife She	**is**	an American. friendly. a City College. in Chicago. a student. busy.	Use *is* with *he, she, it,* and singular subjects (*teacher, wife, college*).
We You The students They	**are**	students. the teacher. from all over the world. immigrants.	Use *are* with *we, you, they,* and plural subjects.

EXERCISE 1 Fill in the blanks with *is, are,* or *am.*

EXAMPLE My name ___is___ Rolando Lopez.

1. I ___am___ from Guatemala.

2. My wife ___is___ from Mexico.

3. My wife and I ___are___ students.

4. The University of Illinois ___is___ a four-year college.

5. My classmates ___are___ from many different countries.

6. We ___are___ immigrants.

7. The professors at my college ___are___ friendly and helpful.

8. My major ___is___ engineering.

9. The semester ___is___ 16 weeks long.

The Present Tense of the Verb *Be*; Preposition of Place; *This, That, These, Those*   **3**

Grammar Variation

1. Have students come to the board and write the verbs next to the subjects.

2. Have more advanced students explain grammar chart **1.1.**

Reading (*cont.*)

3. Have students read the text silently. Tell them to pay special attention to the verb *be.* Then play the audio and have students read along.

4. Check students' comprehension. Ask questions, such as: *What is Rolando Lopez' major?* (engineering) *When are his classes?* (at night and on Saturdays) *Why does he like it at Truman College?* (The teachers are friendly and helpful. The students are interesting.)

1.1 | Forms of *Be*

1. Have students cover up grammar chart **1.1** on page 3. Write several subjects from the readings on the board in a column in no particular order. For example, write: *Truman, I, Rolando, it, they, classes,* etc. Activate students' prior knowledge. Ask students if they know what form of the verb goes with each subject. If students have difficulty with this task, have students find the subjects in the reading and ask them to match them to the correct form of the verb *be.* Write them on the board. For example, write: *classes are.*

2. Have students look at grammar chart **1.1.** Review the example sentences in the chart.

EXERCISE 1

1. Tell students that this exercise is about Rolando Lopez, the student who wrote the composition about Truman College. Have students read the direction line. Ask: *What words do we use here?* (is, are, am) Go over the example in the book. Then do #1 with the class. Ask: *What form of be goes here?* (am)

2. Have students complete the rest of Exercise 1 individually. Then have them check their answers in pairs. Circulate and observe the pair work. Check the answers as a class.

3. If necessary, review grammar chart **1.1** on page 3.

1.2 | Uses of *Be*

1. Copy the explanation side of grammar chart **1.2** on page 4 onto the board. Have students cover up grammar chart **1.2** in their books. Ask students to find an example sentence from the readings for the first four explanations in the grammar chart. (Don't ask them to find examples of the verb *be* with age, weather, or time. These are not in the readings.) Have volunteers write sentences from the chart on the board.
2. Have students look at grammar chart **1.2.** Say: *Compare our chart with the chart in the book.*
3. Review the example sentences in the grammar chart, including the examples for age, weather, and time.
4. Go around the room and ask students about their age, the weather, and the time.

EXERCISE 2

1. Have students read the direction line. Go over the example in the book.
2. Have students complete Exercise 2 individually. Then check the answers as a class.
3. If necessary, review grammar chart **1.2** on page 4.

1.2 | Uses of *Be*

Examples	Explanation
The college is **good**. Evening classes are **convenient** for me. The tuition is **low**. The teachers are very **friendly**.	Use a form of *be* with a description of the subject.
Truman College is **a community college**. The University of Illinois is **a four-year college**.	Use a form of *be* with a classification or definition of the subject.
Truman College is **in Chicago**. Chicago is **in Illinois**. The college is **near public transportation**.	Use a form of *be* with the location of the subject.
I am **from Guatemala**. My wife is **from Mexico**.	Use a form of *be* with the place of origin of the subject.
I am **24 years old**. My teacher is **about 40 years old**.	Use a form of *be* with the age of the subject.
It is **cold** in Chicago in the winter. It is **warm** in Guatemala all year.	Use *is* with weather. The subject is *it*.
It is **6 o'clock** now. It is **late**.	Use *is* with time. The subject is *it*.

EXERCISE **2**   Fill in the blanks to make true statements.

EXAMPLE   Chicago is _____*in Illinois*_____.
  (location)

1. Chicago is a ___*Answers will vary.*___. Illinois is a state.
   (classification)

2. My college is _____ public transportation.
   (location)

3. The teacher is about _____ years old.
   (age)

4. The teacher is from _____.
   (place of origin)

5. It is _____ now.
   (time)

6. It is _____ today.
   (weather)

7. This city is _____.
   (description)

Expansion

Exercise 2 Have students make new sentences based on the sentences in Exercise 2. Say: *Change the information in each sentence to make a new sentence. Then give the new sentences to your partner to answer. For example:*

Boston is a _____.

Brazil is a _____.

South America is a continent.

Circulate to observe pair work. Give help as needed.

1.3 | Word Order with *Be*

Examples			Explanation
Subject	**Be**	**Complement**	• The subject is first. The subject tells who or what we are talking about.
I	am	from Guatemala.	• The verb (*am, is, are*) is second.
Guatemala	is	in Central America.	• The complement is third. The complement finishes, or completes, the sentence with a location, classification, description, etc.
It	is	a small country.	
Spanish	is	my native language.	
You	are	from Vietnam.	
It	is	in Asia.	

EXERCISE **3**   Put the words in the correct order to make a statement. Use a capital letter at the beginning and a period at the end.

EXAMPLE   a two-year college / my college / is   *My college is a two-year college.*

1. am / I / a student   *I am a student.*

2. my parents / in Guatemala / are   *My parents are in Guatemala.*

3. high / is / tuition at a four-year college   *Tuition at a four-year college is high.*

4. is / convenient / my college   *My college is convenient.*

5. my teacher / is / 40 years old   *My teacher is 40 years old.*

6. is / from New York / my teacher   *My teacher is from New York.*

7. eight weeks long / the summer semester / is   *The summer semester is eight weeks long.*

8. Rolando / married / is   *Rolando is married.*

The Present Tense of the Verb *Be*; Preposition of Place; *This, That, These, Those*   **5**

1.3 | Word Order with *Be*

1. Have students cover up grammar chart **1.3** on page 5. Elicit the rule. Say: *Look at the reading on page 2. What comes first? The verb? The subject? The complement?* Ask them to find sentences to illustrate. Write the sentences on the board.

2. Have students look at grammar chart **1.3**. Review the example sentences in the chart.

EXERCISE 3

1. Have students read the direction line. Ask: *What is the word order with* be? (subject first, verb second, complement third) Model the exercise. Go over the example in the book. Then do #1 with the class. Ask a volunteer to give an answer.

2. Have students complete the rest of Exercise 3 individually. Then have them compare their answers in pairs. Finally, check the answers as a class.

3. If necessary, review grammar chart **1.3** on page 5.

Grammar Variation

Write five mixed-up sentences from the reading on the board. Tell students they have two minutes to put them in the correct order. Then elicit the rule for sentence order.

Expansion

Exercise 3 Divide the class into two teams. Give each team ten mixed-up sentences (with subject + *be* + complement) on small pieces of paper. Say: *You must put the words in the correct order and write the sentences on the board. The first team to finish is the winner.*

1.4 | The Subject

1. Ask students to underline every subject in the first two paragraphs in the reading on page 2.
2. Activate students' prior knowledge. Say: *Find an example of a pronoun as a subject.* Then ask students to circle all the subject pronouns in the reading on page 2.
3. Now have students double underline the plural subjects. (Note: If possible, check answers with the class using an overhead projector.)
4. Have students look at grammar chart **1.4**. Review the example sentences in the grammar chart. Review all of the subject pronouns. Explain that *you* is both singular and plural. Give examples. Say: *You are all my students.* Indicate this with a sweeping gesture that includes the whole class. Then point to one student in particular and say: *[Student name], you are my student.*

EXERCISE 4

1. Have students read the direction line. Ask: *What words go in the blanks?* (pronouns) Go over the example in the book. Then do #1 with the class. Ask a volunteer to give an answer. Point out the map of Central America.
2. Have students complete the rest of Exercise 4 individually. Have them compare their answers in pairs. Finally, check the answers as a class.
3. If necessary, review grammar chart **1.4** on page 6.

1.4 | The Subject

Examples	Explanation
I am from Guatemala. **You** are an American citizen. **It** is warm in Guatemala. **We** are happy in the U.S.	The subject pronouns are: *I, you, he, she, it, we, they.*
Chicago is very big. **It** is in Illinois. **My wife** is a student. **She** is from Mexico. **My teacher** is American. **She** is a native speaker of English. **My parents** are in Guatemala. **They** are happy. **My wife and I** are in the U.S. **We** are in Chicago.	• Subject pronouns (*it, she, he, we*) can take the place of nouns (*Chicago, sister, father, friend, I*) • A noun can be singular (*my father*) or plural (*my parents*). A plural noun usually ends in *s*. • When the subject is "another person and I," put the other person before *I*. Note: In conversation you sometimes hear "me and my wife" in the subject position. This is very informal.
My classmates are from many countries. **They** are immigrants. **English and math** are my favorite subjects. **They** are useful subjects.	We use *they* for plural people and things.
The U.S. is a big country. **It** is in North America.	*The United States* (*the U.S.*) is a singular noun. Use *the* before United States or U.S.
You are a good teacher. **You** are good students.	*You* can be a singular or plural subject.
It is cold in Chicago in the winter. **It** is 6 o'clock now.	Use *it* to talk about time and weather.

EXERCISE **4**   Fill in the blanks with the correct pronoun.

EXAMPLE   Nicaragua and Guatemala are countries. _____*They*_____ are in Central America.

1. My wife and I are students. _____*We*_____ are at Truman College.
2. Guatemala is a small country. _____*It*_____ is south of Mexico.
3. Some of the students in my class are international students. _____*They*_____ are from China, Japan, and Spain.

Expansion

Exercise 4 Have students write an e-mail to a friend about their English class. Tell them to use the sentences in Exercise 4 as a guide. Say: *Make the information in the sentences true for you.*

4. _____I_____ am a busy person.

5. English is a hard language. _____It_____ is necessary in the U.S.

6. Adult classes at my college are free. _____They_____ are for ESL students.

7. My book is new. _____It_____ is *Grammar in Context.*

8. My parents are in Guatemala. _____They_____ are old.

9. My teacher is a nice woman. _____She_____ is from Boston.

10. My classmates and I are interested in American life. _____We_____ are new in this country.

LETTER FROM COLLEGE

Before You Read

Circle *T* for True or *F* for False and discuss your answers.

1. The students in this class are from the same country.   T   F

2. Most of the students in this class are the same age.   T   F

Answers will vary.

 Read the following letter. Pay special attention to contractions with *am, is, are.*

United States
Atlantic Ocean
Gulf of Mexico
Puerto Rico

Dear Ola,

College **is** so different here. Students in my class **are** all ages. **We're** 22— **that's** a normal age for college students back home. But some students here **are** in their 50s or 60s. One man in my class **is** 74. **He's** from Korea. This **is** very strange for me, but it **is** interesting too. Some students **are** married. Most students have jobs, so **we're** all very busy.

The students **are** from all over the world. One student **is** from Puerto Rico. Her native language **is** Spanish, but Puerto Rico **isn't** a foreign country and it **isn't** a state of the U.S. It **is** a special territory. It **is** a small island near the U.S.

(continued)

The Present Tense of the Verb *Be*; Preposition of Place; *This, That, These, Those*   **7**

Letter from College (Reading)

1. Have students look at the photo and the map. Ask: *Who are the people?* (students, a teacher) *What are they doing?* (They're in class. They're having a discussion.)

2. Have students look at the title of the reading. Ask: *What is the reading about? How do you know?* Have students use the title, photo, and map to make predictions about the reading.

3. Preteach any vocabulary words your students may not know, such as *territory, rows, speech, major,* and *strict.*

BEFORE YOU READ

1. Have students discuss the questions in pairs.

2. Ask for a few volunteers to share their answers with the class.

⏱ To save class time, skip "Before You Read" or have students prepare answers for homework ahead of time.

Reading 🎧 *CD 1, Track 2*

1. Have students read the text silently. Tell them to pay special attention to the contractions with *am, is,* and *are.* Then play the audio and have students read along silently.

2. Check students' comprehension. Ask questions such as: *Are all the students the same age in Maya's class?* (no) *Where are the students from?* (from all over the world) *Are the classrooms comfortable?* (yes)

⏱ To save class time, have students do the reading for homework ahead of time.

Expansion

Theme The topic for this lesson can be enhanced with the following ideas:

1. A map of the world or a globe
2. Photos of different kinds of classroom setups from formal to very informal

---

Reading Variation

To practice listening skills, have students first listen to the audio alone. Ask a few comprehension questions. Repeat the audio if necessary. Then have students open their books and read along as they listen to the audio.

Reading Glossary

major: one's primary subject of study in college
row: a line of things, people, pictures, etc., placed front to back or side by side
speech: the expression of thoughts with spoken words
strict: expecting rules to be followed, requiring obedience
territory: an area of land not totally self-governing or considered a state or province by a central government

1.5 | Contractions with *Be*

1. Have students cover up grammar chart **1.5** on page 8. Ask students to find examples of contractions from the reading. Write them on the board. For example, write: *he's, we're, teacher's, what's.*

2. Have volunteers explain each contraction. Ask: *How do we make the contraction* he's? (*he is* = take out the first letter of *is* and add an apostrophe)

3. Have students look at grammar chart **1.5**. Review the example sentences in the grammar chart. Demonstrate what American speech would sound like if there were no contractions. To illustrate, enunciate each word very carefully.

4. Have students go back to the reading on page 7 to circle words that are not contracted (e.g., *college is, students are, language is*). Write the examples the students give you on the board. Point out that we do not make contractions with *is* if the noun ends in *s*, *z*, *g*, *sh*, or *ch* sounds. Model the pronunciation of each of the sounds. Also point out that we don't make contractions with plural nouns and *are*.

The classrooms **are** different here too. **They're** big and comfortable. But the desks **are** so small. Another strange thing **is** this: The desks **are** in a circle, not in rows.

In our country, **education's** free. But here **it's** so expensive. At my college, the **tuition's** $125 per credit hour. And books **are** expensive too.

The teacher's young and informal. **He's** about my age. His **name's** Rich Weiss, and **he's** very friendly. **We're** always welcome in his office after class. But English **is** so hard. **It's** not hard to read English, but **it's** hard to understand American speech.

I'm in Minneapolis. **It's** in the northern part of the U.S. **It's** very cold here in the winter. But the summers **are** warm and sunny.

Tell me about your life. **Are** you happy with your college classes? **What's** your major now? **How's** the weather? **What's** your favorite class this semester? How are your teachers? **Are** they strict?

Take care,
Maya

1.5 | Contractions with *Be*

Examples		Explanation
I am	**I'm** in Minneapolis.	We can make a **contraction** with a subject pronoun and *am*, *is*, and *are*. We take out the first letter of *am*, *is*, *are* and put an apostrophe (') in its place. We usually use a contraction when we speak. We sometimes write a contraction in informal writing.
You are	**You're** a student of English.	
She is	**She's** a young teacher.	
He is	**He's** 75 years old.	
It is	**It's** cold in winter.	
We are	**We're** so busy.	
They are	**They're** big.	
The United States is a big country.		We don't make a contraction with *is* if the noun ends in these sounds: *s*, *z*, *g*, *sh*, or *ch*.
College is different here.		
English is the language of the U.S.		
Rich is my English teacher.		
Books are expensive.		We don't make a contraction with a plural noun and *are*.
The classrooms are big.		

8 Lesson **1**

Expansion

Reading In groups have students take turns reading parts of the paragraph out loud, first without contractions, then with contractions. Circulate to observe group work. Give help as needed.

Culture Note

Education is free in the United States from kindergarten through high school. Some school districts also offer free preschool for three and four year-olds, but that isn't very common. College and university programs can be very expensive. State-run universities charge lower fees to state residents, but even state institutions can be expensive. Expensive private colleges can cost as much as $35,000 a year!

EXERCISE **5** Fill in the blanks with the correct form of *be* (*am, is, are*). Make a contraction whenever possible. Not every sentence can have a contraction.

EXAMPLE The United States _____*is*_____ a big country. It _____*'s*_____ between Canada and Mexico.

1. Puerto Rico _____*'s*_____ an island. Puerto Ricans _____*are*_____ American citizens.

2. English _____*is*_____ the main language of the U.S. Spanish and English _____*are*_____ the languages of Puerto Rico.

3. My classmates and I _____*are*_____ immigrants. We _____*'re*_____ in the U.S.

4. Maya _____*'s*_____ in Minneapolis. She _____*'s*_____ at a city college there.

5. Minneapolis _____*is*_____ a big city. It _____*'s*_____ in the northern part of the U.S.

6. The teacher _____*'s*_____ informal. He _____*'s*_____ friendly.

7. The students _____*are*_____ from all over the world. They _____*'re*_____ nice people.

8. The classroom _____*'s*_____ on the first floor. It _____*'s*_____ big.

EXERCISE **6** Fill in the blanks. Make a contraction whenever possible. Not every sentence can have a contraction.

I _____*'m*_____ a student of English at Truman College. _____*I*_____ 'm
(example)   (1)

happy in the U.S. My teacher _____*'s*_____ American. His
(2)

name _____*'s*_____ Charles Madison. Charles _____*is*_____ an
(3)   (4)

experienced teacher. _____*He's*_____ patient with foreign students.
(5)

My class _____*is*_____ big. _____*It's*_____ interesting. All the students
(6)   (7)

_____*are*_____ immigrants, but we _____*'re*_____ from many different
(8)   (9)

countries. Five students _____*are*_____ from Asia. One woman _____*'s*_____
(10)   (11)

from Poland. _____*She's*_____ from Warsaw, the capital of Poland. Many
(12)

students _____*are*_____ from Mexico.
(13)

The Present Tense of the Verb *Be*; Preposition of Place; *This, That, These, Those*   **9**

EXERCISE 5

1. Tell students that the information in the exercise is based on the letter they just read. Have students read the direction line. Ask: *Do all sentences have contractions?* (no) Go over the example in the book.
2. Have students complete the rest of Exercise 5 individually. Check the answers as a class.
3. Assess students' performance. If necessary, review grammar chart **1.5** on page 8.

EXERCISE 6

🎧 *CD 1, Track 3*

1. Tell students that this exercise is about a student from Truman College. Have students read the direction line. Ask: *Do all sentences have contractions?* (no) Go over the example in the book. Then do #1 with the class. Ask a volunteer to give an answer. Remind students that sometimes the verb is missing, sometimes the subject is missing, and sometimes both the subject and the verb are missing.
2. Have students complete Exercise 6 individually. Then check answers as a class.
3. If necessary, review grammar chart **1.5** on page 8.

🕐 To save class time, have students do half of the exercise in class and complete the other half for homework. Or assign the entire exercise for homework.

Exercise 6 Variation

To provide practice with listening skills, have students close their books and listen to the audio. Repeat the audio as needed. Ask comprehension questions, such as: *Where does the student study?* (at Truman College) *Who is Charles Madison?* (the student's teacher) *Is Charles a new teacher?* (no) Then have students open their books and complete Exercise 6.

Expansion

Exercise 6 Have students write a paragraph about their English class. Tell students to use Exercise 6 as a model. Instruct students not to use contractions. Then have students exchange paragraphs with a partner. The partner corrects the paragraph, inserting contractions where they should be used.

1.6 | *Be* with Descriptions

1. Have students cover up grammar chart **1.6** on page 10. Ask volunteers to describe the school and the classroom they're in. As they talk write down adjectives they use on the board. If they need help, prompt: *Is the classroom big or small? Is the school expensive? Are your classmates married?* Ask students if they know what the words you've written on the board are called. (adjectives)

2. Remind students that in English adjectives are not plural.

3. Have students look at grammar chart **1.6**. Review the example sentences in the grammar chart. Point out that adjectives can have many different kinds of endings.

EXERCISE 7

1. Have students read the direction line. Go over the examples. Do #1 with the class. Ask volunteers to model the example.

2. Have students complete Exercise 7 individually. Have students compare work in pairs. Circulate and give help as needed.

3. If necessary, review grammar chart **1.6** on page 10.

We ___'re___ (14) ready to learn English, but English ___is___ (15) a difficult language. I sometimes tell Charles, "You ___'re___ (16) a very kind teacher." Charles says, "___You're___ (17) all good students, and I ___'m___ (18) happy to teach you English."

1.6 | *Be* with Descriptions

Examples	Explanation
Subject　Be　(Very)　Adjective My teacher　is　　　**young.** The desks　are　very　**small.** The weather　is　　　**cold** in winter.	After a form of *be*, we can use a word that describes the subject. Descriptive words are **adjectives.** *Very* can come before an adjective.
The school is **big.** The classrooms are **big.**	Descriptive adjectives have no plural form. 　*Wrong:* The classrooms are bigs.
Some of my classmates are **married.** My class is **interesting.** I'm **interested** in American life.	Some words that end with –*ed* and –*ing* are adjectives: *married, divorced, worried, tired, interested, interesting, bored, boring.*
It's **cold.** I'm **thirsty.** We're **afraid.**	We use a form of *be* with physical or mental conditions: *hungry, thirsty, cold, hot, tired, happy,* etc.

EXERCISE 7 Complete each statement with a subject and the correct form of *be*. Write a contraction wherever possible. Make a *true* statement. Use both singular and plural subjects.

EXAMPLES ___My parents are___ intelligent.　　___The teacher's very___ patient.

1. _____Answers will vary._____ expensive.
2. _____ cheap.
3. _____ new.
4. _____ big.
5. _____ wonderful.
6. _____ difficult.
7. _____ beautiful.
8. _____ famous.

Grammar Variation

Have students circle adjectives in the readings. Elicit the rules for adjectives. Ask: *What do adjectives do?* (describe nouns) *Do adjectives have a plural form?* (no) *What kind of endings do adjectives have?* (some have -*ed* and -*ing* endings)

EXERCISE 8   Write a form of *be* and an adjective to describe each of the following nouns. You may work with a partner.

EXAMPLES   This classroom _is clean._

New York City _is interesting._

1. The teacher _____   Answers will vary.
2. This city _____
3. This college _____
4. Today's weather _____
5. Americans _____
6. American food _____
7. The students in this class _____

1.7 | *Be* with Definitions

Examples				Explanation
Singular Subject	*Be*	*A/An*	Singular Noun	We use a noun after a form of *be* to classify or define the subject.
I	**am**	a	student.	Use *a* or *an* before the definition of a singular noun. Use *a* before a consonant sound. Use *an* before a vowel sound. (The vowels are *a, e, i, o, u*.)
You	**are**	a	teacher.	
Puerto Rico	**is**	an	island.	
Plural Subject	*Be*		Plural Noun	Don't use *a* or *an* before the definition of a plural noun.
You and I	**are**		students.	*Wrong: You and I are a students.*
They	**are**		Americans.	
Subject	*Be*	*(A)*	Adjective Noun	We can include an adjective as part of the definition.
Chicago	is	a	**big** city.	
We	are		**good** students.	

The Present Tense of the Verb *Be*; Preposition of Place; *This, That, These, Those*   **11**

---

1. Have students read the direction line. Go over the examples in the book. Have volunteers model the examples.
2. Have students complete the exercise in pairs. Check the answers as a class.
3. If necessary, review grammar chart **1.6** on page 10.

🕐 To save class time, have students do half of the exercise in class and complete the other half for homework. Or assign the entire exercise for homework.

1.7 | *Be* with Definitions

1. Have students cover up grammar chart **1.7** on page 11. Instruct students to look at you. Point to yourself and say: *I am . . .* Elicit the answer from the students (a teacher). Now say: *You are . . .* Elicit the response from the students (students). Write both phrases on the board. Again, point to yourself and say: *I am an American.* Point to another student (preferably one from another country) and say: *You are . . .*
2. Have students look at grammar chart **1.7.** Review the example sentences in the chart.
3. Remind students to use *an* before a vowel sound. Also, tell students that *a* or *an* is like saying *one*, so plural nouns do not use *a/an*.

EXERCISE 9

1. Tell students that this exercise is to practice writing definitions. Have students read the direction line. Go over the example in the book. Have a volunteer model the example.
2. Have students complete the exercise individually. Check the answers as a class.
3. If necessary, review grammar chart **1.7** on page 11.

EXERCISE 10

1. Have students read the direction line. Ask: *What do we use in front of a vowel sound?* (an) Go over the examples in the book.
2. Have students complete the exercise individually. Check the answers as a class.
3. If necessary, review grammar chart **1.7** on page 11.

EXERCISE 11

1. Have students read the direction line. Ask: *What will you put in the blanks?* (am, is, are, a, or an) *Will all sentences have* a *or* an? (no) Remind students that they should also use contractions wherever possible. Go over the examples in the book.
2. Have students complete the exercise individually. Then have students exchange papers to check answers or check the answers as a class.
3. If necessary, review grammar charts **1.1** on page 3, **1.5** on page 8, and **1.7** on page 11.

To save class time, have students do half of the exercise in class and complete the other half for homework. Or assign the entire exercise for homework.

EXERCISE 9 Fill in the blanks with a form of *be* and a definition of the subject. You may add an adjective. Be careful to add *a* or *an* for singular nouns.

EXAMPLE California _is a state._

1. Canada _is a country._
2. Chicago _is a city._
3. Blue _is a color._
4. Wednesday _is a day._
5. The Pacific and the Atlantic _are oceans._
6. White and green _are colors._
7. January and February _are months._

EXERCISE 10 Add an adjective to each statement. Be careful to use *a* before a consonant and *an* before a vowel sound.

EXAMPLE July 4 is a holiday.
July 4 is an important holiday.

Answers will vary.
1. August is a month.
2. Puerto Rico is an island.
3. A rose is a flower.
4. I'm a student.
5. Los Angeles and Chicago are cities.
6. John is a name.

EXERCISE 11 Fill in the blanks with the correct form of *be*. Add *a* or *an* for singular nouns only. Don't use an article with plural nouns.

EXAMPLES The U.S. _is a_ big country.
The U.S. and Canada _are_ big countries.

1. English and Spanish _are_ languages.
2. England and Spain _are_ countries.
3. The University of Illinois _is a_ state university.
4. It _'s an_ old university.
5. Chicago _'s an_ interesting city.
6. Chicago and Minneapolis _are_ big cities.
7. I _'m a_ student.
8. You _'re an_ English teacher.
9. Some students _are_ immigrants.

12   Lesson 1

Expansion

Exercise 11 Break the class up into groups. Have each group develop a quiz of ten questions on the verb *be* for another group. After the quizzes are made, distribute them to the other groups and set a time limit to take the quiz. Return the quizzes to the groups that wrote them for assessment. Circulate to observe group work. Give help as needed.

EXERCISE 12   Complete each statement. Give a subject and the correct form of *be*. Add *a* or *an* for singular nouns only. Don't use an article with plural nouns. You may work with a partner.

EXAMPLES   *Russia is a* big country.

Canada and Brazil are big countries.

1. _____ Answers will vary. _____ nice person.
2. _____ expensive item.
3. _____ American holiday.
4. _____ warm months.
5. _____ big cities.
6. _____ famous people.
   (NOTE: *people* is plural)
7. _____ American cars.

EXERCISE 13   Fill in the blanks to talk about this city. Make true statements. Remember to add *a* or *an* for a singular noun. You may work with a partner.

EXAMPLES   *Chez Paul is an* expensive restaurant in this city.

January and February are cold months in this city.

1. _____ Answers will vary. _____ popular tourist attraction.
2. _____ big stores.
3. _____ beautiful months.
4. _____ beautiful park.
5. _____ inexpensive restaurant.
6. _____ busy streets.
7. _____ good college.

EXERCISE 14   Fill in the blanks to make true statements about the U.S. or another country.

EXAMPLES   *Rock music is* popular *in the U.S.*

Politicians are rich *in my native country.*

1. ____ Answers will vary. ____ the biggest city _____.
2. _____ the language(s) _____.
3. _____ a popular sport _____.
4. _____ a common last name _____.
5. _____ a beautiful place _____.

The Present Tense of the Verb *Be*; Preposition of Place; *This, That, These, Those*   **13**

Expansion

Exercise 13 In pairs have students write brochures about the city they're living in or a city they're from. Tell them to use the sentences from Exercise 13 as a model. Then have pairs exchange brochures with other pairs to compare cities. Finally, display all the brochures in the room. Vote on the best city brochure.

Exercise 14 Have students develop presentations on their country/city using the sentences from Exercise 14 as a model. Ask students to bring in pictures and other items to enhance their presentations.

EXERCISE 12

1. Have students read the direction line. Ask: *What will you put in the blanks?* (a subject, *a*, or *an*) *Will all sentences have* a *or* an? (no) *Which sounds don't have* a *or* an? (plural nouns) Go over the examples in the book. Have a volunteer model the example.
2. Have students complete the exercise in pairs. Circulate to observe pair work. Give help as needed.
3. If necessary, review grammar charts **1.4** on page 6 and **1.7** on page 11.

🕐 To save class time, have students do half of the exercise in class and complete the other half for homework. Or assign the entire exercise for homework.

EXERCISE 13

1. Tell students that this exercise is about their city. Have students read the direction line. Ask: *What will you put in the blanks?* (a subject, *a*, or *an*). *Will all sentences have* a *or* an? (no) *Which sounds don't have* a *or* an? (plural nouns) Go over the examples. Have volunteers model the examples.
2. Have students complete the exercise in pairs. Circulate to observe pair work. Give help as needed.
3. If necessary, review grammar charts **1.4** on page 6 and **1.7** on page 11.

🕐 To save class time, have students do half of the exercise in class and complete the other half for homework. Or assign the entire exercise for homework.

EXERCISE 14

1. Have students read the direction line. Say: *You can write these questions about the U.S. or another country.* Go over the examples in the book. Have volunteers model the examples.
2. Have students complete Exercise 14 individually. Then have them check their answers in pairs. Circulate and observe the pair work. If necessary, check the answers as a class.
3. If necessary, review grammar charts **1.1.** on page 3, **1.4** on page 6, **1.6** on page 10, and **1.7** on page 11.

🕐 To save class time, have students do half of the exercise in class and complete the other half for homework. Or assign the entire exercise for homework.

1.8 | Prepositions

1. Have students cover up grammar chart **1.8** on pages 14–15. Activate students' prior knowledge. Ask: *What prepositions do you know?* As students call them out, write them on the board.
2. Then ask students to demonstrate the prepositions. First model an example. (Point to the book on the desk.) Say: *On. My book is on the desk.*
3. Have students look at grammar chart **1.8**. Review the examples in the grammar chart. Point out the illustrations that show the meanings of the prepositions. As you go down the chart, demonstrate the prepositions yourself or have volunteers demonstrate them.

1.8 | Prepositions

We use prepositions to show location and origin.

Preposition	Examples	
On	The book is **on** the table. The cafeteria is **on** the first floor.	
At (a general area)	I am **at** school. My brother is **at** home. They are **at** work.	
In (a complete or partial enclosure)	The students are **in** the classroom. The wastebasket is **in** the corner.	
In front of	The blackboard is **in front of** the student.	
In back of / Behind	The teacher is **in back of** the desk. The blackboard is **behind** the teacher.	
Between	The empty desk is **between** the two students.	
Over / Above	The exit sign is **over** the door. The clock is **above** the exit sign.	
Below / Under	The textbook is **below** the desk. The dictionary is **under** the textbook.	
By / Near / Close to	The pencil sharpener is **by** the window. The pencil sharpener is **near** the window. The pencil sharpener is **close to** the window.	
Next to	The light switch is **next to** the door.	
Far from	Los Angeles is **far from** New York.	

(continued)

14   Lesson 1

Grammar Variation

Brainstorm a list of prepositions on the board. Then have students cover up everything except the pictures on grammar chart **1.8.** Ask students to try and guess the prepositions from the picture.

Preposition	Examples
Across from	Room 202 is **across from** Room 203.
In (a city)	The White House is **in** Washington, D.C.
On (a street)	The White House is **on** Pennsylvania Avenue.
At (an address)	The White House is **at** 1600 Pennsylvania Avenue.
From	Mario is **from** Brazil. He is **from** São Paulo.

EXERCISE **15** ABOUT YOU Use a form of *be* and a preposition to tell the location of these things or people in your classroom or school.

EXAMPLE
My dictionary
My dictionary is in my book bag.

Answers will vary.
1. My classroom
2. I
3. The library
4. The cafeteria
5. The parking lot
6. The teacher
7. We
8. My books

1.9 | Negative Statements with *Be*

Examples	Explanation
I am **not** married. Peter is **not** at home. We are **not** doctors.	We put *not* after a form of *be* to make a negative statement.
I'm not late. English **isn't** my native language. My friends **aren't** here now.	We can make contractions for the negative.

Language Note: There is only one contraction of *I am not*. There are two negative contractions for all the other combinations. Study the negative contractions:

I am not	I'm not	—
you are not	you're not	you aren't
he is not	he's not	he isn't
she is not	she's not	she isn't
it is not	it's not	it isn't
we are not	we're not	we aren't
they are not	they're not	they aren't
Tom is not	Tom's not	Tom isn't

The Present Tense of the Verb *Be*; Preposition of Place; *This, That, These, Those* **15**

Expansion

Exercise 15 Divide students into groups. At the front of the room, create an interesting still life with fruit and other objects. Say: *Describe this still life using prepositions.* Circulate to observe group work. Give help when needed. Have a volunteer from each group read the description. Then have the groups compare.

Exercise 15 Divide students into groups. Line up a number of interesting objects on a table in front of the classroom. Ask the groups to design a still life using prepositions. Say: *Don't draw a picture. Just describe it using prepositions.* Have groups exchange descriptions and take turns trying to build the other groups' still life. The group that builds the most accurate still life wins.

1. Tell students that this exercise is about their classroom and their school. Have students read the direction line. Go over the example with the students. (Put your dictionary in your book bag to demonstrate.) Have a volunteer model #1.
2. Have students complete the exercise individually. Have students check answers in pairs or check answers as a class.
3. If necessary, review grammar chart **1.8** on pages 14–15.

1.9 | Negative Statements with *Be*

1. Have students cover up grammar chart **1.9**. Elicit a negative statement with *be*. Turn to a student who is not married and say, for example: *Jenny is married.* Help Jenny, or another student say: *I'm not married* or *She's not married.* Offer more examples to elicit a negative response (e.g., *You're tired; you're late; he's Japanese*). Write the negative sentences on the board.
2. Have students look at grammar chart **1.9**. Review the example sentences in the chart.
3. Explain to students that there are two ways to make contractions. Say: *You can use both contractions. Both are common.* Ask volunteers to demonstrate how to make a negative contraction on the board. Review how to make both contractions with the students. *You're not*—remove the first letter in the verb *be* and replace with an apostrophe. *You aren't*—remove the *o* from *not* and replace with an apostrophe.
4. Point out that there is only one way to contract *I am not—I'm not.*

EXERCISE 16

1. Tell students that this exercise is for practicing the negative with *be*. Have students read the direction line. Go over the examples in the book.
2. Have students complete the exercise individually. Check the answers as a class.
3. If necessary, review grammar chart **1.9** on page 15.

EXERCISE 17

1. Tell students that this exercise is about the class. Have students read the direction line. Ask: *What do we put in the blanks?* (*be* in the affirmative or negative) Remind students to use both forms of contractions. Go over the example sentences in the book.
2. Have students complete the exercise individually. Then have students compare answers with a partner.
3. If necessary, review grammar chart **1.9** on page 15.

🕐 To save class time, have students do half of the exercise in class and complete the other half for homework. Or assign the entire exercise for homework.

EXERCISE **16**   Fill in the blanks with a pronoun and a negative verb. Practice using both negative forms.

EXAMPLE   The classroom is clean and big.
__*It isn't*__ dirty. __*It's not*__ small.

1. We're in the classroom.
   __*We're not*__ in the library. __*We aren't*__ in the cafeteria.
2. Today's a weekday.
   __*It isn't*__ Saturday. __*It's not*__ Sunday.
3. I'm a student. __*I'm not*__ a teacher.
4. The students are busy.
   __*They aren't*__ lazy. __*They're not*__ tired.
5. You're on time.
   __*You aren't*__ early. __*You're not*__ late.
6. My classmates and I are in an English class.
   __*We aren't*__ in the cafeteria. __*We're not*__ in the library.

EXERCISE **17**   ABOUT YOU Fill in the blanks with a form of *be* to make a true affirmative statement or negative statement.

EXAMPLES   I __*am*__ busy on Saturdays.
My English class __*isn't*__ in the morning.

Answers will vary.
1. My class _____ small.
2. The students _____ all the same age.
3. The students _____ from many countries.
4. Books in the U.S. _____ expensive.
5. The teacher _____ from my native country.
6. The seats in this class _____ in a circle.
7. I _____ a full-time student.
8. My classes _____ easy.
9. We _____ in the computer room now.

Expansion

Exercise 17 Have students write an e-mail to a friend describing their class. Say: *Use the negative and the affirmative in your e-mail. Also, remember to use contractions.* Tell students to use Exercise 17 as a model, but to add more information.

EXERCISE **18** True or False. Tell if you think the following statements are true or false. Discuss your opinions.

Answers will vary.

	True	False
1. English is easy for me.		
2. English is easy for children.		
3. American teachers are very strict.[2]		
4. This school is in a nice area.		
5. This course is expensive.		
6. All Americans are rich.		
7. Baseball is popular in the U.S.		
8. January and February are nice months.		

EXERCISE **19** ABOUT YOU If you are from another country, tell your classmates about life there. Fill in the blanks with a form of *be* to make an affirmative or negative statement.

EXAMPLES   I ____'m____ from the capital city.

I ____'m not____ from a small town.

Answers will vary.

1. I _____ happy with the government of my country.
2. I _____ from the capital city.
3. American cars _____ common in my country.
4. Teachers _____ strict.
5. Most people _____ rich.
6. Gas _____ cheap.
7. Apartments _____ expensive.
8. Bicycles _____ a popular form of transportation.
9. Public transportation _____ good.
10. A college education _____ free.
11. The president (prime minister) _____ a woman.
12. My hometown _____ in the mountains.
13. My hometown _____ very big.
14. It _____ very cold in the winter in my hometown.
15. Cell phones _____ popular in my country.

[2]A *strict* teacher has a lot of rules.

EXERCISE 18

1. Tell students that this exercise is about their opinions. Have students read the direction line. Then have a volunteer model #1.
2. Have students complete the rest of the exercise individually. Then put students into groups to discuss their responses. Circulate to observe group work. Give help when needed.
3. If necessary, review grammar chart **1.9** on page 15.

🕐 To save class time, have students do half of the exercise in class and complete the other half for homework. Or assign the entire exercise for homework. If time allows, have students discuss their opinions in class.

EXERCISE 19

1. Tell students that this exercise is about their native countries. Have students read the direction line. Ask: *What do we put in the blanks?* (*be* in the affirmative or negative) Remind students to use both forms of contractions. Go over the example sentences in the book.
2. Have students complete the exercise individually. Then have students compare answers with a partner.
3. If necessary, review grammar chart **1.9** on page 15.

🕐 To save class time, have students do half of the exercise in class and complete the other half for homework. Or assign the entire exercise for homework. If time allows, have students share a few answers in class.

Expansion

Exercise 18 Have groups report their groups' opinions to the class. Compile all the information on the board for a survey of the whole class. Discuss the results.

Exercise 19 If possible, pair students from different countries. Ask each partner to do the same exercise for their partner's country. Have them write their guesses in their notebooks. Then have partners compare their answers. Circulate to observe pair work. Give help as needed.

1. Have students read the direction line. Ask: *What kind of statements will we write?* (negative statements) Remind students to use both forms of contractions. Go over the example in the book.
2. Have students complete the exercise individually. Collect for assessment or check answers as a class.
3. If necessary, review grammar chart **1.9** on page 15.

🕐 To save class time, have students do half of the exercise in class and complete the other half for homework. Or assign the entire exercise for homework.

1. Tell students that this exercise is about their class. Have students read the direction line. Ask: *What do we put in the blanks?* (*be* in the affirmative or negative) Remind students to use both forms of contractions. Go over the example in the book.
2. Have students complete the exercise individually. Then have students compare answers with a partner.
3. If necessary, review grammar charts **1.1** on page 3 and **1.9** on page 15.

🕐 To save class time, have students do half of the exercise in class and complete the other half for homework. Or assign the entire exercise for homework.

EXERCISE **20** Use the words in parentheses ( ) to change each sentence into a negative statement.

EXAMPLE My teacher is American. (Canadian)
He isn't Canadian.

1. Los Angeles and Chicago are cities. (states)
   They aren't states. Or They're not states.
2. I'm from Mexico. (the U.S.)
   I'm not from the U.S.
3. The U.S. is a big country. (Cuba)
   It isn't Cuba. Or It's not Cuba.
4. We're in class now. (in the library)
   We aren't in the library. Or We're not in the library.
5. You're an English teacher. (a math teacher)
   You aren't a math teacher. Or You're not a math teacher.
6. Chicago and Springfield are in Illinois. (Miami)
   They aren't in Miami. They're not in Miami.
7. January is a cold month. (July and August)
   They aren't cold months. They're not cold months.

EXERCISE **21** ABOUT YOU Fill in the blanks with the affirmative or negative of the verb *be* to make a true paragraph.

Answers will vary.

My name _____*is*_____ (example) _____ (your name). I _____ (1) from an

English-speaking country. I _____ (2) a student at City College.

I _____ (3) in my English class now. The class _____ (4)

big. My teacher _____ (5) a man. He/She _____ (6) very

young. The classroom _____ (7) very nice. It _____ (8) clean.

My classmates _____ (9) all very young students. We _____ (10)

all from the same country. We _____ (11) all immigrants.

Expansion

Exercise 20 Have students create an exercise like Exercise 20. Instruct students to change the names of the places. Then have students exchange exercises with a partner. After completing the exercises, partners compare answers. Circulate to observe pair work. Give help as needed.

INSTANT MESSAGE FROM A STUDENT IN THE U.S.

Before You Read

1. Is your family in this city?

2. Do you communicate with your family and friends by e-mail?

Read the following instant message between Mohammad (MHD), a student in the U.S., and his brother, Ali (AL27), back home. Pay special attention to questions.

AL27: Hi, Mohammad.
MHD: Hi, Ali. **How are you?**
AL27: I'm fine.
MHD: **Where are you now?**
AL27: I'm in the college computer lab. **Are you at home?**
MHD: Yes, I am. It's late.

AL27: It's 4:15 p.m. here. **What time is it there?**
MHD: It's 1:15 a.m. here.
AL27: **Why are you still up[3]?**
MHD: I'm not sleepy.
AL27: **Why aren't you sleepy?**
MHD: I'm nervous about my test tomorrow.
AL27: **Why are you nervous?**
MHD: Because my class is very hard.
AL27: **How's college life in the U.S.? Is it very different from here?**
MHD: Yes, it is. But it's exciting for me. My new classmates are so interesting. They're from many countries and are all ages. One man in my class is very old.
AL27: **How old is he?**
MHD: He's 75.
AL27: **Are you serious?**
MHD: Of course, I'm serious. He's an interesting man and a great student.

AL27: **Where's he from?**
MHD: Korea.
AL27: All my classmates are young.
MHD: **Where are Mom and Dad?**
AL27: They're at work.
MHD: **Are they worried about me?**

(continued)

[3]To *be up* means to be awake.

The Present Tense of the Verb *Be*; Preposition of Place; *This, That, These, Those*   **19**

Instant Message from a Student in the U.S. (Reading)

1. Have students look at the photo. Ask: *Who is in the photo?* (a man, a student) *What is he doing?* (He's working on the computer.)
2. Have students look at the title of the reading. Ask: *What is the reading about? How do you know?* Have students make predictions.
3. Preteach any vocabulary words your students may not know, such as *sleepy* or *nervous*.

BEFORE YOU READ

1. Have students discuss the questions in pairs.
2. Ask for a few volunteers to share their answers with the class.

To save class time, skip "Before You Read" or have students prepare answers for homework ahead of time.

Reading 🎧 CD 1, Track 4

1. Have students read the text silently. Tell them to pay special attention to questions. Then play the audio and have students read along silently.
2. Check students' comprehension. Ask questions such as: *Is Ali up late?* (no) *Why is Mohammad nervous?* (He has a test tomorrow.) *How old is the Korean man in Mohammad's class?* (75)

To save class time, have students do the reading for homework ahead of time.

Reading Variation

To practice listening skills, have students first listen to the audio alone. Ask a few comprehension questions. Repeat the audio if necessary. Then have students open their books and read along as they listen to the audio.

Reading Glossary

nervous: worried about a future event
sleepy: needing sleep, tired

Culture Note

Instant Messaging was created in 1996 by four Israelis. They created a company called Mirabilis. Their instant messaging tool was called ICQ (*I seek you*).

1.10 | Be in Yes/No Questions and Short Answers

1. Have students cover up grammar chart **1.10**. Ask students to find *yes/no* questions in the reading. Write examples on the board. (*Are you at home? Are you serious?*)

2. Have students look at grammar chart **1.10**. Review the example sentences in the grammar chart.

3. Explain to students that in a question you put the verb—*am, is, are*—before the subject.

4. Point out that *yes/no* questions are usually answered with a short answer such as *Yes, it is.* Or *No, it isn't.* Affirmative short answers are not contracted. (*Yes, it is.*) Negative short answers are usually contracted. (*No, it isn't; No it's not.*)

5. Direct students' attention to the Pronunciation Note. Demonstrate the rising intonation of *yes/no* questions. Lead students in a choral practice of the intonation.

EXERCISE 22

1. Tell students that this exercise is about Ali and Mohammad from the last reading. Have students read the direction line. Ask: *What kind of sentences will we write?* (short answers) Go over the example in the book. Have students complete the exercise individually. Check answers as a class.

3. If necessary, review grammar chart **1.10** on page 20.

AL27: A little.
MHD: **Why?**
AL27: Because there's so much freedom in the U.S.
MHD: Tell them I'm a good student. I'm on the dean's list.
AL27: **What's that?**
MHD: It's a list of students with a high grade point average.
AL27: That's great. Bye for now.
MHD: Bye.

1.10 | Be in *Yes/No* Questions and Short Answers

Compare statements, *yes/no* questions, and short answers.

Statement	Yes/No Question	Short Answer	Explanation
I am a student.	**Am I** a good student?	Yes, you are.	• In a *yes/no* question, we put *am, is, are* before the subject.
You are in bed.	**Are you** sleepy?	No, I'm not.	
He is old.	**Is he** a good student?	Yes, he is.	• We usually answer a *yes/no* question with a short answer. A short answer contains a pronoun. We don't use a contraction for a short *yes* answer. We usually use a contraction for a short *no* answer.
She is from Africa.	**Is she** from Nigeria?	No, she isn't.	
It is cold today.	**Is it** windy?	Yes, it is.	
We are here.	**Are we** late?	No, you aren't.	
They are worried.	**Are they** angry?	No, they aren't.	

Pronunciation Note: We usually end a *yes/no* question with rising intonation. Listen to your teacher pronounce the questions above.

EXERCISE 22 Answer the questions based on the last reading (the instant message).

EXAMPLES   Is Ali in the U.S.?
No, he isn't.

Is Mohammad in the U.S.?
Yes, he is.

1. Are Ali's parents at work?   *Yes, they are.*

2. Are they worried about Mohammad?   *Yes, they are.*

3. Is Mohammad a good student?   *Yes, he is.*

4. Is it the same time in the U.S. and in Mohammad's native country?
No, it isn't.

5. Is Ali at home?   *No, he isn't.*

6. Are all the students in Mohammad's class from the same country?
No, they're not.

7. Is Mohammad tired?   *No, he isn't.*

Expansion

Grammar Put students in pairs. Ask students to look at Exercise 18 on page 17. Say: *Ask your partner* yes/no *questions. For example: Is English easy for you? Take turns asking and answering.*

EXERCISE 23   ABOUT YOU Close your book. The teacher will ask you some questions. Answer with a true short answer. If the answer is negative, you may add more information.

EXAMPLE   Is your book new?
Yes, it is. OR No, it isn't. It's a used book.

Answers will vary.
1. Is your hometown big?
2. Is Spanish your native language?
3. Is English hard for you?
4. Are you a citizen of the U.S.?
5. Is my pronunciation clear to you?
6. Am I a strict teacher?
7. Are all of you from the same country?
8. Are all of you the same age?

EXERCISE 24   Ask questions about this school and class with the words given. Another student will answer. Use the correct form of *be*.

EXAMPLE   school / big
A: Is this school big?
B: Yes, it is.

1. it / near public transportation
   Is it near public transportation?
2. the cafeteria / on this floor
   Is the cafeteria on this floor?
3. it / open now
   Is it open now?
4. the library / in this building
   Is the library in this building?
5. it / closed now
   Is it closed now?
6. this course / free
   Is this course free?
7. the textbooks / free
   Are the textbooks free?
8. the teacher / strict
   Is the teacher strict?
9. this room / clean
   Is this room clean?
10. it / big
    Is it big?

EXERCISE 25   Ask questions about the U.S. with the words given. Another student will answer. If no one knows the answer, ask the teacher.

EXAMPLE   movie stars / rich
A: Are American movie stars rich?
B: Yes, they are. They're very rich.

1. a high school education / free
   Is a high school education free?
2. college books / free
   Are college books free?
3. medical care / free
   Is medical care free?
4. doctors / rich
   Are doctors rich?
5. blue jeans / popular
   Are blue jeans popular?
6. houses / expensive
   Are houses expensive?
7. Americans / friendly
   Are Americans friendly?
8. Japanese cars / popular
   Are Japanese cars popular?
9. fast-food restaurants / popular
   Are fast-food restaurants popular?
10. movie tickets / cheap
    Are movie tickets cheap?

The Present Tense of the Verb *Be*; Preposition of Place; *This, That, These, Those*   21

EXERCISE 23
1. Tell students that you will ask them some questions. Have students read the direction line. Say: *If you answer in the negative, please give me more information.* Go over the example in the book. Model the example with a student.
2. If necessary, review grammar chart **1.10** on page 20.

EXERCISE 24
1. Tell students that this exercise is about their school and class. Have students read the direction line. Ask: *What kind of questions are we going to ask?* (*yes/no* questions) Go over the example in the book. Model the example with a volunteer. Then have two volunteers model #1.
2. Have students complete the exercise in pairs. Students take turns asking and answering questions. Circulate to observe pair work. Check for correct intonation of questions. Give help as needed.
3. If necessary, review grammar chart **1.10** on page 20.

EXERCISE 25
1. Have students read the direction line. Ask: *What kind of questions are we going to ask?* (*yes/no* questions) Go over the example in the book. Model the example with a volunteer. Then have two volunteers model #1.
2. Have students complete the exercise in pairs, taking turns asking and answering questions. Circulate to observe pair work. Check for correct intonation of questions. Give help as needed.
3. If necessary, review grammar chart **1.10** on page 20.

To save class time, have students do half of the exercise in class and complete the other half in writing for homework. Or if students do not need speaking practice, the entire exercise may be skipped or done in writing.

Exercise 23 Variation
1. To decrease stress for students, ask the questions to students in small groups. Don't ask every question to every student.
2. Use this exercise as an oral assessment. Ask individual students the questions in a quiet setting.

Expansion

Exercise 23 Have students ask and answer questions 1–5 from Exercise 23. Instruct students to write three more questions to ask their partners. Circulate to observe pair work. Give help as needed.

Exercises 24 and 25 Create two rings of students. Have half of the students stand in an outer ring around the classroom. Have the other half stand in an inner ring, facing the outer ring. Instruct students to ask and answer the questions from Exercise 24 and/or Exercise 25. Call out "*turn*" every minute or so. Students in the inner ring should move one space clockwise. Students now ask and answer with their new partners. Make sure students look up at each other when they're speaking.

1.11 | Wh- Questions with Be

1. Have students cover up grammar chart **1.11**. Activate students' prior knowledge. Say: *What wh- questions do you know?* (e.g., *What's your name? Where are you from?*) Write students' examples on the board. Then ask students to find *wh-* questions in the reading on pages 19 and 20. Write examples on the board. (*How are you? Where are you now?*)

2. Have students look at grammar chart **1.11**. Review the example sentences in the chart. Explain that *wh-* questions ask for information. In contrast, *yes/no* questions ask only for a *yes* or *no* response.

3. Explain the Language Notes. Write the contractions for *wh-* words and *is* on the board. Explain that there is no contraction for *which is* and that there is no written contraction for *wh-* words and *are*, but that it's acceptable in informal speech. Then ask students to find contractions with *wh-* words in the reading on pages 19 and 20. Write the examples on the board.

4. Model the pronunciation of *wh-* questions in the chart. Be sure to exaggerate a falling intonation. Lead the class in a choral practice of the *wh-* question intonation.

1.11 *Wh-* Questions with *Be*

Examples				Explanation
Wh-Word	Be	Subject	Complement	A *wh-* question asks for information.
Where	**are**	Mom and Dad?		
Why	**are**	they	worried?	
How old	**is**	the teacher?		
Where	**is**	he	from?	
Why	**aren't**	you	sleepy?	

Question Words

Question	Answer	Meaning of Question Word
Who is your teacher? **Who** are those people?	My teacher is Rich Weiss. They're my parents.	Who = person
What is your classmate's name? **What** is that?	His name is Park. It's a cell phone.	What = thing
When is your test? **When** is the class over?	It's on Friday. It's over at 10 o'clock.	When = time
Why are they worried? **Why** aren't you in bed?	They're worried because you're alone. I'm not in bed because I'm not tired.	Why = reason
Where is your classmate from? **Where** are Mom and Dad now?	He's from Korea. They're at work.	Where = place
How is your life in the U.S.? **How** are you?	It's great! I'm fine.	How = description or health

Language Notes:
1. The *wh-* word + *is* can form a contraction: *who's, what's, when's, where's, how's, why's*
   We can't make a contraction for *which is*.
   We can't make a written contraction for a *wh-* word + *are*.
2. We usually end a *wh-* question with falling intonation. Listen to your teacher say the questions in the above boxes.

Grammar Variation

Activate students' prior knowledge. Say: *What wh- questions do you know?* (e.g., *What's your name? Where are you from?*) Write students' examples on the board. Have students cover up the questions column in grammar chart **1.11**. Ask volunteers to create questions from the answers in the chart (e.g., *Who is your teacher?*). Write examples on the board.

EXERCISE 26 Fill in the blanks with the correct question word and a form of *be*.

EXAMPLE _____*What's*_____ your name?
My name is Frank.

1. _____*Where's*_____ Los Angeles?
It's in California.

2. _____*When's*_____ your birthday?
It's in June.

3. _____*Who's*_____ your teacher?
My teacher is Martha Simms.

4. _____*What's*_____ a rose?
A rose is a flower.

5. _____*Why are*_____ you late?
I'm late because of traffic.

6. _____*Where are*_____ your sisters and brothers?
They're in my country.

7. _____*How are*_____ you?
I'm fine. And you?

8. _____*Where's*_____ the teacher's office?
It's on the second floor.

9. _____*Where are*_____ the restrooms?
The restrooms are at the end of the hall.

10. _____*When's*_____ Labor Day in the U.S.?
It's in September.

11. _____*Why are*_____ we here?
We're here because we want to learn English.

EXERCISE 27 Test your knowledge. Circle the correct answer to the following questions. The answers are at the end of the exercise. You may work with a partner.

1. Where's Dallas?
   a. in California   **b. in Texas**   c. in Illinois

2. When is American Independence Day?
   a. July 4   b. May 31   c. December 25

3. It's 8 a.m. in New York. What time is it in Los Angeles?
   a. 11 a.m.   **b. 5 a.m.**   c. 10 a.m.

4. On what day is Thanksgiving?
   a. on Friday   b. on Sunday   **c. on Thursday**

EXERCISE 26

1. Have students read the direction line. Ask: *What do we write in the blanks?* (question words and the verb *be*) Remind students to use contractions wherever possible. Go over the example in the book. Have a volunteer do #1. Students complete the exercise individually. Check the answers as a class.
2. If necessary, review grammar chart **1.11** on page 22.

EXERCISE 27

1. Tell students that this exercise is to test their knowledge of the U.S. Have students read the direction line. Say: *If you need to, you can use the map of the U.S. on page 24.* Point out the features of the map (e.g., state abbreviations, capital cities, time zones).
2. Have students complete the exercise in pairs. Then have pairs compare answers with other pairs. Circulate to observe pair work. Give help as needed.
3. If necessary, review grammar chart **1.11** on page 22.

To save class time, have students do half of the exercise in class and complete the other half for homework. Or assign the entire exercise for homework.

Expansion

Exercise 26 Have students practice asking and answering the questions from Exercise 26. Say: *Answer the questions with your own information.*

5. Which one of these is the name of a Great Lake?
   a. Mississippi   b. Missouri   (c. Michigan)

6. Where is the Statue of Liberty?
   a. in San Francisco   (b. in New York City)   c. in Los Angeles

7. What is the first day of summer?
   a. June 1   (b. June 21)   c. June 30

8. When is Labor Day in the U.S.?
   a. in May   b. in June   (c. in September)

9. What's the biggest state?
   (a. Alaska)   b. Texas   c. New York

Answers: 1b, 2a, 3b, 4c, 5c, 6b, 7b, 8c, 9a,

The United States of America

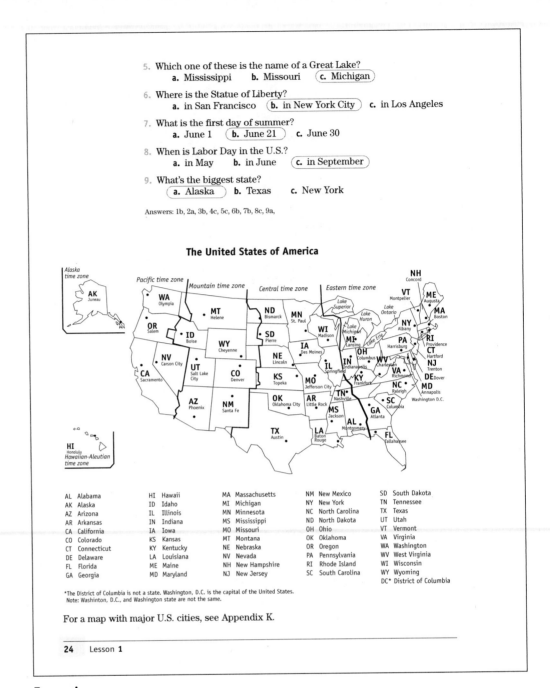

AL	Alabama	HI	Hawaii	MA	Massachusetts	NM	New Mexico	SD	South Dakota
AK	Alaska	ID	Idaho	MI	Michigan	NY	New York	TN	Tennessee
AZ	Arizona	IL	Illinois	MN	Minnesota	NC	North Carolina	TX	Texas
AR	Arkansas	IN	Indiana	MS	Mississippi	ND	North Dakota	UT	Utah
CA	California	IA	Iowa	MO	Missouri	OH	Ohio	VT	Vermont
CO	Colorado	KS	Kansas	MT	Montana	OK	Oklahoma	VA	Virginia
CT	Connecticut	KY	Kentucky	NE	Nebraska	OR	Oregon	WA	Washington
DE	Delaware	LA	Louisiana	NV	Nevada	PA	Pennsylvania	WV	West Virginia
FL	Florida	ME	Maine	NH	New Hampshire	RI	Rhode Island	WI	Wisconsin
GA	Georgia	MD	Maryland	NJ	New Jersey	SC	South Carolina	WY	Wyoming
								DC*	District of Columbia

*The District of Columbia is not a state. Washington, D.C. is the capital of the United States.
Note: Washinton, D.C., and Washington state are not the same.

For a map with major U.S. cities, see Appendix K.

Expansion

Exercise 27 Have students create a similar quiz with information from their own native countries. Have students exchange quizzes with a partner.

1.12 | Comparing Statements and Questions with *Be*

Affirmative Statements and Questions

Wh-Word	Be	Subject	Be	Complement	Short Answer
		Mom and Dad	are	out.	
	Are	they		at the store?	No, they aren't.
Where	are	they?			
		It	is	late.	
	Is	it		1 a.m.?	No, it isn't.
What time	is	it?			

Negative Statements and Questions

Wh-Word	Be + n't	Subject	Be + n't	Complement
		You	aren't	in bed.
Why	aren't	you		sleepy?
		He	isn't	in the U.S.
Why	isn't	he		with his parents?

EXERCISE 28 Respond to each statement with a question.

EXAMPLE Mom and Dad are not here. Where __*are they?*__

1. Mom and Dad are worried about you. Why __*are they worried?*__
2. I'm not sleepy. Why __*aren't you sleepy?*__
3. My teacher is great. Who __*'s your teacher?*__
4. My classes are early. When __*are they?*__
5. My roommate's name is hard to pronounce.
   What __*'s his name?*__
6. My cell phone isn't on. Why __*isn't it on?*__
7. Mom isn't in the kitchen. Where __*is she?*__

The Present Tense of the Verb *Be*; Preposition of Place; *This, That, These, Those*   **25**

1.12 | Comparing Statements and Questions with *Be*

1. Have students cover up grammar chart **1.12**. On the board, write: *Mom and Dad are out.* Ask: *What is the subject of this statement?* (*Mom and Dad*) Then write: *Are they at the store?* Ask: *What is the subject of this question?* (*they*) Write: *No, they aren't.* Ask: *What is the subject of the answer?* (*they*) Then write: *Where are they?* Ask: *What is the subject of this question?* (*they*)

2. Now have students look at grammar chart **1.12**. Point out that in questions, the verb comes before the subject. In information questions, question words always come at the beginning of the sentence.

3. Point out that negative statements and questions work the same way. The verb comes before the subject. Question words go at the beginning of a sentence.

EXERCISE 28

1. Have students read the direction line. Ask: *What are we going to write in the blanks?* (a verb and a subject) Go over the example.

2. Have students complete the exercise individually. Then have students compare answers in pairs. Check answers as a class.

3. If necessary, review grammar chart **1.12** on page 25.

Expansion

Exercise 28 Have students write three new statements. Students say their statement to a partner, the partner replies with a question. Then they switch roles. Circulate to observe pair work. Give help as needed.

1.13 | Questions with *What* and *How*

1. Have students cover up grammar chart **1.13.** Activate students' prior knowledge. Say: *Think of all the kinds of questions you can make with* what. Write examples from the students on the board. If students have trouble thinking of examples, give them hints. For example, point at a book and ask: *What questions can you ask about that book? (What color? What kind?)* Do the same thing with *how.* Or point at a student and say: *What questions can you ask about Suzy? (How old? How tall?)*

2. On the board, summarize all of the *what* and *how* questions students came up with (*What time? What color? What day?*).

3. Have students look at grammar chart **1.13,** and have them compare their lists on the board with the lists in the grammar chart. Review the examples. Point out that *what* can ask for a description. Review the nouns that can be followed by *what* (*nationality, day, time,* etc.). Do the same with *how.* Point out that *how* is used to ask for descriptions and to ask about the weather. Review the adjectives and adverbs that can follow *how* (*old, tall, long,* etc.).

4. Go over the Usage Notes. Remind students that Americans still use inches, feet, miles, etc., to measure length and distance. Ask a student: *How tall are you?* If a student doesn't know his/her height in feet and inches, offer to measure him/her. Demonstrate the typical way Americans say their height: *I'm 5 foot 8* (i.e., *not* 5 feet 8). Other students might want to know their height in inches. Have students measure each other's height.

5. Mention that asking *How are you?* is often another way of saying *hello.*

1.13 | Questions with *What* and *How*

Examples	Explanation

What is a verb?
   It's an action word.
 	
 What is the Dean's List?
   It's a list of the best students.
	What can ask for a definition.

What nationality is the teacher?
   She's American.
 	
 What day is today?
   It's Friday.
 	
 What time is it?
   It's 4:15 p.m.
 	
 What color is the dictionary?
   It's yellow.
 	
 What kind of book is this?
   It's a grammar book.
	A noun can follow *what:*
	 • *what nationality*
	 • *what day*
	 • *what time*
	 • *what color*
	 • *what kind (of)*
	 • *what month*

How is your new class?
   It's great.
 	
 How is the weather today?
   It's cool.
	We can use *how* to ask for a description.
	
	 We use *how* to ask about the weather.

How old is your brother?
   He's 16 (years old).
 	
 How tall are you?
   I'm 5 feet, 3 inches tall.
 	
 How long is this course?
   It's 16 weeks long.
 	
 How long is the table?
   It's 3 feet long.
 	
 How much is the college tuition?
   It's $75 per credit hour.
	An adjective or adverb can follow *how:*
	 • *how old*
	 • *how tall*
	 • *how long*
	 • *how much*
	 • *how big*
	 • *how fast*

Usage Notes:
1. For height, Americans use feet (') and inches (").
 He's 5 feet, 8 inches tall. OR He's five-eight. OR He's 5'8".[4]
2. *How are you?* is often just a way to say hello. People usually answer, "Fine, thanks. How are you?"

[4]See Appendix G for conversion from feet and inches to centimeters.

Grammar Variation

Have students cover up grammar chart **1.13.** Write the statements from the grammar chart on the board (e.g., *She's American, It's Friday, It's 4:15*) and have students try to guess the question word and/or question for the statement.

EXERCISE **29**   Fill in the blanks to complete the questions.

EXAMPLE   How ___old are___ your parents? They're in their 50s.

1. What _____time is_____ it? It's 3 o'clock.
2. What ___kind of___ car ___is___ that?
That's a Japanese car.
3. What ___kind of___ words ___are___ *tall, old,*
new, and *good?* They're adjectives.
4. What ___color's___ your new car? It's dark blue.
5. How ___old's your son___ ? My son is 10 years old.
6. How ___tall is your brother___ ? My brother is 6 feet tall.
7. How ___old are you___ ? I'm 25 years old.
8. How ___much is that car___ ? That car is $10,000.
9. How ___long is that movie___ ? The movie is 2 ½ hours long.

EXERCISE **30**   ABOUT YOU Fill in the blanks to make true statements about
yourself. Then find a partner from a different country, if possible,
and interview your partner by asking questions with the words in
parentheses ( ).

EXAMPLE   I'm from ___Bosnia___. (Where)

A: I'm from Bosnia. Where are you from?
B: I'm from Taiwan.

1. My name is _____Answers will vary._____. (What)
2. I'm from _____. (Where)
3. The president / prime minister of my country is _____
_____. (Who)
4. The flag from my country is _____. (What colors)
5. My country is in _____. (Where)
   (continent or region)
6. I'm _____ feet, _____ inches tall. (How tall)
7. My birthday is in _____. (When)
   (month)
8. My favorite TV show is _____. (What)

The Present Tense of the Verb *Be*; Preposition of Place; *This, That, These, Those*   **27**

EXERCISE 29

1. Have students read the direction
line. Go over the example in the
book. Do #1 as a class.
2. Have students complete the
exercise individually. Then check
the answers as a class.
3. If necessary, review grammar chart
1.13 on page 26.

EXERCISE 30

1. Tell students that this exercise is
about them and their native
countries. Have students read the
direction line. Say: *Complete the*
statements with your own
information. Go over the example.
Model the example with a volunteer.
2. Have students complete the
statements individually. Then have
students ask and answer questions
in pairs. If possible, put students
from different countries in pairs.
Circulate to observe pair work. Give
help as needed.
3. If necessary, review grammar chart
1.13 on page 26.

To save class time, have
students do half of the exercise
in class and complete the other half for
homework. Or assign the entire
exercise for homework. If time allows,
have students interview a partner in
class.

Expansion

Exercise 30 Create two rings of students. Have half of the students stand in an outer ring
around the classroom. Have the other half stand in an inner ring, facing the outer ring. Instruct
students to ask and answer the questions from Exercise 30. Call out *"turn"* every minute or so.
Students in the inner ring should move one space clockwise. Students now ask and answer
with their new partners. Say: *Ask questions in random order.* Make sure students look up at
each other when they're speaking.

1. Tell students that in this exercise Cindy and Maria talk about their classes. Have students read the direction line. Say: *Complete the statements with your own information.* Go over the example.

2. Have students complete Exercise 31 individually. Check answers as a class.

3. Then have students practice the conversation. Circulate to observe pair work. Give help as needed.

4. If necessary, review grammar chart **1.13** on page 26.

🕐 To save class time, have students do half of the exercise in class and complete the other half for homework. Or assign the entire exercise for homework.

EXERCISE 31 Complete the following phone conversation between Cindy (C) and Maria (M).

🎧

C: Hello?

M: Hi, Cindy. This is Maria.

C: Hi, Maria. ___How are you___ ?
　　　　　　　　(example)

M: I'm fine.

C: ___Is this___ your first day of class?
　　　(1)

M: Yes, it is. I'm at school now, but I'm not in class.

C: Why ___aren't you___ in class?
　　　　(2)

M: Because it's break time now.

C: How ___long's___ the break?
　　　　(3)

M: It's 10 minutes long.

C: How ___'s your English class___ ?
　　　　(4)

M: My English class is great. My classmates are very interesting.

C: Where ___are they___ from?
　　　　(5)

M: They're from all over the world.

C: ___Is your teacher___ American?
　　　(6)

M: Yes. My teacher is American. What time ___is it___ ?
　　　　　　　　　　　　　　　　　　(7)

C: It's 3:35.

M: Oh, I'm late.

C: Let's get together soon. ___Are you___ free this weekend?
　　　　　　　　　　　　　　　(8)

M: I'm free on Saturday afternoon.

C: I have a class on Saturday.

M: When ___are you___ free?
　　　　　(9)

C: How about Sunday afternoon?

M: Sunday's fine. Talk to you later.

Exercise 31 Variation

To provide practice with listening skills, have students close their books and listen to the audio. Say: *You will hear a phone conversation between Cindy and Maria.* Repeat the audio as needed. Ask comprehension questions, such as: *Where is Maria right now?* (at school) *Is she in class?* (no) *What is she doing?* (taking a break) Then have students open their books and complete Exercise 31.

Expansion

Exercise 31 Have students create a new conversation for Cindy and Maria. Cindy and Maria are going to get together on Sunday afternoon. Maria is going to ask questions about Cindy's class on Saturday. Have volunteers do a role-play in front of the class.

IN THE SCHOOL CAFETERIA

Before You Read

1. Do you like American food?

2. Do you eat in the school cafeteria?

Read the following conversation between an American (A) student and his Chinese (C) roommate. Pay special attention to *this, that, these, those*.

A: Is **this** your first time in an American college?
C: Yes, it is.
A: Let me show you around the cafeteria. **This** is the cafeteria for students. **That's** the cafeteria for teachers. The vending machines are in **that** room. When the food service is closed, **that** room is always open.
C: The food is in a machine?
A: Yes. And **that's** the change machine. **This** is the line for hot food.
C: What are **those**?
A: They're tacos.
C: **Tacos**? What are **tacos**?
A: They're Mexican food.
C: What's **that**?
A: It's pizza. It's Italian food.
C: What's **this**?
A: It's chop suey. It's a Chinese dish.
C: I'm from China, and I'm sure **this** is not a Chinese dish. Where's the American food in America?
A: This *is* American food—Mexican, Italian, Chinese—it's all American food.
C: Where are the chopsticks?
A: Uh . . . chopsticks? **Those** are the forks and knives, but there are no chopsticks here.

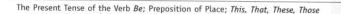

The Present Tense of the Verb *Be*; Preposition of Place; *This, That, These, Those*   **29**

Reading Variation

To practice listening skills, have students first listen to the audio alone. Ask a few comprehension questions. Repeat the audio if necessary. Then have students open their books and read along as they listen to the audio.

Reading Glossary

chopsticks: two thin sticks used to take hold of food and put it in the mouth
vending machine: a machine that gives packaged food, soft drinks, or other items after coins are placed in it

In the School Cafeteria (Reading)

1. Have students look at the illustrations. Ask: *Who are the people?* (two students) *What are they doing?* (They're going to the cafeteria. They're getting lunch in the cafeteria.)
2. Have students look at the title of the reading. Ask: *What is the reading about? How do you know?* Have students make predictions.
3. Pre-teach any vocabulary words your students may not know, such as *vending machine* and *chopsticks*.

BEFORE YOU READ

1. Have students discuss the questions in pairs.
2. Ask for a few volunteers to share their answers with the class.

To save class time, skip "Before You Read" or have students prepare answers for homework ahead of time.

Reading CD 1, Track 6

1. Have students read the text silently. Point out that this is a conversation between an American student and his Chinese roommates. Tell students to pay special attention to *this, that, these,* and *those*. Then play the audio and have students read along silently.
2. Check students' comprehension. Ask questions, such as: *Is there a cafeteria for teachers?* (yes) *What kind of food do they have in the cafeteria?* (Mexican, Italian, and Chinese) *Does the cafeteria have chopsticks?* (no)

To save class time, have students do the reading for homework ahead of time.

1.14 | This, That, These, Those

1. Have students cover up grammar chart **1.14**. Activate students' prior knowledge. Ask volunteers to demonstrate *this, that, these,* and *those*. Write their examples on the board. Say: This, that, these, *and* those *are used to identify nouns.*

2. Have students look at grammar chart **1.14**. Review the example sentences in the grammar chart. Demonstrate the adjectives again—exaggerating distances. Point out that once you identify a noun—you can use a pronoun in the second sentence.

3. Direct students to the Language Note. Explain that *that is* can be contracted to *that's.* Point out that you cannot contract *this, these,* or *those.*

4. Explain that you use *this, that, these, those* in front of nouns to indicate specific nouns.

EXERCISE 32

1. Tell students that in this exercise they are showing a new student the cafeteria. Have students read the direction line. Ask: *What do we put in the blanks?* (*this, that, these,* or *those* and a verb). Remind students to use contractions where they can. Go over the example.

2. Have students complete the exercise individually. Check answers as a class.

3. If necessary, review grammar chart **1.14** on page 30.

1.14 | *This, That, These, Those*

Examples		Explanation
Singular	**This** is pizza.	Use *this* and *these* to identify near objects and people.
Plural	**These** are tacos.	
Singular	**That** is the change machine.	Use *that* and *those* to identify far objects and people.
Plural	**Those** are forks and knives.	
This is pizza. **It's** an Italian food.		After we identify a noun, we can use subject pronouns.
Those are knives and forks. **They're** clean.		
That's my teacher. **She's** a nice woman.		
That room is for the teachers.		A noun can follow *this, that, these, those.*
Those forks are clean.		

Language Note: Only *that is* can form a contraction in writing: ***That's*** the change machine.

EXERCISE 32   Imagine that you are showing a new student the school cafeteria. Use *this, that, these,* and *those,* and a form of *be* to complete each statement. The arrows indicate if the item is near or far.

EXAMPLES   _____This is_____ the school cafeteria. →

    _____Those are_____ the clean dishes. ——————→

1. _____These are_____ the trays. →
2. _____This is_____ today's special. →
3. _____These are_____ the napkins. →
4. _____Those are_____ the forks, knives, and spoons. ——————→
5. _____This is_____ the cashier. →
6. _____Those are_____ the vending machines. ——————→
7. _____That is_____ the eating area. ——————→
8. _____That is_____ the teachers' section. ——————→

Grammar Variation

Have students go through the reading to find one example of *this, that, these,* or *those.* Ask volunteers to explain the usage.

Expansion

Exercise 32 Have students do a role-play. One partner is a new student and the other partner is showing him or her around. Say: *You can create a dialogue about any place in the school: this classroom, the computer or language lab, the gym, etc.* Circulate to observe pair work. Give help as needed. Have volunteers perform in front of the class.

1. Uses of *Be*

DESCRIPTION:	Chicago **is** big.
IDENTIFICATION / CLASSIFICATION:	This **is** Chicago. It **is** a city.
LOCATION:	Chicago **is** in Illinois.
PLACE OF ORIGIN:	The teacher **is** from Chicago.
AGE:	I **am** 25 (years old).
PHYSICAL OR MENTAL CONDITION:	He **is** hungry. I **am** thirsty. She **is** worried.
TIME:	It **is** 6 p.m.
WEATHER:	It **is** warm today.

2. Subject Pronouns

I we he she it you they

3. Contractions

Subject pronoun + form of *be:* I'm, you're, he's, she's, it's, we're, they're
Subject noun + *is:* the teacher's, Tom's, Mary's
Is or *are* + *not:* isn't, aren't
Wh- word + *is:* what's, when's, where's, why's, how's

4. *This / That / These / Those*

This is an English book.
These are pencils.
That is a pen.
Those are pens.

5. Articles *a / an*

Chicago is **a** big city.
Puerto Rico is **an** island.

6. Statements and Questions with *Be*

AFFIRMATIVE:	She **is** busy.
NEGATIVE:	She **isn't** lazy.
YES/NO QUESTION:	**Is** she busy on Saturday?
SHORT ANSWER:	No, she **isn't.**
WH- QUESTION:	When **is** she busy?
NEGATIVE QUESTION:	Why **isn't** she busy on Saturday?
AFFIRMATIVE:	You **are** late.
NEGATIVE:	You **aren't** on time.
YES/NO QUESTION:	**Are** you OK?
SHORT ANSWER:	Yes, I **am.**
WH- QUESTION:	Why **are** you late?
NEGATIVE QUESTION:	Why **aren't** you on time?

The Present Tense of the Verb *Be*; Preposition of Place; *This, That, These, Those*   **31**

Summary of Lesson 1

1. **Uses of *Be*** Review the uses of *be*. Say: *Go to the reading on page 2. Find a sentence for each use of* be. If necessary, have students review:
   1.2   Uses of *Be* (p. 4)
   1.6   *Be* with Descriptions (p. 10)
   1.7   *Be* with Definitions (p. 11)
   1.8   Prepositions (pp. 14-15).

2. **Subject Pronouns** Have students close their books. Instruct students to write a sentence for each subject pronoun. If necessary, have students review:
   1.4   The Subject (p. 6).

3. **Contractions** Have students write eight negative sentences with the verb *be* with different pronouns using both forms of negative contractions. Then, have students write one question for each *wh-* question word. If necessary, have students review:
   1.5   Contractions with *Be* (p. 8)
   1.9   Negative Statements with *Be* (p. 15)
   1.11 Question Words (p. 22).

4. ***This / That / These / Those*** Have students practice *this, that, these, those* in pairs. Say: *Your partner is a new student in this classroom. Show him or her around the classroom.* If necessary, have students review:
   1.14 *This, That, These, Those* (p. 30).

5. **Articles *a / an*** Play a chain game. Have students sit in a circle. The first person says his/her name and some other information (e.g., *I'm John. I'm a mechanic.*) The second person repeats the first person's information and adds his/her own (e.g., *He's John. He's a mechanic. I'm Marta; I'm a…*). If necessary, have students review:
   1.7   *Be* with Definitions (p. 11).

6. **Statements and Questions with *Be*** Have pairs create a dialogue using forms of *be*. Say: *Use affirmative and negative statements,* yes/no *questions, information questions, and short answers. Use contractions wherever possible.* Have students practice their dialogues. If necessary, have students review:
   1.9   Negative Statements with *Be* (p. 15)
   1.10 *Be* in *Yes/No* Questions and Short Answers (p. 20)
   1.11 *Wh-* Questions with Be (p. 22)
   1.13 Questions with *What* and *How* (p. 26).

Editing Advice

Have students close their books. Write the example sentences without editing marks or corrections on the board. For example:

1. *My father he lives in Australia.*
2. *Is small Cuba.*

Ask students to correct each sentence and explain the grammar rule that applies. This activity can be done individually, in pairs, or as a class. After students have corrected each sentence, tell them to turn to pages 32–33. Say: *Now compare your work with the Editing Advice in the book.*

EDITING ADVICE

1. Don't repeat the subject with a pronoun.

   My father ~~he~~ lives in Australia.

2. Use correct word order. Put the subject at the beginning of the statement.

   ~~Cuba is small.~~
   ~~Is small Cuba.~~

3. Use the correct word order. Put the adjective before the noun.

   ~~small country.~~
   Cuba is a ~~country small.~~

4. Use the correct word order in a question.

   ~~is he~~
   Where ~~he is~~ from?

5. Every sentence has a verb. Don't omit *be*.

   is
   My sister ⌃ a teacher.

6. Every sentence has a subject. For time and weather, the subject is *it*.

   It's
   ~~Is~~ 6 o'clock now.
   It's
   ~~Is~~ very cold today.

7. Don't confuse *your* (possession) with *you're*, the contraction for *you are*.

   You're
   ~~Your~~ a good teacher.

8. Don't confuse *this* and *these*.

   This
   ~~These~~ is my coat.
   These
   ~~This~~ are my shoes.

9. The plural of the subject pronoun *it* is *they*, not *its*.

   They're
   Dogs are friendly animals. ~~Its~~ good pets.

10. Use *the* before *U.S.* and *United States*.

    the
    My sister is in ⌃ U.S.

11. Use a singular verb after *the U.S.*

    The U.S. ~~are~~ *is* a big country.

12. Do not use a contraction for *am not.*

    ~~I amn't~~ *I'm not* an American.

13. Put the apostrophe in place of the missing letter.

    She ~~is'nt~~ *isn't* here today.

14. Use an apostrophe, not a comma, for a contraction.

    ~~I,m~~ *I'm* a good student.

15. Use the article *a* or *an* before a singular noun.

    New York is *a* big city.

    San Francisco is *an* interesting city.

16. Don't use *a* before plural nouns.

    July and August are a warm months.

17. Don't use the article *a* before an adjective with no noun.

    New York is a big.

18. Use *an* before a vowel sound.

    Puerto Rico is *an* ~~a~~ island.

19. Don't make an adjective plural.

    My daughters are beautifuls.

20. Don't make a contraction with *is* after *s, z, sh,* or *ch* sounds.

    Los Angeles~~'s~~ *is* a big city.

21. For age, use a number only or a number + *years old.*

    He's 12 years. **OR** *He's 12 years old.*

22. Don't use a contraction for a short *yes* answer.

    Are you from Mexico? Yes, ~~I'm~~ *I am*.

23. Don't separate *how* from the adjective or adverb.

    ~~How is he old?~~ *old is he?*

Lesson 1 Test/Review

For additional practice, review, and assessment materials, see Assessment CD-ROM with *ExamView Pro, More Grammar Practice* Workbook 1, Interactive CD-ROM, and Web site http://elt.thomson.com/gic

PART 1

1. Part 1 may be used in addition to the Assessment CD-ROM with *ExamView Pro* as an in-class test to assess student performance. Have students read the direction line. Ask: *Does every sentence have a mistake?* (no) Review the examples.
2. Collect for assessment.
3. If necessary, have students review: **Lesson 1.**

PART 1 Find the mistakes with the underlined words and correct them. Not every sentence has a mistake. If the sentence is correct, write *C*.

EXAMPLES He,s my brother. *(He's)*

Chicago's a big city. *C*

1. New York and Los Angeles are a big cities.
2. The teacher's not here today. *C*
3. She is'nt in the library.
4. I amn't from Pakistan. I'm from India. *(I'm not)*
5. The students they are very smart.
6. We are intelligents students.
7. We're not hungry. We aren't thirsty. *C*
8. It's warm today. *C*
9. I'm from Ukraine. My wife from Poland. *(is)*
10. My little brother is 10 years. *(old)*
11. French's a beautiful language. *(is)*
12. It's 4:35 now. *C*
13. Your in the U.S. now. *(You're)*
14. These is a good book. *(This)*
15. These are my pencils. *C*
16. Those dogs are beautiful. Its friendly. *(They're)*
17. I live in U.S. *(the)*
18. January is cold month. *(a)*
19. My father is a tall.
20. New York City and Los Angeles are bigs. *(cities)*
21. This is a interesting book. *(an)*
22. Is he from Peru? Yes, he's. *(he is)*
23. Chicago it's a big city. *(is)*

Lesson Review

To use Part 1 as a review, assign it as homework or use it as an in-class activity to be completed individually or in pairs. Check answers and review errors as a class. Reteach grammar points that students haven't mastered. Then student learning may be assessed using a test generated from the Assessment CD-ROM with *ExamView Pro*.

PART **2** Find the mistakes with word order and correct them. Not every sentence has a mistake. If the sentence is correct, write *C.*

EXAMPLES I have a book new.
She is 25 years old. *C*

1. Is very long this book.
2. She has a car very beautiful.
3. Why you are late?
4. How old are you? *C*
5. What nationality your wife is?
6. What color is your new coat? *C*
7. Why the teacher is absent?
8. Is your father a doctor? *C*

PART **3** Fill in the blanks to complete this conversation. Not all blanks need a word. If the blank doesn't need a word, write Ø.

A: Where are you ___from___ ?
(example)

B: I'm from ___Ø___ Mexico.
(example)

A: Are you happy in ___the___ U.S.?
(1)

B: Yes. I ___am___ . The U.S. is ___a___ great country.
(2)   (3)

A: ___Are you___ from ___a___ big city?
(4)   (5)

B: Yes. I'm from Mexico City. It's ___a___ very big city. This city is
(6)

___Ø___ big and beautiful too. But ___it's___ cold in the winter.
(7)   (8)

A: ___Is your roommate___ from Mexico too?
(9)

B: No, my roommate ___'s___ from Taiwan. I'm happy in the
(10)

U.S., but he ___isn't___ happy here.
(11)

A: Why ___isn't he___ happy?
(12)

The Present Tense of the Verb *Be*; Preposition of Place; *This, That, These, Those* **35**

---

1. Part 2 may also be used as an in-class test to assess student performance, in addition to the Assessment CD-ROM with *ExamView Pro.* Have students read the direction line. Ask: *What kind of mistakes will we find?* (word order) *Are there mistakes in every sentence?* (no) Review the example.
2. Have students complete the exercise individually. Collect for assessment.
3. If necessary, have students review: **1.3** Word Order with *Be* (p. 5).

PART 3

1. Part 3 may also be used as an in-class test to assess student performance, in addition to the Assessment CD-ROM with *ExamView Pro.* Tell students that this is a conversation between two students. Review the example.
2. Have students complete individually. Collect for assessment.
3. If necessary, have students review: **Lesson 1.**

Lesson Review

To use Parts 2 and 3 as a review, assign them as homework or use them as in-class activities to be completed individually or in pairs. Check answers and review errors as a class. For Part 3, have students practice the conversation in pairs. Circulate to observe pair work. Give help as needed. Reteach grammar points that students haven't mastered. Then student learning may be assessed using a test generated from the Assessment CD-ROM with *ExamView Pro.*

1. Part 4 may also be used as an in-class test to assess student performance, in addition to the Assessment CD-ROM with *ExamView Pro*. Have students read the direction line. Ask: *Do we make a contraction for everything?* (no) Review the examples.
2. Have students complete the exercise individually. Collect for assessment.
3. If necessary, have students review:
   1.5 Contractions with *Be* (p. 8)
   1.9 Negative statements with *Be* (p. 15)
   1.11 Question Words (p. 22)
   1.14 *This, That, These, Those* (p. 30).

1. Part 5 may also be used as an in-class test to assess student performance, in addition to the Assessment CD-ROM with *ExamView Pro*. Tell students that this is a conversation between two students. Review the example.
2. Have students complete individually. Collect for assessment.
3. If necessary, have students review: **Lesson 1.**

B: He ___'s___ homesick. His parents ___are___ in Taiwan.
(13)   (14)

He ___'s___ alone here.
(15)

A: How ___old is he___ ?
(16)

B: He's very young. He ___'s___ only 18 years ___old___ .
(17)   (18)

A: What ___'s___ his name?
(19)

B: His name ___'s___ Lu.
(20)

PART 4 Write a contraction of the words shown. If it's not possible to make a contraction, put an *X* in the blank.

EXAMPLES   she is ___she's___
English is ___X___

1. we are ___we're___
2. you are not ___you aren't/you're not___
3. I am not ___I'm not___
4. they are ___they're___
5. this is ___X___
6. Los Angeles is ___X___
7. Mary is not ___Mary isn't/Mary's not___
8. he is not ___he isn't/he's not___
9. what is ___what's___
10. what are ___X___

PART 5 Read the conversation between two students, Sofia (S) and Danuta (D). They are talking about their classes and teachers. Fill in the blanks.

D: Hi, Sofia. How's your English class?

S: Hi, Danuta. It___'s___ wonderful. I ___'m___ very happy with it.
(example)   (1)

D: ___I___'m in level 3. What level ___are you___ in?
(2)   (3)

S: I'___m___ in level 2.
(4)

D: My English teacher ___'s___ Ms. Kathy James. ___She's___ a very
(5)   (6)

good teacher. Who ___'s your English teacher___ ?
(7)

Lesson Review

To use Part 4 as a review, assign it as homework or use it as an in-class activity to be completed individually or in pairs. Check answers and review errors as a class. Reteach grammar points that students haven't mastered. Then student learning may be assessed using a test generated from the Assessment CD-ROM with *ExamView Pro*.

S: Mr. Bob Kane is my English teacher. __He's__ very good, too.
(8)

D: __Is he__ an old man?
(9)

S: No, he __isn't__. He's __a__ young man. He __'s__
(10)   (11)   (12)

about 25 years __old__. How __old is Ms. James__?
(13)   (14)

D: Ms. James __is__ about 50 years old.
(15)

S: How __tall is she__?
(16)

D: She's about 5 feet, 6 inches tall.

S: Is she American?

D: Yes, she __is__. She's from New York.
(17)

S: __Is your class big__?
(18)

D: Yes. My class is very big. The students __are__ from many
(19)

countries. Ten students __are__ from Asia, six students
(20)

__are__ from Europe, one student __'s__ from Africa, and
(21)   (22)

five are __from__ Central America. Is your class big?
(23)

S: No, it __isn't__.
(24)

D: Where __are the students from__?
(25)

S: The students __are__ all from the same country. We __'re__
(26)   (27)

from Russia.

D: __Is Mr. Kane__ Russian?
(28)

S: No. Mr. Kane isn't Russian. He's from Canada, but he's __an__
(29)

American citizen now.

The Present Tense of the Verb *Be*; Preposition of Place; *This, That, These, Those*   **37**

Lesson Review

To use Part 5 as a review, assign it as homework or use it as an in-class activity to be completed individually or in pairs. Check answers and review errors as a class. Then practice the conversation in pairs. Circulate to observe pair work. Give help as needed. Reteach grammar points that students haven't mastered. Then student learning may be assessed using a test generated from the Assessment CD-ROM with *ExamView Pro*.

Expansion Activities

These expansion activities provide opportunities for students to interact with one another and further develop their speaking and writing skills. Encourage students to use grammar from this Lesson whenever possible.

🕐 To save class time, assign parts of the activities as homework. Then use class time for interaction and communication. If students do not need additional speaking practice, some of the activities may be assigned as writing activities for homework, or skipped altogether.

CLASSROOM ACTIVITIES

1. Ask: *What verb do we use to describe ourselves?* (be) Have students complete their descriptions individually.
2. Instruct students to choose a famous person that the class would know. Have students complete the descriptions with a partner. Circulate to observe pair work. Give help as needed.
3. Try to pair students of different nationalities, if possible. If necessary, provide the option of writing out the questions before asking a partner. Ask volunteers to share what they learned about their partners.

D: _____ Is that Mr. Kane _____?
(30)

S: No. That's not Mr. Kane. That ____'s____ my husband. I ____'m____
(31)   (32)

late! See you later.

EXPANSION ACTIVITIES

Classroom Activities

1. Write a few sentences about yourself. Give your height, a physical description, your nationality, your occupation, your age (optional), your gender (man or woman). Put the papers in a box. The teacher will read each paper. Guess which classmate is described.

   EXAMPLE   I'm 5 feet, 8 inches tall.
   I'm Mexican.
   I'm thin.
   I'm 21 years old.

2. Work with a partner. Describe a famous person (an actor, a singer, an athlete, a politician). Report your description to the class. Do not give the person's name. See if your classmates can guess who it is.

   EXAMPLE   He is a former basketball player.
   He's tall.
   He's famous.
   He's an African American.

3. Check the words that describe you. Find a partner and ask each other questions using these words. See how many things you have in common. Tell the class something interesting you learned about your partner.

   a. ____ happy
   b. ____ from Africa
   c. ____ from Asia
   d. ____ from Europe
   e. ____ interested in politics
   f. ____ a grandparent
   g. ____ under 20 years old
   h. ____ in love
   i. ____ afraid to speak English
   j. ____ an only child[5]
   k. ____ from the capital of my country
   l. ____ an American citizen
   m. ____ hungry
   n. ____ married
   o. ____ athletic

   [5]An *only child* has no sisters or brothers.

Classroom Activities Variation

Activity 1 Have students write additional information about their families (e.g., *My husband is a pilot.*).

---

4. Fill in the blanks. Then find a partner and read your sentences to your partner. See how many times you match your partner's sentence.

a. Love is _____

b. This city is _____

c. Children are _____

d. The teacher is _____

e. Money is _____

f. The American president is _____

g. My friends are _____

h. I am _____

i. Public transportation in this city is _____

j. This book is _____

5. Work with a partner from the same country, if possible. Fill in a few items for each category. Report some information to the class.

EXAMPLE Typical of the U.S.

Common last names	Common cars	Popular tourist attractions	Popular sports	Language(s)	Capital city	Other big cities
Johnson Wilson	Ford Chevy Toyota	Disneyland Grand Canyon	baseball basketball football	English	Washington	New York Los Angeles Chicago

Typical of _____ (your country)

Common last names	Common cars	Popular tourist attractions	Popular sports	Language(s)	Capital city	Other big cities

The Present Tense of the Verb *Be*; Preposition of Place; *This, That, These, Those*   **39**

CLASSROOM ACTIVITIES (*cont.*)

4. Have students write their sentences individually. Then have students compare their opinions with a partner. Say: *Raise your hand if your partner's opinions are the same as yours.* Circulate to observe pair work. Give help as needed.

5. Ask: *How much do you know about your native country?* Have students work in pairs. If possible, put students from the same country together. Have volunteers report interesting information to the class (e.g., Disneyland is a popular tourist attraction in the U.S.).

Classroom Activities Variation

Activity 5 Have students make brochures about their countries. Encourage students to use drawings, pictures, photos, and other materials to illustrate their brochures. Display the brochures around the class for everyone to see. Ask volunteers to talk about their countries.

WRITE ABOUT IT

Ask students to turn to Exercise 21 on page 18. Say: *Write a paragraph using this information about yourself. Write both negative and affirmative sentences.* Review the model with the students. Collect for assessment and/or have students present their paragraphs to a group.

OUTSIDE ACTIVITY

Tell students that they will be interviewing a native English speaker. Students can report their interview to the class or hand in a written report.

INTERNET ACTIVITY

Ask: *How did you find out about this class? Did anyone find out information by looking on the Internet?* Tell students to find information on the Internet about other schools, colleges, or universities they're interested in. Ask them to visit the Web site of at least one program. Say: *Write down the information from their home page.* Have students discuss programs in groups.

Write About it

Write a paragraph using Exercise 21 as a model. For every negative statement that you write, add an affirmative statement. You may add other information, too.

EXAMPLE

> My name is Mohammad. I'm not from an English speaking country. I'm from Iran. I'm not a student at City College. I'm a student at Roosevelt University. I'm in English class now....

Outside Activity

Interview a native speaker of English (a neighbor, a coworker, another student or a teacher at this college). Ask him or her the following questions. Report this person's answers to the class.

  a. What city are you from?
  b. Are your parents or grandparents from another country? Where are they from?
  c. Is most of your family in this city?
  d. Are you happy with this city? Why or why not?
  e. What are your favorite places in this city?

Internet Activity

Using the Internet, find the Web site of a college you are interested in. Or find the Web site of the college or school you are at now. What information is on the home page? What links are on the home page?

 Additional Activities at http://elt.thomson.com/gic

Write About it Variation

Have students exchange first drafts with a partner. Ask students to help their partners edit their drafts. Refer students to the Editing Advice on pages 32–33.

Outside Activity Variation

As an alternative, you may invite a guest to your classroom (e.g., an administrator, a librarian, or a service worker at your school) and have students do a class interview. Students should prepare their interview questions ahead of time.

Internet Activity Variation

Have students develop a Web site home page on paper about your class. Say: *When you write the Web site, try to use all that we have learned about* be.

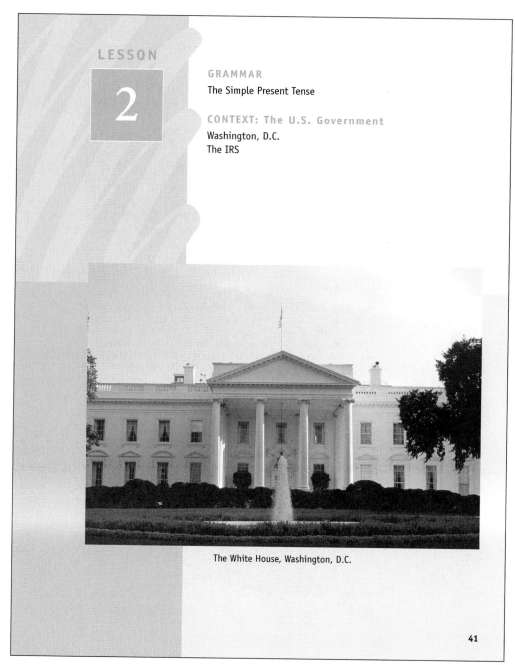

LESSON

2

GRAMMAR
The Simple Present Tense

CONTEXT: The U.S. Government
Washington, D.C.
The IRS

The White House, Washington, D.C.

41

Lesson | 2

Lesson Overview

GRAMMAR

1. Ask: *What tense did we study in Lesson 1?* (the present tense of the verb *be*) *What tense are we going to study in this lesson?* (the simple present tense) *Can anyone make a sentence in the simple present tense?* Have students give examples. Write them on the board.

CONTEXT

1. Ask: *What will we learn about in this lesson?* (the U.S. government; Washington, D.C.; the IRS) Activate students' prior knowledge. Ask: *What do you know about the U.S. government? Has anyone been to Washington, D.C.? What is the IRS?* (the Internal Revenue Service)
2. Have students share their knowledge and personal experiences.

Photo

1. Direct students' attention to the photo. Ask: *What is this building?* (the White House) *Where is it?* (1600 Pennsylvania Ave., Washington, D.C.) *Who lives there?* (the president and his family) Bring in a street map of Washington, D.C., and have students locate the White House and other points of interest they may know on the map.
2. Ask: *Have you ever visited the White House? What is the presidential home like in your native country?*

To save class time, have students do the Test/Review at the end of the lesson, or administer a lesson test generated from the Assessment CD-ROM with *ExamView® Pro.* Skip sections of the lesson that students have already mastered. You may also assign some sections for self-study for extra credit.

Expansion

Theme The topic for this lesson can be enhanced with the following ideas:

1. Postcards from Washington, D.C.
2. Brochures/books about the White House
3. Street map of Washington, D.C.

Culture Note

George Washington, the first president of the U.S., never resided in the White House, although he did oversee its construction. John Adams, the second president of the U.S., was the first resident of the White House. The White House is the only private residence of a head of state to be open to the public free of charge. This practice has been in place since Thomas Jefferson's presidency.

Washington, D.C. (Reading)

1. Have students look at the photos. Ask: *Do you know who Lincoln is?* (the sixteenth president of the United States) *Do you know what the Capitol is?* (the building where the U.S. Congress meets) *Do you know what the Vietnam War Memorial looks like?* (a large wall with a list of all the names of the people who died in the Vietnam War) *Have you visited any of these places?*

2. Have students look at the title of the reading. Ask: *What is the reading about? How do you know?* Have students use the title, pictures, and the map to make predictions about the reading.

3. Preteach any vocabulary words your students may not know, such as *capital, district, factories, subway,* and *law.*

BEFORE YOU READ

1. Have students discuss the questions in pairs.

2. Ask for a few volunteers to share their answers with the class.

🕐 To save class time, skip "Before You Read" or have students prepare answers for homework ahead of time.

Reading 🎧 *CD 1, Track 7*

1. Have students read the text silently. Tell them to pay special attention to the present tense verbs. Then play the audio and have students read along silently.

2. Check students' comprehension. Ask questions such as: *Is Washington, D.C., a state?* (no) *Are there tall buildings in Washington?* (no) *Who works in the Capitol?* (state senators and representatives)

🕐 To save class time, have students do the reading for homework ahead of time.

WASHINGTON, D.C.

 Before You Read

1. What capital cities do you know?
2. What do you know about Washington, D.C.?

 The Lincoln Memorial    The Capitol    The Vietnam War Memorial

🎧 Read the following article. Pay special attention to the present-tense verbs.

Washington, D.C., **is** the capital of the United States. "D.C." **means** District of Columbia. The District of Columbia **is** not a state; it **is** a special government district. It **is** very small. It **is** only 61 square miles (158 square kilometers.) More than half a million people **live** in Washington. Washington **doesn't have** factories. Government and tourism **are** the main businesses of Washington. Washington **doesn't have** tall buildings like other big cities.

Some people who work in Washington **don't live** there. They **live** in the nearby states: Virginia and Maryland. Washington **has** a good subway (metro) system. It **connects** Washington to nearby cities in Virginia and Maryland.

The Capitol, the building where Congress **meets, is** on a hill. State senators and representatives **work** in the capital. They **make** the country's laws.

Tourists from all over the United States and many other countries **visit** Washington. They **come** to see the White House and the Capitol building. Many visitors **want** to see the Vietnam War Memorial. This wall of dark stone **lists** all the names of American soldiers who died in the war in Vietnam.

Delaware
Maryland
Virginia
Washington, D.C.

Reading Variation

To practice listening skills, have students first listen to the audio alone. Ask a few comprehension questions. Repeat the audio if necessary. Then have students open their books and read along as they listen to the audio.

Reading Glossary

capital: the official city where a state, provincial, or national government is located
district: an area officially marked for a purpose
factory: a building or group of buildings where goods are produced
law: a rule made by a government body that must be followed by the people in a nation, state, etc.
subway: a public transportation system with trains that run underground

Besides government buildings, Washington also **has** many important museums and monuments to presidents. The Smithsonian Institution **has** 16 museums and galleries and a zoo. The Smithsonian **includes** the Air and Space Museum. This very popular museum **shows** visitors real spaceships, such as the Apollo 11, which landed on the moon in 1969.

Tourists **don't pay** to see government buildings and museums. However, they **need** tickets to see many places because these places **are** crowded. Government buildings and museums **have** a lot of security. Guards **check** visitors' bags as they **enter** these buildings.

A trip to Washington **is** an enjoyable and educational experience.

Did You
Know?
The first location of the U.S. capital was in New York City.

2.1 | Simple Present Tense—Forms

A simple present-tense verb has two forms: the base form and the *-s* form.

Examples			Explanation
Subject	Base Form	Complement	We use the base form when the subject is *I, you, we, they,* or a plural noun.
I			
You			
We	**live**	in Washington.	
They			
My friends			
Subject	-s Form	Complement	We use the *-s* form when the subject is *he, she, it,* or a singular noun.
He			*Family* is a singular subject.
She			
It	**lives**	in Washington.	
The president			
My family			
Washington **has** many museums.			Three verbs have an irregular *-s* form.
The metro **goes** to Virginia.			have → has (pronunciation /hæz/)
The president **does** a lot of work.			go → goes
			do → does (pronunciation /dʌz/)

DID YOU KNOW?
New York City was the capital of the U.S. until 1790. Philadelphia temporarily served as the nation's capital from 1790 to 1800, when the capital was permanently moved to Washington, D.C.

2.1 | Simple Present Tense—Forms

1. Have students cover up grammar chart **2.1** on page 43. Write the verb *live* at the top of the board. Then write the subject pronouns on the board in the same order they are in the book. Ask: *How do you form the simple present tense?* (use *live* or *lives*) Write students' responses on the board.

2. Have students look at grammar chart **2.1**. Explain that the simple present tense has two forms: the base form and the -s form, and that the subject determines which form we use. Say: *We use the base form when the subject is* I, you, we, they, *or a plural noun. We use the* -s *form when the subject is* he, she, it, *or a singular subject.* Point out that *family* is a singular subject. Read the example sentences.

3. Explain that three verbs (*have, go, do*) have irregular -s forms. Go over the example sentences.

Expansion

Grammar Have students go back to the reading on pages 42–43. Ask students to circle the regular *-s* form verbs and to underline the irregular *-s* form verbs.

1. Tell students that this exercise is about Washington, D.C. Have students read the direction line. Go over the example in the book. Then do #1 with the class. Ask: *Which form of the verb goes here? (lives)* Say: *If you need help, you can look back at the reading on page 43.*

2. Have students complete the rest of Exercise 1 individually. Check the answers as a class. If necessary, review grammar chart **2.1** on page 43.

2.2 | Simple Present Tense—Uses

1. Have students cover up grammar chart **2.2** on page 44. Activate students' prior knowledge. Ask students if they know when to use the simple present tense. Write students' responses on the board.

2. Have students look at grammar chart **2.2**. Explain that one use of the simple present tense is to show truths or facts. Read the example sentences. Ask a volunteer to make a similar sentence about the class (e.g., *Ms. Grant teaches English. English class meets in this room.*).

3. Explain that another use of the simple present is with customs. Read the example. Point out the picture of the man waving. Then have a volunteer make a similar statement about an American custom or a custom from his or her country (e.g., *Americans shake hands when they greet each other.*).

4. Explain that the simple present tense is used to describe regular or repeated actions. Read the example and then ask a volunteer to make a similar sentence about the class (e.g., *We have English class twice a week.*).

5. Explain that the simple present tense is also used to show a place of origin. Read the example and then ask a volunteer to make a similar sentence about himself or herself (e.g., *I come from Colombia.*).

EXERCISE **1**   Fill in the blanks with the correct form of the verb.

EXAMPLE   Visitors ___*like*___ the museums.
                  (like/likes)

1. The president ___*lives*___ in the White House.
               (live/lives)

2. Many people in Washington ___*work*___ for the government.
               (work/works)

3. Washington ___*has*___ many beautiful museums.
           (have/has)

4. Millions of tourists ___*visit*___ Washington every year.
           (visit/visits)

5. The metro ___*connects*___ Washington to nearby cities.
         (connect/connects)

6. The Vietnam War Memorial ___*lists*___ the names of men and women who died in the war.
         (list/lists)

7. "D.C." ___*means*___ District of Columbia.
        (mean/means)

2.2 | Simple Present Tense—Uses

Examples	Uses
The president **lives** in the White House. Washington **has** a good subway (metro) system.	With general truths, to show that something is consistently true
The president **shakes** hands with many people. He **waves** to people.	With customs
We **take** a vacation every summer. We sometimes **go** to Washington.	To show regular activity (a habit) or repeated action
I **come** from Bosnia. He **comes** from Pakistan.	To show place of origin

44   Lesson **2**

EXERCISE **2** ABOUT YOU Write the correct form of the verb. Add more words to give facts about you.

EXAMPLE I _come from Colombia_ .
(come)

Answers will vary.

1. The capital of my country _____ .
(have)

2. Most people in my country _____ .
(have)

3. In my native city, I especially _____ .
(like)

4. Tourists in my country _____ .
(visit)

5. My native city _____ .
(have)

6. My family _____ .
(live)

7. In the U.S., I _____ .
(live)

8. The U.S. _____ .
(have)

9. I _____ College/School.
(attend)

10. This school _____ .
(have)

2.3 | Spelling of the -s Form

Rule	Base Form	-s Form
Add **s** to most verbs to make the -s form.	hope eat	hopes eats
When the base form ends in *ss, sh, ch,* or *x,* add **es** and pronounce an extra syllable.	miss wash catch mix	misses washes catches mixes
When the base form ends in a consonant + *y,* change the *y* to *i* and add **es.**	carry worry	carries worries
When the base form ends in a vowel + *y,* add **s.** Do not change the *y.*	pay enjoy	pays enjoys

The Simple Present Tense **45**

Expansion

Exercise 2 Play a guessing game. Read (or have a volunteer read) a student's answers for items 1–7. Then have the class guess who the student is (and the student's country and native city).

1. Have students read the direction line. Tell students that they have to give facts about themselves, their countries, and other places. Go over the example in the book. Model the exercise using your own information.
2. Have students complete Exercise 2 individually. Then have students compare answers with a partner. Circulate to observe pair work. Give help as needed.
3. If necessary, review grammar chart **2.2** on page 44.

2.3 | Spelling of the -s Form

1. Copy the lists of verbs (base forms and -s forms) from grammar chart **2.3** on the board. Make sure you separate the four sets of verbs. For example:

hope	*hopes*
eat	*eats*
miss	*misses*
wash	*washes*
catch	*catches*
mix	*mixes*

2. Have students cover up grammar chart **2.3** in their books. Say: *There are four rules for adding an s to verbs. Do you know what they are?* If students have difficulty, give them hints. Say: *Look at the endings of these four verbs* (miss, wash, catch, mix). *What do you add along with the s?* (e) *So what's the rule for these verbs?* (When the base form ends in *ss, sh, ch,* or *x* add *es* . . . etc.) Continue with the other verbs.
3. Have students look at grammar chart **2.3**. Say: *Compare our rules with the rules in the book.* Review the rules in the grammar chart.

EXERCISE 3

1. Have students read the direction line. Ask: *What do we write in the blanks?* (the *-s* form of the verb) Go over the examples in the book. Ask students to tell you what the rules are for the spelling of each verb in the examples. (*eat*—add *-s* to most verbs; *study*—consonant + *y*, change the *y* to *i* and add *-es*; *watch*—ends in *ch*, add *-es*)

2. Have students complete Exercise 3 individually. Check answers as a class.

3. If necessary, review grammar chart **2.3** on page 45.

2.4 | Pronunciation of the *-s* Form

1. Have students cover up grammar chart **2.4** in their books. Say: *There are three ways to pronounce the* s. List them across the board:

   1. /s/, **2.** /z/, **3.** /əz/

   Pronounce each sound. Give an example from each list. Remind students that this is about pronunciation, not spelling or writing. Then say: *Listen to each word as I say it. Tell me which sound I'm making.* Say words from the grammar chart lists on page 46 in random order. Pronounce each word carefully. Have students guess where the word belongs and write it under the sound they tell you.

2. Have students look at grammar chart **2.3**. Say: *Compare our lists with the lists in the book.* Go over any errors. Have students practice pronouncing the *-s* form chorally as a class as needed.

3. Direct students to the Language Note. Pronounce *do/does* and *say/says* for the students. Tell them that these verbs end in a vowel sound and have a change in the vowel sound when the *-s* is added.

EXERCISE **3**   Write the *-s* form of the following verbs.

EXAMPLES   eat _____ *eats* _____

study _____ *studies* _____

watch _____ *watches* _____

1. try	*tries*	11. say	*says*
2. play	*plays*	12. change	*changes*
3. have	*has*	13. brush	*brushes*
4. go	*goes*	14. obey	*obeys*
5. worry	*worries*	15. reach	*reaches*
6. finish	*finishes*	16. fix	*fixes*
7. do	*does*	17. work	*works*
8. push	*pushes*	18. raise	*raises*
9. enjoy	*enjoys*	19. charge	*charges*
10. think	*thinks*	20. see	*sees*

2.4 | Pronunciation of the *-s* Form

Pronunciation	Rule	Examples	
/s/	Pronounce /s/ after voiceless sounds: /p, t, k, f/.	hope—hopes eat—eats	pick—picks laugh—laughs
/z/	Pronounce /z/ after voiced sounds: /b, d, g, v, m, n, ŋ, l, r/ and all vowel sounds.	grab—grabs read—reads hug—hugs live—lives hum—hums run—runs	sing—sings fall—falls hear—hears see—sees borrow—borrows
/əz/	Pronounce /əz/ when the base form ends in *ss, ce, se, sh, ch, ge, x*.	miss—misses dance—dances use—uses wash—washes	watch—watches change—changes fix—fixes

Language Note: The following verbs have a change in the vowel sound. Listen to your teacher pronounce these examples.
do/du/—does/dʌz/
say/sei/—says/sɛz/

Grammar Variation

Have students cover up grammar chart **2.4.** Read the verbs in the first list in the grammar chart (*hopes, eats, picks, laughs*). Ask students to repeat what they think the /s/ sound is for that group of words. Then read the verbs from the second list and ask the students to repeat what they think the /s/ sound is for that group of words and so on. After the last group of verbs, ask students to look at the chart. Go over the rules for pronunciation.

Expansion

Grammar For additional practice with pronunciation, make flashcards with the base form of the verbs in grammar chart **2.4** (or other verbs). Show students a flashcard, and have them pronounce the *-s* form. As an alternative to flashcards, you may simply say the base form of the verb and have students say the *-s* form.

EXERCISE **4** Go back to Exercise 3 and pronounce the base form and *-s* form of each verb.

EXERCISE **5** Fill in the blanks with the *-s* form of the verb in parentheses ( ). Pay attention to the spelling rules on page 45. Then say each sentence.

EXAMPLE   A teacher _____*tries*_____ to help students learn.
(try)

1. A pilot _____*flies*_____ an airplane.
(fly)

2. A dishwasher _____*washes*_____ dishes.
(wash)

3. A babysitter _____*watches*_____ children.
(watch)

4. A soldier _____*obeys*_____ an officer.
(obey)

5. A citizen _____*pays*_____ taxes.
(pay)

6. A mechanic _____*fixes*_____ machines.
(fix)

7. A student _____*studies*_____ .
(study)

8. A student _____*does*_____ homework.
(do)

9. A carpenter _____*uses*_____ a hammer.
(use)

10. A teacher _____*teaches*_____ students.
(teach)

EXERCISE **6** Choose one of the following professions. Write at least three sentences to tell what someone in this profession does. You may work with a partner.

mechanic	teacher	bus driver
secretary	cook	tour guide
carpenter	banker	salesperson
plumber	writer	lawyer

Answers will vary.

_____

_____

_____

_____

EXERCISE 4

Have students read the direction line. Turn to Exercise 3 on page 46. Ask: *What are we going to say?* (the base form and the *-s* form) Have a volunteer say #1. Have students finish the exercise in pairs. Circulate to help with pronunciation.

EXERCISE 5

1. Have students read the direction line. Go over the example in the book. Then do #1 with the class. Ask a volunteer to give an answer.

2. Have students complete the rest of Exercise 5 individually. Point out the picture of a carpenter using a hammer. Then have students practice saying the sentences in pairs. Circulate to listen to students practice the pronunciation. Finally, check the answers as a class.

3. If necessary, review grammar chart 2.4 on page 46.

EXERCISE 6

1. Have students read the direction line. Make sure students know the meaning of the professions. Point out the pictures of the carpenter and plumber. Remind students that they only have to write about one profession. Model one example for the students (e.g., *A mechanic fixes cars.*).

2. Have students complete Exercise 6 individually. Then have students read each other their sentences. Circulate to observe pair work. Give help as needed.

3. If necessary, review grammar chart 2.4 on page 46.

To save class time, have students do half of the exercise in class and complete the other half for homework. Or assign the entire exercise for homework.

Expansion

Exercise 4 Have a Spelling and Pronunciation Bee. Make a list of 40 or so verbs. Divide the class into Team A and Team B. Give one team member from Team A a verb and tell them to spell the *-s* form on the board. Do the same with Team B. Then give Team A another verb and ask one member to pronounce the *-s* form, and so on. Make sure team members take turns. To make the exercise more challenging, give extra points if the team can say (or act out) what the word means.

2.5 | Comparing Affirmative Statements— *Be* and Other Verbs

1. Have students cover up grammar chart **2.5.** Write the following on the board:
   a. *I / student*
   b. *I / study / English*
   c. *you / right*
   d. *you / know / the answer*
   e. *he / busy*
   f. *he / work / hard*

2. Tell students to write sentences using the words above. Then have volunteers write them on the board.

3. Have students look at grammar chart **2.5.** Compare the work on the board with the sentences in the chart. Explain to students that they can't use the verb *be* with the simple present tense of other verbs. Briefly review grammar points on the verb *be* from Lesson 1 if needed.

EXERCISE 7

1. Have students read the direction line. Ask: *Do all sentences have the verb* be*?* (no) Go over the examples in the book. Explain that this exercise is about a student comparing himself to his friend.

2. Have students complete Exercise 7 individually. Check the answers as a class. Have volunteers read the sentences aloud. Check for correct pronunciation of the *-s* form.

3. If necessary, review grammar chart **2.5** on page 48.

2.5 | Comparing Affirmative Statements—*Be* and Other Verbs

Examples	Explanation
I **am** a student. I **study** English. You **are** right. You **know** the answer. He **is** busy. He **works** hard.	Don't include a form of *be* with a simple present-tense verb. *Wrong: I'm study English.* *Wrong: You're know the answer.* *Wrong: He's works hard.*

EXERCISE 7 A student is comparing himself to his friend. Fill in the blanks with the correct form of the underlined verb.

EXAMPLES My friend and I are very different.

I <u>get</u> up at 7 o'clock. He ___*gets*___ up at 10.

I'm a good student. He ___*'s*___ a lazy student.

1. I <u>study</u> every day. He ___*studies*___ only before a test.
2. I always <u>get</u> A's on my tests. He ___*gets*___ C's.
3. I <u>have</u> a scholarship. He ___*has*___ a government loan.
4. I'm a good student. He ___*'s*___ an average student.
5. He <u>lives</u> in a dormitory. I ___*live*___ in an apartment.
6. He's from Japan. I ___*'m*___ from the Philippines.
7. He <u>studies</u> with the radio on. I ___*study*___ in a quiet room.
8. He <u>watches</u> a lot of TV. I ___*watch*___ TV only when I have free time.
9. He <u>eats</u> a lot of meat. I ___*eat*___ a lot of fish.
10. He <u>uses</u> a laptop computer. I ___*use*___ a desktop computer.

Expansion

Exercise 7 Have students make six true statements about themselves using verbs in the simple present tense. Tell them they can use Exercise 7 as a model. Then have students read their statements to a partner. Say: *If your partner's information is different from your own, write it down. For example, write:* I live in an apartment. He lives in a hotel. If possible, try to put students of different nationalities together.

2.6 | Negative Statements with the Simple Present Tense

Examples	Explanation
The president **lives** in the White House. The vice president **doesn't live** in the White House. Washington **has** many government buildings. It **doesn't have** tall buildings.	Use *doesn't* + the base form with *he, she, it,* or a singular noun. Compare: lives → doesn't **live** has → doesn't **have** *Doesn't* is the contraction for *does not.*
Visitors **pay** to enter museums in most cities. They **don't pay** in Washington museums. We **live** in Maryland. We **don't live** in Washington.	Use *don't* + the base form with *I, you, we, they,* or a plural noun. Compare: pay → don't **pay** live → don't **live** *Don't* is the contraction for *do not.*

Usage Note: American English and British English use different grammar to form the negative of *have*. Compare:

American: He *doesn't have* a dictionary.

British: He *hasn't* a dictionary. OR He *hasn't got* a dictionary.

EXERCISE 8 Fill in the blanks with the negative form of the underlined verb.

EXAMPLE You need tickets for some museums. You _____*don't need*_____ money for the museums.

1. Washington has tourism. It ___*doesn't have*___ factories.

2. Tourists need to pass through security in Washington museums. They ___*don't need*___ to pay to enter a museum.

The Simple Present Tense **49**

Expansion

Grammar Ask students to find examples of negative statements in the reading on page 42. (*Washington doesn't have factories; some people who work in Washington don't live there.*) Write the examples on the board. Ask students to change the sentences to the affirmative form.

1. Have students cover up grammar chart **2.6.** Activate students' prior knowledge. Ask students if they know how to make negative statements with the simple present tense. Write students' responses on the board.

2. Have students look at grammar chart **2.6.** Review the examples. On the board, write: *lives* and *does not live.* Explain how to form the negative form with *he, she, it,* or a singular noun. (*does + not* + base form) Then show the contraction. (*doesn't* + base form) Say: *The contraction is more common than the long form.*

3. Write on the board: *pay* and *don't pay.* Explain how to form the negative form with *I, you, we, they,* or a plural noun. (*do + not* + base form) Then show the contraction. (*don't* + base form) Say: *The contraction is more common than the long form.*

4. Point out the Usage Note. Explain that in British English the grammar is different for the negative of *have.* Point out the examples in the book. Explain that both mean the same thing.

EXERCISE 8

1. Tell students that this exercise contains information about Washington, D.C. Have students read the direction line. Ask: *What are we going to replace the underlined word with?* (the negative form of the verb) Go over the example in the book. Point out the photo of the security guard in the museum. Have a volunteer do #1.

2. Have students complete the rest of Exercise 8 individually. Check the answers as a class.

3. If necessary, review grammar chart **2.6** on page 49.

1. Tell students that this exercise is about their school. Have students read the direction line. Go over the examples in the book. Have a volunteer model the example.
2. Have students complete Exercise 9 individually. Check the answers as a class.
3. If necessary, review grammar chart **2.6** on page 49.

🕐 To save class time, have students do half of the exercise in class and complete the other half in writing for homework. Or if students do not need speaking practice, the entire exercise may be skipped or done in writing.

1. Tell students that this exercise is about you, their teacher. Have students read the direction line. Go over the example in the book. Have a volunteer model the example.
2. Have students complete Exercise 10 individually. Check the answers as a class.
3. If necessary, review grammar charts **2.3** on page 45 and **2.6** on page 49.

🕐 To save class time, have students do half of the exercise in class and complete the other half in writing for homework. Or if students do not need speaking practice, the entire exercise may be skipped or done in writing.

---

3. The metro runs all day. It ___doesn't run___ after midnight.
4. You need a car in many cities. You ___don't need___ a car in Washington.
5. Washington has a subway system (the metro). Miami ___doesn't have___ a subway system.
6. My friend lives in Virginia. He ___doesn't live___ in Washington.
7. I like American history. I ___don't like___ geography.
8. The president lives in Washington. He ___doesn't live___ in New York.
9. The president serves for four years. He ___doesn't serve___ for six years.
10. We have a president. We ___don't have___ a prime minister.
11. The U.S. Congress makes the laws. The president ___doesn't make___ the laws.
12. Many Washingtonians work in tourism. They ___don't work___ for the government.

EXERCISE 9 Tell if this school has or doesn't have the following items.

EXAMPLES   ESL courses
This school has ESL courses.

classes for children
It doesn't have classes for children.

Answers will vary.
1. a library
2. a cafeteria
3. copy machines
4. a parking lot
5. a swimming pool
6. a gym
7. a student newspaper
8. a theater
9. dormitories
10. classes for children
11. a computer lab
12. e-mail for students

EXERCISE 10 Make an affirmative statement or a negative statement with the words given to state facts about the teacher. Use the correct form of the verb.

EXAMPLE   speak Arabic
The teacher speaks Arabic.
OR
The teacher doesn't speak Arabic.

Answers will vary.
1. talk fast
2. speak English well
3. speak my language
4. give a lot of homework
5. give tests
6. pronounce my name correctly
7. wear glasses
8. wear jeans to class
9. teach this class every day
10. watch the students during a test

50   Lesson 2

Expansion

Exercise 8 Tell students to make questions 3, 4, 5, 8, 9, and 10 true for their native country. Say: *Write negative and affirmative statements.* Then have students compare information in pairs. If possible, put together students from different countries. Circulate to observe pair work. Give help as needed.

Exercise 9 Have students complete this exercise for the last school they attended or for a school their children are attending. Have students compare schools in groups or collect for assessment.

EXERCISE **11** ABOUT YOU Check (✓) the items that describe you and what you do. Exchange your book with another student. Make statements about the other student.

EXAMPLES

_____ I have children.
Marta doesn't have children.

____✓ I like cold weather.
Marta likes cold weather.

Answers will vary.

1. _____ I speak Chinese.
2. _____ I live alone.
3. _____ I live near school.
4. _____ I walk to school.
5. _____ I speak Spanish.

6. _____ I like summer.
7. _____ I like cold weather.
8. _____ I have a laptop.
9. _____ I use the Internet.
10. _____ I have a dog.

2.7 | Comparing Negative Statements with *Be* and Other Verbs

Examples	Explanation
I'm **not** from Mexico. I **don't speak** Spanish. You **aren't** sick. You **don't need** a doctor. He **isn't** hungry. He **doesn't want** dinner.	Don't use *be* to make the negative of a simple present-tense verb. *Wrong:* I *am* don't speak Spanish. *Wrong:* You *aren't* need a doctor. *Wrong:* He *isn't want* dinner.

EXERCISE **12** ABOUT YOU Check (✓) the items that describe you and what you do. Exchange your book with another student. Make statements about the other student.

EXAMPLES

_____ I'm an immigrant.
Margarita isn't an immigrant. She comes from Puerto Rico.

____✓ I have a laptop.
Margarita has a laptop.

Answers will vary.

1. _____ I'm married.
2. _____ I have children/a child.
3. _____ I have a laptop.
4. _____ I'm an American citizen.
5. _____ I like this city.
6. _____ I have a job.

7. _____ I'm a full-time student.
8. _____ I have a pet.[1]
9. _____ I'm an immigrant.
10. _____ I'm happy in the U.S.
11. _____ I like baseball.
12. _____ I understand American TV.

[1] A *pet* is an animal that lives in someone's house. Dogs and cats are common pets.

The Simple Present Tense   **51**

Expansion

Exercise 11 Have students do the same exercise for another student in the class. Say: *For each statement, change* I *to* he *or* she. *Guess the answer for your classmate. If the answer is negative, write the sentence out (e.g.,* He doesn't speak Chinese. He doesn't live alone.*). Remember to use the* -s *form of the verb.*

For an extra challenge, have students write an alternative answer. For example: *He doesn't speak Chinese. He speaks Korean.*

Exercise 12 Have students do the same exercise for another student in the class. Say: *For each statement, change* I *to* he *or* she. *Guess the answer for your classmate. If the answer is negative, write the sentence out (e.g.,* He's not married. He doesn't have children.*). Remember that in this exercise, there are sentences with* be *and sentences with other verbs.*

For an extra challenge, have students write an alternative answer. For example: *He isn't married. He's single.*

EXERCISE 11

1. Tell students that this exercise is about them. Have students read the direction line. Ask: *Do you check every item?* (No. Check only the items that are true for you.) Go over the examples in the book. Model #1 with another student.
2. Have students complete the rest of Exercise 11 individually. Then have partners exchange information and say sentences about their partner.
3. If necessary, review grammar charts **2.3** on page 45 and **2.6** on page 49.

2.7 | Comparing Negative Statements with *Be* and Other Verbs

1. Have students cover up grammar chart **2.7**. Write the following on the board:
   a. I / not / from Mexico
   b. I / not / speak / Spanish
   c. you / not / sick
   d. you / not / need a doctor
   e. he / not / hungry
   f. he / not / want dinner
2. Tell students to write negative statements using the words above. Then have volunteers write them on the board.
3. Have students look at grammar chart **2.7**. Compare the work on the board with the sentences in the chart. Explain to students that they can't use the verb *be* to make a negative of the simple present of other verbs.

EXERCISE 12

1. Tell students that this exercise is about them and the things they do. Have students read the direction line. Ask: *What do you check?* (things that are true) Go over the examples in the book. Have a volunteer model the example.
2. Have students complete the rest of Exercise 12 individually. Then have partners exchange information. Have students say sentences about their partners. Circulate to observe pair work. Give help as needed.
3. If necessary, review grammar charts **2.3** on page 45, **2.6** on page 49, and **2.7** on page 51.

EXERCISE 13

1. Have students read the direction line. Ask: *Do you write sentences on every topic?* (No. Choose one.) Remind students to include some negative statements. Go over the example in the book.
2. Have students complete the rest of Exercise 13 individually. Have students compare sentences in groups. Circulate to observe group work. Give help as needed. Have volunteers read their sentences to the class.
3. If necessary, review grammar charts **2.2** on page 44, **2.3** on page 45, **2.5** on page 48, **2.6** on page 49, and **2.7** on page 51.

🕐 To save class time, have students do half of the exercise in class and complete the other half for homework. Or assign the entire exercise for homework.

EXERCISE 14

🎧 **CD 1, Track 8**

1. Have students read the direction line. Go over the example in the book. Do #1 and #2 with the class. Say: *When you see* not/live, *you need to write the negative. How do we write the negative?* (doesn't live)
2. Have students complete Exercise 14 individually. Then check answers as a class.
3. If necessary, review grammar charts **2.2** on page 44, **2.3** on page 45, **2.5** on page 48, **2.6** on page 49, and **2.7** on page 51.

🕐 To save class time, have students do half of the exercise in class and complete the other half for homework. Or assign the entire exercise for homework.

EXERCISE **13**   Choose one of the items from the list below. Write sentences telling what this person does or is. Include negative statements. You may work with a partner. Read some of your sentences to the class.

EXAMPLE   a good teacher

A good teacher explains the lesson.

A good teacher doesn't get angry at students.

A good teacher doesn't walk away after class when students have questions.

A good teacher is patient.

1. a good friend   3. a good doctor
2. a good mother or father   4. a good adult son or daughter

Answers will vary.

EXERCISE **14**   Fill in the blanks with the correct form of the verb in parentheses ( ).

🎧

Sara Harris ____is____ a 30-year-old woman. She ____lives____ in
      Example: (be)   *(1 live)*

Arlington, Virginia. She ____doesn't live____ in Washington because rent is
                        (2 not/live)

cheaper in Arlington. Arlington ____isn't____ far from Washington.
                                    (3 be/not)

Sara ____doesn't need____ a car because her apartment ____'s____ near
      (4 not/need)   *(5 be)*

a metro stop. She ____uses____ the metro to go to work every day.
                  (6 use)

Sara works in Washington, but she ____doesn't work____ for the government.
                                    (7 not/work)

She ____'s____ a tour guide. She ____takes____ groups on tours of
      (8 be)   *(9 take)*

the Capitol. Tour groups ____don't need____ to pay to enter the Capitol,
                          (10 not/need)

but they ____need____ a reservation.
          (11 need)

52   Lesson 2

Expansion

Exercise 13 Have group discussions. Group people together who wrote on the same topic. Say: *Read your sentences to each other and discuss them.* Groups then report their findings to the class (e.g., *In our group, everyone thinks that a good mother stays home with her children.*).

Exercise 14 Variation

To provide practice with listening skills, have students close their books and listen to the audio. Repeat the audio as needed. Ask comprehension questions, such as: *Who is Sara Harris?* (a 30-year-old woman) *Where does she live?* (in Arlington, Virginia) *Is rent cheaper in Washington or Arlington?* (in Arlington) Then have students open their books and complete Exercise 14.

Expansion

Exercise 14 Have students write a paragraph about their lives. Tell students to use Exercise 14 as a model.

Sara _____ isn't _____ married. She _____ has _____ two
      (12 be/not)   (13 have)

roommates. They _____ work _____ in government offices. Sara and her
          (14 work)

roommates _____ work _____ hard, so they _____ don't have _____ much time to
        (15 work)   (16 not/have)

visit the museums. When Sara's friends _____ visit _____ from out of town,
                    (17 visit)

Sara _____ takes _____ them to museums and other tourist attractions.
      (18 take)

THE IRS

Before You Read

1. Do you pay income tax?
2. What other kinds of taxes do you pay?

Read the following conversation between Annie (A) and Barbara (B) in Washington, D.C. Pay special attention to questions.

A: **Do** you **live** in Washington?
B: No, I don't. I live in Virginia.
A: **Do** you **work** in Washington?
B: Yes, I do.
A: How **do** you **go** to work?
B: I use the metro.
A: How much **does** it **cost**?
B: That depends on how far you ride. I pay $1.50 per ride.
A: Where **do** you **work**?
B: I work at the IRS.

(continued)

The Simple Present Tense   **53**

Expansion

Theme The topic for this lesson can be enhanced with the following ideas:

1. A complete 1040EZ form from the IRS
2. Tax forms for your state

Reading Variation

To practice listening skills, have students first listen to the audio alone. Ask a few comprehension questions. Repeat the audio if necessary. Then have students open their books and read along as they listen to the audio.

Reading Glossary

lottery: a game of chance in which people buy tickets with numbers and the winner is the one whose numbers match those drawn by the lottery organizer
paycheck: a salary or wage check
percentage: an amount of something understood as a part of a whole that equals 100
social security: in the USA, a government program that pays a monthly amount of money to older, nonworking people and others who can't work
tax: a mandatory payment on income, sales, etc. to the government

The IRS (Reading)

1. Have students look at the form. Ask: *Do you recognize this form? What is it?* (a form to report income for tax purposes) *Have you ever filled this out?*
2. Have students look at the title of the reading. Ask: *What is the reading about? How do you know?* Have students make predictions.
3. Preteach any vocabulary words your students may not know, such as *tax, social security, percentage, paycheck,* and *lottery.*

BEFORE YOU READ

1. Have students discuss the questions in pairs.
2. Ask for a few volunteers to share their answers with the class.

🕐 To save class time, skip "Before You Read" or have students prepare answers for homework ahead of time.

Reading 🎧 CD 1, Track 9

1. Have students read the text silently. Tell them to pay special attention to questions. Point out that this is a conversation between two women, Annie and Barbara, and takes place in Washington, D.C. Then play the audio and have students read along silently.
2. Check students' comprehension. Ask questions such as: *How does Barbara get to work?* (by metro) *What does the IRS do?* (collect taxes) *Why does every one give Barbara funny looks when she says where she works?* (because people don't like the IRS, the government agency that collects taxes)

🕐 To save class time, have students do the reading for homework ahead of time.

2.8 | Yes/No Questions and Short Answers with the Present Tense

1. Have students cover up grammar chart **2.8** on pages 54 and 55. Ask students if they remember how to write *yes/no* questions with *be*. Ask volunteers to write them on the board. Remind students that in a question, the verb goes before the subject.

2. Ask: *How do you write questions with the simple present tense?* If students have difficulty, write: *You speak English* on the board. Say: *Try to make a question out of this sentence.* (Do you speak English?) Ask: *Is the verb before the subject?* (No, it's after the subject.) *What comes before the subject?* (Do)

3. Have students look at grammar chart **2.8**. Review the example sentences. Point out that *does* and *do* go before the subject and that the verb does not take an *s* in the third person. Ask: *When do we use* does? (with *he, she, it, everyone, family,* or a singular subject) *When do we use* do? (with *I, we, you, they,* or a plural subject)

4. Have students go back to the reading on page 53. Ask them to find two *yes/no* questions with *do* (*Do you live in Washington? Do you work in Washington?*) and two *yes/no* questions with *does* (*Does everyone pay the same amount of tax? Does everyone get a refund?*).

A: What **does** IRS **mean**?
B: It means Internal Revenue Service. This is the government agency that collects taxes. Whenever I tell people that I work at the IRS, they give me funny looks or say funny things.
A: Why?
B: Because everyone hates the IRS. No one likes to pay taxes. But taxes are necessary.
A: How **does** the IRS **use** the money?
B: For the military, education, health care, social security, and many other things.
A: **Does** everyone **pay** the same amount of tax?
B: No. Poor people pay a smaller percentage. Middle income people pay more. The tax law is very complicated[2].
A: When **do** people in the U.S. **pay** tax?
B: They pay little by little. Money comes out of their paychecks. Then they fill out a form and send it to the IRS every year by April 15.
A: My friend gets a refund[3] every year. **Does** everyone **get** a refund?
B: No. Only people who pay too much during the year get a refund. If we pay too little, we send a check to the IRS by April 15.
A: I hope to win the lottery some day. Then I won't need to pay taxes.
B: You're wrong! The IRS takes a percentage from every lottery winning.
A: How **does** the IRS **know** who wins the lottery?
B: The lottery reports the winner's name to the IRS. A famous American, Benjamin Franklin, said, "In this world nothing is certain but death and taxes."

2.8 | Yes/No Questions and Short Answers with the Present Tense

Examples				Explanation
Does	*Subject*	*Verb*	*Complement*	To form a question with *he, she, it, everyone, family,* or a singular subject, use:
Does	Barbara	**work**	in Washington?	
Does	she	**live**	in Virginia?	*Does* + subject + base form
Does	everyone	**pay**	taxes?	*Wrong:* Does she *works* in Washington?
Does	your family	**visit**	you?	
Do	*Subject*	*Verb*	*Complement*	To form a question with *I, we, you, they,* or a plural noun, use:
Do	you	**work**	hard?	
Do	they	**pay**	taxes?	*Do* + subject + base form
Do	Americans	**like**	the IRS?	

(continued)

[2] *Complicated* means not simple.
[3] A *refund* is money that the government returns to you if you pay too much in taxes.

Culture Note

In 2003, the IRS collected more than 987 billion dollars in taxes from individuals! The IRS also collected more than 194 billion dollars from businesses for a total of more than 1.1 trillion dollars

Grammar Variation

1. Have students go back to the reading on page 53. Ask students to find two *yes/no* questions with *do* (*Do you live in Washington? Do you work in Washington?*) and two *yes/no* questions with *does* (*Does everyone pay the same amount of tax? Does everyone get a refund?*).

2. Then have students look at grammar chart **2.8**. Review the example sentences in the grammar chart. Point out that *does* and *do* go before the subject and that the verb does not take an *s* in the third person. Ask: *When do we use* does? (with *he, she, it, everyone, family,* or a singular subject) *When do we use* do? (with *I, we, you, they,* or a plural subject)

Examples	Explanation

Do lottery winners pay taxes?
Yes, they do.
 	
Do Americans like taxes?
No, they don't.
 	
Does Barbara use the metro?
Yes, she does.
 	
Does she live in Washington?
No, she doesn't.
	We usually answer a *yes/no* question with a short answer.
	
	Short answer:
	   Yes, + subject pronoun + *do/does*.
	   No, + subject pronoun + *don't/doesn't*.

Usage Note: American English and British English use different grammar to form a question with *have*. Compare:
   American: Does she *have* a car? Yes, she *does*.
   British: *Has* she a car? OR *Has* she *got* a car? Yes, she *has*.

Compare Statements and Questions

Do/Does	Subject	Verb	Complement	Short Answer
	Barbara	works	in Washington.	
Does	she	work	for the government?	No, she doesn't.
	You	pay	taxes.	
Do	you	pay	a lot?	Yes, I do.

EXERCISE 15   Answer with a short answer.

EXAMPLE   Does Barbara work in Washington, D.C.? _____*Yes, she does.*_____

1. Does Barbara live in Washington, D.C.? _____*No, she doesn't.*_____
2. Does she work for the government? _____*No, she doesn't.*_____
3. Does the Washington metro go to Virginia? _____*Yes, it does.*_____
4. Does tax money pay for the military? _____*Yes, it does.*_____
5. Do poor people pay taxes? _____*No, they don't.*_____
6. Do people like to pay taxes? _____*No, they don't.*_____
7. Do lottery winners pay taxes? _____*Yes, they do.*_____
8. Does Annie have a lot of questions for Barbara? _____*Yes, she does.*_____

The Simple Present Tense   **55**

Expansion

Exercise 15 Have students write five *yes/no* questions about another country to ask a partner. Use questions from Exercise 15 as a model. Have students ask and answer questions. Circulate to observe pair work. Give help as needed.

2.8 | *Yes/No* Questions and Short Answers with the Present Tense (*cont.*)

5. Ask students to look for short answers in the reading on page 53. (*No, I don't. Yes, I do.*) Then have students look at the grammar chart at the top of page 55. Review the examples. Explain how to form the short answer. (*Yes, + subject pronoun + do/does* and *No, + subject pronoun + don't/doesn't*)

6. Direct students to the Usage Note. Explain that the British form questions and short answers differently with *have*. Say: *Americans use* do/does *as in* Does she have a car? Yes, she does/No, she doesn't. *The British say:* Has she a car? *Or* Has she got a car? No, she hasn't./Yes, she has.

7. Review the structures for statements, *yes/no* questions, and short answers with the simple present tense in the grammar chart on pages 54 and 55. Point out where *do* and *does* come in questions and answers. Point out that the *-s* form of the verb is used for *he, she, it,* etc., in statements, but in questions the base form is used.

EXERCISE 15

1. Tell students that the information in the exercise is based on the reading on pages 53 and 54. Have students read the direction line. Ask: *What do we write on the blanks?* (short answers) Go over the example in the book.

2. Have students complete Exercise 15 individually. Check the answers as a class.

3. If necessary, review grammar chart 2.8 on pages 54 and 55.

Lesson 2   55

1. Tell students that in this exercise they will ask you, the teacher, questions. Have students read the direction line. Go over the example in the book. Then model the example. Choose a volunteer to ask you a question.

2. Have students interview you in groups. Review some of the questions and answers as a class.

3. If necessary, review grammar chart 2.8 on pages 54 and 55.

🕐 To save class time, have students do half of the exercise in class and complete the other half in writing for homework (you may give a *yes/no* answer for the remaining questions and have students write out the short answer). Or if students do not need speaking practice, the entire exercise may be skipped or done in writing.

1. Tell students that this is an activity about their native countries and customs. Have students read the direction line. Ask: *What do we check?* (customs in our native countries) Go over the example with the class. Then model #1 with the class. Ask a volunteer to give an answer. Point out the pictures of people bowing and chopsticks.

2. Have students check their customs individually. (If needed, students may write out the statements and questions before asking another student.) Then have students ask and answer questions in pairs. Circulate and give help as needed.

3. If necessary, review grammar chart 2.8 on pages 54 and 55.

🕐 To save class time, have students do half of the exercise in class and complete the other half in writing for homework (writing out the statements/questions). Or if students do not need speaking practice, the entire exercise may be skipped or done in writing.

EXERCISE 16 Ask your teacher a question with "Do you . . . ?" and the words given. Your teacher will respond with a short answer.

EXAMPLE drive to school

A: Do you drive to school?
B: Yes, I do. OR No, I don't.

1. like your job
   Do you like your job?
2. teach in the summer
   Do you teach in the summer?
3. have another job
   Do you have another job?
4. speak another language
   Do you speak another language?
5. learn English from TV
   Do you learn English from TV?
6. know my language
   Do you know my language?
7. like to read students' homework.
   Do you like to read students' homework?
8. live far from the school
   Do you live far from the school?
9. have a fax machine
   Do you have a fax machine?
10. have trouble with English spelling
    Do you have trouble with English spelling?
11. have a scanner
    Do you have a scanner?
12. like soccer
    Do you like soccer?

EXERCISE 17 ABOUT YOU Put a check (✓) next to customs from your native country. Then make an affirmative or negative statement about your native country or culture. Ask another student if this is a custom in his or her native country or culture.

EXAMPLE ✓ People take off their shoes before they enter a house.

A: Russians take off their shoes before they enter a house. Do Mexicans take off their shoes before they enter a house?
B: No, we don't.

Answers will vary.

1. ____ People take off their shoes before they enter a house.

2. ____ People bow when they say hello.

3. ____ People shake hands when they say hello.

4. ____ People bring a gift when they visit a friend's house.

5. ____ People eat with chopsticks.

6. ____ On the bus, younger people stand up to let an older person person sit down.

7. ____ High school students wear a uniform.

8. ____ People visit friends without calling first.

9. ____ Men open doors for women.

10. ____ Men give flowers to women for their birthdays.

11. ____ People celebrate children's day.

12. ____ Women cover their faces with a veil.

56 Lesson **2**

Exercise 16 Variation

Have students write the questions and their guesses for your answers. Then have students ask you the questions. Survey the class to see how many guessed *yes/no*. Then tell the class your real answer to the question.

Expansion

Exercise 16 Have students ask a partner questions 4, 5, 6, 8, 9, 10, 11, and 12 from Exercise 16.

EXERCISE 18   A tourist in Washington, D.C., has a lot of questions. Fill in the blanks to make questions.

EXAMPLE   Most big cities have tall buildings. _Does Washington have_ tall buildings?
No, it doesn't.

1. The metro trains run all day. _Do they run_ 24 hours a day?
No, they don't. They only run from early morning to midnight. On weekends they run later.

2. In my city, all passengers pay the same fare on the metro.
Do passengers pay the same fare in the metro in Washington?
No, they don't. Passengers pay according to the distance they ride.

3. I need a ticket to enter museums back home. _Do you_
need a ticket to enter museums in Washington?
Yes, you do, but the museums are free.

4. The Washington Monument is very tall. _Does it have_ an elevator?
Yes, it has an elevator.

5. The president works in Washington. _Does he work_ on Capitol Hill?
No, he doesn't. He works in the White House.

6. _Does he make_ the laws?
No, he doesn't. The president doesn't make the laws. Congress makes the laws.

EXERCISE 19   Two students are comparing teachers. Fill in the blanks to complete this conversation.

A: Do you _like_ your English class?
   (example: like)

B: Yes, I _do_ . I _have_ a very good teacher.
      (1)   (2 have)
Her name is Ms. Lopez.

A: _Does she speak_ Spanish?
         (3)

B: No, she doesn't. She comes from the Philippines. She _speaks_
English and Tagalog.   (4 speak)

A: My teacher is very good too. But he _talks_ fast, and sometimes
                                        (5 talk)

I _don't understand_ him. He _gives_ a lot of homework.
   (6 not / understand)   (7 give)

Does your teacher give a lot of homework?
         (8)

The Simple Present Tense   57

Exercise 19 Variation

To provide practice with listening skills, have students close their books and listen to the audio. Repeat the audio as needed. Ask comprehension questions, such as: *Who is Ms. Lopez?* (person B's English teacher) *Is Ms. Lopez a good teacher?* (yes) *Where is Ms. Lopez from?* (the Philippines) Then have students open their books and complete Exercise 19.

EXERCISE 18

1. Tell students that this exercise is about Washington, D.C. A tourist is asking questions about the city. Have students read the direction line. Go over the example with the class. Point out the photo of the Washington Monument.
2. Have students complete the exercise individually. Check the answers as a class.
3. If necessary, review grammar chart **2.8** on pages 54 and 55.

To save class time, have students do half of the exercise in class and complete the other half for homework. Or assign the entire exercise for homework.

EXERCISE 19

CD 1, Track 10

1. Tell students that this exercise is a conversation two students are having about teachers. Have students read the direction line. Go over the example with the class.
2. Have students complete Exercise 19 individually. Then have students check answers in small groups.
3. Then have students practice the conversation in pairs. Circulate and give help as needed
4. If necessary, review grammar charts **2.3** on page 45, **2.4** on page 46, **2.6** on page 49, and **2.8** on pages 54 and 55.

To save class time, have students do half of the exercise in class and complete the other half for homework. Or assign the entire exercise for homework.

2.9 | Comparing *Yes/No* Questions—*Be* and Other Verbs

1. Have students cover up grammar chart **2.9**. Write the following on the board:
   a. *you / lost?*
   b. *you / need help?*
   c. *I / right?*
   d. *I / have / the answer?*
   e. *he / from Haiti?*
   f. *he / speak French?*

2. Tell students to write *yes/no* questions using the words above. Then have volunteers write the questions on the board.

3. Have students look at grammar chart **2.9**. Compare the work on the board with the sentences in the chart. Say: *You can't use the verb be to make questions with a simple present tense verb.*

EXERCISE 20

1. Have students read the direction line. Ask: *What do we write on the blanks?* (a question and a short answer) Go over the examples in the book.

2. Have students complete the exercise individually. Check the answers as a class.

3. If necessary, review grammar chart **2.9** on page 58.

B: Yes, she does. And she _____gives_____ a test once a week.

(9 give)

A: My teacher _____wears_____ jeans to class. He's very informal.

(10 wear)

_____Does your teacher wear_____ jeans to class?

(11)

B: No, she doesn't. She always wears a dress.

A: My teacher always _____talks_____ to us about American culture.

(12 talk)

_____Does_____ your teacher _____talk_____ to you about American culture?

(13)   (14)

B: Yes, she _____does_____.

(15)

2.9 | Comparing *Yes/No* Questions—*Be* and Other Verbs

Examples		Explanation
Are you lost?	No, I'm not.	Don't use *be* to make a question with a simple present-tense verb.
Do you **need** help?	No, I **don't**.	
Am I right?	Yes, you **are**.	*Wrong: Are you need help?*
Do I **have** the answer?	Yes, you **do**.	*Wrong: Am I have the answer?*
Is he from Haiti?	Yes, he **is**.	*Wrong: Is he speak French?*
Does he speak French?	Yes, he **does**.	

EXERCISE 20   Read each statement. Write a *yes/no* question about the words in parentheses ( ). Then write a short answer.

EXAMPLES   Workers pay tax. (lottery winners) (yes)
Do lottery winners pay tax? Yes, they do.

Washington, D.C., is on the east coast. (New York) (yes)
Is New York on the east coast? Yes, it is.

1. Sara works from Monday to Friday. (on the weekend) (no)
Does Sara work on the weekend? No, she doesn't.

2. You are interested in American culture. (the American government) (yes)
Are you interested in the American government? Yes, I am.

3. The president lives in the White House. (the vice president) (no)
Does the vice president live in the White House? No, he doesn't.

Expansion

Exercise 19 Have students write a similar dialogue about their teachers. Have students work in pairs. Circulate to observe pair work. Give help as needed. Ask volunteers to perform a role-play of their dialogue in front of class.

4. The museums are free. (the metro) (no)

   Is the metro free? No, it isn't.

5. Washington has a space museum. (a zoo) (yes)

   Does Washington have a zoo? Yes, it does.

6. Taxes are necessary. (popular) (no)

   Are taxes popular? No, they aren't.

7. Security is high in government offices. (in airports) (yes)

   Is security high in airports? Yes, it is.

8. People hate the IRS. (you) (yes)

   Do you hate the IRS? Yes, I do.

9. The metro runs all day. (after midnight) (no)

   Does the metro run after midnight? No, it doesn't.

10. The metro in Washington is clean. (quiet) (yes)

    Is the metro in Washington quiet? Yes, it is.

Washington, D.C. Subway Map

2.10 | *Or* Questions

Examples	Explanation

Do you study English **or** French?
  I study English.
 	
Is Washington, D.C., on the east coast **or** the west coast?
  It's on the east coast.
	An *or* question gives a choice of answers.

Pronunciation Note: The first part of an *or* question has rising intonation; the second part has falling intonation. Listen to your teacher pronounce the examples above.	

2.10 | *Or* Questions

1. Have students cover up grammar chart **2.10** on page 59. Say: *Listen. At what point in the sentence does my voice go up when I say these sentences?*
   Do you like tea or coffee?
   Is your apartment big or small?
   Do you like the city or the country?

2. Then ask students to look at grammar chart **2.10** on page 59. Explain that *or* questions give you a choice and that the intonation rises on the first choice and falls on the second. Write an example on the board with arrows to demonstrate the intonation. Review the examples in the grammar chart. As you go down the chart, demonstrate the intonation of the questions.

3. Have students practice saying the *or* questions in the chart chorally as a class. Guide students to use correct intonation. If necessary, have students continue to practice in small groups or pairs. Circulate and provide help as needed.

Expansion

Exercise 20 Have students work in pairs. Put students from different countries or cities together. Have each student write five questions about their partner's country or city. Then students take turns asking and answering questions. Circulate and give help as needed.

EXERCISE 21

1. Tell students that this exercise is about them. Have students read the direction line. Ask: *What do we write on the blanks?* (a true statement about ourselves) Point out that students must choose one of the choices listed (e.g., coffee or tea).
2. Have students complete the exercise individually. Then have students ask and answer questions in pairs. Model the example with a volunteer. Say: *Don't forget to use correct intonation when you ask the questions.* If necessary, students may first write out the questions before pairing up.
3. If necessary, review grammar chart **2.10** on page 59.

EXERCISE 21 ABOUT YOU Circle the words that are true for you, and make a statement about yourself. Then ask an *or* question. Another student will answer.

EXAMPLE I drink (coffee) / *tea* in the morning. _I drink coffee in the morning_ .

A: Do you drink coffee or tea in the morning?
B: I drink coffee, too.

Answers will vary.

1. I speak *English / my native language* at home.

   _____

2. I prefer *classical music / popular music*.

   _____

3. I'm *a resident of the U.S. / a visitor*.

   _____

4. I'm *married / single*.

   _____

5. I live in *a house / an apartment / a dormitory*.

   _____

6. I write with my *right hand / left hand*.

   _____

7. I'm from *a big city / a small town*.

   _____

8. I prefer *morning classes / evening classes*.

   _____

9. I prefer to *eat out / eat at home*.

   _____

10. English is *easy / hard* for me.

    _____

11. I live *with someone / alone*.

    _____

Expansion

Exercise 21 Create two rings of students. Have half of the students stand in an outer ring around the classroom. Have the other half stand in an inner ring, facing the outer ring. Instruct students to ask and answer the questions from Exercise 21. Call out *"turn"* every minute or so. Students in the inner ring should move one space clockwise. Students now ask and answer with their new partners. Have students ask questions in random order. Make sure students look at each other when they're speaking.

2.11 | *Wh-* Questions with the Simple Present Tense

Examples					Explanation
Wh-Word	*Does*	*Subject*	*Verb*	*Complement*	To form a question with *he, she, it, everyone, family*, or a singular subject, use:
Where	**does**	Barbara	**work?**		*Wh-* word + *does* + subject + base form
When	**does**	she	**use**	the metro?	Use the base form after *do* or *does*.
How	**does**	the IRS	**use**	your money?	*Wrong:* Where does Barbara *works?*
Wh-Word	*Do*	*Subject*	*Verb*	*Complement*	To form a question with *I, you, we, they*, or a plural subject, use:
When	**do**	we	**pay**	taxes?	*Wh-* word + *do* + subject + base form
Where	**do**	they	**work?**		
Why	**do**	I	**get**	a refund?	
Wh-Word	*Do/Does*	*Subject*	*Verb*	*Preposition*	In informal written and spoken English, we usually put the preposition at the end of a *wh-* question.
Where	do	you	come	**from?**	
Who	does	she	live	**with?**	
What floor	do	you	live	**on?**	
Preposition	*Wh-Word*	*Do/Does*	*Subject*	*Verb*	In formal written and spoken English, we put the preposition before the question word.
With	whom	does	she	live?	
On	what floor	do	you	live?	

Language Note:
We use *whom*, not *who*, after a preposition. We often use *who* when the preposition is at the end of the sentence. Compare:
     Formal: **With whom** do you study?
     Informal: **Who** do you study **with**?

EXERCISE 22 ABOUT YOU Answer the questions.

EXAMPLE   Where do you live?
            I live near the school.

Answers will vary.

1. Who do you live with?
2. What do you bring to class?
3. What does the teacher bring to class?
4. What do you do after class?

5. How do you come to school?
6. Where do you live?
7. What do you like to do on weekends?
8. Why does the teacher give homework?

Expansion

Exercise 22 Create two rings of students. Have half of the students stand in an outer ring around the classroom. Have the other half stand in an inner ring, facing the outer ring. Instruct students to ask and answer the questions from Exercise 22. Call out *"turn"* every minute or so. Students in the inner ring should move one space clockwise. Students now ask and answer with their new partners. Have students ask questions in random order. Make sure students look at each other when they're speaking.

2.11 | *Wh-* Questions with the Simple Present Tense

1. Have students cover up grammar chart **2.11** on page 61. Activate students' prior knowledge. Ask students to tell you all the *wh-* question words they know. Write them on the board.
2. Have students look at grammar chart **2.11**. Ask students to compare the *wh-* question words they remembered with the ones in the chart. Ask: *Did we forget any?*
3. Explain that making a question with a *wh-* word is not much different than making a *yes/no* question. The *wh-* word goes in front of *do* or *does*. Write on the board:

    <u>*Does Barbara work?*</u>
    <u>*Where does Barbara work?*</u>

    (Make sure *does* lines up in each sentence.) Remind students that the verb is in the base form in a question. Review the examples with *does* and *do*.
4. Write the following on the board: *Where . . . from? Who . . . with? What floor . . . on?*

    Say: *There are two ways to write questions with these prepositions—informally and formally. With the informal, the preposition comes at the end of the sentence:*
    Where do you come **from**?
    Who does she live **with**?
    What floor do you live **on**?

    With the formal, the preposition comes BEFORE the question word.
    With whom does she live?
    On what floor do you live?

    Direct students to the Language Note. Explain that we use *whom* (and not *who*) after a preposition.

EXERCISE 22

1. Tell students that this exercise is about them. Have students read the direction line. Then have a volunteer demonstrate the example.
2. Do the exercise as a class, or have students ask and answer questions in pairs. Circulate and give help as needed. If students need practice writing the grammar structure, have them do the exercise in writing instead of orally.
3. If necessary, review grammar chart **2.11** on page 61.

2.12 | Comparing Statements and Questions in the Simple Present Tense

1. Have students cover grammar chart **2.12** on page 62. Ask a volunteer to make a statement in the simple present tense. Write it on the board or have a volunteer write it on the board. Then ask another volunteer to make a *yes/no* question from the statement. Write it on the board, underneath the statement. Ask another volunteer to answer the question with a short answer. Finally have one more volunteer make a *wh-* question for the statement and write it on the board.

2. Have students look at grammar chart **2.12** on page 62. Say: *Compare your work on the board with the chart.* Review the examples of affirmative statements and questions in the chart.

3. Review the negative statements and questions in the second chart. Tell students that they should use contractions (*don't/doesn't*) in negative questions. Explain that if they don't use contractions, they must change the word order: *Why do they <u>not</u> like taxes? Why does she <u>not</u> get a tax refund?*

EXERCISE 23

1. Tell students that this exercise is about them. Have students read the direction line. Ask: *What kind of question do you ask first?* (a *yes/no* question) Go over the examples with the class.

2. Have students complete the exercise with a partner. Circulate to observe pair work. Give help as needed If needed, students may write out the questions before asking another student.

3. If necessary, review grammar chart **2.12** on page 62.

2.12 Comparing Statements and Questions in the Simple Present Tense

Affirmative Statements and Questions

Wh- Word	Do/Does	Subject	Verb	Complement	Short Answer
		My sister	works	in Washington.	
	Does	she	work	for the IRS?	No, she doesn't.
Where	does	she	work?		
		You	pay	tax.	
	Do	you	pay	income tax?	Yes, I do.
Why	do	you	pay	tax?	

Negative Statements and Questions

Wh- Word	Don't/Doesn't	Subject	Verb	Complement
		People	don't like	taxes.
Why	don't	they	like	taxes?
		Sara	doesn't get	a tax refund.
Why	doesn't	she	get	a tax refund?

EXERCISE 23   ABOUT YOU Ask and answer questions with the words given. First ask another student a *yes/no* question. Then use the words in parentheses ( ) to ask a *wh-* question, if possible.

EXAMPLES
   live near school (where)   have cable TV (why)
   A: Do you live near school?   A: Do you have cable TV?
   B: Yes, I do.   B: No, I don't.
   A: Where do you live?   A: Why don't you have cable?
   B: I live on Green and Main.   B: Because it's too expensive.

1. speak Spanish (what language)   *Do you speak Spanish?*

2. have American friends (how many)   *Do you have American friends?*

3. live near the school (where)   *Do you live near the school?*

4. plan to go back to your country (when) (why)
  Do you plan to go back to your country?
5. live alone (with whom OR who . . . with)   *Do you live alone?*

6. practice English outside of class (with whom OR who . . . with)
  Do you practice English outside of class?
7. bring your dictionary to class (why)
  Do you bring your dictionary to class?
8. have a cell phone (why)   *Do you have a cell phone?*

EXERCISE 24   First ask the teacher a *yes/no* question. After you get the answer, use the words in parentheses ( ) to ask a *wh-* question, if possible. Your teacher will answer.

EXAMPLE   teach summer school (why)

A: Do you teach summer school?
B: No, I don't.
A: Why don't you teach summer school?
B: Because I like to travel in the summer.

1. have a laptop computer (what kind of computer)
   Do you have a lap top computer?
2. speak another language (what language)
   Do you speak another language?
3. teach summer school (why)
   Do you teach summer school?
4. correct the homework in school (where)
   Do you correct the homework in school?
5. drive to school (how . . . get to⁴ school)
   Do you drive to school?
6. like to teach English (why)
   Do you like to teach English?
7. come from this city (what city . . . from)
   Do you come from this city?

EXERCISE 25   Ask and answer questions about another teacher with the words given. First ask another student a *yes/no* question. Then use the words in parentheses ( ) to ask a *wh-* question, if possible.

EXAMPLE   speak your language (what languages)

A: Does your teacher speak your language?
B: No, he doesn't.
A: What languages does he speak?
B: He speaks English and French.

1. give a lot of homework (why)
   Does your teacher give a lot of homework?
2. write on the chalkboard (when)
   Does your teacher write on the chalkboard?
3. come to class late (what time)
   Does your teacher come to class late?
4. pronounce your name correctly (how)
   Does your teacher pronounce your name correctly?
5. use a textbook (what textbook)
   Does your teacher use a textbook?
6. wear jeans to class (what)
   Does your teacher wear jeans to class?

⁴*Get to* means arrive at.

EXERCISE 24

1. Tell students that in this exercise they will ask you, the teacher, questions. Have students read the direction line. Ask: *What kind of question do you ask first?* (a *yes/no* question) Model the example with another student.
2. Put students into groups. Have students write out questions if necessary. Go around to each group and answer students' questions.
3. If necessary, review grammar chart **2.12** on page 62.

🕐 To save class time, have students do half of the exercise in class and complete the other half in writing for homework. Or if students do not need speaking practice, the entire exercise may be skipped or done in writing.

EXERCISE 25

1. Tell students that they will be asking and answering questions about another teacher. Have students read the direction line. Model the example with another student.
2. Have students complete Exercise 25 in pairs. Circulate and observe the pair work. Give help as needed. Go over answers as a class.
3. If necessary, review grammar chart **2.12** page 62.

🕐 To save class time, have students do half of the exercise in class and complete the other half in writing for homework. Or if students do not need speaking practice, the entire exercise may be skipped or done in writing.

Expansion

Exercise 24 Use this exercise as an oral assessment. Ask individual students the questions in a quiet setting.

2.13 | Questions About Meaning, Spelling, and Cost

1. Have students cover up grammar chart **2.13**. Elicit question words. Ask students: *When you want to know the meaning of a word, what do you say?* (What does X mean?) *When you want to know how to spell something, what do you say?* (How do you spell X?) *When you want to know how to say something in another language, what do you say?* (How do you say X in your language.) *When you want to know how much something costs, what do you say?* (How much does X cost?)

2. Have students look at grammar chart **2.13**. Review the example sentences.

3. Explain to students that *mean, spell, say,* and *cost* are all verbs that go in the verb position in a question. For example, it's incorrect to say *What means "D.C."?*

EXERCISE 26

1. Have students read the direction line. Remind students to read the answer for help in writing the question. Go over the example in the book.

2. Have students complete the exercise individually. Then have students practice the conversation in pairs. Circulate to observe pair work. Give help as needed. Go over the answers as a class.

3. If necessary, review grammar chart **2.13** on page 64.

2.13 | Questions About Meaning, Spelling, and Cost

Wh- Word	Do/Does	Subject	Verb	Complement	Explanation
What	does	"D.C."	mean?		*Mean, spell, say,* and *cost* are verbs and should be in the verb position of a question.
How	do	you	spell	"government"?	
How	do	you	say	"government" in your language?	
How much	does	a metro ticket	cost?		

EXERCISE 26 Fill in the blanks in the conversation below with the missing words.

A: What ___'s___ your name?
    (example)

B: My name is Martha Gomez.

A: How ___do you___ spell "Gomez"?
    (1)

B: G-O-M-E-Z. It's a Spanish name.

A: Are you ___from___ Spain?
    (2)

B: No, I'm ___not___ .
    (3)

A: What country ___do___ you come ___from___ ?
    (4)   *(5)*

B: I come from Guatemala.

A: What language ___do___ they ___speak___ in Guatemala?
    (6)   *(7)*

B: They speak Spanish in Guatemala.

A: ___Is your___ your family here?
    (8)

B: No. My family is still in Guatemala. I call them once a week.
A: Isn't that expensive?

B: No, it ___isn't___ . I use a phone card.
    (9)

A: How much ___does it___ cost?
    (10)

B: It ___costs___ five dollars. We can talk for 35 minutes. I like
    (11)
to say hello to my family every week.

A: How ___do you say___ "hello" in Spanish?
    (12)

Expansion

Exercise 26 Have pairs rewrite the conversation making it true for them. Then have them practice the conversation. Ask volunteers to share their conversations with the class.

B: We say "hola." Please excuse me now. I'm late for my class. *Hasta luego.*

A: What ___does___ "hasta luego" ___mean___?
  (13)   (14)

B: It means "see you later" in Spanish.

2.14 | Comparing *Wh-* Questions—*Be* and Other Verbs

Examples	Explanation

Who **is** she?
Where **does** she live?
 	
How **are** you?
How **do** you **feel**?
 	
Where **am** I?
What **do** I **need**?
	Don't forget to use *do* or *does* in a question with a simple present-tense verb.
	
	   Wrong: Where she lives?
	   Wrong: How you feel?
	
	Don't use *be* to form a simple present-tense question.
	
	   Wrong: What am I need?

EXERCISE 🎧 Read this conversation between two new students, Ricardo (R) and Alexander (A). Fill in the blanks with the missing words.

R: Hi. My name ___'s___ Ricardo.
          (example)

   What ___'s your name___?
              (1)

A: Alexander.

R: Nice to meet you, Alexander. Where ___are you from/do you come from___?
                                              (2)

A: I ___'m/come___ from Ukraine.
        (3)

R: What languages ___do you speak___?
                        (4)

A: I speak Ukrainian and Russian.

R: ___Are you___ a new student?
        (5)

A: Yes, I am. What about you? Where ___are you/do you come from___ from?
                                          (6)

R: I ___'m/come___ from Peru.
        (7)

The Simple Present Tense **65**

Exercise 27 Variation

To provide practice with listening skills, have students close their books and listen to the audio. Repeat the audio as needed. Ask comprehension questions, such as: *Who are the two people talking?* (Ricardo and Alexander) *Where is Alexander from?* (Ukraine) *Does Alexander speak Russian?* (yes) Then have students open their books and complete Exercise 27.

2.14 | Comparing *Wh-* Questions—*Be* and Other Verbs

1. Have students cover up grammar chart **2.14.** Write the following on the board:
   a. *who / she?*
   b. *where / she / live?*
   c. *how / you?*
   d. *how / you / feel?*
   e. *where / I?*
   f. *what / I / need?*

2. Tell students to write *wh-* questions using the words above. Say: *Write the missing verbs.* Then have volunteers write them on the board.

3. Have students look at grammar chart **2.14.** Compare the work on the board with the sentences in the chart. Say: *Don't forget to use do or does in a question. Also, remember that you can't use the verb* be *to make questions with a simple present tense verb.*

EXERCISE 27

🎧 *CD 1, Track 11*

1. Have students read the direction line. Tell students that this is a conversation between two new students, Ricardo and Alexander. Remind students to look at the answer for help writing the question. Go over the example in the book.

2. Have students complete Exercise 27 individually. Then check answers as a class.

3. Have students practice the conversation in pairs. Circulate to observe pair work. Give help as needed.

4. If necessary, review grammar chart **2.14** on page 65.

A: Where _____ 's Peru _____?
(8)

R: It's in South America. We speak Spanish in Peru. I want to learn English and then go back to my country.

A: Why _____ do you want _____ to go back to Peru?
(9)

R: Because my father has an export business there, and I want to work with him.

A: What _____ does "export" mean _____?
(10)

R: "Export" means to sell your products in another country.

A: Why _____ do you need _____ to know English?
(11)

R: I need to know English because we have many American customers.

A: How many languages _____ does your father speak _____?
(12)

R: My father speaks four languages: English, French, German, and Spanish.

A: Tell me about your English class. _____ Do you like _____ your English teacher?
(13)

R: Oh, yes. I like her very much.

A: Who _____ 's _____ your English teacher?
(14)

R: Barbara Nowak.

A: _____ How do you spell "Nowak" _____?
(15)

R: N-O-W-A-K. It's a Polish name.

A: How many students _____ does your class have _____?
(16)

R: It has about 35 students. The classroom is very big.

A: What floor _____ is it on _____?
(17)

R: It's on the second floor.

A: When _____ does _____ your class _____ begin _____?
(18)   (19)

R: It begins at 6 o'clock. I'm late. See you later.

A: _____ How do you say _____ "see you later" in Spanish?
(20)

R: We say "hasta luego."

Expansion

Exercise 27 Have pairs rewrite the conversation making it true for them. Tell students they can change information and make it shorter. Have the pairs practice their new conversation. Circulate to observe pair work. Give help as needed. Ask volunteers to share their conversations with the class.

66 *Grammar in Context 1* Teacher's Edition

1. The simple present tense has two forms: the base form and the -s form:

Base Form		-s Form	
I		Everyone	
You		He	
We	eat.	She	eats.
They		It	
(Plural noun)		(Singular noun)	

2. Simple present-tense patterns with the -s form:

AFFIRMATIVE:	The president **lives** in Washington, D.C.
NEGATIVE:	He **doesn't live** in New York.
YES/NO QUESTION:	**Does** he **live** in the White House?
SHORT ANSWER:	Yes, he **does.**
WH- QUESTION:	Where **does** the vice president **live?**
NEGATIVE QUESTION:	Why **doesn't** the vice president **live** in the White House?

3. Simple present-tense patterns with the base form:

AFFIRMATIVE:	We **study** English in class.
NEGATIVE:	We **don't study** American history in class.
YES/NO QUESTION:	**Do** we **study** grammar?
SHORT ANSWER:	Yes, we **do.**
WH- QUESTION:	Why **do** we **study** grammar?
NEGATIVE QUESTION:	Why **don't** we **study** history?

4. Present-tense patterns with the verb be:

AFFIRMATIVE:	The teacher **is** absent.
NEGATIVE:	She **isn't** here today.
YES/NO QUESTION:	**Is** she sick?
SHORT ANSWER:	No, she **isn't.**
WH- QUESTION:	Where **is** she?
NEGATIVE QUESTION:	Why **isn't** she here?

5. We use the simple present tense with:

General truths and facts	Washington, D.C., **has** over half a million people. Americans **speak** English.
Customs	Japanese people **take** off their shoes when they enter a house. Americans **don't visit** friends without an invitation.
Regular activities (*More on this use in Lesson 3*)	He **visits** his parents every summer. I **play** soccer once a week.

Summary of Lesson 2

1. **Forms of the simple present tense** Have students make sentences for each subject in the chart. If necessary, review:
   - **2.1** Simple Present Tense— Forms (p. 43).

2. **Simple present-tense patterns with the -s form** Have students close their books. Say: *Write one sentence for each sentence type listed. Use a subject that takes the -s form. Then compare your sentences with those in the book.* If necessary, review:
   - **2.3** Spelling of the -s Form (p. 45)
   - **2.6** Negative Statements with the Simple Present Tense (p. 49)
   - **2.8** *Yes/No* Questions and Short Answers with the Present Tense (pp. 54–55)
   - **2.10** *Or* Questions (p. 59)
   - **2.11** *Wh-* Questions with the Simple Present Tense (p. 61).

3. **Simple present-tense patterns with the base form** Have students close their books. Say: *Write one sentence for each sentence type listed. Use a subject that takes the base form. Then compare your sentences with those in the book.* If necessary, review:
   - **2.6** Negative Statements with the Simple Present Tense (p. 49)
   - **2.8** *Yes/No* Questions and Short Answers with the Present Tense (pp. 54–55)
   - **2.10** *Or* Questions (p. 59)
   - **2.11** *Wh-* Questions with the Simple Present Tense (p. 61).

4. **Present-tense patterns with the verb *be*** Have students close their books. Say: *Write one sentence for each sentence type listed. Use the verb* be. *Then compare your sentences with those in the book.* If necessary, review:
   - **2.5** Comparing Affirmative Statements—*Be* and Other Verbs (p. 48)
   - **2.7** Comparing Negative Statements with *Be* and Other Verbs (p. 51)
   - **2.9** Comparing *Yes/No* Questions—*Be* and Other Verbs (p. 58)
   - **2.14** Comparing *Wh-* Questions— *Be* and Other Verbs (p. 65).

5. **Uses of the simple present tense** Have students write an affirmative sentence in the simple present tense for each use. If necessary, review:
   - **2.2** Simple Present Tense—Uses (p. 44).

Editing Advice

Have students close their books. Write the example sentences without editing marks or corrections on the board. For example:

1. He need more money.

   This school have a big library.

2. My father doesn't has a car.
   Does your mother speaks English well?

Ask students to correct each sentence. This activity can be done individually, in pairs, or as a class. After students have corrected each sentence, tell them to turn to pages 68–69. Say: *Now compare your work with the Editing Advice in the book.*

EDITING ADVICE

1. Don't forget to use the *-s* form when the subject is *he, she, it,* or a singular noun.

   He need more money.
   ^s

   has
   This school have a big library.

2. Use the base form after *does* and *doesn't*.

   have
   My father doesn't has a car.

   Does your mother speaks English well?

3. If you are living in the U.S., use the American form, not the British form, with *have*.

   doesn't have
   He hasn't a car.

   Do you have
   Have you a car?

4. Don't forget *do/does* in a question.

   do
   Where your parents live?

5. Use correct word order in a question.

   your brother live
   Where does live your brother?

   does your father have
   What kind of car has your father?

   don't you
   Why you don't like pizza?

6. Don't use *be* with another verb to form the simple present tense.

   I
   I'm have three brothers.
   She's lives in New York.

   I don't
   I'm not have a car.

7. Don't use *be* in a simple present-tense question that uses another verb.

   Does
   Is your college have a computer lab?

   Do
   Are you speak French?

8. Use correct spelling for the *-s* form.

    studies
She studys in the library.

    watches
He watchs TV every evening.

9. Use the correct negative form.

    doesn't
He not know the answer.

    don't
They no speak English.

10. Don't use an *-ing* form for simple present tense.

    write
I writing a letter to my family once a week.

11. *Family* is a singular word. Use the *-s* form.

    s
My family live in Germany.

12. Use the same auxiliary verb in a short answer as in a *yes/no* question.

    am
Are you hungry? Yes, I do.

    do
Do you like baseball? Yes, I am.

13. Use the correct word order with questions about meaning, spelling, and cost.

    does "wonderful" mean
What means "wonderful"?

    do bananas cost
How much cost bananas this week?

    do you
How spell "opportunity"?

    do you
How say "opportunity" in your language?

Lesson 2 Test/Review

For additional practice, review, and assessment materials, see Assessment CD-ROM with *ExamView Pro*, *More Grammar Practice* Workbook 1, Interactive CD-ROM, and Web site http://elt.thomson.com/gic

PART 1

1. Part 1 may be used as an in-class test to assess student performance, in addition to the Assessment CD-ROM with *ExamView Pro*. Have students read the direction line. Ask: *Does every sentence have a mistake?* (no) Go over the examples with the class.
2. Have students complete the assignment individually. Collect for assessment.
3. If necessary, have students review: **Lesson 2.**

PART **1** Find the mistakes with the underlined words and correct them. Not every sentence has a mistake. If the sentence is correct, write *C*.

EXAMPLES *I don't*
I'm not speak English well.
What does the teacher want? *C*

1. My mother washes my clothes every Sunday. *C*
2. I *don't have* haven't a dictionary.
3. Where *do* you live?
4. He *doesn't* no need help from you.
5. My sister talks a lot. *C*
6. You *don't* aren't need a dictionary for the test.
7. My brother goes to a state university. *C*
8. *Do* Are you want to buy a new computer?
9. Does your apartment have a dishwasher? Yes, it *does* is.
10. What kind of computers *does* has this school *have*?
11. How *do you* spell "computer"?
12. What does the teacher want? *C*
13. Why you don't *you* want to practice English at home?
14. How many children *does* do your sister have?
15. How much *does a stamp cost* costs a stamp?
16. The teacher doesn't speak my language. *C*
17. My mother worries a lot about me. *C*
18. Miami *doesn't* don't have cold winters.
19. *I don't* I'm not like to use public transportation.
20. How *do you* say "potato" in your language?

Lesson Review

To use Part 1 as a review, assign it as homework or use it as an in-class activity to be completed individually or in pairs. Check answers and review errors as a class. Reteach grammar points that students haven't mastered. Then student learning may be assessed using a test generated from the Assessment CD-ROM with *ExamView Pro*.

                                                goes
21. My friend ~~going~~ to Puerto Rico every winter.

22. My family <u>has</u> a big house. *c*

23. How many states <u>does</u> the U.S. have? *c*

                does "adjective" mean
24. What ~~means "adjective"~~?

PART 2 Write the -s form of the following verbs. Use correct spelling.

EXAMPLE   take _____*takes*_____

1. go _____*goes*_____

2. carry _____*carries*_____

3. mix _____*mixes*_____

4. drink _____*drinks*_____

5. play _____*plays*_____

6. study _____*studies*_____

7. catch _____*catches*_____

8. say _____*says*_____

PART 3 Fill in the first blank with the affirmative form of the verb in parentheses ( ). Then write the negative form of this verb.

EXAMPLES   A monkey _____*lives*_____ in a warm climate.
                              (live)

          It _____*doesn't live*_____ in a cold climate.

          Brazil _____*is*_____ a big country.
                        (be)

          Haiti _____*isn't*_____ a big country.

1. The English language _____*uses*_____ the Roman alphabet.
                                          (use)

   The Chinese language _____*doesn't use*_____ the Roman alphabet.

2. We _____*speak*_____ English in class.
            (speak)

   We _____*don't speak*_____ our native languages in class.

3. March _____*has*_____ 31 days.
                  (have)

   February _____*doesn't have*_____ 31 days.

The Simple Present Tense 71

PART 2

1. Part 2 may also be used as an in-class test to assess student performance, in addition to the Assessment CD-ROM with *ExamView Pro*. Have students read the direction line. Go over the example with the class.
2. Have students complete the exercise individually. Collect for assessment.
3. If necessary, have students review:
   2.3 Spelling of the -s Form (p. 45).

PART 3

1. Part 3 may also be used as an in-class test to assess student performance, in addition to the Assessment CD-ROM with *ExamView Pro*. Have students read the direction line. Ask: *Is the first or second sentence in the negative?* (second) Go over the examples with the class.
2. Have students complete the exercise individually. Collect for assessment.
3. If necessary, have students review:
   2.5 Comparing Affirmative Statements—*Be* and Other Verbs (p. 48)
   2.7 Comparing Negative Statements with *Be* and Other Verbs (p. 51).

Lesson Review

To use Parts 2 and 3 as a review, assign them as homework or use them as in-class activities to be completed individually or in pairs. Check answers and review errors as a class. Reteach grammar points that students haven't mastered. Then student learning may be assessed using a test generated from the Assessment CD-ROM with *ExamView Pro*.

1. Part 4 may also be used as an in-class test to assess student performance, in addition to the Assessment CD-ROM with *ExamView Pro*. Have students read the direction line. Ask: *Do we use* wh- *words in these questions?* (no) Go over the examples as a class.

2. Have students complete the exercise individually. Collect for assessment.

3. If necessary, have students review:

   2.8 *Yes/No* Questions and Short Answers with the Present Tense (pp. 54–55)

   2.9 Comparing *Yes/No* Questions—*Be* and Other Verbs (p. 58).

---

4. Mexico and Canada _____ *are* _____ in North America.
   (be)

   Colombia and Ecuador _____ *aren't* _____ in North America.

5. You _____ *pronounce* _____ the "k" in "bank."
   (pronounce)

   You _____ *don't pronounce* _____ the "k" in "knife."

6. The teacher _____ *teaches* _____ the English language.
   (teach)

   He/She _____ *doesn't teach* _____ American history.

7. A green light _____ *means* _____ "go."
   (mean)

   A yellow light _____ *doesn't mean* _____ "go."

8. I _____ *come* _____ from another country.
   (come)

   I _____ *don't come* _____ from the U.S.

9. English _____ *is* _____ hard for me.
   (be)

   My language _____ *isn't* _____ hard for me.

PART **4**   Write a *yes/no* question about the words in parentheses ( ). Then write a short answer.

EXAMPLES   January has 31 days. (February) (no)

Does February have 31 days? No, it doesn't.

China is in Asia. (Korea) (yes)

Is Korea in Asia? Yes, it is.

1. The U.S. has 50 states. (Mexico) (no)

   Does the U.S. have 50 states? Yes, it does.

2. The post office sells stamps. (the bank) (no)

   Does the bank sell stamps? No, it doesn't.

3. San Francisco is in California. (Los Angeles) (yes)

   Is Los Angeles in California? Yes, it is.

4. The metro runs all day. (all night) (no)

   Does the metro run all night? No, it doesn't.

5. January and March have 31 days. (April and June) (no)

   Do April and June have 31 days? No, they don't.

72   Lesson **2**

Lesson Review

To use Part 4 as a review, assign it as homework or use it as an in-class activity to be completed individually or in pairs. Check answers and review errors as a class. Reteach grammar points that students haven't mastered. Then student learning may be assessed using a test generated from the Assessment CD-ROM with *ExamView Pro*.

6. The president lives in the White House. (the vice president) (no)

    Does the vice president live in the White House? No, he doesn't.

7. Americans speak English. (Canadians) (yes)

    Do Canadians speak English? Yes, they do.

8. We come to class on time. (the teacher) (yes)

    Does the teacher come to class on time? Yes, she does.

9. The museums have good security. (the White House) (yes)

    Does the White House have good security? Yes, it does.

PART **5** Read each statement. Then write a *wh-* question about the words in parentheses ( ). You don't need to answer the question.

EXAMPLES   February has 28 days. (March)

    How many days does March have?

    Mexico is in North America. (Venezuela)

    Where is Venezuela?

1. Mexicans speak Spanish. (Canadians)

    What language do Canadians speak?

2. The U.S. has 50 states. (Mexico)

    How many states does Mexico have?

3. The president lives in the White House. (the vice president)

    Where does the vice president live?

4. Thanksgiving is in November. (Christmas)

    When is Christmas?

5. You spell "occasion" O-C-C-A-S-I-O-N: ("tomorrow")

    How do you spell "tomorrow"?

6. "Occupation" means job or profession. ("occasion")

    What does "occasion" mean?

7. The president doesn't make the laws. (why)

    Why doesn't the president make the laws?

8. Marek comes from Poland. (you)

    What country do you come from?

1. Part 5 may also be used as an in-class test to assess student performance, in addition to the Assessment CD-ROM with *ExamView Pro*. Have students read the direction line. Point out that it isn't necessary to answer the question. Go over the examples with the class.

2. Have students complete the exercise individually. Collect for assessment.

3. If necessary, have students review:

    2.11 *Wh-* Questions with the Simple Present Tense (p. 61)

    2.12 Comparing Statements and Questions in the Simple Present Tense (p. 62).

Lesson Review

To use Part 5 as a review, assign it as homework or use it as an in-class activity to be completed individually or in pairs. Check answers and review errors as a class. Reteach grammar points that students haven't mastered. Then student learning may be assessed using a test generated from the Assessment CD-ROM with *ExamView Pro*.

1. Part 6 may also be used as an in-class test to assess student performance, in addition to the Assessment CD-ROM with *ExamView Pro*. Have students read the direction line. Point out that this conversation is an interview. Go over the examples with the class.

2. Have students complete the interview individually. Collect for assessment.

3. If necessary, have students review:

    2.8 *Yes/No* Questions and Short Answers with the Present Tense (pp. 54–55)

    2.9 Comparing *Yes/No* Questions—*Be* and Other Verbs (p. 58)

    2.11 *Wh-* Questions with the Simple Present Tense (p. 61)

    2.12 Comparing Statements and Questions in the Simple Present Tense (p. 62)

    2.13 Questions About Meaning, Spelling, and Cost (p. 64)

    2.14 Comparing *Wh-* Questions —*Be* and Other Verbs (p. 65).

PART 6   Read this interview. Fill in the blanks with the missing word.

A: How old _____*are you*_____?
(example)

B: I'm 30 years old.

A: _____*Are you*_____ married?
(1)

B: No I'm single.

A: _____*Do you live*_____ with your parents?
(2)

B: No, I don't live with my parents.

A: Why _____*don't you live*_____ with your parents?
(3)

B: I don't live with my parents because they live in another city.

A: Where _____*do they live*_____?
(4)

B: They live in Chicago.

A: ___*Do*___ you ___*like*___ Washington?
(5)   (6)

B: Yes, I like it very much.

A: Why _____*do you like*_____ Washington?
(7)

B: I like it because it has so many interesting museums and galleries. But I don't have time to visit these places very often. I work every day. When my parents visit, we go to galleries and museums.

A: When _____*do they visit you*_____?
(8)

B: They visit me in the spring. They love Washington.

A: Why _____*do they love*_____ Washington?
(9)

B: They love it because it's a beautiful, interesting city. And they love it because I'm here.

A: What kind of job _____*do you have*_____?
(10)

B: I have a job with the government. I work in the Department of Commerce.

A: What _____*does "commerce" mean*_____?
(11)

B: Commerce means "business."

A: How _____*do you spell it*_____?
(12)

B: C-O-M-M-E-R-C-E.

74 Lesson **2**

Lesson Review

To use Part 6 as a review, assign it as homework or use it as an in-class activity to be completed individually or in pairs. Check answers and review errors as a class. Reteach grammar points that students haven't mastered. Then student learning may be assessed using a test generated from the Assessment CD-ROM with *ExamView Pro*.

A: _____ Do you like _____ your job?
                              (13)

B: Yes, I like my job very much.

A: _____ Where do you live _____?
                              (14)

B: I live a few blocks from the White House.

A: _____ Do you _____ have a car?
                              (15)

B: No, I don't. I don't need a car.

A: How _____ do you go _____ to work?
                              (16)

B: I go to work by metro. If I'm late, I take a taxi.

A: How much _____ does a taxi ride cost _____?
                              (17)

B: A taxi ride from my house to work costs about $12.

A: _____ Is the metro _____ clean?
                              (18)

B: Oh, yes. The metro is very clean.

A: _____ Do the trains run _____ all night?
                              (19)

B: No, the trains don't run all night. They run until midnight.

A: In my city, we don't say "metro." We use a different word.

B: How _____ do you say _____ "metro" in your city?
                              (20)

A: We say "subway."

EXPANSION ACTIVITIES

Classroom
   Activities

1. Check (✓) all the items below that are true of you. Find a partner and compare your list to your partner's list. Write three sentences telling about differences between you and your partner. (You may read your list to the class.)

a. ____ I have a cell phone.   g. ____ I play a musical instrument.

b. ____ I own a home.   h. ____ I sing well.

c. ____ I live in an apartment.   i. ____ I'm a good driver.

d. ____ I exercise regularly.   j. ____ I like pizza.

e. ____ I'm a vegetarian.   k. ____ I use an electronic calendar.

f. ____ I live with my parents.   l. ____ I write with my left hand.

The Simple Present Tense **75**

Expansion Activities

These expansion activities provide opportunities for students to interact with one another and further develop their speaking and writing skills. Encourage students to use grammar from this Lesson whenever possible.

🕐 To save class time, assign parts of the activities as homework. Then use class time for interaction and communication. If students do not need additional speaking practice, some of the activities may be assigned as writing activities for homework, or skipped altogether.

CLASSROOM ACTIVITIES

1. Have students read the direction line. Model the first item with a student. Have students complete the checklist on their own. Then instruct students to compare lists and write sentences about themselves and their partners (*I have a cell phone. Pedro doesn't have a cell phone.*). Circulate to observe pair work. Give help as needed.

Classroom Activities Variation

Activity 1 Do a class survey. In groups, have students compare information. Have students report their results to the class. Record the information on the board for selected categories (e.g., *All of the students in the class have a cell phone.*).

2. Have students read the direction line. Go over the sample questions and briefly model the activity. Before the game, brainstorm *wh-* question words and write them on the board. Point out that both *yes/no* questions and *wh-* questions may be asked.

3. Have students read the direction line. Go over the example and briefly model the activity. Point out that the answer to the example is a lion.

4. Tell students that this activity is about making comparisons between schools. Have students read the direction line. Go over the example with the class. Have students work in groups. Circulate to observe group work. Give help as needed.

WRITE ABOUT IT

Briefly model the activity with the class. Choose a tourist attraction in the U.S. and elicit sentences about it from the students (e.g., *I love New York City. It's very exciting. It has tall buildings. It has wonderful stores and restaurants.*). Collect for assessment and/or have students present their paragraphs to a group.

OUTSIDE ACTIVITY

Tell students that they will be interviewing a native English speaker about his or her favorite tourist place. Students can report their interview to the class or hand in a written report.

INTERNET ACTIVITIES

1. Tell students: *You're going to find out about tourist places on the Internet.* Write the ideas from the book on the board and any other ideas students might have. Ask: *What questions will you answer about the tourist attraction?* (What is it? Where is it? What does it cost to enter? What does it have?)

2. Brainstorm places of interest in your city. Write them on the board. Ask: *What questions will you answer about the tourist attraction?* (What is it? Where is it? What does it cost to enter? What does it have?)

---

2. **Game:** One student thinks of the name of a famous person and writes this person's initials on the chalkboard. Other students ask questions to try to guess the name of this person.

   SAMPLE QUESTIONS
   Is he an athlete?   Is he tall?
   Where does he come from?   How old is he?

3. **Game:** One student comes to the front of the room. He or she thinks of an animal and writes the name of this animal on a piece of paper. The other students try to guess which animal it is by asking questions. The person who guesses the animal is the next to come to the front of the room.

   EXAMPLE
   lion
   Does this animal fly? No, it doesn't.
   Does it live in water? No, it doesn't.
   What does it eat? It eats meat.
   Does this animal live in Africa? Yes, it does.

4. In a small group, discuss differences between classes and teachers in this school and another school you know.

   EXAMPLES
   In my college back home, students stand up when they speak. This class has some older people. In my native country, only young people study at college.

Write About it — Write about a tourist attraction in your country (or in another country you know something about).

Outside Activity — Interview an American about his or her favorite tourist place in the U.S. Why does he or she like this place? What does this place have?

Internet Activities

1. Using the Internet, find information about one of the following places: Disneyland, the White House, the Holocaust Museum, Ellis Island, Epcot Center, the Alamo, or any other American tourist attraction that interests you. Then answer these questions:

What is it?	What does it cost to enter?
Where is it?	What does it have?

2. Using the Internet, find information about a museum or place of special interest in this city. Then answer these questions:

What is it?	What does it cost to enter?
Where is it?	What does it have?

 Additional Activities at http://elt.thomson.com/gic

76 Lesson **2**

Write About it Variation

Have students make brochures about the tourist attractions. Encourage students to use drawings, pictures, photos, and other materials to illustrate their brochures. Display the brochures around the class for everyone to see. Ask volunteers to talk about the tourist attractions. Have each student exchange first drafts with a partner. Ask students to help their partners edit their drafts. Refer students to the Editing Advice on pages 68–69.

Outside Activity Variation

As an alternative, you may invite a guest to your classroom (e.g., an administrator, a librarian, or a service worker at your school) and have students do a class interview. Students should prepare their interview questions ahead of time.

Internet Activities Variation

Activity 2 If students don't have access to the Internet, they may find the information needed in local telephone books or resources at a local public library.

LESSON

3

GRAMMAR
Frequency Words with the Simple Present Tense
Prepositions of Time

CONTEXT: American Holidays
Three Special Days
The Fourth of July

77

Lesson | 3

Lesson Overview

1. Briefly review other tenses students have learned. Ask: *What tense did we study in Lesson 1?* (present tense of the verb *be*) *What tense did we study in Lesson 2?* (simple present tense)
2. Ask: *What tense are we going to study in this lesson?* (simple present tense) *What else will we study?* (frequency words and prepositions of time) *Do you know any frequency words or prepositions of time that we use with the simple present tense?* (e.g., *sometimes* and *in the morning*) Have students give examples. Write the examples on the board.

CONTEXT

1. Ask: *What are we going to learn about in this lesson?* (American holidays, celebrating holidays) Activate students' prior knowledge. Ask: *What do you know about holidays in the United States?*
2. Have students share their knowledge and personal experiences.

Photo

1. Direct students' attention to the photo. Ask: *Who are the people?* (a mother and her son and daughter) *Why do they have gifts? Why are the children kissing and hugging their mother?* (because it's Mother's Day)
2. Have students share similar experiences.

To save class time, have students do the Test/Review at the end of the lesson, or administer a lesson test generated from the Assessment CD-ROM with *ExamView®* *Pro*. Skip sections of the lesson that students have already mastered. You may also assign some sections for self-study for extra credit.

Expansion

Theme The topic for this lesson can be enhanced with the following ideas:

1. A homemade card that your children gave you for Mother's or Father's Day
2. A typical store-bought Mother's Day card
3. Advertisements from stores featuring Mother's Day sales with gift suggestions
4. Catalog from florist shop with different bouquets for Mother's Day

Three Special Days (Reading)

1. Have students look at the photo. Ask: *Who are the people?* (a couple; a wife and husband; a boyfriend and girlfriend; sweethearts) *What are they doing?* (The woman is giving the man flowers.)
2. Have students look at the title of the reading. Ask: *What is the reading about? How do you know?* Have students use the pictures, photo, and title to make predictions about the reading.
3. Pre-teach any vocabulary words your students may not know, such as *sweethearts, manufacturers, valentines, florist, parade, shamrock,* and *greeting card.* For *sweethearts, valentines, shamrock,* and *greeting card,* point out the pictures on page 78. For *parade,* direct students to the picture on page 79.

BEFORE YOU READ

1. Have students discuss the questions in pairs. Try to pair students of different cultures together.
2. Ask for a few volunteers to share their answers with the class.

🕐 To save class time, skip "Before You Read" or have students prepare answers for homework ahead of time.

Reading 🎧 *CD 1, Track 12*

1. Have students read the text silently. Tell them to pay special attention to frequency words such as *always* and *often.* Then play the audio and have students read along silently.
2. Check students' comprehension. Ask questions such as: *What kinds of gifts do people give on Valentine's Day?* (flowers, candy, and cards called valentines) *Who celebrates St. Patrick's Day?* (Irish people and many other Americans) *When is Mother's Day?* (the second Sunday in May)

🕐 To save class time, have students do the reading for homework ahead of time.

DID YOU KNOW?

Explain that several holidays have their origins in Ancient Rome, including Easter and Christmas. Say: *Describe any holidays celebrated in your native country. Are any connected to ancient rituals?*

Before You Read

1. What is your favorite holiday? When is it?
2. Do you celebrate Mother's Day? When?
3. Do you send cards for special occasions?

🎧 Read the following article. Pay special attention to the frequency words.

Did You Know?

Valentine's Day began in ancient Rome to honor Juno, the Roman goddess of women and marriage.

Valentine's Day is a day of love. It is **always** on February 14. On this day, people **often** give flowers or candy to their spouses or sweethearts. Candy manufacturers make candy or candy boxes in the shape of a heart. People **sometimes** send cards, called valentines, to close friends and relatives. Red is the color associated with Valentine's Day. A valentine **usually** has a red heart and a message of love. It **often** has a picture of Cupid, a symbol of romantic love. Florists sell a lot of red roses on Valentine's Day. Young children **usually** have a party at school and exchange cards.

Another special day is Saint Patrick's Day. It is **always** on March 17. It is really an Irish holiday, but many Americans like St. Patrick's Day even if they are not Irish. We **sometimes** say that on St. Patrick's Day everybody is Irish. In New York City, there is **always** a parade on St. Patrick's Day. Green is the color associated with St. Patrick's Day. People **often** wear green clothes on this day. One symbol of St. Patrick's Day is the shamrock.

Businesses are **never** closed for Valentine's Day or St. Patrick's Day. People **never** take a day off from work for these days. Schools and government offices are **always** open (except if these days fall on a Sunday).

Another special day is Mother's Day. It is **always** in May, but it isn't **always** on the same date. It is **always** on the second Sunday in May. People **usually** buy presents for their mothers and grandmothers or send special cards. Families **often** have dinner in a restaurant. Florists sell a lot of flowers on Mother's Day.

People enjoy these holidays. Greeting card companies also enjoy these holidays. They **always** sell a lot of cards and make a lot of money at these times.

78   Lesson 3

Reading Variation

To practice listening skills, have students first listen to the audio alone. Ask a few comprehension questions. Repeat the audio if necessary. Then have students open their books and read along as they listen to the audio.

Reading Glossary

florist: a person who owns or runs a flower shop

greeting card: a card, usually folded and printed with a message inside, such as "Get well" or "Happy Birthday"

manufacturer: a business that makes things

parade: an orderly movement of people in fanciful or formal dress or in uniforms, usually to show pride or to honor a special day or event

shamrock: a tiny green plant with three leaves; the symbol of Ireland

sweetheart: someone who is loved with tender affection and feels the same

valentine: a love letter or greeting card given to a person to show affection or love on Saint Valentine's Day

3.1 | Frequency Words with the Simple Present Tense

Frequency Word	Frequency	Examples
Always	100%	Mother's Day is **always** in May.
Usually	↑	I **usually** take my mother out to dinner.
Often		People **often** wear green on St. Patrick's Day.
Sometimes		I **sometimes** watch the parade.
Rarely/Seldom	↓	We **rarely** give flowers to children.
Never	0%	Businesses are **never** closed for Valentine's Day.

EXERCISE 1 Choose the correct word to fill in the blanks.

EXAMPLE People _____*often*_____ give flowers or candy on Valentine's
(never, seldom, often)

Day.

1. Valentine's Day is _____*always*_____ on February 14.
(always, sometimes, never)

2. People _____*often*_____ send valentine cards to their
(rarely, often, never)

sweethearts.

3. A valentine card _____*usually*_____ has a red heart and a
(never, rarely, usually)

message of love.

4. Young children _____*usually*_____ have a Valentine's Day party
(usually, always, never)

at school.

5. Saint Patrick's Day is _____*always*_____ on March 17.
(always, sometimes, never)

St. Patrick's Day Parade

Frequency Words with the Simple Present Tense; Prepositions of Time **79**

Grammar Variation

Have students come to the board and write the frequency words on the scale. Or have students draw a scale from 0 percent to 100 percent in their notebooks. Have them look at the reading and try to write the frequency words on the scale.

3.1 | Frequency Words with the Simple Present Tense

1. Have students cover up grammar chart **3.1** on page 79. Write all the frequency words on the board in scrambled order. Have students find sentences from the reading that contain frequency words. Write a few of the sentences on the board. For example, write: *It is always on February 14.*

2. On the board, draw a scale from 0 percent to 100 percent. Ask students to place the frequency words on the scale. Ask: *Where is* never *on the scale?*

3. Have students look at grammar chart **3.1.** Ask students to compare the scale on the board with the scale in the book. Ask: *Is our scale the same as the scale in the book?* Point out that *rarely* and *seldom* have the same frequency.

4. Review the example sentences in the grammar chart. Remind students that frequency words are used with the simple present tense.

EXERCISE 1

1. Tell students that this exercise is about the special days they just read about. Have students read the direction line. Ask: *What words do we use here?* (frequency words) Go over the example in the book. Then do #1 with the class.

2. Have students complete Exercise 1 individually. Then have them check their answers in pairs and compare their answers with the reading. Circulate to observe the pair work. If necessary, check the answers as a class.

3. If necessary, review grammar chart **3.1** on page 79.

EXERCISE 2

1. Tell students that this exercise is about this class or this school. Have students read the direction line. Ask: *What words do we use here?* (frequency words) Go over the example in the book. Ask: *What frequency word do we use here?* (answers will vary) Point out the picture of the man and woman wearing suits for #1.

2. Have students complete Exercise 2 individually. Then have them check their answers in pairs. Circulate to observe the pair work. If necessary, check the answers as a class.

3. If necessary, review grammar chart **3.1** on page 79.

🕐 To save class time, have students do half of the exercise in class and complete the other half for homework. Or assign the entire exercise for homework.

---

6. A St. Patrick's Day card _____*never*_____ has a red heart.
    (always, usually, never)

7. In New York City, there is _____*always*_____ a parade on Saint
    (always, seldom, never)
    Patrick's Day.

8. Card companies _____*always*_____ do a lot of business before
    (never, always, seldom)
    holidays.

9. Businesses are _____*never*_____ closed for St. Patrick's Day
    (always, usually, never)
    and Valentine's Day.

10. Mother's Day is _____*always*_____ in May.
    (always, usually, never)

11. Mother's Day is _____*never*_____ on a Saturday in the U.S.
    (always, never, sometimes)

EXERCISE 2   Fill in the blank with an appropriate frequency word about this class or this school.

EXAMPLE   We *sometimes* use a dictionary in class.

1. The teacher _____Answers will vary._____ wears a suit to class.

2. The school is _____ closed on Labor Day.

3. The students _____ ask questions in class.

4. The windows of the classrooms are _____ open.

5. The students _____ talk to each other during a test.

6. The door of the classroom is _____ open.

7. We _____ write a composition in class.

8. The teacher _____ writes on the blackboard (chalkboard).

9. The students _____ write on the blackboard (chalkboard).

10. The students _____ stand up when the teacher enters the room.

11. The teacher is _____ late to class.

12. We _____ read stories in class.

Expansion

Exercise 2 In pairs, have students tell each other how they spend Mother's Day in their native country. Say: *Tell your partner about Mother's Day in your home or in your native country. Your partner wants to know what your family does for Mother's Day. Your partner says, "Please tell me about Mother's Day in your home." Say three sentences about Mother's Day. Use frequency words to talk about what you do or do not do.* Instruct students to switch roles and repeat.

3.2 | Position of Frequency Words and Expressions

Examples	Explanation
Businesses *are* **never** closed for St. Patrick's Day. Mother's Day *is* **always** in May.	The frequency word comes after the verb *be*.
I **usually** *buy* a card for my mother. I **sometimes** *wear* green on St. Patrick's Day.	The frequency word comes before other verbs.
Sometimes I take my mother to a restaurant. **Usually** the weather is nice in May. **Often** we give gifts.	*Sometimes*, *usually*, and *often* can come at the beginning of the sentence, too.

EXERCISE 3   ABOUT YOU Add a frequency word to each sentence to make a **true** statement about yourself.

EXAMPLE   I eat fish.
I usually eat fish on Fridays.

Answers will vary. 1. I cook the meals in my house.

2. I stay home on Sundays.

3. I buy the Sunday newspaper.

4. I read the newspaper in English.

5. I use public transportation.

6. I'm tired in class.

7. I use my dictionary to check my spelling.

8. I buy greeting cards.

Grammar Variation

Ask students to cover up the Explanation side of the grammar chart. Elicit the rules from the students. Ask: *Does the frequency verb come before or after the verb* be? *Does the frequency verb come before or after other verbs? Do* usually *and* sometimes *always come at the beginning of the sentence?*

Expansion

Exercise 3 Have students survey the answers to Exercise 3 in groups. Ask: *How many cook meals? How many stay home on Sundays?* and so on. Circulate to observe the group work. Give help as needed. Then put the results of the survey on the board.

3.2 | Position of Frequency Words and Expressions

1. Have students cover up grammar chart **3.2** on page 81. Then have students find sentences from the reading on page 78 that contain frequency words and the verb *be*. Have them find sentences with other verbs and frequency words. Write several of the sentences with *be* and several sentences with other verbs on the board. For example, write:
   It is always on February 14. Businesses are never closed for Valentine's Day or St. Patrick's Day.
   A valentine usually has a red heart and a message of love.
   (Make sure the verbs of each sentence line up on the board.)

2. Ask students to guess the rule for the position of frequency words with *be* and other verbs. If students have difficulty guessing the rule, ask: *Do frequency words come before or after* be? *Do frequency words come before or after other verbs?*

3. Have students look at grammar chart **3.2**. Review the example sentences in the grammar chart. Point out to students that *sometimes*, *usually*, and *often* can also come at the beginning of the sentence.

EXERCISE 3

1. Tell students that this exercise is about their personal customs and routines. Have students read the direction line. Ask: *What words do we use here?* (frequency words)

2. Go over the example in the book. Then do #1 with the class. Ask a volunteer to give an answer.

3. If students need speaking practice, have them say true statements in pairs. If students need writing practice, have them complete the exercise in writing. Then have them compare their answers in pairs. Finally, check the answers as a class.

4. If necessary, review grammar chart **3.2** on page 81.

1. Tell students that this exercise is about customs and routines from their countries or cultural groups. Have students read the direction line. Go over the example. Then do #1 with the class. Ask a volunteer to give an answer.

2. Have students complete the rest of Exercise 4 individually. Then have them compare their answers in pairs. Try to pair students from different cultural groups. Finally, check the answers as a class.

3. If necessary, review grammar chart **3.2** on page 81.

🕐 To save class time, have students do half of the exercise in class and complete the other half for homework. Or assign the entire exercise for homework.

EXERCISE 5

1. Tell students that this exercise is about their personal customs and routines. Have students read the direction line. Go over the example in the book. Ask: *What tense is the first example in?* (simple present tense) *And the second example?* (present tense of *be*) Encourage students to use both the verb *be* and other verbs in their statements.

2. Have students complete the rest of Exercise 5 individually. Then have them compare their answers in pairs. Finally, check the answers as a class.

3. If necessary, review grammar chart **3.2** on page 81.

🕐 To save class time, have students do half of the exercise in class and complete the other half for homework. Or assign the entire exercise for homework.

EXERCISE **4** Add a verb (phrase) to make a **true** statement about people from your country or cultural group.

EXAMPLE people / often
Russian people often go to the forest on the weekends to pick mushrooms.

1. people / often
   _____
                 Answers will vary.

2. people / seldom
   _____

3. women / usually
   _____

4. women / rarely
   _____

5. men / usually
   _____

6. men / rarely
   _____

EXERCISE **5** ABOUT YOU Add a verb phrase to make a **true** statement about yourself.

EXAMPLE I / never
I never go to bed after 11 o'clock.
OR
I'm never in a good mood in the morning.

1. I / never
   _____
                 Answers will vary.

2. I / always / in the morning
   _____

3. I / usually / on Sunday
   _____

4. I / often / on the weekend
   _____

5. I / sometimes / in class
   _____

82 Lesson 3

Expansion

Exercise 4 Try and find similarities between cultures. Ask volunteers to talk about what they wrote in Exercise 4. Write examples on the board and ask students if there are similarities with other cultures.

Exercise 5 Put students in groups. Ask students to make true or false statements about themselves. Have the other students guess if the statements are true or false. Model an example. Say: *I always wake up early on Sundays. True or false?* Students guess if you're telling the truth.

EXERCISE **6** Use the words below to make sentences.

EXAMPLE mechanics / sometimes
Mechanics sometimes charge too much money.

1. American doctors / rarely

_____
Answers will vary.

2. American teachers / sometimes

_____

3. students at this school / often

_____

4. this classroom / never

_____

5. American hospitals / always

_____

6. people in this country / often

_____

THE FOURTH OF JULY

Before You **Read**

1. Do you like to see fireworks?
2. Do you celebrate any American holidays? What's your favorite American holiday?

Frequency Words with the Simple Present Tense; Prepositions of Time **83**

EXERCISE 6

1. Tell students that this exercise is about their observations and opinions. Have students read the direction line. Go over the example in the book.
2. Have students complete the rest of Exercise 6 in pairs. Circulate to observe pair work. Give help as needed.
3 If necessary, review grammar chart **3.2** on page 81.

To save class time, have students do half of the exercise in class and complete the other half for homework. Or assign the entire exercise for homework.

The Fourth of July (Reading)

1. Have students look at the photo. Ask: *Who are the people?* (families, friends) *What are they doing?* (They're having a picnic.)
2. Pre-teach any vocabulary words your students may not know, such as *barbecue, grill, backyard,* and *fireworks*. For *barbecue* and *grill*, point out the photo on page 83. For *fireworks*, direct students to the picture on page 84.

BEFORE YOU READ

1. Activate students' prior knowledge of American customs. Quickly brainstorm a list of American holidays with the class and write them on the board. Ask: *What other American holidays do you know?* (e.g., April Fool's Day, Memorial Day, Labor Day, Halloween, and Thanksgiving)
2. Have students discuss the questions in pairs.
3. Ask for a few volunteers to share their answers with the class.

To save class time, skip "Before You Read" or have students prepare answers for homework ahead of time.

Expansion

Exercise 6 Take a survey of the class. How did students complete the statements?

Theme The topic for this lesson can be enhanced with the following ideas:
1. Magazine pictures of Fourth of July picnics and celebrations
2. Photos from home of family Fourth of July picnics

Culture Note

Here are some other interesting American holidays:

April Fool's Day is celebrated on April 1. People play practical jokes on each other.

Memorial Day is a day of remembrance for those who died in military service. It is celebrated on the last Monday of May.

Labor Day is celebrated on the first Monday in September. It is a day that honors American workers.

Halloween is celebrated on October 31. Children dress up in costumes and go through their neighborhoods collecting candy and other treats.

Thanksgiving is celebrated on the fourth Thursday in November. Americans get together with family and friends to give thanks.

Reading *CD 1, Track 13*

1. Have students read the text silently. Tell them to pay special attention to prepositions of time such as *in* and *at*. Then play the audio and have students read along.
2. Check students' comprehension. Ask questions such as: *What is another name for Independence Day?* (the Fourth of July) *What do the writer and her family eat on the Fourth of July?* (hamburgers and hot dogs) *When do they usually eat?* (at about three o'clock) *Where do they go in the evening?* (to the park)

To save class time, have students do the reading for homework ahead of time.

3.3 | Prepositions of Time

1. Have students cover up grammar chart **3.3** on page 84. Then have students find sentences from the reading that contain prepositions of time. Write several of the sentences on the board. For example, write: *We celebrate it on July 4; We usually start to eat at about three o'clock*, etc.
2. Have students look at grammar chart **3.3**. Review the example sentences in the grammar chart. Then have students underline some of the prepositions. For example, say: *Find a sentence with* at.

 Read the following student composition. Pay special attention to prepositions of time.

My favorite holiday in the U.S. is American Independence Day. We celebrate it **on** July 4. In fact, we often call this holiday "The Fourth of July."

In the morning, my family and I prepare hamburgers for a barbecue. Our guests arrive **in** the afternoon, and we cook hamburgers and hotdogs on the grill in the backyard. We usually start to eat **at** about three o'clock. We have a lot of barbecues **in** the summer, but my favorite is **on** the Fourth of July.

We usually stay in our yard **from** about two o'clock **to** six o'clock p.m. Then **in** the evening, we usually go to the park. Most of our town goes there too, so we visit with each other while we wait for the fireworks. Finally, **at** night when it's completely dark, the fireworks show begins.

This is an exciting time for all of us. We celebrate our nation's independence and we have a lot of fun.

3.3 | Prepositions of Time

Preposition	Examples	Explanation
in	We prepare for the barbecue **in the morning.** We eat **in the afternoon.** We go to the park **in the evening.**	Use *in* with morning, afternoon, and evening.
in	Americans elect a president every four years: **in 2004, 2008, 2012,** etc.	Use *in* with years.
in	We often have a barbecue **in the summer.** It's too cold to have a barbecue **in the winter.**	Use *in* with seasons: summer, fall, winter, spring.
in	We celebrate Independence Day **in July.** We celebrate Mother's Day **in May.**	Use *in* with months.
on	We celebrate Independence Day **on July 4.** This year the holiday is **on Tuesday.**	Use *on* with dates and days.
at	We start to eat **at three o'clock.** We start the grill **at noon.** We go to bed **at midnight.**	Use *at* with a specific time of day.
at	The firework show starts **at night.**	Use *at* with night.
from . . . to	We stay in the backyard **from** two **to** six o'clock.	Use *from . . . to* with a beginning and an ending time. We can also say *from . . . till* or *until.*

84   Lesson **3**

Reading Variation

To practice listening skills, have students first listen to the audio alone. Ask a few comprehension questions. Repeat the audio if necessary. Then have students open their books and read along as they listen to the audio.

Reading Glossary

barbecue: a party where food is grilled or barbecued
fireworks: light, colorful explosives used for celebrations
grill: a frame of metal bars on which food is cooked, usually outside.
yard: an outdoor area usually behind or in front of a house

Culture Note

Many towns and cities have Fourth of July parades with floats, marching bands, military veterans, and other attractions.

Grammar Variation

Have students underline every prepositional phrase of time in the reading. For example, *on July 4*. Then have them match the preposition with the explanation in the grammar chart.

EXERCISE **7** ABOUT YOU Answer these questions. Use the correct preposition.

Answers will vary.
1. What time do you get up in the morning?
2. What time do you go to bed at night?
3. What time does your English class begin?
4. What days does your English class meet?
5. What time do you get to school?
6. When do students have vacation?
7. When do you do your homework?
8. What hours do you go to school?
9. When is your birthday?

3.4 | Questions with *Ever*

We use *ever* in a question when we want an answer that has a frequency word.

Do/Does	Subject	Ever	Verb	Complement	Short Answer
Do	you	**ever**	cook	outside?	Yes, we **sometimes** do.
Does	your brother	**ever**	work	on a holiday?	Yes, he **often** does.

Be	Subject	Ever	Complement	Short Answer
Are	the stores	**ever**	open on a holiday?	Yes, they **sometimes** are.
Is	the park	**ever**	crowded on the Fourth of July?	Yes, it **always** is.

Language Notes:
1. In a short answer, the frequency word comes between the subject and the verb.
2. If the frequency word is *never,* don't use a negative verb.
    Is the school **ever** open on the Fourth of July?
        No, it **never** is.
    Do you **ever** buy fireworks?
        No, I **never** do.

Frequency Words with the Simple Present Tense; Prepositions of Time   **85**

Expansion

Exercise 7 Create two rings of students. Have half of the students stand in an outer ring around the classroom. Have the other half stand in an inner ring, facing the outer ring. Instruct students to interview each other using the questions from Exercise 7. Call out *"turn"* every minute or so. Students in the inner ring should move one space clockwise. Students now interview their new partner. Make sure students look up at each other when they're asking and answering questions.

1. Tell students that this exercise is about their personal routines and customs. Have students read the direction line. Ask: *What kind of questions are these?* (information questions or *wh-* questions) Model the exercise. Do #1 with the class. Ask a volunteer to give an answer. Remind students to use the appropriate preposition in their answer.
2. Have students complete the rest of Exercise 7 individually. Then have them interview each other in pairs. Say: *Now ask your partner the questions and write down his or her answers.* Finally, check the answers as a class.
3. If necessary, review grammar chart **3.3** on page 84.

3.4 | Questions with *Ever*

1. Have students cover up grammar chart **3.4** on page 85. Review *yes/no* questions with students. Write statements on the board based on the reading. For example, write:
The Fourth of July is my favorite holiday.
We cook hamburgers and hot dogs on the grill.
Then have students write questions in their notebooks for the statements. Check answers with the class. (*Is the Fourth of July your favorite holiday? Do you cook hamburgers and hot dogs on the grill?*)
2. Have students look at grammar chart **3.4.** Say: *We use ever in a question when we want an answer that has a frequency word.* Review the example sentences in the grammar chart.
3. Review the Language Notes. Ask students to look at the frequency word in short answers. Ask: *Where is the frequency word?* (It's between the subject and the verb.) Remind students not to use a negative verb with *never.* Write on the board:
Correct: No, it never is.
Wrong: No, it never isn't.

EXERCISE 8

1. Tell students that this exercise is about personal preferences and customs. Have students read the direction line. Ask: *What word do we add to the questions?* (ever) Ask: *What words are in the answers?* (frequency words)
2. Direct students to the examples in the book. Point out that students can answer *yes* or *no* with just a frequency word or they can answer with a longer sentence. (*Yes, often.* OR *Yes, I often do.*) Model the first example with a student. Then have two other students model the next example.
3. Have students complete the exercise in pairs. Check the answers as a class.
4. If necessary, review grammar chart **3.4** on page 85.

EXERCISE 9

1. Tell students that this exercise is about American customs. Have students read the direction line. Ask: *What word do we add to the questions?* (ever) Ask: *What words are in the answers?* (frequency words) Go over the examples in the book. Model the first example with a student. Then have two other students model the next example.
2. Have students complete the exercise in pairs. Point out the pictures of chopsticks and men shaking hands. Check the answers as a class.
3. If necessary, review grammar chart **3.4** on page 85.

🕐 To save class time, have students do half of the exercise in class and complete the other half in writing for homework. Or if students do not need speaking practice, the entire exercise may be skipped or done in writing.

EXERCISE **8** ABOUT YOU Add *ever* to ask these questions. Another student will answer.

EXAMPLES Do you eat in a restaurant?

A: Do you ever eat in a restaurant?
B: Yes, I often do. OR Yes, often.

Are you bored in class?

A: Are you ever bored in class?
B: No, I never am. OR No, never.

Answers will vary.
1. Do you use public transportation?
2. Do you drink coffee at night?
3. Do you drink tea in the morning?
4. Do you speak English at home?
5. Do you watch TV at night?
6. Do you rent DVDs?
7. Are you late to class?
8. Do you drive and use your cell phone at the same time?
9. Are you homesick?
10. Are you lazy on Saturdays?
11. Does it snow in March?
12. Do you ask for directions on the street?

EXERCISE **9** Add *ever* to these questions to ask about Americans. Another student will answer.

EXAMPLES Do Americans eat fast food?

A: Do Americans ever eat fast food?
B: Yes, they sometimes do.

Are Americans friendly to you?

Answers will vary.
A: Are Americans ever friendly to you?
B: Yes, they usually are.

1. Do Americans eat with chopsticks?
2. Do Americans carry radios?
3. Do Americans say, "Have a nice day"?
4. Do Americans kiss when they meet?
5. Do Americans pronounce your name incorrectly?
6. Are Americans impolite to you?
7. Do Americans shake hands when they meet?
8. Do Americans ask you what country you're from?
9. Are Americans curious about your native country?

86 Lesson **3**

Expansion

Exercise 9 If possible, select students of different nationalities to be interviewed. Tell interviewers to ask questions 1–4, 7, and 9 from Exercise 9. Say: *Substitute the word* American *for your partner's nationality. For example: Do Colombians ever eat with chopsticks?* Circulate to observe the pair work. Give help when needed.

EXERCISE **10** ABOUT YOU Fill in the blanks with a frequency word to make a statement about yourself. Then ask a question with *ever*. Another student will answer.

EXAMPLE I _____*never*_____ jog in the morning.

A: Do you ever jog in the morning?
B: No, I never do.

Answers will vary.

1. I _____ ride a bike in the summer.
2. I _____ visit relatives on Sunday.
3. I _____ go to sleep before 9 p.m.
   (Women: Do A. Men: Do B.)
4. A. I _____ wear high heels.
   B. I _____ wear a suit and tie.
5. I _____ do exercises.
6. I _____ eat meat.
7. I _____ drink colas.
8. I _____ buy the Sunday newspaper.
9. I _____ put sugar in my coffee.
10. I _____ take a nap in the afternoon.
11. I _____ eat in a restaurant.
12. I _____ use a fax machine.
13. I _____ bake bread.
14. I _____ use cologne or perfume.
15. I _____ take a bubble bath.
16. I _____ check my e-mail in the morning.
17. I _____ borrow money from a friend.
18. I _____ leave a light on when I sleep.
19. I _____ drink coffee at night.
20. I _____ listen to the radio when I'm driving.

EXERCISE 10

1. Tell students that this exercise is about their personal customs and habits. Have students read the direction line. Ask: *What word do we put in the blank?* (a frequency word) Ask: *Then what do we do?* (Write a question with *ever*.) Model the example with a student. Then have two other students model #1. Point out the pictures of high heels, the Sunday newspaper, and a bubble bath.
2. Have students fill in the blanks and write the questions individually. Then have students ask and answer questions in pairs. Check the answers as a class.
3. If necessary, review grammar chart **3.4** on page 85.

To save class time, have students do half of the exercise in class and complete the other half in writing for homework (with students using their own information to answer the questions). Or if students do not need speaking practice, the entire exercise may be skipped or done in writing.

Expansion

Exercise 10 Ask students to choose three interesting questions from Exercise 10. Have students travel around the room asking the questions. Say: *Find three students who answer* no *and three students who answer* yes *to your questions. Write down their names and their responses.*

3.5 | Questions with *How Often* and Answers with Frequency Expressions

1. Have students cover up grammar chart **3.5** on page 88. Write frequency expressions from the chart on the board. For example, write: *every day, every month,* and *twice a week.* Ask: *What do you do every day? What do you do every other day? What do you do twice a week?* Have volunteers answer. Write their responses on the board.

every day	every month	twice a week
take a shower	go to the movies	go to the gym

2. Write *How often* on the board. Make a sentence with one of the students' sentences. Write: *How often do you take a shower?* Write the answer. (*every day*) Ask volunteers to make sentences with *how often* and the information on the board.

3. Have students look at grammar chart **3.5**. Say: *We ask a question with* how often *when we want to know the frequency of an activity.* Review the example sentences and the expressions that show frequency in the grammar chart. Tell students that frequency expressions can come at the beginning or at the end of a sentence.

EXERCISE 11

1. Tell students that this exercise is about their personal customs and habits. Have students read the direction line. Ask: *What words do we use to make the question?* (*How often do you*) Model the example with a student. Then have two other students model #1. Point out the picture of the man shopping for groceries.

2. Have students ask and answer questions in pairs. If necessary, students may write the questions before working with a partner. Check the answers as a class.

3. If necessary, review grammar chart **3.5** on page 88.

3.5 | Questions with *How Often* and Answers with Frequency Expressions

We ask a question with *how often* when we want to know the frequency of an activity.

Examples	Explanation

How often do you eat hamburgers?
   Once in a while.
How often do you visit your mother?
   Once a week.
How often do you go to the park?
   Every week.
	Expressions that show frequency are:
	 • every day (week, month, year)
	 • every other day (week, month, year)
	 • from time to time
	 • once in a while

I learn more about life in America **every day.** **Every day** I learn more about life in America. **From time to time,** I eat hamburgers. I eat hamburgers **from time to time.**	Frequency expressions can come at the beginning or the end of the sentence.

EXERCISE **11**   ABOUT YOU Ask a question with "How often do you . . . ?" and the words given. Another student will answer.

EXAMPLE   get a haircut

A: How often do you get a haircut?
B: I get a haircut every other month.

1. come to class
   How often do you come to class?
2. shop for groceries
   How often do you shop for groceries?
3. wash your clothes
   How often do you wash your clothes?
4. use your cell phone
   How often do you use your cell phone?
5. go out to dinner
   How often do you go out to dinner?
6. use public transportation
   How often do you use public transportation?
7. renew your driver's license
   How often do you renew your driver's license?
8. buy the newspaper
   How often do you buy the newspaper?
9. go to the movies
   How often do you go to the movies?
10. check your e-mail
    How often do you check your e-mail?

88   Lesson 3

Expansion

Exercise 11 Create two rings of students. Have half of the students stand in an outer ring around the classroom. Have the other half stand in an inner ring, facing the outer ring. Instruct students to interview each other using the questions from Exercise 11. Call out *"turn"* every minute or so. Students in the inner ring should move one space clockwise. Students now interview their new partner. Make sure students look at each other when they're asking and answering questions.

EXERCISE **12** Linda has a list to remind her of the things she has to do on a regular basis. Write questions and answers about her activities.

> • drive daughter to ballet lessons—Tu, Th
> • pick up son at baseball practice—Mon, Wed
> • shop for groceries—Sat
> • take the dog for a haircut—3rd day of every month
> • go to the beauty salon—5th day of every month
> • visit Mom—Fri
> • go to the gym—Mon, Wed, Fri morning
> • prepare the kids' lunches—Mon to Fri
> • change oil in car—Jan, April, July, Oct

EXAMPLE   *How often does she drive her daughter to ballet lessons?*

She drives her daughter to ballet lessons twice a week.

1. _____ **Answers will vary.** _____

2. _____

3. _____

4. _____

5. _____

6. _____

7. _____

8. _____

EXERCISE 12

1. Tell students that this exercise is about Linda's activities. Have students read the direction line. Ask: *What question words will you use in the question?* (*how often*) Model the example with a student. Then have two other students model #1.
2. Have students complete the exercise individually. Then have them check answers in pairs.
3. If necessary, review grammar chart **3.5** on page 88.

🕐 To save class time, have students do half of the exercise in class and complete the other half for homework. Or assign the entire exercise for homework.

Expansion

Exercise 12 Have students write their own list of things they do on a regular basis. Tell students not to include when or how often they do the activity. Have students exchange lists and interview each other. Ask students to report interesting activities to the class (e.g., *John goes to Karate class every other day.*). Circulate to observe pair work. Give help when needed.

EXERCISE 13

1. Tell students that this exercise is about their family members' habits and routines. Have students read the direction line. Ask: *What words will we use in the sentences?* (frequency words) Go over the example in the book.

2. Have students complete the exercise individually. Collect for assessment or have students read their sentences to a partner.

3. If necessary, review grammar charts **3.1** on page 79 and **3.5** on page 88.

🕐 To save class time, have students do the exercise for homework.

EXERCISE 14

🎧 *CD 1, Track 14*

1. Tell students that this exercise is a conversation between two friends. Have students read the direction line. Remind students that the verbs should be in the simple present tense. Go over the example in the book. Point out the picture of someone knitting.

2. Have students complete Exercise 14 individually. Then check answers as a class.

3. Have students practice the dialogue in pairs.

4. If necessary, review grammar charts **3.1** on page 79 and **3.5** on page 88.

🕐 To save class time, have students do half of the exercise in class and complete the other half for homework. Or assign the entire exercise for homework.

EXERCISE 13 ABOUT YOU Write a few sentences about a member of your family or another person you know. Use frequency words.

EXAMPLE
My sister never helps with the housework.

She sometimes leaves dirty dishes in the sink.

She always gets good grades.

Answers will vary.

EXERCISE 14 Use the words in parentheses ( ) to complete this conversation. Put the words in the correct order. Use the correct form of the verb.

🎧

A: Let's go to a movie tonight.

B: I can't. My mother ___*always makes*___ dinner for me on Fridays.
(example: make/always)

If I don't visit her, she ___*usually complains*___.
(1 complain/usually)

And if I don't call her, she worries.

A: ___*How often do you call*___ her?
(2 how/often/you/call)

B: ___*I call her every day*___.
(3 I/every day/call her)

A: Why do you call her so often?

B: She's old now, and she ___*'s often*___ lonely.
(4 often/be)

A: Well, invite your mother to go to the movies.

B: Thanks, but she has a favorite TV show on Friday nights.

She ___*always watches*___ it.
(5 watch/always)

A: ___*Does she ever*___ go out?
(6 ever/she)

B: She ___*rarely does*___. She prefers to stay home.
(7 rarely/do)

She likes to cook, knit, and watch TV.

A: Is she a good cook?

B: Not really. She ___*usually cooks*___ the
(8 usually/cook)

same thing every week: chicken on Friday, fish on Saturday, meatloaf

on Sunday. . . . Her routine ___*never changes*___.
(9 change/never)

Only Mother's Day is different.

90   Lesson 3

Exercise 14 Variation

To provide practice with listening skills, have students close their books and listen to the audio. Repeat the audio as needed. Ask comprehension questions, such as: *What does person A want to do tonight?* (go to a movie) *What does person B's mother do on Friday nights?* (make dinner for person B) *Is person B's mother young or old?* (old) Then have students open their books and complete Exercise 14.

A: What ___*do you usually do*___ on Mother's Day?
         (10 you/do/usually)

B: My sister and I ___*usually buy*___ her flowers
              (11 usually/buy)

and take her to a restaurant.

A: Does she like that?

B: Not really. She ___*usually says*___ ,
                (12 usually/say)

"Don't waste your money. Flowers ___*always die*___ in a day
                                  (13 die/always)

or two. And my cooking is better than restaurant food."

A: ___*Is she always*___ hard to please?
     (14 be/she/always)

B: Yes, she is.

A: ___*Is she ever*___ satisfied?
     (15 be/she/ever)

B: Not usually. She ___*always says*___ ,
                  (16 always/say)

"I don't want Mother's Day once a year. I want it every day."

EXERCISE **15** *Combination Exercise.* Read a student's composition about the Fourth of July. Find the mistakes with the underlined words and correct them. Add a form of the verb *be* where necessary. If the underlined words are correct, write *C*.

My favorite holiday in the U.S. <u>is</u> the Fourth of July. My
                                    C
family <u>puts always</u> an American flag in front of the house.
     always puts

My friends and relatives <u>always get</u> together for a BBQ.
                            C

We usually <u>cook</u> hamburgers and hotdogs on the grill.
           C

<u>Sometimes we</u> cook fried chicken and steaks. The men in
       C

the family usually <u>cooking</u>. (They <u>rarely cook</u> the rest of
                   cook   *C*

the year!) We <u>usually have</u> the BBQ at my house, but
              C

sometimes <u>we're have</u> the BBQ in a park. We always <u>has</u>
           we   *have*

a potluck; everyone <u>brings</u> a different dish. My mother
                    C

always <u>bake</u> a delicious apple pie.
       bakes

Frequency Words with the Simple Present Tense; Prepositions of Time   **91**

EXERCISE 15

1. Tell students that this exercise is about how one person celebrates the Fourth of July. Have students read the direction line. Ask: *Does every sentence have a mistake?* (no) Go over the examples. Point out the photo of the house with an American flag in front.
2. Have students complete the exercise individually. Collect for assessment or check answers as a class.
3. If necessary, review Lessons 1, 2, and 3.

⏱ To save class time, have students do half of the exercise in class and complete the other half for homework. Or assign the entire exercise for homework.

Culture Note

Americans often show patriotism on special days by hanging the American flag outside their homes. You will often see flags out on Memorial Day (the last Monday in May), the Fourth of July (July 4) and on Flag Day (June 14). Some people even hang their flags out all year round.

Summary of Lesson 3

1. **Frequency Words** Have students practice frequency words in pairs using the reading on page 78. Say: *Go back to the reading on page 78. One student says, "True or false? St. Patrick's Day is sometimes on March 17." The other student says, "False. St. Patrick's Day is always on March 17." Each partner makes four true or false statements.*
   If necessary, have students review:
   3.1 Frequency Words with the Simple Present Tense (p. 79)
   3.2 Position of Frequency Words and Expressions (p. 81).

2.–3. **The Position of Frequency Words and Expressions** Have students close their books. Instruct students to write down at least five frequency words and five frequency expressions on a piece of paper. Have students practice in pairs. Say: *One student says, "Every other day." The other student gives an example about him or herself, such as, "I have English class every other day" or "Every other day I have English class."* Instruct students to switch roles and repeat.
   If necessary, have students review:
   3.2 Position of Frequency Words and Expressions (p. 81)
   3.5 Questions with *How Often* and Answers with Frequency Expressions (p. 88).

4. **Frequency Questions and Answers** Have students write ten questions using *ever* and *how often*. Remind students to use *ever* with the simple present tense and also with the present tense of *be*. Then have students ask and answer the questions in pairs.
   If necessary, have students review:
   3.4 Questions with *Ever* (p. 85)
   3.5 Questions with *How Often* and Answers with Frequency Expressions (p. 88).

5. **Prepositions of Time** Write three to five questions on the board to elicit prepositions of time. For example, write:
   What time do you eat breakfast/ dinner?
   When do you go shopping?
   When do you do your homework?
   When do you go to work/school?
   What time do you get home?
   Have students answer the questions in their notebooks. Then instruct students to go around the room and

---

Our city always has a parade ~~at~~ on the Fourth of July ~~from~~ C noon ~~at~~ to one o'clock. ~~In the~~ At night, we usually go to see the fireworks at the main park. The park ~~always is~~ is always crowded. The weather usually is nice, but ~~it's~~ it sometimes rains and the fireworks show is canceled. When that ~~happen~~ happens, we are very disappointed. Luckily, that seldom ~~happens~~ C happens.

Most businesses and schools ~~is~~ are closed on the Fourth of July. The library, banks, and offices are always C closed. ~~I'm~~ I never work on this holiday, but my brother is a police officer and he sometimes ~~work~~ works on the Fourth of July. Some businesses, such as supermarkets, ~~stays~~ stay open for half the day. People often ~~forgets~~ forget to buy something and need to get some last minute items.

I always look forward to this holiday because I see all my family and we ~~has~~ have a lot of fun together. Also my birthday is ~~on~~ in July and I get a lot of presents.

SUMMARY OF LESSON 3

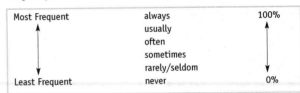

1. Frequency Words:

Most Frequent	always	100%
↑	usually	↑
	often	
	sometimes	
	rarely/seldom	↓
Least Frequent	never	0%

2. The Position of Frequency Words:
   AFTER THE VERB *BE*: He is **always** late.
   BEFORE A MAIN VERB: I **usually** walk to work.

3. The Position of Frequency Expressions:
   Every day I watch TV.
   I watch TV **every day.**

4. Frequency Questions and Answers:
   Do you **ever** wear a suit? I seldom do.
   Are you **ever** bored in class? Yes, sometimes.
   How often do you go to the library? About once a month.

5. Review prepositions of time on page 84. Review the simple present tense in Lessons 1 and 2.

EDITING ADVICE

1. Put the frequency word in the correct place.
   am never
   I never am bored in class.
   I always
   Always I drink coffee in the morning.

2. Don't separate the subject and the verb with a frequency phrase.
   once in a while
   She once in a while visits her grandmother.
   Every other day we
   We every other day write a composition.

3. Don't use a negative verb with *never.*
   do
   Do you ever take the bus to school? No, I never don't.
   We never don't eat in class.

4. Use *ever* in questions. Answer the question with a frequency word.
   sometimes
   Do you ever listen to the radio in the morning? Yes, I ever do.

LESSON 3 TEST/REVIEW

PART 1   Find the mistakes with the underlined words and correct them (including mistakes with word order). Not every sentence has a mistake. If the underlined words are correct, write C.

EXAMPLES   Do you ever drink coffee? No, I never don't.
            do
            I never eat spaghetti.   *C*

Lesson Review

To use Part 1 as a review, assign it as homework or use it as an in-class activity to be completed individually or in pairs. Check answers and review errors as a class. Reteach grammar points that students haven't mastered. Then student learning may be assessed using a test generated from the Assessment CD-ROM with *ExamView Pro.*

---

5. **Prepositions of Time (*cont.*)** ask other students the same questions. Ask: *How many students have the same information as you?*

   The Simple Present Tense Divide the class into Team A and Team B. Write a verb in the base form on the board. For example, write: *Celebrate.* Say: *One member from each team comes up to the board and writes a sentence in the simple present tense with* celebrate. Let the team help members with the sentence. If necessary, have students review: **Lessons 1 and 2.**

Editing Advice

Have students close their books. Write the example sentences without editing marks or corrections on the board. For example:

1. *I never am bored in class.*
2. *Always I drink coffee in the morning.*

Ask students to correct each sentence. This activity can be done individually, in pairs, or as a class. After students have corrected each sentence, tell them to turn to page 93. Say: *Now compare your work with the Editing Advice in the book.*

Lesson 3 Test/Review

For additional practice, review, and assessment materials, see Assessment CD-ROM with *ExamView Pro, More Grammar Practice* Workbook 1, Interactive CD-ROM, and Web site http://elt.thomson.com/gic

PART 1

1. Part 1 may be used as an in-class test to assess student performance, in addition to the Assessment CD-ROM with *ExamView Pro.* Have students read the direction line. Ask: *Does every sentence have a mistake?* (no) Collect for assessment.
2. If necessary, have students review: **Lessons 1, 2, and 3.**

PART 2

1. Part 2 may also be used as an in-class test to assess student performance, in addition to the Assessment CD-ROM with *ExamView Pro*. Tell students that this is a conversation between two students. Words and phrases are missing. Review the example. Then do #1 as a class. Ask: *What goes in the first blank? (is)*
2. Collect for assessment.
3. If necessary, have students review: **Lessons 1, 2, and 3.**

1. ~~Always I~~ give my mother a present for Mother's Day.
   I always

2. I rarely go downtown.   *C*

3. ~~They never are~~ on time.
   They're never

4. ~~It snows seldom~~ in April.
   It seldom snows

5. Do you ever take the bus? Yes, I never do.
   No

6. Are you ever late to class? Yes, ~~always I am~~.
   I always am

7. Do you ever use chopsticks? Yes, ~~I ever do~~.
   I always do

8. ~~What often~~ do you go to the library? I go to the library twice a month.
   How often

9. ~~I once in a while~~ eat in a restaurant.
   Once in a while I

10. Every other day she cooks chicken.   *C*

PART **2**   This is a conversation between two students. Fill in the blanks to complete the conversation.

A: Who _____is_____ your English teacher?
   (example)

B: His name _____'s_____ David.
   (1)

A: _____Do you like_____ David?
   (2)

B: Yes. I like him very much.

A: _____Does_____ he wear a suit to class?
   (3)

B: No, he _____doesn't_____. He always _____wears_____
   (4)   *(5)*

   jeans and running shoes.

A: _____How old is he_____?
   (6)

B: He _____'s_____ about 60 years old.
   (7)

A: _____Does he speak_____ your language?
   (8)

B: No, he doesn't speak Spanish, but he _____speaks_____ Polish
   (9)

   and Russian. And English, of course.

A: _____How often_____ does your class meet?
   (10)

B: It meets three days a week: Monday, Wednesday, and Friday.

94   Lesson **3**

Lesson Review

To use Part 2 as a review, assign it as homework or use it as an in-class activity to be completed individually or in pairs. Check answers and review errors as a class. Reteach grammar points that students haven't mastered. Then student learning may be assessed using a test generated from the Assessment CD-ROM with *ExamView Pro*.

A: My class _____meets_____ two days a week: Tuesday and
   (11)
Thursday.

B: Tell me about your English teacher.

A: Her name _____name is_____ Dr. Misko. She never
   (12)

_____wears_____ jeans to class. She _____only_____
   (13)   (14)

wears a dress or suit. She _____doesn't speak_____ my language.
   (15)

She only _____speaks_____ English.
   (16)

B: Do you like her?

A: Yes, but she _____gives_____ a lot of homework and tests.
   (17)

B: _____How often_____ does she give a test?
   (18)

A: Once a week. She gives a test every Friday. I _____don't_____
   (19)
like tests.

B: My teacher sometimes teaches us American songs.

_____Does_____ your teacher _____ever_____
   (20)   (21)

_____teach_____ you American songs?
   (22)

A: No, she never _____does_____.
   (23)

B: What book _____does your class use_____?
   (24)

A: My class uses *Grammar in Context*.

B: What _____does "context" mean_____?
   (25)

A: "Context" means the words that help you understand a new word or
idea.

B: How _____do you spell "context"_____?
   (26)

A: C-O-N-T-E-X-T.

PART 3   Fill in the blanks with the correct preposition.

EXAMPLE   Many people go to church _____on_____ Sundays.

1. We have classes _____in_____ the evening.

2. Valentine's Day is _____in_____ February.

3. Valentine's Day is _____on_____ February 14.

Frequency Words with the Simple Present Tense; Prepositions of Time   **95**

PART 3

1. Part 3 may also be used as an in-class test to assess student performance, in addition to the Assessment CD-ROM with *ExamView Pro*. Tell students that prepositions of time are missing. Review the example. Then do #1 as a class. Ask: *What goes in the first blank? (on)*

2. Collect for assessment.

3. If necessary, have students review:
   3.3   Prepositions of Time (p. 84).

Lesson Review

To use Part 3 as a review, assign it as homework or use it as an in-class activity to be completed individually or in pairs. Check answers and review errors as a class. Reteach grammar points that students haven't mastered. Then student learning may be assessed using a test generated from the Assessment CD-ROM with *ExamView Pro*.

1. Part 4 may also be used as an in-class test to assess student performance, in addition to the Assessment CD-ROM with *ExamView Pro*. Tell students that this is a composition a student wrote about his teacher. Have students read the direction line. Ask: *Does every sentence have a mistake?* (no)
2. Collect for assessment.
3. If necessary, have students review: **Lessons 1, 2, and 3.**

---

4. A news program begins __*at*__ 6 o'clock.
5. I watch TV __*at*__ night.
6. We have vacation __*in*__ the summer.
7. Many Americans work __*from*__ 9 __*to*__ 5 o'clock.
8. I drink coffee __*in*__ the morning.
9. I study __*in*__ the afternoon.

PART 4 Read this student's composition about his teacher. Find the mistakes with the underlined words, and correct them. Add the verb *be* where necessary. If the underlined words are correct, write *C*.

    My English teacher ^*is* Barbara Nowak. She teach *teaches* grammar and composition at City College. She very *She's very* nice, but she's *C* very strict. She give *gives* a lot of homework, and we take *C* a lot of tests. If I pass the test, I very *I'm very* happy. English's *English is* hard for me.

    Every day *C*, at the beginning of the class, she takes *C* attendance and we hand *C* in our homework. Then she's explains *she explains* the grammar. We do *C* exercises in the book. The book have *has* a lot of exercises. Most exercises is *are* easy, but some are hard. Sometimes we says *say* the answers out loud, but sometimes we write *C* the answers. Sometimes the teacher asks *C* a student to write the answers on the chalkboard.

    The students like *C* Barbara because she make *makes* the class interesting. She brings often *often brings* songs to class, and we learn *C* the words. Sometimes we watch *C* a movie in class. Always I *I always* enjoy her lessons.

    After class I sometimes going *sometimes go* to her office if I want more help. She very *She's very* kind and always try *tries* to help me.

    Barbara dresses *C* very informally. Sometimes she wears *C* a skirt, but she wears usually *she usually wears* jeans. She about *She's about* 35 years old, but she's looks *she looks* like a teenager. (In my country, never a teacher wear *a teacher never wears* jeans.) I very *I'm very* happy with my teacher. She understand *understands* the problems of a foreigner because she's *C* also a foreigner. She's comes *She comes* from Poland, but she speaks *C* English very well. She know *knows* it's hard to learn another language.

Lesson Review

To use Part 4 as a review, assign it as homework or use it as an in-class activity to be completed individually or in pairs. Check answers and review errors as a class. Reteach grammar points that students haven't mastered. Then student learning may be assessed using a test generated from the Assessment CD-ROM with *ExamView Pro*.

EXPANSION ACTIVITIES

Classroom Activities

1. Find a partner. Interview your partner about one of his or her teachers, friends, or relatives. Ask about this person's usual activities.

   EXAMPLE   A: What's your math teacher's name?
            B: Her name is Kathy Carlson.
            A: Does she give a lot of homework?
            B: No, she doesn't.
            A: What does she usually wear to class?
            B: She usually wears a skirt and blouse.
            A: Does she ever wear jeans to class?
            B: No, she never does.

2. In a small group or with the entire class, use frequency words to talk about the activities of a famous person (the president, a singer, an actor, etc.).

   EXAMPLE   The president of the U.S. often meets with leaders of other countries.

3. Find a partner. Talk about a special holiday that you and your family celebrate. Ask your partner questions about the date of the holiday, food, clothing, preparations, activities, and so on.

   EXAMPLE   A: We celebrate the Lunar New Year.
            B: Do you wear special clothes?
            A: Yes, we do.
            B: What kind of clothes do you wear?

4. Look at the list of Linda's activities on page 89. Write a list to remind yourself of things you do on a regular basis. Find a partner. Compare your list to your partner's list.

5. Describe your favorite holiday to your classmates.

Frequency Words with the Simple Present Tense; Prepositions of Time   **97**

Classroom Activities Variation

Activity 2 Bring in magazine pictures of famous people from all over the world. Distribute three to five pictures to each group. Ask students to make statements about these well-known people.

Activity 3 Bring in photos from home of special occasions. Tell students about your family's traditions. Or have students ask you questions about your pictures.

Expansion Activities

These expansion activities provide opportunities for students to interact with one another and further develop their speaking and writing skills. If time is short, have students do parts of the activities at home. Save the class time for interaction and communication.

To save class time, assign parts of the activities as homework. Then use class time for interaction and communication. If students do not need additional speaking practice, some of the activities may be assigned as writing activities for homework, or skipped altogether.

CLASSROOM ACTIVITIES

1. Tell students that this activity is about usual activities. Ask: *What tense do we use to talk about usual activities?* (the simple present tense) Remind students to use frequency words and expressions, prepositions of time, and questions with *ever*. If necessary, provide the option of writing out the questions before asking a partner. Have two volunteers read the example interview.

2. As a class, brainstorm a list of famous people from the U.S. and from other parts of the world. Write the names on the board. Say: *Let's find out how much we know about well-known people. Who should we talk about? How about Prince Charles?* Elicit other names. In groups, or as a class, have students make statements about the activities of the list of people you brainstormed.

3. Try to pair students of different nationalities, if possible. If necessary, provide the option of writing out the questions before asking a partner.

4. Instruct students to write only a list of activities, but not to when or how often they do them. Tell students to read their partners' lists and ask questions. Say: *Remember to ask your partners how often and when they do the activity.*

5. Do a quick class survey. Find out students' favorite holidays. Have students talk about their holidays in groups or ask volunteers to talk to the class about their holidays.

6. Tell students this is an activity about customs. Have students cover up the chart. Activate students' prior knowledge of American customs. Ask: *How much do you know about American customs? For example, what do Americans say when someone sneezes?* ("God bless you.") Ask students to complete the activity individually and then discuss their responses in a group. If necessary, go over any vocabulary students might not understand.

6. In the left column is a list of popular customs in the U.S. Do people in your native country or cultural group have similar customs? If so, put a check (✓) in Column A. If not, put a check (✓) in Column B. Discuss your answers in a group.

American Customs	A Similar custom in my native country or cultural group	B Completely different custom in my native country or cultural group
1. Americans often say, "Have a nice day."		
2. When someone sneezes, Americans usually say, "God bless you."		
3. Americans often ask, "How are you?" People usually reply, "I'm fine, thanks. How are you?"		
4. Americans rarely visit their friends without calling first.		
5. Americans are often in a hurry. They rarely have free time.		
6. Americans often eat popcorn in a movie theater.		
7. Americans often eat in fast-food restaurants.		
8. Americans often say, "OK."		
9. Americans often wear shorts and sandals in the summer.		
10. Americans often listen to a personal stereo.		
11. When eating, Americans usually hold a fork in the right hand and a knife in the left hand.		
12. Banks in the U.S. often have a time/temperature sign.		
13. American restaurants usually have salt and pepper shakers on the table.		
14. When a radio or TV breaks down, Americans often buy a new one. They rarely try to repair it.		
15. Americans often send greeting cards to close friends and relatives for birthdays, anniversaries, holidays, and illnesses.		
16. The Sunday newspaper often has store coupons.		
17. There is a special day for sweethearts, like Valentine's Day.		

98   Lesson 3

Write About it

1. Write about one of your teachers. Describe your teacher and tell about his or her classroom behavior and activities.
2. Write about a holiday that you celebrate. Explain how you celebrate this holiday. Or write about how you celebrate your birthday or another special day.

Outside Activities

1. Ask an American-born person to do Exercise 4. See how your answers compare to this person's answers. Report this person's answers to the class.
2. Go to a drugstore, supermarket, or card store. Is there a special holiday at this time (for example, Father's Day, Thanksgiving, Christmas, Chanukah)? Read the messages in a few cards. Make a card for someone you know. Write your own message.

Internet Activities

1. Find a greeting card site on the Internet. Send an electronic greeting card to someone you know.
2. Using the Internet, find the answers to these questions:
   a. When is Father's Day in the U.S.?
   b. What is the origin of Mother's Day?
   c. When is Thanksgiving?
   d. What is the history of the Fourth of July?

 Additional Activities at http://elt.thomson.com/gic

Frequency Words with the Simple Present Tense; Prepositions of Time   **99**

Write About it Variation

Item 2 Have students exchange first drafts with a partner. Ask students to help their partners edit their drafts. Refer students to the Editing Advice on page 93.

Outside Activities Variation

Activity 2 Bring in a number of cards from home to show students. Show cards of varying styles that celebrate different occasions, such as humorous, romantic, blank, holiday, or birthday cards. Bring in materials for students to make cards in class.

WRITE ABOUT IT

1. Brainstorm classroom activities. Ask: *What kinds of activities does your teacher do in class?* (e.g., *teach, talk, write on the board, give homework, correct papers, prepare assignments*) Write them on the board. Say: *Now use these ideas to write about one of your teachers.* Encourage students to use frequency words and expressions in their writing.
2. Have students write a paragraph about a holiday or special occasion. Say: *Write about the way you celebrate birthdays or a special holiday in your family. Give details about what you usually do, always do, never do, and sometimes do.* Collect for assessment and/or have students present their paragraphs to a group.

OUTSIDE ACTIVITIES

1. Instruct students to ask an American-born person to complete Exercise 4 on page 82. Then have the class compare their findings.
2. Have students look at cards in a store to get ideas to make their own card. Have students design their cards at home. If necessary, provide appropriate phrases and words for the message in the card.

INTERNET ACTIVITIES

1. Survey the class to see how many students have sent electronic greeting cards. Ask: *Who uses electronic greeting cards? What greeting card sites do you use?* On the board, write the names of the sites they have used. Add your own favorite sites. Ask students to send you a greeting card. Point out that greeting card Web sites are typically free.
2. a. Father's Day is always on the third Sunday in June.
   b. Mother's Day has its origins in Ancient Greece and Rome. "Mothering Sunday" was an English holiday celebrated from the seventeenth century.
   c. Thanksgiving is always on the fourth Thursday in November.
   d. The United States Declaration of Independence was adopted in Philadelphia on July 4, 1776. It became customary to celebrate the signing every July fourth.

LESSON

4

GRAMMAR

Singular and Plural
Articles and Quantity Words
There + Be + Noun

CONTEXT: Americans and Where They Live

Americans and Where They Live
Finding an Apartment
Calling About an Apartment

101

Lesson Overview

GRAMMAR

Ask: *What did we study in Lesson 3?* (frequency words and prepositions of time) *What are we going to study in this lesson?* (the singular and plural; articles and quantity words; *there + be + noun*) Activate students' prior knowledge. Have volunteers give examples. Write them on the board. Ask: *What's the plural of teacher?* (*teachers*) *What about child?* (*children*) *Name two articles that we've already studied.* (*a, an*) *Do you know any quantity words?* (*some, many*)

CONTEXT

1. Ask: *What will we learn about in this lesson?* (where Americans live, finding an apartment) Activate students' prior knowledge. Ask: *Which of you live in an apartment? A house?*
2. Have students share their knowledge and personal experiences.

Photo

1. Direct students' attention to the photos. Ask: *What is this?* (a house) *And this?* (an apartment building) *And this other building?* (a brownstone)
2. Ask: *What is your house or apartment like? Is it big or small? New or old?*

🕐 To save class time, have students do the Test/Review at the end of the lesson, or administer a lesson test generated from the Assessment CD-ROM with *ExamView® Pro.* Skip sections of the lesson that students have already mastered. You may also assign some sections for self-study for extra credit.

Expansion

Theme The topic for this lesson can be enhanced with the following ideas:

1. Interior and exterior pictures of your house or apartment
2. Classified ads from the newspaper for apartments and houses

4.1 | Singular and Plural—An Overview

1. Have students close their books. Write a brief list of nouns in the singular on the board. (*kid, beach, American, man*) Ask: *Are these nouns singular or plural?* (singular)
2. Ask volunteers to write the plural of each word on the board. (*kids, beaches, Americans, men*) Explain that the plural usually ends in *-s* or *-es*, although some plural forms are irregular, for example, *men*.

Americans and Where They Live (Reading)

1. Have students look at the illustration. Ask: *Who are these people?* (a family) *Where are they?* (in front of a house) *How do you know they're in front of their house?* (the house number behind them)
2. Have students look at the title of the reading. Ask: *What is the reading about? How do you know?* Have students make predictions.
3. Preteach any vocabulary words your students may not know, such as *household, homeowner,* and *renters.*

BEFORE YOU READ

1. Have students discuss the questions in pairs.
2. Ask for a few volunteers to share their answers with the class.

To save class time, skip "Before You Read" or have students prepare answers for homework ahead of time.

Reading 🎧 CD 1, Track 15

1. Have students read the text silently. Tell them to pay special attention to plural nouns. Then play the audio and have students read along silently.
2. Check students' comprehension. Ask questions such as: *How many people live in the U.S.?* (about 295 million) *How many have pets?* (58 percent) *Are homes in San Diego inexpensive?* (no)

To save class time, have students do the reading for homework ahead of time.

4.1 | Singular and Plural—An Overview

Examples	Explanation
Some kids live with one **parent.** Some kids live with two **parents.** Everyone pays **taxes.**	Singular means one. Plural means more than one. Plural nouns usually end in *-s* or *-es*.
Some young **men** and **women** live with their parents. Some **children** live with their grandparents.	Some plural forms are irregular. They don't end in *-s*. Examples: man → men woman → women child → children

AMERICANS AND WHERE THEY LIVE[1]

Before You Read

1. Do you know anyone who lives alone?
2. Does your family own a house or rent an apartment?

Read the following information. Pay special attention to plural nouns.

There are about 295 million **people** in the U.S.
- The average family has 3.17 **people.**
- 5.5% of **children** live in **households** run by one or both **grandparents.**
- 69% of **children** live with two **parents.**
- 15% of **males** 25–34 live at home with one or both **parents.**
- 8% of **females** 25–34 live at home with one or both **parents.**
- 26% of **Americans** live alone. (Compare this to 8% in 1940.)
- 31% of **households** have a dog.
- 27% of **households** have a cat.

Homes
- 67% of American **families** own their **homes.**
- 25% of **homeowners** are over 65 **years** old.
- The price of **homes** depends on the city where you live. Some **cities** have very expensive **homes:** San Francisco, Boston, San Diego, Honolulu, and New York.
- The average American moves a lot. In a five-year period, 46% of **Americans** change their address. **Renters** move more than **owners.** Young **people** move more than older people.

[1] Statistics are from the 2000 census.

Reading Variation

To practice listening skills, have students first listen to the audio alone. Ask a few comprehension questions. Repeat the audio if necessary. Then have students open their books and read along as they listen to the audio.

Reading Glossary

homeowner: a property owner, especially of a house or apartment
household: the person or people living together in one home
renter: a person or business that rents things, such as apartments, from the owner(s)

Average home prices in the most expensive American cities (2002)	
San Francisco	$541,000
Boston	$398,000
San Diego	$362,000
Honolulu	$330,000
New York City	$304,000

EXERCISE **1** Tell if the statement is true (*T*) or false (*F*).

EXAMPLE Homes in Boston are very expensive. T

1. Most children live with their grandparents. F
2. Houses in New York City are more expensive than houses in San Francisco. F
3. Most people rent an apartment. F
4. Americans stay in the same house for most of their lives. F
5. Cats are more popular than dogs in American homes. F
6. Families in the U.S. are small (under five people). T
7. Most children live with both parents. T
8. The price of homes depends on where you live. T

Singular and Plural; Articles and Quantity Words; *There + Be* + Noun   **103**

1. Tell students that this true or false exercise is based on the reading on page 102. Have students read the direction line. Go over the example in the book. Say: *If you need help, you can look back at the reading on page 102.*
2. Have students complete Exercise 1 individually. Check the answers as a class.
3. If necessary, review grammar chart **4.1** on page 102.

Expansion

Exercise 1 Have students research similar statistics for their native countries. If possible, put students of the same nationality in the same group. Have group members compare information. Finally, have groups present their information to the class.

4.2 | Regular Noun Plurals

1. Copy the lists of nouns (example words and plural forms) from grammar chart **4.2** on the board. Keep nouns in the same groups and in the same order as in the chart in the book. For example:

Singular	Plural
bee	*bees*
banana	*bananas*
pie	*pies*
bed	*beds*
pin	*pins*
month	*months*

2. Have students cover up grammar chart **4.2** in their books. Say: *Study these spelling changes. Can you guess what the rules for adding an -s are?* If students have difficulty, give them hints. Say: *Look at the endings of the four nouns in row 3 (ss, sh, ch, and x). What do you add? (es) So what's the rule?* (When the noun ends in *ss, sh, ch,* or *x,* add *es.*)

3. Have students look at grammar chart **4.2**. Say: *Compare our rules with the rules in the book.* Review the rules in the grammar chart.

4. Point out the exceptions. Some nouns ending in a consonant + *o* that do not add an *-e* are: *photos, pianos, solos, altos, sopranos, autos,* and *avocados.* Nouns that end in *f* or *fe* that don't change to *-ves* are: *beliefs, chiefs, roofs,* and *chefs.*

EXERCISE 2

1. Have students read the direction line. Ask: *What do we write in the blanks?* (the plural form of the noun) Go over the examples in the book. Ask students to tell you what the rules are for the spelling of each noun in the examples. (Words that end in *f,* add *-ves*; vowel + *y,* add *–s*; etc.)

2. Have students complete Exercise 2 individually. Check answers as a class.

3. If necessary, review grammar chart **4.2** on page 104.

4.2 | Regular Noun Plurals

Word Ending	Example Words	Plural Addition	Plural form
Vowel	bee banana pie	+ s	bees bananas pies
Consonant	bed pin month	+ s	beds pins months
ss, sh, ch, x	class dish church box	+ es	classes dishes churches boxes
Vowel + y	boy day monkey	+ s	boys days monkeys
Consonant + y	lady story party	y + ies	ladies stories parties
Vowel + o	patio stereo radio	+ s	patios stereos radios
Consonant + o	mosquito tomato potato	+ es	mosquitoes tomatoes potatoes
Exceptions: photos, pianos, solos, altos, sopranos, autos, avocados.			
f or fe	leaf calf knife	f + ves fe + ves	leaves calves knives
Exceptions: beliefs, chiefs, roofs, chefs			

EXERCISE 2 Write the plural form of each noun.

EXAMPLES   leaf ___*leaves*___

toy ___*toys*___

1. dish ___*dishes*___
2. country ___*countries*___
3. half ___*halves*___
4. book ___*books*___
5. boy ___*boys*___
6. girl ___*girls*___

Grammar Variation

Have students cover up grammar chart **4.2**. Write the singular nouns from the chart on the board. Ask students to go up to the board and write the plural forms next to them. Then ask students to look at grammar chart **4.2** and check the board. Go over the rules for spelling.

7. bench _benches_	20. cow _cows_
8. box _boxes_	21. table _tables_
9. shark _sharks_	22. roach _roaches_
10. stereo _stereos_	23. fox _foxes_
11. knife _knives_	24. house _houses_
12. story _stories_	25. turkey _turkeys_
13. sofa _sofas_	26. chicken _chickens_
14. key _keys_	27. wolf _wolves_
15. movie _movies_	28. dog _dogs_
16. squirrel _squirrels_	29. bath _baths_
17. mosquito _mosquitos_	30. pony _ponies_
18. lion _lions_	31. duck _ducks_
19. fly _flies_	32. moth _moths_

4.3 | Pronunciation of Plural Nouns

The plural ending has three pronunciations: /s/, /z/, and /əz/

Pronunciation	Rule	Examples	
/s/	Pronounce /s/ after voiceless sounds: /p, t, k, f, θ/	lip—lips cat—cats rock—rocks cuff—cuffs month—months	
/z/	Pronounce /z/ after voiced sounds: /b, d, g, v, m, n, ŋ, l, r/ and all vowels	cab—cabs lid—lids bag—bags stove—stoves sum—sums	can—cans thing—things bill—bills car—cars bee—bees
/əz/	Pronounce /əz/ when the base form ends in s, ss, ce, se, sh, ch, ge, x	bus—buses class—classes place—places cause—causes dish—dishes beach—beaches garage—garages tax—taxes	

4.3 | Pronunciation of Plural Nouns

1. Have students cover up grammar chart **4.3** in their books. Say: *There are three ways to pronounce the endings of plural nouns.* Across the board, write:
   1. /s/
   2. /z/
   3. /əz/
   Then pronounce each sound. Remind students that this is about pronunciation, not spelling or writing. Then say: *Listen to each word as I say it. Tell me which sound I'm making.* Say words from the grammar chart lists on page 105 in random order. Pronounce each word carefully. Have students guess where the word belongs and write it under the sound they tell you.

2. Have students look at grammar chart **4.3.** Say: *Compare our lists with the lists in the book.* Go over any errors. Have volunteers pronounce words.

Have students read the direction line. Turn to Exercise 2 on page 104. Have students complete the exercise in pairs. Circulate to help with pronunciation. Go over pronunciation in class, if necessary.

4.4 | Irregular Noun Plurals

1. Have students cover up grammar chart **4.4**. Activate students' prior knowledge. Write the list of the singular nouns from the chart on the board. Ask volunteers to come up to the board and write the plural spellings.

2. Have students look at grammar chart **4.2**. Say: *Compare our nouns on the board with the plurals in the book. How many did we get right?* Review the information in the grammar chart. Explain to students that there are no rules for spelling changes with these nouns. English learners have to memorize the plural forms.

3. Point out that some nouns do not have a singular form (e.g., *pajamas, clothes,* and *pants/slacks*). Point out that exact numbers use the singular form, and the plural form of a number such as *thousand,* i.e., *thousands,* is not exact.

4. Go over the Language Notes. Demonstrate the pronunciation differences between *woman* and *women.* Say them several times and have students guess if you're saying the singular or plural. Explain that sometimes you can use *persons* as the plural for *person*—but that it's not common.

EXERCISE 3 Go back to Exercise 2 and pronounce the plural form of each word.

4.4 | Irregular Noun Plurals

Singular	Plural	Explanation
man woman mouse tooth foot goose	men women mice teeth feet geese	Some nouns have a vowel change in the plural form. Singular: Do you see that old **woman?** Plural: Do you see those young **women?**
sheep fish deer	sheep fish deer	Some plural forms are the same as the singular form. Singular: I have one **fish** in my tank. Plural: She has ten **fish** in her tank.
child person mouse	children people (OR persons) mice	For some plurals we change to a different form. Singular: She has one **child.** Plural: They have two **children.**
	pajamas clothes pants/slacks (eye)glasses scissors	Some words have no singular form. Example: My **pants** are new. Do you like them?
dozen (12) hundred thousand million		Exact numbers use the singular form. Examples: The U.S. has over 290 **million** people. I need to buy **a dozen** eggs.
	dozens hundreds thousands millions	The plural form of a number is *not* an exact number. Example: **Thousands** of people live alone.

Language Notes:
1. You hear the difference between *woman* (singular) and *women* (plural) in the first syllable.
2. The plural of *person* can also be *persons,* but *people* is more common.

106 Lesson 4

EXERCISE **4**   The following nouns have an irregular plural form. Write the plural.

EXAMPLE   man ___men___

1. foot ___feet___   5. fish ___fish___
2. woman ___women___   6. mouse ___mice___
3. policeman ___policemen___   7. sheep ___sheep___
4. child ___children___   8. tooth ___teeth___

EXERCISE **5**   Fill in the blanks with the correct plural form of the noun in parentheses.

EXAMPLE   Some ___people___ like to live alone.
                    (person)

1. Most ___families___ in the U.S. own a house.
        (family)

2. The U.S. has over 290 million ___people___.
                                        (person)

3. Americans move many ___times___.
                            (time)

4. Most single ___parents___ are ___women___.
                  (parent)   *(woman)*

5. Some ___women___ earn more money than their ___husbands___.
        (woman)   *(husband)*

6. ___Homes___ are very expensive in some ___cities___.
    (Home)   *(city)*

7. Divorce is very high in some ___countries___.
                                    (country)

8. Some ___children___ live with only one parent.
        (child)

9. How many square ___feet___ does your house or apartment have?
                      (foot)

10. Some ___children___ live with ___grandparents___.
          (child)   *(grandparent)*

11. The average family has 3.17 ___people___.
                                  (person)

12. Some apartments have a problem with ___mice___.
                                          (mouse)

Singular and Plural; Articles and Quantity Words; *There + Be* + Noun   **107**

EXERCISE 4

1. Have students read the direction line. Ask: *What do we write in the blanks?* (the plural form of the noun) Go over the example in the book.
2. Have students complete Exercise 4 individually. Check answers as a class.
3. If necessary, review grammar chart **4.4** on page 106.

EXERCISE 5

1. Have students read the direction line. Go over the example. Then do #1 with the class. Ask a volunteer to give an answer.
2. Have students complete the rest of Exercise 5 individually. Then have students practice saying the sentences in pairs. Finally, check the answers as a class.
3. If necessary, review grammar charts **4.2** on page 104, **4.3** on page 105, and **4.4** on page 106.

To save class time, have students do half of the exercise in class and complete the other half for homework. Or assign the entire exercise for homework.

Expansion

Exercise 4 Have a spelling and pronunciation bee. Make a list of approximately 40 nouns. Divide the class into Team A and Team B. Give one member from Team A a noun, and tell them to write the plural form on the board. Do the same with Team B. Then give a member from Team A a plural noun to pronounce. Do the same with Team B. To make the exercise more challenging, give extra points if the team can say (or act out) what the word means.

Exercise 5 Have students write an e-mail to a friend in another country. Say: *Talk about life here in the U.S. How many people are there? Where do people live?* Tell students to use information from the reading and from Exercise 5.

Finding an Apartment (Reading)

1. Have students look at the artwork. Ask: *What does the sign say?* (Apartment for Rent) *Do you live in an apartment? Does this look like a nice apartment to live in?*

2. Have students look at the title of the reading. Ask: *What is the reading about? How do you know?* Have students use the pictures and the title to make predictions about the reading.

3. Preteach any vocabulary words your students may not know, such as *ad, listing, appointment,* and *janitor.*

BEFORE YOU READ

1. Have students discuss the questions in pairs.
2. Ask for a few volunteers to share their answers with the class.

To save class time, skip "Before You Read" or have students prepare answers for homework ahead of time.

Reading CD 1, Track 16

1. Have students read the text silently. Tell them to pay special attention to *there + be* followed by singular and plural nouns. Then play the audio and have students read along silently.

2. Check students' comprehension. Say: *Name two ways to look for an apartment.* (ads in a newspaper, "For Rent" signs in front of buildings) *What are some questions you should ask about the apartment* (Is there a lease? Are there smoke detectors?)

To save class time, have students do the reading for homework ahead of time.

FINDING AN APARTMENT

Before You **Read**

1. Do you live in a house, an apartment, or a dorm?[2] Do you live alone?

2. Do you like the place where you live? Why or why not?

 Read the following article. Pay special attention to *there + be* followed by singular and plural nouns.

There are several ways to find an apartment. One way is to look in the newspaper. **There is** an "Apartments for Rent" section in the back of the newspaper. **There are** many ads for apartments. **There are** also ads for houses for rent and houses for sale. Many newspapers also put their listings online.

Another way to find an apartment is by looking at the buildings in the neighborhood where you want to live. **There are** often "For Rent" signs on the front of the buildings. **There is** usually a phone number on the sign. You can call and ask for information about the apartment that you are interested in. You can ask:

- How much is the rent?
- Is heat included?
- What floor is the apartment on?
- **Is there** an elevator?
- How many bedrooms **are there** in the apartment?
- How many closets **are there** in the apartment?
- Is the apartment available[3] now?

If an apartment interests you, you can make an appointment to see it. When you go to see the apartment, you should ask some more questions, such as the following:

- **Is there** a lease?[4] How long is the lease?

[2] *Dorm* is short for *dormitory,* a building where students live.
[3] *Available* means ready to use now.
[4] A *lease* is a contract between the owner (landlord or landlady) and the renter (tenant). It tells how much the rent is, how long the tenant can stay in the apartment, and other rules.

Reading Variation

To practice listening skills, have students first listen to the audio alone. Ask a few comprehension questions. Repeat the audio if necessary. Then have students open their books and read along as they listen to the audio.

Reading Glossary

ad: short for advertisement
appointment: a time, place, and date to see someone
janitor: a person in charge of cleaning and fixing things in a building
listing: an advertisement

APARTMENTS FOR RENT

5 rooms, 2 baths, fenced yard, pets allowed. References required. Call 555-112-3345 after 6:00 p.m.

4 rooms, 1 bath, quiet dead end street. 2 car driveway. Call 555-122-3445 for appointment.

5 rooms, 1 bath, new kitchen and ~~~ting. Dish wash-

* **Is there a** janitor or manager?
* **Is there a** parking space for each tenant? Is it free, or do I have to pay extra?
* **Are there** smoke detectors? (In many places, the law says that the landlord must put a smoke detector in each apartment and in the halls.)
* **Is there a** laundry room in the building? Where is it?

The landlord may ask you a few questions, such as:

* How many people **are there** in your family?
* Do you have any pets?

You should check over the apartment care-fully before you sign the lease. If **there are** some problems, you should talk to the landlord to see if he will take care of them before you move in.

Singular and Plural; Articles and Quantity Words; *There + Be + Noun*   **109**

4.5 | Using *There + Is/Are*

1. Have students turn to the reading on pages 108 and 109. Ask students to find examples of *there is* and *there are* in the reading (e.g., *There is usually a number on the sign. There are also ads for houses for rent and houses for sale.*). Write students' responses on the board. Now have students identify the nouns that follow *there is* and *there are* (*a number, ad*). Ask: *Which ones are plural and which ones are singular?*

2. Have students look at grammar chart **4.5**. Review the examples. Point out the contraction *there's*. Explain that there are two forms of contraction for the negative: *there isn't* and *there's no*. Tell students that there is no contraction for *there are*. However, there is a contraction for the negative of *there are*: *there aren't*. Tell students that they can also use *there are no*.

3. Have students cover up grammar chart **4.5** again. Write on the board:
   _____ *a dining room and living room.*
   _____ *three bathrooms and a laundry room.*
   _____ *a closet in the hall and two closets in the master bedroom.*
   Ask students to complete the sentences using *there is* or *there are*.

4. Ask students to look at grammar chart **4.5** on page 110. Review the Language Notes at the bottom. Say: *When two nouns follow* there, *use the singular if the first noun is singular and use the plural if the first noun is plural.*

5. Explain that *there is* and *there are* are not used before nouns preceded by the definite article *the*. Review the example in the Language Notes.

4.5 | Using *There + Is/Are*

We use *there + is* or *there + are* to introduce a subject into the conversation when we show location or time.

	Examples				
Singular	*There*	*is*	*a/an/one*	singular subject	location/time
	There	is	a	janitor	in my building.
	There	is	an	open house	at 1:00.
	There	is	one	dryer	in the basement.
	There	is	a	rent increase	this year.
	Note: *There's* is the contraction for *there is*.				
Negative Singular	*There*	*isn't*	*a*	singular subject	location/time
	There	isn't	a	back door	in my apartment.
	There's	*no*		singular subject	location/time
	There's	no		balcony	in my apartment.
	There's	no		heat	this month.
Plural	*There*	*are*	*plural word*	plural subject	location/time
	There	are	several	windows	in the bedroom.
	There	are	many	children	in the building.
	There	are	some	cats	in the building.
	There	are	two	closets	in the hall.
	There	are	—	curtains	on the windows.
	Note: We don't write a contraction for *there are*.				
Negative Plural	*There*	*aren't*	*plural word*	plural subject	location/time
	There	aren't	any	shades	on the windows.
	There	aren't	any	new tenants	this month.
	There	*are*	*no*	plural subject	location/time
	There	are	no	cabinets	in the kitchen.

Language Notes:
1. When two nouns follow *there*, use a singular verb (*is*) if the first noun is singular. Use a plural verb (*are*) if the first noun is plural.
   There is a closet in the bedroom and two closets in the hall.
   There are two closets in the hall and one closet in the bedroom.
   There is a washer and dryer in the basement.
2. *There* never introduces a specific or unique noun. Don't use a noun with the definite article (*the*) after *there*.
   Wrong: There's the Eiffel Tower in Paris.
   Right: The Eiffel Tower is in Paris.

110 Lesson 4

Expansion

Grammar Ask students to describe the classroom. Say: *Describe the classroom. Tell me what's in here.* Model an example (*There are desks in the classroom.*).

EXERCISE **6** ABOUT YOU Use the words given to make a statement about the place where you live (house or apartment). If you live in a dorm, use Exercise 7 instead. **Answers will vary.**

EXAMPLES carpet / in the living room
There's a carpet in the living room.

trees / in front of the building
There are no trees in front of the building.

1. porch
2. blinds / on the windows
3. door / in every room
4. window / in every room
5. lease
6. closet / in the living room
7. number / on the door of the apartment
8. overhead light / in every room
9. microwave oven / in the kitchen
10. back door
11. fireplace
12. smoke detector

EXERCISE **7** ABOUT YOU Make a statement about your dorm and dorm room with the words given. (If you live in an apartment or house, skip this exercise.)

Answers will vary.

EXAMPLES window / in the room
There's a window in the room.

curtains / on the window
There are no curtains on the window.
There are shades.

1. closet / in the room
2. two beds / in the room
3. private bath / for every room
4. men and women / in the dorm
5. cafeteria / in the dorm
6. snack machines / in the dorm
7. noisy students / in the dorm
8. numbers / on the doors of the rooms
9. elevator(s) / in the dorm
10. laundry room / in the dorm

Singular and Plural; Articles and Quantity Words; *There* + *Be* + Noun **111**

EXERCISE 6

1. Tell students that this exercise is about them and where they live. Have students read the direction line. Ask: *Who should do this exercise?* (people who live in a house or an apartment) Go over the examples in the book. Have a volunteer model #1. Point out the pictures of the porch, blinds, and fireplace.
2. Have students complete the rest of Exercise 6 individually. Check the answers as a class.
3. If necessary, review grammar chart **4.5** on page 110.

EXERCISE 7

1. Tell students that this exercise is about them and where they live. Have students read the direction line. Ask: *Who should do this exercise?* (people who live in a dorm) Go over the examples in the book. Have a volunteer model #1. Point out the picture of the shade.
2. Have students complete the rest of Exercise 7 individually. Check the answers as a class.
3. If necessary, review grammar chart **4.5** on page 110.

To save class time, have students do half of the exercise in class and complete the other half in writing for homework. Or if students do not need speaking practice, the entire exercise may be skipped or done in writing.

Expansion

Exercises 6 and 7 Have students compare information about their house, apartment, or dorm with a partner. Say: *You tell your partner:* There's carpet in the living room. *Your partner says:* There's no carpet in my living room. Circulate to observe pair work. Give help as needed.

4.6 | Questions and Short Answers Using *There*

1. Have students turn to the reading on pages 108 and 109. Ask students to find examples of *is there* and *are there* in the reading (e.g., *Is there an elevator? Are there smoke detectors?*). Write students' examples on the board.

2. Have students look at grammar chart **4.6**. Review the examples for both singular and plural statements. Go over the word order for *yes/no* questions with *there + be*. Review short answers. Point out that *Yes, there is* doesn't have a contraction. There are two contractions for short negative answers in the singular: *No, there isn't* and *No, there's not*. In the plural, *Yes, there are* is not contracted. The contraction for the negative is *No, there aren't*.

3. Explain that *any* is often used in questions and negatives with plural nouns. *Any*, which means *some*, is not used in affirmative statements.

4. Have students ask and answer questions about the classroom or school using *there is/there are*. Model an example: *Is there a library at this school? Yes, there is.*

5. Review word order with information questions. (*How many + plural noun + are there...?*)

EXERCISE 8

1. Tell students that this exercise is about their apartments. Have students read the direction line. Ask: *Do students who live in dorms do this exercise?* (No. Students who live in dorms should do Exercise 9.) Go over the examples. Have two volunteers model the examples.

2. Have students complete Exercise 8 in pairs. Circulate to observe pair work. Give help as needed.

3. If necessary, review grammar chart **4.6** on page 112.

4.6 | Questions and Short Answers Using *There*

Compare statements (S) and questions (Q) with *there*. Observe short answers (A).

	Examples	Explanation
Singular Statement Yes/No Question	S: **There is** a laundry room in the building. Q: **Is there** an elevator in the building? A: Yes, there is. S: **There's** a closet in the bedroom. Q: **Is there** a closet in the hall? A: No, there isn't.	Question word order: *Is + there + a/an + singular noun . . . ?* Short answers: Yes, there is. (no contraction) No, there isn't. OR No, there's not.
Plural Statement Yes/No Question	S: **There are** some children in the building. Q: **Are there** (any) children on your floor? A: Yes, there are. S: **There are** trees in back of the building. Q: **Are there** (any) trees in front of the building? A: No, there aren't.	Question word order: *Are + there + (any) + plural noun . . . ?* We often use *any* to introduce a plural noun in a *yes/no* question. Short answers: No, there aren't.
Plural Statement Information Question	S: **There are** ten apartments in my building. Q: **How many** apartments **are there** in your building? A: Thirty.	Question word order: *How many + plural noun + are there . . . ?*

EXERCISE 8 ABOUT YOU Ask and answer questions with *there* and the words given to find out about another student's apartment and building. (If you live in a dorm, use Exercise 9 instead.)

EXAMPLES a microwave oven / in your apartment

A: Is there a microwave oven in your apartment?
B: No, there isn't.

closets / in the bedroom

A: Are there any closets in the bedroom?
B: Yes. There's one closet in the bedroom.

Expansion

Exercise 8 Create two rings of students. Have half of the students stand in an outer ring around the classroom. Have the other half stand in an inner ring, facing the outer ring. Instruct students to ask and answer the questions from Exercise 8. Call out *"turn"* every minute or so. Students in the inner ring should move one space clockwise. Students now ask and answer with their new partner. Have students ask questions in random order. Make sure students look at each other when they're speaking.

1. children / in your building
Are there any children in your building?
2. a dishwasher / in the kitchen
Is there a dishwasher in the kitchen?
3. a yard / in front of your building
Is there a yard in front of your building?
4. trees / in front of your building
Are there any trees in front of your building?
5. a basement / in the building
Is there a basement in the building?
6. a laundry room / in the basement
Is there a laundry room in the basement?
7. a janitor / in the building
Is there a janitor in the building?
8. noisy neighbors / in the building
Are there any noisy neighbors in the building?
9. nosy[5] neighbors / in the building
Are there any nosy neighbors in the building?
10. an elevator / in the building
Is there an elevator in the building?
11. parking spaces / for the tenants
Are there any parking spaces for the tenants?
12. a lot of closets / in the apartment
Are there a lot of closets in the apartment?
13. how many apartments / in your building
How many apartments are there in your building?
14. how many parking spaces / in front of your building
How many parking spaces are there in front of your building?

EXERCISE 9

1. Tell students that this exercise is about their dorms. Have students read the direction line. Ask: *Do students who live in apartments do this exercise?* (No. Students who live in apartments should do Exercise 8.) Go over the example. Have two volunteers model the example. Point out the picture of the bulletin board.
2. Have students complete Exercise 9 in pairs. Circulate to observe pair work. Give help as needed.
3. If necessary, review grammar chart 4.6 on page 112.

EXERCISE **9**   ABOUT YOU Ask and answer questions with *there* and the words given to find out about another student's dorm. (If you live in an apartment or house, skip this exercise.)

EXAMPLE   a bicycle room / in your dorm

A: Is there a bicycle room in your dorm?
B: No, there isn't.

1. married students   *Are there any married students in your dorm?*
2. private rooms   *Are there any private rooms in your dorm?*
3. a bicycle room
Is there a bicycle room in your dorm?
4. a computer room   *Is there a computer room in your dorm?*
5. an elevator
Is there an elevator in your dorm?
6. a bulletin board   *Is there a bulletin board in your dorm?*
7. graduate students   *Are there any graduate students in your dorm?*
8. a quiet place to study   *Is there a quiet place to study in your dorm?*
9. an air conditioner / in your room
Is there an air conditioner in your room?
10. a parking lot / for your dorm
Is there a parking lot for your dorm?
11. how many rooms / in your dorm
How many rooms are in your dorm?
12. how many floors / in your dorm
How many floors are in your dorm?

[5] A *nosy* person is a person who wants to know everyone's business.

Singular and Plural; Articles and Quantity Words; *There + Be* + Noun   **113**

Expansion

Exercise 9 Create two rings of students. Have half of the students stand in an outer ring around the classroom. Have the other half stand in an inner ring, facing the outer ring. Instruct students to ask and answer the questions from Exercise 9. Call out *"turn"* every minute or so. Students in the inner ring should move one space clockwise. Students now ask and answer with their new partner. Have students ask questions in random order. Make sure students look at each other when they're speaking.

EXERCISE 10

1. Tell students that in this exercise they will ask you, the teacher, questions. Have students read the direction line. Go over the examples in the book. Then model the examples. Ask a volunteer to ask you the questions. Point out the picture of the file cabinet.

2. Have students interview you in groups. Review some of the questions and answers as a class.

3. If necessary, review grammar chart 4.6 on page 112.

To save class time, have students write the questions for homework. Then have a few volunteers ask you the questions in class.

EXERCISE 11

🎧 *CD 1, Track 17*

1. Have students read the direction line. Go over the example in the book. Explain that this is a phone conversation between a student who is looking for an apartment and the landlady. Remind students to use contractions wherever possible.

2. Have students complete Exercise 11 individually. Check answers as a class.

3. If necessary, review grammar chart 4.6 on page 112.

To save class time, have students do half of the exercise in class and complete the other half for homework. Or assign the entire exercise for homework.

EXERCISE **10** Use the words given to ask the teacher a question about his or her office. Your teacher will answer.

EXAMPLES   pencil sharpener

A: Is there a pencil sharpener in your office?
B: No, there isn't.

books

A: Are there any books in your office?
B: Yes. There are a lot of books in my office.

1. phone
   Is there a phone in your office?
2. file cabinet
   Is there a file cabinet in your office?
3. photos of your family   *Are there any photos of your family in your office?*
4. radio
   Is there a radio in your office?
5. copy machine
   Is there a copy machine in your office?
6. windows
   Are there any windows in your office?

7. calendar
   Is there a calendar in your office?
8. bookshelves   *Are there any bookshelves in your office?*
9. plants
   Are there any plants in your office?
10. voice mail
    Is there voice mail in your office?
11. fax machine   *Is there a fax machine in your office?*
12. computer
    Is there a computer in your office?

EXERCISE **11** A student is calling about an apartment for rent. Fill in the blanks with *there is, there are, is there, are there,* and other related words to complete this phone conversation between the student (S) and the landlady (L).

S: I'm calling about an apartment for rent on Grover Street.

L: We have two apartments available. ___*There's*___ a four-room
   (example)
   apartment on the first floor and a three-room apartment on the fourth floor. Which one are you interested in?

S: I prefer the smaller apartment. ___*Is there*___ an elevator in the building?
   (1)

L: Yes, there is. How many people ___*are there*___ in your family?
   (2)

S: It's just for me. I live alone. I'm a student. I need a quiet apartment. Is this a quiet building?

L: Oh, yes. ___*There are*___ no kids in the building.
   (3)
   This is a very quiet building.

S: That's good. I have a car. ___*Are there (any)*___ parking spaces?
   (4)

L: Yes. ___*There are*___ 20 spaces in back of the building.
   (5)

S: How ___*many*___ apartments ___*are there*___ in the building?
   (6)   *(7)*

L: ___*There are*___ 30 apartments.
   (8)

Expansion

Exercise 10 Have students pair up and ask each other questions about their living rooms or bedrooms. Students can use ideas from Exercise 10.

Exercise 11 Variation

To provide practice with listening skills, have students close their books and listen to the audio. Explain that this is a phone conversation between a student who is looking for an apartment and the landlady. Repeat the audio as needed. Ask comprehension questions, such as: *Where is the apartment?* (on Grover Street) *How many bedrooms does the apartment on the first floor have?* (four) *Does the student want a large apartment?* (no) Then have students open their books and complete Exercise 11.

S: Twenty parking spaces for 30 apartments? Then _____
_____ there aren't _____ enough spaces for all the tenants.
(9)

L: Don't worry. Not everyone has a car. Parking is on a first-come,
first-served basis.[6] And _____ there are _____ plenty
(10)
of[7] spaces on the street.

S: _____ Is there _____ a laundry room in the building?
(11)

L: Yes. There are washers and dryers in the basement.
S: How much is the rent?
L: It's $850 a month.
S: I hear a dog. Is that your dog?
L: Yes, but don't worry. I don't live in the building. ___ There are ___
(12)
no dogs in the building.
S: When can I see the apartment?
L: How about tomorrow at six o'clock?
S: That'll be fine. Thanks.

4.7 | *There* vs. *They* and Other Pronouns

Examples		Explanation
There's a *janitor* in the building.	**He's** in the basement.	To introduce a new noun, we use *there* + *is/are*. When we use this noun again as the subject of another sentence, we use *he, she, it,* or *they*.
There's a little *girl* in the next apartment.	**She's** cute.	
There's an empty *apartment* on the first floor.	**It's** available now.	
There are two washing *machines*.	**They're** in the basement.	

Pronunciation Note: We pronounce *there* and *they're* exactly the same. Listen to your teacher pronounce the sentences from the box above.

Spelling Note: Don't confuse *there* and *they're*.
There are dogs in the next apartment.
They're very friendly.

[6] A *first-come, first-served* basis means that people who arrive first will get something first (parking spaces, theater tickets, classes at registration).
[7] *Plenty of* means "a lot of."

4.7 | *There* vs. *They* and Other Pronouns

1. Have students look at grammar chart **4.7**. Explain that *there* + *is/are* is used to introduce new nouns. When we use the noun again, we use a pronoun: *he, she, it,* or *they*.

2. Review the examples in the chart. Have volunteers make sentences using *there is/are* and pronouns with *be*. For example: *There is a big chalkboard in the room. It is at the front of the room.*

3. Go over the Pronunciation Note and the Spelling Note. Point out that people often get confused with *there are* and *they are*—especially since their pronunciations are similar. Demonstrate their pronunciations. Have students practice the pronunciation chorally.

Expansion

Exercise 11 Have students practice the conversation in pairs. Circulate to observe pair work and give help as needed. Ask volunteers to role-play all or part of the conversation in front of the class.

EXERCISE 12

1. Have students read the direction line. Go over the examples in the book. Have a volunteer do #1.
2. Have students complete the rest of Exercise 12 individually. Check the answers as a class.
3. If necessary, review grammar chart **4.7** on page 115.

EXERCISE 13

1. Tell students that this exercise is about their school. Have students read the direction line. Ask: *What kind of question do you ask if the answer is "yes" to the first question?* (a question with *where*) Go over the examples with the class. Have two students model the example.
2. Have students complete the exercise in pairs. Circulate to observe pair work. Give help as needed.
3. If necessary, review grammar chart **4.6** on page 112.

🕐 To save class time, have students do half of the exercise in class and complete the other half in writing for homework. Or if students do not need speaking practice, the entire exercise may be skipped or done in writing.

EXERCISE **12** Fill in the blanks with *there's, there are, it's,* or *they're*.

EXAMPLE _____There's_____ a small apartment for rent in my building.
_____It's_____ on the fourth floor.

1. _____There are_____ two apartments for rent. _____They're_____ not on the same floor.
2. _____There's_____ a laundry room in the building. _____It's_____ in the basement.
3. The parking spaces are in the back of the building. _____ _____They're_____ for the tenants with cars.
4. The parking spaces don't cost extra. _____They're_____ free for the tenants.
5. The apartment is small. _____It's_____ on the fourth floor.
6. The building has 30 apartments. _____It's_____ a big building.
7. The student wants to see the apartment. _____It's_____ on Grover Street.
8. The building is quiet because _____there are_____ no kids in the building.
9. How much is the rent? _____It's_____ $850 a month.
10. Is the rent high? No, _____It's_____ not high.
11. _____There are_____ no dogs in the building.
12. _____It's_____ a quiet building.

EXERCISE **13** Ask a question about this school using *there* and the words given. Another student will answer. If the answer is "yes," ask a question with *where*.

EXAMPLE lockers
A: Are there any lockers at this school?
B: Yes, there are.
A: Where are they?
B: They're near the gym.

1. a library
   Is there a library at this school?
2. vending machines *Are there any vending machines at this school?*
3. public telephones *Are there any public telephones at this school?*
4. a computer room *Is there a computer room at this school?*
5. a cafeteria *Is there a cafeteria at this school?*
6. a gym *Is there a gym at this school?*
7. a swimming pool *Is there a swimming pool at this school?*
8. tennis courts *Are there any tennis courts at this school?*
9. dormitories *Are there any dormitories at this school?*
10. a parking lot *Is there a parking lot at this school?*
11. a bookstore *Is there a bookstore at this school?*
12. copy machines *Are there any copy machines at this school?*
13. a student lounge *Is there a student lounge at this school*
14. a fax machine *Is there a fax machine at this school?*

Expansion

Exercise 13 Have students ask and answer questions about their last school. Tell students to use the words from Exercise 13.

CALLING ABOUT AN APARTMENT

Before You Read

1. Does your neighborhood have more apartment buildings or houses?
2. Do you prefer to live alone, with a roommate, or with your family? Why?

Read the following phone conversation between a student (S) and the manager (M) of a building. Pay special attention to the definite article (*the*), the indefinite articles (*a, an*), and indefinite quantity words (*some, any*).

S: Hello? I want to speak with **the landlord.**
M: I'm **the manager** of **the building.** Can I help you?
S: I need to find **a** new **apartment.**
M: Where do you live now?
S: I live in **a** big **apartment** on Wright Street. I have **a roommate**, but he's graduating, and I need **a** smaller **apartment.** Are there **any** small **apartments** for rent in your building?
M: There's one.
S: What floor is it on?
M: It's on **the** third **floor.**
S: Does it have **a bedroom?**
M: No. It's **a** studio **apartment.** It has **a living room** and **a kitchen.**
S: Is **the living room** big?
M: So-so.
S: Does **the kitchen** have **a stove** and **a refrigerator?**
M: Yes. **The refrigerator** is old, but it works well. **The stove** is pretty new.
S: Can I see **the apartment?**
M: I have a question for you first. Do you have **a dog?** We don't permit **dogs. Dogs** make a lot of noise.
S: I don't have **a dog.**
M: I'm happy to hear that.
S: But I have **a snake.**
M: **A snake?**
S: **Snakes** are quiet.
M: Yes, but . . .
S: Don't worry. I keep **the snake** in a glass box.
M: I hope **the box** is always closed.
S: It is. I only open it to feed **the snake.** I feed it **mice.**
M: Oh.
S: When can I see **the apartment?**
M: I have to speak to **the landlord.** I'm not sure if you can have **snakes** and **mice** in **the apartment.**

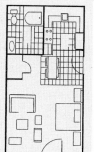

Singular and Plural; Articles and Quantity Words; *There + Be +* Noun   **117**

Expansion

Theme The topic for this lesson can be enhanced with the following ideas:

1. Online listings of apartments
2. Real estate brochures of apartment listings with full descriptions of the apartments for rent
3. Floor plans of apartments

Reading Variation

To practice listening skills, have students first listen to the audio alone. Ask a few comprehension questions. Repeat the audio if necessary. Then have students open their books and read along as they listen to the audio.

Reading Glossary

landlord: a man or business that owns real estate, especially that which is rented to others
permit: an official document giving someone the freedom to do something or go somewhere
roommate: a person who lives with one in a room, apartment, or house
snake: a long, slender reptile with no legs that moves with a curvy, winding motion

---

Calling About an Apartment (Reading)

1. Have students look at the floor plan. Ask: *What is this?* (the floor plan to a house or an apartment) *Is there a bathroom?* (yes) *Is there a bedroom?* (no) *Is there a living room?* (yes)
2. Have students look at the title of the reading. Ask: *What is the reading about? How do you know?* Have students use the title and the illustrations to make predictions about the reading.
3. Preteach any vocabulary words your students may not know, such as *landlord, roommate, snake,* and *permit.* For *snake,* point out the illustration on page 117.

BEFORE YOU READ

1. Have students discuss the questions in pairs.
2. Ask for a few volunteers to share their answers with the class.

To save class time, skip "Before You Read" or have students prepare answers for homework ahead of time.

Reading ∩ *CD 1, Track 18*

1. Have students read the text silently. Explain that this is a phone conversation between a student and the manager of a building. Tell students to pay special attention to the definite article (*the*), the indefinite articles (*a, an*), and indefinite quantity words (*some, any*). Then play the audio and have students read along silently.
2. Check students' comprehension. Ask questions such as: *Why does the student want a new apartment?* (because his roommate is moving out) *Is there an apartment available in the manager's building?* (Yes, there's one on the third floor.) *What kind of pet does the student have?* (a snake)

To save class time, have students do the reading for homework ahead of time.

4.8 | Articles with Definite and Indefinite Nouns

1. Have students go to the reading on page 117. Ask them to:
   a. underline articles *a/an* + noun
   b. double underline definite article *the* + noun
   c. circle nouns without articles
2. Ask volunteers to discuss why a noun in the reading has *a/an* and not *the* and vice versa.
3. Ask why some of the nouns don't have an article.
4. Have students look at grammar chart **4.8** on page 118. Read through the examples and explanations.
5. Explain that *a/an* are used for general nouns and that *the* is used for specific nouns. Singular nouns are introduced with *a/an*. Later, when they are referred to again, we use *the*. Plural nouns are introduced with *some, any,* or no article. Later, when they are referred to again, we use *the*.
6. Explain that *the* is also used if this noun is the only one or if the speaker and listener share the same experience. Review the examples in the chart. Point out that when students refer to you, they may say "the teacher" because they share the same experience (same classroom, same teacher).

EXERCISE 14

1. Have students read the direction line. Point out that the conversations are between two students. Ask: *What words go in the blanks?* (*the, a, an, some,* or *any*) Go over the example in the book.
2. Have students complete the exercise individually. Check answers as a class. Then have students practice the conversations in pairs. Circulate to observe pair work.
3. If necessary, review grammar chart **4.8** on page 118.

4.8 | Articles with Definite and Indefinite Nouns

Singular		
Indefinite	**Definite**	**Explanation**
I live in **a** big building. There's **a** janitor in the building.	**The** building is near the college. **The** janitor lives on the first floor.	We introduce a singular noun with the indefinite articles (*a* or *an*). When we refer to this noun again, we use the definite article *the*.
	May I speak to **the** landlord? He lives on **the** third floor. **The** basement is dirty.	We use *the* before a singular noun if this noun is the only one or if the speaker and listener share an experience and are referring to the same one. (In this case, they are talking about the same building.)

Plural		
Indefinite	**Definite**	**Explanation**
My building has **(some)** washing machines. Are there **(any)** dryers?	**The** washing machines are in the basement. Where are **the** dryers?	We introduce a plural noun with *some, any,* or no article. When we refer to this noun again, we use the definite article *the*.
	The tenants are angry. **The** washing machines don't work.	We use *the* before a plural noun if the speaker and the listener share the same experience. (In this case, they are talking about the same building.)

EXERCISE 14 Fill in the blanks in the conversations between two students. Use *the, a, an, some,* or *any*.

CONVERSATION 1

A: Is there ____a____ cafeteria at this school?
          (example)

B: Yes, there is.

A: Where's ____the____ cafeteria?
          (1)

B: It's on ____the____ first floor.
          (2)

A: Are there ____any____ snack machines in ____the____ cafeteria?
          (3)   *(4)*

B: Yes, there are.

A: I want to buy ____a____ soft drink.
          (5)

B: ____The____ soft drink machine is out of order today.
     (6)

Grammar Variation

Have students close their books. Write a part of the conversation from the reading on page 117 on the board. However, change the articles. For example, write:

M: I'm **a manager** of **a building**.

S: I need to **find new apartment**.

Ask students to correct the mistakes.

CONVERSATION 2

A: Is there _____a_____ bookstore for this college?
     (1)

B: Yes, there is.

A: Where's _____the_____ bookstore?
      (2)

B: It's on Green Street.

A: I need to buy _____a_____ dictionary.
       (3)

B: Today's _____a_____ holiday. _____The_____ bookstore is closed today.
    (4)   (5)

EXERCISE 15   Fill in the blanks in the conversation about apartment problems.
Use *the, a, an, some,* or *any.*

A: I have _____a_____ problem in my apartment.
    (example)

B: What's _____the_____ problem?
     (1)

A: _____The_____ landlord doesn't provide enough heat. I have
   (2)

to wear _____a_____ sweater or _____a_____ coat all the
    (3)   (4)

time in the apartment.

B: Why don't you talk to _____the_____ building manager?
         (5)

Maybe _____the_____ heating system is broken. If he doesn't
    (6)

solve _____the_____ problem, you can send _____a_____
    (7)   (8)

letter to _____the_____ Department of Housing.
    (9)

A: That's _____a_____ good idea. There's one more problem.
    (10)

I have _____a_____ neighbor who has _____a_____ small dog.
   (11)   (12)

_____The_____ dog barks all the time when _____the_____ neighbor isn't
 (13)   (14)

home. We share _____a_____ wall, and I can hear _____the_____ dog
     (15)   (16)

barking through _____the_____ wall.
     (17)

CD 1, Track 19

1. Have students read the direction line. Go over the example in the book. Have a volunteer do #1.
2. Have students complete Exercise 15 individually. Check answers as a class.
3. Then have students practice the conversations in pairs. Circulate to observe pair work.
4. If necessary, review grammar chart **4.8** on page 118.

To save class time, have students do half of the exercise in class and complete the other half for homework. Or assign the entire exercise for homework.

Exercise 15 Variation

To provide practice with listening skills, have students close their books and listen to the audio. Repeat the audio as needed. Ask comprehension questions, such as: *What is person A's problem?* (The landlord doesn't provide enough heat.) *What does person A have to wear in the apartment?* (a sweater or a coat) *Who should person A write a letter to?* (the Department of Housing) Then have students open their books and complete Exercise 15.

Expansion

Exercise 15 Have students write a new conversation based on the one in Exercise 15. Ask students to change some details (e.g., the air-conditioning is broken, not the heat). Then have volunteers role-play the new conversation in front of the class. Circulate to observe pair work. Give help as needed.

4.9 | Making Generalizations

1. Explain to students that a generalization says that something is true of all members of a group. Give an example. Say: *Students are noisy. That means that all students, everywhere are noisy. Is this true?* (no)

2. Have students look at grammar chart **4.9**. Review the information. Say: *To make a generalization about a singular noun, use* a *or* an. *To make a generalization about a plural noun, don't use any article. To make a generalization about an object, use a plural noun with no article.*

3. Write the following words on the board:
   1. houses
   2. cat
   3. sharks
   4. subway
   5. bus
   6. taxes
   Ask students to write two sentences for each item. Say: *Write a generalization and write a sentence about something specific.* Have volunteers write their sentences on the board.

EXERCISE 16

1. Have students read the direction line. Ask: *What do you change from singular to plural?* (the subject) *What else are we going to change?* (articles and verbs) Go over the example in the book.

2. Have students complete Exercise 16 individually. Check answers as a class.

B: Talk to ___the___ neighbor. Tell him there are dog services. For
   (18)
   ___a___ price, someone can go to his house every day and play
   (19)
   with ___the___ dog and take it out for a walk.
   (20)

A: I don't think he wants to pay ___the___ price for this service.
   (21)

B: Then talk to ___the___ landlord. Tell him about ___the___ problem.
   (22)   (23)

4.9 | Making Generalizations

A generalization says that something is true of all members of a group.

Singular	Plural	Explanation
A snake is quiet. **A dog** makes noise.	**Snakes** are quiet. **Dogs** make noise.	To make a generalization about the **subject**, use the indefinite article (*a* or *an*) with a singular subject or no article with a **plural** subject.
	I don't like **snakes.** Snakes eat **mice.**	To make a generalization about the **object**, use the plural form with no article.

EXERCISE 16   The following sentences are generalizations. Change the subject from singular to plural. Make other necessary changes.

EXAMPLE: A single parent has a difficult life.
           Single parents have a difficult life.

1. A house in San Diego is expensive.
   Houses in San Diego are expensive.

2. A homeowner pays property tax.
   Homeowners pay property tax.

3. A dog is part of the family.
   Dogs are part of the family.

4. A renter doesn't have freedom to make changes.
   Renters don't have freedom to make changes.

5. An owner has freedom to make changes.
   Owners have freedom to make changes.

Grammar Variation

Have students close their books. Write the second part of the conversation from the reading on page 117 on the board. However, change the articles. For example, write:

> *Do you have **the dog**?*
> *We don't permit **the dogs**.*

Have students correct the errors.

EXERCISE **17** ABOUT YOU Use the noun in parentheses ( ) to give general information about your native country or hometown. Use the plural form with no article.

EXAMPLE (woman)
Generally, women don't work outside the home in my native country.

Answers will vary.
1. (person)   5. (house)
2. old (person)   6. poor (person)
3. (women)   7. (car)
4. (man)   8. (doctor)

EXERCISE **18** Add a plural subject to these sentences to make a generalization.

EXAMPLE _____*Small children*_____ need a lot of sleep.
1. _____Answers will vary._____ make a lot of money.
2. _____ have a hard life.
3. _____ talk on the phone a lot.
4. _____ are in good physical condition.
5. _____ believe in Santa Claus.
6. _____ worry about children.

EXERCISE **19** ABOUT YOU Use the plural form of each noun to tell if you like or don't like the following living conditions.

Answers will vary.

EXAMPLE tall building
I like tall buildings.

1. white wall   7. high ceiling
2. curtain on the window   8. bright light
3. picture on the wall   9. two-story house
4. plant   10. digital clock
5. friendly neighbor   11. carpet
6. blind on the window   12. hardwood floor

Expansion

Exercise 17 Have students compare answers in groups. If possible, put students with different nationalities together.

Exercise 18 Take a class survey. Compare answers as a class. Write the results of the survey on the board.

EXERCISE 17

1. Tell students that they will be making generalizations about their native countries or hometowns. Have students read the direction line. Ask: *Will you use plural or singular nouns?* (plural) *Will you use an article?* (no) Go over the example. Have a volunteer model the example.
2. Have students complete Exercise 17 individually. Collect for assessment.
3. If necessary, review grammar chart **4.9** on page 120.

EXERCISE 18

1. Have students read the direction line. Remind students that this exercise is about making generalizations. Go over the example in the book.
2. Have students complete Exercise 18 individually. Check answers with the class. Have volunteers read their sentences aloud.
3. If necessary, review grammar chart **4.9** on page 120.

To save class time, have students do half of the exercise in class and complete the other half for homework. Or assign the entire exercise for homework.

EXERCISE 19

1. Tell students that this exercise is about their likes and dislikes. Have students read the direction line. Ask: *Do you use singular or plural nouns?* (plural) *Do you use articles?* (no) Go over the example in the book. Have a volunteer model the example. Point out the pictures of curtains, blinds, a digital clock, and hardwood floor.
2. Have students complete Exercise 19 individually. Then have students compare answers in pairs. Circulate to observe pair work. Give help as needed.
3. If necessary, review grammar chart **4.9** on page 120.

To save class time, have students do half of the exercise in class and complete the other half in writing for homework. Or if students do not need speaking practice, the entire exercise may be skipped or done in writing.

EXERCISE 20

1. Tell students that this exercise is about their likes and dislikes. Have students read the direction line. Go over the examples in the book. Have two volunteers model #1.
2. Have students complete the rest of Exercise 20 in pairs. Circulate to observe pair work. Give help as needed.
3. If necessary, review grammar chart **4.9** on page 120.

🕐 To save class time, have students do half of the exercise in class and complete the other half in writing for homework (answering the questions themselves). Or if students do not need speaking practice, the entire exercise may be skipped or done in writing.

EXERCISE 21

🎧 *CD 1, Track 20*

1. Have students read the direction line. Explain that this is a conversation between two students. Ask: *Will you always use an article?* (no) Go over the example in the book. Point out the picture of the pirate on page 123.
2. Have students complete Exercise 21 individually. Check answers as a class.
3. Then have students practice the conversation in pairs. Circulate to observe pair work. Give help as needed.
4. If necessary, review grammar chart **4.8** on page 118.

🕐 To save class time, have students do half of the exercise in class and complete the other half for homework. Or assign the entire exercise for homework.

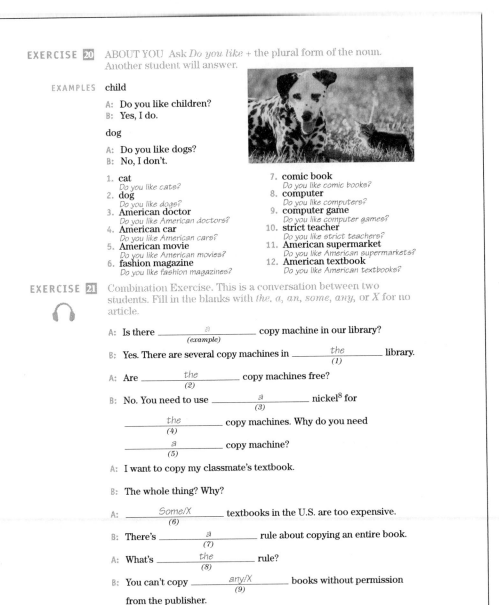

EXERCISE 20 ABOUT YOU Ask *Do you like* + the plural form of the noun. Another student will answer.

EXAMPLES child
A: Do you like children?
B: Yes, I do.

dog
A: Do you like dogs?
B: No, I don't.

1. cat
   Do you like cats?
2. dog
   Do you like dogs?
3. American doctor
   Do you like American doctors?
4. American car
   Do you like American cars?
5. American movie
   Do you like American movies?
6. fashion magazine
   Do you like fashion magazines?
7. comic book
   Do you like comic books?
8. computer
   Do you like computers?
9. computer game
   Do you like computer games?
10. strict teacher
    Do you like strict teachers?
11. American supermarket
    Do you like American supermarkets?
12. American textbook
    Do you like American textbooks?

EXERCISE 21 🎧 Combination Exercise. This is a conversation between two students. Fill in the blanks with *the, a, an, some, any,* or *X* for no article.

A: Is there _____*a*_____ copy machine in our library?
   (example)

B: Yes. There are several copy machines in _____*the*_____ library.
   (1)

A: Are _____*the*_____ copy machines free?
   (2)

B: No. You need to use _____*a*_____ nickel[8] for
   (3)
   _____*the*_____ copy machines. Why do you need
   (4)
   _____*a*_____ copy machine?
   (5)

A: I want to copy my classmate's textbook.

B: The whole thing? Why?

A: _____*Some/X*_____ textbooks in the U.S. are too expensive.
   (6)

B: There's _____*a*_____ rule about copying an entire book.
   (7)

A: What's _____*the*_____ rule?
   (8)

B: You can't copy _____*any/X*_____ books without permission
   (9)
   from the publisher.

[8] A *nickel* is a five-cent coin.

122 Lesson 4

Expansion

Exercise 20 Take a class survey. Compare answers as a class. Write the results of the survey on the board.

Exercise 21 Variation

To provide practice with listening skills, have students close their books and listen to the audio. Explain that this is a conversation between two students. Repeat the audio as needed. Ask comprehension questions, such as: *How many copy machines are there in the library?* (several) *Does it cost money to use the copy machines?* (yes) *What does person A want to copy?* (a classmate's textbook) Then have students open their books and complete Exercise 21.

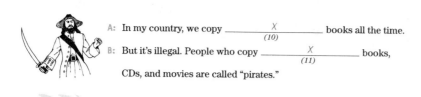

A: In my country, we copy _____X_____ books all the time.
                                        (10)

B: But it's illegal. People who copy _____X_____ books,
                                           (11)

CDs, and movies are called "pirates."

SUMMARY OF LESSON 4

1. Singular and Plural
   boy—boys
   box—boxes
   story—stories
   (Exceptions: men, women, people, children, feet, teeth)

2. *There + be*
   There's an empty apartment in my building.
   There are two washing machines in the basement.
   Are there any parking spaces?

3. Articles

   • To make a generalization:
   SINGULAR   **A dog** has good hearing.
   PLURAL   **Dogs** have good hearing.
                  I like **dogs.**

   • To introduce a new noun into the conversation:
   SINGULAR   I have **a dog.**
   PLURAL   I have **(some) turtles.**
                  I don't have **(any) birds.**

   • To talk about a previously mentioned noun:
   SINGULAR   I have a dog. **The dog** barks when the letter
                  carrier arrives.
   PLURAL   I have some turtles. I keep **the turtles** in the
                  bathroom.

   • To talk about specific items or people from our experience:
   SINGULAR   **The janitor** cleans the basement once a week.
   PLURAL   **The tenants** have to take out their own garbage.

   • To talk about the only one:
   The president lives in Washington, D.C.
   The Statue of Liberty is in New York.

Singular and Plural; Articles and Quantity Words; *There + Be* + Noun   **123**

Summary of Lesson 4

1. **Singular and Plural** Review the rules for forming the plural of nouns. Go over the examples in the book. If necessary, have students review:
   4.1   Singular and Plural—An Overview (p. 102)
   4.2   Regular Noun Plurals (p. 104)
   4.4   Irregular Noun Plurals (p. 106).

2. *There + be* Have students close their books. On the board, write:
   affirmative
   negative
   yes/no *question with short answer*
   how many
   Instruct students to write two affirmative sentences (singular and plural); two negative sentences (singular and plural); two *yes/no* questions with short answers (singular and plural); and one question using *how many.* Say: *You can write the questions about this classroom or about where you live.* Then go over the examples in the book. If necessary, have students review:
   4.5   Using *There + Is/Are* (p. 110)
   4.6   Questions and Short Answers Using *There* (p. 112).

3. **Articles** Have students read the examples and write sentences of their own. Then put students in pairs to compare work. Circulate to observe and give help as needed. If necessary, have students review:
   4.8   Articles with Definite and Indefinite Nouns (p. 118)
   4.9   Making Generalizations (p. 120).

Expansion

Exercise 21 Have volunteers role-play the conversation in front of the class.

Summary Have a spelling and pronunciation bee. Make a list of approximately 40 nouns. Divide the class into Team A and Team B. Give one member from Team A a noun, and tell them to write the plural form on the board. Do the same with Team B. Then give a member from Team A a plural noun to pronounce. Do the same with Team B. To make the exercise more challenging, give extra points if the team can say (or act out) what the word means.

Editing Advice

Have students close their books. Write the example sentences without editing marks or corrections on the board. For example:

1. *People in my country is very poor.*

2. *The dogs are friendly animals.*

Ask students to correct each sentence and provide a rule or explanation for each correction. This activity can be done individually, in pairs, or as a class. After students have corrected each sentence, tell them to turn to page 124. Say: *Now compare your work with the Editing Advice in the book.*

EDITING ADVICE

1. *People* is a plural noun. Use a plural verb form.

                  are
   People in my country is very poor.

2. Don't use *the* with a generalization.

     D
   The dogs are friendly animals.

3. Don't confuse *there* with *they're*.

                        They're
   I have two brothers. There in Florida.

4. Use *there* + *is/are* to introduce a new subject.

              there are
   In my class five students from Haiti.
                  ^

5. Don't confuse *it's* and *there's*.

     There's
   It's a closet in my bedroom.

6. Don't confuse *have* and *there*.

     There's
   Have a closet in my bedroom.

7. Don't use *the* + a unique noun after *there*.

         T   *is*
   There's the Golden Gate Bridge in California.
                           ^

8. Don't use *the* with the first mention of a noun when you and the listener do not share a common experience with this noun.

            a
   I have the new watch.

9. Don't use an apostrophe for a plural ending.

                   brothers
   She has three brother's.

PART **1** A woman is showing her new apartment to her friend. Find the mistakes with the underlined words in this conversation and correct them. If the sentence is correct, write *C*.

A: Let me show you around my new apartment.

B: It's a big apartment.   *C*

A: It's big enough for my family. ~~They're~~ *There* are four bedrooms and two bathrooms. ~~Has~~ *E* each bedroom ~~a~~ *has* large closet. Let me show you my
        (1)
kitchen too.

B: Oh. ~~It's~~ *There's* a new dishwasher in your kitchen.
        (2)

A: It's wonderful. You know how I hate to wash dishes.   *C*
        (3)

B: Is there a microwave oven?   *C*
        (4)

A: No, there isn't.   *C*
        (5)

B: Are ~~any~~ *there* washers and dryers for clothes?
        (6)

A: Oh, yes. They're in the basement. In the laundry room ~~are~~ *there* five
        (7)   (8)
washers and five dryers. I never have to wait.

B: ~~There are~~ *Are there* a lot of people in your building?
        (9)

A: In my building ~~30 apartments~~ *there are*.
        (10)

B: ~~Is~~ *there* a janitor in your building?
        (11)

A: Yes. There's a very good janitor. He keeps the building very clean.   *C*
        (12)

B: I suppose this apartment costs a lot.

A: Well, yes. The rent is high. But I share the apartment with my
cousins.   *C*   (13)

Lesson 4 Test/Review

For additional practice, review, and assessment materials, see Assessment CD-ROM with *ExamView Pro*, *More Grammar Practice* Workbook 1, Interactive CD-ROM, and Web site http://elt.thomson.com/gic

PART 1

1. Part 1 may be used in addition to the Assessment CD-ROM with *ExamView Pro* as an in-class test to assess student performance. Have students read the direction line. Explain that this conversation is about a woman who is showing her new apartment to her friend. Ask: *Does every sentence have a mistake?* (no) Review the examples.

2. Have students complete the assignment individually. Collect for assessment.

3. If necessary, have students review: **Lesson 4.**

Lesson Review

To use Part 1 as a review, assign it as homework or use it as an in-class activity to be completed individually or in pairs. Check answers and review errors as a class. Reteach grammar points that students haven't mastered. Then student learning may be assessed using a test generated from the Assessment CD-ROM with *ExamView Pro*.

PART 2

1. Part 2 may also be used as an in-class test to assess student performance, in addition to the Assessment CD-ROM with *ExamView Pro*. Have students read the direction line. Review the example.
2. Have students complete the exercise individually. Collect for assessment.
3. If necessary, have students review:
   4.2 Regular Noun Plurals (p. 104).

PART 3

1. Part 3 may also be used as an in-class test to assess student performance, in addition to the Assessment CD-ROM with *ExamView Pro*. Have students read the direction line. Review the example. Point out the pictures of the mummy and the dinosaur.
2. Have students complete the exercise individually. Collect for assessment.
3. If necessary, have students review:
   4.5 Using *There + Is/Are* (p. 110)
   4.6 Questions and Short Answers Using *There* (p. 112)
   4.7 *There* vs. *They* and Other Pronouns (p. 115).

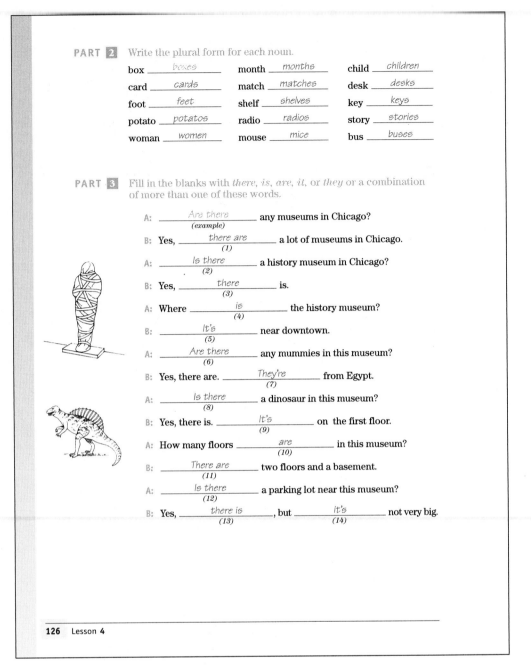

PART **2** Write the plural form for each noun.

box ___boxes___   month ___months___   child ___children___
card ___cards___   match ___matches___   desk ___desks___
foot ___feet___   shelf ___shelves___   key ___keys___
potato ___potatos___   radio ___radios___   story ___stories___
woman ___women___   mouse ___mice___   bus ___buses___

PART **3** Fill in the blanks with *there, is, are, it,* or *they* or a combination of more than one of these words.

A: ___Are there___ any museums in Chicago?
     (example)

B: Yes, ___there are___ a lot of museums in Chicago.
         (1)

A: ___Is there___ a history museum in Chicago?
     (2)

B: Yes, ___there___ is.
        (3)

A: Where ___is___ the history museum?
        (4)

B: ___It's___ near downtown.
   (5)

A: ___Are there___ any mummies in this museum?
     (6)

B: Yes, there are. ___They're___ from Egypt.
               (7)

A: ___Is there___ a dinosaur in this museum?
     (8)

B: Yes, there is. ___It's___ on the first floor.
          (9)

A: How many floors ___are___ in this museum?
           (10)

B: ___There are___ two floors and a basement.
   (11)

A: ___Is there___ a parking lot near this museum?
     (12)

B: Yes, ___there is___, but ___it's___ not very big.
      (13)   *(14)*

Lesson Review

To use Parts 2 and 3 as a review, assign them as homework or use them as in-class activities to be completed individually or in pairs. Check answers and review errors as a class. Reteach grammar points that students haven't mastered. Then student learning may be assessed using a test generated from the Assessment CD-ROM with *ExamView Pro*.

PART **4**   Fill in the blanks with *the, a, an, some, any,* or *X* for no article.

A: Do you like your apartment?

B: No, I don't.

A: Why not?

B: There are many reasons. First, I don't like _____*the*_____ janitor.
   (example)
   He's impolite.

A: Anything else?

B: I want to get _____*a*_____ dog.
   (1)

A: So?

B: It's not permitted. _____*The*_____ landlord says that _____*X*_____ dogs
   (2)   (3)
   make a lot of noise.

A: Can you get _____*a*_____ cat?
   (4)

B: Yes, but I don't like _____*X*_____ cats.
   (5)

A: Is your building quiet?

B: No. There are _____*X*_____ children in _____*the*_____ building. When
   (6)   (7)
   I try to study, I can hear _____*the*_____ children in the next apartment.
   (8)
   They watch TV all the time.

A: You need to find _____*a*_____ new apartment.
   (9)

B: I think you're right.

PART 4

1. Part 4 may also be used as an in-class test to assess student performance, in addition to the Assessment CD-ROM with *ExamView Pro*. Have students read the direction line. Ask: *Will all nouns have an article?* (no) Review the example.

2. Have students complete the exercise individually. Collect for assessment.

3. If necessary, have students review:
   4.8 Articles with Definite and Indefinite Nouns (p. 118)
   4.9 Making Generalizations (p. 120).

Lesson Review

To use Part 4 as a review, assign it as homework or use it as an in-class activity to be completed individually or in pairs. Check answers and review errors as a class. Reteach grammar points that students haven't mastered. Then student learning may be assessed using a test generated from the Assessment CD-ROM with *ExamView Pro*.

Expansion Activities

These expansion activities provide opportunities for students to interact with one another and further develop their speaking and writing skills. Encourage students to use grammar from this lesson whenever possible.

To save class time, assign parts of the activities as homework. Then use class time for interaction and communication. If students do not need additional speaking practice, some of the activities may be assigned as writing activities for homework, or skipped altogether.

CLASSROOM ACTIVITIES

1. Have students read the direction line. Go over the list of items to make sure everyone knows the meanings of the words. Point out the pictures of a scale and an orange juice squeezer. Model the activity for the class. Have students complete the chart on their own. Then instruct students to compare lists. Circulate to observe pair work. Give help as needed.

2. Have students bring in the classifieds section of a newspaper. Put students in groups to compare apartments. Circulate to observe pair work. Give help as needed. Have groups report "good apartment deals" to the class (e.g., *There's a really nice apartment by the park. It's only $600 a month.*).

3. Instruct groups to explore the rest of the newspaper. Go over the examples in the book. Have volunteers report their findings to the class.

EXPANSION ACTIVITIES

Classroom Activities

1. Make a list of things you have, things you don't have but would like to have, and things you don't need. Choose from the list below and add any other items you can think of. Then find a partner and compare lists.

a computer	a house	a credit card
a DVD player	a diamond ring	a speaker phone
a digital camera	a CD player	a cell phone
an encyclopedia	an electric can opener	a big-screen TV
a pager	a microwave oven	a letter opener
an electric toothbrush	a waterbed	a blow dryer
a scale	an electronic calendar	an orange juice squeezer

I have:	I don't have, but I would like to have:	I don't need:

Discuss your chart with a partner. Tell why you need or don't need some things. Tell why you want some things that you don't have.

2. People often use the newspaper to look for an apartment. The Sunday newspaper has the most ads. Bring in a copy of the Sunday newspaper. Look at the section of the newspaper that has apartments for rent. Ask the teacher to help you understand the abbreviations.

3. What other sections are there in the Sunday newspaper? Work with a partner and make a list of everything you can find in the Sunday paper.

EXAMPLE There's a TV schedule for this week's programs.
There are a lot of ads and coupons.
There's a crossword puzzle.

Classroom Activities Variation

Activity 1 Do a class survey. In groups, have students compare information. Have students report their results to the class. Record the information on the board for selected categories (e.g., *All of the students in the class have a blow dryer.*).

Activity 2 Find or create ads for apartments and houses for half of the class. Make sure the ads include some details. Make copies of each ad. Put each of the ads on small identical cards. Pass out the cards randomly to students. Ask students to circulate around the room to find their match. Say: *Don't show your card to anyone. Describe the apartment or house. For example, say: There's a backyard, a swimming pool, etc.*

---

4. Look at the information about two apartments for rent below. What are some of the advantages and disadvantages of each one? Discuss your answers with a partner or with the entire class.

Apartment 1	Apartment 2
a view of a park	on a busy street
rent = $950	rent = $750
fifth floor (an elevator in the building)	third floor walk-up
a new kitchen with a dishwasher	old appliances in the kitchen
pets not allowed	pets allowed
hardwood floors	a carpet in the living room
the janitor lives in the building	the owner lives in the building on the first floor
management controls the heat	the tenant controls the heat
no air conditioners	air conditioners in the bedroom and living room
faces north only	faces east, south, and west
a one-year lease	no lease
a large building—50 apartments	a small building—6 apartments
washers and dryers on each floor	a laundry room in the basement
parking spaces on first-come, first-served basis	a parking space for each tenant

5. Do you have a picture of your house, apartment, or apartment building? Bring it to class and tell about it.

6. Find a partner and pretend that one of you is looking for an apartment and the other person is the landlady, landlord, or manager. Ask and answer questions about the apartment, the building, parking, laundry, and rent. Write your conversation. Then read it to the class.

7. In a small group or with the entire class, discuss the following:
   a. How do people rent apartments in your hometown? Is rent high? Is heat usually included in the rent? Does the landlord usually live in the building?
   b. What are some differences between a typical apartment in this city and a typical apartment in your hometown?

4. Have students read the direction line. Briefly model the activity with a volunteer.

5. Instruct students to bring in pictures of their homes. Ask volunteers to describe their homes to a group or to the class.

6. Have students read the direction line. Say: *Ask and answer questions about the apartment.* Brainstorm questions to ask a landlord (e.g., *Is there an elevator? Is there a garage?*). Then have students work in pairs to write the conversations. Circulate to observe pair work. Give help as needed.

7. Tell students that this activity is about making comparisons. Have students read the direction line. Put students in groups. Try to mix students who are from different towns and/or countries. Circulate to observe group work. Give help as needed.

Expansion

Classroom Activities For activity 6, have volunteers role-play their conversations in front of the class.

8. Tell students that they'll be making generalizations in this activity. Have students read the direction line. Ask: *Which word do we make plural?* (the word in parentheses) Have students work in pairs. Circulate to observe pair work. Give help as needed.

WRITE ABOUT IT

1. Have students read the direction line. Go over the example. Have students complete the assignment individually. Collect for assessment and/or have students present their paragraph to a group.

2. Tell students that for this activity they'll write a comparison. Have students read the direction line. Instruct students to work individually.

INTERNET ACTIVITY

Tell students: *You're going to look on the Internet for apartments for rent and houses for sale in the area.* Ask: *What questions will you answer about the real estate market here?* (Where are the highest rent and housing prices?)

---

8. Use the plural form of the word in parentheses ( ) to make a generalization. Remember, don't use an article with the plural form to make a generalization. You may work with a partner.

EXAMPLES (child)

Children like to watch cartoons.

American (highway)

American highways are in good condition.

1. (American)
2. American (child)
3. big (city) in the U.S.
4. (teacher) at this college
5. (student) at this college
6. American (doctor)
7. old (person) in the U.S.
8. American (woman)

1. Write a description of a room or place that you like very much. (Review prepositions in Lesson 1.)

EXAMPLE My favorite place is my living room. There are many pictures on the walls. There's a picture of my grand-parents above the sofa. There are a lot of pictures of my children on the wall next to the sofa.

There's a TV in the corner. Under the TV there is a DVD player. There's a box of movies next to the DVD player . . . .

2. Write a comparison of your apartment in this city and your apartment or house in your hometown.

EXAMPLE There are many differences between my apartment here and my apartment in Kiev, Ukraine. In my Kiev apartment, there is a door on every room. In my apartment here, only the bedrooms and bathrooms have doors. In my Kiev apartment, there is a small window inside each large window. In the winter, I can open this small window to get some fresh air. My apartment here doesn't have this small window. I have to open the whole window to get air. Sometimes the room becomes too cold. . . .

Use the Internet to look for apartments for rent and houses for sale in this city (or nearby suburbs). What parts of this city or the suburbs have the highest rents and housing prices?

Additional Activities at http://elt.thomson.com/gic

130   Lesson 4

Write About it Variation

Have students exchange first drafts with a partner. Ask students to help their partners edit their drafts. Refer students to the Editing Advice on page 124.

LESSON

5

GRAMMAR

Possession
Object Pronouns
Questions About the Subject

CONTEXT: Families and Names

Names
William Madison's Name
Who Helps Your Parents?

131

Lesson Overview

GRAMMAR

Ask: *What did we study in Lesson 4?* (singular and plural nouns; articles and quantity words; *there + be + noun*) *What are we going to study in this lesson?* (possession; object pronouns; questions about the subject) Activate students' prior knowledge. Have volunteers give examples. Write them on the board. Ask: *Can you give me examples of possessives?*

CONTEXT

1. Ask: *What will we learn about in this lesson?* (families and names) Activate prior knowledge. Ask a few students their names. Ask them if their last name is their father's, mother's, husband's, etc.
2. Have students share their knowledge and personal experiences.

Photo

1. Direct students' attention to the photo. Ask: *Who are these people?* (a family; parents, children, family dog)
2. Ask students about their families: *Are you married? Do you have a family? Do you have children? Who lives with you?*

To save class time, have students do the Test/Review at the end of the lesson, or administer a lesson test generated from the Assessment CD-ROM with *ExamView*® *Pro*. Skip sections of the lesson that students have already mastered. You may also assign some sections for self-study for extra credit.

Expansion

Theme The topic for this lesson can be enhanced with the following ideas:

1. Pictures of your family or someone else's family
2. Pictures of extended families
3. A family tree

Names (Reading)

1. Have students look at the photo. Ask: *Who is this man?* (Michael)
2. Have students look at the title of the reading. Ask: *What is the reading about? How do you know?* Have students use the title and photo to make predictions about the reading.
3. Preteach any vocabulary words your students may not know, such as *surname, initial,* and *hyphen.*

BEFORE YOU READ

1. Have students discuss the questions in pairs.
2. Ask for a few volunteers to share their answers with the class.

To save class time, skip "Before You Read" or have students prepare answers for homework ahead of time.

Reading ∩ *CD 1, Track 21*

1. Have students read the text silently. Tell them to pay special attention to possessive forms. Then play the audio and have students read along silently.
2. Check students' comprehension. Ask questions such as: *How many names do Americans usually have?* (three) *Do women always change their last names when they get married?* (No; some keep their maiden names.) *Do men usually change their last names?* (no)

To save class time, have students do the reading for homework ahead of time.

DID YOU KNOW?

In 1900, the most popular male name was John, and the most popular female name was Mary. In 2000, the most popular male and female names were Jacob and Emily.

NAMES

Before You Read

1. What is your complete name? What do your friends call you?
2. Do you like your name?

 Read the following article. Pay special attention to possessive forms.

Americans usually have three names: a first name, a middle name, and a last name (or surname). For example: Marilyn Sue Ellis or Edward David Orleans. Some people use an initial when they sign **their** names: Marilyn S. Ellis, Edward D. Orleans. Not everyone has a middle name.

American women often change **their** last names when they get married. For example, if Marilyn Ellis marries Edward Orleans, **her** name becomes Marilyn Orleans. Not all women follow this custom. Sometimes a woman keeps **her** maiden name[1] and adds **her husband's** name, with or without a hyphen (-): For example, Marilyn Ellis-Orleans or Marilyn Ellis Orleans. Sometimes a woman does not use **her husband's** name at all. In this case, if the couple has children, they have to decide if **their** children will use **their father's** name, **their mother's** name, or both. A man does not usually change **his** name when he gets married.

Some people have **their mother's** last name as a middle name: John Fitzgerald Kennedy, Franklin Delano Roosevelt.[2]

Did You Know?

The five most common last names in the U.S. are Smith, Johnson, Williams, Jones, and Brown.

[1] A *maiden name* is a woman's family name before she gets married.
[2] These are the names of two American presidents.

132 Lesson 5

Reading Variation

To practice listening skills, have students first listen to the audio alone. Ask a few comprehension questions. Repeat the audio if necessary. Then have students open their books and read along as they listen to the audio.

Reading Glossary

hyphen: the punctuation mark (-)
initial: the first letter of a word or name
surname: family name or last name

5.1 | Possessive Form of Nouns

We use the possessive form to show ownership or relationship.

Noun	Ending	Examples
Singular Noun father mother dog	Add apostrophe + *s*	I use my **father's** last name. I don't use my **mother's** last name. My **dog's** name is PeeWee.
Plural Noun Ending in -s parents boys	Add apostrophe only	My **parents'** names are Ethel and Herman. My **sons'** names are Ted and Mike.
Irregular Plural Noun children women	Add apostrophe + *s*	What are your **children's** names? Marilyn and Sandra are **women's** names.
Names That End in -s Mr. Harris Charles	Add apostrophe only OR Add apostrophe + *s*	Do you know **Charles'** wife? OR Do you know **Charles's** wife?
Inanimate Objects the classroom the school	Use "*the* _____ *of* _____." Do not use apostrophe + *s*.	**The door of the classroom** is closed. Washington College is **the name of my school.**

EXERCISE **1** Fill in the blanks with the possessive form of a noun to make a true statement.

EXAMPLE I use my _____*father's*_____ last name.

Answers will vary.

1. I use my _____ last name.

2. I don't use my _____ last name.

3. An American married woman often uses her _____ last name.

4. A married woman in my native culture uses her _____ last name.

5. A single American woman usually uses her _____ last name.

6. An American man rarely uses his _____ last name.

7. John Kennedy had his _____ maiden name as a middle name.

5.1 | Possessive Forms of Nouns

1. Have students close their books. Put students into pairs. Write grammar chart **5.1** on the board. Keep the middle column ("Ending") empty. Say: *Study the nouns and the examples of possessives, and try to guess the rule for the endings.* Have volunteers write the rules on the board.

2. Then ask students to look at grammar chart **5.1** to compare their chart with the chart in the book.

3. Make sure to point out that possession by inanimate objects is expressed in the following way: *the _____ of _____.*

EXERCISE 1

1. Tell students that this exercise is based on the reading on page 132. Have students read the direction line. Review the example. Have a volunteer model #1.

2. Have students complete Exercise 1 individually. Check the answers as a class.

3. If necessary, review grammar chart **5.1** on page 133.

EXERCISE 2

1. Have students read the direction line. Ask: *Do we always use 's or '?* (No. Some of the sentences have inanimate objects.) Review the examples.
2. Have students complete Exercise 2 individually. Then have them compare answers in pairs. Circulate to observe pair work. Give help as needed. Check answers as a class.
3. If necessary, review grammar chart **5.1** on page 133.

🕐 To save class time, have students do half of the exercise in class and complete the other half for homework. Or assign the entire exercise for homework.

EXERCISE 2   Some of the following sentences can show possession with 's or '. Rewrite these sentences. Write "no change" for the others.

EXAMPLES   The teacher knows the names of the students.
The teacher knows the students' names.

The door of the classroom is usually closed.
No change.

1. The teacher always corrects the homework of the students.
   The teacher always corrects the students' homework.
2. The name of the textbook is *Grammar in Context*.
   No change.
3. The job of the teacher is to explain the grammar.
   The teacher's job is to explain the grammar.
4. What are the names of your parents?
   What are your parents' names?
5. The color of this book is blue.
   No change.
6. Do you use the last name of your father?
   Do you use your father's last name?
7. What is the name of your dog?
   What is your dog's name?
8. The names of the children are Jason and Jessica.
   The children's names are Jason and Jessica.

Expansion

Exercise 2 Have students make questions from the statements in Exercise 2. Then have pairs ask and answer the questions. Circulate to observe pair work. Give help as needed.

5.2 | Possessive Adjectives

Possessive adjectives show ownership or relationship.

Examples	Explanation	
Compare subject pronouns and possessive adjectives	Subject Pronouns	Possessive Adjectives
I like **my** name.	I	my
You're a new student. What's **your** name?	you	your
He likes **his** name.	he	his
She doesn't like **her** name.	she	her
Is this your dog? Is *it* friendly? What's **its** name?	it	its
We use **our** nicknames.	we	our
They are my friends. **Their** last name is Jackson.	they	their
Be careful not to confuse *his* and *her*.		
My sister loves **her** husband.	*Wrong:* My sister loves *his* husband.	
My uncle lives with **his** daughter.	*Wrong:* My uncle lives with *her* daughter.	
My sister's name is Marilyn. **Her son's** name is David.	We can use a possessive adjective (*my, her*) and a possessive noun (*sister's, son's*) together.	
My **sister's husband's** name is Edward.	We can use two possessive nouns together (*sister's husband's*).	

EXERCISE 3   Fill in the blanks with the possessive adjective that relates to the subject.

EXAMPLE   I like _____*my*_____ teacher.

1. He loves _____*his*_____ mother.
2. She loves _____*her*_____ father.
3. A dog loves _____*its*_____ master.
4. Many American women change _____*their*_____ names when they get married.
5. Sometimes a woman keeps _____*her*_____ maiden name and adds _____*her*_____ husband's name.
6. American men don't usually change _____*their*_____ names when they get married.
7. Do you use _____*your*_____ father's last name?
8. I bring _____*my*_____ book to class.
9. We use _____*our*_____ books in class.
10. The teacher brings _*his* **or** *her*_ book to class.
11. Some students do _____*their*_____ homework in the library.

Possession; Object Pronouns; Questions About the Subject   **135**

5.2 | Possessive Adjectives

1. Have students cover up grammar chart **5.2** in their books. Activate prior knowledge. Ask: *What are the subject pronouns?* (I, you, he, etc.) Write them on the board. Then ask: *Do you know what the possessive adjectives are for these pronouns?* (my, your, his, etc.) Write them on the board next to the subject pronouns.
2. Have students look at grammar chart **5.2**. Say: *Compare our lists with the grammar chart.* Go over any errors.
3. Review the examples in the chart. Point out that English learners sometimes confuse *his* and *her*. Point out the difference between *its* (the possessive adjective) and *it's* (the contraction for *it is*). Show how we can use possessive adjectives and nouns together.

EXERCISE 3

1. Have students read the direction line. Ask: *What will we write in the blanks?* (possessive adjectives) Review the example in the book. Have a volunteer do #1.
2. Have students complete the rest of Exercise 3 individually. Check the answers as a class.
3. If necessary, review grammar chart **5.2** on page 135.

Expansion

Grammar Play a chain game. Have students sit in a circle. The first person says his or her name and a relative's name (e.g., *My name is Maria and my aunt's name is Sophia.*). The person sitting next to her repeats her information and then adds his or her own information (e.g., *Her name is Maria and her aunt's name is Sophia. My name is Oscar and my father's name is Juan.*). The last person in the circle tries to repeat everyone's information.

5.3 | Questions with *Whose*

1. Have students cover up grammar chart **5.3**. Pick up book from a student's desk. Ask: *Whose book is this?* (Tina's book) Write it on the board. Then ask: *What was the question I asked?* Have a volunteer write it on the board.
2. Have students look at grammar chart **5.3**. Say: Whose + *noun asks about possession or ownership.* Go over the pattern for questions with *whose.*

EXERCISE 4

1. Have students read the direction line. Review the examples in the book. Have a volunteer do #1.
2. Have students complete the rest of Exercise 4 individually. Check the answers as a class.
3. If necessary, review grammar chart **5.3** on page 136.

5.3 | Questions with *Whose*

Whose + noun asks about possession or ownership.

Questions					Answers
Whose + noun + aux. verb + subject + verb					
Whose	name	do	you	use?	I use **my father's** name.
Whose	composition	do	you	like?	I like **Lisa's** composition.
Whose + noun + *be* verb + subject					
Whose	book	is	that?		It's **Bob's** book.
Whose	glasses	are	those?		They're **my** glasses.

EXERCISE 4 Write a question with *whose* and the words given. Answer with the words in parentheses ( ).

EXAMPLES **wife / that (Robert)**
Whose wife is that? That's Robert's wife.

children / these (Robert)
Whose children are these? These are Robert's children.

1. office / this (the dean)
Whose office is this? This is the dean's office.

2. offices / those (the teachers)
Whose offices are those? Those are the teachers' offices.

3. dictionary / that (the teacher)
Whose dictionary is that? That's the teacher's dictionary.

4. books / those (the students)
Whose books are those? Those are the students' books?

5. car / that (my parents)
Whose car is that? That's my parents' car.

6. house / this (my cousin)
Whose house is this? This is my cousin's house.

7. papers / those (Mr. Ross)
Whose papers are those? Those are Mr. Ross' papers.

8. CDs / these (the programmer)
Whose CDs are these? These are the programmer's CDs.

Expansion

Exercise 4 Play a guessing game. Have students select something of their own to put in a bag. Say: *Don't let the other group members see what you put in the bag.* Place the bag in front of the group. The students take out an object and try to guess whose it is. Say: *First, ask: Whose comb is this? Each group member tries to guess. It's Luisa's comb. It's Muhamud's comb, etc.*

5.4 | Possessive Pronouns

We use possessive pronouns to avoid repetition of a noun.

Examples	Explanation
You don't know my name. I know **yours**. (*yours = your name*) Your name is easy for Americans. **Mine** is hard. (*mine = my name*) My parents are in the U.S. **Theirs** are in Russia. (*theirs = their parents*)	When we omit the noun, we use the possessive pronoun. Compare:

Possessive Adjectives	Possessive Pronouns
my	mine
your	yours
his	his
her	hers
our	ours
their	theirs

Examples	Explanation
Robert's wife speaks English. **Peter's** doesn't. (*Peter's = Peter's wife*)	After a possessive noun, we can omit the noun.

EXERCISE 5 In each pair of sentences below, replace the underlined words with a possessive pronoun.

EXAMPLE   Your book is new. <u>My book</u> is old.
Your book is new. Mine is old.

1. His name is Charles. <u>Her name</u> is Paula.
   His name is Charles. Hers is Paula.
2. My teacher comes from Houston. <u>Paula's teacher</u> comes from El Paso.
   My teacher comes from Houston. Hers comes from El Paso.
3. I like my English teacher. Does your brother like <u>his English teacher</u>?
   I like my English teacher. Does your brother like his?
4. I have my dictionary today. Do you have <u>your dictionary</u>?
   I have my dictionary today. Do you have yours?
5. Please let me use your book. I don't have <u>my book</u> today.
   Please let me use your book. I don't have mine today.
6. My parents' apartment is big. <u>Our apartment</u> is small.
   My parents' apartment is big. Ours is small.
7. My car is old. <u>Your car</u> is new.
   My car is old. Yours is new.

1. Have students cover up grammar chart **5.4** in their books. Activate prior knowledge. Say: *OK. Let's review. What are the subject pronouns?* Write them on the board. *What are the possessive adjectives?* (*my, your, his*, etc.) Write them on the board. Then ask: *Do you know what the possessive pronouns are?* (*mine, yours, his, hers*, etc.) Write them on the board next to the possessive adjectives.
2. Have students look at grammar chart **5.4.** Say: *Compare our lists with the grammar chart.* Go over any errors.
3. Review the examples in the chart. Say: *We use possessive pronouns to avoid repetition of a noun.* Direct students to the first example in the chart. Say: *Instead of repeating* name (*i.e.*, my name, your name), *we can just say* yours.
4. Explain that after a possessive noun, the noun can be omitted. Review the example in the book.

EXERCISE 5

1. Have students read the direction line. Ask: *What do we replace the underlined words with?* (a possessive pronoun) Go over the example in the book. Have a volunteer do #1.
2. Have students complete the rest of Exercise 5 individually. Check the answers as a class.
3. If necessary, review grammar chart **5.4** on page 137.

Expansion

Exercise 5 Have students work in pairs to create sentences. Say: *Write sentences similar to those in Exercise 5, but use your own information.* Circulate to observe pair work. Give help as needed.

CD 1, Track 22

1. Have students read the direction line. Go over the example in the book. Have a volunteer do #1.
2. Have students complete Exercise 6 individually. Check answers as a class.
3. Then have pairs practice the conversation.
4. If necessary, review grammar chart **5.4** on page 137.

🕐 To save class time, have students do half of the exercise in class and complete the other half for homework. Or assign the entire exercise for homework.

5.5 | The Subject and the Object

1. Have students turn to Exercise 3 on page 135. Say: *Underline the subject in each sentence.* Then say: *Find the object in each sentence and circle it.* If students have difficulty, say: *The object is the noun after the verb.* Check that students have found all the subjects and objects. Go over any errors.
2. Have students look at grammar chart **5.5**. Review the examples in the chart.
3. Point out that pronouns can be used for both subjects and objects. Explain that a sentence with two clauses will have more than one subject and more than one object.

EXERCISE **6** Circle the correct word in parentheses ( ) to complete this conversation.

A: Do you live with (*your*, *yours*) parents?
   (example)
B: No, I don't. Do you live with (*your*, *yours*)?
   (1)
A: No. I live with (*my*, *mine*) sister. (*Our*, *Ours*) parents are back
   (2)   *(3)*
   home. They live with (*my*, *mine*) brother.
   (4)
B: (*Your*, *Yours*) brother is single, then?
   (5)
A: No, he's married. He lives with his wife and (*our*, *ours*) parents.
   (6)
B: If he's married, why does he live with (*your*, *yours*) parents?
   (7)
A: In (*our*, *ours*) country, it's an honor to live with parents.
   (8)
B: Not in (*my*, *mine*). Grown children don't usually want to live with
   (9)
   (*their*, *theirs*) parents, and parents don't usually want to live with
   (10)
   (*their*, *theirs*) grown children.
   (11)
A: Where do (*your*, *yours*) parents live?
   (12)
B: They live in another state.
A: Isn't that hard for you?
B: Not really. I have (*my*, *mine*) own life, and they have (*their*, *theirs*).
   (13)   *(14)*

5.5 | The Subject and the Object

Examples	Explanation
S V O Bob likes Mary. We like movies.	The **subject** (S) comes before the verb (V). The **object** (O) comes after the verb. The object is a person or a thing.
S V O S V O Bob likes Mary because **she** helps **him**.	We can use pronouns for the **subject** and the **object.**
S V O S V O I like movies because **they** entertain **me**.	

Exercise 6 Variation

To provide practice with listening skills, have students close their books and listen to the audio. Repeat the audio as needed. Ask comprehension questions, such as: *Where are person A's parents?* (back home) *Is person A's brother married?* (yes) *Does person A live with his wife or his parents?* (both) Then have students open their books and complete Exercise 6.

WILLIAM MADISON'S NAME

Before You Read

1. What are common American names?

2. What is a very common first name in your country or native culture? What is a very common last name? Is your name common in your country or native culture?

🎧 Read the following conversation. Pay special attention to object pronouns.

A: I have many questions about American names. Can you answer **them** for me?

B: Of course.

A: Tell **me** about your name.

B: My name is William, but my friends call **me** Bill.

A: Why do they call **you** Bill?

B: Bill is a common nickname for William.

A: Is William your first name?

B: Yes.

A: What's your full name?

B: William Michael Madison.

A: Do you ever use your middle name?

B: I only use **it** for very formal occasions. I sign my name William M. Madison, Jr. (junior).

A: What does "junior" mean?

B: It means that I have the same name as my father. His name is William Madison, Sr. (senior).

A: What's your wife's name?

B: Anna Marie Simms-Madison. I call **her** Annie.

A: Why does she have two last names?

B: Simms is her father's last name, and Madison is mine. She uses both names with a hyphen (-) between **them.**

A: Do you have any children?

B: Yes. We have a son and a daughter. Our son's name is Richard, but we call **him** Dick. Our daughter's name is Elizabeth, but everybody calls **her** Lizzy.

A: What do your children call **you**?

B: They call **us** Mommy and Daddy, of course.

Possession; Object Pronouns; Questions About the Subject   **139**

William Madison's Name (Reading)

1. Have students look at the photo. Ask: *Who are these people?* (a family and grandparents)

2. Have students look at the title of the reading. Ask: *What is the reading about? How do you know?* Have students use the title and photo to make predictions about the reading.

3. Preteach any vocabulary words your students may not know, such as *nickname*.

BEFORE YOU READ

1. Have students discuss the questions in pairs.

2. Ask for a few volunteers to share their answers with the class.

🕐 To save class time, skip "Before You Read" or have students prepare answers for homework ahead of time.

Reading 🎧 *CD 1, Track 23*

1. Have students first read the text silently. Tell them to pay special attention to object pronouns. Then play the audio and have students read along silently.

2. Check students' comprehension. Ask questions such as: *How many names does William have?* (three) *Why do William's friends call him Bill?* (It's a common nickname for William.) *Why does William sign his name with "junior"?* (because he has the same name as his father)

🕐 To save class time, have students do the reading for homework ahead of time.

Reading Variation

To practice listening skills, have students first listen to the audio alone. Ask a few comprehension questions. Repeat the audio if necessary. Then have students open their books and read along as they listen to the audio.

Reading Glossary

nickname: an informal name given to a person in addition to a legal one

5.6 | Object Pronouns

1. Have students cover up grammar chart **5.6** in their books. Write the subject pronouns on the board. Activate prior knowledge. Say: *OK. Here are the subject pronouns. Can you write the object pronouns?* If students have difficulty, have them look back at the reading and find the object pronouns. Have a volunteer write them on the board.

2. Have students look at grammar chart **5.6**. Say: *Compare our list with the grammar chart.* Go over any errors.

3. Review the examples in the chart. Say: *We can use an object pronoun after the verb or after a preposition.* Then go back to the reading on page 139. Ask students to circle the verbs and the object pronouns.

4. Explain that after a preposition, an object pronoun is used. Ask: *What prepositions do you know?* (*of, about, to, from, in,* etc.) Go over the examples in the chart. Point out that we use *them* for both plural people and plural things.

5.6 | Object Pronouns

Subject	Object	Examples		
		Subject	Verb	Object
I →	me	You	love	me.
you →	you	I	love	you.
he →	him	She	loves	him.
she →	her	He	loves	her.
it →	it	We	love	it.
we →	us	They	love	us.
they →	them	We	love	them.

They love us

He loves her

We can use an object pronoun after the verb or after a preposition.		
Object Noun	**Object Pronoun**	**Explanation**
I have a **middle name.**	I use **it** when I sign my name.	We can use an object pronoun to substitute for an object noun.
He loves **his wife.**	The kids love **her** too.	
You know **my son.**	Friends call **him** Dick.	
We have **two children.**	We love **them.**	We use *them* for plural people and things.
I need **my books.**	I use **them** in class.	
I have **two last names.**	I use both *of* **them.**	An object pronoun can follow a preposition (*of, about, to, from, in,* etc.).
My sister has **a son.**	She always talks *about* **him.**	

EXERCISE 7 Fill in the blanks. Substitute an object pronoun for the underlined words.

EXAMPLE   I look like <u>my father</u>, but my brother doesn't look like _____*him*_____.

1. <u>My brother's</u> name is William, but we call _____*him*_____ Bill.
2. <u>I</u> understand the teacher, and the teacher understands _____*me*_____.
3. I use <u>my dictionary</u> when I write, but I don't use _____*it*_____ when I speak.
4. I like <u>this city</u>. Do you like _____*it*_____ too?
5. I talk to <u>Americans</u>, but I don't always understand _____*them*_____.
6. We listen to <u>the teacher</u>, and we talk to _*him or her*_.
7. When <u>we</u> make a mistake, the teacher corrects _____*us*_____.
8. <u>The president</u> has advisers. They help _____*him*_____ make decisions.
9. <u>You</u> understand me, and I understand _____*you*_____.
10. <u>My friends</u> sometimes visit me, and I sometimes visit _____*them*_____.

EXERCISE 8   This is a conversation between two students, one from China (A), one from the U.S. (B). Fill in the blanks with an appropriate object pronoun.

A: Americans are very informal about names. The teacher calls

_____*us*_____ by our first names.
(example)

B: What does the teacher call _____*you*_____ in your country?
(1)

A: In my country, when a teacher talks to a woman, he calls

_____*her*_____ "Miss" or "Madam." When he talks to a man, he calls
(2)
_____*him*_____ "Sir."
(3)

B: I like it when the teacher calls _____*me*_____ by my first name.
(4)

A: I don't. There's another strange thing: In my country, we never use a

first name for our teachers. We call _____*them*_____ "Professor" or
(5)

"Teacher." Our teacher here gets mad when we call _____*her*_____
(6)

"Teacher." She doesn't like _____*it*_____. She says it's impolite. But in
(7)

my country, "Teacher" is a term of great respect.

B: Only small children in the U.S. call their teacher "Teacher." If you

know your teacher's name, use _____*it*_____.
(8)

Possession; Object Pronouns; Questions About the Subject   **141**

EXERCISE 7

1. Have students read the direction line. Ask: *What do we replace the underlined words with?* (an object pronoun) Review the example. Have a volunteer do #1.
2. Have students complete the rest of Exercise 7 individually. Check the answers as a class.
3. If necessary, review grammar chart **5.6** on page 140.

EXERCISE 8

🎧 *CD 1, Track 24*

1. Tell students that this is a conversation between a Chinese student and an American student. Have students read the direction line. Ask: *What do we put on the blank?* (an object pronoun) Review the example.
2. Have students complete Exercise 8 individually. Then check answers as a class or in small groups.
3. Then have students practice the conversation in pairs. Circulate to observe pair work. Give help as needed.
4. If necessary, review grammar chart **5.6** on page 140.

🕐 To save class time, have students do half of the exercise in class and complete the other half for homework. Or assign the entire exercise for homework.

Exercise 8 Variation

To provide practice with listening skills, have students close their books and listen to the audio. Repeat the audio as needed. Ask comprehension questions, such as: *How do American teachers call their students?* (by their first names) *How do Chinese teachers call their students?* (using *miss, madam, sir,* etc.) *Do Chinese students call their teachers by their first names?* (no) Then have students open their books and complete Exercise 8.

EXERCISE 9

1. Have students read the direction line. Ask: *What do we write on the blanks?* (*I, I'm, my, mine,* or *me*) Review the examples in the book.
2. Have students complete Exercise 9 individually. Check the answers as a class.
3. If necessary, review grammar charts **5.4** on page 137, **5.5** on page 138, and **5.6** on page 140.

🕐 To save class time, have students do half of the exercise in class and complete the other half for homework. Or assign the entire exercise for homework.

A: Do you mean I should call ___*her*___ Dawn?
(9)

B: If that's what she likes.

A: I'm sorry. I can't do ___*that*___. She's about 50 years old, and
(10)
I'm only 20.

B: Then call ___*her*___ Ms. Paskow.
(11)

A: She doesn't like to use her last name. She says everyone
mispronounces ___*it*___. Sometimes I call ___*her*___ Ms. Dawn, but
(12) (13)
she says no one does that here.

B: We have an expression, "When in Rome, do as the Romans do."[3]

A: It's hard for ___*me*___ to change my customs after a lifetime of
(14)
following ___*them*___.
(15)

EXERCISE 9   Fill in the blanks with *I, I'm, my, mine,* or *me*.

EXAMPLES   ___*I'm*___ a foreign student. ___*I*___ come from Japan.
___*My*___ roommate's parents live in the U.S., but ___*mine*___ live in
Japan. ___*My*___ parents write to ___*me*___ twice a month.

1. ___*My*___ roommate's name is Kelly. ___*Mine*___ is Yuki.
2. ___*My*___ roommate helps ___*me*___ with my English.
3. ___*We*___ study at the University of Wisconsin.
4. ___*My*___ major is engineering.
5. ___*I*___ have a roommate.
6. ___*I'm*___ 20 years old.
7. ___*My*___ parents don't live in
the U.S.

[3] This expression means that you should follow the customs of the country you are in.

Expansion

Exercise 8 Have pairs rewrite the conversation. Say: *You can change the information to make it true for you.*

EXERCISE **10**   Fill in the blanks with *he, he's, his,* or *him.*

EXAMPLE   I have a good friend. ___His___ name is Paul. ___He's___ Puerto Rican.

___He___ lives in New York. I like ___him___.

1. ___He's___ married.
2. ___He___ works in an office.
3. ___He's___ an accountant.
4. ___His___ son helps ___him___ in ___his___ business.
5. ___He's___ 37 years old. ___His___ wife is 35.
6. My wife and ___his___ wife are friends.
7. My wife is a doctor. ___His___ is a computer programmer.

EXERCISE **11**   Fill in the blanks with *she, she's, her,* or *hers.*

EXAMPLE   I have a friend. ___Her___ name's Diane. ___She's___ American.

___She___ lives in Boston. My native language is Korean. ___Hers___ is English.

1. ___She's___ an interesting person.
2. I like ___her___ very much.
3. ___She's___ married.
4. ___She___ has two children.
5. My children go to Dewey School. ___Hers___ go to King School.
6. ___She's___ a nurse. ___She___ likes ___her___ job.
7. ___Her___ husband is a teacher.

EXERCISE **12**   Fill in the blanks with *they, they're, their, theirs,* or *them.*

EXAMPLE   Diane and Richard are my friends. ___They___ live in Boston. ___Their___ house is beautiful. ___They're___ happy. I see ___them___ on the weekends.

1. ___They're___ Americans.
2. ___They___ both work.
3. ___They___ have two children.
4. ___Their___ children go to public school.
5. My house is small. ___Theirs___ is big.
6. ___They're___ interested in art.
7. I talk to ___them___ once a week.

Possession; Object Pronouns; Questions About the Subject   **143**

Expansion

Exercises 9, 10, 11, and 12 Have students write an e-mail to a friend in another city or country. Say: *Write about yourself, or a friend or friends. Use the sentences in Exercises 9, 10, 11, and 12 as models.* Remind students to use all forms of pronouns. Collect for assessment.

EXERCISE 10

1. Have students read the direction line. Ask: *What do we write on the blanks?* (he, he's, his, or him) Go over the examples in the book.
2. Have students complete Exercise 10 individually. Check the answers as a class.
3. If necessary, review grammar charts **5.4** on page 137, **5.5** on page 138, and **5.6** on page 140.

🕐 To save class time, have students do half of the exercise in class and complete the other half for homework. Or assign the entire exercise for homework.

EXERCISE 11

1. Have students read the direction line. Ask: *What do we write on the blanks?* (she, she's, her, or hers) Review the examples in the book.
2. Have students complete Exercise 11 individually. Check the answers as a class.
3. If necessary, review grammar charts **5.4** on page 137, **5.5** on page 138, and **5.6** on page 140.

🕐 To save class time, have students do half of the exercise in class and complete the other half for homework. Or assign the entire exercise for homework.

EXERCISE 12

1. Have students read the direction line. Ask: *What do we write on the blanks?* (they, they're, their, theirs, or them) Review the examples in the book.
2. Have students complete Exercise 12 individually. Check the answers as a class.
3. If necessary, review grammar charts **5.4** on page 137, **5.5** on page 138, and **5.6** on page 140.

🕐 To save class time, have students do half of the exercise in class and complete the other half for homework. Or assign the entire exercise for homework.

EXERCISE 13

1. Have students read the direction line. Ask: *What do we write on the blanks?* (*it, it's, or its*) Review the examples in the book.
2. Have students complete Exercise 13 individually. Check the answers as a class.
3. If necessary, review grammar charts **5.4** on page 137, **5.5** on page 138, and **5.6** on page 140.

🕐 To save class time, have students do half of the exercise in class and complete the other half for homework. Or assign the entire exercise for homework.

EXERCISE 14

1. Have students read the direction line. Ask: *What do we write on the blanks?* (*we, we're, our, ours, or us*) Review the examples in the book.
2. Have students complete Exercise 14 individually. Check the answers as a class.
3. If necessary, review grammar charts **5.4** on page 137, **5.5** on page 138, and **5.6** on page 140.

🕐 To save class time, have students do half of the exercise in class and complete the other half for homework. Or assign the entire exercise for homework.

EXERCISE 15

1. Have students read the direction line. Ask: *What do we write on the blanks?* (*you, you're, your,* or *yours*) Review the examples in the book.
2. Have students complete Exercise 15 individually. Check the answers as a class.
3. If necessary, review grammar charts **5.4** on page 137, **5.5** on page 138, and **5.6** on page 140.

🕐 To save class time, have students do half of the exercise in class and complete the other half for homework. Or assign the entire exercise for homework.

EXERCISE 13   Fill in the blanks about a cat. Use *it, it's,* or *its.*

EXAMPLE ___It's___ an independent animal. ___It___ always lands on ___its___ feet.

1. ___It___ likes to eat fish.
2. ___It's___ a small animal.
3. ___Its___ fur is soft.
4. ___It___ catches mice.
5. ___Its___ claws are sharp.
6. ___It's___ a clean animal.
7. Do you see that cat? Yes, I see ___it___.

EXERCISE 14   Fill in the blanks with *we, we're, our, ours,* or *us.*

EXAMPLE ___We___ study English. ___We're___ foreign students. ___Our___ teacher is American. He helps ___us___.

1. ___We___ come from different countries.
2. ___We're___ in class now.
3. ___Our___ classroom is comfortable.
4. The teacher asks ___us___ a lot of questions.
5. The teacher's textbook has the answers. ___We___ don't have the answers.
6. ___We're___ interested in English.

EXERCISE 15   Fill in the blanks with *you, you're, your,* or *yours.*

EXAMPLE ___You're___ a good teacher. Students like ___you___. My other teacher's name is hard to pronounce. ___Yours___ is easy to pronounce.

1. ___You___ explain the grammar well.
2. We all understand ___you___.
3. Our pronunciation is sometimes hard to understand. ___Yours___ is clear.
4. ___You're___ a kind teacher.
5. ___Your___ class is very interesting.
6. ___You___ have a lot of experience with foreign students.

144 Lesson 5

Expansion

Exercises 13 and 14 Have students write an e-mail to a friend in another city or country. Say: *Write about yourself, or a friend or friends. Use the sentences in Exercises 13 and 14 as models.* Remind students to use all forms of pronouns. Have students exchange e-mails with a partner. Say: *Correct your partner's e-mail.* Circulate to give help as needed.

WHO HELPS YOUR PARENTS?

Before You Read

1. At what age should adult children leave home if they're not married?
2. Should adult children take care of their parents?

Read the following conversation. Pay special attention to questions.

A: **Where does your dad live?**
B: He lives back in our country.
A: **Is he in good health?**
B: His health is so-so.
A: **Who takes care of him?**
B: My brother and his wife do.
A: **Do they go to his house every day?**
B: No. They live with him.
A: **Why do they live with him?**
B: It's the custom in my country. What about in America? Do you live with your parents?
A: Of course not. I'm 25. I live with my roommate.
B: **Where do your parents live?**
A: My parents are divorced. My mother lives just a couple of miles from me. My dad lives in another state.
B: **How often do you see your parents?**
A: I see my dad a couple of times a year. I see my mom about once or twice a month.
B: Is that all? **Who helps them? Who shops for them? Who cooks for them?**
A: They're in their 60s and in great health. They can do everything. No one takes care of them. **What's wrong with that?**
B: What about when they get older?
A: I never think about it. **Who knows about the future?** I have my life to live, and they have theirs.

Possession; Object Pronouns; Questions About the Subject **145**

Who Helps Your Parents? (Reading)

1. Have students look at the photo. Ask: *Who are these people?* (a couple, their daughter, and her grandfather)
2. Have students look at the title of the reading. Ask: *What is the reading about? How do you know?* Have students use the title and the photo to make predictions about the reading.
3. Preteach any vocabulary words your students may not know such as *health, so-so,* and *take care of.*

BEFORE YOU READ

1. Have students discuss the questions in pairs.
2. Ask for a few volunteers to share their answers with the class.

To save class time, skip "Before You Read" or have students prepare answers for homework ahead of time.

Reading ∩ *CD 1, Track 25*

1. Have students read the text silently. Tell them to pay special attention to questions. Then play the audio and have students read along silently.
2. Check students' comprehension. Ask questions such as: *Where does the person B's dad live?* (with person B's brother and brother's wife) *Do Americans typically live with their parents after the age of 25?* (no) *Where does person A's dad live?* (in another state)

To save class time, have students do the reading for homework ahead of time.

Reading Variation

To practice listening skills, have students first listen to the audio alone. Ask a few comprehension questions. Repeat the audio if necessary. Then have students open their books and read along as they listen to the audio.

Reading Glossary

health: the condition of a living thing's body and mind
so-so: not wonderful; fair, mediocre
take care of: to attend to or provide for the needs, operation, or treatment of

Culture Note

Most senior citizens in the U.S. do not live with their children after retirement. They usually live with their spouses or alone. Most senior citizens (80 percent) live in houses that they own. Only 4.5 percent of the population lives in nursing homes. About 5 percent of the elderly lives in senior housing of various types, which typically offers services for the elderly such as transportation, meals, and even social events.

5.7 | Questions About the Subject or About the Complement

1. Have students turn to the reading on page 145. Ask them to look at the questions in the reading. Say: *Underline the questions with* do *or* does. *Circle the questions with a verb in the* -s *form.*

2. Have students look at grammar chart **5.7** on page 146. Explain that when we use *do* or *does* in a question, we are asking about the complement of the sentence not the subject. Read the examples and the explanation. Then explain that when we use the *-s* form in a question, we are asking a question about the subject. Read the examples and the explanation.

3. Have students look back again at the reading on page 145 to compare.

EXERCISE 16

1. Have students read the direction line. Go over the examples in the book. Have volunteers model the examples. Point out the pictures of people dusting, making the bed, vacuuming the carpet, and sweeping the floor.

2. Have students complete Exercise 16 in pairs. Circulate to observe pair work. Give help as needed.

3. If necessary, review grammar chart **5.7** on page 146.

EXERCISE 17

🎧 *CD 1, Track 26*

1. Have students read the direction line. Go over the examples with the class.

2. Have students complete Exercise 17 individually. Check answers as a class.

3. If necessary, review grammar chart **5.7** on page 146.

🕐 To save class time, have students do half of the exercise in class and complete the other half for homework. Or assign the entire exercise for homework.

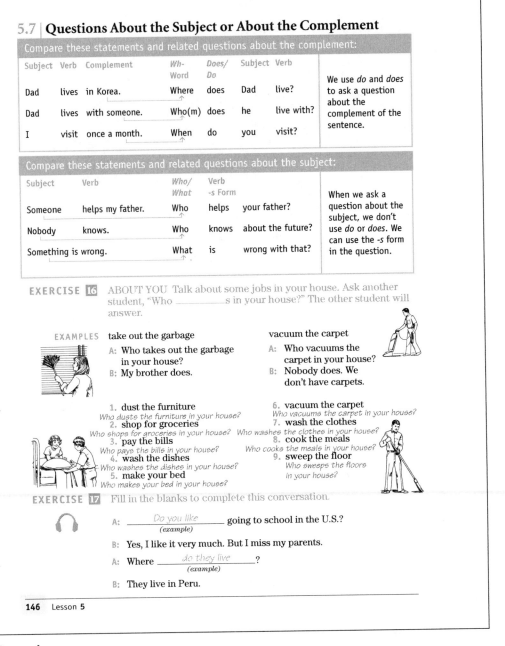

5.7 | Questions About the Subject or About the Complement

Compare these statements and related questions about the complement:

Subject	Verb	Complement	Wh-Word	Does/Do	Subject	Verb	
Dad	lives	in Korea.	Where	does	Dad	live?	We use *do* and *does* to ask a question about the complement of the sentence.
Dad	lives	with someone.	Who(m)	does	he	live with?	
I	visit	once a month.	When	do	you	visit?	

Compare these statements and related questions about the subject:

Subject	Verb		Who/What	Verb -s Form		
Someone	helps my father.		Who	helps	your father?	When we ask a question about the subject, we don't use *do* or *does*. We can use the *-s* form in the question.
Nobody	knows.		Who	knows	about the future?	
Something is wrong.			What	is	wrong with that?	

EXERCISE 16 ABOUT YOU Talk about some jobs in your house. Ask another student, "Who _____s in your house?" The other student will answer.

EXAMPLES
take out the garbage
A: Who takes out the garbage in your house?
B: My brother does.

vacuum the carpet
A: Who vacuums the carpet in your house?
B: Nobody does. We don't have carpets.

1. dust the furniture
Who dusts the furniture in your house?
2. shop for groceries
Who shops for groceries in your house?
3. pay the bills
Who pays the bills in your house?
4. wash the dishes
Who washes the dishes in your house?
5. make your bed
Who makes your bed in your house?

6. vacuum the carpet
Who vacuums the carpet in your house?
7. wash the clothes
Who washes the clothes in your house?
8. cook the meals
Who cooks the meals in your house?
9. sweep the floor
Who sweeps the floors in your house?

EXERCISE 17 Fill in the blanks to complete this conversation.

A: ___*Do you like*___ going to school in the U.S.?
        (example)

B: Yes, I like it very much. But I miss my parents.

A: Where ___*do they live*___?
              (example)

B: They live in Peru.

Expansion

Exercise 16 Create two rings of students. Have half of the students stand in an outer ring around the classroom. Have the other half stand in an inner ring, facing the outer ring. Instruct students to ask and answer the questions from Exercise 16. Call out *"turn"* every minute or so. Students in the inner ring should move one space clockwise. Students now ask and answer with their new partners. Have students ask questions in random order. Make sure students look at each other when they're speaking.

Exercise 17 Variation

To provide practice with listening skills, have students close their books and listen to the audio. Repeat the audio as needed. Ask comprehension questions, such as: *Where does person B go to school?* (in the U.S.) *Where do person B's parents live?* (in Peru) *How old are they?* (in their sixties) Then have students open their books and complete Exercise 17.

A: How old ___are they___?
(example)

B: They're in their 60s.

A: Who ___takes care___ of them?
(1)

B: No one takes care of them. They're in great health.

A: ___Do they live___ alone?
(2)

B: No, they don't. They live with my oldest sister.

A: ___Is she single___?
(3)

B: No, she isn't single. She's married. She's a nurse and her husband is a doctor.

A: How many ___kids do they have___?
(4)

B: They have three kids. The girl is seven, and the boys are six and two.

A: Who ___takes care of___ the kids when your sister and her
(5)
husband go to work?

B: The older two are in school. My parents take care of the youngest boy.

A: How often ___do you talk to___ your parents?
(6)

B: I talk to them about once a week.

A: Is it expensive to call your country?

B: Not really. I buy a phone card.

A: How much ___does it cost___?
(7)

B: It costs $5.00 We can talk for 30 minutes.

A: Do you plan to see them soon?

B: Who ___knows___? Maybe yes, maybe no. I hope so.
(8)

5.8 | Who, Whom, Who's, Whose

Examples	Explanation
Compare: Who needs the teacher's help? We do. Who(m)* do you love? I love my parents. Who's that man? He's my dad. Whose book is this? It's mine.	*Who* = Subject *Who(m)* = Object *Who's* = *Who is* *Whose* = Possession (ownership)
*Note: Many native speakers use *who* in place of *whom*.	

5.8 | Who, Whom, Who's, Whose

1. Have students cover up grammar chart **5.8**. Write the following on the board:
   1. who   a. who is
   2. whose   b. object
   3. who's   c. possession (ownership)
   4. who(m)   d. subject
   Ask students to match the columns.

2. Have students look at grammar chart **5.8**. Go over the examples. Point out that *whom* is now considered formal and that it is more common to hear *who* as the object.

Expansion

Exercise 17 Have students practice the conversation from Exercise 17 in pairs. Ask volunteers to role-play all or part of the conversation in front of the class.

EXERCISE 18

1. Have students read the direction line. Ask: *What do we write in the blanks?* (*who, whom, who's,* or *whose*) Review the example.
2. Have students complete Exercise 18 individually. Check the answers as a class.
3. If necessary, review grammar chart **5.8** on page 147.

EXERCISE 19

1. Have students read the direction line. Go over the example.
2. Have students complete Exercise 19 individually. Check the answers as a class. Then have students practice the conversation in pairs.
3. If necessary, review Lesson 5.

🕐 To save class time, have students do half of the exercise in class and complete the other half for homework. Or assign the entire exercise for homework.

EXERCISE **18** Fill in the blanks with *who, whom, who's,* or *whose.*

EXAMPLE __Who__ likes ice cream? I like ice cream.

1. __Whose__ last name do you use? I use my father's last name.
2. __Whose__ composition is this? It doesn't have a name on it. It's mine.
3. __Who__ is your best friend? My best friend is Nina.
4. __Who__ has my dictionary? I do. Do you need it now?
5. __Who(m)__ do you call when you have a problem? I call my parents.
6. __Who__ needs more practice with pronouns? We all do!

EXERCISE **19** *Combination exercise.* Circle the correct word to complete this conversation between two students.

EXAMPLE A: (Who, (Who's,) Whose, Whom) your English teacher?
  (example)

  B: ((My,) Mine, Me) teacher's name is Charles Flynn.
  (1)

  A: (My, (Mine,) Me) is Marianne Peters. She's Mr. Flynn's wife.
  (2)

  B: Oh, really? His last name is different from (she, her, (hers)).
  (3)

  A: Yes. She uses ((her,) hers, his, he's) father's last name, not her
  (4)

  ((husband's,) husbands', husbands, husband).
  (5)

  B: Do they have children?

  A: Yes.

  B: ((Whose,) Who's, Who, Whom) name do the children use?
  (6)

  A: (They, They're, (Their,) Theirs) children use both last names.
  (7)

  B: How do you know so much about (you, you're, (your,) yours) teacher
  (8)

  and (she, she's, (her,) hers) children?
  (9)

  A: We talk about (we, us, (our,) ours) names in class. We also talk about
  (10)

  American customs. She explains her customs, and we explain
  (our, (ours,) us).
  (11)

  B: Mr. Flynn doesn't talk about (her, (his,) he's, hers) family in class.
  (12)

  A: Do you call (her, his, (him,) he) "mister"?
  (13)

B: Of course. (He, He's, His) the teacher. We show respect.
(14)

A: But we call Marianne by (her, hers, she) first name. (She, She's, Her)
(15)   (16)

prefers that.

B: I prefer to call (our, us, ours) teachers by (they, they're, their, theirs)
(17)   (18)

last names. That's the way we do it in my country.

A: And in (me, my, mine) too. But (we, we're, us) in the U.S. now.
(19)   (20)

There's an expression: When in Rome, do as the Romans do.

SUMMARY OF LESSON 5

1. Pronouns and Possessive Forms

Subject Pronoun	Object Pronoun	Possessive Adjective	Possessive Pronoun
I	me	my	mine
you	you	your	yours
he	him	his	his
she	her	her	hers
it	it	its	—
we	us	our	ours
they	them	their	theirs
who	whom	whose	whose

Subject	I come from Cuba.	They come from Korea.	Who comes from Poland?
Object	The teacher helps me.	The teacher helps them.	Who(m) does the teacher help?
Possessive Adjective	My name is Rosa.	Their names are Kim and Park.	Whose name do you use?
Possessive Pronoun	Your book is new. Mine is used.	Your book is new. Theirs is used.	This is your book. Whose is that?

2. Possessive Forms of Nouns
Jack's car is old.
His parents' car is new.
The children's toys are on the floor.
What's the name of our textbook?

Summary Of Lesson 5

1. **Pronouns and Possessive Forms**
Have students close their books. Write the chart headings across the top of the board. Write the subject pronouns in the first column. Have students come up to the board to fill in the chart with pronouns and possessive forms. Then have volunteers write sentences and questions with the pronouns and possessive forms. Have students open their books and compare their charts with the charts in the book. Go over the example sentences in the book. If necessary, have students review:
    5.2   Possessive Adjectives (p. 135)
    5.4   Possessive Pronouns (p. 137)
    5.6   Object Pronouns (p. 140).
2. **Possessive Forms of Nouns**
Review the example sentences. Then have students talk about things in the classroom using possessive pronouns (e.g., *Maria's notebook is blue and white.*). If necessary, have students review:
    5.1   Possessive Forms of Nouns (p. 133).

Expansion

Exercise 19 Have pairs write a conversation using subject pronouns, object pronouns, possessive pronouns, possessive nouns, and possessive adjectives. Ask volunteers to role-play their conversations in front of the class.

Editing Advice

Have students close their books. Write the example sentences without editing marks or corrections on the board. For example:

1. *Your a good person.*
   Where's you're book?

Ask students to correct each sentence and provide a rule or an explanation for each correction. This activity can be done individually, in pairs, or as a class. After students have corrected each sentence, tell them to turn to pages 150–151. Say: *Now compare your work with the Editing Advice in the book.*

EDITING ADVICE

1. Don't confuse *you're* (you are) and *your* (possessive form).
   You're
   Your a good person.
   your
   Where's you're book?

2. Don't confuse *he's* (he is) and *his* (possessive form).
   His
   He's name is Paul.
   He's
   His a good student.

3. Don't confuse *it's* (it is) and *its* (possessive form).
   It's
   Its a beautiful day today.
   its
   A monkey uses it's tail to climb trees.

4. Don't confuse *his* (masculine) and *her* (feminine).
   his
   My brother loves her daughter.
   her
   My sister loves his son.

5. Don't confuse *my* and *mine*.
   my
   I don't have mine book today.

6. Don't confuse *they're* and *their*.
   Their
   I have two American friends. They're names are Bob and Sue.

7. Use the correct pronoun (subject or object).
   her
   I have a daughter. I love she very much.
   I
   My father and me like to go fishing.

8. Don't use *the* with a possessive form.
   M
   The my friend is very tall.

   I need the your dictionary.

---

9. Don't use *do* or *does* in a *who* question about the subject.

    has
    Who does ̶have a Spanish dictionary?

10. Don't separate *whose* from the noun.

    book
    Whose is this book?

11. Don't confuse *whose* and *who's*.

    Whose
    Who's coat is that?

12. Use the correct word order for possession.

    My neighbor's dog
    Dog my neighbor makes a lot of noise.

13. Put the apostrophe in the right place.

    parents'
    My parent's car is new.

14. Don't use the possessive form for nonliving things.

    name of the book
    Grammar in Context is the book's name.

LESSON 5 TEST/REVIEW

PART **1** Find the mistakes with the underlined words and correct them. Not every sentence has a mistake. If the sentence is correct, write C.

EXAMPLES
Whose
Who's book is that?

Who's your best friend? *C*

1. Where does *your* you're brother live?

2. Paul is in my English class, but *he's* his not in my math class.

3. *It's* Its important to know a second language.

4. Whose name do you use, your father's or your mother's? *C*

5. Who wants to leave early today? We all do. *C*

6. Maria's son goes to a bilingual school. Her son's teacher comes from Cuba. *C*

Possession; Object Pronouns; Questions About the Subject   **151**

Lesson 5 Test/Review

For additional practice, review, and assessment materials, see Assessment CD-ROM with *ExamView Pro*, *More Grammar Practice* Workbook 1, Interactive CD-ROM, and Web site http://elt.thomson.com/gic

PART 1

1. Part 1 may be used as an in-class test to assess student performance, in addition to the Assessment CD-ROM with *ExamView Pro*. Have students read the direction line. Ask: *Does every sentence have a mistake?* (no) Review the examples with the class.

2. Have students complete the assignment individually. Collect for assessment.

3. If necessary, have students review: **Lesson 5.**

Lesson Review

To use Part 1 as a review, assign it as homework or use it as an in-class activity to be completed individually or in pairs. Check answers and review errors as a class. Reteach grammar points that students haven't mastered. Then student learning may be assessed using a test generated from the Assessment CD-ROM with *ExamView Pro*.

1. Part 2 may also be used as an in-class test to assess student performance, in addition to the Assessment CD-ROM with *ExamView Pro*. Have students read the direction line. Review the example.
2. Have students complete the exercise individually. Collect for assessment.
3. If necessary, have students review: **Lesson 5.**

7. I visit my girlfriend once a week. ~~His~~ *Her* son likes to play with <u>mine</u>.

8. <u>The door of the classroom</u> is open.   *C*

9. Do you know ~~the first name the teacher~~ *the teacher's first name*?

10. I have two married brothers. <u>My brother's wives</u> are wonderful women.   *C*

11. ~~Your~~ *You're* always late to class.

12. <u>My ~~the~~ brother's</u> car is new.

13. <u>Whose ~~is this umbrella~~</u> *umbrella is this*?

14. She likes her mother-in-law because ~~mother her husband~~ *her husband's mother* always helps her.

15. Do they visit ~~theirs~~ *their* parents often?

16. A dog wags (moves) <u>its</u> tail when <u>it's</u> happy.   *C*

17. Susan and Linda are <u>women's</u> names.   *C*

18. Who ~~does have~~ *has* a red pen?

19. <u>My friend and ~~me~~ *I*</u> eat dinner together once a week.

20. <u>Whose pen</u> is this?   *C*

PART **2**   Choose the correct word to complete these sentences.

EXAMPLE   Most American women change _____*c*_____ names when they get married, but not all do.

    a. her   **b.** hers   **c.** their   **d.** theirs

1. I have two _____*a*_____.
    a. sisters   **b.** sister's   **c.** sisters'   **d.** sister

2. _____*a*_____ names are Marilyn and Charlotte.
    a. Their   **b.** Theirs   **c.** They're   **d.** They   **e.** Hers

3. _____*b*_____ both married.
    a. Their   **b.** They're   **c.** They   **d.** Them   **e.** There

4. Marilyn uses _____*c*_____.
    a. the last name her husband
    b. the last name of his husband
    c. her husband's last name
    d. his husband's last name

5. Charlotte uses _____*b*_____ father's last name.
   a. we **b.** our **c.** ours **d.** us

6. I have one brother. _____*a*_____ married.
   a. He's **b.** His **c.** He **d.** Him

7. _____*c*_____ wife is very nice.
   a. Him **b.** Her **c.** His **d.** He's

8. _____*a*_____ first name is Sandra.
   a. My **b.** Mine **c.** I'm **d.** Me

9. My friends call _____*a*_____ "Sandy."
   a. me **b.** my **c.** mine

10. My sister often uses her middle name, but I rarely use _____*b*_____.
    a. my **b.** mine **c.** me **d.** I'm

11. You have a dog, but I don't know _____*c*_____ name.
    a. it **b.** it's **c.** its

12. _____*d*_____ your teacher?
    a. Whom **b.** Who **c.** Whose **d.** Who's

13. Her _____*b*_____ names are Ricky and Eddie.
    a. childs' **b.** children's **c.** childrens **d.** childrens'

14. _____*c*_____ has the newspaper?
    a. Whom **b.** Whose **c.** Who **d.** Who's

15. Who _____*c*_____ more time with the test?
    a. need **b.** does need **c.** needs **d.** does needs

16. The teacher's name is on _____*a*_____.
    a. the door of her office
    b. her office's door
    c. the door her office
    d. her the office's door

17. _____*d*_____
    a. Who's is that office?
    b. Whose is that office?
    c. Who's office is that?
    d. Whose office is that?

Lesson Review

To use Part 2 as a review, assign it as homework or use it as an in-class activity to be completed individually or in pairs. Check answers and review errors as a class. Reteach grammar points that students haven't mastered. Then student learning may be assessed using a test generated from the Assessment CD-ROM with *ExamView Pro*.

1. Part 3 may also be used as an in-class test to assess student performance, in addition to the Assessment CD-ROM with *ExamView Pro*. Have students read the direction line. Explain that this conversation is between two women who are talking about names. Review the example.

2. Have students complete the exercise individually. Collect for assessment.

3. If necessary, have students review:
   - 5.1 Possessive Forms of Nouns (p. 133)
   - 5.2 Possessive Adjectives (p. 135)
   - 5.4 Possessive Pronouns (p. 137)
   - 5.5 The Subject and the Object (p. 138)
   - 5.6 Object Pronouns (p. 140).

PART 3 Two women are talking about names. Fill in the blanks with possessive forms, subject pronouns, or object pronouns. Some blanks need an apostrophe or an apostrophe + s.

A: What's your last name?

B: It's Woods.

A: Woods sounds like an American name. But __you're__ Polish, aren't you?
   (example)

B: Yes, but Americans have trouble pronouncing __my__ name, so I use the name "Woods."
   (1)

A: What's __your__ real last name?
   (2)

B: Wodzianicki.

A: My name is hard for Americans too, but __I__ like my name, and I don't want to change __it__. I'm proud of it.
   (3)   *(4)*

B: What's __your__ last name?
   (5)

A: Lopez Hernandez.

B: Why do __you__ have two last names?
   (6)

A: I come from Mexico. Mexicans have two last names. Mexicans use both parents __'__ names.
   (7)

B: What happens when a woman get married? Does she use __her__
   (8)
   parents __'__ names and __her__ husband __'s__
   (9)   *(10)*   *(11)*
   name too?

A: No. When a woman gets married, she usually drops __her__
   (12)
   mother __'s__ name. She adds "of" (in Spanish, "de") and
   (13)
   __her__ husband __'s__ name. My sister is married.
   (14)   *(15)*
   __Her__ name is Maria Lopez de Castillo. Lopez is __my__
   (16)   *(17)*
   father __'s__ name and Castillo is her husband __'s__
   (18)   *(19)*
   name. __Her__ kids __'__ last name is Castillo Lopez.
   (20)   *(21)*

Lesson Review

To use Part 3 as a review, assign it as homework or use it as an in-class activity to be completed individually or in pairs. Check answers and review errors as a class. Reteach grammar points that students haven't mastered. Then student learning may be assessed using a test generated from the Assessment CD-ROM with *ExamView Pro*.

B: That's confusing. Everybody in the family has a different last name.

A: It's not confusing for us. You understand your customs, and we understand _____ours_____.
          (22)

B: Do your sister _____'s_____ kids have American first names?
          (23)

A: My sister gave _____them_____ Spanish names, but _____their_____ friends
          (24)   (25)

gave them American names. Her daughter _____'s_____ name is Rosa,
          (26)

but _____he_____ friends call her Rose. _____Her_____ son _____'s_____
     (27)   (28)   (29)

name is Eduardo, but _____his_____ friends call _____him_____
          (30)   (31)

Eddie. Ricardo is the youngest one. _____He's_____ still a baby, but
          (32)

when he goes to school, _____his_____ friends will probably call
          (33)

_____him_____ Rick.
  (34)

EXPANSION ACTIVITIES

Classroom Activities

1. Find a partner. Compare yourself to your partner. Compare physical characteristics, clothes, family, home, job, car, and so on. Report some interesting facts to the class.

   EXAMPLE My hair is straight. Mark's is curly.
   His eyes are blue. Mine are brown.
   My family lives in this city. Mark's family lives in Romania.

2. One student will ask these *who* questions. Raise your hand if this is a fact about you. The first student will answer the question after he or she sees raised hands.

   EXAMPLE Who has kids?
   Ben, Maria, and Lidia have kids.
   Who has a cell phone?
   No one has a cell phone.

   1. Who has kids?

   2. Who likes cartoons?

   3. Who plays soccer?

   4. Who has a laptop computer?

Expansion Activities

These expansion activities provide opportunities for students to interact with one another and further develop their speaking and writing skills. Encourage students to use grammar from this lesson whenever possible.

🕐 To save class time, assign parts of the activities as homework. Then use class time for interaction and communication. If students do not need additional speaking practice, some of the activities may be assigned as writing activities for homework, or skipped altogether.

CLASSROOM ACTIVITIES

1. Review the example. Model the activity with a volunteer. Have pairs make comparisons and present their facts to a group or to the class. Circulate to observe pair work. Give help as needed.

2. This activity can be done as a whole class activity or in groups. If necessary, review the meanings of vocabulary such as *cartoons*, *vegetarian*, etc. Point out the photo of the sports fans on page 156. Have different volunteers ask the questions.

CLASSROOM ACTIVITIES (*cont.*)

3. Decide if the class is going to do the original activity or the variation. Have students read the direction line. Review the examples.

4. This activity can be done as a whole class activity or in groups. Have students read the direction line. Then tell the students about your own name. If possible, put students into groups from different countries.

5. Who is a sports fan?
6. Who likes to swim?
7. Who is a vegetarian?
8. Who wants a grammar test?
9. Who has American friends?
10. Who has a pet?
11. Who lives in a house?
12. Who is over 6 feet tall?
13. Who has a motorcycle?
14. Who has an e-mail address?
15. Who gets a lot of junk mail?
16. Who exercises every day?
17. Who watches TV in the morning?
18. Who has a middle name?
19. Who wants to become an American citizen?
20. Who plays a musical instrument?

3. Think of something unusual that you do or are. Write a sentence telling what you do or are. Then ask a question to find out who else does or is this.

EXAMPLES I have a pet snake. Who else has a pet snake?
I play volleyball. Who else plays volleyball?
I am a Buddhist. Who else is a Buddhist?

(Variation: On a piece of paper, write something unusual that you do or are. Give the papers to the teacher. The teacher reads a statement. Other students—and the teacher—try to guess who wrote it. Example: Someone has a pet snake. Who has a pet snake?)

4. Discuss naming customs in your native culture. Do people have a middle name? Do fathers and sons ever have the same name? Tell about your name. Does it mean something?

156 Lesson 5

Joke

A woman is outside her house. A dog is near her. A man walks by and is interested in the dog. He wants to pet the dog. He asks the woman, "Does your dog bite?" The woman answers no. The man pets the dog, and the dog bites him. He says, "You told me that your dog doesn't bite." The woman answers, "This is not my dog. Mine is in the house."

Outside Activity

Ask an American to tell you about his or her name. Tell the class something interesting you learned from this American.

Internet Activity

Find a phone directory on the Internet. Look up your last name in a major American city, such as New York City, or in the city where you live. How many people in this city have your last name?

Additional Activities at http://elt.thomson.com/gic

Possession; Object Pronouns; Questions About the Subject   **157**

Have students read through the joke silently. Then ask if everyone understands it. Finally, have volunteers try out their stand-up skills by performing the joke in front of the class.

OUTSIDE ACTIVITY

Brainstorm questions to ask an American about his or her name. Write them on the board (e.g., *Your name is interesting—tell me about it. Do you have your father's name? Is your last name your father's name or your mother's name?*).

INTERNET ACTIVITY

Tell students: *You're going to look for phone directories on the Internet. Then you're going to find out how many people in this city have your last name.* Ask students if they ever look for phone numbers on the Internet. Write on the board phone directory Web sites you and your students use.

Outside Activity Variation

As an alternative, you may invite a guest to your classroom (e.g., an administrator, a librarian, or a service worker at your school) and have students do a class interview. Students should prepare their interview questions ahead of time.

Internet Activity Variation

If students don't have access to the Internet, they may find the information needed in a local phone directory. In addition to looking up their last names, students may look up the most common American last names *(Smith, Johnson, Williams, Jones,* and *Brown).*

LESSON

6

GRAMMAR

The Present Continuous Tense[1]

CONTEXT: Observations About American Life

Observations in the Park
Observations in the School Cafeteria

[1]The present continuous tense is sometimes called the present progressive tense.

159

Expansion

Theme The topic for this lesson can be enhanced with the following ideas:

1. Information about local parks
2. A menu from your school's or another school's cafeteria

Lesson | 6

Lesson Overview

GRAMMAR

Ask: *What did we study in Lesson 5?* (possession; object pronouns; questions about the subject) *What are we going to study in this lesson?* (the present continuous tense) Point out the footnote that says the present continuous tense is also called the present progressive tense. Activate prior knowledge that students may have. Have volunteers give examples. Write them on the board. Walk across the room. Ask: *What am I doing now?* (walking)

CONTEXT

1. Ask: *What will we learn about in this lesson?* (things about American life, parks, school cafeterias) Activate students' prior knowledge. Ask students if they go to or know of any parks in the area. If applicable, ask students if they ever eat in the school cafeteria. Ask: *Do you like the food?*
2. Have students share their knowledge and personal experiences.

Photos

Direct students' attention to the photos. Ask: *What's happening in the bottom picture?* (A girl is playing with a dog in a park.) *Are there any parks like this where you live? What's happening in the top picture?* (Two boys are skateboarding.) *Do children in your neighborhood skateboard?*

To save class time, have students do the Test/Review at the end of the lesson, or administer a lesson test generated from the Assessment CD-ROM with *ExamView*® *Pro.* Skip sections of the lesson that students have already mastered. You may also assign some sections for self-study for extra credit.

Observations in the Park (Reading)

1. Have students look at the photo. Ask: *What's going on in the picture?* (There's a boy playing baseball. There are people watching the baseball game.)
2. Have students look at the title of the reading. Ask: *What is the reading about? How do you know?* Have students make predictions.
3. Preteach any vocabulary words your students may not know, such as *journal, observe,* and *behavior.*

BEFORE YOU READ

1. Have students discuss the questions in pairs.
2. Ask for a few volunteers to share their answers with the class.

To save class time, skip "Before You Read" or have students prepare answers for homework ahead of time.

Reading 🎧 *CD 1, Track 27*

1. Have students read the text silently. Tell them to pay special attention to the present continuous tense. Then play the audio and have students read along silently.
2. Check students' comprehension. Ask questions such as: *What is Dan doing?* (writing in his journal) *Why is he writing in a journal?* (He is doing homework for his ESL class.) *Who is making a lot of noise?* (teenagers)

To save class time, have students do the reading for homework ahead of time.

Before You Read

1. Do you ever write in a journal?
2. Do you ever compare the behavior of Americans to the behavior of people from your native culture?

 Read the following entry from Dan's journal. Pay special attention to the present continuous tense.

September 9

I'm **taking** an ESL course this semester. Our teacher wants us to write in a journal every day. I'm **beginning** my journal now. I'm in the park now. It's a beautiful day. The sun **is shining.** I'm **sitting** on a park bench and **observing** the behavior of people around me.

It's warm and most of the people **are wearing** shorts, but I'm **wearing** long pants. Even old people **are wearing** shorts. This surprises me. Some people **are jogging.** They **are** all **carrying** a personal stereo and **wearing** headphones. They **are** all **jogging** alone. A lot of people **are going** by on rollerskates. Some young kids **are using** a skateboard. It seems that these are popular activities here.

A group of young men **is playing** soccer. I don't think they're Americans. I think Americans don't like soccer. I hear them speaking Spanish. Americans prefer baseball. In another part of the park, small children **are playing** baseball. Their parents **are watching** them. This is called Little League. Little League is very popular here.

One man **is riding** a bike and **talking** on a cell phone at the same time. Some people **are having** a picnic. They **are barbecuing** hamburgers.

There is a group of teenagers nearby. They **are talking** very loudly. They have a big boombox and **are listening** to hip-hop music. They**'re making** a lot of noise.

I'm **learning** a lot about the American lifestyle.

160 Lesson 6

Reading Variation

To practice listening skills, have students first listen to the audio alone. Ask a few comprehension questions. Repeat the audio if necessary. Then have students open their books and read along as they listen to the audio.

Reading Glossary

behavior: a way of acting
journal: a written record, a diary
observe: to view, watch, especially for anything unusual

6.1 | The Present Continuous Tense

To form the present continuous tense, use a form of *be* (*is, am, are*) + verb *-ing*. We use the present continuous tense to describe an action in progress at this moment.

Examples				Explanation
Subject	Be	Verb + -ing	Complement	

Subject	Be	Verb + -ing	Complement
I	am	taking	an ESL class.
The sun	is	shining.	
A man	is	jogging.	
He	is	wearing	shorts.
You	are	reading	Dan's journal.
Kids	are	listening	to music.
They	are	talking	very loudly.
We	are	learning	about American life.

Explanation
I → am
He/She/It → is
Singular Subject → is + verb -ing
We/You/They → are
Plural Subject → are

Examples	Explanation
I'm taking an ESL class this semester. **They're** listening to music. **We're** observing the American lifestyle. **Dan's** writing in his journal.	We can make a contraction with the subject pronoun and a form of *be*. Most nouns can also form a contraction with *is*.[2]

Dan **isn't** writing a composition. He's writing in his journal.
The teenagers **aren't** paying attention to other people.
	To form the negative, put *not* after the verb *am/is/are*.
	Negative contractions:
	  is not = isn't
	  are not = aren't
	There is no contraction for *am not*.

A man **is riding** his bike **and talking** on his cell phone.	When the subject is doing two or more things, we don't repeat the verb *be* after *and*.

EXERCISE **1** Fill in the blanks with the missing part of each sentence.

EXAMPLE   I' __in__ writing in my journal.

1. Most people are wear __ing__ shorts.
2. Some young men __are__ playing soccer.
3. Some children are play __ing__ baseball.
4. Teenagers __are__ listening to music.
5. I' __m__ looking at people in the park.
6. The sun __is__ shining.
7. A man is riding his bike and talk __ing__ on his cell phone.
8. I'm learn __ing__ about life in the U.S.

[2]See Lesson 1, page 8 for exceptions.

Expansion

Grammar Put students in groups. Say: *One member mimes an activity and the other students in the group guess.* Tell students to use the present continuous tense to describe the activity (e.g., *Pedro's watching TV.*).

6.1 | The Present Continuous Tense

1. Have students look at the reading on page 160. Say: *All the words in bold in the reading are in the present continuous.* Write several examples on the board. (*I'm taking an ESL course. The sun is shining. They are barbecuing.*) Say: *Study these verbs and try to guess the rule for forming the present continuous tense.* Have volunteers write their guesses on the board.

2. Then ask students to compare their guesses with grammar chart **6.1**. Review how to form the present continuous: *be* + verb + *-ing*. Explain that the present continuous is used to describe an action in progress at this moment. Demonstrate, or have volunteers demonstrate, various actions. Narrate the actions (e.g., *I'm running. He's writing.*). Review all of the examples and explanations.

3. Explain that contractions are made with the pronoun and the verb *be*. Also point out that most nouns can form a contraction with *is*.

4. Review how to form the negative: *be* + *not* + verb + *-ing*. Remind students to use contractions in the negative (*isn't* and *aren't*). Explain that there is no contraction for *am not*.

5. Point out to students that when the subject is doing two or more things, we don't repeat the verb *be* after *and*.

EXERCISE 1

1. Have students read the direction line. Go over the example in the book. Say: *The verb might be missing or the* -ing *might be missing.*

2. Have students complete Exercise 1 individually. Review the answers as a class.

6.2 | Spelling of the -ing Form

1. Copy the lists of verbs (base form and -ing form) from grammar chart **6.2** on the board. Make sure you separate the six sets of verbs. For example:

    eat eating
    go going
    study studying

    plan planning
    stop stopping
    sit sitting

2. Have students cover up grammar chart **6.2** in their books. Say: *There are six rules for spelling the -ing form. Can you guess what they are?* Give them hints. Say: *The first row is the category that most verbs belong to. In the second row, pay attention to syllables and consonant and vowel patterns. The verbs in the third row are exceptions to the verbs in the second row. In the fourth and fifth rows, pay attention to syllables and consonant and vowel patterns.* Write the rules the students come up with on the board.

3. Have students look at grammar chart **6.2.** Say: *Compare our rules with the rules in the book.* Review the rules in the grammar chart.

EXERCISE 2

1. Have students read the direction line. Ask: *What do we write in the blanks?* (the -ing form of the verb) Point out that the accent marks show which syllable is stressed. Go over the examples in the book. Ask students to tell you what the rules are for the spelling of each noun in the examples (*Do not double a final y; ends in consonant + e drop e add -ing.*).

2. Have students complete Exercise 2 individually. Check answers as a class.

3. If necessary, review grammar chart **6.2** on page 162.

6.2 | Spelling of the -ing Form

Rule	Verbs	-ing Form
Add -ing to most verbs. (Note: Do not drop the *y* of the base form.)	eat go study	eating going studying
For a one-syllable verb that ends in a consonant + vowel + consonant (CVC), double the final consonant and add -ing.	p l a n ↓ ↓ ↓ C V C s t o p ↓ ↓ ↓ C V C s i t ↓ ↓ ↓ C V C	planning stopping sitting
Do not double a final *w, x,* or *y.*	show mix stay	showing mixing staying
For a two-syllable verb that ends in CVC, double the final consonant only if the last syllable is stressed.	refér admít begín	referring admitting beginning
When the last syllable of a two-syllable verb is not stressed, do not double the final consonant.	lísten ópen óffer	listening opening offering
If the verb ends in a consonant + *e*, drop the *e* before adding -ing.	live take write	living taking writing

EXERCISE 2 Write the -ing form of the verb. (Two-syllable verbs that end in CVC have accent marks to show which syllable is stressed.)

EXAMPLES   play _____ *playing*

make _____ *making*

1. plan _____ *planning*
2. ópen _____ *opening*
3. sit _____ *sitting*
4. begín _____ *beginning*
5. hurry _____ *hurrying*
6. háppen _____ *happening*

7. stay _____ *staying*
8. grow _____ *growing*
9. marry _____ *marrying*
10. grab _____ *grabbing*
11. write _____ *writing*
12. fix _____ *fixing*

Grammar Variation

Have students cover up grammar chart **6.2.** Write the base form of the verbs from the chart on the board. Ask students to go up to the board and write the -ing form next to it. (Have students go up in groups so that their answers remain somewhat anonymous.) Then ask students to look at grammar chart **6.2** and check what's on the board. Go over the rules for spelling.

---

13. wipe	wiping	17. wait	waiting
14. carry	carrying	18. serve	serving
15. drink	drinking	19. visit	visiting
16. drive	driving	20. prefér	preferring

EXERCISE 3   Fill in the blanks with the present continuous tense of the verb in parentheses ( ). Use correct spelling.

EXAMPLE   Dan ____is observing____ people in the park.
              (observe)

1. He ____'s writing____ about his observations.
        (write)

2. Some men ____are playing____ soccer.
           (play)

3. A man ____'s riding____ a bike.
        (ride)

4. Some people ____are jogging____ .
              (jog)

5. The sun ____'s shining____ .
         (shine)

6. He ____'s sitting____ on a park bench.
      (sit)

7. Some people ____are going____ by on rollerskates and skate-boards.
              (go)

8. Some people ____are carrying____ a personal stereo.
              (carry)

6.3 | The Present Continuous Tense—Uses

Examples	Explanation
I **am writing** in my journal now. I **am observing** the American lifestyle. Children **are playing** baseball. Teenagers **are listening** to music.	To show that an action is in progress now, at this moment.
I'm **learning** about the American lifestyle. I'm **taking** an ESL course this semester.	To show a long-term action that is in progress. It may not be happening at this exact moment.
Most people **are wearing** shorts. I'm **sitting** on a park bench.	To describe a state or condition, using the following verbs: *sit, stand, wear, sleep*.

The Present Continuous Tense   **163**

EXERCISE 3

1. Have students read the direction line. Go over the example. Then do #1 with the class. Ask a volunteer to give an answer.
2. Have students complete Exercise 3 individually. Then have students practice saying the sentences in pairs. Finally, check the answers as a class.
3. If necessary, review grammar chart **6.2** on page 162.

To save class time, have students do half of the exercise in class and complete the other half for homework. Or assign the entire exercise for homework.

6.3 | The Present Continuous Tense—Uses

1. Have students cover up grammar chart **6.3** in their books. Write the following sentences and explanations from the grammar chart on the board:
   a. *I am writing in my journal now.*
   b. *I'm taking an ESL course this semester.*
   c. *Most people are wearing shorts.*

   1. *To show a long-term action that is in progress.*
   2. *To describe a state or condition.*
   3. *To show that an action is in progress now, at this moment.*
   Say: *Match the examples to the rule.*
2. Have students look at grammar chart **6.3.** Say: *Compare our answers with the grammar chart.* Go over any errors.
3. Review the examples in the chart.

Expansion

Grammar In pairs, have students write two sentences for each of the three rules. Say: *Look at the classroom right now. What is happening?* Circulate to observe pair work. Have volunteers write their sentences on the board.

EXERCISE 4

1. Tell students that this exercise is about what they're doing in the classroom now. Have students read the direction line. Go over the examples in the book. Have volunteers model the examples.
2. Have students complete Exercise 4 individually. Then have pairs compare answers. Circulate to observe pair work. Give help as needed.
3. If necessary, review grammar chart **6.3** on page 163.

EXERCISE 5

1. Have students read the direction line. Say: *You're going to be making affirmative or negative sentences based on what's true for you.* Go over the examples in the book. Have volunteers model the examples.
2. Have students complete Exercise 5 individually. Then have pairs compare answers. Circulate to observe pair work. Give help as needed.
3. If necessary, review grammar chart **6.3** on page 163.

⊘ To save class time, have students do half of the exercise in class and complete the other half in writing for homework. Or if students do not need speaking practice, the entire exercise may be skipped or done in writing.

EXERCISE **4** ABOUT YOU Make a **true** affirmative statement or negative statement about your activities now with the words given.

EXAMPLES wear a watch
I'm not wearing a watch (now).

drink coffee
I'm drinking coffee (now).

Answers will vary.
1. sit in the back of the room
2. speak my native language
3. pay attention
4. ask questions
5. learn the present continuous tense
6. look out the window
7. look at the chalkboard
8. write a composition
9. use my textbook
10. wear jeans

EXERCISE **5** ABOUT YOU Make a true affirmative statement or negative statement about yourself with the words given. Talk about a long-term action.

EXAMPLES look for a job
I'm looking for a job.

live in a hotel
I'm not living in a hotel.

Answers will vary.
1. look for a new apartment
2. learn a lot of English
3. gain weight
4. lose weight
5. spend a lot of money
6. save my money
7. write a term paper[3]
8. try to understand American customs
9. meet Americans
10. learn how to drive
11. live in a dorm
12. plan to return to my hometown

[3]A *term paper* is a paper that students write for class. The student researches a topic. It often takes a student a full semester (or term) to produce this paper.

164 Lesson 6

Expansion

Exercises 4 and 5 Have students write an e-mail to a friend. Say: *Tell your friend what you're doing now, at this moment, and what your long-term actions are.*

6.4 | Questions with the Present Continuous Tense

Affirmative Statements and Questions

Wh- Word	Be	Subject	Be	Verb + -ing	Complement	Short Answer
		Dan	is	writing.		
	Is	he		writing	a composition?	No, he isn't.
What	is	he		writing?		A page in his journal.
		The kids	are	playing.		
	Are	they		playing	soccer?	No, they aren't.
What	are	they		playing?		Baseball.

Negative Statements and Questions

Wh- Word	Be + n't	Subject	Be + n't	Verb + -ing	Complement
		The kids	aren't	playing	soccer.
Why	aren't	they		playing	soccer?
		Dan	isn't	using	his computer.
Why	isn't	he		using	his computer?

Language Note:
When the question is "What . . . doing?" we usually answer with a different verb.
    What is Dan **doing?** He's **writing** in his journal.
    What are those kids **doing?** They're **playing** baseball.

EXERCISE 6 Use the words given to ask a question about what this class is doing now. Another student will answer.

EXAMPLE we / use the textbook now

  A: Are we using the textbook now?
  B: Yes, we are.

1. the teacher / wear a sweater
  Is the teacher wearing a sweater now?
2. the teacher / write on the chalkboard
  Is the teacher writing on the chalkboard now?
3. the teacher / erase the chalkboard
  Is the teacher erasing the chalkboard now?
4. the teacher / sit at the desk
  Is the teacher sitting at the desk now?
5. the teacher / take attendance
  Is the teacher taking attendance now?
6. the teacher / explain the grammar
  Is the teacher explaining the grammar now?
7. the teacher / help the students
  Is the teacher helping the students now?
8. we / practice the present continuous tense
  Are we practicing the present continuous tense now?
9. we / practice the past tense
  Are we practicing the past tense now?
10. we / review Lesson 5
  Are we reviewing Lesson 5 now?
11. we / make mistakes
  Are we making mistakes now?
12. what / the teacher / wear
  What is the teacher wearing now?
13. where / the teacher / stand or sit
  Where is the teacher standing or sitting now?
14. what exercise / we / do
  What exercise are we doing now?
15. what / you / think about
  What are you thinking about now?

Exercise 6 Variation

If students have difficulty with this exercise, have them write out the questions before asking and answering questions with a partner.

6.4 | Questions with the Present Continuous Tense

1. Have students cover up grammar chart **6.4** in their books. Write on the board: *Dan is writing.* Underneath write: *composition.* Now say: *Write a yes/no question about Dan writing a composition.* Have a volunteer write it on the board. Then say: *Now write a wh-question about Dan writing.* Ask another volunteer to write it on the board.

2. Have students look at grammar chart **6.4**. Say: *Compare our answers with the grammar chart.* Review all of the examples, including negative statements and questions. Go over contractions with the negative.

3. Direct students to the Language Note. Demonstrate *what . . . doing?* Ask the class about the actions of different students. Elicit responses. Ask: *What's Farid doing? What's Karmen doing? What are Sylvia and Andrea doing?* Write the questions on the board and their responses. Explain that when we ask a *what . . . doing?* question, we usually respond with another verb.

EXERCISE 6

1. Tell students that this exercise is about the class. Have students read the direction line. Say: *Some of the questions are* yes/no *questions, and some are* wh- *questions.* Go over the example with the class. Have two students model #1.

2. Have students complete the exercise in pairs. Tell students to alternate asking and answering questions. Circulate to observe pair work. Give help as needed.

3. If necessary, review grammar chart **6.4** on page 165.

EXERCISE 7

1. Tell students that this exercise is about them and their long-term actions. Have students read the direction line. Ask: *What kind of questions are we asking?* (yes/no questions) Go over the example with the class. Have two students model the example.

2. Have students complete the exercise in pairs. Tell students to alternate asking and answering questions. Circulate to observe pair work. Give help as needed.

3. If necessary, review grammar chart **6.4** on page 165.

🕐 To save class time, have students do half of the exercise in class and complete the other half in writing for homework, answering the question themselves. Or if students do not need speaking practice, the entire exercise may be skipped or done in writing.

EXERCISE 8

1. Have students read the direction line. Say: *You're going to write what's true for you. And then you're going to ask your partner the same questions.* Go over the example with the class. Have two students model the example.

2. First have students fill in the blanks individually. Then tell students to ask and answer questions in pairs. Circulate to observe pair work. Give help as needed.

3. If necessary, review grammar chart **6.4** on page 165.

🕐 To save class time, have students fill in the blanks and write out the questions for homework. Then they may ask/answer the questions in class. Or if students do not need speaking practice, the entire exercise may be skipped.

EXERCISE 7 ABOUT YOU Ask a question about a long-term action with the words given. Another student will answer.

EXAMPLE   you / study math this semester

A: Are you studying math this semester?
B: Yes, I am.

1. you / plan to buy a car
   Are you planning to buy a car?
2. you / study biology this semester
   Are you studying biology this semester?
3. you / take other courses this semester   *Are you taking other courses this semester?*
4. you / look for a new apartment
   Are you looking for a new apartment?
5. you / look for a job
   Are you looking for a job?

6. your English / improve
   Is your English improving?
7. your vocabulary / grow
   Is your vocabulary growing?
8. the teacher / help you
   Is the teacher helping?
9. the students / make progress
   Are the students making progress?
10. you / learn about other students'
    countries   *Are you learning about other students' countries?*

EXERCISE 8 ABOUT YOU Fill in the blanks with *I'm* or *I'm not* + the *-ing* form of the verb in parentheses ( ) to tell if you are doing these things now or at this general point in time. Then ask another student if he or she is doing this activity now. The other student will answer.

EXAMPLES   (plan) _____*I'm planning*_____ to buy a computer.

A: Are you planning to buy a computer?
B: Yes, I am.

(learn) _____*I'm not learning*_____ to drive a car.

A: Are you learning to drive a car?
B: No, I'm not.

Answers will vary.

1. (wear) _____ jeans.
2. (hold) _____ a pencil.
3. (chew) _____ gum.
4. (think) _____ about the weekend.
5. (live) _____ in a dorm.
6. (plan) _____ to take a vacation.
7. (look) _____ for a job.
8. (plan) _____ to buy a computer.
9. (take) _____ a computer class this semester.
10. (get) _____ tired.
11. (gain) _____ weight.

Expansion

Exercise 7 Create two rings of students. Have half of the students stand in an outer ring around the classroom. Have the other half stand in an inner ring, facing the outer ring. Instruct students to ask and answer the questions from Exercise 7. Call out *"turn"* every minute or so. Students in the inner ring should move one space clockwise. Students now ask and answer with their new partner. Have students ask questions in random order. Make sure students look at each other when they're speaking.

12. (learn) _____ about the history of the U.S.

13. (learn) _____ how to drive.

EXERCISE 9 ABOUT YOU Read each sentence. Then ask a *wh-* question about the words in parentheses ( ). Another student will answer.

EXAMPLE   We're doing an exercise. (What exercise)

A: What exercise are we doing?
B: We're doing Exercise 9.

1. We're practicing a tense. (What tense)
   What tense are we practicing?
2. We're using a textbook. (What kind of book)
   What kind of textbook are we using?
3. You're listening to the teacher. (Why)
   Why are you listening to the teacher?
4. The teacher's helping the students. (Why)
   Why is the teacher helping the students?
5. I'm answering a question. (Which question)
   Which question are you answering?
6. We're practicing questions. (What kind of questions)
   What kind of questions are we practicing?
7. Your English is improving. (Why)
   Why is your English improving?
8. Your life is changing. (How)
   How is your life changing?
9. You're taking courses. (How many courses)
   How many courses are you taking?

EXERCISE 10   A woman is calling her husband from a cell phone in her car. Fill in the blanks to complete the conversation.

A: Hello?
B: Hi. It's Betty.
A: Oh, hi, Betty. This connection is so noisy. Where ___*are you calling*___ from?
                                                          (example)
B: I ___*'m calling*___ from the car. I ___*'m using/on*___
      (1)   (2)
   the cell phone.
A: ___*Are you coming*___ home now?
              (3)
B: No, I'm not. I'm driving to the airport.
A: Why ___*are you driving*___ to the airport?
              (4)
B: I'm going to pick up a client.
A: I can't hear you. There's so much noise.
B: Airplanes ___*are flying*___ overhead. They're very low.
                    (5)
A: I can't hear you. Talk louder please.

Exercise 10 Variation

To provide practice with listening skills, have students close their books and listen to the audio. Repeat the audio as needed. Ask comprehension questions, such as: *Why is Betty driving to the airport?* (to pick up a client) *Why is it so noisy at the airport?* (because airplanes are flying overhead and they're very low) *Why is Betty late?* (because she's stuck in traffic) Then have students open their books and complete Exercise 10.

EXERCISE 9

1. Have students read the direction line. Ask: *What kind of question do we ask?* (a *wh-* question) Go over the example with the class. Have two students model #1.
2. Have students complete the exercise in pairs. Circulate to observe pair work. Give help as needed.
3. If necessary, review grammar chart **6.4** on page 165.

🕐 To save class time, have students do half of the exercise in class and complete the other half in writing for homework. Or if students do not need speaking practice, the entire exercise may be skipped or done in writing.

EXERCISE 10

🎧 *CD 1, Track 28*

1. Have students read the direction line. Point out that this conversation is between a woman (Betty) and her husband. Direct students to the picture on page 167. Ask: *Where is Betty calling from?* (her car; the airport; her cell phone) Direct students to the picture on page 168. Ask: *Where is Betty's husband?* (at home with the children)
2. Go over the example in the book. Remind students to use contractions wherever possible.
3. Have students complete Exercise 10 individually. Then check answers as a class.
4. Then have students practice the conversation in pairs. Circulate to observe pair work. Give help as needed.
5. If necessary, review grammar chart **6.4** on page 165.

🕐 To save class time, have students do half of the exercise in class and complete the other half for homework. Or assign the entire exercise for homework.

B: I ___'m talking___ as loud as I can. I ___'m going___
               (6)   (7)

to the airport to pick up a client. I'm late. Her plane ___is landing___
                                                              (8)

now, and I'm stuck[4] in traffic. I'm getting nervous. Cars aren't moving.

A: Why ___aren't they___ moving?
                (9)

B: There's an accident on the highway.

A: I worry about you. ___Are you wearing your seat belt___?
                                   (10)

B: Of course, I'm wearing my seat belt.
A: That's good.

B: What ___are you doing___ now?
                  (11)

A: I ___'m using___ the computer. I ___'m looking___
         (12)   (13)

for information about cars on the Internet.

B: What ___are the kids___ doing?
                  (14)

A: The kids? I can't hear you.
B: Yes, the kids.

A: Meg ___'s watching___ TV. Pam ___'s doing___ her
            (15)   (16)

homework.

B: Why ___isn't___ Meg doing her homework?
               (17)

A: She doesn't have any homework today.

B: ___Are you making___ dinner for the kids?
            (18)

A: No, I'm not making dinner. I ___'m waiting___ for you to come
                                      (19)

home and make dinner.
B: Please don't wait for me. Oh. Traffic is finally moving. Talk to you
later.

[4] When you are stuck in traffic, you can't move because other cars aren't moving.

Expansion

Exercise 10 Have volunteers role-play all or part of the conversation in Exercise 10 in front of the class.

Observations in the School Cafeteria (Reading)

1. Have students look at the illustration. Ask: *Where are these people?* (in a cafeteria) *What are they doing?* (eating, talking, reading, etc.)
2. Have students look at the title of the reading. Ask: *What is the reading about? How do you know?* Have students use the title and the picture to make predictions about the reading.
3. Preteach any vocabulary words your students may not know, such as *kiss, feed,* and *bother.*

Before You Read

1. When you observe the students at this school, do you see any strange behaviors?

2. Is your behavior in this school different from your behavior when you are with your family or people from your native culture?

Read the following entry from Dan's journal. Pay special attention to verbs—simple present and present continuous.

October 8

I'm **sitting** in the school cafeteria now. I'm **writing** in my journal. I **want** to know about American customs, so I'm **observing** the behavior of other students. I **see** many strange behaviors and customs around me.

I'm **looking** at a young couple at the next table. The young man and woman **are touching, holding** hands, and even **kissing.** It looks strange because people never **kiss** in public in our country. At another table, a young man and woman **are sitting** with a baby. The man **is feeding** the baby. Men never **feed** the baby in our country. Why **isn't** the woman **feeding** the baby? Students in our country are usually single, not married with children.

Two women **are putting** on makeup. I **think** this is bad public behavior. These women **are wearing** shorts. In our country, women never **wear** shorts.

A group of students **is listening** to the radio. The music is very loud. Their music **is bothering** other people, but they **don't care.** I'm **sitting** far from them, but I **hear** their music.

A young man **is resting** his feet on another chair. His friend **is eating** a hamburger with his hands. Why **isn't** he **using** a fork and knife?

These kinds of behaviors **look** bad to me. I'm **trying** to understand them, but I'm **having** a hard time. I still **think** many of these actions are rude.[5]

---

[5]*Rude* means impolite.

The Present Continuous Tense   **169**

BEFORE YOU READ

1. Have students discuss the questions in pairs.
2. Ask for a few volunteers to share their answers with the class.

To save class time, skip "Before You Read" or have students prepare answers for homework ahead of time.

Reading ⌒ *CD 1, Track 29*

1. Have students read the text silently. Tell them to pay special attention to verbs: simple present and present continuous. Then play the audio and have students read along silently.
2. Check students' comprehension. Ask questions such as: *What is Dan doing?* (observing people) *Who is feeding the baby?* (the man) *Is Dan surprised at the behavior of the people in the cafeteria?* (Yes. He thinks they're being rude.)

To save class time, have students do the reading for homework ahead of time.

Reading Variation

To practice listening skills, have students first listen to the audio alone. Ask a few comprehension questions. Repeat the audio if necessary. Then have students open their books and read along as they listen to the audio.

Reading Glossary

bother: to disturb or give unwanted attention
feed: to provide with food
kiss: to press the lips against someone or something

6.5 | Contrast of Present Continuous and Simple Present

1. Have students go to the reading on page 169. Say: *Underline the verbs in the simple present and circle the verbs in the present continuous.* Have volunteers give examples of what they circled and underlined. Elicit students' prior knowledge. Ask: *For what do we use the simple present tense?* (to talk about a habitual activity, a custom, or a general truth or fact) *What do we use the present continuous for?* (to show actions in progress at this moment, to show long-term action in progress, to describe a state or condition)

2. Have students look at grammar chart **6.5**. Go over the examples and the explanations.

3. Review the examples in the chart. Say: *We can use an object pronoun after the verb or after a preposition.* Then go back to the reading on page 169. Ask students to circle the verb and the object pronoun.

4. Explain that the question *What does she do?* is used to ask about a profession or job. *What is she doing?* asks about a present activity. Review the example sentences. Go around the room asking students both questions: *What are you doing?* and *What do you do?*

EXERCISE 11

🎧 *CD 1, Track 30*

1. Have students read the direction line. Point out that this conversation takes place in a cafeteria and is between two students discussing American customs and those of their native countries. Go over the example in the book. Remind students to use contractions wherever possible.

2. Have students complete Exercise 11 individually. Check answers as a class.

3. If necessary, review grammar chart **6.5** on Page 170.

6.5 | Contrast of Present Continuous and Simple Present

Form

Simple Present	Present Continuous
Dan sometimes **wears** a suit. He **doesn't** usually **wear** shorts. **Does** he ever **wear** a hat? Yes, he **does.** When **does** he **wear** a hat? Who **wears** a hat?	He **is wearing** jeans now. He **isn't wearing** a belt. **Is** he **wearing** a T-shirt? No, he **isn't.** What **is** he **wearing**? Who **is wearing** a T-shirt?

Uses

Examples	Explanation
a. Dan **writes** in his journal once a week in the college cafeteria. b. People **eat** hamburgers with their hands. c. The college cafeteria **has** inexpensive food.	We use the *simple present tense* to talk about: a. a habitual activity b. a custom c. a general truth or fact
a. Dan **is writing** in his journal now. b. He **is learning** more and more about life in the U.S.	We use the *present continuous tense* for: a. an action that is in progress at this moment b. a longer action that is in progress at this general time
Compare: Dan's family **lives** in another country. Dan **is living** in a dorm this semester.	When we use *live* in the simple present, we mean that this is a person's home. In the present continuous, it shows a temporary, short-term residence.
Compare: What **does** she **do** for a living? She's a nurse. What **is** she **doing**? She's waiting for the bus.	*What does she do?* asks about a profession or job. *What is she doing?* asks about her present activity.

EXERCISE 11 🎧 Two students meet in the cafeteria and discuss American customs and the customs of their native countries. Fill in the blanks with the correct form of the verb in parentheses ( ). Practice the simple present and the present continuous.

A: Hi. What _____ *are you doing* _____ here?

          (example: you/do)

B: I _____ *'m eating* _____ lunch. I always _____ *eat* _____

          (1 eat)   (2 eat)

lunch at this time. But I _____ *also observe* _____ behaviors and

          (3 also/observe)

customs in this country.

170 Lesson **6**

Exercise 11 Variation

To provide practice with listening skills, have students close their books and listen to the audio. Repeat the audio as needed. Ask comprehension questions, such as: *Why does person B think the man looks strange?* (because he's wearing an earring) *Do women in person B's country wear earrings?* (yes) *Why does person A think the woman looks strange?* (because she's wearing three earrings in one ear) Then have students open their books and complete Exercise 11.

A: What do you mean?

B: Well, look at that man over there. He ___'s wearing___ an
                                            (4 wear)

earring. It looks so strange. Only women ___wear___
                                              (5 wear)

earrings in my country.

A: It *is* strange. And look at that woman. She ___'s wearing___
                                                   (6 wear)

three earrings in one ear.

B: And she ___'s wearing___ running shoes with a dress. In my
              (7 wear)

country, people only ___use___ running shoes for sports
                        (8 use)

activities.

A: Look at that student over there. He ___'s using___ a colored
                                          (9 use)

pen to mark his textbook. In my country, we never ___write___
                                                      (10 write)

in our textbooks because they ___belong___ to the college,
                                 (11 belong)

not to the students.

B: Many college activities are different here. For example, my English

teacher usually ___sits___ at the desk in class. In my
                   (12 sit)

country, the teacher always ___stands___ in class. And the
                               (13 stand)

students always ___stand up___ when the teacher
                   (14 stand up)

___enters___ the room.
  (15 enter)

A: And college students always ___study___ English or
                                  (16 study)

another foreign language. Here, nobody knows another language.

My American roommate ___is taking___ five courses this
                         (17 take)

semester, but no foreign language.

B: By the way, how many classes ___are you taking___ this semester?
                                   (18 you/take)

The Present Continuous Tense   **171**

6.6 | Nonaction Verbs

1. Have students cover up grammar chart **6.6**. Ask: *What are nonaction verbs? Can you give me any examples?* If students have difficulty, tell them that nonaction words describe a state or condition, not an action. Then ask them to go to the reading on page 169. Say: *Double underline the nonaction verbs. (want, see, think, care, hear,* and *look)* Have volunteers give examples of what they underlined. Write them on the board.

2. Have students look at grammar chart **6.6**. Say: *Are the verbs you found in the reading on this list?* Go over the examples and the explanations.

3. Direct students to the Language Notes. Say: *Compare the verbs* hear, see, listen, *and* look. Hear *and* see *are nonaction verbs because they are involuntary—you do them without necessarily wanting to.* Listen *and* look *are action verbs because they are voluntary actions.* Go over the examples.

A: Four. In my country, I usually _____ take _____ eight courses a
(19 take)
semester, but my adviser here says I can only take four.

B: I have to go now. My girlfriend _____ 's waiting _____ for me at the
(20 wait)
library.

6.6 | Nonaction Verbs

Some verbs are nonaction verbs. Nonaction verbs describe a state or condition, not an action.

Examples	Explanation
He **hears** the music now. The music is bothering Dan, but the other students **don't care.** Dan **needs** a quiet place to write. He **doesn't understand** the behavior of some students. He **thinks** these behaviors are rude.	We do not usually use the present continuous tense with nonaction verbs. We use the *simple present tense,* even if we are talking about now.

Nonaction Verbs

like	know	see	cost
love	believe	smell	own
hate	think (that)	hear	have (for possession)
want	care (about)	taste	
need	understand	feel	
prefer	remember	seem	

Compare action and nonaction verbs.

Action (uses the present continuous tense)	Nonaction (uses the simple present tense)
The music **is bothering** Dan.	He **prefers** soft music.
Dan **is learning** about American customs.	He **cares** about good behavior.
He **is looking** at two people kissing.	This behavior **looks** strange to him.
He **is writing** about the students.	He **wants** to understand their customs.
He **is using** a laptop.	He **has** a PC in his dorm room.
The students **are listening** to the music.	Dan **hears** the music.
Dan **is looking** at students in the cafeteria.	He **sees** some strange behaviors.

Language Notes:
Hear and *see* are nonaction verbs. *Listen* and *look* are action verbs.
Hear and *see* are involuntary. *Listen* and *look* are voluntary.

Expansion

Exercise 11 Have students role-play all or part of the conversation in front of the class. If possible, have students go to the cafeteria to observe people. Then have them work in pairs to create a similar dialogue.

EXERCISE **12** Fill in the blanks with the simple present or the present continuous tense of the verb in parentheses ( ).

EXAMPLES I ___*understand*___ the explanation now.
             (understand)

I ___*am writing*___ now.
   (write)

1. I ___*'m studying*___ English this semester.
      (study)

2. We ___*'re using*___ the textbook now.
       (use)

3. We ___*need*___ a lot of practice with verb tenses.
       (need)

4. We ___*'re comparing*___ action and nonaction verbs.
       (compare)

5. I ___*don't remember*___ every grammar rule.
      (not/remember)

6. I ___*see*___ the chalkboard.
      (see)

7. I ___*'m not looking*___ at the clock now. I ___*'m looking*___
      (not/look)   *(look)*
at my book.

8. I ___*don't need*___ my dictionary now.
      (not/need)

9. We ___*'re not writing*___ a composition now.
       (not/write)

10. We ___*don't hear*___ the students in the next room.
        (not/hear)

11. We ___*'re learning*___ about nonaction verbs.
        (learn)

12. We ___*know*___ a lot of grammar.
        (know)

1. Have students read the direction line. Say: *You have to decide between using the present continuous and the simple present.* Go over the examples.
2. Have students complete Exercise 12 individually. Check the answers as a class.
3. If necessary, review grammar chart **6.6** on page 172.

Expansion

Exercise 12 Have students explain why they used the simple present or the present continuous in each statement in Exercise 12 (e.g., 1. *understand*—simple past because *understand* is a nonaction word).

6.7 | *Think, Have,* and the Sense Perception Verbs

1. Have students cover up grammar chart **6.7**. Write on the board all of the example sentences from the grammar chart. Write them without the verb in place. Don't label the sentences with "action" or "nonaction." Don't write the explanations. For example:
   (think)
   He _____ about his mother's cooking.
   He _____ it is wrong to kiss in public.

2. Say: *Some verbs can be action or nonaction verbs depending on the use. Study these sentences. Which sentence needs an action verb, and which sentence needs a nonaction verb?* (action—*He is thinking about his mother's cooking;* nonaction—*He thinks it is wrong to kiss in public.*)

3. Have students look at grammar chart **6.7**. Say: *Compare our sentences on the board with the chart.* Review the examples and the explanations. Go over any errors.

EXERCISE 13

1. Have students read the direction line. *You have to decide between using the present continuous and the simple present.* Go over the examples.

2. Have students complete Exercise 13 individually. Check the answers as a class.

3. If necessary, review grammar chart **6.7** on page 174.

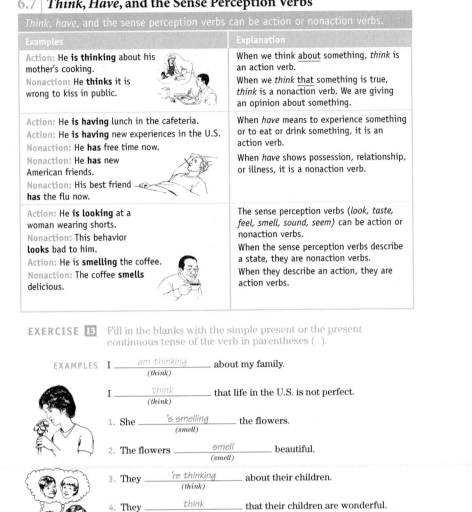

6.7 | *Think, Have,* and the Sense Perception Verbs

Think, have, and the sense perception verbs can be action or nonaction verbs.

Examples	Explanation
Action: He **is thinking** about his mother's cooking. **Nonaction:** He **thinks** it is wrong to kiss in public.	When we think <u>about</u> something, *think* is an action verb. When we *think* <u>that</u> something is true, *think* is a nonaction verb. We are giving an opinion about something.
Action: He **is having** lunch in the cafeteria. **Action:** He **is having** new experiences in the U.S. **Nonaction:** He **has** free time now. **Nonaction:** He **has** new American friends. **Nonaction:** His best friend **has** the flu now.	When *have* means to experience something or to eat or drink something, it is an action verb. When *have* shows possession, relationship, or illness, it is a nonaction verb.
Action: He **is looking** at a woman wearing shorts. **Nonaction:** This behavior **looks** bad to him. **Action:** He is **smelling** the coffee. **Nonaction:** The coffee **smells** delicious.	The sense perception verbs (*look, taste, feel, smell, sound, seem*) can be action or nonaction verbs. When the sense perception verbs describe a state, they are nonaction verbs. When they describe an action, they are action verbs.

EXERCISE 13 Fill in the blanks with the simple present or the present continuous tense of the verb in parentheses ( ).

EXAMPLES I ___*am thinking*___ about my family.
(think)

I ___*think*___ that life in the U.S. is not perfect.
(think)

1. She ___*'s smelling*___ the flowers.
(smell)

2. The flowers ___*smell*___ beautiful.
(smell)

3. They ___*'re thinking*___ about their children.
(think)

4. They ___*think*___ that their children are wonderful.
(think)

5. I ___*'m having*___ a good time in the U.S.
(have)

Grammar Variation

Have students cover up the examples side of grammar chart **6.7**. Write the sentences without the verbs in place (as described above). Go over the explanations in the book. Then have students complete the sentences on the board using the right form of each verb.

6. I _____have_____ a lot of new friends.
(have)

7. I _____don't have_____ a lot of free time.
(not/have)

8. My friend _____has_____ a cold now and she can't go out
(have)

today, so I _____'m having_____ lunch alone now.
(have)

9. He _____'s looking_____ at a car now.
(look)

10. The car _____looks_____ new.
(look)

EXERCISE 14 Fill in the blanks with the simple present or the present continuous of the verb in parentheses ( ). Use the simple present for regular activity and with nonaction verbs.

EXAMPLES Dan _____wants_____ to understand American behavior.
(want)

He _____is looking_____ at some Americans in the cafeteria now.
(look)

1. Dan _____'s writing_____ in his journal now.
(write)

2. He _____'s sitting_____ in the school cafeteria now.
(sit)

3. He _____sees_____ a couple with a baby.
(see)

4. He often _____goes_____ to the cafeteria between classes.
(go)

5. He _____writes_____ in his journal once a week.
(write)

6. He _____thinks_____ that his family _____wants_____
(think)   (want)

to know about American customs.

7. He _____'s looking_____ at a young man and woman. They
(look)

_____are holding_____ hands.
(hold)

8. This behavior _____looks_____ bad in his country.
(look)

The Present Continuous Tense **175**

1. Have students read the direction line. Point out that students should use the simple present with action verbs that are regular activities (e.g., *He thinks about his mother's cooking every night.*) and with nonaction verbs (e.g., *He thinks it is wrong to kiss in public.*). Go over the examples.

2. Have students complete Exercise 14 individually. Check the answers as a class.

3. If necessary, review grammar charts **6.5** on page 170, **6.6** on page 172, and **6.7** on page 174.

To save class time, have students do half of the exercise in class and complete the other half for homework. Or assign the entire exercise for homework.

Expansion

Exercise 13 Have students explain why they used the simple present or the present continuous in each statement in Exercise 13 (e.g., 1. *smelling*—present continuous because *smell* is an action word here. I'm smelling the flowers right now.).

1. Have students read the direction line. Ask: *What do we write in the blanks?* (the negative form of the verb) Go over the examples in the book. Remind students to use contractions wherever possible.

2. Have students complete Exercise 15 individually. Then have students compare answers in pairs. Circulate to observe pair work. Give help as needed.

3. If necessary, review grammar chart **6.1** on page 161.

🕐 To save class time, have students do half of the exercise in class and complete the other half for homework. Or assign the entire exercise for homework.

---

9. He _____'s thinking_____ about American customs now.
       (think)

10. Some women _____are wearing_____ shorts now.
         (wear)

11. Women in Dan's country never _____wear_____ shorts.
                                    (wear)

12. American customs _____seem_____ strange to him.
                        (seem)

EXERCISE 15 Read each sentence. Write the negative form of the underlined word, using the word(s) in parentheses ( ).

EXAMPLES Dan <u>is looking</u> at Americans. (people from his country)
He isn't looking at people from his country.

He <u>knows</u> about customs from his country. (American customs)
He doesn't know about American customs.

1. The father <u>is feeding</u> the baby. (the mother)
   The mother isn't feeding the baby.

2. Dan's <u>sitting</u> in the cafeteria. (in class)
   Dan isn't sitting in class.

3. He <u>understands</u> customs from his country. (American customs)
   He doesn't understand American customs.

4. American men and women sometimes <u>kiss</u> in public. (men and women in his country)
   Men and women in his country don't kiss in public.

5. Americans <u>use</u> their hands to eat a hamburger. (to eat spaghetti)
   Americans don't use their hands to eat spaghetti.

6. A man <u>is wearing</u> an earring in one ear. (in both ears)
   A man isn't wearing an earring in both ears.

7. Americans <u>seem</u> strange to him. (to me)
   Americans don't seem strange to me.

8. American men <u>like</u> to take care of babies. (Dan)
   Dan doesn't like to take care of babies.

9. American women often <u>wear</u> shorts in the summer. (women in Dan's country never)
   Women in Dan's country never wear shorts in the summer.

176 Lesson **6**

EXERCISE **16**   Read each sentence. Then write a *yes/no* question about the words in parentheses ( ). Write a short answer.

EXAMPLES   American women sometimes wear earrings. (American men/ever)

Do American men ever wear an earring? Yes, they do.

The women are wearing shorts. (the men)

Are the men wearing shorts? No, they aren't.

1. Dan is writing. (his homework)

     Is Dan doing his homework? Yes, he is.

2. He's watching people. (American people)

     Is he watching American people? Yes, he is.

3. He understands his own customs. (American customs)

     Does he understand American customs? No, he doesn't.

4. American men wear shorts in the summer. (American women)

     Do American women wear shorts in the summer? Yes, they do.

5. The man is eating. (a hot dog)

     Is the man eating a hot dog? No, he isn't.

EXERCISE **17**   Read each statement. Then write a *wh-* question about the words in parentheses ( ). An answer is not necessary.

EXAMPLES   A young man is resting his feet on a chair. (why)

Why is he resting his feet on a chair?

Dan lives in the U.S. (where/his family)

Where does his family live?

1. Dan is writing a letter. (to whom) OR (who . . . to)

     To whom is he writing a letter? Or Who is he writing a letter to?

2. Dan wants to know about American customs. (why)

     Why does he want to know about American customs?

3. Two women are putting on makeup. (where)

     Where are they putting on make up?

4. American men and women touch and hold hands in public. (why)

     Why are they touching and holding hands in public?

5. Dan writes to his family. (how often)

     How often does Dan write to his family?

The Present Continuous Tense   **177**

EXERCISE 16

1. Have students read the direction line. Ask: *What do we write in the blanks?* (a *yes/no* question and a short answer) Go over the examples in the book.
2. Have students complete the exercise individually. Check the answers as a class.
3. If necessary, review grammar chart **6.4** on page 165.

🕐 To save class time, have students do half of the exercise in class and complete the other half for homework. Or assign the entire exercise for homework.

EXERCISE 17

1. Have students read the direction line. Ask: *What do we write in the blanks?* (a *wh-* question) Point out that students do not need to write an answer. Go over the examples in the book.
2. Have students complete the exercise individually. Then have students compare answers in pairs. Circulate to observe pair work. Give help as needed.
3. If necessary, review grammar chart **6.4** on page 165.

🕐 To save class time, have students do half of the exercise in class and complete the other half for homework. Or assign the entire exercise for homework.

1. Have students read the direction line. Explain that this is a phone conversation between Dan and his mother. Point out the pictures of Dan and his mother on pages 178 and 179. Go over the example in the book. Remind students to use contractions wherever possible.

2. Have students complete Exercise 18 individually. Check answers as a class.

3. Then have students practice the conversation in pairs. Circulate to observe pair work. Give help as needed.

4. If necessary, review grammar charts **6.5** on page 170, **6.6** on page 172, and **6.7** on page 174.

🕐 To save class time, have students do half of the exercise in class and complete the other half for homework. Or assign the entire exercise for homework.

---

6. The man isn't using a fork. (why/not)

   Why isn't he using a fork?

7. Women don't wear shorts in some countries. (why)

   Why don't women wear shorts in some countries?

8. Americans often wear blue jeans. (why)

   Why do Americans often wear blue jeans?

9. "Custom" means tradition or habit. (what/"behavior")

   What does behavior mean?

EXERCISE 18 🎧 *Combination exercise.* This is a phone conversation between Dan (D) and his mother (M). Fill in the blanks with the correct form of the words in parentheses ( ) to complete the conversation.

D: Hello?
M: Hi. This is Mom.
D: Hi, Mom. How ___*are you doing*___?
    (example: you/do)

M: We ___*'re doing*___ fine. And you?
    (1 do)

  How ___*do you like*___ college in the U.S.?
    (2 you/like)

D: Great. I ___*like*___ it a lot. I ___*'m having*___
    (3 like)   *(4 have)*

  a lot of fun.

M: Fun? ___*Why aren't you studying*___?
    (5 why/you/not/study)

D: I *am* studying. But I ___*'m also meeting*___ new people from all over
    (6 also/meet)

  the world. I ___*'m thinking*___ about getting an earring.
    (7 think)

M: What? Earrings are for women.

D: But, Mom, all the guys ___*are doing*___ it these days.
    (8 do)

M: I ___*don't care*___. You ___*don't need*___ an earring in your
  (9 not/care)   *(10 not/need)*

  ear. You just ___*need*___ to study. ___*Are you getting*___
    (11 need)   *(12 you/get)*

  good grades?

Exercise 18 Variation

To provide practice with listening skills, have students close their books and listen to the audio. Repeat the audio as needed. Ask comprehension questions, such as: *Where is Dan's college?* (in the U.S.) *What does Dan think of college?* (He thinks it's great, fun.) *What is Dan thinking of doing?* (getting an earring) Then have students open their books and complete Exercise 18.

D: You _____*know*_____ I'm a good student. Of course,
     (13 know)

   I _____*'m getting*_____ good grades.
     (14 get)

M: _____*Are you practicing*_____ your guitar these days?
     (15 you/practice)

D: Yes, I am. But I _____*don't have*_____ as much time as before.
     (16 not/have)

   I _____*'m taking*_____ five classes this semester.
     (17 take)

M: Only five? Students here _____*usually take*_____ eight classes.
     (18 usually/take)

D: The system is different here. Freshmen only take four or five classes.

M: What _____*does "freshman" mean*_____?
     (19 freshman/mean)

D: A freshman is a student in the first year of college.

M: How's the food? _____*Are you getting*_____ enough to eat?
     (20 you/get)

D: Yes, I am. In fact, I _____*'m gaining*_____ weight. But I
     (21 gain)

   _____*don't like*_____ the food here.
     (22 not/like)

M: Why _____*don't you like*_____ the food?
     (23 not/like)

D: It's too greasy. And it _____*doesn't taste*_____ like food back home.
     (24 not/taste)

   I really _____*miss*_____ your food.
     (25 miss)

M: I _____*'m making*_____ your favorite dish now.
     (26 make)

D: Really? I _____*'m getting*_____ hungry just thinking about it.
     (27 get)

M: You and Dad _____*always think*_____ that my food is the best.
     (28 always/think)

D: Where's Dad?

M: He _____*'s working*_____ in the garden now. He's planting a new tree.
     (29 work)

D: Thanks for sending me the sweater. I _____*'m wearing*_____ it now.
     (30 wear)

M: _____ Do you have _____ enough warm clothes?
(31 you/have)

D: For now, I do. But it _____ 's starting _____ to get cold these days.
(32 start)

And the days _____ are getting _____ shorter. Fall is beautiful here.
(33 get)

The trees _____ are changing/change _____ color. I _____ 'm looking _____
(34 change)   (35 look)

out my window now and I _____ see _____ a beautiful maple
(36 see)

tree with red leaves. But I _____ prefer _____ the climate back
(37 prefer)

home. It's warm all year. Here it's really cold in December and January.

M: I _____ 'm making _____ a new sweater for you now. Your sister Ruby
(38 make)

_____ is making _____ you a scarf.
(39 make)

D: Thanks, Mom. Where's Ruby? _____ Does she want _____ to talk to me now?
(40 she/want)

M: I _____ don't think _____ so. She _____ 's watching _____ a video
(41 not/think)   (42 watch)

with her friends.

D: _____ Is she getting _____ good grades this semester?
(43 she/get)

M: She _____ 's spending/spends _____ too much time with her friends these days.
(44 spend)

D: Well, she's 16. Friends are really important when you're 16.
M: I'm worried about her.
D: Don't worry so much, Mom.
M: Of course I worry. I'm a mother. Dad _____ 's coming _____ in now.
(45 come)

He _____ wants _____ to talk to you now.
(46 want)

D: OK, Mom. Bye.

Expansion

Exercise 18 Have pairs write their own conversations. Tell students they can use Exercise 18 as a model. Circulate to observe pair work. Give help as needed. Have volunteers role-play their conversations in front of the class.

Uses of Tenses

Simple Present Tense	
General truths	Americans **speak** English. Oranges **grow** in Florida.
Regular activity, habit	I always **speak** English in class. I sometimes **eat** in the cafeteria. I **visit** my parents every Friday.
Customs	Americans **shake** hands. Japanese people **bow.**
Place of origin	Miguel **comes** from El Salvador. Marek **comes** from Poland.
With nonaction verbs	She **has** a new car. I **like** the U.S. You **look** great today.

Present Continuous (with action verbs only)	
Now	We **are reviewing** now. I **am looking** at page 181 now.
A long action in progress at this general time	Dan **is learning** about American customs. He **is studying** English.
A descriptive state	She **is wearing** shorts. He **is sitting** near the door. The teacher **is standing.**

Summary of Lesson 6

Uses of Tenses Have students close their books. Create two matching exercises. Write the sentences from the simple present tense chart on the board. Choose one sentence from each row and write them in random order. Then write the uses in random order. For example:

Oranges grow in Florida. Customs Japanese people bow. General truths Etc.

Do the same with the present continuous chart. Have students match the uses with the example sentences. Then have students open their books and compare their work with the charts in the book. Go over the example sentences in the book. If necessary, have students review:

6.1 The Present Continuous Tense (p. 161)
6.3 The Present Continuous Tense— Uses (p. 163)
6.5 Contrast of Present Continuous and Simple Present (p. 170)
6.6 Nonaction Verbs (p. 172)
6.7 *Think, Have,* and the Sense Perception Verbs (p. 174)
Lesson 2.

Editing Advice

Have students close their books. Write the example sentences without editing marks or corrections on the board. For example:

1. *He working now.*

2. *Where you're going?*

Ask students to correct each sentence and provide a rule or explanation for each correction. This activity can be done individually, in pairs, or as a class. After students have corrected each sentence, tell them to turn to page 182. Say: *Now compare your work with the Editing Advice in the book.*

EDITING ADVICE

1. Include *be* with a continuous tense.
   He _is_ working now.

2. Use the correct word order in a question.
   Where _are you_ you're going?
   Why you _don't you_ don't like New York?

3. Don't use the present continuous with a nonaction verb.
   She is _has_ having her own computer.

4. Use the *-s* form when the subject is *he*, *she*, or *it*.
   He _has_ have a new car. He like_s_ to drive.

5. Don't use *be* with a simple present-tense verb.
   I'm need a new computer.

6. Use *do* or *does* in a simple present-tense question.
   Where _does_ lives your mother _live_?

7. Don't use the *-s* form after *does*.
   Where does he takes the bus?

Review the Editing Advice for the simple present tense on pages 68–69.

PART 1 Find the mistakes with the underlined words and correct them. Not every sentence has a mistake. If the sentence is correct, write C.

EXAMPLES
owns
She's <u>owning</u> a new bike now.
<u>I'm not studying</u> math this semester.   *C*

1. Why <u>you aren't</u> listening to me?   *aren't you*

2. Usually <u>I'm go</u> home after class.   *I go*

3. I think that <u>he's having</u> trouble with this lesson.   *C*

4. She's <u>thinking</u> about her family now.   *C*

5. Does she <u>needs</u> help with her homework?   *need*

6. What kind of car <u>do you have</u>?   *C*

7. What <u>he's</u> studying now?   *is he*

8. Does he <u>has</u> any children?   *have*

9. He's <u>wearing</u> jeans now.   *C*

10. My teacher <u>speak</u> English well.   *speaks*

11. I'm <u>speak</u> my native language at home.   *speaking*

12. The baby <u>sleeping</u> now.   *is sleeping*

13. When <u>begins summer</u>?   *does summer begin*

14. Where <u>does your family lives</u>?   *live*

PART 2 This is a conversation between two students, Alicia (A) and Teresa (T), who meet in the school library. Fill in the blanks with the simple present or the present continuous form of the verb in parentheses ( ).

T: Hi, Alicia.

A: Hi, Teresa. What <u>are you doing</u> here?
(example: you/do)

T: I <u>'m looking</u> for a book on American geography. What
(1 look)
about you?

A: I <u>'m returning</u> a book. <u>Do you want</u> to go for
(2 return)   *(3 you/want)*
a cup of coffee?

The Present Continuous Tense   **183**

Lesson 6 Test/Review

For additional practice, review, and assessment materials, see Assessment CD-ROM with *ExamView Pro, More Grammar Practice* Workbook 1, Interactive CD-ROM, and Web site http://elt.thomson.com/gic

PART 1

1. Part 1 may be used as an in-class test to assess student performance, in addition to the Assessment CD-ROM with *ExamView Pro*. Have students read the direction line. Ask: *Does every sentence have a mistake?* (no) Go over the examples with the class.

2. Have students complete the assignment individually. Collect for assessment.

3. If necessary, have students review: **Lesson 6.**

PART 2

1. Part 2 may also be used as an in-class test to assess student performance, in addition to the Assessment CD-ROM with *ExamView Pro*. Have students read the direction line. Explain that this is a conversation between two students, Alicia and Teresa, and takes place in the school library. Go over the example with the class.

2. Have students complete the exercise individually. Collect for assessment.

3. If necessary, have students review: **Lesson 6.**

Lesson Review

To use Parts 1 and 2 as a review, assign them as homework or use them as in-class activities to be completed individually or in pairs. Check answers and review errors as a class. For Part 2, have students practice the conversation in pairs. Circulate to observe pair work. Give help as needed. Reteach grammar points that students haven't mastered. Then student learning may be assessed using a test generated from the Assessment CD-ROM with *ExamView Pro*.

T: I can't. I _____'m waiting_____ for my friend. We _____'re working_____
       (4 wait)   (5 work)

on a geography project together, and we _____need_____ to
                                              (6 need)

finish it by next week.

A: _____Do you like_____ your geography class?
          (7 you/like)

T: Yes. I especially _____like_____ the teacher, Bob. He's a
                            (8 like)

handsome young man. He's very casual. He always

_____wears_____ jeans and a T-shirt to class. He
      (9 wear)

_____has_____ an earring in one ear.
      (10 have)

A: That _____seems_____ very strange to me.
              (11 seem)

I _____think_____ that teachers in the U.S. are very informal.
         (12 think)

How _____'s Bob teaching_____ the class? By lecturing?
            (13 Bob/teach)

T: No. We _____usually work_____ in small groups, and he
                 (14 usually/work)

_____helps_____ us by walking around the classroom.
      (15 help)

A: _____Does he give_____ hard tests?
          (16 he/give)

T: No. He _____doesn't believe_____ in tests.
                 (17 not/believe)

A: Why _____doesn't he believe_____ in tests?
              (18 he/not/believe)

T: He _____thinks_____ that students get too nervous during a test.
            (19 think)

He _____says_____ it's better to work on projects. This week
          (20 say)

we _____are working_____ on city maps.
          (21 work)

A: That _____sounds_____ interesting.
              (22 sound)

T: Why _____are you asking_____ me so many questions about my teacher?
              (23 you/ask)

A: I _____'m thinking_____ about taking a geography course next
            (24 think)

semester.

T: Bob's very popular. Be sure to register early because his classes

always _____fill_____ quickly. Oh. I _____see_____
         (25 fill)   (26 see)

my friend now. She _____'s walking_____ toward us. I have to go now.
                        (27 walk)

A: Good luck on your project.

T: Thanks. Bye.

PART 3   Fill in the blanks with the negative form of the underlined word.

EXAMPLE   Teresa is in the library. She _____isn't_____ at home.

1. Alicia wants to go for a cup of coffee. Teresa _____doesn't want_____ to
   go for a cup of coffee.

2. Teresa is looking for a book. Alicia _____isn't looking_____ for a book.

3. They are talking about school. They _____aren't talking_____ about the
   news.

4. They have time to talk now. They _____don't have_____ time for a cup
   of coffee.

5. Students in the geography class work in small groups.
   They _____don't work_____ alone.

6. Alicia's teacher gives tests. Teresa's teacher _____doesn't give_____ tests.

7. Teresa is waiting for a friend. Alicia _____isn't waiting_____ for a friend.

8. The teacher seems strange to Alicia. He _____doesn't seem_____ strange
   to Teresa.

9. Alicia is returning a book. Teresa _____isn't returning_____ a book.

PART 4   Read each sentence. Then write a *yes/no* question about the
         words in parentheses ( ). Write a short answer.

EXAMPLE   Teresa is looking for a book. (a geography book)
          Is she looking for a geography book? Yes, she is.

1. Bob likes projects. (tests)
   Does he like tests? No, he doesn't.

2. Alicia has time now. (Teresa)
   Does Teresa have time now? No, she doesn't.

1. Part 3 may also be used as an in-class test to assess student performance, in addition to the Assessment CD-ROM with *ExamView Pro*. Have students read the direction line. Point out that students need to use the negative form of the underlined word. Go over the example with the class.

2. Have students complete the exercise individually. Collect for assessment.

3. If necessary, have students review:
   6.1   The Present Continuous Tense (p. 161)
   6.5   Contrast of Present Continuous and Simple Present (p. 170).

1. Part 4 may also be used as an in-class test to assess student performance, in addition to the Assessment CD-ROM with *ExamView Pro*. Have students read the direction line. Explain that students should write a *yes/no* question and a short answer. Go over the example with the class.

2. Have students complete the exercise individually. Collect for assessment.

3. If necessary, have students review:
   6.4   Questions with the Present Continuous Tense (p. 165)
   6.5   Contrast of Present Continuous and Simple Present (p. 170).

Lesson Review

To use Parts 3 and 4 as a review, assign them as homework or use them as in-class activities to be completed individually or in pairs. Check answers and review errors as a class. Reteach grammar points that students haven't mastered. Then student learning may be assessed using a test generated from the Assessment CD-ROM with *ExamView Pro*.

1. Part 5 may also be used as an in-class test to assess student performance, in addition to the Assessment CD-ROM with *ExamView Pro*. Have students read the direction line. Ask: *Do we write answers?* (no) Go over the example with the class.
2. Have students complete the exercise individually. Collect for assessment.
3. If necessary, have students review:
   - **6.4** Questions with the Present Continuous Tense (p. 165)
   - **6.5** Contrast of Present Continuous and Simple Present (p. 170).

---

3. They are talking about their classes. (their teachers)

   Are they talking about their teachers? Yes, they are.

4. Bob wears jeans to class. (ever / a suit)

   Does he ever wear a suit to class? No, he doesn't.

5. Alicia wants to go for coffee. (Teresa)

   Does Teresa want to go for coffee? No, she doesn't.

6. American teachers seem strange to Alicia. (to Teresa)

   Do American teachers seem strange to Teresa? No, they don't.

7. Teresa is working on a geography project. (Alicia)

   Is Alicia working on a geography project? No, she isn't.

PART **5**   Read each sentence. Then write a question with the words in parentheses ( ). An answer is not necessary.

EXAMPLE   Bob is popular. (Why)

Why is he popular?

1. Bob sounds interesting. (Why)

   Why does he sound interesting?

2. Bob doesn't like tests. (Why)

   Why doesn't he like tests?

3. Teresa and her friend are working on a project. (What kind of project)

   What kind of project are they working on?

4. Teresa studies in the library. (How often)

   How often does Teresa study in the library?

5. Teresa is looking for a book. (What kind)

   What kind of book is she looking for?

6. Teresa is waiting for her friend. (Why)

   Why is she waiting for her friend?

7. Her classmates aren't writing a term paper. (Why)

   Why aren't her classmates writing a term paper?

186   Lesson 6

Lesson Review

To use Part 5 as a review, assign it as homework or use it as an in-class activity to be completed individually or in pairs. Check answers and review errors as a class. Reteach grammar points that students haven't mastered. Then student learning may be assessed using a test generated from the Assessment CD-ROM with *ExamView Pro*.

Classroom Activities

1. Think of a place (cafeteria, airport, train station, bus, playground, church, opera, movie theater, laundry, office at this school, kindergarten classroom, restaurant, department store, etc.). Pretend you are at this place. Write three or four sentences to tell what people in this place are doing. Other students will guess where you are.

EXAMPLE   People are walking fast.
People are carrying suitcases.
People are standing in long lines.
They're buying tickets.
Guess: Are you at the airport?

2. Pretend you are calling from your cell phone. You are telling your family where you are. Fill in the blanks to tell what you and other people are doing. Then find a partner and see how many of your sentences match your partner's sentences.

   a. I'm at the supermarket. I'm _____.
   Do you need anything while I'm here?

   b. I'm in my car. I'm _____.

   c. I'm in the school library. I'm _____.

   People _____ me to be quiet because

   I'm _____ to you on my cell phone.

   d. I'm in a taxi. I'm on my way home. I'm _____

   you to let you know that _____.

   e. I'm at the bus stop. I _____ for the bus, but it's late. I don't want you to worry.

   f. I'm at a shoe store. I _____.

   g. I'm at the playground with the kids. The kids _____

   _____

   h. I'm at the movies. I can't talk now because the movie _____

   _____

   i. I'm in the bedroom. I have to talk softly because my roommate

   _____

   j. I'm in class now. I can't talk. The teacher _____

   _____

Expansion Activities

These expansion activities provide opportunities for students to interact with one another and further develop their speaking and writing skills. If time is short, have students do parts of the activities at home. Save the class time for interaction and communication.

🕐 To save class time, assign parts of the activities as homework. Then use class time for interaction and communication. If students do not need additional speaking practice, some of the activities may be assigned as writing activities for homework, or skipped altogether.

CLASSROOM ACTIVITIES

1. This guessing activity can be done in groups or as a whole class. Have students read the direction line. Go over the example. Model the activity with a volunteer.

2. Have students read the direction line. Model letter "a" for the class. Say: *First complete the sentences on your own. Then compare your sentences with a partner.*

Expansion

Classroom Activities Have students create mini cell phone dialogues based on the ideas from Activity 2. Ask volunteers to role-play their dialogues in front of the class.

CLASSROOM ACTIVITIES (*cont.*)

3. In groups, have students discuss behaviors that are strange to them. Then have groups report the results of their discussions to the class (e.g., *We think it's strange that Americans don't have much physical contact when they greet each other.*). If possible, put students from different countries together in the same group.

OUTSIDE ACTIVITY

Ask students to observe behaviors in public places. Say: *Write down all the actions you see.* Have students report their observations in groups or have volunteers report their observations to the class.

INTERNET ACTIVITY

Tell students: *Research a college in this area. Answer the questions listed in the book.* Have students brainstorm a list of local colleges. Go over the questions to make sure students understand everything.

Outside Activity

Internet Activity

3. In a small group or with the entire class, discuss behaviors that are strange to you. What American behaviors are not polite in your native culture?

Go to the school cafeteria, student union, or other crowded place. Sit there for a while and look for unusual behaviors. Write down some of the unusual things you see. Report back to the class.

Find the Web site of a college in this city. Answer the following questions:

1. Where is it?
2. What's the tuition?
3. Does this college have evening classes?
4. Does this college have more than one location?
5. Does it have a graduate program?
6. Does it have dormitories?
7. Does it have ESL classes?
8. When is the next registration?
9. What are the vacation days?

 Additional Activities at http://elt.thomson.com/gic

Internet Activity Variation

If students don't have access to the Internet, they may find the information needed using resources at a local public library.

Expansion

Internet Activity Have students create a poster for the college they research. Display the posters around the room.

LESSON

7

GRAMMAR
Future Tenses—*Will* and *Be Going To*
Comparison of Tenses

CONTEXT: Weddings
Planning for a Wedding
Jason and Katie—Starting a Married Life

189

Lesson Overview

GRAMMAR

1. Briefly review other tenses students have learned. Ask: *What tense did we study in Lessons 1, 2, and 3?* (simple present tense) *What tense did we study in Lesson 6?* (present continuous tense)
2. Ask: *What tenses are we going to study in this lesson?* (future tenses) *What words do we use to talk about the future?* (*will* and *be going to*) Have volunteers give examples. Write the examples on the board.

CONTEXT

1. Ask: *What will we learn about in this lesson?* (planning a wedding, starting a married life) Elicit students' prior knowledge. Ask: *Have you ever planned or helped to plan a wedding?*
2. Have students share their knowledge and personal experiences.

Photo

1. Direct students' attention to the photo. Ask: *Who are the people in the photo?* (a couple; a bride and a groom) *Why are they wearing special clothes? Why are they smiling?* (because they're getting married)
2. Have students share similar experiences.

⏱ To save class time, have students do the Test/Review at the end of the lesson, or administer a lesson test generated from the Assessment CD-ROM with *ExamView® Pro*. Skip sections of the lesson that students have already mastered. You may also assign some sections for self-study for extra credit.

Expansion

Theme The topic for this lesson can be enhanced with the following ideas:

1. Photos of your wedding or of another wedding
2. Newspaper articles about weddings or wedding announcements
3. A registry list from a department store
4. Newspaper articles on unusual weddings or honeymoon trips

Planning for a Wedding (Reading)

1. Have students look at the photo. Ask: *Who are the people?* (a couple) *Where are they?* (at a store) *What are they doing?* (choosing gifts for their gift registry)
2. Have students look at the title of the reading. Ask: *What is the reading about?* Have students use the title and photo to make predictions.
3. Preteach any vocabulary words students may not know, such as *engaged, invitations, reception, rehearsal, honeymoon, duplicate,* and *debt.* For *invitation,* direct students to the graphic on page 191. For *reception,* point out the footnote at the bottom of the page.

BEFORE YOU READ

1. Have students discuss the questions in pairs. Try to pair students of different cultures together.
2. Ask for a few volunteers to share their answers with the class.

To save class time, skip "Before You Read" or have students prepare answers for homework ahead of time.

Reading 🎧 *CD 1, Track 32*

1. Have students read the reading silently. Tell them to pay special attention to the future tense verbs *will* and *be going to.* Then play the audio and have students read along.
2. Check students' comprehension. Ask questions such as: *What do Karyn and Steve need to do before the wedding?* (choose photographers, invitations, a wedding dress, etc.)
3. Direct students to the wedding cost chart on page 191. Ask: *Are American weddings expensive? Are weddings in your native country expensive?*

To save class time, have students do the reading for homework ahead of time.

DID YOU KNOW?

There are name change kits that brides (and grooms) may purchase. These kits include helpful forms and information on changing one's name.

DID YOU KNOW?

About 43 percent of couples exceed their wedding budget.

PLANNING FOR A WEDDING

Before You Read

1. In your native culture, what kind of gifts do people give to a bride and groom?

2. Are weddings expensive in your native culture?

🎧 Read the following article. Pay special attention to future-tense verbs.

Did You Know?
Most brides (83 percent) take their husband's last name.

Did You Know?
Over 2 million couples get married in America each year. About half of these couples will get divorced. For many couples getting married today, their debt will last longer than their marriage.

Karyn and Steve are engaged now and are planning their wedding. They need a lot of time to plan. They**'re going to graduate** from college next year, and the wedding **will take** place a year and a half after they graduate from college. They **will need** time to choose a photographer, invitations, a place for the reception,[1] a wedding dress, flowers, rings, a wedding cake, entertainment, and more. The wedding **is going to be** very expensive. In addition to paying for the wedding and reception, they **will need** to rent a limousine and pay for a rehearsal dinner and a honeymoon. They **are going to invite** about 250 people, including many friends and relatives from out of town. They **are going to pay** for the hotel rooms for their grandparents, aunts, and uncles. It **is going to take** a lot of time and energy to plan for the wedding.

Before their wedding, they **will register** for gifts. They **will go** to stores and select the gifts they want to receive. When guests go to the stores, they **will choose** a gift from this list. This way, Karyn and Steve **are going to receive** exactly what they want. They **won't receive** duplicate presents. About six or seven weeks before the wedding, they **will send** out their invitations. After they return from their honeymoon in Hawaii, they **are going to send** thank-you cards to all the guests.

Who**'s going to pay** for all this? After they graduate, they **will work** and **save** money for their dream wedding. But their parents **are going to help** too. Like many young couples, they **will have** credit card debt for years after the wedding. This is in addition to college debt.

[1] A *reception* is a party after a wedding.

190 Lesson **7**

Reading Variation

To practice listening skills, have students first listen to the audio alone. Ask a few comprehension questions. Repeat the audio if necessary. Then have students open their books and read along as they listen to the audio.

Reading Glossary

debt: a sum of money owed to another
duplicate: an exact copy
engaged: having a formal agreement to get married
honeymoon: a trip people take after they get married
invitation: a card or spoken request asking someone to come to an event
reception: a type of party planned so people can meet a special guest and each other
rehearsal: a practice session

Culture Note

Bridal registries usually include items for the kitchen, the bedroom, and the bathroom. They don't usually include large pieces of furniture or personal items, such as clothing.

Average Wedding Cost in the U.S. (2003) = $22,000

Typical Costs

Wedding dress = $800
Engagement ring = $3,500
Flowers = $1,000
Reception = $11,000
Invitations = $500

Mr. and Mrs. David K. Smith
and
Mr. and Mrs. John H. Gilbert
invite you to join in the marriage
of their children
Karyn Ann
and
Steven James
Saturday, March 26
Three O'Clock
St. Luke's Church
Westford, New York

7.1 | Future with *Will*

Examples				Explanation
Subject	Will	Verb	Complement	We use *will* + the base form for the future tense. *Will* doesn't have an *-s* form.
They	**will**	**rent**	a limousine.	
There	**will**	**be**	a reception.	
The bride	**will**	**wear**	a white dress.	
They'll register for gifts. **She'll** buy a white dress. **He'll** rent a tuxedo. **It'll** take them a long time to plan for the wedding.				We can make a contraction with the subject pronoun and *will*. I will = I'll It will = It'll You will = You'll We will = We'll He will = He'll They will = They'll She will = She'll
They **will not receive** duplicate presents. They **won't pay** for everything. Their parents will help them.				Put *not* after *will* to form the negative. The contraction for *will not* is *won't*.
I will **always** love you. I will **never** leave you. We will **probably** give money as a gift.				You can put an adverb (*always, never, probably, even*) between *will* and the main verb.

Grammar Variation

Draw a time line on the board. Draw a mark in the center and label it *present (now)/Karyn and Steve—engaged*. Label the right side *future/Karyn and Steve—married*.

7.1 | Future with *Will*

1. Have students cover up grammar chart **7.1**. Then have students find sentences from the reading that contain *will*. Write a few of the sentences on the board. For example, write: *They will need to rent a limousine.* Then below that write: *They will register for gifts.* Make sure the subject, *will*, and the verb line up. Ask: *What do all the sentences have?* (subject + *will* + verb) Write these labels above the sentences.

2. Demonstrate how to form the contraction of *will* (by adding *'ll*). On the board, write: *They will register for gifts.* Ask: *How can we make a contraction with the subject and* will? (subject + *'ll*) Write: *They'll register for gifts.* Elicit contractions for other subject pronouns. Write them on the board.

3. Demonstrate how to form the negative. On the board, write: *They will register for gifts.* Ask: *How can we make this sentence negative?* (add *not* after *will*) Write: *They will not register for gifts.* Then ask: *How can we make a contraction?* (*will* + *not* = *won't*) Write: *will* + *not* = *won't. They won't register for gifts.*

4. Demonstrate the use of an adverb in sentences with *will*. Say: *We want to use* probably *in the sentence* They will register for gifts. *Where does it go?* (after *will*) On the board, write: *They will probably register for gifts.*

5. Have students look at grammar chart **7.1**. Review the forms of *will*. Point out that, unlike the simple present and present continuous tenses, there is only one form of *will* for different subject pronouns.

6. Discuss the function of the future tenses. Ask: *In the reading, are Karyn and Steve married?* (no) *When do they want to marry?* (a year and a half after they graduate from college) Say: *The reading says, "The wedding will take place a year and a half after they graduate from college." When do we use* will? (to talk about future events)

EXERCISE 1

1. Tell students that this exercise is about Karyn and Steve's wedding plans. Have students read the direction line. Ask: *What do we write on the blanks?* (*will* + verb) Go over the example.

2. Have students complete Exercise 1 individually. Then have them check their answers in pairs. Finally, check the answers as a class.

3. If needed, review grammar chart **7.1** on page 191.

7.2 | Future with *Be Going To*

1. Have students cover up grammar chart **7.2**. Then have students find sentences from the reading on page 190 that contain *be going to*. Write a few of the sentences on the board. For example, write: *They're going to graduate from college next year.* Then below that, write: *The wedding cake is going to be very expensive.* Make sure the subject, *be*, *going to*, and the verb line up. Ask: *What do all the sentences have?* (subject + *be* + *going to* + verb) Write these labels above the sentences.

2. Review how to form contractions with *be*. On the board, write: *The bride is going to wear a white dress.* Ask: *How can we make a contraction with the subject and be?* (subject + *'s*) Write: *The bride's going to wear a white dress.*

3. Review how to form the negative. On the board, write: *They are not going to graduate this year.* Ask: *How do we form the negative?* (add *not* after *be*) Then ask: *How can we make a contraction?* (*they're not* or *they aren't*)

4. Demonstrate the use of an adverb in sentences with *be going to*. Say: *Put the adverb between* be *and* going to. On the board, write: *They are probably going to open their gifts at home.*

5. Have students look at grammar chart **7.2** on page 192. Review the examples and explanations. Point out that, in informal speech, *going to* in front of another verb often sounds like *gonna*. Demonstrate the pronunciation of these two sentences:
   I'm going to have breakfast now.
   I'm going to the restaurant now.

EXERCISE **1**   Fill in the blanks with an appropriate verb in the future tense. Practice *will*.

EXAMPLE   Karyn and Steve's wedding _____*will be*_____ in a church.

1. They _____*will invite*_____ 250 guests.
2. The wedding _____*will be*_____ expensive.
3. They _____*will go*_____ to Hawaii on their honeymoon.
4. They _____*will be in*_____ debt for many years after the wedding.
5. Guests _____*will choose*_____ presents that the bride and groom want.
6. The bride and groom _____*will rent*_____ a limousine.
7. Their parents _____*will help*_____ them pay for the wedding.

7.2 | Future with *Be Going To*

Examples					Explanation
Subject	*Be*	*Going To*	Verb	Complement	Use *is/am/are* + *going to* + the base form for the future tense.
I	**am**	**going to**	**buy**	a gift.	We can make a contraction with the subject pronoun and *is, am, are*:
You	**are**	**going to**	**attend**	the wedding.	**I'm** going to buy a gift.
They	**are**	**going to**	**send**	invitations.	We can make a contraction with a singular noun + *is*:
The bride	**is**	**going to**	**wear**	a white dress.	The **bride's** going to wear a white dress.

They **are not going to graduate** this year. Their parents **aren't going to pay** for everything.	To make a negative statement, put *not* after *is/am/are*.
They **are going to go** on a honeymoon. OR They **are going** on a honeymoon.	When the main verb is *to go*, we often delete it.
They **are probably going** to open their gifts at home. They **are always going** to remember their wedding day.	We can put an adverb (*always, never, probably, even*) between *is, am, are* and *going*.

Pronunciation Notes:

1. In informal speech, *going to* before another verb often sounds like "gonna." We don't write "gonna."
2. We only pronounce "gonna" before a verb. We don't pronounce "gonna" in the following sentence: They are going to Hawaii.

Listen to your teacher pronounce the sentences in the above boxes.

Expansion

Exercise 1 Have students do a role-play in pairs. Say: *You will take turns being Karyn/Steve and a friend. The friend wants to know about the wedding plans. The friend says, "Please tell me about your wedding plans." Then Karyn/Steve says three sentences about the wedding plans. Use* will *to talk about the plans. Then switch roles and repeat.*

EXERCISE **2**   Fill in the blanks with an appropriate verb in the future tense.
Practice *be going to*.

EXAMPLE   They __*are going to send*__ thank-you cards to the guests.

1. Musicians __*are going to play*__ at the wedding.
2. A professional photographer __*is going to take*__ pictures.
3. There __*are going to be*__ a lot of people at the wedding.
4. The bride __*is going to wear*__ a white dress.
5. The wedding __*is going to cost*__ a lot of money.
6. They __*are going to have*__ wedding debt and college debt for many years.
7. The wedding cake __*is going to be*__ very expensive.

7.3 | Choosing *Will* or *Be Going To*

Examples	Explanation
I think the newlyweds **will** be very happy together. I think the newlyweds **are going to** be very happy together.	For a prediction, we can use either *will* or *be going to*.
The wedding **will** be in a church. The wedding **is going to** be in a church. They **will** send out 250 invitations. They **are going to** send out 250 invitations.	For a simple fact about the future, we can use either *will* or *be going to*.
I **will** always love you. I **will** never leave you.	For a promise, use *will*.
A: What gift are you planning to give your cousin for the wedding? B: I don't know. Maybe I**'ll** just give money.	Use *will* when you don't have a previous plan, but you decide what to do at the time of speaking.
A: This gift box is heavy. B: I**'ll** carry it for you.	When you offer to help someone, use *will*.
They **are going to** get married on May 6. I **am going to** buy a gift. Guests **are going to** come from out of town.	When we have a previous plan to do something, we usually use *be going to*. *I'm **going** to buy a gift.* = *I'm **planning** to buy a gift.*

Expansion

Exercise 2 Ask students to write about their wedding plans. Say: *What will your wedding be like? Write five to ten sentences using the sentences from Exercises 1 and 2 as models.* Have students discuss their wedding plans in groups.

---

1. Tell students that this exercise is based on the reading on page 190. Have students read the direction line. Ask: *What do we write on the blanks?* (*be going to* + verb) Go over the example in the book.
2. Have students complete Exercise 2 individually. Check the answers as a class.
3. If necessary, review grammar chart **7.2** on page 192.

7.3 | Choosing *Will* or *Be Going To*

1. Have students cover up the explanations side of grammar chart **7.3**. Write the following categories across the board:
   promises
   no previous plans
   predictions
   facts about the future
   previous plans
   offers to help
2. Have students read the sentences in the grammar chart (without looking at the explanations). Say: *Find the sentences that match the category. For example, which sentences are promises?* Write the sentences on the board under the correct categories. Then have students guess the rules for using *will* or *be going to*. Tell students that sometimes you can use both *will* and *be going to*. Ask: *Do you use* will *or* be going to *for promises?* (*will*)
3. Have students look at the explanations in grammar chart **7.3**. Ask students to compare their work on the board with the chart.

EXERCISE 3

1. Tell students that this exercise is about them and what they're going to be doing. Have students read the direction line. Ask: *Which future tense will we use here?* (*be going to*) Go over the example in the book. Have a volunteer model the example.

2. Have students complete Exercise 3 individually. Point out the photo of the woman shopping for groceries. Then have pairs compare answers. Circulate to observe pair work. Give help as needed.

3. If necessary, review grammar chart **7.2** on page 192.

EXERCISE 4

1. Tell students that this exercise is about their predictions for this class. Have students read the direction line. Ask: *Which future tense do we use with predictions?* (*be going to* or *will*) *Which one are we going to use for this exercise?* (*be going to*) Go over the example in the book. Have a volunteer model the example.

2. Have students complete Exercise 4 individually. Then have pairs compare answers. Circulate to observe pair work. Give help as needed.

3. If necessary, review grammar chart **7.3** on page 193.

EXERCISE 5

1. Tell students that this exercise is about Karyn and Steve's wedding plans. Have students read the direction line. Ask: *What do we write on the blanks?* (*will* + verb) Go over the example.

2. Have students complete Exercise 5 individually. Then have them check their answers in pairs. Finally, check the answers as a class.

3. If needed, review grammar chart **7.1** on page 191.

🕐 To save class time, have students do half of the exercise in class and complete the other half for homework. Or assign the entire exercise for homework.

EXERCISE 3 ABOUT YOU Tell if you have plans to do these things or not. Use *be going to*.

EXAMPLE meet a friend after class.
I'm (not) going to meet a friend after class.

Answers will vary.
1. get something to eat after class
2. watch TV tonight
3. eat dinner at home tonight
4. go to the library this week
5. go shopping for groceries this week
6. stay home this weekend
7. take a vacation this year
8. move (to a different apartment) this year
9. buy a car this year

EXERCISE 4 ABOUT YOU Tell if you predict that these things are going to happen or not in this class. Use *be going to*.

EXAMPLE we / finish this lesson today
We are going to finish this lesson today.

Answers will vary.
1. the teacher / give a test soon
2. the test / be hard
3. most students / pass the test
4. I / pass the test
5. the teacher / give everyone an A
6. my English / improve
7. we / finish this book by the end of the semester
8. the next test / cover the future tense
9. we / have a party at the end of the semester

EXERCISE 5 Fill in the blanks to complete these statements. Use *be going to*.

EXAMPLE I don't understand the meaning of a word. _I'm going to look it up in_ my dictionary.

1. It's hot in here. I ____'m going to open____ a window.

2. It's too noisy in this house. I can't study. I ___'m going to go to___ the library.

3. She's hungry. She ____'s going to have____ dinner now.

4. My mother in Poland always worries about me. I ___'m going to tell___ her that I'm fine.

194 Lesson 7

Expansion

Exercise 3 Take a class survey. How many people are going to do the same thing? Write the results on the board.

Exercise 4 Take a class survey. How many people predicted the same thing? Write the results on the board.

---

5. We don't have any milk in the house. When I go out shopping, I
   _____'m going to buy_____ some milk.

6. She plans to be a doctor. She _____'s going to_____ medical
   school next year.

7. I'm not happy with my job. I _____'m going to quit_____
   and look for another one.

8. I _____'m moving_____ next week. Here's my new address.

9. My parents miss me very much. They _____'re going to come_____
   next month to visit for three weeks.

10. There's a great new movie at the Garden Theater. My friends and
    I _____are going to go_____
    tomorrow night. Do you want to go with us?

EXERCISE ⑥   Tell if you predict that these things will happen or not in the next 50
             years. Use *will*. You may work with a partner or in a small group.

EXAMPLE   people / have more free time
          I think people won't have more free time. They will spend more time at
          their jobs and less time with their families.

Answers will vary.   1. there / another world war

                     2. the economy of the U.S. / get worse

                     3. people in the U.S. / have fewer children

                     4. Americans / live longer

Expansion

Exercise 6 Have students complete the exercise again using *be going to*.

---

1. Tell students that this exercise is
   about their predictions for the next
   50 years. Have students read the
   direction line. Ask: *Which future
   tense do we use with predictions?*
   (*be going to* or *will*) *Which one are
   we going to use for this exercise?*
   (*will*) Go over the example in the
   book. Have a volunteer model the
   example.

2. Have students complete Exercise 6
   in pairs. Circulate to observe pair
   work. Give help as needed.

3. If necessary, review grammar chart
   7.1 on page 191.

   🕐 To save class time, have
   students do half of the exercise
   in class and complete the other half in
   writing for homework. Or if students
   do not need speaking practice, the
   entire exercise may be skipped or done
   in writing.

EXERCISE 7

1. Ask: *What are you going to buy your friends for their birthdays?* Have students read the direction line. Ask: *Which future tense do we use when we don't have a plan?* (*will*) Go over the example in the book. Have a volunteer model the example.

2. Have students complete Exercise 7 individually. Have students compare answers in pairs. Circulate to observe pair work. Give help as needed.

3. If necessary, review grammar chart **7.1** on page 191.

🕐 To save class time, have students do half of the exercise in class and complete the other half in writing for homework. Or if students do not need speaking practice, the entire exercise may be skipped or done in writing.

EXERCISE 8

1. Explain that this exercise is about a man proposing to a woman. Have students read the direction line. Ask: *Which future tense do we use for promises?* (*will*) Go over the example.

2. Have students complete Exercise 8 individually. Check the answers as a class.

3. If needed, review grammar chart **7.1** on page 191.

🕐 To save class time, have students do half of the exercise in class and complete the other half for homework. Or assign the entire exercise for homework.

---

5. health care / improve
6. cars / use solar energy[2]
7. divorce / increase
8. crime / get worse
9. people / get tired of computers
10. technology / continue to grow

EXERCISE **7** Some friends of yours are going to have a birthday soon, and you want to buy them a present or do something special for them. What will you buy or do for these people?

EXAMPLE Maria's birthday is in the winter.
I'll buy her a sweater. OR I'll take her skiing.

Answers will vary.
1. Bill loves to go fishing.
2. Tina loves to eat in restaurants.
3. Carl needs a new radio.
4. Jim has a new CD player.
5. Lisa loves the beach in the summer.
6. Tom loves movies.

EXERCISE **8** A man is proposing marriage to a woman. He is making promises. Fill in the blanks to complete these statements.

EXAMPLE I _____will be_____ a good husband to you.

1. I love you very much. I (always) ___'ll always love___ you.
2. I want to make you happy. I ___'ll do___ everything I can to make you happy.
3. I don't have a lot of money, but I ___'ll work___ and try to make money.
4. We ___'ll have___ children, and I ___'ll be___ a good father to them.
5. We ___'ll grow___ old together.
6. We ___'ll be___ best friends and take care of each other.
7. You are the only woman for me. I (not) ___won't look___ at another woman.

[2] *Solar energy* comes from the sun.

Expansion

Exercise 7 Have students write a list of friends and family. Say: *Now write what they like to do or what they need. Then write down what you're going to get them for their birthdays.*

196 *Grammar in Context 1* Teacher's Edition

EXERCISE **9** Offer to help in these situations using *will* + an appropriate verb.

EXAMPLE
A: I have to move next Sunday. It's so much work.

B: *Don't worry. I'll help you pack.*

1. A: My hands are full. I need to open the door.

   B: *Don't worry. I'll open the door.*

2. A: I need stamps, but I have no time to go to the post office.

   B: I'm going to the post office. *I'll buy you stamps.*

3. A: I cook every night. I'm tired of cooking.

   B: Take a break. *I'll cook* _____ tonight.

4. A: I don't have experience with computers. I have to write my composition on the computer.

   B: Come to my house after class. *I'll help you.*

5. A: I always drive when we go to the country. I'm tired.

   B: No problem. *I'll drive* _____ this time.

6. A: Let's go out to dinner tonight.

   B: I can't. I don't have any money.

   A: That's okay. *I'll pay.*

7. A: I can't pay my phone bill. I'm not working now and don't have much money.

   B: Don't worry. *I'll pay it.* _____. You can pay me back next month.

8. A: The phone's ringing and I'm eating a sandwich. My mouth is full.

   B: Finish your lunch. *I'll answer the phone.*

1. Have students read the direction line. Ask: *Which future tense do we use offers of help?* (*will*) Go over the example.
2. Have students complete Exercise 9 individually. Check the answers as a class.
3. If needed, review grammar chart **7.1** on page 191.

🕐 To save class time, have students do half of the exercise in class and complete the other half for homework. Or assign the entire exercise for homework.

Expansion

Exercise 9 Create two rings of students. Have half of the students stand in an outer ring around the classroom. Have the other half stand in an inner ring, facing the outer ring. Instruct students to ask and answer the questions from Exercise 9. Call out *"turn"* every minute or so. Students in the inner ring should move one space clockwise. Students now ask and answer with their new partners. Have students ask questions in random order. Make sure students look at each other when they're speaking.

7.4 | Questions with *Be Going To*

1. Have students cover up grammar chart **7.4**. Say: *We're going to review statements, questions, and short answers.* Write on the board: *You are going to send a gift.* Ask a volunteer to write a *yes/no* question for this statement using the word *money* (e.g., *Are you going to send money?*). Ask another volunteer to give a negative short answer (e.g., *No, I'm not.*). Ask a volunteer to write a *wh-* question with *what* (e.g., *What are you going to send?*). Write *Towels* on the board. Then ask a volunteer to write a question using *who* and *money.* (e.g., *Who is going to send money?*).

2. Have students look at grammar chart **7.4** and ask them to compare their work on the board with the chart. Go over any errors. Review the other sentences.

3. Review negative questions and statements. Explain that the contraction for the negative statement can be written *you aren't* or *you're not,* but the contraction with the *wh-* question can only be written as *aren't you.*

EXERCISE 10

1. Tell students that this exercise is about them. Have students read the direction line. Ask: *What kind of question do you ask first?* (a *yes/no* question) Then ask: *What kind of questions do you ask next?* (a *wh-* question) Go over the example with the class. Model the example with a volunteer.

2. Have students complete the exercise in pairs.

3. If necessary, review grammar chart **7.4** on page 198.

7.4 | Questions with *Be Going To*

Compare Affirmative Questions and Statements

Wh-Word	Be	Subject	Be	Going To + Base Form	Complement	Short Answer
		You	are	going to send	a gift.	
	Are	you		going to send	money?	No, I'm not.
What	are	you		going to send?		Towels.
		Who	is	going to send	money?	Her uncle is.
		She	is	going to wear	a white dress.	
	Is	she		going to wear	white shoes?	Yes, she is.
		Who	is	going to wear	a tuxedo?	The groom is.

Compare Negative Questions and Statements

Wh-Word	Be + n't	Subject	Be + n't	Going To + Base Form	Complement
		You	aren't	going to attend	the wedding.
Why	aren't	you		going to attend?	

EXERCISE 10 ABOUT YOU Ask another student a *yes/no* question with *are you going to* about a time later today. Then ask a *wh-* question with the words in parentheses ( ) whenever possible.

EXAMPLE   listen to the radio (when)
A: Are you going to listen to the radio tonight?
B: Yes, I am.

A: When are you going to listen to the radio?
B: After dinner.

1. watch TV (what show)
   Are you going to watch TV tonight?
2. listen to the radio (when)
   Are you going to listen to the radio tonight?
3. read the newspaper (what newspaper)
   Are you going to read the newspaper tonight?
4. go shopping (why)
   Are you going to go shopping tonight?
5. take a shower (when)
   Are you going to take a shower tonight?
6. eat dinner (with whom) OR (who . . . with)
   Are you going to eat dinner tonight?

Expansion

Exercise 10 Create two rings of students. Have half of the students stand in an outer ring around the classroom. Have the other half stand in an inner ring, facing the outer ring. Instruct students to ask and answer the questions from Exercise 10. Call out *"turn"* every minute or so. Students in the inner ring should move one space clockwise. Students now ask and answer with their new partners. Have students ask questions in random order. Make sure students look at each other when they're speaking.

7. call someone (whom)
   Are you going to call someone tonight?
8. check your e-mail (when)
   Are you going to check your email tonight?
9. do your homework (when)
   Are you going to do your homework tonight?

EXERCISE **11**   Ask another student a *yes/no* question with *be going to* and the words given. Then ask a *wh-* question with the words in parentheses ( ) whenever possible.

EXAMPLE   study another English course after this one (which course)

A: Are you going to study another English course after this one?
B: Yes, I am.

A: Which course are you going to study?
B: I'm going to study level 4.

1. stay in this city (why)
   Are you going to stay in this city?
2. study something new (what)
   Are you going to study something new?
3. look for a job (when)
   Are you going to look for a job?
4. get an A in this course (what grade)
   Are you going to get an A in this course?
5. buy a computer (why) (what kind)
   Are you going to buy a computer?
6. visit other American cities (which cities)
   Are you going to visit other American cities?
7. transfer to another school (why) (which school)
   Are you going to transfer to another school?

7.5 | Questions with *Will*

Compare Affirmative Questions and Statements

Wh-Word	Will	Subject	Will	Base Form	Complement	Short Answer
		The wedding	will	begin	soon.	
	Will	the wedding		begin	in 15 minutes?	Yes, it will.
When	will	the wedding		begin?		At 8 o'clock.
		Who	will	begin	the wedding?	The groom will.

Compare Negative Questions and Statements

Wh-Word	Won't	Subject	Won't	Base Form	Complement
		The groom	won't	pay	for the whole wedding.
Why	won't	the groom		pay	for the whole wedding?

Future Tenses—*Will* and *Be Going To*; Comparison of Tenses   **199**

---

1. Tell students that this exercise is about what they're going to do after this course ends. Have students read the direction line. Ask: *What kind of question do you write first?* (a *yes/no* question) Then ask: *What kind of question do you write?* (a *wh-* question) Go over the example with the class. Model the example with a volunteer.
2. Have students complete the exercise in pairs.
3. If necessary, review grammar chart **7.4** on page 198.

7.5 | Questions with *Will*

1. Have students cover up grammar chart **7.5**. Write on the board: *The wedding will begin soon.* Ask a volunteer to write a *yes/no* question for this statement using the words *in fifteen minutes* (e.g., *Will the wedding begin in 15 minutes?*). Ask another volunteer to give an affirmative short answer (e.g., *Yes, it will.*). Ask a volunteer to write a *wh-* question using *when* (e.g., *When will the wedding begin?*). Write *At 8 o'clock* on the board. Then write the last question and answer on the board (*Who will begin the wedding? The groom.*).
2. Have students look at grammar chart **7.5** and ask them to compare their work on the board with the chart. Go over any errors.
3. Review negative questions and statements. Remind students that the contraction for *will not* is *won't*.

Expansion

Exercise 11 Have students write five more *yes/no* questions to ask their partners. Wherever possible, they should also follow up with a *wh-* question.

EXERCISE 12

1. Have students read the direction line. Go over the example in the book. Explain that sometimes they will have to write the pronoun in the blanks as well. Remind students to use contractions wherever possible. Complete conversation #1 with the class.

2. Have students complete the exercise individually. Then have students practice the conversations in pairs. Circulate to observe pair work. Give help as needed.

3. If necessary, review grammar chart **7.5** on page 199.

EXERCISE **12**   Fill in the blanks with the correct form of the verb in ( ).
Use *will* for the future.

1. **A:** I don't have time to shop for a wedding gift, and the wedding is to-morrow.

   B: What ___will you do___ ?
   (example: you/do)

   A: I ___'ll probably send___ a check.
   (probably/send)

2. **A:** What time ___will the wedding start___ ?
   (the wedding/start)

   B: The invitation says it ___will start___ at 5:30 p.m., but
   (start)

   usually weddings don't start exactly on time.

3. **A:** Where ___will the wedding be___ ?
   (the wedding/be)

   B: It'll be in a hotel.

4. **A:** What ___will you wear___ to the wedding?
   (you/wear)

   B: I don't know. I ___'ll probably wear___ my blue suit. Oh. I just
   (probably/wear)

   remembered my blue suit is dirty. I ___won't have___ time
   (not/have)

   to take it to the cleaners. I ___'ll have to___ wear my gray suit.
   (have to)

5. **A:** How many people ___will attend___ the wedding?
   (attend)

   B: About 200 people ___will attend___ the wedding.
   (attend)

6. **A:** What kind of food ___will they serve___ at the reception?
   (they/serve)

   B: There ___will be___ a choice of chicken or fish.
   (be)

7. **A:** Do you think the bride and groom ___will be___ happy
   (be)

   together?

   B: Yes, I think they ___will___ . They love each other
   (be)

   very much.

---

8. A: I'm going to a store to check the wedding registry.

   B: I _____ 'll go _____ with you.

(go)

   A: It's late. The store __ will probably be __ closed by the time we

(probably/ be)

   arrive. I _____ 'll go _____ tomorrow morning instead.

(go)

9. A: How long _____ will the wedding last _____?

(the wedding/last)

   B: The ceremony __ will probably last __ about a half hour. Then

(probably/last)

   there's a dinner. People __ will probably stay __ for hours after

(probably/stay)

   the dinner to dance.

10. A: _____ Will the bride and groom leave _____ for their

(the bride and groom/leave)

    honeymoon immediately?

    B: Probably not. They _____ 'll be _____ tired after the

(be)

    wedding. They _____ 'll probably leave _____ the next day.

(probably/leave)

EXERCISE **13** In this conversation, fill in the blanks using the words in
parentheses ( ). Choose *will* or *be going to* for the future tenses.
In some cases, both answers are possible.

A: I'm so excited. My sister __ is going to get __ married

(example: get)

next year.

B: Why are *you* so excited?

A: I'm going to be a bridesmaid.

B: How many bridesmaids __ is she going to have/will she have __?

(1 she/have)

A: Three.

B: What kind of dresses __ are the bridesmaids going to wear/will the bridesmaids wear __?

(2 the bridesmaids/wear)

A: All the bridesmaids __ are going to wear/will wear __ blue dresses,

(3 wear)

but each one __ is going to choose/will choose __ her own style.

(4 choose)

B: __ Is the wedding going to be/Will the wedding be __ in your church?

(5 the wedding/be)

Future Tenses—*Will* and *Be Going To*; Comparison of Tenses **201**

🎧 *CD 1, Track 33*

1. Have students read the direction
line. Say: *In this exercise, you're
going to choose* be going to *or* will.
Review briefly when to use *will*
(promises, no previous plans, and
offers of help) and when to use *be
going to* (previous plans). Remind
students that in all other cases, they
can use both *will* or *be going to*
(predictions and simple facts about
the future). Give examples
whenever necessary. Go over the
example in the book.

2. Have students complete Exercise
13 individually. Point out the photo
of the bride with her bridesmaids.
Check answers as a class.

3. Have student practice the
conversation in pairs.

4. If necessary, review grammar chart
7.3 on page 193.

🕐 To save class time, have
students do half of the exercise
in class and complete the other half for
homework. Or assign the entire
exercise for homework.

Exercise 13 Variation

To provide practice with listening skills, have students close their books and listen to the
audio. Repeat the audio as needed. Ask comprehension questions, such as: *Who is getting
married next year?* (person A's sister) *How many bridesmaids is her sister going to have?*
(three) *What are the bridesmaids going to wear?* (blue dresses) Then have students open
their books and complete Exercise 13.

A: No, it isn't. It's going to be outdoors, in a garden. After that, there

_____is going to be/there will be_____ a dinner at a restaurant.
                                  (6 be)

B: Why _____are they going to wait_____ to get married?
                        (7 they/wait)

A: They're both in college now, and they want to get married after they
   finish college.

B: Where _____are they going to live/will they live_____ after they get married?
                              (8 live)

A: Probably here for a while. But then they _____'re going to look/will look_____
                                                            (9 look)

   for jobs in the Boston area.

B: How many people _____are they going to invite_____ to the wedding?
                                  (10 invite)

A: It _____'s going to be/will be_____ a big wedding because we have a large
          (11 be)

   family, and so does her boyfriend, Joe. They _____'re going to invite_____
                                                            (12 invite)

   about 400 people.

B: Wow! The wedding _____is going to be/will be_____ expensive.
                                  (13 be)

   Who _____'s going to pay_____ for it?
                    (14 pay)

A: Our parents and Joe's parents _____are going to pay_____. They
                                            (15 pay —)

   _____are going to split/will split_____ the cost 50/50. A lot of relatives
                  (15 split)

   and friends _____are going to come/will come_____ here from out of town.
                              (16 come)

B: Where _____are they going to stay/will they stay_____?
                        (17 they/stay)

A: In hotels.

B: It's _____going to be_____ expensive for the guests too. They
              (18 be)

   _____are going to have to/will have to_____ pay for their flights,
                  (19 have to)

   hotels, and a wedding gift.

A: I know. But they want to come. Of course, some people

   _____won't come_____ because it _____'ll be_____ too
          (20 not come)   (21 be)

   expensive for them.

Expansion

Exercise 13 Have students talk about the wedding that is being discussed in the conversation. Ask questions such as: *Do you think this is a typical wedding? Why? Have you been to a wedding like this in the U.S.? What was it like? Was is very different from weddings in your country? If so, why? Do you think this wedding is big? Expensive?* Have students discuss the wedding in groups. Then have groups report their impressions to the class.

7.6 | Future Tense + Time/*If* Clause[3]

Time or *If* Clause (Simple Present Tense)	Main Clause (Future Tense)	Explanation
After they **graduate,**	they **are going to work.**	The sentences on the left have two clauses, a time or *if* clause and a main clause.
Before they **get** married,	they **are going to send** out invitations.	
When they **return** from the honeymoon,	they **will send** thank-you cards.	We use the *future* only in the main clause; we use the *simple present tense* in the time/*if* clause.
If their grandparents **come** from out of town,	they **will pay** for their hotel.	

Main Clause (Future Tense)	Time or *If* Clause (Simple Present Tense)	Explanation
They **are going to work**	after they **graduate.**	We can put the main clause before the time/*if* clause.
Their grandparents **will stay** in a hotel	if they **come.**	

Punctuation Note:

If the time/*if* clause comes before the main clause, we use a comma to separate the two parts of the sentence. If the main clause comes first, we don't use a comma.

Compare:

If I get an invitation, I'll go to the wedding.

I'll go to the wedding if I get an invitation.

Usage Note:

There is a proverb that means "I will decide when I need to decide." The proverb is:

I'll cross that bridge when I get to it.

---

[3] A clause is a group of words that has a subject and a verb. Some sentences have more than one clause.

7.6 | Future Tense + Time/*If* Clause

1. Have students go back to the reading on page 190. Read through the second paragraph and draw students' attention to the time clauses (e.g., *Before their wedding, they will register for gifts.*). Point out that these sentences are made up of two clauses: the time clause and the main clause. Have students underline the time clause and double underline the main clause. Ask: *What tense is used in the time clause?* (simple present) *What tense is used in the main clause?* (future)

2. Have students look at grammar chart **7.6.** Review all of the examples and explanations. Ask students if they know the meaning of *if.* Tell students that *if* creates a condition. Action *X* will happen if action *Y* happens.

3. Direct students to the Punctuation Note. Point out that the main clause can come before or after the time/*if* clause. Explain that when the time/*if* clause goes first, they must use a comma. Go over the examples.

4. Go over the meaning of the proverb. If possible, demonstrate the use of the proverb by explaining a difficult decision you will need to make in the future.

EXERCISE 14

1. Have students read the direction line. Point out that this exercise is about an old fable. Briefly introduce the fable. Then ask a volunteer to review time/*if* clauses briefly. (The verb in the time/*if* clause is always in the simple present tense. The verb in the main clause is in the future.) Go over the example in the book.

2. Have students complete the exercise individually. Point out the picture of the young lady carrying a pail of milk. Go over the answers with the class.

3. If necessary, review grammar chart **7.3** on page 193.

EXERCISE 15

1. Tell students that this exercise is about future plans. Go over the examples in the book. Tell students that they can use *be going to* if they have a plan, or *will* if they did not have a plan and are deciding what to do now. Model the exercise with your own information.

2. Have students complete Exercise 15 individually. Then have students compare answers with a partner. Circulate to observe pair work. Give help as needed.

3. If necessary, review grammar chart **7.6** on page 203.

⏱ To save class time, have students do half of the exercise in class and complete the other half for homework. Or assign the entire exercise for homework.

EXERCISE 14   This is an old fable.[4] It's the story of a young lady. She is carrying a pail of milk to the market. As she walks there, she thinks about what she will do with the money that the milk will bring. Fill in the blanks with the correct form of the verb to complete this story.

EXAMPLE   When I _____*sell*_____ this milk, I _____*will buy*_____ some eggs.
(sell)   (buy)

1. When the eggs _____*hatch*_____, I _____*'ll have*_____
(hatch)   (have)
many chickens.

2. I _____*'ll sell*_____ the chickens when they _____*'re*_____
(sell)   (be)
big.

3. When I _____*sell*_____ the chickens, I _____*'ll have*_____
(sell)   (have)
money to buy a pretty new dress.

4. I _____*'ll go*_____ to a party when I _____*have*_____
(go)   (have)
my new dress.

5. All the young men _____*will notice*_____ me when I
(notice)
_____*wear*_____ the dress.
(wear)

6. When the men _____*see*_____ how pretty I am, they
(see)
_____*will want*_____ to marry me.
(want)

Suddenly the young woman drops the milk pail and all the milk spills.
What lesson does this story try to teach us?

EXERCISE 15   ABOUT YOU Complete each statement.

EXAMPLES   When this class is over, _____*I'll go home.*_____
When this class is over, _____*I'm going to get something to eat.*_____

1. When this semester is over, _____**Answers will vary.**_____
2. When this class is over, _____
3. When I get home today, _____
4. When I graduate (or finish my courses at this school), _____
_____

[4] A *fable* is an old story. It usually teaches us a lesson, called a moral.

Expansion

Exercise 14 Discuss the fable. Ask students if they've ever heard this story before or if their culture has a similar fable or story. Ask volunteers to tell the rest of the class their fable.

Culture Note

The moral of this famous fable is "Don't count your chickens before they are hatched."

---

5. When I return to my country / become a citizen, _____

6. When I retire, _____

7. When I speak English better, _____

EXERCISE 16 ABOUT YOU Complete each statement.

EXAMPLES If I drink too much coffee, ___*I won't sleep tonight.*___

If I drink too much coffee, ___*I'm going to feel nervous.*___

1. If I practice English, ___**Answers will vary.**___

2. If I don't study, _____

3. If I don't pay my rent, _____

4. If I pass this course, _____

5. If we have a test next week, _____

6. If the teacher is absent tomorrow, _____

7. If I find a good job, _____

EXERCISE 17 On the first day of class, a teacher is explaining the course to the students. Fill in the blanks to complete this conversation between a teacher (T) and her students (S).

T: In this course, you ___*are going to study*___ English grammar. You
  _____(example: study)_____

  ___*are going to write*___ a few short compositions. Tomorrow,
  _____(1 write)_____

  I ___*'m going to give*___ you a list of assignments. Do you
  _____(2 give)_____

  have any questions about this course?

S: Yes. How many tests ___*will we have*___ ?
  _____(3 have)_____

T: You will have 14 tests, one for each lesson in the book. If you're

  absent from a test, you can make it up.[5] If you ___*don't take*___
  _____(4 not take)_____

  the test, you ___*'ll get*___ an F on that test.
  _____(5 get)_____

S: ___*Will you tell*___ us about the tests ahead of time?
  _____(6 tell)_____

T: Oh, yes. I'll always tell you about a test a few days before.

[5] If you are absent on the day of a test, the teacher expects you to take it at a later time.

Future Tenses—*Will* and *Be Going To*; Comparison of Tenses   **205**

Expansion

Exercise 15 Take a quick class survey. What are everyone's plans?

Exercise 17 Variation

To provide practice with listening skills, have students close their books and listen to the audio. Repeat the audio as needed. Ask comprehension questions, such as: *What are the students going to study in this course?* (English grammar) *What are they going to write?* (a few short compositions) *What is the teacher going to give the students tomorrow?* (a list of assignments) Then have students open their books and complete Exercise 17.

EXERCISE 16

1. Remind students that *if* introduces a condition. Go over the examples in the book. Model the exercise with your own information.

2. Have students complete Exercise 16 individually. Then have students compare answers with a partner. Circulate to observe pair work. Give help as needed.

3. If necessary, review grammar chart **7.6** on page 203.

To save class time, have students do half of the exercise in class and complete the other half for homework. Or assign the entire exercise for homework.

EXERCISE 17

CD 1, Track 34

1. Tell students that this exercise is a conversation between a teacher and students on the first day of class. Have students read the direction line. Say: *In this exercise, you're going to choose to use* be going to *or* will. Review briefly when to use *will* (promises, no previous plans, offers of help) and when to use *be going to* (previous plans). Remind students that in all other cases, they can use both *will* or *be going to* (predictions and simple facts about the future). Give examples whenever necessary. Go over the example in the book.

2. Have students complete Exercise 17 individually. Then check answers as a class.

3. Have students practice the conversation in pairs. Circulate to observe pair work. Give help as needed.

4. If necessary, review grammar charts **7.3** on page 193, **7.4** on page 198, **7.5** on page 199, and **7.6** on page 203.

To save class time, have students do half of the exercise in class and complete the other half for homework. Or assign the entire exercise for homework.

1. Have students read the direction line. Ask: *Do we use* will *or* be going to *when we're asking about simple facts in the future?* (both *will* and *be going to*) Go over the examples in the book.
2. Have students write the questions individually on pieces of paper. Then read the questions out loud and answer them in front of the class.
3. If necessary, review grammar charts **7.4** on page 198, and **7.5** on page 199.

🎧 *CD 2, Track 1*

1. Have students read the direction line. Explain that this is a conversation between a young woman who is going to leave her country to go to the U.S. and her friend. Say: *In this exercise, you're going to choose to use* be going to *or* will. Review briefly when to use *will* (promises, no previous plans, offers of help) and when to use *be going to* (previous plans). Remind students that in all other cases, they can use both *will* or *be going to* (predictions and simple facts about the future). Give examples whenever necessary. Go over the example in the book.
2. Have students complete Exercise 19 individually. Point out the map of the U.S. on page 207 and the location of Ann Arbor, Michigan.
3. Then have students practice the conversation in pairs. Circulate to observe pair work. Give help as needed.
4. If necessary, review grammar charts **7.3** on page 193, **7.4** on page 198, **7.5** on page 199, and **7.6** on page 203.

🕐 To save class time, have students do half of the exercise in class and complete the other half for homework. Or assign the entire exercise for homework.

S: When ___are you going to give/will you give___ the midterm exam?
   (7 give)

T: I'm going to give you the midterm exam in April.

S: ___Will it be___ very hard?
   (8 be)

T: If you ___study___, it won't be hard.
   (9 study)

S: What ___will we study___ in this course?
   (10 study)

T: You'll study verb tenses, count and noncount nouns, and comparison of adjectives.

S: ___Will we finish___ everything in this book?
   (11 finish)

T: Yes, I think we'll finish everything.

S: ___When will the semester be___ over?
   (12 be)

T: The semester will be over[6] in June. Tomorrow I ___'m going to give/___
   (13 give)
   ___will give___ you a course outline with all this information.

EXERCISE **18** Write two questions to ask your teacher about this course.

EXAMPLES *Will there be a test on this lesson?*

When will you give us the next test?

Answers will vary.

EXERCISE **19** A young woman (A) is going to leave her country to go to the U.S. Her friend (B) is asking her questions. Fill in the blanks to complete this conversation.

A: I'm so happy! I'm going to the U.S.

B: When ___are you going to leave?___
   (example: leave)

A: I'm going to leave next month.

B: So soon? ___Are you going to buy/Will you buy___ anything
   (1 buy)
   before you ___leave___?
   (2 leave)

[6] To *be over* means to be finished.

Exercise 19 Variation

To provide practice with listening skills, have students close their books and listen to the audio. Repeat the audio as needed. Ask comprehension questions, such as: *When is the young woman going to leave for the U.S.?* (next month) *Why is she going to buy warm clothes?* (because winter in Ann Arbor, Michigan, is very cold) *Does she know where she's going to live?* (No, she's not sure.) Then have students open their books and complete Exercise 19.

A: Yes. I'm going to buy warm clothes for the winter. I hear the winter there is very cold.

B: Where _____ are you going to be/will you be _____ ?
(3 be)

A: I'll be in Ann Arbor, Michigan.

B: Where _____ are you going to live/will you live _____ ?
(4 live)

A: I'm not sure. When I _____ get _____ there,
(5 get)

I _____ 'll decide _____ where to live.
(6 decide)

B: _____ Are you going to work/Will you work _____ in the U.S.?
(7 work)

A: No, I'm not going to work. I have a scholarship. I'm going to study at the University of Michigan.

B: What _____ are you going to study/will you study _____ ?
(8 study)

A: I'm going to study to be a computer analyst.

B: When _____ are you going to return/will you return _____ to our country?
(9 return)

A: I _____ 'm going to return/will return _____ when I _____ graduate _____ .
(10 return)   (11 graduate)

B: When _____ are you going to graduate/will you graduate _____ ?
(12 you/graduate)

A: In four years.

B: That's a long time! _____ Will you miss _____ me?
(13 miss)

A: Of course, I'll miss you.

B: _____ Will you write _____ to me?
(14 write)

A: Of course. I _____ 'll write _____ to you when I _____ find _____
(15 write)   (16 find)

a place to live.

Ann Arbor, Michigan

Expansion

Exercise 19 Have students work in pairs to write a conversation similar to the one in Exercise 19. Tell students to use the conversation in Exercise 19 as a model, but to make the information true for them, if possible. Ask volunteers to role-play their conversation in front of the class.

EXERCISE 20

🎧 **CD 1, Track 36**

1. Have students read the direction line. Explain that this is a conversation between a young Korean woman who is getting married and her friends. Say: *In this exercise, you're going to choose to use* be going to *or* will. *Remind students that in some cases, they can use both* will *or* be going to *(predictions and simple facts about the future). Go over the example in the book.*

2. Have students complete Exercise 20 individually. Point out the photo of a Korean bride in a traditional wedding dress. Check answers as a class.

3. Have students practice the conversation in pairs. Circulate to observe pair work. Give help as needed.

4. If necessary, review grammar charts **7.3** on page 193, **7.4** on page 198, **7.5** on page 199, and **7.6** on page 203.

🕐 To save class time, have students do half of the exercise in class and complete the other half for homework. Or assign the entire exercise for homework.

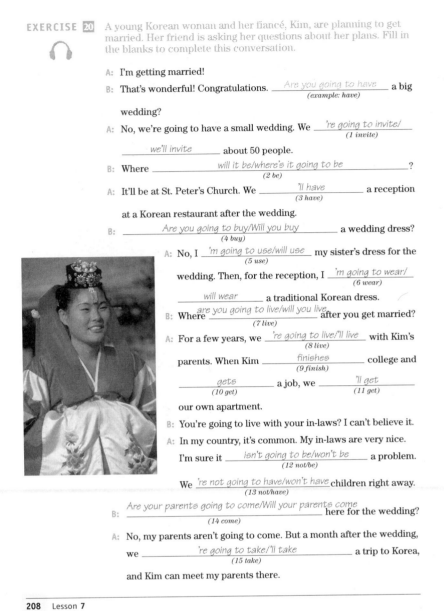

EXERCISE **20**   A young Korean woman and her fiancé, Kim, are planning to get married. Her friend is asking her questions about her plans. Fill in the blanks to complete this conversation.

A: I'm getting married!

B: That's wonderful! Congratulations. __*Are you going to have*__ a big
   (example: have)
   wedding?

A: No, we're going to have a small wedding. We __*'re going to invite/*__
   (1 invite)
   __*we'll invite*__ about 50 people.

B: Where __*will it be/where's it going to be*__?
   (2 be)

A: It'll be at St. Peter's Church. We __*'ll have*__ a reception
   (3 have)
   at a Korean restaurant after the wedding.

B: __*Are you going to buy/Will you buy*__ a wedding dress?
   (4 buy)

A: No, I __*'m going to use/will use*__ my sister's dress for the
   (5 use)
   wedding. Then, for the reception, I __*'m going to wear/*__
   (6 wear)
   __*will wear*__ a traditional Korean dress.

B: Where __*are you going to live/will you live*__ after you get married?
   (7 live)

A: For a few years, we __*'re going to live/'ll live*__ with Kim's
   (8 live)
   parents. When Kim __*finishes*__ college and
   (9 finish)
   __*gets*__ a job, we __*'ll get*__
   (10 get)   *(11 get)*
   our own apartment.

B: You're going to live with your in-laws? I can't believe it.

A: In my country, it's common. My in-laws are very nice.
   I'm sure it __*isn't going to be/won't be*__ a problem.
   (12 not-be)
   We __*'re not going to have/won't have*__ children right away.
   (13 not-have)

B: __*Are your parents going to come/Will your parents come*__ here for the wedding?
   (14 come)

A: No, my parents aren't going to come. But a month after the wedding,
   we __*'re going to take/'ll take*__ a trip to Korea,
   (15 take)
   and Kim can meet my parents there.

Exercise 20 Variation

To provide practice with listening skills, have students close their books and listen to the audio. Repeat the audio as needed. Ask comprehension questions, such as: *Is the Korean woman going to have a big wedding or a small wedding?* (a small wedding) *How many people is she going to invite?* (about 50) *Where will the wedding be?* (at St. Peter's Church) Then have students open their books and complete Exercise 20.

Expansion

Photo Have students discuss wedding attire. Ask students to look at the photo on page 208. Say: *This is a traditional Korean wedding dress. The photo on page 189 shows a couple in traditional Western wedding attire. What is traditional for brides and grooms to wear in your countries?*

B: _____When are you going to get/When will you get_____ married?
     (16 get)

A: On May 15. I hope you'll be able to attend. We _____'ll send_____
                                                       (17 send)
   you an invitation.

B: I _____'ll be_____ glad to attend.
        (18 be)

JASON AND KATIE—STARTING A MARRIED LIFE

Before You Read

1. Do you think life is hard for newlyweds? In what way?
2. In your community, do parents help their children after they get married?

Read the following article. Pay special attention to verb tenses: simple present, present continuous, and future.

Jason and Katie are newlyweds. The wedding is over, the honeymoon was great, the gifts are opened, and their life as a married couple **is beginning.** They **are learning** that they have many responsibilities as a married couple.

Katie **works** as a nurse full-time. She **doesn't work** in a hospital. She **goes** to people's homes and **helps** them there. Jason **isn't working** now. He's still **attending** college. He's in his last year. He's **studying** to be a lawyer. After classes every day, he **studies** at home or **goes** to the law library at his college. He's **going to graduate** next June. When he **graduates,** he **will have** to take a special exam for lawyers. If he **passes** it, he'**ll get** a good job and **make**

(continued)

Future Tenses—*Will* and *Be Going To*; Comparison of Tenses   **209**

Reading Variation

To practice listening skills, have students first listen to the audio alone. Ask a few comprehension questions. Repeat the audio if necessary. Then have students open their books and read along as they listen to the audio.

Reading Glossary

attend: to be present at
loan: a sum of money borrowed at a rate of interest
newlyweds: people who have just been married
suburb: the general term for an area outside a big city

Jason and Katie— Starting a Married Life (Reading)

1. Have students look at the photo. Ask: *Who are the people?* (a young couple, newlyweds) *Do you think they were married a long time ago or recently?* (recently) *Do they look happy?* (yes)
2. Have students look at the title of the reading. Ask: *What is the reading about?* Have students use the title and the photo to make predictions.
3. Preteach any vocabulary words students may not know such as *newlyweds, attend, loan,* and *suburb.*

BEFORE YOU READ

1. Have students discuss the questions in pairs. Try to pair students of different cultures together.
2. Ask for a few volunteers to share their answers with the class.

🕐 To save class time, skip "Before You Read" or have students prepare answers for homework ahead of time.

Reading 🎧 *CD 1, Track 37*

1. Have students read the reading silently. Tell them to pay special attention to verb tenses: simple present, present continuous, and future. Then play the audio and have students read along.
2. Check students' comprehension. Ask questions such as: *Does Katie work?* (Yes. She's a nurse.) *What does Jason do?* (He's a law student.) *When is he going to graduate?* (next June) *When are they thinking about having children?* (in the future; after they are financially stable)

🕐 To save class time, have students do the reading for homework ahead of time.

7.7 | Comparison of Tenses

1. Have students go back to the reading on pages 209–210. Ask students to find one example for each tense. Say: *Underline the simple present tense, double underline the present continuous, and circle the future tense.* Ask volunteers to write examples of each tense on the board.

2. Have students look at grammar chart **7.7**. Ask students to compare their work on the board with the chart. Review all of the examples and explanations of uses.

good money. But when he **starts** to work, he**'ll have** to pay back student loans. For now, they**'re** both **living** on Katie's salary.

Katie and Jason **are saving** money little by little. They**'re planning** to buy a house in a suburb some day. They **are** also **thinking** about having two children in the future. But they want to be financially stable before they **have** children. Their parents sometimes **offer** to help them, but they **don't want** to depend on their parents. Because Jason is so busy with his studies and Katie is so busy with her job, they rarely **go** out. Staying at home **helps** them save money.

7.7 | Comparison of Tenses

Uses

Examples	Explanation
a. Katie **works** as a nurse. Jason **studies** law. Lawyers **make** a lot of money in the U.S. b. Grown children **don't like** to depend on their parents. c. Jason **goes** to the library almost every day. d. Jason and Katie **have** a lot of responsibilities now. e. When Jason **graduates,** he will look for a job.	Use the **simple present tense:** a. with facts b. with customs c. with habits and regular activities d. with nonaction verbs e. in a time clause or an *if* clause when talking about the future
a. I **am reviewing** verb tenses now. b. Jason and Katie **are saving** money to buy a house. They **are planning** to move to a suburb.	Use the **present continuous tense:** a. with an action in progress now, at this moment b. with a long-term action that is in progress; it may not be happening at this exact moment
a. Katie thinks Jason **will be** a good lawyer. b. The law exam **will be** in March. c. "I**'ll always** love you, Katie," says Jason. d. "I**'ll help** you in the kitchen," says Katie. e. What will you do next year? I**'ll** cross that bridge when I get to it.	Use *will* for the **future:** a. with predictions b. with facts c. with promises d. with an offer to help e. when you don't have a previous plan; when you decide what to do at the time of speaking
a. I think they **are going to have** a wonderful life. b. For many years, they **are going to receive** bills for student loans. c. Jason **is going to look** for a job next year.	Use *be going to* for the **future:** a. with predictions b. with facts c. with plans

Grammar Variation

To review the uses of the verb tenses, have students cover up grammar chart **7.7**. Write each example sentence from the chart on a slip of paper, and pass them out to students. On the board, write the headings *simple present tense, present continuous tense, future with* will, and *future with* be going to. Have students read their sentences, decide the tense of the sentence, and write the sentence under the proper heading. Then write the list of explanations (e.g., *with facts, with customs,* etc.) from chart **7.7** next to the sentences on the board. Have students match the example sentences with the explanations.

Forms

Simple Present Tense	Present Continuous Tense
Jason **studies** law.	They **are saving** money to buy a house.
He **doesn't study** medicine.	They **aren't saving** to buy a new car.
Does he **study** every day?	**Are** they **saving** for a vacation?
Yes, he **does.**	No, they **aren't.**
Where **does** he **study?**	How **are** they **saving** money?
Why **doesn't** he **study** medicine?	Why **aren't** they **saving** to buy a car?
Who **studies** medicine?	Who **is saving** money?

Future with *Will*	Future with *Be Going To*
Jason **will graduate** next year.	They **are going to buy** a house.
He **won't graduate** this year.	They **aren't going to buy** a new car.
Will he **graduate** in January?	**Are** they **going to buy** a house in the city?
No, he **won't.**	No, they **aren't.**
When **will** he **graduate?**	Where **are** they **going to buy** a house?
Why **won't** he **graduate** in January?	Why **aren't** they **going to buy** a house in the city?
Who **will graduate** in January?	Who **is going to buy** a house?

EXERCISE **21** Fill in the blanks with the correct tense and form of the verb in parentheses ( ).

EXAMPLE   Jason _____is going to graduate_____ next year.
(graduate)

1. He _____'ll have_____ a good job when he _____graduates_____ .
(have)   (graduate)

2. He _____often studies_____ in the library.
(often/study)

3. Jason and Katie _____rarely go_____ out.
(rarely/go)

4. They _____'re saving_____ their money now.
(save)

5. They _____'re thinking_____ about buying a house.
(think)

6. They _____think_____ it's better to live in a suburb.
(think)

Future Tenses—*Will* and *Be Going To*; Comparison of Tenses   **211**

7.7 | Comparison of Tenses (*cont.*)

3. Review the forms of the verb tenses. Go over affirmative and negative statements, *yes/no* questions, short answers, and *wh-* questions (including negative questions and questions about the subject) for each tense. Have students provide other examples for each form.

EXERCISE 21

1. Tell students that this exercise is a review of all the tenses they've learned. Have students read the direction line. Go over the example.
2. Have students complete the rest of Exercise 21 individually. Then have students practice saying the sentences in pairs. Finally, check the answers as a class.
3. If necessary, review grammar chart **7.7** on pages 210–211.

EXERCISE 22

1. Have students read the direction line. Ask: *What do we replace the underlined words with?* (the negative) Go over the example in the book.
2. Have students complete the rest of Exercise 22 individually. Check the answers as a class.
3. If necessary, review grammar chart **7.7** on pages 210–211.

🕐 To save class time, have students do half of the exercise in class and complete the other half for homework. Or assign the entire exercise for homework.

EXERCISE 23

1. Have students read the direction line. Ask: *What do we write in the blanks?* (a question and a short answer) Go over the examples in the book. Point out the photo of a nurse.
2. Have students complete the exercise individually. Check the answers as a class.
3. If necessary, review grammar chart **7.7** on pages 210–211.

🕐 To save class time, have students do half of the exercise in class and complete the other half for homework. Or assign the entire exercise for homework.

EXERCISE 22   Fill in the blanks with the negative form of the underlined verb.

EXAMPLE   They are young. They ___aren't___ old.

1. They have an apartment now. They ___don't have___ a house.
2. They want children, but they ___don't want___ children right now.
3. Katie is working. Jason ___isn't working___ now. He's going to school.
4. They depend on each other. They ___don't depend___ on their parents.
5. Jason will graduate in June. He ___won't graduate___ in January.

EXERCISE 23   Read each statement. Then write a *yes/no* question with the words in parentheses ( ). Write a short answer.

EXAMPLE   Katie works as a nurse. (in a hospital)
Does she work in a hospital? No, she doesn't.

1. Jason is a student. (Katie)
   Is Katie a student? No, she's not.
2. Jason is attending college now. (Katie)
   Is Katie attending college now? No, she's not.
3. Jason will have a job. (a good job)
   Will Jason have a good job? Yes, he will.
4. They are thinking about buying a house. (about having children)
   Are they thinking about having children? Yes, they are.
5. They are going to have children. (five children)
   Are they going to have five children? No, they're not.

212   Lesson 7

Expansion

Exercise 23 Have each student write questions about their partner's life. Say: *Use the sentences in Exercise 23 as a model. Take turns asking and answering questions.*

EXERCISE **24** Read each statement. Then write a *wh-* question about the words in parentheses ( ). An answer is not necessary.

EXAMPLE Katie <u>works</u> as a nurse. (Where)
Where does she work as a nurse?

1. They <u>are saving</u> their money. (why)
Why are they saving their money?

2. They <u>don't want</u> to depend on their parents. (why)
Why don't they want to depend on their parents?

3. Jason <u>will make</u> good money. (when)
When will Jason make good money?

4. Jason <u>wants</u> to be a lawyer. (why)
Why does Jason want to be a lawyer?

5. Katie <u>isn't going to work</u> when her children are small. (why)
Why isn't Katie going to work when her children are small?

6. Jason <u>will pay</u> back his student loans. (when)
When will Jason pay back his student loans?

7. They <u>don't go</u> out very much. (why)
Why don't they go out very much?

8. Jason <u>is attending</u> college. (what college)
What college is Jason attending?

9. He <u>is going to graduate</u>. (when)
When is he going to graduate?

10. Jason <u>isn't earning</u> money now. (who)
Who isn't earning money now?

11. Someone <u>wants</u> to help them. (who)
Who wants to help them?

12. They <u>are learning</u> about responsibilities. (how)
How are they learning about responsibilities?

1. Have students read the direction line. Ask students what kind of questions they will be writing (*wh-* or information questions). Ask: *Are you going to write answers?* (no) Go over the example in the book.
2. Have students complete Exercise 24 individually. Check answers as a class.
3. If necessary, review grammar chart **7.7** on pages 210–211.

🕐 To save class time, have students do half of the exercise in class and complete the other half for homework. Or assign the entire exercise for homework.

Expansion

Exercise 24 Have students ask and answer the questions in Exercise 24 in pairs. Tell students that the questions are based on the reading on pages 209–210.

Summary of Lesson 7

1. **Future patterns with *will*** Have students practice forms of *will* in pairs. Say: *One student says, "Affirmative." The other student gives an example, such as, "Sally will wear a white wedding dress."* Instruct students to continue with the other forms of *will*. Then have pairs switch roles and repeat. If necessary, have students review:

   7.1 Future with *Will* (p. 191)
   7.5 Questions with *Will* (p. 199).

2. **Future patterns with *be going to*** Have students practice forms of *be going to* in pairs using the same suggestion above for *will*. If necessary, have students review:

   7.2 Future with *Be Going To* (p. 192)
   7.4 Questions with *Be Going To* (p. 198).

3. **Uses of *be going to* and *will*** Have students close their books. Then read an example from the chart. Have students identify the use. For example, say: *I will help you tomorrow.* Students say: *promise.* On the board, write: *promise.* If necessary, have students review:

   7.3 Choosing *Will* or *Be Going To* (p. 193).

4. **The simple present tense and the present continuous tense** Say examples of the uses of these two tenses. Have students identify the uses. Then have students practice the uses in pairs. (See suggestion for uses of *be going to* and *will* above.) If necessary, have students review:

   7.7 Comparison of Tenses (pp. 210–211).

Editing Advice

Have students close their books. Write the example sentences without editing marks or corrections on the board. For example:

1. *I will be go.*
2. *He will angry.*

Ask students to correct each sentence and provide a rule or explanation for each correction. Then have them turn to pages 214–215. Say: *Now compare your work with the Editing Advice in the book.*

SUMMARY OF LESSON 7

1. Future patterns with *will*

AFFIRMATIVE:	He **will buy** a car.
NEGATIVE:	He **won't buy** a used car.
YES/NO QUESTION:	**Will** he **buy** a new car?
SHORT ANSWER:	Yes, he **will.**
WH- QUESTION:	When **will** he **buy** a car?
NEGATIVE QUESTION:	Why **won't** he **buy** a used car?
SUBJECT QUESTION:	Who **will buy** a car?

2. Future patterns with *be going to*

AFFIRMATIVE:	He **is going to buy** a car.
NEGATIVE:	He **isn't going to buy** a used car.
YES/NO QUESTION:	**Is** he **going to buy** a new car?
SHORT ANSWER:	Yes, he **is.**
WH- QUESTION:	When **is** he **going to buy** a car?
NEGATIVE QUESTION:	Why **isn't** he **going to buy** a used car?
SUBJECT QUESTION:	Who **is going to buy** a car?

3. Uses of *be going to* and *will*

Use	Will	Be Going To
Prediction	You **will become** rich and famous.	You **are going to become** rich and famous.
Fact	The sun **will set** at 6:32 p.m. tonight	The sun **is going to set** at 6:32 p.m. tonight.
Plan		I'm **going to buy** a new car next month.
Promise	I **will help** you tomorrow.	
Offer to help	A: I can't open the door. B: **I'll open** it for you.	
No previous plan	A: I need to go to the store. B: **I'll go** with you.	

4. Review the simple present tense and the present continuous tense on page 181.

EDITING ADVICE

1. Don't use *be* with a future verb.

   I will be ~~go~~.

---

2. Use *be* in a future sentence that has no other verb.

           be
      He will ⌃ angry.
                  be
      There will ⌃ a party soon.

3. Don't combine *will* and *be going to*.

          is
      He ~~will~~ going to leave.   OR   *He will leave.*

4. Don't use the present tense for a future action.

                            'll
      I'm going home now. I ⌃ see you later.

5. Don't use the future tense after *when* or *if*.

      When they will go home, they will watch TV.

6. Use a form of *be* with *going to*.

         is
      He ⌃ going to help me.

7. Use *to* after *going*.

                to
      I'm going ⌃ study on Saturday.

8. Use correct word order for questions.

             aren't you
      Why you ~~aren't~~ going to eat lunch?

LESSON 7 TEST / REVIEW

PART **1**   Find the mistakes with the underlined words and correct them. Not every sentence has a mistake. If the sentence is correct, write C.

                    am
  EXAMPLES   I <u>will going to</u> buy a newspaper.
                If you're too tired to cook, <u>I'll do it.</u>   *C*

               will you
  1. When <u>you will</u> write your composition?

  2. We <u>will be buy</u> a new car soon.

Future Tenses—*Will* and *Be Going To*; Comparison of Tenses   **215**

Lesson 7 Test/Review

For additional practice, review, and assessment materials, see Assessment CD-ROM with *ExamView Pro*, *More Grammar Practice* Workbook 1, Interactive CD-ROM, and Web site http://elt.thomson.com/gic

1. Part 1 may be used as an in-class test to assess student performance, in addition to the Assessment CD-ROM with *ExamView Pro*. Have students read the direction line. Ask: *Does every sentence have a mistake?* (no) Go over the examples with the class.
2. Have students complete the assignment individually. Collect for assessment.
3. If necessary, have students review: **Lesson 7.**

Lesson Review

To use Part 1 as a review, assign it as homework or use it as an in-class activity to be completed individually or in pairs. Check answers and review errors as a class. Reteach grammar points that students haven't mastered. Then student learning may be assessed using a test generated from the Assessment CD-ROM with *ExamView Pro*.

Lesson 7   215

1. Part 2 may also be used as an in-class test to assess student performance, in addition to the Assessment CD-ROM with *ExamView Pro*. Have students read direction line. Remind students that in some cases, both *will* and *be going to* can be used. Go over the examples with the class.

2. Have students complete the exercise individually. Collect for assessment.

3. If necessary, have students review:
   7.3 Choosing *Will* or *Be Going To* (p. 193).

---

3. <u>Are</u>
   ~~Will~~ you going to eat dinner tonight?

4. When he <u>leaves</u>
   will ~~leave~~, he will turn off the light.

5. <u>I'm going</u>
   ~~I going~~ to take a vacation soon.

6. Is he going to use the computer? *C*

7. They're going <u>to</u> graduate soon.

8. I will <u>be</u> happy when I will <u>know</u> more English.

9. I'm going on vacation. I ~~will~~ <u>am</u> going to leave next Friday.

10. I'll write you a letter when I <u>arrive</u>. *C*

11. There will <u>be</u> a test soon.

12. I'll help you tomorrow. *C*

PART **2** Fill in the blanks with *will* or a form of *be + going to*. In some cases, both answers are possible.

EXAMPLES I believe the next president _____ <u>will OR is going to</u> _____ be a Democrat.

You can't move your piano alone. I _____ <u>'ll</u> _____ help you do it.

1. We _____ <u>want to</u> _____ eat in a new restaurant tomorrow. Do you want to go with us?

2. My friend is planning her wedding. She _____ <u>'s going to</u> _____ invite 150 guests to her wedding.

3. I promise I _____ <u>'ll</u> _____ clean my room tomorrow.

4. If you come to work late every day, you _____ <u>won't</u> _____ lose your job.

5. You don't know anything about computers? Come to my house. I _____ <u>'ll</u> _____ teach you.

6. The teacher _____ <u>will **or** is going to</u> _____ give a test next Friday.

7. Next week we _____ <u>will **or** are going to</u> _____ begin Lesson Eight.

8. Mother: Please call me when you arrive.
   Daughter: Don't worry, Mom. I _____ <u>'ll</u> _____ call you as soon as I arrive.

9. We're planning a picnic, but I think it _____ <u>will **or** is going to</u> _____ rain tomorrow.

216 Lesson 7

Lesson Review

To use Part 2 as a review, assign it as homework or use it as an in-class activity to be completed individually or in pairs. Check answers and review errors as a class. Reteach grammar points that students haven't mastered. Then student learning may be assessed using a test generated from the Assessment CD-ROM with *ExamView Pro*.

PART 3

PART **3** Fill in the blanks with the negative form of the underlined word.

EXAMPLE She <u>will get</u> married in church. She _____won't get_____
married at home.

1. She <u>is going to invite</u> all her relatives. She ___'s not going to invite___
all her friends.

2. He <u>will wear</u> a tuxedo. He _____won't wear_____
a suit.

3. I <u>am going to buy</u> a gift. I _____'m not going to buy_____
dishes.

4. <u>I'll help</u> you tomorrow. I _____won't help_____
you today.

5. You <u>are going to meet</u> my parents. You ___'re not going to meet___
my brothers.

PART **4** Read each statement. Then write a *yes/no* question about the
words in parentheses ( ). Write a short answer.

EXAMPLE She <u>will write</u> a letter. (a postcard) (no)
Will she write a postcard? No, she won't.

1. They <u>will send</u> a gift. (money) (no)
Will they send money? No, they won't.

2. You're <u>going to invite</u> your friends. (relatives) (yes)
Are you going to invite your relatives? Yes, I am.

3. They <u>are going to receive</u> gifts. (open the gifts) (yes)
Are they going to open the gifts? Yes, they are.

4. They <u>will need</u> things for their kitchen. (for their bathroom) (yes)
Will they need things for their bathroom? Yes, they will.

5. There <u>will be</u> a party after the wedding. (food at the party) (yes)
Will there be food at the party? Yes, there will.

PART **5** Read each statement. Then write a question with the words in
parentheses ( ). No answer is necessary.

EXAMPLE <u>I'm going to buy</u> something. (What)
What are you going to buy?

1. They <u>will use</u> the money. (How)
How will they use the money?

Future Tenses—*Will* and *Be Going To*; Comparison of Tenses **217**

Lesson Review

To use Parts 3, 4, and 5 as a review, assign them as homework or use them as in-class activities to be completed individually or in pairs. Check answers and review errors as a class. Reteach grammar points that students haven't mastered. Then student learning may be assessed using a test generated from the Assessment CD-ROM with *ExamView Pro*.

PART 3

1. Part 3 may also be used as an in-class test to assess student performance, in addition to the Assessment CD-ROM with *ExamView Pro*. Have students read the direction line. Ask: *What will you replace the underlined words with?* (the negative) Go over the example with the class.
2. Have students complete the exercise individually. Collect for assessment.
3. If necessary, have students review:
   7.1 Future with *Will* (p. 191)
   7.2 Future with *Be Going To* (p. 192).

PART 4

1. Part 4 may also be used as an in-class test to assess student performance, in addition to the Assessment CD-ROM with *ExamView Pro*. Have students read the direction line. Point out that students need to write a *yes/no* question as well as a short answer. Go over the example with the class.
2. Have students complete the exercise individually. Collect for assessment.
3. If necessary, have students review:
   7.4 Questions with *Be Going To* (p. 198)
   7.5 Questions with *Will* (p. 199).

PART 5

1. Part 5 may also be used as an in-class test to assess student performance, in addition to the Assessment CD-ROM with *ExamView Pro*. Have students read the direction line. Ask: *What kind of questions will you be writing?* (wh-questions) Remind students that an answer is not necessary. Go over the example with the class.
2. Have students complete the exercise individually. Collect for assessment.
3. If necessary, have students review:
   7.4 Questions with *Be Going To* (p. 198)
   7.5 Questions with *Will* (p. 199).

Test on Comparison of Tenses

1. Part 1 may be used as an in-class test to assess student performance, in addition to the Assessment CD-ROM with *ExamView Pro*. Have students read the direction line. Point out that this is a letter from Barbara to Judy. Go over the example with the class.
2. Have students complete the assignment individually. Collect for assessment.
3. If necessary, have students review:
   7.7   Comparison of Tenses (pp. 210–211).

---

2. I'm going to send a gift. (What kind of gift)

   What kind of gift are you going to send?

3. They will thank us. (When)

   When will they thank us?

4. They're going to get married. (Where)

   Where are they going to get married?

5. They aren't going to open the gifts at the wedding. (Why)

   Why aren't they going to open the gifts at the wedding?

6. There will be a lot of people at the wedding. (How many people)

   How many people will there be at the wedding?

7. Some people will give money. (Who)

   Who will give money?

TEST ON COMPARISON OF TENSES

PART **1**   Read the following letter. Fill in the blanks with the simple present, the present continuous, or the future tense.

Dear Judy,

Please excuse me for not writing sooner. I rarely _____*have*_____
(example: have)

time to sit and write a letter. My husband _____*'s working*_____ on his
(1 work)

car now, and the baby _____*'s sleeping*_____. So now I
(2 sleep)

_____*have*_____ a few free moments.
(3 have)

I _____*'m*_____ a student now. I _____*go*_____
(4 be)   (5 go)

to Kennedy College twice a week. The school _____*is*_____ a
(6 be)

few blocks from my house. I usually _____*walk*_____ to school,
(7 walk)

but sometimes I _____*drive*_____. My mother usually
(8 drive)

_____*watches*_____ the baby when I'm in school. This semester
(9 watch)

I _____*'m studying*_____ English and math. Next semester
(10 study)

I _____*'m going to take*_____ a computer course. I _____*think*_____
(11 take)   (12 think)

knowledge about computers _____*will help or is going to help*_____ me find a good job.
(13 help)

When the semester _____is_____ over, we _____'re going_____
(14 be)   (15 go)
to Canada for vacation. We _____'re going to visit_____ my husband's sister.
(16 visit)
She _____lives_____ in Montreal. We _____'re going to spend_____
(17 live)   (18 spend)
Christmas with her family this year. When we _____get_____ to
(19 get)
Montreal, I _____'ll send_____ you a postcard.
(20 send)
Please write and tell me what is happening in your life.
Love,
Barbara

PART 2 Fill in the blanks with the negative form of the underlined verb.

EXAMPLE Barbara's a student. She _____isn't_____ a teacher.

1. She's writing a letter now. She _____isn't writing_____ a composition.

2. Her mother sometimes takes care of her baby. Her father _____
   _____doesn't take_____ care of her baby.

3. They're going to visit her husband's sister. They _____aren't_____
   _____going to visit_____ her mother.

4. She goes to Kennedy College. She _____doesn't go_____ to Truman
   College.

5. Barbara and her husband live in the U.S. They _____don't live_____
   in Canada.

6. Her family will go to Montreal. They _____won't go_____ to
   Toronto.

PART 3 Read each statement. Then write a yes/no question with the words
in parentheses ( ). Write a short answer, based on the letter.

EXAMPLE Barbara's studying English. (math)
         Is she studying math? Yes, she is.

1. The baby's sleeping. (her husband)
   Is her husband sleeping? No, he isn't.

2. She sometimes drives to school. (ever/walk to school)
   Does she ever walk to school? Yes, she does.

3. She's going to take a computer course next semester. (a math class)
   Is she going to take a math class? No, she isn't.

PART 2

1. Part 2 may be used as an in-class test to assess student performance, in addition to the Assessment CD-ROM with *ExamView Pro*. Have students read the direction line. Ask: *What will you replace the underlined words with?* (the negative) Go over the example with the class.
2. Have students complete the assignment individually. Collect for assessment.
3. If necessary, have students review:
   7.7   Comparison of Tenses (pp. 210–211).

PART 3

1. Part 3 may be used as an in-class test to assess student performance, in addition to the Assessment CD-ROM with *ExamView Pro*. Tell students that this exercise is based on the letter in Part 1 on page 218. If necessary, review the letter before students begin Part 3.
2. Have students read the direction line. Instruct students to write a *yes/no* question, as well as a short answer that is based on the information in the letter. Go over the example with the class.
3. Have students complete the assignment individually. Collect for assessment.
4. If necessary, have students review:
   7.7   Comparison of Tenses (pp. 210–211).

PART 4

1. Part 4 may be used as an in-class test to assess student performance, in addition to the Assessment CD-ROM with *ExamView Pro*. Tell students that this exercise is based on the letter in Part 1 on page 218. If necessary, review the letter before students begin Part 4.
2. Have students read the direction line. Instruct students to write a *wh*-question, as well as a short answer that is based on the information in the letter. Go over the example with the class.
3. Have students complete the assignment individually. Collect for assessment.
4. If necessary, have students review:
   7.7 Comparison of Tenses (pp. 210–211).

4. She'll go to Canada. (Montreal)

   Is she going to go to Montreal? Yes, she is.

5. She's going to send Judy a postcard. (a letter)

   Is she going to send Judy a letter? No, she isn't.

6. She sometimes writes letters. (write a letter/now)

   Is she writing a letter now? Yes, she is.

7. Her sister-in-law lives in Canada. (in Toronto)

   Does her sister-in-law live in Toronto? No, she doesn't.

PART **4**   Read each statement. Then write a *wh*- question with the words in parentheses ( ). Write an answer, based on the letter.

EXAMPLE   She goes to college. (Where)

   A: *Where does she go to college?*

   B: *She goes to Kennedy College.*

1. Her baby's sleeping. (What/her husband/do)

   A: *What is her husband doing?*

   B: *He's working on his car.*

2. She's taking two courses this semester. (What courses)

   A: *What courses is she taking this semester?*

   B: *She's taking English and Math.*

3. Someone watches her baby. (Who)

   A: *Who is watching her baby?*

   B: *Her mother is watching her baby.*

4. She's going to take a course next semester. (What course)

   A: *What course is she going to take next semester?*

   B: *She's going to take a computer course next semester.*

5. They'll go on vacation for Christmas. (Where)

   A: *Where will they go on vacation for Christmas?*

   B: *They'll go to Canada on vacation for Christmas.*

6. Her husband's sister lives in another city. (Where/she)

   A: *Where does her husband's sister live?*

   B: *She lives in Montreal.*

7. She doesn't usually drive to school. (Why)

   A: *Why doesn't she usually drive to school?*

   B: *She usually walks to school.*

EXPANSION ACTIVITIES

Classroom Activities

1. Check (✓) the activities that you plan to do soon. Find a partner. Ask your partner for information about the items he or she checked off. Report something interesting to the class about your partner's plans.

   EXAMPLE ✓ move
   When are you going to move?
   Why are you going to move?
   Are your friends going to help you?
   Are you going to rent a truck?
   Where are you going to move to?

   a. _____ get married

   b. _____ go back to my country

   c. _____ spend a lot of money

   d. _____ write a letter

   e. _____ buy something (a computer, a DVD player, a TV, an answering machine, etc.)

   f. _____ go to a party

   g. _____ have a job interview

   h. _____ transfer to another college

   i. _____ become a citizen

   j. _____ eat in a restaurant

2. Role-play the following characters. Practice the future tense.

   a. Fortune-teller and young woman. The woman wants to know her future.

   b. Man proposing marriage to a woman. The man is making promises.

   c. Teenager and parents. The teenager wants to go to a party on Saturday night.

   d. Politician and voter. The politician wants votes.

   e. Landlord and a person who wants to rent an apartment. The person wants to know what the landlord will do to fix up the apartment.

Future Tenses—*Will* and *Be Going To*; Comparison of Tenses   **221**

Expansion Activities

These expansion activities provide opportunities for students to interact with one another and further develop their speaking and writing skills. Encourage students to use grammar from this Lesson whenever possible.

🕐 To save class time, assign parts of the activities as homework. Then use class time for interaction and communication. If students do not need additional speaking practice, some of the activities may be assigned as writing activities for homework, or skipped altogether.

CLASSROOM ACTIVITIES

1. Tell students that this activity is about future plans. Ask: *Do we use* will *or* be going to *when we talk about future plans?* (*be going to*) First have students check the activities they're going to do. Then put students in pairs to ask and answer questions.

2. Review the uses of the future tense for each item (a. prediction; b. promise; c. plan, promise; d. plan, promise; e. promise). Have students work in pairs to create dialogues. Then have volunteers role-play the dialogues in front of the class.

Classroom Activities Variation

Activity 2 Have students do a role-play of an interview between a news reporter and a famous person. The news reporter asks questions and takes notes. Then the reporter writes a news article on the interview. Have students switch roles and repeat.

CLASSROOM ACTIVITIES (*cont.*)

3. After students complete their charts, have students give their partners advice about their concerns. Say: *Listen to your friend's concerns about the future. Tell your friend what he/she should do. For example, if your friend is worried about money, help him/her think of ways to save money.*

4. After students have completed the activity, survey the class to find out the most popular choices for each situation. Then share with students the type of gifts that Americans would typically get.

TALK ABOUT IT

1. Model this activity by telling the class about gift-giving customs in the U.S. Use the occasions in Classroom Activity 4 for ideas.

2. Have students debate whether a man should support a woman or whether a woman should support a man. Divide the class into two teams. Tell each team to list five reasons supporting their views. Have each team present their arguments. Then give each team an opportunity to respond to the other team's arguments. At the end of the debate, survey the class to see which opinion is more popular.

OUTSIDE ACTIVITY

Tell students that they will be interviewing an American about his or her concerns for the future. Some students can report their interview to the class and others can choose to hand in a written report.

INTERNET ACTIVITY

Tell students: *You're going to find out about wedding or bridal registries on the Internet. Ask: What questions will you answer about the registry? (What kind of gifts can a couple register for? What are the prices?)*

---

3. What are your concerns and plans for the future? Write one or two sentences (statements or questions) for each of the categories in the box below. Then find a partner. Discuss your concerns and plans with your partner.

Job/Career	*Where will I work if I lose my present job?*
Money	
Learning English	
Home	
Family and children	
Health	
Fun and recreation	
Other	

4. Imagine that you are going to buy a gift for someone in the following circumstances. What gift would you buy? Find a partner and compare your list of gifts to your partner's list.

a. a friend in the hospital after surgery _____

b. a couple with a new baby _____

c. a nephew graduating from high school _____

d. a friend getting married for the second time _____

e. a friend moving into a new apartment _____

f. a family that invites you to dinner at their house _____

Talk About it

1. In a small group or with the entire class, talk about gift-giving customs in your native culture. What kind of gifts do people give for weddings? How much money do they spend? Do newlyweds open presents at the wedding? Do they send thank-you cards? What kind of gifts do people give for other occasions?

2. Once a couple marries, both people often work. Sometimes only the man or only the woman works. In your native culture, does a woman ever support a man financially? Discuss.

Outside Activity

Use the third classroom activity above to interview an American about his or her concerns about the future. What is he or she worried about?

Internet Activity

Find a bridal or wedding registry on the Internet. What kind of gifts can a couple register for? What are the prices?

 Additional Activities at http://elt.thomson.com/gic

222 Lesson **7**

Outside Activity Variation

As an alternative, you may invite a guest to your classroom (e.g., an administrator, a librarian, or a service worker at your school) and have students do a class interview. Students should prepare their interview questions ahead of time.

Expansion

Classroom Activities For Activity 3, have students write a future plan based on the advice they get from their partners. Remind them to use *be going to*.

Internet Activity Variation

1. For a more structured task, have students choose one store that offers a bridal registry. Tell them to choose ten items they want on their registry. Have them write down the name of the store, the URL of the store's Web site, the names of the items, the quantities desired, and the prices.

2. If students don't have Internet access, you may bring in department store or discount store flyers. In pairs, have students make a list of gifts they would like for their bridal registry. Have them include the quantity and the prices.

GRAMMAR
The Simple Past Tense

CONTEXT: Flying
The Wright Brothers—Men with a Vision
Charles Lindbergh and Amelia Earhart
Robert Goddard

223

Lesson | 8

Lesson Overview

GRAMMAR

Ask: *What did we study in Lesson 7?* (the future tenses: *will* and *be going to*) *What tense are we going to study in this lesson?* (the simple past tense) *Can anyone make a sentence in the simple past tense?* Have students give examples. Write them on the board.

CONTEXT

1. Ask: *What are we going to learn about in this lesson?* (flying) Activate students' prior knowledge. Ask: *Is anyone here familiar with the history of flying? Who invented the airplane?*
2. Have students share their knowledge and personal experiences. Ask: *What kinds of airplanes have you flown in? Has anyone here flown very small planes? Is anyone a pilot? How old were you when you first flew on a plane?*

Photo

1. Direct students' attention to the photo. Ask: *What is this a picture of?* (an early airplane)
2. Ask: *When do you think this photo was taken?*

🕐 To save class time, have students do the Test/Review at the end of the lesson, or administer a lesson test generated from the Assessment CD-ROM with *ExamView® Pro.* Skip sections of the lesson that students have already mastered. You may also assign some sections for self-study for extra credit.

Expansion

Theme The topic for this lesson can be enhanced with the following ideas:

1. Books with pictures of the Wright brothers, early airplanes, and famous aviators
2. Books with pictures of early space travel

The Wright Brothers— Men with a Vision (Reading)

1. Have students look at the photo. Ask: *Why are the Wright brothers famous?* (They invented the airplane.)
2. Have students look at the title of the reading. Ask: *What is the reading about? How do you know?* Have students use the title and photo to make predictions about the reading.
3. Preteach any vocabulary words students may not know, such as *glider, aspect, construct, design, crash, fail, fix, invent, investigate,* and *gather.*

BEFORE YOU READ

1. Have students discuss the questions in pairs.
2. Ask for a few volunteers to share their answers with the class.

🕐 To save class time, skip "Before You Read" or have students prepare answers for homework ahead of time.

Reading 🎧 *CD 2, Track 1*

1. Have students read the text silently. Tell them to pay special attention to the simple past tense verbs. Then play the audio and have students read along silently.
2. Check students' comprehension. Ask questions such as: *When did the Wright brothers first start thinking about flying?* (as young boys when they received a flying toy from their father) *When did they construct their first flying machine?* (in 1899) *Who was the pilot for their first flight?* (Orville Wright) *Who offered them a contract to build planes?* (President Theodore Roosevelt)

🕐 To save class time, have students do the reading for homework ahead of time.

THE WRIGHT BROTHERS—MEN WITH A VISION

Before You Read

1. Do you like to travel by airplane? Why or why not?
2. What are the names of some famous inventors?

Wilbur Wright, 1867–1912; Orville Wright, 1871–1948

 Read the following article. Pay special attention to simple past-tense verbs.

Over 100 years ago, people only **dreamed** about flying. The Wright brothers, Wilbur and Orville, **were** dreamers who **changed** the world.

Wilbur Wright **was** born in 1867 and Orville **was** born in 1871. In 1878, they **received** a paper flying toy from their father. They **started** to think about the possibility of flight. They **played** with kites and **studied** everything they could about glider planes.

When they were older, they **started** a bicycle business in Dayton, Ohio. They **used** the bicycle shop to design their airplanes. They **studied** three aspects of flying: lift, control, and power. In 1899, they **constructed** their first flying machine—a kite made of wood, wire, and cloth. It **had** no pilot.

224 Lesson **8**

Reading Variation

To practice listening skills, have students first listen to the audio alone. Ask a few comprehension questions. Repeat the audio if necessary. Then have students open their books and read along as they listen to the audio.

Reading Glossary

aspect: point of view, consideration
construct: to build; to put together piece by piece
crash: a violent hit against something, usually with damage; an accident, smashup
design: style, form
fail: to not succeed
fix: to repair something
gather: to meet
glider: a type of airplane that rides air currents without an engine
invent: to create something new
investigate: to look at something carefully; examine

Because of wind, it was difficult to control. They **continued** to study aerodynamics.[1] Finally Wilbur **designed** a small machine with a gasoline engine. Wilbur **tried** to fly the machine, but it **crashed.** They **fixed** it and **flew** it for the first time on December 17, 1903, with Orville as the pilot. The airplane **remained** in the air for twelve seconds. It **traveled** a distance of 120 feet. It **weighed** over 600 pounds. This historic flight **changed** the world. However, only four newspapers in the U.S. **reported** this historic moment.

The Wright brothers **offered** their invention to the U.S. government, but the government **rejected**[2] their offer at first. The government **didn't believe** that these men **invented** a flying machine. Finally, President Theodore Roosevelt **investigated** their claims and **offered** the inventors a contract to build airplanes for the U.S. Army.

December 17, 2003 **marked** 100 years of flight. There **was** a six-day celebration at Kitty Hawk, North Carolina, the location of the first flight. A crowd of 35,000 people **gathered** to see a replica[3] of the first plane fly. The cost to recreate the plane **was** $1.2 million. However, it **rained** hard that day and the plane **failed** to get off the ground.

You can now see the Wright brothers' original airplane in the Air and Space Museum in Washington, D.C.

Did You Know?
The Wright brothers never married. Their only love was aviation.

8.1 | The Simple Past Tense of Regular Verbs

1. Have students go back to the reading on pages 224 and 225. Say: *Find verbs in the past that end in -ed (dreamed, changed, received, started,* etc.). Write the verbs on the board. Then ask students to tell you the base form of the verbs. Write them next to the past tense (*dream, change, receive, start,* etc.).
2. Have students look at grammar chart **8.1**. Explain that to form the simple past of regular verbs, you add *-ed*. Review the examples in the chart.
3. Explain that verbs that come after *to* are in the base form, not the past, so their endings do not change. Explain the use of *ago*, which means *before now*.

8.1 | The Simple Past Tense of Regular Verbs

Examples	Explanation
The Wright brothers **started** a bicycle business in Ohio. They **dreamed** about flying. They **designed** an airplane. The president **offered** them a contract.	To form the simple past tense of regular verbs, we add *-ed* to the base form. Base Form — Past Form start — start**ed** dream — dream**ed** design — design**ed** offer — offer**ed** The past form is the same for all persons.
The Wright brothers **wanted** *to fly.* They **continued** *to study* about flying.	The verb after *to* does **not** use the past form.
The Wright brothers **invented** the airplane over 100 years **ago.** We **celebrated** the one-hundredth anniversary of flight a few years **ago.**	We often use *ago* in sentences about the past. *Ago* means *before now.*

[1] *Aerodynamics* is the branch of mechanics that deals with the motion of air and its effect on things.
[2] *Reject* means not accept.
[3] A replica is a copy of an original.

The Simple Past Tense   **225**

EXERCISE 1

1. Tell students that this exercise is about the reading on pages 224–225. Have students read the direction line. Ask: *What are you going to underline?* (the past tense verbs) Go over the example in the book.
2. Have students complete the rest of Exercise 1 individually. Check the answers as a class.
3. If necessary, review grammar chart **8.1** on page 225.

8.2 | Spelling of the Past Tense of Regular Verbs

1. Copy the lists of verbs (base form and past form) from grammar chart **8.2** on the board. Make sure you separate the eight sets of verbs. For example:

   start started
   rain rained
   die died
   live lived
   etc.

2. Have students cover up grammar chart **8.2** in their books. Say: *There are eight rules for spelling the past tense of regular verbs. Can you list them?* If students have difficulty, give them hints. For example, say: *Look at the endings of these two verbs:* die *and* live. *What do you add?* (d) *So what's the rule?* (When the base form ends in *e*, add *d*.)
3. Have students look at grammar chart **8.2**. Say: *Compare our rules with the rules in the book.* Review the rules in the grammar chart.

EXERCISE **1** Underline the past tense verbs in the following sentences.

EXAMPLE   The Wright brothers <u>lived</u> in Dayton, Ohio.

1. Their father <u>worked</u> as a Christian minister.
2. The boys <u>learned</u> mechanical things quickly.
3. They <u>loved</u> bicycles.
4. They <u>opened</u> the Wright Cycle Company repair shop, where they <u>repaired</u> bicycles.
5. They <u>started</u> to produce their own bicycle models.
6. They <u>used</u> the bike shop to build airplane parts.
7. They <u>succeeded</u> in flying the first airplane in 1903.
8. Wilbur <u>died</u> nine years later, of typhoid.[4]
9. Orville <u>lived</u> to be 76 years old.

8.2 | Spelling of the Past Tense of Regular Verbs

Rule	Base Form	Past Form
Add -ed to most regular verbs.	start rain	started rained
When the base form ends in e, add -d only.	die live	died lived
When the base form ends in a consonant + y, change y to i and add -ed.	carry study	carried studied
When the base form ends in a vowel + y, add -ed. Do not change the y.	stay enjoy	stayed enjoyed
When a one-syllable verb ends in a consonant-vowel-consonant, double the final consonant and add -ed.	stop hug	stopped hugged
Do not double a final w or x.	fix show	fixed showed
When a two-syllable verb ends in a consonant-vowel-consonant, double the final consonant and add -ed only if the last syllable is stressed.	occúr permít	occurred permitted
When the last syllable of a two-syllable verb is not stressed, do not double the final consonant.	ópen óffer	opened offered

[4]*Typhoid* is a serious infection causing a fever and often death.

226   Lesson **8**

Expansion

Grammar Have students cover up the rules in grammar chart **8.2.** Write the rules in random order on the board. Ask students to match the rules on the board with the verbs in the chart.

EXERCISE 2   Write the past tense of these regular verbs. (Accent marks show you where a word is stressed.)

EXAMPLES   learn _____ learned _____   clap _____ clapped _____

love _____ loved _____   lísten _____ listened _____

1. play _____ played _____   11. enjoy _____ enjoyed _____
2. study _____ studied _____   12. drag _____ dragged _____
3. decide _____ decided _____   13. drop _____ dropped _____
4. want _____ wanted _____   14. start _____ started _____
5. like _____ liked _____   15. follow _____ followed _____
6. show _____ showed _____   16. prefér _____ preferred _____
7. look _____ looked _____   17. like _____ liked _____
8. stop _____ stopped _____   18. mix _____ mixed _____
9. háppen _____ happened _____   19. admít _____ admitted _____
10. carry _____ carried _____   20. devélop _____ developed _____

8.3 | Pronunciation of -ed Past Forms

Pronunciation	Rule	Examples	
/t/	Pronounce /t/ after voiceless sounds: /p, k, f, s, š, č/	jump—jumped cook—cooked cough—coughed	kiss—kissed wash—washed watch—watched
/d/	Pronounce /d/ after voiced sounds: /b, g, v, ð, z, ž, ǰ, m, n, ŋ, l, r/ and all vowels.	rub—rubbed drag—dragged love—loved bathe—bathed use—used massage—massaged charge—charged	name—named learn—learned bang—banged call—called care—cared free—freed
/əd/	Pronounce /əd/ after /d/ or /t/ sounds.	wait—waited hate—hated want—wanted	add—added decide—decided

Grammar Variation

Have students cover up grammar chart **8.3.** Read the past forms of the verbs in the first list in the chart (*jumped, cooked, coughed, kissed, washed,* and *watched*). Ask students to repeat what they think the *-ed* sound is for that group of words. Then read the verbs from the second list and ask the students to repeat what they think the *-ed* sound is for that group of words, and so on. After the last group of verbs, ask students to look at the chart. Go over the rules for pronunciation. If necessary, practice the pronunciation of the past forms chorally as a class.

1. Have students read the direction line. Ask: *What do we write in the blanks?* (the past tense of the regular verbs) Go over the examples in the book. Ask students to tell you what the rules are for the spelling of each verb in the examples (*learned:* add *-ed* to most regular verbs; *loved:* ends in *e*, add *-d*; *clapped:* one syllable, ends in consonant-vowel-consonant, double the final consonant, add *-ed*; *listened:* two-syllable verb, not stressed, don't double final consonant). Point out that the accent marks show which syllable is stressed.
2. Have students complete Exercise 2 individually. Check answers as a class.
3. If necessary, review grammar chart **8.2** on page 226.

8.3 | Pronunciation of -ed Past Forms

1. Have students cover up grammar chart **8.3** in their books. Say: *There are three ways to pronounce the -ed ending.* Write:
   1. /t/   2. /d/   3. /_d/
   across the board, and pronounce each sound. Give an example of each from the chart. Remind students that this is about pronunciation, not spelling or writing. Then say: *Listen to each word as I say it. Tell me which sound I'm making.* Say words from the grammar chart lists on page 227 in random order. Pronounce each word carefully. Have students guess where the word belongs and write it under the sound they tell you.
2. Have students look at grammar chart **8.3.** Say: *Compare our lists with the lists in the book.* Go over any errors. Have volunteers pronounce words. If necessary, practice the pronunciation of the past forms chorally as a class.

EXERCISE 3

Have students read the direction line. Turn to Exercise 3 on page 228. Ask: *What are we going to pronounce?* (the base form and the past form) Have a volunteer pronounce #1. Have students finish the exercise in pairs. Circulate to help with pronunciation.

EXERCISE 4

1. Have students read the direction line. Go over the example in the book. Then do #1 with the class. Ask a volunteer to give an answer.
2. Have students complete Exercise 4 individually. Then have students practice saying the sentences in pairs. Circulate to listen to students practice their pronunciation. Finally, check the answers as a class.
3. If necessary, review grammar chart 8.3 on page 227.

EXERCISE 3 Go back to Exercise 2 and pronounce the base form and past form of each verb.

EXERCISE 4 Fill in the blanks with the past tense of the verb in parentheses ( ). Use the correct spelling.

EXAMPLE The Wright brothers _received_ a flying toy from their father.
(receive)

1. They _played_ with kites.
(play)

2. They _dreamed_ about flying.
(dream)

3. They _studied_ everything they could about flying.
(study)

4. They _started_ a bicycle business.
(start)

5. They _used_ the bicycle shop to design airplanes.
(use)

6. They _tried_ to fly their first plane in 1899.
(try)

7. Their first plane _crashed_ .
(crash)

8. They _fixed_ it.
(fix)

9. In 1903, their plane _stayed_ in the air for 12 seconds.
(stay)

10. They _offered_ their invention to the U.S. government.
(offer)

11. The government _decided_ to offer them a contract.
(decide)

12. Wilbur Wright _died_ in 1912.
(die)

13. Orville Wright _lived_ for many more years.
(live)

14. Their invention _changed_ the world.
(change)

Charles Lindbergh and Amelia Earhart (Reading)

CHARLES LINDBERGH AND AMELIA EARHART

Before You Read

1. When was the first time you traveled by airplane?
2. Do you recognize the people in these photos?

Charles Lindbergh, 1902–1974

Amelia Earhart, 1897–1937

🎧 *Read the following article. Pay special attention to the past-tense forms of* be.

At the beginning of the twentieth century, flight **was** new. It **was** not for everyone. It **was** only for the brave and adventurous. Two adventurers **were** Charles Lindbergh and Amelia Earhart.

Charles Lindbergh loved to fly. He **was** born in 1902, one year before the Wright brothers' historic flight. In 1927, a man offered a $25,000 reward for the first person to fly from New York to Paris nonstop. Lindbergh **was** a pilot for the United States Mail Service at that time. He wanted to win the prize. He became famous because he **was** the first person to fly alone across the Atlantic Ocean. His plane **was** in the air for 33 hours. The distance of the flight **was** 3,600 miles. There **were** thousands of people in New York to welcome him home. He **was** an American hero. He **was** only 25 years old.

Another famous American aviator[5] **was** Amelia Earhart. She **was** the first woman to fly across the Atlantic Ocean alone. She **was** 34 years old. Americans **were** in love with Earhart. In 1937, however, she **was** on a flight around the world when her plane disappeared somewhere in the Pacific Ocean. No one really knows what happened to Earhart.

[5]*Aviator* means pilot.

The Simple Past Tense   **229**

Charles Lindbergh and Amelia Earhart (Reading)

1. Have students look at the title of the reading and the photos. Ask: *What is the reading about?* Have students use the title and the photos to make predictions about the reading.
2. Preteach any vocabulary words students may not know such as, *brave, adventurous, historic,* and *disappear.*

BEFORE YOU READ

1. Have students discuss the questions in pairs.
2. Ask for a few volunteers to share their answers with the class.

🕐 To save class time, skip "Before You Read" or have students prepare answers for homework ahead of time.

Reading 🎧 *CD 2, Track 2*

1. Have students read the text silently. Tell them to pay special attention to the past tense forms of *be.* Then play the audio and have students read along silently.
2. Check students' comprehension. Ask questions such as: *What kind of people flew in airplanes at the beginning of the twentieth century?* (brave and adventurous people) *Whom did Charles Lindbergh work for?* (the U.S. Mail Service) *Why did he become famous?* (He was the first person to fly alone across the Atlantic Ocean.) *How old was Earhart when she flew across the Atlantic alone?* (34 years old) *Where did she disappear?* (somewhere over the Pacific Ocean)

🕐 To save class time, have students do the reading for homework ahead of time.

Expansion

Theme The topic for this lesson can be enhanced with the following ideas:

1. Books with photos of Lindbergh and Earhart
2. A world map

Reading Variation

To practice listening skills, have students first listen to the audio alone. Ask a few comprehension questions. Repeat the audio if necessary. Then have students open their books and read along as they listen to the audio.

Reading Glossary

adventurous: daring; bold
brave: unafraid of danger
disappear: to go out of sight
historic: important in history; famous

8.4 | Past Tense of *Be*

1. Have students go back to the reading on page 229. Say: *Find all of the past forms of* be *(was, were).* Write students' responses on the board.
2. Have students look at grammar chart **8.4.** Explain that, as they just discovered, there are only two past forms of *be.* Go through the example sentences.
3. Explain that with *there,* we use *was* for singular and *were* for plural.
4. Explain that the negative is formed by putting *not* after *was* or *were.*
5. Write the contractions for *was not* (*wasn't*) and *were not* (*weren't*) on the board.

EXERCISE 5

1. Have students read the direction line. Ask: *When do we use* was? (with *I, he, she, it,* singular subject) *When do we use* were? (with *we, you, they,* plural subject) Go over the example in the book.
2. Have students complete Exercise 5 individually. Check the answers as a class.
3. If necessary, review grammar chart **8.4** on page 230.

8.4 | Past Tense of *Be*

The verb *be* has two forms in the past: *was* and *were.*

Examples			Explanation
Subject	*Was*	Complement	
I	**was**	interested in the story.	*I, he, she, it,* singular subject → *was*
Charles	**was**	a pilot too.	
He	**was**	brave.	
Amelia	**was**	a pilot.	
She	**was**	popular.	
The airplane	**was**	new in 1903.	
It	**was**	in the air for 12 seconds.	
Subject	*Were*	Complement	
We	**were**	interested in the story.	*We, you, they,* plural subject → *were*
You	**were**	in class yesterday.	
Amelia and Charles	**were**	brave.	
They	**were**	heroes.	
There	*Was*	Singular Subject	
There	**was**	a celebration in 2003.	*There* + *was* + singular noun
There	*Were*	Plural Subject	
There	**were**	thousands of people.	*There* + *were* + plural noun
Charles **was not** the first person to fly. We **were not** at the 2003 celebration.			To make a negative statement, put *not* after *was* or *were.*
I **wasn't** here yesterday. You **weren't** in class yesterday.			The contraction for *was not* is *wasn't.* The contraction for *were not* is *weren't.*

EXERCISE **5** Fill in the blanks with *was* or *were.*

EXAMPLE Lindbergh and Earhart __were__ very famous.

1. The Wright brothers __were__ the inventors of the airplane.
2. The first airplane __was__ in the air for 12 seconds.
3. Lindbergh and Earhart __were__ aviators.
4. There __were__ thousands of people in New York to welcome Lindbergh home.
5. Earhart __was__ the first woman to fly across the Atlantic Ocean.

Expansion

Exercise 5 Have students write sentences about a famous historical person from their country. Instruct students to use the past form of *be.* If possible, have students from the same country work together in pairs or groups. Ask volunteers to share their information with the class.

6. I ___was___ interested in the story about Earhart and Lindbergh.

7. ___Were___ you surprised that Earhart was a woman?

8. Lindbergh ___was___ in Paris.

9. We ___were___ happy to read about flight.

10. There ___was___ a celebration of 100 years of flight in 2003.

11. There ___were___ thousands of people at the celebration.

8.5 | Uses of *Be*

Examples	Explanation
Lindbergh **was** an aviator.	Classification of the subject
Lindbergh **was** brave.	Description of the subject
Lindbergh **was** in Paris.	Location of the subject
Earhart **was** from Kansas.	Place of origin of the subject
She **was** born in 1897.	With *born*
There **were** thousands of people in New York to welcome Lindbergh.	With *there*
Lindbergh **was** 25 years old in 1927.	With age

EXERCISE 6 Read each statement. Then write a negative statement with the words in parentheses ( ).

EXAMPLE The Wright brothers were inventors. (Earhart and Lindbergh)

Earhart and Lindbergh weren't inventors.

1. The train was common transportation in the early 1900s. (the airplane)

   The airplane wasn't common transportation in the early 1900s.

2. Earhart was from Kansas. (Lindbergh)

   Lindbergh wasn't from Kansas.

3. Lindbergh's last flight was successful. (Earhart's last flight)

   Earhart's last flight wasn't successful.

8.5 | Uses of *Be*

1. Have students cover up grammar chart **8.5** on page 231. Make a matching exercise on the board. Write the example sentences from grammar chart **8.5** in random order on the board. Then write the explanations in random order on the board. Ask students to match the example sentences to the appropriate explanations.

2. Have students look at grammar chart **8.5.** Say: *Now check your work against the grammar chart.* Go over any errors.

3. Go over each example and each explanation.

EXERCISE 6

1. Have students read the direction line. Ask: *What kind of statement are we going to write?* (a negative statement) Quickly review the contractions for *was not* and *were not* on the board. Go over the example in the book.

2. Have students complete Exercise 6 individually. Check the answers as a class.

3. If necessary, review grammar chart **8.5** on page 231.

8.6 | Questions with *Was/Were*

1. Have students cover up grammar chart **8.6**. Write the following statements on the board:
   The first flight was long.
   The first flight was successful.
   The Wright brothers were inventors.
   There were a lot of people at the 100 year celebration.
   There was a lot of rain that day.
   Say: *Write a yes/no question and a short answer for each statement.*

2. Then write the following statements on the board:
   The first flight was 12 seconds.
   The first flight was in Kitty Hawk, North Carolina.
   Say: *Write a wh- question for each statement.*

3. Then write the following statements on the board:
   She wasn't successful because her plane disappeared somewhere in the Pacific Ocean.
   I wasn't there because I missed the plane.
   Say: *Write a negative wh- question for each statement.*

4. Then write the following statements on the board:
   No one was with Earhart when she disappeared.
   There was one person in the airplane.
   Say: *Write a subject question for each statement.*

5. Have students look at grammar chart **8.6** on page 232. Say: *Check your work against the chart in the book.* Go over the examples and explanations.

4. Lindbergh's plane was in the air for many hours. (the Wright brothers' first plane)

   The Wright brothers' first plane wasn't in the air for many hours.

5. The Wright brothers were inventors. (Earhart)

   Earhart wasn't an inventor.

6. There were a lot of trains 100 years ago. (planes)

   There weren't a lot of planes 100 years ago.

7. Lindbergh was born in the twentieth century. (the Wright brothers)

   The Wright brothers weren't born in the twentieth century.

8. The 1903 flight at Kitty Hawk was successful. (the 2003 flight)

   The 2003 flight at Kitty Hawk wasn't successful.

8.6 | Questions with *Was/Were*

Examples	Explanation

Was the first flight long?
  No, it **wasn't.**
Was the first flight successful?
  Yes, it **was.**
Were the Wright brothers inventors?
  Yes, they **were.**
	Yes/No Questions
	  Was/were + subject . . . ?
	
	Answer with a short answer, containing a pronoun + *was, wasn't, were, weren't.*

Were there a lot of people at the 100 year celebration?
  Yes, there **were.**
Was there a lot of rain that day?
  Yes, there **was.**
	In a question with *there*, use *there* + *was/were* in the short answer.

How long **was** the first flight? Where **was** the first flight?	*Wh- Questions* *Wh-* word + *was/were* + subject . . . ?
Why **wasn't** Amelia successful? Why **weren't** you there?	*Negative Questions* Why + *wasn't/weren't* + subject . . . ?

Who **was** with Earhart when she disappeared?
How many people **were** in the airplane?
	Subject Questions
	  Who + *was* . . . ?
	  How many . . . + *were* . . . ?

Compare statements and questions

Affirmative Statements and Questions

Wh- Word	Was/Were	Subject	Was/Were	Complement	Short Answer
		Amelia	was	born before 1903.	
	Was	she		born in the U.S.?	Yes, she was.
When	was	she		born?	In 1897.
		Charles and Amelia	were	famous.	
	Were	they		inventors?	No, they weren't.
		Someone	was	with Amelia.	
		Who	was	with Amelia?	A copilot.
		Many people	were	at the celebration of flight.	
		How many people	were	at the celebration?	Thousands.

Negative Statements and Questions

Wh- Word	Wasn't/Weren't	Subject	Wasn't/Weren't	Complement
		Air travel	wasn't	safe 100 years ago.
Why	wasn't	it		safe?
		The Wright brothers	weren't	afraid of flying.
Why	weren't	they		afraid?

6. Review the comparison of statements and questions on page 233. Have students cover the chart with a piece of paper. Ask students to look only at the first statement *(Amelia was born before 1903.)*. Then say: *Ask a* yes/no *question about the country she was born in (Was she born in the U.S.?)*. Then have students reveal the answer by moving their papers down one line. Use this method for the whole chart.

EXERCISE 7

1. Have students read the direction line. Ask: *What do we write on the blanks?* (a *yes/no* question and a short answer) Go over the example in the book.
2. Have students complete the exercise individually. Check the answers as a class.
3. If necessary, review grammar chart **8.6** on pages 232–233.

EXERCISE 8

1. Tell students they will be interviewing their partners about leaving his or her country and coming to the U.S. Have students read the direction line. Say: *Write down your partner's information.* Model #1 with a student.
2. Have students complete the exercise in pairs. Circulate to observe pair work. Give help as needed.
3. If necessary, review grammar chart **8.6** on pages 232–233.

EXERCISE **7** Read each statement. Then write a *yes/no* question with the words in parentheses ( ). Give a short answer.

EXAMPLE The Wright brothers were inventors. (Lindbergh)

Was Lindbergh an inventor? No, he wasn't.

1. The airplane was an important invention. (the telephone)

   Was the telephone an important invention? Yes, it was.

2. Thomas Edison was an inventor. (the Wright brothers)

   Were the Wright brothers inventors? Yes, they were.

3. Amelia Earhart was American. (Lindbergh)

   Was Lindbergh American? Yes, he was.

4. Travel by plane is common now. (100 years ago)

   Was travel by plane common 100 years ago? No, it wasn't.

5. There were telephones 100 years ago. (airplanes)

   Were there airplanes 100 years ago? Yes, there were.

6. You are in class today. (yesterday)

   Were you in class yesterday? **(Answers will vary.)**

7. I was interested in the story about the aviators. (you)

   Were you interested in the story about the aviators? **(Answers will vary.)**

8. I wasn't born in the U.S. (you)

   Were you born in the U.S? **(Answers will vary.)**

EXERCISE **8** ABOUT YOU Interview a classmate who is from another country.

Answers will vary.
1. Where were you born?
2. Were you happy or sad when you left your country?
3. Who was with you on your trip to the U.S.?
4. Were you happy or sad when you arrived in the U.S.?
5. What was your first impression of the U.S.?
6. Were you tired when you arrived?
7. Who was there to meet you?
8. How was the weather on the day you arrived?

234 Lesson **8**

Expansion

Exercise 8 Do a survey with the class. Have students report the results of their interviews in small groups. Then have the groups report their results to the class (e.g., *Three students were born in Ecuador, one was born in Egypt, and one was born in Japan.*). Record the results on the board.

EXERCISE 9   Read each statement. Then write a *wh-* question with the words in parentheses ( ). Answer the question.

EXAMPLE   Lindbergh was very famous. (why)

A: Why was Lindbergh famous?

B: He was one of the first aviators.

1. Lindbergh was a hero. (why)

   A: Why was Lindbergh a hero?

   B: He was the first person to fly across the Atlantic Ocean.

2. Lindbergh was American. (what nationality/Earhart)

   A: What nationality was Earhart?

   B: She was American.

3. Earhart was 34 years old when she crossed the ocean. (Lindbergh)

   A: How old was Lindbergh when he crossed the ocean?

   B: He was 25 years old.

4. Lindbergh was a famous aviator. (who/the Wright brothers)

   A: Who were the Wright brothers?

   B: They were famous inventors.

5. Lindbergh was born in 1902. (Earhart) (answer: 1897)

   A: When was Earhart born?

   B: She was born in 1897.

6. The Wright brothers were famous. (why)

   A: Why were the Wright brothers famous?

   B: They invented the first airplane.

7. The flight at Kitty Hawk in 2003 wasn't successful. (why)

   A: Why wasn't the flight in 2003 at Kitty Hawk successful?

   B: It rained hard and the plane failed to get off the ground.

EXERCISE 10   Fill in the blanks with the correct past-tense form of *be*. Add any other necessary words.

A: I tried to call you last weekend. I ___was___ worried about you.
                                          (example)

B: I ___wasn't___ home. I ___was___ out of town.
        (1 not)   *(2)*

The Simple Past Tense   **235**

EXERCISE 9

1. Have students read the direction line. Ask: *What kind of questions will we write?* (*wh-* or information questions) Say: *Write the question with the information in the parentheses.* Go over the example. Then say: *If the parentheses contain a different subject, write the question with the new subject.* Point out that #2 has a different subject in parentheses. Do #2 as a class.

2. Have students complete the exercise individually. Then have them practice asking and answering the questions in pairs. Circulate to observe pair work. Give help as needed.

3. If necessary, review grammar chart **8.6** on pages 232–233.

To save class time, have students do half of the exercise in class and complete the other half for homework. Or assign the entire exercise for homework.

EXERCISE 10

CD 2, Track 3

1. Have students read the direction line. Go over the example with the class. Remind students that they might need to use other words in the blanks.

2. Have students complete Exercise 10 individually. Check answers as a class.

3. If necessary, review grammar chart **8.6** on pages 232–233.

To save class time, have students do half of the exercise in class and complete the other half for homework. Or assign the entire exercise for homework.

Exercise 10 Variation

To provide practice with listening skills, have students close their books and listen to the audio. Repeat the audio as needed. Ask comprehension questions, such as: *Where was person B last week?* (out of town; in Washington, D.C.) *Was the trip expensive?* (no) *How did person B get to Washington, D.C.?* (by plane) Then have students open their books and complete Exercise 10.

Lesson **8**   **235**

A: Where _____were you_____?
      (3)

B: In Washington, D.C.

A: _____Were you_____ alone?
        (4)

B: No, I _____wasn't_____.
             (5)
I was with my brother.

A: _Was your trip_ expensive?
      (6)

B: No. Our trip wasn't expensive at all.

A: Really? Why _____wasn't it_____ expensive?
                           (7)

B: The flight from here to Washington _____was_____ cheap. And we
                                          (8)

stayed with some friends in their apartment. They _____were_____
                                                       (9)

very helpful. They showed us a lot of beautiful places in Washington.
But my favorite place was the Air and Space Museum.

A: _____Were there_____ a lot of people at the museum?
                  (10)

B: Yes, there were. It _____was_____ very crowded. But it _____was_____
                          (11)   (12)

wonderful to see the Wright brothers' airplane and the airplane that

Lindbergh used when he crossed the Atlantic. Also it _____was_____
                                                         (13)

interesting to see the spacecraft of the astronauts. We _____weren't_____
                                                           (14 not)

bored for one minute in that museum.

A: How long _____was_____ your flight to Washington?
                (15)

B: It _____was_____ only 2 hours and 15 minutes from here. We don't think
         (16)

about flying as anything special anymore. But just a little over

100 years ago, flight _____was_____ just a dream of two brothers.
                          (17)

Can you believe it? There _____were_____ only 66 years between the first
                             (18)

flight in 1903 and the trip to the moon in 1969!

A: That's amazing!

Expansion

Exercise 10 Have students create their own conversations in pairs. Say: *Use Exercise 10 as a model.* Then have volunteers role-play all or part of their conversations in front of the class.

8.7 | Simple Past Tense of Irregular Verbs—An Overview

Examples	Explanation
I **came** to the U.S. by plane. My flight **took** six hours. I **felt** happy when I arrived.	Many verbs are irregular in the past tense. An irregular verb does not use the *-ed* ending.

ROBERT GODDARD

Before You **Read**

1. Did you ever see the first moon landing in 1969?
2. Are you interested in astronauts and rockets?

Robert Goddard with early rocket

Apollo 11 on the moon

 Read the following article. Pay special attention to past-tense verbs.

firecracker

Robert Goddard **was** born in 1882. When he **was** a child, he **became** interested in firecrackers and **thought** about the possibility of space travel. He later became a physics professor at a university. In his free time, he **built** rockets and **took** them to a field, but they **didn't fly**. When he **went** back to his university after his failed attempts, the other professors **laughed** at him.

(continued)

Reading Variation

To practice listening skills, have students first listen to the audio alone. Ask a few comprehension questions. Repeat the audio if necessary. Then have students open their books and read along as they listen to the audio.

Reading Glossary

firecracker: a light, often colorful explosive intended for celebration
grow: to develop; mature
last: to continue to exist
light: to set on fire
prove: to show that something is true or genuine

8.7 | Simple Past Tense of Irregular Verbs—An Overview

1. Have students cover up grammar chart **8.7** on page 237. Write the following sentences on the board:

   I _____ (come) to the U.S. by plane.

   My flight _____ (take) six hours.

   I _____ (feel) happy when I arrived.

   Explain that some verbs are irregular and have irregular past tense endings. Say: *You already learned at least one important irregular verb in the past.* Elicit a response (*be = was/were*). Elicit any prior knowledge students may have. Ask: *Do you know the past tense of the irregular verbs in parentheses?* Have volunteers write them on the board.

2. Then have students look at grammar chart **8.7.** Review the example sentences in the grammar chart.

Robert Goddard (Reading)

1. Have students look at the photo. Ask: *Why is Robert Goddard famous?* (He invented the rocket.)

2. Have students look at the title of the reading. Ask: *What is the reading about? How do you know?* Have students use the title and the photos to make predictions about the reading.

3. Preteach any vocabulary words students may not know such as, *firecracker, prove, light, last,* and *grow.* Use the picture on page 237 to help students understand the meaning of *firecracker.*

BEFORE YOU READ

1. Have students discuss the questions in pairs.

2. Ask for a few volunteers to share their answers with the class.

To save class time, skip "Before You Read" or have students prepare answers for homework ahead of time.

🎧 *CD 2, Track 4*

1. Have students read the text silently. Tell them to pay special attention to the past tense verbs. Then play the audio and have students read along silently.

2. Check students' comprehension. Ask questions such as: *What did Goddard teach at the university?* (physics) *Where did Goddard think people could travel to with rockets?* (the moon) *How long did the first rocket flight last?* (2½ seconds)

🕐 To save class time, have students do the reading for homework ahead of time.

DID YOU KNOW?

After her flight into space, Valentina Tereshkova was honored with the title Hero of the Soviet Union.

Did You Know?

The first woman in space was a Russian, Valentina Tereshkova, in 1963.

In 1920, Goddard **wrote** an article about rocket travel. He **believed** that one day it would be possible to go to the moon. When the *New York Times* **saw** his article, a reporter **wrote** that Goddard **had** less knowledge about science than a high school student. Goddard **wanted** to prove that the *New York Times* **was** wrong.

In 1926, he **built** a ten-foot rocket, **put** it into an open car, and **drove** to his aunt's nearby farm. He **put** the rocket in a field and **lit** the fuse. Suddenly the rocket **went** into the sky. It **traveled** at 60 mph to an altitude of 41 feet. Then it **fell** into the field. The flight **lasted** 2½ seconds, but Goddard **was** happy about his achievement. Over the years, his rockets **grew** to 18 feet and **flew** to 9,000 feet in the air. No one **made** fun of him after he was successful.

When Goddard **died** in 1945, his work **did not stop.** Scientists **continued** to build bigger and better rockets. In 1969, when the American rocket Apollo 11 **took** the first men to the moon, the *New York Times* **wrote:** "The *Times* regrets[6] the error."

1920	Goddard **published** a paper on rockets.
1926–1939	Goddard **built** and **flew** rockets.
1944	Germany **used** the first rockets in World War II.
1957	The Russians **sent** up their first satellite, Sputnik 1.
1958	The Americans **sent** up their first satellite, Explorer 1.
1961	Yuri Gagarin, a Russian, **became** the first person in space.
1961	Alan Shepard **became** the first American in space.
1969	The United States **put** the first men on the moon.
2004	A spacecraft on Mars **sent** color photos to Earth.

Mars Rover

[6]*Regret* means to be sorry for.

238 Lesson **8**

List of Irregular Past Tense Verbs[7]

Verbs with No Change		Final *d* Changes to *t*	
bet—bet	hurt—hurt	bend—bent	send—sent
cost—cost	let—let	build—built	spend—spent
cut—cut	put—put	lend—lent	
fit—fit	quit—quit		
hit—hit	shut—shut		

Verbs with a Vowel Change			
feel—felt	lose—lost	bring—brought	fight—fought
keep—kept	mean—meant[8]	buy—bought	teach—taught
leave—left	sleep—slept	catch—caught	think—thought
break—broke	steal—stole	begin—began	sing—sang
choose—chose	speak—spoke	drink—drank	sink—sank
freeze—froze	wake—woke	ring—rang	swim—swam
dig—dug	spin—spun	drive—drove	shine—shone
hang—hung	win—won	ride—rode	write—wrote
blow—blew	grow—grew	bleed—bled	meet—met
draw—drew	know—knew	feed—fed	read—read[9]
fly—flew	throw—threw	lead—led	
sell—sold	tell—told	find—found	wind—wound
shake—shook	mistake—mistook	lay—laid	pay—paid
take—took		say—said[10]	
tear—tore	wear—wore	bite—bit	hide—hid
		light—lit	
become—became	eat—ate	fall—fell	hold—held
come—came			
give—gave	lie—lay	run—ran	see—saw
forgive—forgave		sit—sat	
forget—forgot	get—got	stand—stood	
shoot—shot		understand—understood	

Miscellaneous Changes			
be—was/were	go—went	hear—heard	
do—did	have—had	make—made	

[7]For an alphabetical list of irregular verbs, see Appendix D.
[8]There is a change in the vowel sound. *Meant* rhymes with *sent*.
[9]The past form of *read* is pronounced like the color *red*.
[10]*Said* rhymes with *bed*.

The Simple Past Tense   **239**

8.8 | List of Irregular Past Tense Verbs

1. Have students cover up grammar chart **8.8**. Ask students to go back to the reading on pages 237 and 238. Ask: *How many of these verbs do you know? Write the base form above or next to the past tense form.* Ask for volunteers to tell you the base form of the verbs in the reading.

2. Tell students to look at grammar chart **8.8**. Say: *Check your work with the grammar chart.* Point out any errors.

3. Explain that some irregular verbs don't have any changes in the past; they're spelled the same and they're pronounced the same. Quickly go through the first list in the chart to demonstrate the pronunciation. Elicit a response. Ask: *If the spelling and the pronunciation don't change, how do we know which one is in the past, and which one is in the present or base form?* (by the context of the rest of the sentence)

4. Review the verbs with vowel changes. Explain that the verbs are grouped according to vowel change similarities. Say: *English language learners must memorize the past form of irregular verbs.* Point out that there is an alphabetical list of irregular verbs in the Appendix on pages AP6 and AP7. Demonstrate the pronunciation of the base form and the past form of each verb. Have students repeat after you.

5. Finally, the last chart shows irregular verbs with miscellaneous changes. Review those verbs and demonstrate their pronunciation. Have students repeat after you. Point out that past tense verbs only have one form except for *be*, which has two (*was/were*).

EXERCISE 11

1. Have students read the direction line. Ask: *What do we write in the blanks?* (the past tense of one of the verbs from the box) Go over the example.
2. Have students complete the exercise individually. Go over the answers with the class.
3. If necessary, review grammar chart **8.8** on page 239.

EXERCISE 12

1. Have students read the direction line. Go over the example in the book.
2. Have students complete Exercise 12 individually. Check the answers as a class.
3. If necessary, review grammar chart **8.8** on page 239.

🕐 To save class time, have students do half of the exercise in class and complete the other half for homework. Or assign the entire exercise for homework.

EXERCISE **11**   Fill in the blanks with the past tense of one of the words from the box below.

fly	think	drive	be	fall
write	put	✓become	see	

EXAMPLE   Goddard ___became___ interested in rockets when he was a child.

1. He ___was___ a professor of physics.
2. People ___thought___ that space travel was impossible.
3. Goddard ___put___ his first rocket in a car and ___drove___ to his aunt's farm.
4. The rocket ___flew___ for 2¹/₂ seconds and then it ___fell___ to the ground.
5. Goddard never ___saw___ the first moon landing.
6. The *New York Times* ___wrote___ about their mistake 49 years later.

EXERCISE **12**   Fill in the blanks with the past tense of the verb in parentheses ( ).

EXAMPLE   The Wright brothers' father ___gave___ them a flying toy.
(give)

1. They ___had___ a dream of flying.
(have)

2. They ___became___ interested in flying after seeing a flying toy.
(become)

3. They ___read___ many books on flight.
(read)

4. They ___sold___ bicycles.
(sell)

5. They ___built___ the first airplane.
(build)

6. At first they ___had___ problems with wind.
(have)

7. They ___made___ some changes to the airplane.
(make)

Expansion

Exercises 11 and 12 Have students practice telling another student the stories of the Wright brothers or Goddard. Have them practice in pairs. Then have volunteers tell their stories to the class.

---

8. They ___flew___ for the first time in 1903.
   (fly)

9. Only a few people ___saw___ the first flight.
   (see)

10. President Theodore Roosevelt ___heard___ about their airplane.
    (hear)

11. The airplane was an important invention because it ___brought___
    (bring)
    people from different places closer together.

12. Thousands of people ___went___ to North Carolina for the 100th
    (go)
    anniversary of flight.

8.9 | Negative Forms of Past Tense Verbs

Compare affirmative (A) and negative (N) statements with past-tense verbs.

Examples	Explanation
A. Lindbergh **returned** from his last flight. N. Earhart **didn't return** from her last flight.	For the negative past tense, we use *didn't* + the base form for ALL verbs, regular and irregular.
A. The Wright brothers **flew** in their airplane. N. Goddard **didn't fly** in his rocket.	Compare returned—didn't return flew—didn't fly built—didn't build put—didn't put
A. Goddard **built** rockets. N. He **didn't build** airplanes.	
A. The Russians **put** a woman in space in 1963. N. The Americans **didn't put** a woman in space until 1983.	Remember: *Put* and a few other past-tense verbs are the same as the base form.

8.9 | Negative Forms of Past Tense Verbs

1. Have students cover up grammar chart **8.9.** Ask students to go back to the reading on pages 237 and 238. Say: *Circle the negative verbs in the past tense.* Write students' examples on the board (*didn't fly* and *did not stop*).

2. Tell students to look at grammar chart **8.9.** Write on the board: *didn't + base form.* Explain that this is how the negative is formed for all verbs—regular and irregular.

3. Review all of the example sentences in the chart.

1. Have students read the direction line. Ask: *What do we write in the blanks?* (the negative of the underlined verb) Go over the example in the book.

2. Have students complete Exercise 13 individually. Check the answers as a class.

3. If necessary, review grammar chart **8.9** on page 241.

EXERCISE **13**   Fill in the blanks with the negative form of the underlined words.

EXAMPLE   Goddard <u>believed</u> in space flight. Other people _____*didn't believe*_____ in space flight.

1. In 1926 his rocket <u>flew</u>. Before that time, his rockets _____*didn't fly*_____.

2. He <u>wanted</u> to build rockets. He _____*didn't want*_____ to build airplanes.

3. In 1920, a newspaper <u>wrote</u> that he was foolish. The newspaper _____*didn't write*_____ about the possibility of rocket travel.

4. The first rocket <u>stayed</u> in the air for $2\frac{1}{2}$ seconds. It _____*didn't stay*_____ in the air for a long time.

5. Goddard <u>thought</u> his ideas were important. His colleagues _____*didn't think*_____ his ideas were important.

6. Goddard <u>saw</u> his rockets fly. He _____*didn't see*_____ rockets go to the moon.

7. A rocket <u>went</u> to the moon in 1969. A rocket _____*didn't go*_____ to the moon during Goddard's lifetime.

8. In 1957, the Russians <u>put</u> the first man in space. The Americans _____*didn't put*_____ the first man in space.

9. In 1969, the first Americans <u>walked</u> on the moon. Russians _____*didn't walk*_____ on the moon.

10. The Wright brothers <u>dreamed</u> about flying. They _____*didn't dream*_____ about rockets.

11. They <u>sold</u> bicycles. They _____*didn't sell*_____ cars.

12. Their 1903 airplane <u>had</u> a pilot. Their first airplane _____*didn't have*_____ a pilot.

13. The Wright brothers <u>built</u> the first airplane. They _____*didn't build*_____ the first rocket.

14. The Wright brothers <u>wanted</u> to show their airplane to the U.S. government. The government _____*didn't want*_____ to see it at first.

EXERCISE **14** ABOUT YOU If you are from another country, fill in the blanks with the affirmative or negative form of the verb in parentheses to tell about the time before you came to the U.S. Add some specific information to tell more about each item.

EXAMPLES   I _____*studied*_____ English before I came to the U.S.
                         (study)

I studied with a private teacher for three months.

OR

I _____*didn't study*_____ English before I came to the U.S.
                         (study)

I didn't have enough time.

Answers will vary.   1. I _____ my money for dollars before I came to
                                    (exchange)
the U.S.

2. I _____ a passport.
          (get)

3. I _____ for a visa.
          (apply)

4. I _____ English.
          (study)

5. I _____ some things (house, furniture, etc.).
          (sell)

6. I _____ goodbye to my friends.
          (say)

7. I _____ an English dictionary.
          (buy)

8. I _____ a clear idea about life in the U.S.
          (have)

9. I _____ afraid about my future.
          (be)

10. I _____ to another country first.
           (go)

11. I _____ English well.
        (understand)

12. I _____ a lot about Americans.
          (know)

1. Tell students that this exercise is about their experiences before coming to the U.S. Have students read the direction line. Ask: *What do we write in the blanks?* (the affirmative or negative of the verb) Say: *Make sure the information is true for you.* Instruct students to add specific information for each item whenever possible. Go over the examples in the book.

2. Have students complete Exercise 14 individually. Then have students compare answers in pairs. If possible have students from different countries work together. Circulate to observe pair work. Give help as needed.

3. If necessary, review grammar chart 8.9 on page 241.

To save class time, have students do half of the exercise in class and complete the other half for homework. Or assign the entire exercise for homework.

Expansion

Exercise 14 Have students write three more sentences in the past tense about their lives before coming to the U.S. Have students compare their new statements with a partner.

EXERCISE 15

1. Tell students that this exercise is about their experiences after coming to this city or country. Have students read the direction line. Say: *Make the sentences affirmative or negative, according to what's true for you.* Go over the examples in the book. Have a student model #1. Point out the photos of a Social Security card and a driver's license.

2. Have students complete Exercise 15 in pairs. Then have students compare answers with their partners. If possible, have students from different countries work together. Circulate to observe pair work. Give help as needed.

3. If necessary, review grammar chart **8.9** on page 241.

🕐 To save class time, have students do half of the exercise in class and complete the other half in writing for homework. Or if students do not need speaking practice, the entire exercise may be skipped or done in writing.

EXERCISE 16

1. Tell students that this exercise is about their experiences this week. Have students read the direction line. Say: *Make the sentences affirmative or negative, according to what's true for you.* Go over the examples in the book. Have a student model #1. Point out the picture of a phone card.

2. Have students complete Exercise 16 in pairs. Then have students compare answers with their partners. If possible, have students from different countries work together. Circulate to observe pair work. Give help as needed.

3. If necessary, review grammar chart **8.9** on page 241.

🕐 To save class time, have students do half of the exercise in class and complete the other half in writing for homework. Or if students do not need speaking practice, the entire exercise may be skipped or done in writing.

EXERCISE **15**   If you come from another city or country, tell if these things happened or didn't happen after you moved to this city. Add some specific information to tell more about each item.

EXAMPLE   find an apartment
I found an apartment two weeks after I arrived in this city.
OR
I didn't find an apartment right away. I lived with my cousins for two months.

Answers will vary.
1. find a job
2. register for English classes
3. rent an apartment
4. buy a car
5. get a Social Security card
6. go to the bank
7. visit a museum
8. see a relative
9. buy clothes
10. get a driver's license

EXERCISE **16**   ABOUT YOU Tell if you did or didn't do these things in the past week. Add some specific information to tell more about each item.

EXAMPLE   go to the movies
I went to the movies last weekend with my brother. We saw a great movie.
OR
I didn't go to the movies this week. I didn't have time.

Answers will vary.
1. receive a letter
2. write a letter
3. go to the library
4. do laundry
5. buy groceries
6. use a phone card
7. buy a magazine
8. work hard
9. look for a job
10. rent a DVD
11. send an e-mail
12. read a newspaper

Expansion

Exercises 15 and 16 Have students write a time line based on either Exercise 15 or 16. Then have students practice telling their partners the events that happened to them. Ask volunteers to present their time lines to the class.

8.10 | Questions with Past Tense Verbs

Yes/No Questions and Short Answers

Examples	Explanation

Did Goddard **invent** the rocket?
  Yes, he **did.**
Did Goddard **live** to see man land on the moon?
  No, he **didn't.**
Did Lindbergh **fly** across the ocean alone?
  Yes, he **did.**
	Did + subject + base form . . . ?
	
	Use the base form for both regular and irregular verbs.
	
	Short Answers
	  Yes, + subject pronoun + *did.*
	  No, + subject pronoun + *didn't.*

Wh- Questions

Wh- Questions	
When **did** Lindbergh **cross** the ocean? How **did** Earhart's **plane** disappear? When **did** Goddard **become** a professor?	*Wh-* word + *did* + subject + base form . . . ?
Negative Questions	
Why **didn't** the Wright brothers' first plane **fly?** Why didn't Earhart **return?**	*Why* + *didn't* + subject + base form . . . ?

Compare affirmative statements and questions

Wh- Word	Did	Subject	Verb	Complement	Short Answer
		Goddard	studied	physics.	
	Did	he	study	hard?	Yes, he did.
When	did	he	study	physics?	In the beginning of the twentieth century.
		Lindbergh	flew	across the Atlantic.	
	Did	he	fly	alone?	Yes, he did.
Why	did	he	fly	alone?	Because he was brave.

Compare negative statements and questions

Wh- Word	Didn't	Subject	Verb	Complement
		Goddard	didn't see	the rocket go to the moon.
Why	didn't	he	see	the rocket go to the moon?
		Amelia	didn't return	from her last trip.
Why	didn't	she	return?	

The Simple Past Tense   **245**

1. Have students cover up grammar chart **8.10.** Write the following sentences on the board: *Goddard invented the rocket. Lindbergh flew across the ocean alone.* Say: *Write yes/no questions and short answers for these two sentences.*

2. Write the following sentences on the board: *Lindbergh crossed the ocean. (when) Earhart's plane disappeared. (how) Goddard became a professor. (when)* Say: *Write* wh- *questions for these three sentences.*

3. Write the following sentences on the board: *The Wright brothers' first plane didn't fly. (why) Earhart didn't return. (why)* Say: *Write negative* wh- *questions for these two sentences.*

4. Have students look at grammar chart **8.10.** Say: *Now compare your sentences with the sentences in the grammar chart.* Write on the board: Did + *subject* + *base form* . . . ? Explain that this is how questions are formed in the simple past for all verbs—regular and irregular. Review negative and affirmative short answers. Then write on the board: Wh- *word* + did + *subject* + *base form* . . . ? Explain that this is how *wh-* questions are formed in the simple past for all verbs—regular and irregular. Finally, write: Wh- *word* + didn't + *subject* + *base form* . . . ? Explain that this is how negative questions are formed in the simple past for all verbs—regular and irregular.

5. Quickly review the comparison of affirmative statements and questions.

EXERCISE 17

1. Tell students that they will be interviewing a partner about his or her life before coming to the U.S. Have students read the direction line. Model #1 with another student.
2. Have students complete Exercise 17 in pairs. If possible have students from different countries work together. Circulate to observe pair work. Give help as needed.
3. If necessary, review grammar chart **8.10** on page 245.

EXERCISE 18

1. Have students read the direction line. Ask: *What do we write on the blanks?* (a *yes/no* question and a short answer) Go over the example in the book.
2. Have students complete the exercise individually. Check the answers as a class.
3. If necessary, review grammar chart **8.10** on page 245.

🕐 To save class time, have students do half of the exercise in class and complete the other half for homework. Or assign the entire exercise for homework.

EXERCISE **17**   ABOUT YOU Use these questions to ask another student about the time when he or she lived in his or her native country.

Answers will vary.

1. Did you study English in your country?
2. Did you live in a big city?
3. Did you live with your parents?
4. Did you know a lot about the U.S.?
5. Were you happy with the political situation?
6. Did you finish high school?
7. Did you own a car?
8. Did you have a job?
9. Did you think about your future?
10. Were you happy?

EXERCISE **18**   Read each statement. Write a *yes/no* question about the words in parentheses ( ). Write a short answer.

EXAMPLE   The Wright brothers had a dream. (Goddard) (yes)
Did Goddard have a dream? Yes, he did.

1. Wilbur Wright died in 1912. (his brother) (no)
   Did his brother die in 1912? No, he didn't.

2. The Wright brothers built an airplane. (Goddard) (no)
   Did Goddard build an airplane? No, he didn't.

3. Earhart loved to fly. (Lindbergh) (yes)
   Did Lindbergh love to fly? Yes, he did.

4. Lindbergh crossed the ocean. (Earhart) (yes)
   Did Earhart cross the ocean? Yes, she did.

5. Lindbergh worked for the U.S. Mail Service. (Earhart) (no)
   Did Earhart work for the U.S. Mail Service? No, she didn't.

6. Lindbergh became famous. (Earhart) (yes)
   Did Earhart become famous? Yes, she did.

7. Earhart disappeared. (Lindbergh) (no)
   Did Lindbergh disappear? No, he didn't.

Expansion

Exercise 17 Create two rings of students. Have half of the students stand in an outer ring around the classroom. Have the other half stand in an inner ring, facing the outer ring. Instruct students to ask and answer the questions from Exercise 17. Call out *"turn"* every minute or so. Students in the inner ring should move one space clockwise. Students now ask and answer with their new partners. Have students ask questions in random order. Make sure students look at each other when they're speaking.

8. Lindbergh was born in the twentieth century. (Earhart) (no)

Was Earhart born in the twentieth century? No, she wasn't.

9. Lindbergh won money for his first flight. (the Wright brothers) (no)

Did the Wright brothers win money for their first flight? No, they didn't.

10. People didn't believe the Wright brothers at first. (Goddard) (no)

Did people believe Goddard at first? No, they didn't.

11. The Wright brothers dreamed about flight. (Goddard) (yes)

Did Goddard dream about flight? Yes, he did.

12. The Russians sent a rocket into space in 1957. (the Americans) (no)

Did the Americans send a rocket into space in 1957? No, they didn't.

13. The Russians put a man in space in 1961. (Americans) (yes)

Did the Americans put a man in space in 1961? Yes, they did.

14. Americans saw the first moon landing. (Goddard) (no)

Did Goddard see the first moon landing? No, he didn't.

EXERCISE 19   Fill in the blanks with the correct words.

EXAMPLE   What kind of engine *did the first airplane have?*
The first airplane had a gasoline engine.

1. Where *did the Wright brothers build their plane*?
The Wright brothers built their plane in their bicycle shop.

2. Why *did the first plane crash*?
The first plane crashed because of the wind.

3. Why *was the plane* difficult to control?
The plane was difficult to control because of the wind.

4. Why *didn't newspapers report* the first flight in 1903?
Newspapers didn't report it because they didn't believe it.

5. Where *did Lindbergh work*?
Lindbergh worked for the U.S. Mail Service.

6. Why *did he cross the ocean*?
He crossed the ocean to win the prize money.

7. How much money *did he win*?
He won $25,000.

1. Have students read the direction line. Say: *Complete the questions.* Ask: *What kind of questions are they?* (*wh-* or information questions) Go over the example in the book.
2. Have students complete the exercise individually. Check the answers as a class.
3. If necessary, review grammar chart **8.10** on page 245.

To save class time, have students do half of the exercise in class and complete the other half for homework. Or assign the entire exercise for homework.

8. How old _was he_ _____ when he crossed the ocean?
   Lindbergh was 25 years old when he crossed the ocean.

9. Where _did his plane land_ _____?
   His plane landed in Paris.

10. When _did Lindbergh die_ _____?
    Lindbergh died in 1974.

11. Where _was Earhart born_ _____?
    Earhart was born in Kansas.

12. Where _did she disappear_ _____?
    She disappeared in the Pacific Ocean.

13. Why _didn't Earhart return_ _____?
    Nobody knows why Earhart didn't return.

14. Who _was Earhart_ _____ with?
    Earhart was with a copilot.

15. When _did the first man walk on the moon_ _____?
    The first man walked on the moon in 1969.

16. Why _didn't Goddard see_ _____ the first moon landing?
    Goddard didn't see the first moon landing because he died in 1945.

Expansion

Exercise 19 Have students practice asking and answering the questions in pairs.

EXERCISE 20 Read each statement. Then write a question with the words in parentheses ( ). Answer with a complete sentence. (The answers are at the bottom of the page.)

EXAMPLE The Wright brothers were born in the nineteenth century. (Where)
Where were they born? They were born in Ohio.

1. The Wright brothers were born in the nineteenth century. (When/Lindbergh)
   When was Lindbergh born? He was born in 1902.

2. Their father gave them a toy. (What kind of toy)
   What kind of toy did their father give them? He gave them a flying toy.

3. They had a shop. (What kind of shop)
   What kind of shop did they have? They had a bicycle shop.

4. They designed airplanes. (Where)
   Where did they design airplanes? They designed airplanes in their bicycle shop.

5. They flew their first plane in North Carolina. (When)
   When did they fly their first plane? They flew their first plane in 1903.

6. The first plane stayed in the air for a few seconds. (How many seconds)
   How many seconds did it stay in the air? It stayed in the air for 12 seconds.

7. The U.S. government didn't want to see the airplane at first. (Why)
   Why didn't the U.S. government want to see the airplane at first? They didn't believe it.

8. The Wright brothers invented the airplane. (What/Goddard)
   What did Goddard invent? He invented the rocket.

9. Goddard took his rocket to his aunt's farm. (Why)
   Why did Goddard take his rocket to his aunt's farm? He took the rocket to his aunt's farm to see if it would fly.

10. People laughed at Goddard. (Why)
    Why did people laugh at Goddard? They didn't believe him or they thought he was a fool.

ANSWERS TO EXERCISE 20:
(1) 1902, (2) a flying toy, (3) a bicycle shop, (4) in their bicycle shop, (5) in 1903, (6) 12 seconds, (7) they didn't believe it, (8) the rocket, (9) to see if it would fly, (10) they didn't believe him (they thought he was a fool)

The Simple Past Tense **249**

1. Have students read the direction line. Ask: *What kind of questions are we going to write?* (wh- or information questions) Go over the example in the book. Tell students to try to answer the questions without looking at the answers.
2. Have students complete the exercise individually. Check the answers as a class.
3. If necessary, review grammar chart **8.10** on page 245.

To save class time, have students do half of the exercise in class and complete the other half for homework. Or assign the entire exercise for homework.

Expansion

Exercise 20 Have students practice asking and answering the questions in pairs.

EXERCISE 21

1. Tell students that this activity is about them. Have students read the direction line. Ask: *What do we check?* (events that happened to them) Go over the examples with the class. Then have volunteers model the examples.

2. Have students check the statements individually. Then have students ask and answer questions in pairs. Circulate and give help as needed.

3. If necessary, review grammar chart **8.10** on page 245.

EXERCISE 22

1. Tell students that this activity is about things they did when they were children. Have students read the direction line. Ask: *What do we check?* (things that happened when we were young) Go over the example with the class. Then have volunteers model the example. Point out the photo of the child taking music lessons on page 251.

2. Have students check the statements individually. Then have students ask and answer questions in pairs. Circulate and give help as needed.

3. If necessary, review grammar chart **8.10** on page 245.

EXERCISE **21**   ABOUT YOU Check (✓) all statements that are true for you. Then read aloud one statement that you checked. Another student will ask a question with the words in parentheses ( ). Answer the question.

EXAMPLES   ✓ I did my homework. (where)

B: Where did you do your homework?
A: I did my homework in the library.

✓ I got married. (when)

B: When did you get married?
A: I got married six years ago.

Answers will vary.
1. ____ I graduated from high school. (when)
2. ____ I studied biology. (when)
3. ____ I bought an English dictionary. (where)
4. ____ I left my country. (when)
5. ____ I came to the U.S. (why)
6. ____ I brought my clothes to the U.S. (what else)
7. ____ I rented an apartment. (where)
8. ____ I started to study English. (when)
9. ____ I chose this college. (why)
10. ____ I found my apartment. (when)
11. ____ I needed to learn English. (when)
12. ____ I got married. (when)

EXERCISE **22**   ABOUT YOU Check (✓) which of these things you did when you were a child. Make an affirmative or negative statement about one of these items. Another student will ask a question about your statement.

EXAMPLE   ____ I attended public school.

A: I didn't attend public school.
B: Why didn't you attend public school?
A: My parents wanted to give me a religious education.

Expansion

Exercise 21 Create two rings of students. Have half of the students stand in an outer ring around the classroom. Have the other half stand in an inner ring, facing the outer ring. Instruct students to ask and answer the questions from Exercise 21. Call out *"turn"* every minute or so. Students in the inner ring should move one space clockwise. Students now ask and answer with their new partners. Have students ask questions in random order. Make sure students look at each other when they're speaking.

Answers will vary.
1. _____ I participated in a sport.
2. _____ I enjoyed school.
3. _____ I got good grades in school.
4. _____ I got an allowance.[11]
5. _____ I lived with my grandparents.
6. _____ I took music lessons.
7. _____ I had a pet.
8. _____ I lived on a farm.
9. _____ I played soccer.
10. _____ I studied English.
11. _____ I had a bike.
12. _____ I thought about my future.

8.11 | Questions About the Subject

Examples			Explanation
Subject	Verb	Complement	When we ask a question about the subject, we use the past-tense form, not the base form. We don't use *did* in the question.
Someone	invented	the rocket.	
Who	invented	the rocket?	
			Compare
Some people	laughed	at Goddard.	What **did** the Wright Brothers **invent?**
How many people	laughed	at Goddard?	Who **invented** the airplane?
Something	happened	to Amelia's plane.	Why **did** people **laugh** at Goddard?
What	happened	to Amelia's plane?	Who **laughed** at Goddard?
			When **did** the accident **happen?**
			What **happened?**

[11]An *allowance* is money children get from their parents, usually once a week.

The Simple Past Tense   **251**

8.11 | Questions About the Subject

1. Have students cover up grammar chart **8.11.** Write the following sentences on the board: *Someone invented the rocket. Some people laughed at Goddard. Something happened to Amelia's plane.* Say: *Write questions about the subjects of these three sentences.* Elicit the pattern for questions about the subject (subject + verb + complement). Ask: *Is this pattern the same as or different from the pattern for statements?* (the same)

2. Have students look at grammar chart **8.11.** Tell students to check their sentences. Go over any errors. Remind students that with questions about the subject, the past tense form is used, not the base form. Also point out that we don't use *did* in questions about the subject. Go over the examples for comparison.

Expansion

Exercise 22 Create two rings of students. Have half of the students stand in an outer ring around the classroom. Have the other half stand in an inner ring, facing the outer ring. Instruct students to ask and answer the questions from Exercise 22. Call out *"turn"* every minute or so. Students in the inner ring should move one space clockwise. Students now ask and answer with their new partners. Have students ask questions in random order. Make sure students look at each other when they're speaking.

EXERCISE 23

1. Tell students to cover up the answers at the bottom of page 252. Have students read the direction line. Ask: *How much have you learned about the history of flight? Let's take a quiz.* Go over the example with the class.
2. Have students complete the exercise individually. Have students check answers in pairs.
3. If necessary, review grammar chart **8.11** on page 251.

EXERCISE 24

1. Have students read the direction line. Say: *You're going to ask your classmates questions.* Ask: *What kind of question is the first one?* (a question about the subject) Say: *Remember, questions about the subject don't use* did. Go over the example with the class. Have volunteers model the example.
2. Have students complete the exercise in groups. Say: *One student will ask a question. The person who answers the question will then ask the next question.* Circulate to observe group work. Give help as needed.
3. If necessary, review grammar chart **8.11** on page 251.

EXERCISE 23 Choose the correct words to answer these questions about the subject. (The answers are at the bottom of the page.)

EXAMPLE Who invented the airplane? (The Wright brothers, Goddard, Lindbergh)

1. Which country sent the first rocket into space? (the U.S., China, Russia)
2. Who walked on the moon in 1969? (an American, a Russian, a Canadian)
3. Who sent up the first rocket? (The Wright brothers, Goddard, Lindbergh)
4. Who disappeared in 1937? (Earhart, Goddard, Lindbergh)
5. Who won money for flying across the Atlantic Ocean? (Earhart, Lindbergh, Goddard)
6. Which president showed interest in the Wright brothers' airplane? (T. Roosevelt, Lincoln, Wilson)
7. Which newspaper said that Goddard was a fool? (*Chicago Tribune*, *Washington Post*, *New York Times*)

EXERCISE 24 Read one of the *who* questions below. Someone will volunteer an answer. Then ask the person who answered "I did" a related question.

EXAMPLES A: Who went to the bank last week?
B: I did.

A: Why did you go to the bank?
B: I went there to buy a money order.

Answers will vary.
1. Who brought a dictionary to class today?
2. Who drank coffee this morning?
3. Who wrote a composition last night?
4. Who watched TV this morning?
5. Who came to the U.S. alone?
6. Who made a long distance call last night?
7. Who studied English before coming to the U.S.?
8. Who bought a newspaper today?

ANSWERS TO EXERCISE 23:
(1) Russia, (2) an American, (3) Goddard, (4) Earhart, (5) Lindbergh, (6) T. Roosevelt, (7) *New York Times*

Expansion

Exercise 23 Tell students to write three more questions to ask their group members. Remind students to write questions about the subject. Have students take turns asking and answering their new questions.

EXERCISE 25

Combination Exercise Fill in the blanks in this conversation between two students about their past.

A: I _____was born_____ in Mexico. I _____came_____
   (example: born)   (1 come)

to the U.S. ten years ago. Where _____were you_____ born?
                                    (2 be)

B: In El Salvador. But my family _____moved_____ to Guatemala
                                    (3 move)

when I _____was_____ ten years old.
         (4 be)

A: Why _____did you move_____ to Guatemala?
         (5 move)

B: In 1998 we _____lost_____ our home.
               (6 lose)

A: What _____happened_____?
          (7 happen)

B: A major earthquake _____hit_____ my town. Luckily,
                        (8 hit)

my family was fine, but the earthquake _____destroyed_____
                                          (9 destroy)

our home and much of our town. We _____went_____
                                    (10 go)

to live with cousins in Guatemala.

A: How long _____did you stay_____ in Guatemala?
             (11 stay)

B: I stayed there for about three years. Then I _____came_____
                                                  (12 come)

to the U.S.

A: What about your family? _____Did they come_____ to the U.S. with you?
                            (13 come)

B: No, they _____didn't_____. I _____found_____ a job,
             (14)   (15 find)

_____saved_____ my money, and _____brought_____
   (16 save)   (17 bring)

them here later.

Exercise 25 Variation

To provide practice with listening skills, have students close their books and listen to the audio. Repeat the audio as needed. Ask comprehension questions, such as: *Where was person A born?* (in Mexico) *Where was person B born?* (in El Salvador) *Where did person B's family move to?* (Guatemala) Then have students open their books and complete Exercise 25.

EXERCISE 25

⌒ *CD 2, Track 5*

1. Have students read the direction line. Ask: *What tense are we going to use in this exercise?* (the past) Say: *Right. The past of* be *and the simple past of other verbs.* Go over the example in the book. Do #1 and 2 with the class.
2. Have students complete Exercise 25 individually. Check answers as a class.
3. If necessary, review **Lesson 8.**

   To save class time, have students do half of the exercise in class and complete the other half for homework. Or assign the entire exercise for homework.

Summary of Lesson 8

1. *Be* Review the forms of the simple past tense of *be*. Have students cover up the sentences in the chart on page 254. Then have students work in pairs to make sentences with *was* and *were*.
Write on the board:
was were
affirmative
negative
yes/no *questions*
short answers
wh- *questions*
negative questions
subject questions
Say: *Write statements and questions for both* was *and* were. Then have students open their books and compare their sentences with the sentences in the chart. If necessary, have students review:
8.4 Past Tense of *Be* (p. 230)
8.5 Uses of *Be* (p. 231)
8.6 Questions with *Was/Were* (pp. 232–233).

A: My parents _____didn't come_____ with me either. But my older
           (18 not/come)

brother did. I _____started_____ to go to school as soon as I
           (19 start)

_____arrived_____.
(20 arrive)

B: Who _____supported_____ you while you were in school?
           (21 support)

A: My brother _____did_____.
           (22)

B: I _____didn't go_____ to school right away because I
           (23 not/go)

_____had_____ to work. Then I _____got_____
       (24 have)   (25 get)

a grant and _____started_____ to go to City College.
                    (26 start)

A: Why _____did you choose_____ City College?
                 (27 choose)

B: I chose it because it has a good ESL program.

A: Me, too.

SUMMARY OF LESSON 8

The Simple Past Tense

1. *Be*

I He She It	was in Paris.	We You They	were in Paris.
There was a problem.		There were many problems.	

AFFIRMATIVE:	He **was** in Poland.	They **were** in France.
NEGATIVE:	He **wasn't** in Russia.	They **weren't** in England.
YES/NO QUESTION:	**Was** he in Hungary?	**Were** they in Paris?
SHORT ANSWER:	No, he **wasn't**.	No, they **weren't**.
WH- QUESTION:	Where **was** he?	When **were** they in France?
NEGATIVE QUESTION:	Why **wasn't** he in Russia?	Why **weren't** they in Paris?
SUBJECT QUESTION:	Who **was** in Russia?	How many people **were** in France?

254 Lesson **8**

Expansion

Exercise 25 Have students create their own dialogues. Say: *Use Exercise 25 as a model.* Ask volunteers to role-play all or part of their dialogues in front of the class.

2. Other Verbs

	Regular Verb *(work)*	Irregular Verb *(buy)*
AFFIRMATIVE:	She **worked** on Saturday.	They **bought** a car.
NEGATIVE:	She **didn't work** on Sunday.	They **didn't buy** a motorcycle.
YES/NO QUESTION:	**Did** she **work** in the morning?	**Did** they **buy** an American car?
SHORT ANSWER:	Yes, she **did.**	No, they **didn't.**
WH- QUESTION:	Where **did** she **work?**	What kind of car **did** they **buy?**
NEGATIVE QUESTION:	Why **didn't** she **work** on Sunday?	Why **didn't** they **buy** an American car?
SUBJECT QUESTION:	Who **worked** on Sunday?	How many people **bought** an American car?

EDITING ADVICE

1. Use the base form, not the past-tense form, after *to*.

   buy
   I wanted to ~~bought~~ a new car.

2. Review the spelling rules for adding *-ed*, and use correct spelling.

   studied
   I ~~studied~~ for the last test.
   dropped
   He ~~droped~~ his pencil.

3. Use the base form after *did* or *didn't*.

   know
   She didn't ~~knew~~ the answer.
   come
   Did your father ~~came~~ to the U.S.?

4. Use correct word order in a question.

   your mother go
   Where did ~~go your mother~~?
   did your sister buy
   What ~~bought your sister~~?

5. Use *be* with *born*. (Don't add *-ed* to *born*.) Don't use *be* with *died*.

   was born
   Her grandmother ~~borned~~ in Russia.

   She ~~was~~ died in the U.S.
   was
   Where ~~did~~ your grandfather born?
   did
   Where ~~was~~ your grandfather died?

Summary of Lesson 8 (*cont.*)

2. **Other Verbs** Review the simple past tense of other verbs—regular and irregular. Have students cover up the sentences in the chart on this page. Then have students work in pairs to make sentences with *work* and *buy*. Write on the board:
regular (work) *irregular* (buy)
affirmative
negative
yes/no *questions*
short answers
wh- *questions*
negative questions
subject questions

Say: *Write statements and questions for* work *and* buy. Then have students compare their sentences with the sentences in the chart. If necessary, have students review:

Editing Advice

Have students close their books. Write the example sentences without editing marks or corrections on the board. For example:

1. I wanted to bought a new car.

2. I studyed for the last test.
He droped his pencil.

Ask students to correct each sentence and provide a rule or explanation for each correction. This activity can be done individually, in pairs, or as a class. After students have corrected each sentence, tell them to turn to pages 255–256. Say: *Now compare your work with the Editing Advice in the book.*

Lesson 8 Test/Review

For additional practice, review, and assessment materials, see Assessment CD-ROM with *ExamView Pro, More Grammar Practice* Workbook 1, Interactive CD-ROM, and Web site http://elt.thomson.com/gic

PART 1

1. Part 1 may be used in addition to the Assessment CD-ROM with *ExamView Pro* as an in-class test to assess student performance. Have students read the direction line. Ask: *Does every sentence have a mistake?* (no) Go over the examples with the class.
2. Have students complete the assignment individually. Collect for assessment.
3. If necessary, have students review: **Lesson 8.**

---

6. Check your list of verbs for irregular verbs.
   brought
   I bringed my photos to the U.S.
   saw
   I seen the accident yesterday.

7. Use *be* with an age.
   was
   My grandfather had 88 years old when he died.

8. Don't confuse *was* and *were*.
   were
   Where was you yesterday?

9. Don't use *did* in a question about the subject.
   took
   Who did take my pencil?

LESSON 8 TEST/REVIEW

PART 1   Find the mistakes with the underlined words, and correct them. Not every sentence has a mistake. If the sentence is correct, write *C*.

EXAMPLES
was
Lindbergh were famous.
Lindbergh <u>was born</u> in 1902.   *C*

1. Lindbergh decided to <u>flew</u> across the Atlantic.
   fly

2. The first plane <u>stay</u> in the air for 12 seconds.
   stayed

3. When <u>Lindbergh crossed</u> the ocean?
   did Lindbergh cross

4. Earhart <u>borned</u> in 1897.
   was born

5. Who <u>invented</u> the first rocket?   *C*

6. When did Goddard <u>invented</u> the rocket?
   invent

7. When <u>was Goddard died</u>?
   did Goddard die

8. When <u>was Goddard born</u>?   *C*

9. Lindbergh <u>won</u> $25,000.   *C*

Lesson Review

To use Part 1 as a review, assign it as homework or use it as an in-class activity to be completed individually or in pairs. Check answers and review errors as a class. Reteach grammar points that students haven't mastered. Then student learning may be assessed using a test generated from the Assessment CD-ROM with *ExamView Pro*.

10. Thousands of people ~~seen~~ *saw* Lindbergh in Paris.

11. Lindbergh ~~had~~ *was* 25 years old when he made his historic flight.

12. Who ~~did walk~~ *walked* on the moon in 1969?

13. How many people <u>walked</u> on the moon?   *c*

14. Earhart ~~didn't returned~~ *didn't return* from her flight across the Pacific.

15. The Wright brothers' father <u>gave</u> his sons a flying toy.   *c*

16. Goddard's colleagues ~~didn't believed~~ *didn't believe* him.

17. The first rocket flight <u>lasted</u> 2½ seconds.   *c*

18. When ~~landed men~~ *did men land* on the moon?

19. What <u>happened</u> to Earhart's plane?   *c*

20. Who <u>saw</u> the first moon landing?   *c*

PART **2**   Write the past tense of each verb.

EXAMPLES   live _____*lived*_____   feel _____*felt*_____

1. eat	*ate*	11. drink	*drank*
2. see	*saw*	12. build	*built*
3. get	*got*	13. stop	*stopped*
4. sit	*sat*	14. leave	*left*
5. hit	*hit*	15. buy	*bought*
6. make	*made*	16. think	*thought*
7. take	*took*	17. run	*ran*
8. find	*found*	18. carry	*carried*
9. say	*said*	19. sell	*sold*
10. read	*read*	20. stand	*stood*

PART **3**   Fill in the blanks with the negative form of the underlined verb.

EXAMPLE   Lindbergh <u>worked</u> for the U.S. Mail Service. Earhart
_____*didn't work*_____ for the U.S. Mail Service.

1. There <u>were</u> trains in 1900. There _____*weren't*_____ any airplanes.

The Simple Past Tense   **257**

PART 2

1. Part 2 may be used in addition to the Assessment CD-ROM with *ExamView Pro* as an in-class test to assess student performance. Say: *Some of these verbs are regular and some are irregular.* Go over the example with the class.

2. Have students complete the exercise individually. Collect for assessment.

3. If necessary, have students review:
   8.2   Spelling of the Past Tense of Regular Verbs (p. 226)
   8.8   List of Irregular Past Tense Verbs (p. 239).

PART 3

1. Part 3 may be used in addition to the Assessment CD-ROM with *ExamView Pro* as an in-class test to assess student performance. Have students read the direction line. Ask: *What do we write on the blanks?* (the negative) Go over the example with the class.

2. Have students complete the exercise individually. Collect for assessment.

3. If necessary, have students review:
   8.4   Past Tense of *Be* (p. 230)
   8.9   Negative Forms of Past Tense Verbs (p. 241).

Lesson Review

To use Parts 2 and 3 as a review, assign them as homework or use them as in-class activities to be completed individually or in pairs. Check answers and review errors as a class. For an extra challenge, have students pronounce the past tense forms in Part 2. Reteach grammar points that students haven't mastered. Then student learning may be assessed using a test generated from the Assessment CD-ROM with *ExamView Pro*.

1. Part 4 may be used in addition to the Assessment CD-ROM with *ExamView Pro* as an in-class test to assess student performance. Have students read the direction line. Ask: *Do we use wh- words in these questions?* (no; we write *yes/no* questions.) Go over the example as a class.

2. Have students complete the exercise individually. Collect for assessment.

3. If necessary, have students review:

   8.6 Questions with *Was/Were* (p. 232–233)

   8.10 Questions with Past Tense Verbs (p. 245).

2. The Wright brothers <u>flew</u> a plane in 1903. They _____*didn't fly*_____ a plane in 1899.

3. Charles Lindbergh <u>was</u> an aviator. He _____*wasn't*_____ a president.

4. The Wright brothers <u>invented</u> the airplane. They _____*didn't invent*_____ the telephone.

5. Wilbur Wright <u>died</u> of typhoid fever. He _____*didn't die*_____ in a plane crash.

6. Lindbergh <u>went</u> to Paris. Earhart _____*didn't go*_____ to Paris.

7. Lindbergh <u>came</u> back from his flight. Earhart _____*didn't come*_____ back from her last flight.

8. Goddard <u>was born</u> in the nineteenth century. He _____*wasn't born*_____ in the twentieth century.

9. Goddard <u>built</u> a rocket. He _____*didn't build*_____ an airplane.

10. Goddard <u>became</u> a physics professor. He _____*didn't become*_____ a pilot.

PART **4** Read each statement. Write a *yes/no* question about the words in parentheses ( ). Write a short answer.

EXAMPLE Lindbergh crossed the ocean. (Earhart) (yes)
Did Earhart cross the ocean? Yes, she did.

1. Wilbur Wright became famous. (Orville Wright) (yes)
Did Orville Wright become famous? Yes, he did.

2. Lindbergh was an aviator. (Goddard) (no)
Was Goddard an aviator? No, he wasn't.

3. Lindbergh flew across the Atlantic Ocean. (Earhart) (yes)
Did Earhart fly across the Atlantic Ocean? Yes, she did.

4. Lindbergh was born in the U.S. (Goddard) (yes)
Was Goddard born in the U.S? Yes, he was.

5. Goddard wrote about rockets. (the Wright brothers) (no)
Did the Wright brothers write about rockets? No, they didn't.

6. The Russians sent a man into space. (the Americans) (yes)
Did the Americans send a man into space? Yes, they did.

7. Goddard died in 1945. (Wilbur Wright) (no)
Did Wilbur Wright die in 1945? No, he didn't.

258　Lesson **8**

Lesson Review

To use Part 4 as a review, assign it as homework or use it as an in-class activity to be completed individually or in pairs. Check answers and review errors as a class. Reteach grammar points that students haven't mastered. Then student learning may be assessed using a test generated from the Assessment CD-ROM with *ExamView Pro*.

8. The U.S. put men on the moon in 1969. (Russia) (no)

Did Russia put men on the moon in 1969? No, they didn't.

9. People laughed at Goddard's ideas in 1920. (in 1969) (no)

Did they laugh at his ideas in 1969? No, they didn't.

10. Goddard thought about rockets. (about computers) (no)

Did Goddard think about computers? No, he didn't.

PART **5** Write a *wh-* question about the words in parentheses ( ). It is not necessary to answer the questions.

EXAMPLE The Wright brothers became famous for their first airplane. (why / Lindbergh)

Why did Lindbergh become famous?

1. Earhart was born in 1897. (when / Lindbergh)

When was Lindbergh born?

2. Thomas Edison invented the phonograph. (what / the Wright brothers)

What did the Wright brothers invent?

3. Thomas Edison invented the phonograph. (who / the airplane)

Who invented the airplane?

4. Lindbergh crossed the ocean in 1927. (when / Earhart)

When did Earhart cross the ocean?

5. Lindbergh got money for his flight. (how much)

How much money did Lindbergh get for his flight?

6. Earhart wanted to fly around the world. (why)

Why did Earhart want to fly around the world?

7. Many people saw Lindbergh in Paris. (how many people)

How many people saw Lindbergh in Paris?

8. Goddard's colleagues didn't believe his ideas. (why)

Why didn't Goddard's colleagues believe his ideas?

9. Wilbur Wright died in 1912. (when / Orville Wright)

When did Orville Wright die?

10. A president examined Goddard's ideas. (which president)

Which president examined Goddard's ideas?

The Simple Past Tense **259**

PART 5

1. Part 5 may be used in addition to the Assessment CD-ROM with *ExamView Pro* as an in-class test to assess student performance. Have students read the direction line. Go over the example with the class. Remind students not to answer the questions.
2. Have students complete the exercise individually. Collect for assessment.
3. If necessary, have students review:
   8.6 Questions with *Was/Were* (p. 232–233)
   8.10 Questions with Past Tense Verbs (p. 245)
   8.11 Questions About the Subject (p. 251).

Lesson Review

To use Part 5 as a review, assign it as homework or use it as an in-class activity to be completed individually or in pairs. Check answers and review errors as a class. Reteach grammar points that students haven't mastered. Then student learning may be assessed using a test generated from the Assessment CD-ROM with *ExamView Pro*.

Expansion Activities

These expansion activities provide opportunities for students to interact with one another and further develop their speaking and writing skills. Encourage students to use grammar from this lesson whenever possible.

🕐 To save class time, assign parts of the activities as homework. Then use class time for interaction and communication. If students do not need additional speaking practice, some of the activities may be assigned as writing activities for homework, or skipped altogether.

CLASSROOM ACTIVITIES

1. Have students work in groups. Say: *Choose a member of the group to interview about his or her first experiences here in the U.S. Take turns asking questions. Then report the results of the interview to the class* (e.g., *When Lina arrived, she lived in Minneapolis. Her cousin, Felipe, picked her up at the airport.*). If it's helpful, brainstorm more questions for the interview and write them on the board.

2. Tell students that they will interview their partners about their experiences before and after they came to the U.S. Go over the sample interview. Have students review Exercise 25 before beginning this activity.

3. Explain the directions for Parts A and B. Have students work in pairs to complete the activity. Have students check their answers for Part A before beginning Part B. Then check the answers to Part B as a class.

EXPANSION ACTIVITIES

Classroom Activities

1. In a small group or with the entire class, interview a foreign student about his or her first experiences in the U.S.

   EXAMPLES Where did you live when you arrived?
   Who picked you up from the airport?
   Who helped you in the first few weeks?
   What was your first impression of the U.S.?

2. Find a partner from another country to interview. Ask questions about the circumstances that brought him or her to the U.S. and the conditions of his or her life after he or she arrived. Write your conversation. Use Exercise 25 as your model.

   EXAMPLE A: When did you leave your country?
   B: I left Ethiopia five years ago.
   A: Did you come directly to the U.S.?
   B: No. First I went to Sudan.
   A: Why did you leave Ethiopia?

3. **Game: Who and When**

   Part A. On left side of the page, there are questions about famous people. On the right side of the page are some names of famous people. Work with a partner and see how many you can match. (You can find the answers on page 262.) The first one has been done for you.

   a. Who invented the rocket? 4
   b. Who discovered America?
   c. Who painted the Mona Lisa?
   d. Who wrote *Romeo and Juliet*?
   e. Who was the first person to walk on the moon?
   f. Who was the first person in space?
   g. Which president freed the slaves?
   h. Who composed *The Magic Flute*?
   i. Who invented the phonograph?
   j. Who was the first president of the U.S.?
   k. Who became president after Reagan and before Clinton?
   l. Who invented the telephone?

   1. Leonardo da Vinci
   2. Yuri Gagarin
   3. William Shakespeare
   4. Robert Goddard
   5. Thomas Edison
   6. George Washington
   7. George Bush
   8. Pablo Picasso
   9. Alexander Graham Bell
   10. Johann Sebastian Bach
   11. Christopher Columbus
   12. Neil Armstrong
   13. Wolfgang Mozart
   14. Abraham Lincoln

Classroom Activities Variation

Activity 3 Have students close their books. Break students up into Team A and Team B. Ask the questions. The teams take turns guessing the answers. For Part B, give the statement and have the teams write the questions on the board. Then say the dates. Have the teams take turns guessing the correct dates.

Part B. Take each question from Part A and write a question using *when*. Try to guess the answer by choosing one of the years given. (You can find the answers on page 262.)

EXAMPLE   When did Goddard invent the rocket?

a. 1903	1914	(1926)	1935
b. 1215	1385	1492	1620
c. 1325	1503	1625	1788
d. 1596	1675	1801	1865
e. 1957	1960	1969	1972
f. 1957	1960	1969	1970
g. 1834	1850	1865	1899
h. 1623	1688	1699	1791
i. 1877	1899	1902	1920
j. 1620	1724	1789	1825
k. 1985	1989	1990	1992
l. 1845	1877	1910	1935

4. Finish these statements five different ways. Then find a partner and compare your sentences to your partner's sentences. Did you have any sentences in common?

EXAMPLE   When I was a child, *I didn't like to do my homework.*

When I was a child, *my parents gave me a bicycle for my tenth birthday.*

When I was a child, *my nickname was "Curly."*

a. When I was a child, _____

_____

_____

_____

b. Before I came to the U.S., _____

_____

_____

_____

1. Interview an American about a vacation he or she took. Find out where he or she went, with whom, for how long, and other related information.

2. Interview an American about a famous person he or she admires. Ask what this famous person did.

Outside Activities

The Simple Past Tense   **261**

4. After students complete their sentences, have them compare responses in pairs. Ask volunteers to talk about their experiences.

OUTSIDE ACTIVITIES

1. Tell students that they will be interviewing an American about a vacation he or she took. Brainstorm interview questions as a class. Students can report their interviews to the class or hand in a written report.

2. Tell students that they will be interviewing an American about a famous person he or she admires. Brainstorm interview questions as a class. Students can report their interviews to the class or hand in a written report.

Outside Activities Variation

As an alternative, you may invite a guest to your classroom (e.g., an administrator, a librarian, or a service worker at your school) and have students do a class interview. Students should prepare their interview questions ahead of time.

INTERNET ACTIVITIES

1. Tell students: *You're going to research one of these famous people on the Internet.* Ask if anyone knows all of the people on the list. If necessary, briefly review the list of people with the class. Ask: *What questions will you answer about the person? (What did he or she do? When did he or she do it? When was he or she born?* etc.)

2. Have students prepare a brief presentation of the 2004 landing on Mars. Have volunteers present their information to the class.

3. Have students prepare a brief presentation of the 2003 anniversary of the Wright brothers' first flight. Have volunteers present their information to the class.

Internet
Activities

1. Using the Internet, find out something about one of the following famous people. What did he or she do? When did he or she do it? When was he or she born? Is he or she still alive? If not, when did he or she die?

   a. Marie Curie
   b. Alexander Fleming
   c. Thomas Edison
   d. Alexander Graham Bell
   e. Bill Gates
   f. Henry Ford
   g. Jonas Salk
   h. Edwin Hubble
   i. Enrico Fermi
   j. John Von Neumann
   k. Leo Baekeland
   l. Ian Wilmut

2. Find a Web site with information about the 2004 landing on Mars. Find a picture of Mars.

3. Find a Web site with information about the 2003 anniversary of the Wright brothers' first flight. What events took place?

 Additional Activities at http://elt.thomson.com/gic

ANSWERS TO CLASSROOM ACTIVITY 3:
Part A: b = 11, c = 1, d = 3, e = 12, f = 2, g = 14, h = 13, i = 5, j = 6, k = 7, l = 9
Part B: a = 1926, b = 1492, c = 1503, d = 1596, e = 1969, f = 1957, g = 1865, h = 1791, i = 1877, j = 1789, k = 1989, l = 1877

262   Lesson **8**

Internet Activities Variation

If students don't have access to the Internet, they may find the information needed in books and other resources at a local public library.

Activity 1 Have students research a famous person from their countries. Ask volunteers to make a brief presentation in front of the class. Encourage students to include time lines and photos.

LESSON

9

GRAMMAR

Infinitives
Modals
Imperatives

CONTEXT: Smart Shopping

Getting the Best Price
Getting a Customer's Attention
Smart Shopping: Coupons, Rain Checks, and Rebates
The Customer Service Counter

263

Expansion

Theme The topic for this lesson can be enhanced with the following ideas:

1. Store flyers
2. Store coupons, rebates, and rain checks

Lesson | 9

Lesson Overview

GRAMMAR

1. Ask: *What did we study in Lesson 8?* (the simple past tense) *What are we going to study in this lesson?* (infinitives, modals, and imperatives) *Can anyone give me examples of infinitives, modals, or imperatives?* Have students give examples. Write them on the board.

CONTEXT

1. Ask: *What will we learn about in this lesson?* (smart shopping) Activate students' prior knowledge. Ask: *What is "smart shopping"? Are you a smart shopper? Where do you like to shop? In your opinion, where can you get the best bargains?*
2. Have students share their knowledge and personal experiences.

Photo

1. Direct students' attention to the photo. Ask: *What's going on in this photo?* (A man is shopping for a camera.) Ask: *What kind of store is he in?* (an electronics store)
2. *Have you shopped for a camera recently? Where did you buy it? Did you get a good price? How do you know? How many cameras did you look at before you bought your camera?*

🕐 To save class time, have students do the Test/Review at the end of the lesson, or administer a lesson test generated from the Assessment CD-ROM with *ExamView®Pro*. Skip sections of the lesson that students have already mastered. You may also assign some sections for self-study for extra credit.

9.1 | Infinitives—An Overview

Have students look at grammar chart **9.1.** Say: *The infinitive of the verb is to + the base form.* Explain that an infinitive never has an ending and that it never shows tense. Read the example sentences from the chart.

Getting the Best Price (Reading)

1. Have students look at the photo. Ask: *Who are the people in the photo?* (a family and a salesperson)
2. Have students look at the title of the reading. Ask: *What is the reading about? How do you know?* Have students use the title and the photo to make predictions about the reading.
3. Preteach any vocabulary words students may not know such as *prove* and *receipt.*

BEFORE YOU READ

1. Have students discuss the questions in pairs.
2. Ask for a few volunteers to share their answers with the class.

To save class time, skip "Before You Read" or have students prepare answers for homework ahead of time.

Reading ○ *CD 2, Track 6*

1. Have students read the text silently. Tell them to pay special attention to infinitives. Then play the audio and have students read along silently.
2. Check students' comprehension. Ask questions such as: *If you find a lower price, what do some stores do?* (match the price) *How can you prove that another store has a cheaper price?* (by showing an advertisement) *What does the salesperson want to do?* (He wants to help his store make money.) *What do you need to keep to prove that you bought an item?* (the receipt)

To save class time, have students do the reading for homework ahead of time.

9.1 | Infinitives—An Overview

Examples	Explanation
I want **to go** shopping. I need **to buy** a new DVD player. It's important **to compare** prices. It's not hard **to be** a good shopper.	An infinitive is *to* + the base form: *to go, to buy, to compare, to be*

GETTING THE BEST PRICE

 Before You Read

1. Do you like to shop for new things such as TVs, DVD players, computers, microwave ovens?
2. Do you try to compare prices in different stores before you buy an expensive item?

Read the following article. Pay special attention to infinitives.

Are you planning **to buy** a new TV, digital camera, or DVD player? Of course you want **to get** the best price. Sometimes you see an item you like at one store and then go to another store **to compare** prices. If you find the same item at a higher price, you probably think it is necessary **to go** back to the first store **to get** the lower price. But it usually isn't. You can simply tell the salesperson in the second store that you saw the item at a better price somewhere else. Usually the salesperson will try **to match**[1] the other store's price. However, you need **to prove** that you can buy it cheaper elsewhere.[2] The proof can be an advertisement from the newspaper. If you don't have an ad, the salesperson can call the other store **to check** the price. The salesperson doesn't want you **to leave** the store without buying anything. He wants his store **to make** money. Some salespeople are happy **to call** the other store **to check** the price.

What happens if you buy something and a few days later see it cheaper at another store? Some stores will give you the difference in price for a limited period of time (such as 30 days). It's important **to keep** the receipt **to show** when you bought the item and how much you paid.

Every shopper wants **to save** money.

[1] To *match* a price means to give you an equal price.
[2] *Elsewhere* means somewhere else, another place.

Reading Variation

To practice listening skills, have students first listen to the audio alone. Ask a few comprehension questions. Repeat the audio if necessary. Then have students open their books and read along as they listen to the audio.

Reading Glossary

prove: to show that something is true or genuine
receipt: a piece of paper showing that a bill is paid

9.2 | Verbs Followed by an Infinitive

We often use an infinitive after certain verbs.

Examples				Explanation
Subject	Verb	Infinitive	Complement	We use an infinitive after these verbs:
I	plan	**to buy**	a camera.	
We	want	**to get**	the best price.	
You	need	**to be**	a smart shopper.	
She	likes	**to save**	money.	

				begin	hope	prefer

We use an infinitive after these verbs:

begin	hope	prefer
continue	like	promise
decide	love	start
expect	need	try
forget	plan	want

They	want	**to buy**	a DVD player.
We	wanted	**to buy**	a new TV.
He	is planning	**to buy**	a microwave oven.

An infinitive never has an ending. It never shows tense. Only the first verb has an ending or shows tense.

Wrong: He wanted to *bought* a new TV.

Pronunciation Notes:

1. In informal speech, *want to* is pronounced "wanna." Listen to your teacher pronounce these sentences:

    I *want to* buy a DVD.

    Do you *want to* go shopping with me?

2. In other infinitives, we often pronounce *to* like "ta" or "da" (after a vowel sound) or "a" (after a "d" sound). Listen to your teacher pronounce these sentences:

    Do you like to watch movies at home? ("ta")

    I plan to buy a new DVD player. ("ta")

    Try to get the best price. ("da")

    We decided to buy a digital camera. ("a")

    I need to compare prices. ("a")

EXERCISE 1 Circle the correct verb form to complete each sentence.

EXAMPLE She wants (*buy*, *to buy*, *buys*) a new microwave oven.

1. I'm planning (*shop*, *shopping*, *to shop*) for a wide-screen TV.

2. I decided (*to spend*, *to spent*, *spent*) about $500.

3. I'm trying (*get*, *to get*, *to getting*) the best price.

4. The saleswoman forgot (*gave*, *to give*, *to gave*) me her business card.

5. Did you decide (*to buy*, *to bought*, *bought*) a DVD player?

6. You need (*be*, *to be*, *are*) a smart shopper.

9.2 | Verbs Followed by an Infinitive

1. Have students go back to the reading on page 264. Say: *Circle all the verbs* (*other than* be) *that come before the infinitives* (*want, go, try,* etc.). Have volunteers give you examples. Go over any errors.

2. Have students look at grammar chart **9.2.** Say: *There are some verbs that are often followed by an infinitive, for example* plan, want, need, *and* like. Go over the examples. Point out the list of other verbs that are often followed by an infinitive. Ask students to go back to the reading to see if they circled any of the verbs from the chart.

3. Review the sentences in the different tenses. Say: *An infinitive can follow a verb that's in the past, present, and future. But notice that the infinitive itself does not show tense or whether the subject is singular or plural.*

4. Direct students to the Pronunciation Notes. Demonstrate the informal pronunciation of *want to* ("wanna"). Explain that most native speakers say *wanna*—but it's never written that way. Have students practice the pronunciation chorally as a class.

5. Explain that often the *to* in infinitives is pronounced "ta" or "da" (after a vowel sound as in *try "ta" get*) or "a" (after a "d" sound as in *decided "a" buy*). Demonstrate the pronunciation. Go over the example sentences. Read the sentences in the top part of the chart as well. Have students practice the pronunciation chorally as a class.

EXERCISE 1

1. Have students read the direction line. Ask: *What are you going to circle?* (the correct verb) Go over the example in the book.

2. Have students complete the rest of Exercise 1 individually. Check the answers as a class.

3. If necessary, review grammar chart **9.2** on page 265.

EXERCISE 2

1. Have students read the direction line. Say: *Write a sentence using the verbs given. You can write a sentence in the present or the past. Remember, these verbs are used with infinitives.* Go over the examples in the book. Ask volunteers to models the examples.

2. Have students complete Exercise 2 individually. Then have students compare answers in pairs. Circulate to observe pair work. Give help as needed.

3. If necessary, review grammar chart **9.2** on page 265.

🕐 To save class time, have students do half of the exercise in class and complete the other half for homework. Or assign the entire exercise for homework.

EXERCISE **2**   ABOUT YOU Make a sentence about yourself with the words given. Use an appropriate tense. You may find a partner, and compare your sentences to your partner's sentences.

EXAMPLES   like / eat
I like to eat pizza.

learn / speak
I learned to speak German when I was a child.

try / find
I'm trying to find a bigger apartment.

1. love / go

   Answers will vary.

2. like / play

3. need / have

4. expect / get

5. want / go

6. plan / buy

7. need / understand

8. not need / have

9. try / learn

Expansion

Exercise 2 Have students write a short paragraph about their partners. Use some of the information from Exercise 2. Say: *Tell the class about your classmate. Write a paragraph about him or her; include interesting information.*

EXERCISE **3** ABOUT YOU Ask a question with the words given in the present tense. Another student will answer.

EXAMPLE like / travel

A: Do you like to travel?
B: Yes, I do. OR No, I don't.

1. expect / pass this course
   Do you expect to pass this course?
2. plan / graduate soon
   Do you plan to graduate soon?
3. plan / transfer to another college
   Do you plan to transfer to another college?
4. like / read
   Do you like to read?
5. like / study grammar
   Do you like to study grammar?
6. try / understand Americans
   Do you try to understand Americans?
7. try / learn idioms
   Do you try to learn idioms?
8. expect / leave this country
   Do you expect to leave this country?

EXERCISE **4** ABOUT YOU Ask a question with "Do you want to . . . ?" and the words given. Another student will answer. Then ask a *wh-* question with the words in parentheses ( ) whenever possible.

EXAMPLE buy a car (why)

A: Do you want to buy a car?
B: Yes, I do. OR No, I don't.

A: Why do you want to buy a car?
B: I don't like public transportation.

1. take a computer course next semester (why)
   Do you want to take a computer course next semester?
2. move (why) (when)
   Do you want to move?
3. leave this country (why) (when)
   Do you want to leave this country?
4. get a job / get another job (what kind of job)
   Do you want to get another job?
5. become an American citizen (why)
   Do you want to become an American citizen?
6. transfer to a different school (why)
   Do you want to transfer to a different school?
7. take another English course next semester (which course)
   Do you want to take another English course next semester?
8. learn another language (which language)
   Do you want to learn another language?
9. review the last lesson (why)
   Do you want to review the last lesson?

Infinitives; Modals; Imperatives **267**

Expansion

Exercise 4 Have students write five more questions to ask a partner. Have students take turns asking and answering. Ask volunteers to share some questions and answers with the class.

1. Have students read the direction line. Say: *Find out more information about your classmate.* Remind students that they should use different tenses. Go over the example in the book. Ask volunteers to model the example.
2. Have students complete Exercise 3 in pairs. Circulate to observe pair work. Give help as needed.
3. If necessary, review grammar chart **9.2** on page 265.

To save class time, have students do half of the exercise in class and complete the other half in writing for homework, answering the questions themselves. Or if students do not need speaking practice, the entire exercise may be skipped or done in writing.

1. Have students read the direction line. Ask: *How are we going to begin the first question?* (with *Do you want to …*) *What kind of question is the second question?* (a *wh-* question) Go over the example in the book. Ask a volunteer to model the example with you. Answer the example question with a negative answer.
2. Have students complete Exercise 4 in pairs. Circulate to observe pair work. Give help as needed.
3. If necessary, review grammar chart **9.2** on page 265.

To save class time, have students do half of the exercise in class and complete the other half in writing for homework, answering the questions themselves. Or if students do not need speaking practice, the entire exercise may be skipped or done in writing.

9.3 | *It + Be* + Adjective + Infinitive

1. Have students go back to the reading on page 264. Say: *There are two phrases in the reading that begin with the impersonal it (it is necessary to go and it's important to keep). Underline them.* Write on the board: It + be + *adjective*. Have volunteers give you examples. Go over any errors.

2. Have students look at grammar chart **9.3**. Say: *We often use an infinitive with sentences beginning with an impersonal* it. Go over the examples. Point out the list of adjectives that are often followed by an infinitive.

EXERCISE 5

1. Tell students that this exercise is about their opinions. Have students read the direction line. Go over the example in the book. Have a volunteer model the example.

2. Have students complete Exercise 5 individually. Quickly go around the class to have students share their answers.

3. If necessary, review grammar chart **9.3** on page 268.

EXERCISE 6

1. Tell students that this exercise is about their opinions. Have students read the direction line. Go over the example in the book. Have a volunteer model the example.

2. Have students complete Exercise 6 individually. Quickly go around the class to have students share their answers.

3. If necessary, review grammar chart **9.3** on page 268.

🕐 To save class time, have students do half of the exercise in class and complete the other half for homework. Or assign the entire exercise for homework.

9.3 | *It + Be* + Adjective + Infinitive

We often use an infinitive with sentences beginning with an impersonal *it*.

Examples				Explanation
It	*Be (+ n't)*	Adjective	Infinitive Phrase	An infinitive can follow these adjectives:
It	is	important	**to save** your receipt.	dangerous hard good
It	is	easy	**to shop.**	possible difficult expensive
It	isn't	necessary	**to go** back to the first store.	impossible easy fun
				important necessary

EXERCISE 5   Complete each statement.

EXAMPLE   It's expensive to own *a big car.*

1. It's important to learn _____ Answers will vary.
2. It's hard to pronounce _____
3. It's hard to lift _____
4. It's necessary to have _____
5. It's easy to learn _____
6. It's hard to learn _____
7. It isn't necessary to know _____

EXERCISE 6   Complete each statement with an infinitive phrase.

EXAMPLE   It's easy *to ride a bike.*

1. It's fun _____ Answers will vary.
2. It's impossible _____
3. It's possible _____
4. It's necessary _____
5. It's dangerous _____
6. It's hard _____
7. It isn't good _____
8. It isn't necessary _____

Expansion

Exercise 6 Have students discuss their ideas in groups. Ask: *Did anyone have the same ideas you had? Do you agree or disagree strongly with what your groups members wrote?*

9.4 | *Be* + Adjective + Infinitive

We often use an infinitive after certain adjectives.

Examples				Explanation
Subject	*Be*	Adjective	Infinitive Phrase	We can use an infinitive after these adjectives:
I	am	ready	**to buy** a camera.	happy afraid lucky
The salesman	is	glad	**to help** you.	sad prepared proud
He	is	prepared	**to make** a sale.	glad ready

EXERCISE 7   Fill in the blanks.

EXAMPLE   I'm lucky *to be in the U.S.* _____

1. Americans are lucky _____ Answers will vary. _____
2. I'm proud _____
3. I'm happy _____
4. I'm sometimes afraid _____
5. I'm not afraid _____
6. Are the students prepared _____
7. Is the teacher ready _____

EXERCISE 8   ABOUT YOU Answer the following questions. (You may work with a partner and ask and answer with your partner.)

Answers will vary.
1. Are you happy to be in this country?
2. Is it important to know English or another language in your country?
3. Are you afraid to make a mistake when you speak English?
4. Is it possible to find a job without knowing any English?
5. Is it easy to learn English grammar?
6. Is it important to wear a seat belt when you are a passenger in a car?
7. Is it necessary to have a computer?
8. Were you sad to leave your country?
9. Are you prepared to have a test on this lesson?

Infinitives; Modals; Imperatives   **269**

Expansion

Exercise 7 Have students discuss their ideas in groups. Ask: *Did anyone have the same ideas you had? Do you agree or disagree strongly with what your groups members wrote?*

Exercise 8 Create two rings of students. Have half of the students stand in an outer ring around the classroom. Have the other half stand in an inner ring, facing the outer ring. Instruct students to ask and answer the questions from Exercise 8. Call out *"turn"* every minute or so. Students in the inner ring should move one space clockwise. Students now ask and answer with their new partners. Have students ask questions in random order. Make sure students look at each other when they're speaking.

9.4 | *Be* + Adjective + Infinitive

Have students look at grammar chart **9.4**. Say: *We often use an infinitive after certain adjectives.* Go over the examples. Point out the list of adjectives that are often followed by an infinitive.

EXERCISE 7

1. Tell students that this exercise is about their opinions. Have students read the direction line. Go over the example in the book. Have a volunteer model the example.
2. Have students complete Exercise 7 individually. Quickly go around the class to have students share their answers.
3. If necessary, review grammar chart **9.4** on page 269.

EXERCISE 8

1. Tell students that they'll first answer the questions themselves and then they'll interview a partner. Have students read the direction line. Tell students to answer the questions with complete sentences.
2. Have students first answer the questions individually. Then have students ask and answer questions in pairs. Circulate to observe pair work. Give help as needed.
3. If necessary, review grammar charts **9.3** on page 268 and **9.4** on page 269.

To save class time, have students do half of the exercise in class and complete the other half in writing for homework. Or if students do not need speaking practice, the entire exercise may be skipped or done in writing.

9.5 | Using an Infinitive to Show Purpose

1. Have students cover up grammar chart **9.5**. Say: *We often use an infinitive to show purpose or to show why we're doing something. For example, I went to the store to buy milk. The infinitive (to buy milk) shows that the purpose of going to the store was to buy milk.* Have students go back to the reading on page 264. Say: *Double underline the infinitives that show purpose or why something is being done.* Have volunteers give you examples. Go over any errors.

2. Have students look at grammar chart **9.5**. Go over the examples. Point out that some people make the mistake of using *for* to show purpose.

3. Explain that the use of *to* to show purpose is a short form of *in order to*. Read through the example sentences. Then go back to the top of the chart and ask volunteers to substitute *in order to* for *to* in the other example sentences.

EXERCISE 9

1. Have students read the direction line. Go over the example in the book. Have a volunteer do #1.

2. Have students complete Exercise 9 individually. Check the answers as a class.

3. If necessary, review grammar chart **9.5** on page 270.

EXERCISE 10

 CD 2, Track 7

1. Have students read the direction line. Ask: *What kind of verb do we write on the blanks?* (infinitives) Go over the example in the book. Ask: *What does the infinitive show here?* (It shows purpose—it shows what person A uses the camera for.)

2. Have students complete Exercise 10 individually. Check answers as a class.

3. Then have students practice the conversation in pairs.

4. If necessary, review grammar chart **9.5** on page 270.

To save class time, have students do half of the exercise in class and complete the other half for homework. Or assign the entire exercise for homework.

9.5 | Using an Infinitive to Show Purpose

Examples	Explanation
I went to a store **to buy** a digital camera. I went to a second store **to compare** prices. The saleswoman called the first store **to check** the price.	We use an infinitive to show the purpose of an action. Do not use *for* to show purpose. *Wrong:* I went to a store *for buy* a digital camera.
I use a digital camera **to** e-mail photos to my friends. I use a digital camera **in order to** e-mail photos to my friends.	*To* for purpose is the short form of *in order to*.

EXERCISE 9 Fill in the blanks to show purpose.

EXAMPLE I bought a phone card to *call my friends.*

1. I use my dictionary to _____ **Answers will vary.**
2. At the end of a concert, people applaud to _____
3. He went to an appliance store to _____
4. She worked overtime to _____
5. I bought the Sunday newspaper to _____
6. You need to show your driver's license to _____
7. You can use a hammer to _____
8. Some people join a health club to _____
9. On a computer, you use the mouse to _____
10. When you return an item to a store, take your receipt to _____
_____

EXERCISE 10 Fill in the blanks to complete this conversation.

A: Do you want to see my new digital camera?
B: Wow. It's so small. Does it take good pictures?
A: Absolutely. I use this camera ___*to take*___ all my pictures
  (example)
  now. I never use my old one anymore.
B: Aren't digital cameras expensive?
A: Not anymore. I went online ___*to compare*___ prices. Then I
  (1)
  went to several stores in this city ___*to get*___ the best price.
  (2)

270 Lesson **9**

Expansion

Exercise 9 Have students practice asking and answering questions based on each item in Exercise 9. Instruct students to use this pattern:
A: Why did you buy a phone card?
B: To call my friends.

Exercise 10 Variation

To provide practice with listening skills, have students close their books and listen to the audio. Repeat the audio as needed. Ask comprehension questions, such as: *What kind of camera does person A have?* (a digital camera) *Is the digital camera big or small?* (small) *Why did person A go to several stores?* (to find the best price) Then have students open their books and complete Exercise 10.

B: Do you take a lot of pictures?

A: Oh, yes. And I put them on my computer _____ *to send* _____

(3)

them by e-mail to my family back home.

B: Do you ever make prints of your pictures?

A: Of course. I bought some high-quality glossy paper

_____ *to make* _____ prints for my family album.

(4)

B: I still like my old camera.

A: But you have to take the film to a photo place and then you have to

wait _____ *to see* _____ if the pictures are good or not. With my

(5)

digital camera, I can see immediately if the pictures are good.

B: Is it hard to use the camera?

A: At first I had to read the manual carefully _____ *to learn* _____

(6)

how to take good pictures and transfer them to my computer.
But now it's easy. I'll take a picture of you. Smile.

B: My eyes are closed in the picture. Take another picture of me.

A: OK. This one's better. But I don't like the background. I can push this

button _____ *to change* _____ the background. It's too dark. I can

(7)

push this button _____ *to make* _____ the color brighter.

(8)

B: Which button do you push _____ *to make* _____ me more handsome?

(9)

Expansion

Exercise 10 Have students write a similar conversation about another new electronic device, such as an mp3 player. Have students work in pairs. Then ask volunteers to role-play their conversations in front of the class.

Getting a Customer's Attention (Reading)

1. Have students look at the photo. Ask: *What kind of store is this?* (a wholesale store like Costco or Sam's Club where customers buy in bulk at cheaper prices) *What's happening in the picture?* (Customers are tasting samples of food.)
2. Have students look at the title of the reading. Ask: *What is the reading about? How do you know?* Have students use the title and photo to make predictions about the reading.
3. Preteach any vocabulary words students may not know such as *technique, encourage, service,* and *competition.*

BEFORE YOU READ

1. Have students discuss the questions in pairs.
2. Ask for a few volunteers to share their answers with the class.

To save class time, skip "Before You Read" or have students prepare answers for homework ahead of time.

Reading ∩ CD 2, Track 8

1. Have students read the text silently. Tell them to pay special attention to objects before an infinitive. Then play the audio and have students read along silently.
2. Check students' comprehension. Ask questions such as: *What are two techniques stores use to get you to buy their products?* (free samples and getting two for the price of one) *What do movie theaters do to get more customers?* (offer lower prices at early hours)

To save class time, have students do the reading for homework ahead of time.

GETTING A CUSTOMER'S ATTENTION

Before You Read

1. Do you try free samples of food in supermarkets?
2. Do you ever go to the movies early in the day to get a cheaper ticket?

 Read the following article. Pay special attention to objects before an infinitive.

Stores use several techniques to get your business. Did you ever go to a food store and see someone giving away free samples? Many supermarkets **encourage you to buy** a product by giving you a free sample. They think that if you try this product, maybe you will buy it. Often they encourage you even more by giving you a coupon for the product.

Sometimes a store will advertise two for the price of one. This is a marketing technique to get your interest. After you come into the store for the sale item, the manager **wants you to do** the rest of your shopping there, too.

Movie theaters lower their price in the early hours. This is because most people don't think of going to a movie early in the day. Both you and the movie theater benefit when you take advantage of the reduced price. You help fill the theater and get a cheap ticket in return.

Another way to get customer attention is with good service. Sometimes as you're leaving a store, a salesperson may ask you, "Do you **want me to take** this out to your car for you?" There is no extra charge for such service.

With so much competition between businesses, owners and managers have to use all kinds of techniques to get our attention and **encourage us to shop** at their store and return often.

272 Lesson 9

Reading Variation

To practice listening skills, have students first listen to the audio alone. Ask a few comprehension questions. Repeat the audio if necessary. Then have students open their books and read along as they listen to the audio.

Reading Glossary

competition: the people, as a group, that one is trying to do better than, especially in business
encourage: to give strength or hope to someone; urge
service: general attention to customers' needs in a business
technique: a method, procedure by which something is performed

---

9.6 | Object Before an Infinitive

Examples	Explanation
They **like you to try** the free sample. Do you **want me to carry** this out to your car for you? They **want us to do** all our shopping in one store. I **expect salespeople to be** courteous. I **expect them to be** helpful, too.	After *like, want, need, expect,* and *encourage,* we can use a noun or object pronoun (*me, you, him, her, it, us, them*) + an infinitive.

EXERCISE 11   Circle the correct words in parentheses ( ) to complete each conversation.

CONVERSATION 1

Salesman: Do you want (**me**, I) (**to help**, help) you find something?
(example) (1)

Mother: Yes. We could use your help. Our daughter wants (we, **us**)
(2)

(bought, **to buy**) her a new cell phone. We don't know which
(3)

plan to buy.

Salesman: How many minutes a month does she talk on the phone?

Mother: She never stops talking on the phone. I want (**her to use**,
(4)

that she use) it just for emergencies, but she chats with her

friends all the time.

Salesman: Here's a plan I want (**you to consider**, *that you consider*).
(5)

It has unlimited calls at night and on weekends.

Mother: You don't understand. We want (**her**, she) to use the phone
(6)

less, not more.

CONVERSATION 2

Man: I'm going to buy a digital camera on Saturday. I need

(*that you*, **you to**) come with me.
(1)

Friend: Why? How do you want (*that I*, **me to**) help you?
(2)

Man: You already have a digital camera, so you can give me
advice.

9.6 | Object Before an Infinitive

1. Have students cover up grammar chart **9.6**. Then ask them to go back to the reading on page 272. Ask them to study the verb phrases that are highlighted in the text. Ask: *Can you find a pattern?* (verb + object + infinitive) Then ask: *What verbs are followed by an object?* (*encourage* and *want*)

2. Have students look at grammar chart **9.6** on page 273. Say: *After like, want, need, expect, and encourage, we can use a noun or object pronoun + infinitive.* If necessary, briefly review object pronouns (see grammar chart **5.6** on page 140). Go over the examples and explanations.

EXERCISE 11

🎧 *CD 2, Track 9*

1. Have students read the direction line. Tell students that they will be circling objects and infinitives.

2. Have students complete Exercise 11 individually. Check answers as a class.

3. Then have students practice the conversations in pairs.

4. If necessary, review grammar chart **9.6** on page 273.

Exercise 11 Variation

To provide practice with listening skills, have students close their books and listen to the audio. Say: *You will hear four short conversations.* Repeat the audio as needed. Ask comprehension questions, such as: *In conversation 1, does the mother need the salesman's help?* (yes) *What does the daughter want her parents to do?* (buy her a new cell phone) *What does the mother need help with?* (choosing a plan to buy) Then have students open their books and complete Exercise 11.

CONVERSATION 3

Husband: Oh, look. There's free food over there. Do you want
(*me to get*, *that I get*) you a little hotdog?
(1)

Wife: No. They just want (*us*, *we*) to spend our money on things
(2)
we don't need.

CONVERSATION 4

Grocery Clerk: Excuse me, miss. You have a lot of bags. Do you want
(*me*, *I*) (*to help*, *helping*) you take them to your car?
(1)   (2)

Shopper: Thanks. My husband's in the car. I wanted (*him*, *he*)
(3)
(*to help*, *helped*) me, but he hates shopping. He prefers
(4)
to wait in the car. Besides, he has a bad back, and I
don't want (*that he*, *him to*) lift anything. We're having a
(5)
dinner party on Saturday and we invited 20 guests, but I . . .

Grocery Clerk: Uh, excuse me. I hear my boss calling me. He needs me
now (*to give*, *giving*) him some help.
(6)

Expansion

Exercise 11 Have volunteers role-play their conversations in front of the class.

EXERCISE **12** Fill in the blanks with an object pronoun and the infinitive of the word in parentheses ( ).

EXAMPLE A: What should we do for homework?

B: I'd like _____*you to write*_____ a composition about shopping.
_____(write)

1. A: Do you want the teacher to explain the grammar again?

    B: Yes. And I want _____*him/her to speak*_____ more slowly.
    _____(speak)

2. A: Do your parents want you to be more independent?

    B: Yes. They want _____*me to learn*_____ how to drive.
    _____(learn)

3. A: Do you expect your parents to buy you a car?

    B: No, but I expect _____*them to pay for*_____ my insurance.
    _____(pay for)

4. A: Do you need my help on Saturday?

    B: Yes. I need _____*you to move*_____ some of my furniture
    _____(move)

    into the basement.

5. A: Where's your girlfriend?

    B: I don't know. I expected _____*her to be*_____ here
    _____(be)

    two hours ago, but she's always late.

6. A: Our teacher gives so much homework. He expects _____*us*_____

    _____*to write*_____ one composition a week.
    _____(write)

    B: And he doesn't want _____*us to come*_____ late
    _____(come)

    to class. If we come ten minutes late, he marks us absent.

7. A: Did your brother go on the trip with you?

    B: No, he didn't. We wanted _____*him to go*_____,
    _____(go)

    but he needed to stay home.

---

1. Have students read the direction line. Ask: *What do we write on the blanks?* (an object pronoun and the infinitive of the word in parentheses) Go over the example in the book.
2. Have students complete the exercise individually. Then have students compare answers and practice the short dialogues in pairs. Circulate to observe pair work. Give help as needed.
3. If necessary, review grammar chart **9.6** on page 273.

To save class time, have students do half of the exercise in class and complete the other half for homework. Or assign the entire exercise for homework.

9.7 | Overview of Modals

1. Have students cover up grammar chart **9.7** on page 276. Write on the board: *can, could, should, will, would, may, might,* and *must.* Activate prior knowledge. Ask: *Does anyone know any of these words?* Then write on the board: *He can sleep late every day.* Ask: *Do you notice anything different about the word* can*? How is it different from other verbs?* (It doesn't have an *-s* form. You don't use the infinitive after *can.*)

2. Then have students look at grammar chart **9.7**. Say: *Modals are different from other verbs in the following ways.* Review the facts about modals.

3. Quickly go over the meanings of the modals in the chart. (*Can* means ability, possibility, and permission. *Should* is used to give or ask for advice. *Must* is a very formal way of expressing necessity. It's used to talk about rules and laws. *Have to* is another way of saying *must,* but it's less formal. *Might* and *may* mean the same thing. They are used to show possibility.) Explain, though, that you will go over each modal in depth later in the lesson.

4. Review the comparison of affirmative and negative statements and questions.

9.7 Overview of Modals

List of Modals	Facts About Modals

can
could
should
will
would
may
might
must
	1. Modals are different from other verbs because they don't have an *-s, -ed,* or *-ing* ending.
	    He **can** compare prices. (NOT: He *cans*)
	2. Modals are different from other verbs because we don't use an infinitive after a modal.[3] We use the base form.
	    Compare:
	    He **wants to buy** a digital camera.
	    He **might buy** a digital camera.
	3. To form the negative, put *not* after the modal.
	    You **should not** throw away the receipt.
	    Hurry! These prices **may not** last.
	4. Some verbs are like modals in meaning: *have to, be able to*
	    You **must** return the item within 30 days. = You **have to** return the item within 30 days.
	    He **can't** get a credit card. = He **is not able to** get a credit card.

Compare Affirmative Statements and Questions

Wh- Word	Modal	Subject	Modal	Base Form	Complement	Short Answer
		You	should	buy	a new TV.	
	Should	you		buy	a DVD player?	No, you shouldn't.
What	should	you		buy?		
		Who	should	buy	a new TV?	
		She	can	compare	prices.	
	Can	she		compare	prices online?	Yes, she can.
How	can	she		compare	prices online?	
		Who	can	compare	prices?	

Compare Negative Statements and Questions

Wh- Word	Modal	Subject	Modal	Base Form	Complement
		He	shouldn't	buy	a digital camera.
Why	shouldn't	he		buy	a digital camera?

[3] Exception: *ought to. Ought to* means *should.*

Before You Read

1. Do you see coupons in magazines and newspapers? Do you use them?
2. Do you see signs that say "rebate" on store products? Do you see signs that say "Buy one, get one free"?

Read the following article. Pay special attention to modals and related expressions.

Do you ever receive coupons in the mail? Manufacturers often send coupons to shoppers. They want people to try their products. If you always use the same toothpaste and the manufacturer gives you a coupon for a different toothpaste, you **might** try the new brand.[4] Coupons have an expiration date. You **should** pay attention to this date because you **cannot** use the coupon after this date.

Stores have weekly specials. But there is usually a limit. If you see a sign that says, "Eggs, 69¢ a dozen. Limit 2," this means you **can** only buy two dozen at this price. If you see a sign that says, "3 for $1.00," you **don't have to** buy three items to get the special price. If you buy only one, you **will** pay 34¢.

What **should** you do if a store has a special but you **can't** find this item on the shelf? If this item is sold out, you **can** go to the customer service desk and ask for a rain check. A rain check allows you to buy this item at the sale price even after the sale is over. A rain check usually has an expiration date. You **must** buy this item by the expiration date if you want to receive the sale price.

If you see a sign that says "rebate," this means that you **can** get money back from the manufacturer. You **have to** mail the proof of purchase and the cash register receipt to the manufacturer to prove that you bought this product. Also you **have to** fill out a small form. The manufacturer **will** return some money to you. It **may** take six to eight weeks to receive this money.

These sales techniques help manufacturers get your attention, but they also help you save money.

[4] The brand is the company name.

Infinitives; Modals; Imperatives **277**

Reading Variation

To practice listening skills, have students first listen to the audio alone. Ask a few comprehension questions. Repeat the audio if necessary. Then have students open their books and read along as they listen to the audio.

Reading Glossary

expiration: a date at which something is no longer valid
limit: the greatest amount or extent allowed
manufacturer: a business that makes things

Smart Shopping: Coupons, Rain Checks, and Rebates (Reading)

1. Have students look at the illustrations. Ask: *What kind of coupon is this?* (a manufacturer's coupon) *What does "do not double" mean?* (the store can't double the value of the coupon) *Have you ever used a rain check?*
2. Have students look at the title of the reading. Ask: *What is the reading about? How do you know?* Have students use the title and the pictures to make predictions about the reading.
3. Preteach any vocabulary words students may not know such as *manufacturer, expiration,* and *limit.*

BEFORE YOU READ

1. Have students discuss the questions in pairs.
2. Ask for a few volunteers to share their answers with the class.

🕐 To save class time, skip "Before You Read" or have students prepare answers for homework ahead of time.

Reading 🎧 CD 2, Track 10

1. Have students read the text silently. Tell them to pay special attention to modals and related expressions. Then play the audio and have students read along silently.
2. Check students' comprehension. Ask questions such as: *Why do manufacturers send coupons to customers?* (to get you to try their products) *What should you do if you can't find a sale item on the shelf?* (ask for a rain check) *When you fill out a rebate form, what does the manufacturer send you?* (some money)

🕐 To save class time, have students do the reading for homework ahead of time.

9.8 | Can

1. Have students cover up grammar chart **9.8**. Make a matching exercise on the board. Write on one side of the board:
   I can't afford to eat in a restaurant every day.
   You can return an item within 30 days.
   If you use coupons, you can save money.
   I can find many ways to save money.

   On the other side of the board write:
   ability
   possibility
   permission
   have enough money to buy something
   Say: *Match the examples with the explanations.*

2. Tell students to look at grammar chart **9.8**. Say: *Check your work with the grammar chart.* Point out any errors. Go over all of the example sentences.

3. Explain that the negative of *can* is *cannot* and the contraction is *can't*.

4. Direct students to the Pronunciation Notes. Go over the pronunciation of *can* and *cannot*. Tell students that they must listen for the sound of the vowel and not the ending because the final *t* in *can't* is difficult to hear. Tell students that this is often confusing for native speakers as well. Point out that in short answers *can* may sound like /kæn/. But tell students that in a short answer they can easily distinguish between the two by listening for *yes* or *no*.

5. Demonstrate the pronunciation with the sentences in the grammar chart. Then read the sentences in Exercise 13. Ask students to hold up their hands if they hear *can* and to keep their hands down if they hear *can't*. Then have students practice the pronunciation chorally as a class.

EXERCISE 13

1. Have students read the direction line. Go over the examples. Point out that in this exercise, *can* is being used to express ability.

2. Have students complete the exercise individually. Then have students practice pronouncing *can* and *can't* in pairs. Circulate to observe pair work. Give help as needed.

3. If necessary, review grammar chart **9.8** on page 278.

9.8 | Can

Examples	Explanation
I **can** find many ways to save money. I **can** explain how to use a rebate.	Ability
If you use coupons, you **can** save money. If the item is sold out, you **can** get a raincheck.	Possibility
The sign says, "Eggs 69¢. Limit 2." You **can** only buy two cartons of eggs at the special price. You **can** return an item within 30 days.	Permission
I **can't afford to** eat in a restaurant every day. **Can** you **afford** to buy lobster?	*Can afford to* means have enough money to buy something.
You **cannot** buy more than the limited quantity. You **can't** use a coupon after the expiration date.	The negative of *can* is *cannot*. The contraction is *can't*.

Pronunciation Notes:

1. In affirmative statements, we usually pronounce *can* /kən/. In negative statements, we pronounce *can't* /kænt/. Sometimes it is hard to hear the final **t**, so we must pay attention to the vowel sound and the stress to hear the difference between *can* and *can't*. Listen to your teacher pronounce these sentences:
   I *can* gó. /kən/
   I *cán't* go. /kænt/

2. In a short answer, we pronounce *can* /kæn/.
   Can you help me later?
   Yes, I *can*. /kæn/

EXERCISE 13   ABOUT YOU Fill in the blanks with *can* or *can't* to tell about your abilities.

EXAMPLES   I ___can___ drive a car.

   I ___can't___ fly a plane.

Answers will vary.
1. I _____ read without glasses.
2. I _____ speak Spanish.
3. I _____ drive a car.
4. I _____ play tennis.
5. I _____ sing well.

---

6. I _____ change a tire.

7. I _____ save money.

8. I _____ read the newspaper
without a dictionary.

EXERCISE 14 ABOUT YOU Ask a question about a classmate's abilities with the
words given. Another student will answer.

EXAMPLE speak Spanish

A: Can you speak Spanish?
B: Yes, I can. OR No, I can't.

1. write with your left hand
   Can you write with your left hand?
2. type without looking at the keyboard
   Can you type without looking at the keyboard?
3. use a computer
   Can you use a computer?
4. play chess
   Can you play chess?
5. ski
   Can you ski?

6. play the piano
   Can you play the piano?
7. speak French
   Can you speak French?
8. bake a cake
   Can you bake a cake?
9. play the guitar
   Can you play the guitar?
10. sew
    Can you sew?

EXERCISE 15 Write down one thing that you can do well. Share your answer
with a partner or with the entire class.

Answers will vary.

EXERCISE 16 These sentences are true about an American supermarket.
Check (✓) which ones are true about a supermarket in
another country.

Answers will vary.
1. _____ You can use coupons.

2. _____ You can sometimes buy two items for the price of one.

3. _____ You can cash a check.

4. _____ You can buy stamps.

5. _____ You can get money back from a manufacturer.

6. _____ You can pay by check or credit card.

EXERCISE 14

1. Tell students that they will interview
a partner. Have students read the
direction line. Ask: *What kind of
questions are we asking? (yes/no*
questions) Go over the example.
Have volunteers model the example.
Point out that in this exercise, *can* is
being used to express ability.

2. Have students complete the
exercise in pairs. Circulate to
observe pair work. Give help as
needed.

3. If necessary, review grammar chart
9.8 on page 278.

EXERCISE 15

1. Have students read the direction
line. Write a model sentence on the
board: *I can _____ (really)
well.*

2. Have students share what they do
well with a partner. Ask volunteers
to tell the class what their partners
can do well.

3. If necessary, review grammar chart
9.8 on page 278.

EXERCISE 16

1. Have students read the direction
line. Say: *Check what's true for
supermarkets in your native
country or a country you lived in
for a long time.* Point out that these
statements are true for American
supermarkets.

2. Have students complete the activity
individually. Then have students
compare answers in pairs or groups.
If possible, put students from
different countries together.

3. If necessary, review grammar chart
9.8 on page 278.

⏱ To save class time, have
students do half of the exercise
in class and complete the other half for
homework. Or assign the entire
exercise for homework.

Expansion

Exercise 13 Take a quick survey of the class. How many students can or can't do the
activities in the exercise?

Exercise 14 Variation

Have students write what they do well on a small piece of paper. Tell students not to write
their names. Ask students to pick a paper from the hat, and then try to find the person who
wrote it. Say: *Go around the class and ask* yes/no *questions* (e.g., *Can you swim well? Can
you ride a bike well?*).

9.9 | Should

1. Have students look at grammar chart **9.9**. Say: *We use* should *to give or ask for advice.* Read the examples in the chart.
2. Go over the negative and the contraction *shouldn't*. Point out that the negative is used to give advice or a warning.

EXERCISE 17

1. Have students read the direction line. Ask: *What do we write in the blanks?* (advice about shopping in the U.S.) Go over the examples in the book.
2. Have students complete Exercise 17 in pairs. Circulate to observe pair work. Give help as needed.
3. If necessary, review grammar chart **9.9** on page 280.

---

7. _____ You can't bargain[5] for the price.
8. _____ You can return an item if you're not satisfied. You can get your money back.
9. _____ You can get free bags (paper or plastic).
10. _____ You can use a shopping cart. Small children can sit in the cart.
11. _____ If you have a small number of items, you can go to a special lane.
12. _____ You can shop 24 hours a day (in some supermarkets).

9.9 | Should

Examples	Explanation
You **should** use coupons to save money. What **should** I do if the item is sold out? You **should** compare prices before you buy.	We use *should* to give or ask for advice.
You **should not** waste your money. You **shouldn't** buy things you don't need.	The negative of *should* is *should not*. The contraction is *shouldn't*. We use the negative to give advice or a warning.

EXERCISE 17 If someone from another country is going to live in the U.S., what advice can you give him or her about shopping? Work with a partner to write six sentences of advice.

EXAMPLES *You should always look at the expiration date on a food product.*

You should shop for summer clothes in July and August. Summer clothes are cheapest at that time.

1. _____ **Answers will vary.** _____
2. _____
3. _____
4. _____
5. _____
6. _____

[5] To *bargain* for a price means to make an offer lower than the price the seller is asking.

Expansion

Exercise 17 Have students compare advice in groups. Then have them compile the best advice from the group and present it to the class.

EXERCISE **18** What should a person do about each of the following health problems? Write a sentence of advice for each one. (You may work with a partner.)

EXAMPLE   He has a headache.

He should take an aspirin and lie down.

1. He has a stomachache. _____ **Answers will vary.** _____

2. She has a cut. _____

3. He has a burn. _____

4. She has a cold. _____

5. He has a fever. _____

6. She has a toothache. _____

7. He's always nervous. _____

8. She has a backache. _____

EXERCISE **19** A father is giving his son advice. What advice do you think he is giving? Write sentences with *should*. (You may work with a partner.)

EXAMPLES   You eat hot dogs, fries, and colas all the time.

You should eat more fruits and vegetables.

You shouldn't eat so much junk food.

1. You spend too much time at the computer.

_____ **Answers will vary.** _____

2. You always ask me for money.

_____

3. You always wait until the last minute to study for a test.

_____

4. Your hair is too long.

_____

5. Your clothes look dirty.

_____

6. You talk for hours on the phone with your friends.

_____

Infinitives; Modals; Imperatives **281**

Expansion

Exercise 18 Survey the class. What was the advice for the different complaints?

1. Tell students that this exercise is about health advice. Have students read the direction line. Go over the example in the book. Ask a volunteer to model the example.
2. Have students complete Exercise 18 individually. Then have students compare answers in pairs. If possible, have students from different countries work together. Circulate to observe pair work. Give help as needed.
3. If necessary, review grammar chart **9.9** on page 280.

To save class time, have students do half of the exercise in class and complete the other half for homework. Or assign the entire exercise for homework.

EXERCISE 19

1. Tell students that this exercise is about a father giving his son advice. Have students read the direction line. Say: *You can use a negative or an affirmative statement.* Go over the example in the book.
2. Have students complete Exercise 19 individually. Then have students compare answers in pairs. If possible, have students from different countries work together. For #7, point out the footnote and the picture on page 282 to explain *mess.* Circulate to observe pair work. Give help as needed.
3. If necessary, review grammar chart **9.9** on page 280.

To save class time, have students do half of the exercise in class and complete the other half for homework. Or assign the entire exercise for homework.

EXERCISE 20

1. Tell students that this exercise is about their opinions on raising children. Have students read the direction line.

2. Have students complete Exercise 20 individually. Then have students compare answers in groups. If possible, have students from different countries work together. Circulate to observe group work. Give help as needed.

3. If necessary, review grammar chart **9.9** on page 280.

🕐 To save class time, have students check the statements for homework. Then students may discuss their answers in class.

7. You never clean your room. It's a mess!⁶

_____

8. You never listen to your mother when she tells you something.

_____

9. You want your driver's license, but you're not responsible.

_____

EXERCISE 20 Check (✓) if you agree or disagree about what schoolchildren should or shouldn't do. Discuss your answers with the whole class or in a small group.

Answers will vary.	I agree.	I disagree.
1. Children should go to a teacher when they have a family problem.		
2. They shouldn't play video games.		
3. They should select their own TV programs.		
4. They shouldn't trust all adults.		
5. They should always tell the truth.		
6. They should be responsible for taking care of younger sisters and brothers.		
7. They should select their own friends.		
8. They should always obey their parents and teachers.		
9. They should learn to use a computer.		
10. They should study a foreign language.		
11. They should help their parents with small jobs in the house.		

⁶ To be a *mess* means to be disorganized.

Expansion

Exercise 20 What else do students think children shouldn't do? Have students discuss other ideas in their groups. Then have groups report to the class.

Exercise 20 What should parents do or not do? Have groups write a list of 5–10 statements. Then have groups exchange lists and say whether they agree or disagree with the statements.

EXERCISE **21** Read each statement. Then ask a question with the word in parentheses ( ). Another student will answer.

EXAMPLE The students should do the homework. (why)

A: Why should they do the homework?
B: It helps them understand the lesson.

1. The students should study the lessons. (why)
2. The teacher should take attendance. (when)
3. The students should bring their textbook to class. (what else)
4. I should study modals. (why)
5. We should register for classes early. (why)
6. The teacher should speak clearly. (why)
7. The students shouldn't talk during a test. (why)
8. We shouldn't do the homework in class. (where)
9. The teacher should announce a test ahead of time. (why)

9.10 | *Must*

Examples	Explanation
To get a rebate, you **must** send the proof of purchase. You **must** include your receipt.	We use *must* to talk about rules and laws. *Must* has a very official, formal tone.
You **must not** use the handicapped parking space if you don't have permission. The store **mustn't** sell a product after its expiration date.	For the negative, use *must not*. The contraction is *mustn't*. *Must not* and *cannot* are very close in meaning. You *must not* park in the handicapped space = You *cannot* park in the handicapped space.

Infinitives; Modals; Imperatives **283**

EXERCISE 21

1. Have students read the direction line. Say: *Make questions out of the statements.* Go over the example. Have volunteers model #1.
2. Have students complete the rest of Exercise 21 in pairs. Make sure students take turns asking and answering. Circulate to observe pair work. Give help as needed.
3. If necessary, review grammar chart **9.9** on page 280.

🕐 To save class time, have students do half of the exercise in class and complete the other half in writing for homework. Or if students do not need speaking practice, the entire exercise may be skipped or done in writing.

9.10 | *Must*

1. Have students look at grammar chart **9.10**. Say: *We use* must *to talk about rules or advice.* Then read the examples in the chart. Have students go back to the reading on page 277. Ask: *How is* must *used in the text?* (It's used to talk about the rules for buying an item with a rain check.)
2. Go over the negative and the contraction *mustn't*. Explain that *must not* and *cannot* mean the same thing. Point out the pictures of the handicapped spaces.

Expansion

Exercise 21 Have students write their own "I should" lists. Say: *What do you think you should do? Make a list:* I should exercise more, I should eat more vegetables, *etc.*

Culture Note

Only people with a special permit can park in handicapped spaces. Permits are obtained through the state's department/registry of motor vehicles and are only granted to those with certain physical limitations. A car parked in a handicapped space without a permit may be ticketed.

EXERCISE 22

1. Say: *These are some rules you might have to follow if you worked in a supermarket.* Have students read the direction line. Point out the photo of the man working behind the deli counter.

2. Have students complete Exercise 22 individually. Go over the answers as a class.

3. If necessary, review grammar chart **9.10** on page 283.

EXERCISE 23

1. Say: *In this exercise, you have to name something you* must have *or do in a certain situation.* Go over the example in the book. Ask a volunteer what else you need to drive (a car, the keys, gas, etc.).

2. Have students complete the exercise individually. Then have students compare answers in groups. Circulate to observe group work. Give help as needed.

3. If necessary, review grammar chart **9.10** on page 283.

🕐 To save class time, have students do half of the exercise in class and complete the other half in writing for homework. Or if students do not need speaking practice, the entire exercise may be skipped or done in writing.

EXERCISE 22 Here are some rules in a supermarket. Fill in the blanks with *must* or *must not*.

1. Employees in the deli department _____ *must* _____ wear a hairnet or a hat.

2. When employees use the washroom, they _____ *must* _____ wash their hands before returning to work.

3. Employees _____ *must not* _____ touch food with their bare hands. They _____ *must* _____ wear plastic gloves.

4. The store _____ *must not* _____ sell food after the expiration date.

5. Customers _____ *must not* _____ take shopping carts out of the parking lot.

EXERCISE 23 Name something.

EXAMPLE
Name something you must have if you want to drive.
You must have a license.

Answers will vary.
1. Name something you must do or have if you want to leave the country.

2. Name something you must not carry onto an airplane.

3. Name something you must not do in the classroom.

4. Name something you must not do during a test.

5. Name something you must not do or have in your apartment.

6. Name something you must do or have to enter an American university.

7. Name something you must do when you drive a car.

8. Name something you must not do when you drive a car.

284 Lesson **9**

Expansion

Exercise 22 Have students write rules for other work situations (e.g., hospital, restaurant, school, etc.). Students can work alone or in pairs or groups.

Exercise 23 Survey the class. Have groups report their answers to the class (e.g., *Everyone in our group said you must have a passport if you want to leave the country.*).

9.11 | *Have To*

	Examples	Explanation
Affirmative	I don't have enough milk. I **have to** go shopping. If you want to return an item, you **have to** show a receipt.	*Have to* is similar in meaning to *must*. *Have to* is less formal. We use it for personal obligations.
Negative	A: The DVD player was cheaper in the first store. Let's go back there. B: You **don't have to** go back there. Just tell the salesperson, and she'll probably give you the same price. If you sample food in a supermarket, you **don't have to** buy it.	*Don't have to* means it's not necessary.

EXERCISE 24   Tell if you *have to* or *don't have to* do these things at this school. (Remember: *don't have to* means it's not necessary.)

EXAMPLES   study before a test
I have to study before a test.

study in the library
I don't have to study in the library. I can study at home.

Answers will vary.

1. wear a suit to school
2. come to class on time
3. stand up to ask a question in class
4. do homework
5. notify the teacher if I'm going to be absent
6. call the teacher "professor"
7. raise my hand to answer
8. take a final exam
9. wear a uniform
10. buy my own textbooks

EXERCISE 25   Ask your teacher what he or she *has to* or *doesn't have to* do.

EXAMPLE   work on Saturdays
A: Do you have to work on Saturdays?
B: Yes, I do. OR No, I don't.

1. take attendance
Do you have to take attendance?
2. give students grades
Do you have to give students grades?
3. call students by their last names
Do you have to call students by their last names?
4. wear a suit
Do you have to wear a suit?
5. work in the summer
Do you have to work in the summer?
6. have a master's degree
Do you have to have a master's degree?
7. work on Saturdays
Do you have to work on Saturdays?
8. come to this school every day
Do you have to come to this school every day?

9.11 | *Have To*

1. Have students look at grammar chart **9.11**. Say: Have to *is similar to* must. Have to *is less formal.* Then read the examples in the chart. Have students go back to the reading on page 277. Say: *See how* have to *is used in the text. It means:* it's necessary.
2. Explain that *don't have to* means *it's not necessary.* Go over the examples in the chart.

EXERCISE 24

1. Ask: *What do you have to do in this class? What don't you have to do in this class?* Have students read the direction line. Go over the example with the class.
2. Have students complete the exercise individually. Go over the answers as a class.
3. If necessary, review grammar chart **9.11** on page 285.

EXERCISE 25

1. Say: *Now you're going to interview me.* Have students read the direction line. Model the example with a student.
2. Have students interview you in groups.
3. If necessary, review grammar chart **9.11** on page 285.

Expansion

Exercise 24 Have students write about what they had to do in their last school. Briefly review the past tense (*I had to . . . I didn't have to . . .*). Collect for assessment or have students exchange papers to compare.

EXERCISE 26

1. Ask: *What do students and teachers have to or don't have to do in your country?* Have students read the direction line. Go over the example with the class.
2. Have students complete the exercise individually. Then have students compare answers in groups. If possible, put students from different countries together.
3. If necessary, review grammar chart **9.11** on page 285.

🕐 To save class time, have students do half of the exercise in class and complete the other half for homework. Or assign the entire exercise for homework.

EXERCISE 27

1. Have students read the direction line. Go over the example with the class. Point out the picture of the "10 items or fewer" lane at the bottom of the page.
2. Have students complete the exercise individually. Go over the answers as a class.
3. If necessary, review grammar chart **9.11** on page 285.

🕐 To save class time, have students do half of the exercise in class and complete the other half for homework. Or assign the entire exercise for homework.

EXERCISE 26 If you are from another country, write four sentences about students and teachers in your country. Tell what they *have to* or *don't have to* do. Use the ideas from the previous exercises. You may share your sentences with a small group or with the class.

EXAMPLE *In my country, a student has to wear a uniform.*

1. _____ **Answers will vary.** _____
2. _____
3. _____
4. _____

EXERCISE 27 Tell what Judy *has to* or *doesn't have to* do in these situations.

EXAMPLE Judy has a coupon for cereal. The expiration date is tomorrow. She has to *use it by tomorrow or she won't get the discount*.

1. The coupon for cereal says "Buy 2, get 50¢ off." She has to _____ *buy 2* _____ in order to get the discount.
2. Judy has no milk in the house. She has to _____ *buy* _____ more milk.
3. Eggs are on sale for 89¢, limit two. She has three cartons of eggs. She has to _____ *put back* _____ one of the cartons of eggs.
4. She has a rebate application. She has to fill out the application if she wants to get money back. She also has to _____ *send* _____ the proof-of-purchase symbol and the receipt to the manufacturer.
5. She wants to pay by check. The cashier asks for her driver's license. She has to _____ *show her license* _____ .
6. She has 26 items in her shopping cart. She can't go to a lane that says "10 items or fewer." She has to _____ *go to* _____ another lane.

Expansion

Exercise 26 Have students make a poster with things you have to or don't have to do in their countries. If possible, have pairs or groups from the same country work together. Display the posters around the classroom. Have a class discussion.

Exercise 27 Have students change the statements about what Judy has to or doesn't have to do into the first person (e.g., *I have to use it by tomorrow or I won't get the discount.*). Then have students practice saying the statements in pairs.

9.12 | *Must* and *Have To*

In affirmative statements, *have to* and *must* are very **similar** in meaning. In negative statements, *have to* and *must* are very **different** in meaning.

	Examples	Explanation
Affirmative	If you wish to return an item, you **must** have a receipt. You **must** send the rebate coupon by October 1. You **have to** send the rebate coupon by October 1.	Use *must* or *have to* for rules. *Must* is more formal or more official, but we can use *have to* for rules too.
	I don't have any milk. I **have to** go to the store to buy some. I need to buy a lot of things. I **have to** use a shopping cart.	Use *have to* for personal obligations or necessities.
Negative	You **must not** park in the handicapped parking space. The store **must not** sell an item after the expiration date.	*Must not* shows that something is prohibited or against the law.
	The sign says, "3 for $1.00," but you **don't have to** buy three to get the sale price. You **don't have to** pay with cash. You can use a credit or debit card.	*Don't have to* shows that something is not necessary, that there is a choice.

EXERCISE **28** Fill in the blanks with *must not* or *don't have to*.

EXAMPLES You _____*must not*_____ take a shopping cart out of the parking lot.

We _____*don't have to*_____ shop every day. We can shop once a week.

1. If you sample a product, you _____*don't have to*_____ buy it.

2. If you have just a few items, you _____*don't have to*_____ use a shopping cart. You can use a basket.

3. If you have a lot of items in your shopping cart, you _____*must*_____ _____*not*_____ use the checkout that says "10 items or fewer."

4. You _____*must not*_____ park in the handicapped parking space if you don't have permission.

5. You _____*don't have to*_____ take your own bags to the supermarket. Someone will give you bags for your groceries.

Infinitives; Modals; Imperatives **287**

9.12 | *Must* and *Have To*

1. Have students look at grammar chart **9.12.** Point out that the affirmative *must* and *have to* have similar meanings, but the negatives *mustn't* and *don't have to* are very different. Go over the examples. *Must* and *have to* can both be used for rules, although *must* sounds much more formal. *Have to* can also be used for personal obligation.

2. Say: Must not *means that something is prohibited or against the law.* Don't have to *simply means that something is not necessary.* Go over the example sentences.

EXERCISE 28

1. Say: *In this exercise, you have to decide when to use* have to, don't have to, must, *or* must not. Have students read the direction line. Say: *Remember that* have to *and* must *are similar in meaning, but* don't have to *and* must not *are different.* Go over the examples with the class.

2. Have students complete the exercise individually. Go over the answers with the class.

3. If necessary, review grammar chart **9.12** on page 287.

Expansion

Exercise 28 Have students write about rules and regulations at their workplace. Make sure students use *have to/don't have to* and *must/must not*.

Lesson **9**   287

9.13 | Might/May and Will

1. Have students look at grammar chart **9.13**. Have students read the example sentences. Explain that *might* and *may* have the same meaning. Both show possibility. The adverb *maybe* also has the same meaning. All three mean: *it's possible*. Tell students not to confuse *maybe* (the adverb) and *may be* (the verb—e.g., *I may be free tomorrow night.*).

2. Have students go back to the reading on page 277. Have them substitute *may* for *might* and *might* for *may* in the text.

3. Explain that the negative of *may* is *may not* and the negative of *might* is *might not*, and that there are no contractions for *may not* or *might not*.

4. *Will* expresses certainty of something happening in the future. Point out the *if* clauses in the two example sentences: *If the price is 3 for $1.00, you will pay 34¢ for one.*

9.13 | Might/May and Will

Examples	Explanation
I have a coupon for a new toothpaste. I **might** buy it. I **may** like it. A rebate check **might** take six to eight weeks.	*May* and *might* have the same meaning. They show possibility. Compare *maybe* (adverb) and *may* or *might* (modal verbs): *Maybe it will rain* tomorrow. It *may rain* tomorrow. It *might rain* tomorrow.
Those cookies taste great, but they **may not** be healthy for you. I **might not** have time to shop next week, so I'll buy enough for two weeks.	The negative of *may* is *may not*. The negative of *might* is *might not*. We do not make a contraction for *may not* and *might not*.
If the price is 3 for $1.00, you **will** pay 34¢ for one. If the sign says "Two for one," the store **will** give you one item for free.	*Will* shows certainty about the future.

EXERCISE 29 Tell what may or might happen in the following situations.

EXAMPLE Meg needs to go shopping. She's not sure what her kids want. They might
_____want a new kind of_____ cereal.

1. She's not sure if she should buy the small size or the large size of
cereal. The large size may _____be_____ cheaper.

2. If she sends in the rebate form today, she might _____get_____
a check in four or five weeks.

3. The store sold all the coffee that was on sale. The clerk said, "We
might _____have_____ more coffee tomorrow."

4. Bananas are so expensive this week. If she waits until next week, the
price may _____go down_____.

5. The milk has an expiration date of June 27. Today is June 27. She's
not going to buy the milk because it might _____expire_____.

6. She's not sure what brand of toothpaste she should buy. She might
buy the one she usually buys, or she might _buy a different brand_

EXERCISE 30 Tell what *may* or *might* happen in the following situations.
If you think the result is certain, use *will*.

EXAMPLES If you don't put money in a parking meter, _____you might get a_____
parking ticket.

If you are absent from tests, _____you may not pass the course._

If you don't pass the tests, _____you'll fail the course._

1. If you drive too fast, _____**Answers will vary.**_____

2. If you get a lot of tickets in one year, _____

3. If you don't water your plants, _____

4. If you don't take the final exam, _____

5. If you don't lock the door of your house, _____

6. If you eat too much, _____

7. If you work hard and save your money, _____

8. If the weather is nice this weekend, _____

9. If you park in the handicapped space without permission, _____

_____

Infinitives; Modals; Imperatives **289**

1. Have students read the direction
line. Ask: *What do you write after*
may *or* might? (a verb in the base
form) Go over the example with the
class.

2. Have students complete the
exercise individually. Go over the
answers with the class.

3. If necessary, review grammar chart
9.13 on page 288.

EXERCISE 30

1. Say: *This time you have to write*
may, might, *or* will. *Remember,
you can use* may *and* might
*interchangeably: they mean the
same thing.* Have students read the
direction line. Go over the examples
with the class.

2. Have students complete the
exercise individually. Then have
students compare statements in
pairs. Circulate to observe pair
work.

3. If necessary, review grammar chart
9.13 on page 288.

To save class time, have
students do half of the exercise
in class and complete the other half for
homework. Or assign the entire
exercise for homework.

9.14 | Making Requests

1. Have students cover up grammar chart **9.14**. Tell one student: *Stand up.* Then say to another student: *Could you stand up?* Explain that imperatives like *stand up, sit down, don't run,* etc., can be used to make a request, but that modals can also be used for requests. They sound softer and more polite. Say: *Could you stand up? Could you sit down?*
2. Have students look at grammar chart **9.14**. Explain that the imperative is the base form of the verb. The subject is *you*, but it's not spoken. For negative, put *don't* in front of the verb. Go over the example sentences.
3. *May* and *could* are both used for requests. Go over the two example sentences.

The Customer Service Counter (Reading)

1. Have students look at the title of the reading. Ask: *What is the reading about?* Have students make predictions.
2. Preteach any vocabulary words students may not know such as *cash, fill out,* and *approval.*

BEFORE YOU READ

1. Have students discuss the questions in pairs.
2. Ask for a few volunteers to share their answers with the class.

To save class time, skip "Before You Read" or have students prepare answers for homework ahead of time.

9.14 | Making Requests

Examples	Explanation
Park over there. **Don't park** in the handicapped space.	We can use imperatives to make a request. The imperative is the base form of the verb. The subject is *you*, but we don't include *you* in the sentence. For a negative, put *don't (do not)* before the verb.
Send the rebate coupon soon. **Do not** wait.	
May I see your driver's license? **Could** you give me change for a dollar?	We also use modals to make requests. Modals give the request a more polite tone.

THE CUSTOMER SERVICE COUNTER

Before You Read

1. Do you have a check-cashing card at a local supermarket?
2. Do you pay with cash when you shop in a supermarket?

Read the following conversation, first between two friends (A and B), and then between A and a customer service representative (C). Pay special attention to requests.

A: I need to cash a check.
B: **Let's go** to the customer service counter at Dominick's. Someone told me they have a check-cashing service there.
A: **Could** you drive?
B: **Why don't we** walk? It's not far.

. . . *At the customer service counter . . .*

C: **Can** I help you?
A: Yes. **I'd like** to cash a check.
C: Do you have a check-cashing card?
A: No, I don't.
C: Here's an application. Please **fill** it out.
A: I don't have a pen. **Could** I use your pen?
C: Here's a pen.
A: Thanks.

Reading Variation

To practice listening skills, have students first listen to the audio alone. Ask a few comprehension questions. Repeat the audio if necessary. Then have students open their books and read along as they listen to the audio.

Reading Glossary

approval: permission; consent
cash: to exchange a check for currency
fill out: to complete

. . . A few minutes later . . .

A: Here's my application.
C: **May** I see your driver's license?
A: Here it is. Did I fill out the application correctly?
C: No. Please **don't write** in the gray box. You made another mistake, too. You wrote the day before the month. Please **write** the month before the day. For August 29, we write 8/29, not 29/8. **Why don't you fill out** another form? Here's a clean one.
A: Thanks.

. . . A few minutes later . . .

A: Here it is. **Could** you check to see if I filled it out right this time?
C: You forgot to sign your name. Please **sign** your name on the bottom line.
A: OK. **Could** you cash my check now?
C: I'm sorry, sir. We have to wait for approval. We'll send you your check-cashing card in the mail in a week to ten days. Can I help you with anything else?
A: Yes. **I'd like** to buy some stamps.
C: Here you are. Anything else?
A: No. That's it.
C: Have a nice day.

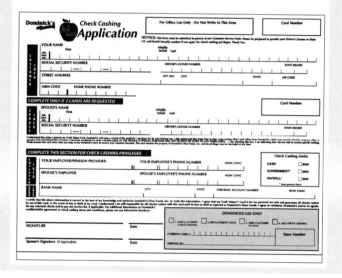

Reading 🎧 *CD 2, Track 11*

1. Before reading, have students fill out the check-cashing application.
2. Have students read the text silently. Tell them to pay special attention to requests. Then play the audio and have students read along silently.
3. Check students' comprehension. Ask questions such as: *Where is there a check-cashing service?* (at the customer service counter at Dominick's) *What does person A need to cash a check?* (a check-cashing card) *What does person A have to fill out to get a check-cashing card?* (an application) *What mistakes did person A make in filling out the application?* (wrote in the gray box; wrote the date incorrectly) *When will person A get the check-cashing card?* (in a week to ten days)
4. Ask students if they think they made any errors filling out the application.

🕐 To save class time, have students do the reading for homework ahead of time.

9.15 | Imperatives

1. Have students cover up grammar chart **9.15**. Remind students that modals can make requests sound more polite. Go over the examples.

2. Have students cover up grammar chart **9.15**. Make a matching exercise on the board. Write the following sentences on one side of the board:
   1. *Please sign your name at the bottom.*
   2. *Don't move!*
   3. *Watch out! There's a bee on your nose.*
   4. *Always do your best.*
   5. *Have a nice day.*
   6. *Shut up!*

   On the other side of the board, write:
   a. *to give a warning*
   b. *in some impolite expressions*
   c. *to give a command*
   d. *to give instructions*
   e. *to give encouragement*
   f. *in certain conversational expressions*

   Say: *Match the examples with the explanations.*

2. Tell students to look at grammar chart **9.15**. Say: *Check your work with the grammar chart.* Point out any errors. Go over all the example sentences.

3. Explain that *let's (let us)* + the base form of a verb is used to make a suggestion. Go over the examples.

EXERCISE 31

1. Have students read the direction line. Go over the example with the class. Point out that students need to choose either an affirmative or negative imperative verb.

2. Have students complete the exercise individually. Then have students compare statements in pairs. Circulate to observe pair work.

3. If necessary, review grammar chart **9.15** on page 292.

9.15 | Imperatives

Imperatives give instructions, warnings, and suggestions.

Examples	Explanation
Please **sign** your name at the bottom. **Write** the month before the day. **Be** careful when you fill out the application. **Don't write** in the gray box.	We use the imperative form to give instructions.
Stand at attention. **Don't move!** You're under arrest.	We use the imperative to give a command.
Watch out! There's a bee on your nose. **Don't move.**	We use the imperative to give a warning.
Always do your best. **Never give** up.	We use the imperative to give encouragement. We can put *always* and *never* before an imperative.
Have a nice day. **Make** yourself at home.	We use the imperative in certain conversational expressions.
Shut up! **Mind** your own business!	We use the imperative in some angry, impolite expressions.
Let's get an application for check cashing. **Let's not** make any mistakes.	*Let's = let us.* We use *let's* + the base form to make a suggestion. The negative form is *let's not. Let's* includes the speaker.

EXERCISE **31** Fill in the blanks with an appropriate imperative verb (affirmative or negative) to give instructions.

EXAMPLE _____*Go*_____ to the customer service desk for an application.

1. _____*Fill*_____ out the application in pen.

2. _____*Don't use*_____ a pencil to fill out an application.

3. _____*Write*_____ all the information in clear letters.

4. If you have a middle name, _____*write*_____ your middle initial.

5. _____*Don't write*_____ anything in the box in the lower right corner.

6. If you are not married, _____*don't fill*_____ out the second part.

7. When you give your telephone number, always _____*give*_____ your area code.

---

8. ____Write____ your last name before your first name on this application.

9. ____Give____ the application to a person at the customer service counter.

EXERCISE 32 Choose one of the activities from the following list (or choose a different one, if you like). Use imperatives to give instructions on how to do the activity. (You may work with a partner.)

EXAMPLE get from school to your house

Take the number 53 bus north from the corner of Elm Street. Ask the driver for a transfer. Get off at Park Avenue. Cross the street and wait for a number 18 bus.

Answers will vary.

1. hang a picture
2. change a tire
3. fry an egg
4. prepare your favorite recipe
5. hem a skirt
6. write a check
7. make a deposit at the bank
8. tune a guitar
9. get a driver's license
10. use a washing machine
11. prepare for a job interview
12. get from school to your house
13. get money from a cash machine (automatic teller)
14. do a search on the Internet
15. send a text message

EXERCISE 33 Work with a partner. Write a list of command forms that the teacher often uses in class. Read your sentences to the class.

EXAMPLES Open your books to page 10.

Don't come late to class.

1. _____ Answers will vary. _____
2. _____
3. _____

Infinitives; Modals; Imperatives **293**

EXERCISE 32

1. Tell students that they will be giving instructions for one of the activities listed. Have students read the direction line. Go over the example with the class. For #2, point out the photo of the woman changing a tire.
2. Have students complete the exercise in pairs. Circulate to observe pair work. If possible, have pairs who wrote about the same activity compare their instructions.
3. If necessary, review grammar chart **9.15** on page 292.

🕐 To save class time, have students do half of the exercise in class and complete the other half in writing for homework. Or if students do not need speaking practice, the entire exercise may be skipped or done in writing.

EXERCISE 33

1. Say: *Think about the things I always ask you to do in class. Think about the instructions, commands, and requests I give you. You're going to write some of them down.* Have students read the direction line. Go over the examples with the class.
2. Have students complete the exercise individually. Then have students read their sentences to the class.
3. If necessary, review grammar chart **9.15** on page 292.

🕐 To save class time, have students do half of the exercise in class and complete the other half for homework. Or assign the entire exercise for homework.

Exercise 32 Variation

Have pairs write each line of their instructions on strips of paper. Then have them exchange strips with another pair. The pairs should try to put the instructions in the correct order, and then guess what the instructions are for.

EXERCISE 34

1. Say: *In this exercise, we're going to practice* let's. Have students read the direction line. Go over the example with the class.
2. Have students complete Exercise 34 individually. Check answers as a class.
3. Then have students practice the conversation in pairs.
4. If necessary, review grammar chart **9.15** on page 292.

To save class time, have students do half of the exercise in class and complete the other half for homework. Or assign the entire exercise for homework.

EXERCISE 35

1. Say: *What things would you like do or would you like me to do in class?* Have students read the direction line. Go over the examples with the class.
2. Have students complete the exercise in pairs. Then have students compare their suggestions in groups. Have groups report to the class.
3. If necessary, review grammar chart **9.15** on page 292.

To save class time, have students do half of the exercise in class and complete the other half for homework. Or assign the entire exercise for homework.

EXERCISE 34   Fill in the blanks with an appropriate verb to complete this conversation.

A: I need to cash a check.

B: We also need to get some groceries. Let's _____go_____ to the
(example)
supermarket.

A: Do you want to drive there?

B: The supermarket is not so far. Let's _____walk_____.
(1)

A: It looks like rain.

B: No problem. Let's _____bring_____ an umbrella.
(2)

A: Let's _____go_____. It's late and the store will close soon.
(3)

B: Don't worry. This store is open 24 hours a day.

A: We're almost out of dog food. Let's _____buy_____ a
(4)
20-pound bag.

B: Let's not _____walk_____ then. I don't want to carry a
(5)
20-pound bag home. Let's _____drive_____ instead.
(6)

EXERCISE 35   Work with a partner. Write a few suggestions for the teacher or other students in this class. Read your suggestions to the class.

EXAMPLES   *Let's review verb tenses.*

Let's not speak our native languages in class.

1. _____**Answers will vary.**_____
2. _____
3. _____
4. _____
5. _____
6. _____

Exercise 34 Variation

To provide practice with listening skills, have students close their books and listen to the audio. Repeat the audio as needed. Ask comprehension questions, such as: *What does person A need to do?* (cash a check) *Where does person B want to go?* (to the supermarket) *Is the supermarket close by or far?* (close by) Then have students open their books and complete Exercise 34.

Expansion

Exercise 34 Have students write dialogues in pairs. Make sure students use *let's* in the dialogues. Tell students to use the dialogue in Exercise 34 as a model.

9.16 | Using Modals to Make Requests and Ask Permission

An imperative form may sound too strong in some situations. Modals can make a request sound more polite.

Examples		Explanation
Would **Could**	you cash my check, please?	We use these modals to make a request. These expressions are more polite than "Cash my check."
May **Could** **Can**	I use your pen, please?	We use these modals to ask permission. These expressions are more polite than "Give me your pen."
I **would like** to cash a check. How **would** you **like** your change?		*Would like* has the same meaning as *want*. *Would like* is softer than *want*. The contraction of *would* after a pronoun is *'d*: I'd like to cash a check.
Why don't you fill out another form? **Why don't we** walk to the supermarket?		Use *why don't you . . . ?* and *why don't we . . . ?* to offer suggestions.
May **Can**	I help you?	Salespeople often use these expressions to offer help to a customer.

EXERCISE 36   Read the following conversation between a salesperson (S) and a customer (C) in an electronics store. Change the underlined words to make the conversation more polite.

S: <u>What do you need?</u>   *May I help you?*
   (example)

C: <u>I want</u> to buy a new computer. <u>Show</u> me your latest models.   *I would like*   *Could you show* ?
   (1)   *(2)*

S: <u>Do you want</u> to see the laptops or the desktops?   *Would you like*
   (3)

C: <u>Show</u> me the desktops.   *Could you show* ?
   (4)

S: This is one of our most popular desktops.

C: <u>Turn</u> it on.   *Could you turn* ?
   (5)

S: It *is* on. Just hit the space bar.

Expansion

Grammar Have students go back to the reading on pages 290–291. Have students read through for modals and imperatives. Ask students to identify the use for the modal or imperative (making a request, offer help, etc.). Have students work in pairs.

9.16 | Using Modals to Make Requests and Ask Permission

1. Have students cover up grammar chart **9.16.** Tell one student: *Raise your hand.* Then say to another student: *Could you raise your hand?* Write the two requests on the board. Ask: *Are both of these requests?* (yes) *Which one is more polite?* (*Could you raise your hand?*) Explain that both imperatives and modals can be used to make a request or ask permission, but that modals sound softer and more polite.

2. Make a matching exercise on the board. Write the examples and explanations from the grammar chart on the board in random order. On one side of the board, write:
   1. May/Can I help you?
   2. Why don't you fill out another form?
   3. Would/Could you cash my check, please?
   4. I would like to cash a check.
   5. May/Could/Can I use your pen, please?
   On the other side of the board, write the following explanations:
   a. Use these modals to make a request.
   b. Use these modals to ask permission.
   c. This modal means "want."
   d. Use this phrase to offer a suggestion.
   e. Use these expressions to offer help.
   Say: *Match the examples with the explanations.*

2. Tell students to look at grammar chart **9.16.** Say: *Check your work with the grammar chart.* Point out any errors. Go over all the example sentences.

EXERCISE 36

1. Say: *This is a conversation between a salesperson and a customer in an electronics store. We're going to make the conversation more polite by using modals.* Have students read the direction line. Go over the example with the class.

2. Have students complete the exercise individually. Go over the answers with the class.

3. If necessary, review grammar chart **9.16** on page 295.

C: I don't know how much memory to buy.

S: How do you use your computer?

C: We like to play games and watch movies.

S: Then ~~buy~~ *why don't you* buy this computer, which has a lot of memory and speed.
    (6)

C: ~~Tell~~ *Could you tell* me the price?
    (7)

S: We have a great deal on this one. It's $1,299. If you buy it this week, you can get a $200 rebate from the manufacturer.

C: ~~Let me take~~ *May I take* it home and try it out?
    (8)

S: No problem. If you're not happy with it, you can return it within 30

    days and get your money back. ~~Do you want~~ *Would you like* to buy a service contract?
    (9)

C: What's that?

S: If you have any problem with the computer for the next two years, we will replace it for free. The contract costs $49.99.

C: ~~Let me see~~ *Can I see* the service contract?
    (10)

S: Here's a copy. Take this card to the customer service desk and someone will bring you your computer.

C: Thanks.

S: Have a nice day.

C: You, too.

Expansion

Exercise 36 Have students practice the conversation or create their similar conversations in pairs. Ask volunteers to role-play the conversation in front of the class.

1. Imperatives
   Sit down. **Don't** be late.

2. *Let's*
   Let's go to the movies. **Let's not** be late.

3. Infinitive Patterns
   He wants **to go.**
   It's necessary **to learn** English.
   I'm afraid **to stay.**
   I use coupons **to save** money.
   I want them **to help** me.

4. Modals

Modal	Examples	Explanation
can	He **can** speak English. An 18-year-old **can** vote. **Can** I borrow your pen?	He has this ability. He has permission. I'm asking permission.
can't	You **can't** park here. It's a bus stop. I **can't** help you now. I'm busy.	It is not permitted. I am not able to.
should shouldn't	You **should** eat healthy food. You **shouldn't** drive if you're sleepy.	It's good advice. It's a bad idea.
may may not	**May** I borrow your pen? I **may** buy a new car. I **may not** be here tomorrow.	I'm asking permission. This is possible. This is possible.
might might not	It **might** rain tomorrow. We **might not** have our picnic.	This is possible. This is possible.
must must not	A driver **must** have a license. I'm late. I **must** hurry. You **must not** drive without a license	This is a legal necessity. This is a personal necessity. This is against the law.
will will not	The manufacturer **will** send you a check. You **will not** receive the check right away.	This is in the future.
would would like	**Would** you help me move? I **would like** to use your pen.	I'm asking a favor. I want to use your pen.
could	**Could** you help me move?	I'm asking a favor.
have to not have to	She **has to** leave. She **doesn't have to** leave.	It's necessary. It's not necessary.

Infinitives; Modals; Imperatives **297**

Summary of Lesson 9

1. **Imperatives** Remind students that for an imperative, you use the base form of the verb. In groups, have students take turns giving each other commands (e.g., *Sit down. Write your name.* If necessary, have students review:
   9.15 Imperatives (p. 292).

2. *Let's* Remind students that *let's* is the contraction of *let us* and that it is used for making suggestions. Have students make a list of things to do and places to go in their countries. Then have students work in pairs to plan a trip and itinerary to each country (e.g., *Let's go to Bogotá. Let's visit the Museum of Gold. Then let's see a bullfight.*). If necessary, have students review:
   9.15 Imperatives (p. 292).

3. **Infinitive Patterns** Review infinitive patterns. Have students write a sentence for each infinitive pattern:
   Sentence 1: verb followed by an infinitive
   Sentence 2: *it* + *be* + adjective + infinitive
   Sentence 3: *be* + adjective + infinitive
   Sentence 4: using an infinitive to show purpose
   Sentence 5: object before an infinitive
   If necessary, have students review:
   9.2 Verbs Followed by an Infinitive (p. 265)
   9.3 *It* + *Be* + Adjective + Infinitive (p. 268)
   9.4 *Be* + Adjective + Infinitive (p. 269)
   9.5 Using an Infinitive to Show Purpose (p. 270)
   9.6 Object Before an Infinitive (p. 273).

4. **Modals** Review modals. Go over examples and explanations in the chart. Have students work in pairs to write sentences for each modal. Circulate to observe pair work. Give help as needed. If necessary, have students review:
   9.7 Overview of Modals (p. 276)
   9.8 *Can* (p. 278)
   9.9 *Should* (p. 280)
   9.10 *Must* (p. 283)
   9.11 *Have To* (p. 285)
   9.12 *Must* and *Have To* (p. 287)
   9.13 *Might/May* and *Will* (p. 288)
   9.14 Making Requests (p. 290)
   9.16 Using Modals to Make Requests and Ask Permission (p. 295).

Editing Advice

Have students close their books. Write the example sentences without editing marks or corrections on the board. For example:

1. *I must to go.*
2. *They like play.*

Ask students to correct each sentence and provide a rule or explanation for each correction. This activity can be done individually, in pairs, or as a class. After students have corrected each sentence, tell them to turn to pages 298–299. Say: *Now compare your work with the Editing Advice in the book.*

EDITING ADVICE

1. Don't use *to* after a modal.

   I must to go.

2. Use *to* between verbs.

   They like ˄*to* play.

3. Always use the base form after a modal.

   He can swims.

   She can't ~~driving~~ *drive* the car.

4. Use the base form in an infinitive.

   He wants to goes.

   I wanted to worked.

5. We can introduce an infinitive with *it* + an adjective.

   It i˄ Is important to get exercise.

6. Don't put an object between the modal and the main verb.

   She can ~~the lesson~~ understand *understand the lesson*.

7. Use the correct word order in a question.

   Why you ~~can't~~ stay? *can't you*

8. Use an infinitive after some adjectives.

   I'm happy ˄*to* meet you.

   It's necessary ˄*to* have a job.

9. Use *not* after *let's* to make a negative.

   Let's ~~don't~~ *not* go to the party.

10. Use *don't* to make a negative imperative.

    Don't: Not come home late.

---

11. Use *to*, not *for*, to show purpose.

                  to

    We went to the theater for see a play.

12. Use the object pronoun and an infinitive after *want*, *expect*, *need*, etc.

             him to close

    I want he closes the door.

LESSON 9 TEST /REVIEW

PART 1   Find the *grammar* mistakes with the underlined words and correct them. Not every sentence has a mistake. If the sentence is correct, write *C*.

EXAMPLES   You <u>should to study</u> more.

              I <u>don't have to work</u> on Saturday. *C*

1. I need <u>cash</u> a check.   [*to*]

2. What <u>I can</u> do for you?   [*can I*]

3. I'm afraid <u>to walk</u> alone at night. *C*

4. She <u>has to</u> leave early today. *C*

5. We wanted <u>to went</u> home early last night.   [*to go*]

6. <u>Is</u> necessary to have a car.   [*It is*]

7. You must <u>to go</u> to court next week.   [*go*]

8. She <u>can English speak</u> very well.   [*can speak English*]

9. Don't <u>to walk</u> so fast.   [*walk*]

10. What <u>I must</u> do to get a driver's license?   [*must I*]

11. He <u>should study</u> harder. *C*

12. We <u>want</u> learn English quickly.   [*to*]

13. My brother <u>can speaks</u> English very well.   [*can speak*]

14. It's impossible <u>learn</u> English in one month. *C*

15. She likes <u>to swim</u> in the ocean. *C*

16. Let's <u>don't</u> make a lot of noise. Dad is sleeping.   [*not*]

Infinitives; Modals; Imperatives   **299**

Lesson 9 Test/Review

For additional practice, review, and assessment materials, see Assessment CD-ROM with *ExamView Pro*, *More Grammar Practice* Workbook 1, Interactive CD-ROM, and Web site http://elt.thomson.com/gic

PART 1

1. Part 1 may be used in addition to the Assessment CD-ROM with *ExamView* Pro as an in-class test to assess student performance. Have students read the direction line. Ask: *Does every sentence have a mistake?* (no) Point out that students are to find the grammar mistakes (not punctuation). Go over the examples with the class.

2. Have students complete the assignment individually. Collect for assessment.

3. If necessary, have students review: **Lesson 9.**

Lesson Review

To use Part 1 as a review, assign it as homework or use it as an in-class activity to be completed individually or in pairs. Check answers and review errors as a class. Reteach grammar points that students haven't mastered. Then student learning may be assessed using a test generated from the Assessment CD-ROM with *ExamView Pro*.

1. Part 2 may also be used in addition to the Assessment CD-ROM with *ExamView Pro* as an in-class test to assess student performance. Have students read the direction line. Say: *In this exercise, you have to decide if the sentence needs a to. Then write the negative form.* Go over the examples with the class.

2. Have students complete the exercise individually. Collect for assessment.

3. If necessary, have students review:

   9.1 Infinitives—An Overview (p. 264)

   9.2 Verbs Followed by an Infinitive (p. 265)

   9.3 *It* + *Be* + Adjective + Infinitive (p. 268)

   9.4 *Be* + Adjective + Infinitive (p. 269)

   9.5 Using an Infinitive to Show Purpose (p. 270).

---

17. I was glad to̶ ̶m̶e̶t̶ *to meet* him yesterday.

18. Don't worry. Everything will be fine.   *C*

19. She went to the school f̶o̶r̶ ̶t̶a̶l̶k̶ *to talk* to her daughter's teacher.

20. You should looking *be* for a new job.

21. The teacher always says, "N̶o̶t̶ *Don't* talk during a test."

22. I use spell check t̶o̶ ̶c̶h̶e̶c̶k̶i̶n̶g̶ *to check* my spelling.

23. My parents want I̶ ̶g̶r̶a̶d̶u̶a̶t̶e̶ *me to graduate* from college.

PART 2 Fill in the first blank with *to* or nothing (*X*). Then write the negative form in the second blank.

EXAMPLES   I'm ready ___*to*___ study Lesson 10.

I __*'m not ready to study*__ Lesson 11.

You should ___*X*___ drive carefully.

You __*shouldn't drive*__ fast.

1. I need ___*to*___ learn English. I __*don't need to learn*__ Polish.

2. You must ___*X*___ stop at a red light. You __*must not stop*__ on the highway.

3. The teacher expects ___*to*___ pass most of the students. She __*doesn't expect to pass*__ all of the students.

4. We want ___*to*___ study grammar. We __*don't want to study*__ literature.

5. The teacher has ___*to*___ give grades. He __*doesn't have to give*__ an A to everyone.

6. We might ___*X*___ have time for some questions later. We __*might not have*__ time for a discussion.

7. It's important ___*to*___ practice American pronunciation now. It __*isn't important to practice*__ British pronunciation.

8. It's easy ___*to*___ learn one's native language. It __*isn't easy to learn*__ a foreign language.

9. Let's ___*X*___ speak English in class. __*Let's not speak*__ our native languages in class.

10. Please attend the meeting. __*Let's*__ be here at six o'clock, please. __*Let's not be*__ late.

Lesson Review

To use Part 2 as a review, assign it as homework or use it as an in-class activity to be completed individually or in pairs. Check answers and review errors as a class. Reteach grammar points that students haven't mastered. Then student learning may be assessed using a test generated from the Assessment CD-ROM with *ExamView Pro*.

PART 3   Change each sentence to a question.

EXAMPLES   I'm afraid to drive.
Why _are you afraid to drive?_

He can help you.
When _can he help me?_

1. You should wear a seat belt.
Why _should I wear a seat belt?_

2. I want to buy some grapes.
Why _do you want to buy some grapes?_

3. He must fill out the application.
When _must he fill out the application?_

4. She needs to drive to New York.
When _does she need to drive to New York?_

5. You can't park at a bus stop.
Why _can't I park at a bus stop?_

6. It's necessary to eat vegetables.
Why _is it necessary to eat vegetables?_

7. She has to buy a car.
Why _is it necessary to buy a car?_

8. They'd like to see you.
When _would they like to see me?_

PART 4   This is a phone conversation between a woman (W) and her
mechanic (M). Choose the correct words to fill in the blanks.

W: This is Cindy Fine. I'm calling about my car.

M: I ___can't___ hear you. ___Could___
   (example: can't, may not)   (1 could, might)
   you speak louder, please?

W: This is Cindy Fine. Is my car ready yet?

M: We're working on it now. We're almost finished.

W: When ___can___ I pick it up?
   (2 would, can)

M: It will be ready by four o'clock.

W: How much will it cost?

M: $375.

Infinitives; Modals; Imperatives   **301**

PART 3

1. Part 3 may also be used in addition to the Assessment CD-ROM with *ExamView Pro* as an in-class test to assess student performance. Have students read the direction line. Remind students that questions without modals or the verb *be* will need *do* or *does*. Go over the examples with the class.

2. Have students complete the exercise individually. Collect for assessment.

3. If necessary, have students review:
   9.7   Overview of Modals (p. 276)
   9.8   *Can* (p. 278)
   9.9   *Should* (p. 280)
   9.10 *Must* (p. 283)
   9.11 *Have To* (p. 285)
   9.12 *Must* and *Have To* (p. 287)
   9.13 *Might/May* and *Will* (p. 288).

PART 4

1. Part 4 may also be used in addition to the Assessment CD-ROM with *ExamView Pro* as an in-class test to assess student performance. Have students read the direction line. Say: *This is a phone conversation between a woman and her mechanic. The mechanic is fixing her car. In this exercise, you have to choose the correct modal.* Go over the example as a class.

2. Have students complete the exercise individually. Collect for assessment.

3. If necessary, have students review:
   9.8   *Can* (p. 278)
   9.9   *Should* (p. 280)
   9.10 *Must* (p. 283)
   9.11 *Have To* (p. 285)
   9.12 *Must* and *Have To* (p. 287)
   9.13 *Might/May* and *Will* (p. 288).

Lesson Review

To use Parts 3 and 4 as a review, assign them as homework or use them as in-class activities to be completed individually or in pairs. Check answers and review errors as a class. Reteach grammar points that students haven't mastered. Then student learning may be assessed using a test generated from the Assessment CD-ROM with *ExamView Pro*.

1. Part 5 may also be used in addition to the Assessment CD-ROM with *ExamView Pro* as an in-class test to assess student performance. Have students read the direction line. Go over the examples with the class.

2. Have students complete the exercise individually. Collect for assessment.

3. If necessary, have students review:
   9.8 *Can* (p. 278)
   9.9 *Should* (p. 280)
   9.10 *Must* (p. 283)
   9.11 *Have To* (p. 285)
   9.12 *Must* and *Have To* (p. 287)
   9.13 *Might/May* and *Will* (p. 288).

W: I don't have that much money right now. ___Can___ *(3 Can, Might)* I pay by credit card?

M: Yes. You ___may___ *(4 may, might)* use any major credit card.

Later, at the mechanic's shop:

M: Your car's ready, ma'am. The engine problem is fixed. But you ___should___ *(5 may, should)* replace your brakes. They're not so good.

W: ___Do I have to___ *(6 Do I have to, May I)* do it right away?

M: No, you ___don't have to___ *(7 must not, don't have to)* do it immediately, but you ___should___ *(8 would, should)* do it within a month or two. If you don't do it soon, you ___may___ *(9 may, would)* have an accident.

W: How much will it cost to replace the brakes?

M: It ___will___ *(10 would, will)* cost about $200.

W: I ___would___ *(11 will, would)* like to make an appointment to take care of the brakes next week. ___Can___ *(12 Can, Will)* I bring my car in next Monday?

M: Yes, Monday is fine. You ___should___ *(13 could, should)* bring it in early because we get very busy later in the day.

W: OK. See you Monday morning.

PART 5 Decide if the sentences have the same meaning or different meanings. Write *S* for same, *D* for different.

EXAMPLES   Would you like to go to a movie? Do you want to go to a movie? *S*
    We will not go to New York. We should not go to New York. *D*

1. You should go to the doctor. You can go to the doctor. *D*

2. I may buy a new car. I must buy a new car. *D*

3. Could you help me later? Would you help me later? *S*

Lesson Review

To use Part 5 as a review, assign it as homework or use it as an in-class activity to be completed individually or in pairs. Check answers and review errors as a class. Reteach grammar points that students haven't mastered. Then student learning may be assessed using a test generated from the Assessment CD-ROM with *ExamView Pro*.

4. She must not drive her car. She doesn't have to drive her car. D
5. She has to leave immediately. She must leave immediately. S
6. We will have a test soon. We may have a test soon. D
7. I can't go to the party. I might not go to the party. D
8. You shouldn't buy a car. You don't have to buy a car. D
9. May I use your phone? Could I use your phone? S
10. He might not eat lunch. He may not eat lunch. S
11. I should go to the doctor. I must go to the doctor. D
12. I have to take my passport with me. I should take my passport with me. D

PART 6 Circle the correct words to complete each sentence.

1. If you sample a product in a supermarket, you (*don't have to*, *shouldn't*) buy it.
2. If you have just a few items, you (*shouldn't*, *don't have to*) use a shopping cart. You (*can*, *must*) use a small basket.
3. You (*must*, *should*) use coupons to save money.
4. You (*shouldn't*, *don't have to*) pay with cash. You can use a credit card.
5. Salesperson to customer: (*May*, *Would*) I help you?
6. You (*must*, *should*) make a list before going shopping.
7. You (*don't have to*, *must not*) take your own bags to the supermarket. Bags are free.
8. Try this new pizza. You (*should*, *might*) like it.
9. You (*can't*, *shouldn't*) use coupons after the expiration date.
10. You (*must not*, *don't have to*) park in the handicapped parking space. It's against the law.

PART 6

1. Part 6 may also be used in addition to the Assessment CD-ROM with *ExamView Pro* as an in-class test to assess student performance. Have students read the direction line. Go over the examples with the class.
2. Have students complete the exercise individually. Collect for assessment.
3. If necessary, have students review:
   9.8 *Can* (p. 278)
   9.9 *Should* (p. 280)
   9.10 *Must* (p. 283)
   9.11 *Have To* (p. 285)
   9.12 *Must* and *Have To* (p. 287)
   9.13 *Might/May* and *Will* (p. 288).

Lesson Review

To use Part 6 as a review, assign it as homework or use it as an in-class activity to be completed individually or in pairs. Check answers and review errors as a class. Reteach grammar points that students haven't mastered. Then student learning may be assessed using a test generated from the Assessment CD-ROM with *ExamView Pro*.

Expansion Activities

These expansion activities provide opportunities for students to interact with one another and further develop their speaking and writing skills. Encourage students to use grammar from this lesson whenever possible.

🕐 To save class time, assign parts of the activities as homework. Then use class time for interaction and communication. If students do not need additional speaking practice, some of the activities may be assigned as writing activities for homework, or skipped altogether.

CLASSROOM ACTIVITIES

1. Have students work individually to fill out the chart. Then put students in pairs to compare charts. If possible, have students from different countries work together.
2. Have students work individually to fill out the chart. Then put students in pairs to compare charts.
3. Have students work in groups to fill out the chart.

EXPANSION ACTIVITIES

Classroom Activities

1. Imagine that a friend of yours is getting married. You are giving him or her advice about marriage. Write some advice for this person. (You may work with a partner or compare your advice to your partner's advice when you are finished.)

It's important	It's not important
It's important to be honest.	It's not important to do everything together.

2. Imagine that a friend of yours is going to travel to the U.S. You are giving him or her advice about the trip and life in the U.S. Write as many things as you can in each box. Then find a partner and compare your advice to your partner's advice.

It's necessary OR It's important OR You should	It's difficult OR You shouldn't
It's necessary to have a passport.	It's difficult to understand American English.

3. Working in a small group, write a list to give information to a new student or to a foreign student. If you need more space, use your notebook.

should or shouldn't	must or have to	don't have to	might or might not	can or can't
You should bring your transcripts to this college.				

Expansion

Classroom Activities For Activity 1, ask: *What other structures can we use to give advice, suggestions, or warnings to people who are getting married?* (should, have to/don't have to, imperatives) *Add more advice to your charts using these structures or modals.*

Classroom Activities For Activities 1 and 2, have students create a dialogue based on the advice they give. Ask volunteers to role-play their dialogues in front of the class.

Classroom Activities Variation

Activity 3 Have students write a letter or e-mail to a friend who is planning to come to the U.S. to study. Tell students to first fill out the chart and then write the letter.

---

4. With a partner, write a few instructions for one of the following situations.

    EXAMPLE using a microwave oven

    You shouldn't put anything metal in the microwave.
    You can set the power level.
    You should rotate the dish in the microwave. If you don't, the food might not cook evenly.

    a. preparing for the TOEFL[7]

    b. taking a test in this class

    c. preparing for the driver's test in this state

5. Bring in an application. (Bring two of the same application, if possible.) It can be an application for a job, driver's license, license plate, apartment rental, address change, check-cashing card, rebate, etc. Work with a partner. One person will give instructions. The other person will fill it out.

6. Bring in ads from different stores. You can bring in ads from supermarkets or any other store. See what is on sale this week. Find a partner and discuss the products and the prices. Compare prices at two different stores, if possible. What do these products usually cost in your native country? Do you have all of these products in your native country?

Talk About it

Discuss: Do you use coupons, rebates, or rain checks? Why or why not?

Write About it

1. Write about the differences between shopping in the U.S. and in another country.

2. Imagine that a new classmate just arrived from another country. Write a composition giving advice about shopping in the U.S.

Internet Activities

1. Use the Internet to compare the prices of a product, such as a DVD player, TV, digital camera, or computer.

2. Use the Internet to find application forms. (Examples: change of address form from the post office; application for a checking account from a bank; application for a credit card; application for a frequent flyer program from an airline; motor vehicle registration form in your state)

 Additional Activities at http://elt.thomson.com/gic

---

[7] The *TOEFL* is the Test of English as a Foreign Language.

Write About it Variation

Have students exchange first drafts with a partner. Ask students to help their partners edit their drafts. Refer students to the Editing Advice on pages 298–299.

4. Have students work in pairs to write instructions for any one of the three situations listed in the book.

5. Ask students ahead of time to bring in any kind of application. If possible, have several applications on hand in case students forget theirs. Circulate to observe pair work and give help as needed.

6. Ask students ahead of time to bring in circulars from stores. If possible, have several store circulars on hand in case students forget theirs.

TALK ABOUT IT

Have students discuss coupons, rebates and rain checks in groups. Then have groups report to the class (e.g., *Only one person in our group uses coupons. No one else uses them.*).

WRITE ABOUT IT

1. If possible, have students from the same country work in pairs. Model an example for the class. Say, for example: *In my country, we don't use rebate checks, and there aren't very many coupons. Most of the time, especially in the small stores, you have to pay in cash.*

2. Have students work on their own to write an e-mail to a friend about shopping in the U.S.

INTERNET ACTIVITIES

1. Tell students: *You're going to comparison shop for electronics on the Internet.* Ask students to find prices for two items. Have students make a chart of the products they looked for and the prices they found. Survey the class. Who found the best prices?

2. Ask students to think about something that they might need to fill out an application for in the near future. Have them look for an application on the Internet. Ask them to print out the application and bring it in to class to fill out.

LESSON

10

GRAMMAR
Count and Noncount Nouns
Quantity Words

CONTEXT: Nutrition and Health
A Healthy Diet
Eat Less, Live Longer

307

Expansion

Theme The topic for this lesson can be enhanced with the following ideas:

1. Pictures of food talked about in the lesson
2. Food packages with nutritional information
3. Food pyramid

Lesson | 10

Lesson Overview

GRAMMAR

1. Ask: *What did we study in Lesson 9?* (infinitives, modals, and imperatives) *What will we study in this lesson?* (count and noncount nouns, quantity words) *Give me examples of count and noncount nouns. What's a quantity word?* Have students give examples. Write them on the board.

CONTEXT

1. Ask: *What are we going to learn about in this lesson?* (nutrition and health) Activate students' prior knowledge. Ask: *Are you a healthy eater? What foods are healthy? What foods are unhealthy?*
2. Have students share their knowledge and personal experiences.

Photo

1. Direct students' attention to the photo. Ask: *What's going on in this photo?* (A large family is having dinner on a special occasion.) *What are they eating? What do you see on the table?*
2. Ask: *Do your family get-togethers look like this?*

🕐 To save class time, have students do the Test/Review at the end of the lesson, or administer a lesson test generated from the Assessment CD-ROM with *ExamView® Pro*. Skip sections of the lesson that students have already mastered. You may also assign some sections for self-study for extra credit.

10.1 | Count and Noncount Nouns—An Overview

1. Write on one side of the board:
   one apple—two apples
   one egg—twelve eggs
   one bean—three beans
   On the other side of the board, write:
   bread
   milk
   cheese
   Ask: *What's the difference between these two groups of nouns?* (The first group has both singular and plural forms. The second group does not have a plural form.) Say: *Nouns can be divided into two groups: count and noncount nouns.* Ask: *Which one is the first group here on the board?* (count) *Which is the second group?* (noncount)
2. Have students look at grammar chart **10.1**. Go over the examples and explanations.

A Healthy Diet (Reading)

1. Have students look at the photo. Ask: *What is this woman doing?* (reading the label on a milk carton) *Why is she doing it?* (to look at the nutritional information)
2. Have students look at the title of the reading. Ask: *What is the reading about?* Have students use the title, the photo, and the pictures to make predictions about the reading.
3. Preteach any vocabulary words students may not know, such as *carbohydrate, supplement, package,* and *ingredient*.

BEFORE YOU READ

1. Have students discuss the questions in pairs.
2. Ask for a few volunteers to share their answers with the class.

To save class time, skip "Before You Read" or have students prepare answers for homework ahead of time.

10.1 | Count and Noncount Nouns—An Overview

Nouns can be divided into two groups: count and noncount nouns.

Examples	Explanation
I eat four **eggs** a week. I eat one **apple** a day. Do you like **grapes**?	Count nouns have a singular and plural form. egg—eggs apple—apples
I like **milk**. I drink **coffee** every day. Do you like **cheese**?	Noncount nouns have no plural form.

A HEALTHY DIET

Before You Read

1. What kind of food do you like to eat? What kind of food do you dislike?
2. What are some popular dishes from your country or native culture?

 Read the following article. Pay special attention to count and noncount nouns.

> It is important to eat well to maintain good **health**. A healthy diet consists of a variety of **foods**.
> You need carbohydrates. The best carbohydrates come from whole grain **bread**, **cereal**, and **pasta**. Brown **rice** is much healthier than white **rice**. **Sugar** is a carbohydrate too, but it has no real nutritional value.

308 Lesson **10**

Reading Variation

To practice listening skills, have students first listen to the audio alone. Ask a few comprehension questions. Repeat the audio if necessary. Then have students open their books and read along as they listen to the audio.

Reading Glossary

carbohydrate: any of a group of nutrients, such as sugar and starch, that provides the body with energy
ingredient: a part of something
package: a container, especially one wrapped up and sealed
supplement: something added to an existing thing to complete or improve it

Of course, you need **fruits** and **vegetables** too. But not all vegetables are equally good. **Potatoes** can raise the sugar in your **blood,** which can be a problem for people with diabetes. It is better to eat **carrots, broccoli, corn,** and **peas.**

You also need protein. Red **meat** is high in protein, but a diet with a lot of red **meat** can cause heart disease, diabetes, and cancer. Better sources of protein are **chicken, fish, beans, eggs,** and **nuts.** Some people worry that **eggs** contain too much **cholesterol.** (Cholesterol is a substance found in animal **foods.**) But recent studies show that eating one **egg** a day is not usually harmful and gives us other nutritional benefits.

Many **people** think that all **fat** is bad. But this is not true. The **fat** in **nuts** (especially **walnuts**) and **olive oil** is very healthy. The **fat** in **butter** and **cheese** is not good.

It is not clear how much **milk** and other dairy **products** an adult needs. It is true that dairy products are a good source of **calcium,** but a calcium supplement can give you what you need without the **fat** and **calories** of milk.

The best way to stay healthy is to eat the right kinds of food. Food **packages** have information about nutrition and calories. You should read the package to avoid artificial **ingredients** and high levels of **fat** and **sugar.** It is also important to control your weight and to exercise every day.

Did You
Know?

Americans spent $16.8 billion on vitamin and mineral supplements in 2002.

Count and Noncount Nouns; Quantity Words **309**

Reading 🎧 *CD 2, Track 13*

1. Have students read the text silently. Tell them to pay special attention to count and noncount nouns. Then play the audio and have students read along silently.

2. Check students' comprehension. Ask questions such as: *What is the best kind of carbohydrate?* (whole grains) *Name some good vegetables to eat.* (broccoli, carrots, peas, and corn) *What kinds of problems can a diet with a lot of red meat cause?* (heart disease, diabetes, and cancer) *Is all fat bad?* (no; fat from olive oil and nuts is very good, for example.)

🕐 To save class time, have students do the reading for homework ahead of time.

10.2 | Noncount Nouns

1. Have students cover up grammar chart **10.2.** Write these four categories across the board:
   A. *Nouns that have no distinct, separate parts. We look at the whole.*
   B. *Nouns that have parts that are too small or insignificant to count.*
   C. *Nouns that are classes or categories of things. The members of the category are not the same.*
   D. *Nouns that are abstractions.*

2. Have students go back to the reading on pages 308–309. Ask: *Which group do the nouns in the reading belong to? Write them in your notebooks under the correct group.* Have volunteers write the words on the board.

3. Then have students look at grammar chart **10.2.** Say: *Now compare your work with the chart.* Go over any errors.

4. Remind students that noncount nouns do not have a plural. Write on the board: *air.* Say: *You can't write airs.*

10.2 | Noncount Nouns

Noncount nouns fall into four different groups.

Group A: Nouns that have no distinct, separate parts. We look at the whole.

milk	air	meat
oil	pork	butter
water	cholesterol	poultry
coffee	paper	cheese
tea	soup	
yogurt	bread	

Group B: Nouns that have parts that are too small or insignificant to count.

rice	snow	hair
sugar	sand	grass
salt	corn	popcorn

Group C: Nouns that are classes or categories of things. The members of the category are not the same.

money (nickels, dimes, dollars)
food (vegetables, meat, spaghetti)
candy (chocolates, mints, candy bars)
furniture (chairs, tables, beds)
clothing (sweaters, pants, dresses)
mail (letters, packages, postcards)
fruit (cherries, apples, grapes)
makeup (lipstick, rouge, eye shadow)
homework (compositions, exercises, reading)

Group D: Nouns that are abstractions.

love	advice	happiness
life	knowledge	education
time	nutrition	experience
truth	intelligence	crime
beauty	unemployment	music
luck	patience	art
fun	noise	work
help	information	health

310   Lesson **10**

EXERCISE **1**   Fill in the blanks with a noncount noun.

EXAMPLE   Brown _____*rice*_____ is healthier than white _____*rice*_____.

1. Babies need a lot of _____*milk*_____, but adults don't.
2. Food from animals contains _____*cholesterol*_____.
3. Children like to eat _____*candy*_____, but it's not good for their teeth.
4. Food packages have information about _____*nutrition*_____.
5. Some people put _____*milk*_____ in their coffee.
6. _____*Olive oil*_____ is a good source of fat.
   _____*Butter*_____ is not a good source of fat.
7. _____*Coffee*_____ contains caffeine. Don't drink it at night.
8. People with high blood pressure shouldn't put a lot of _____*salt*_____ on their food.
9. Soda and candy contain a lot of _____*sugar*_____.

EXERCISE **2**   Fill in the blanks with a noncount noun from the list on page 310.

EXAMPLE   Students at registration need _____*information*_____.

1. I get a lot of _____*mail*_____ every day in my mailbox.
2. In the winter, there is a lot of _____*snow*_____ in the northern parts of the U.S.
3. In the U.S., people eat _____*popcorn*_____ in a movie theater.
4. Students have to do _____*homework*_____ every day.
5. When you walk on the beach, you get _____*sand*_____ in your shoes.
6. Money doesn't buy _____*happiness*_____.
7. Our parents often give us a lot of _____*advice*_____ about how to live our lives.
8. Some cities have a lot of _____*unemployment*_____. Many people are without jobs.
9. I need a quiet place to study. Can you study with _____*noise*_____ in the background?

EXERCISE 1

1. Have students read the direction line. Ask: *What are you going to write on the blanks?* (noncount nouns) Go over the example in the book.
2. Have students complete Exercise 1 individually. Check the answers as a class.
3. If necessary, review grammar chart **10.2** on page 310.

EXERCISE 2

1. Have students read the direction line. Remind students that the noncount nouns for this exercise are in grammar chart **10.2** on page 310. Go over the example in the book.
2. Have students complete Exercise 2 individually. Then have students compare answers in pairs. Circulate to observe pair work. Give help as needed.
3. If necessary, review grammar chart **10.2** on page 310.

To save class time, have students do half of the exercise in class and complete the other half for homework. Or assign the entire exercise for homework.

Expansion

Exercise 2 Have students work in pairs to identify the group from grammar chart **10.2** that each noncount noun in Exercise 2 belongs to (group A, B, C, or D).

10.3 | Count and Noncount Nouns

1. Write on the board:
   rice
   beans
   fruit
   food
   candy

   Ask: *Are these count or noncount nouns?* Say: *Sometimes things in grammar are not logical. Rice is noncount but beans are count. You have to learn the exceptions. Fruit, food, and candy are noncount nouns when they are used as a general term. For example:* The food at this hotel is good. *But if you mean kinds of food or kinds of fruit, they can be count nouns. For example:* Oranges and lemons are fruits that contain a lot of Vitamin C. *Candy is generally noncount, but if you are talking about pieces of candy, then you can use the plural form. For example:* There are three candies on the table.

2. Review the example sentences in the chart.

EXERCISE 3

1. Remind students that some noncount nouns have a plural form when the meaning is different (e.g., *fruit/fruits, candy/candies*). Have students read the direction line. Go over the example in the book.

2. Have students complete Exercise 3 individually. Go over the answers as a class.

3. If necessary, review grammar chart **10.3** on page 312.

10.3 | Count and Noncount Nouns

Examples	Explanation
I eat a lot of **rice** and **beans.** rice = noncount noun beans = count noun	*Count* and *noncount* are grammatical terms, but they are not always logical. *Rice* is very small and is a noncount noun. *Beans* and *peas* are also very small, but they are count nouns.
a. He eats a lot of **fruit.** b. Oranges and lemons are **fruits** that contain Vitamin C. a. She bought a lot of **food** for the party. b. **Foods** that contain a lot of cholesterol are not good for you.	a. Use *fruit* and *food* as noncount nouns when you mean fruit and food in general. b. Use *fruits* and *foods* as count nouns when you mean kinds of fruit or categories of food.
a. Children like to eat **candy.** b. There are three **candies** on the table.	a. When you talk about candy in general, *candy* is noncount. b. When you look at individual pieces of candy, you can use the plural form.

EXERCISE 3 Fill in the blanks with the singular or plural form of the word in parentheses ( ). Use the singular for noncount nouns. Use the plural for count nouns.

EXAMPLE Add ___*peas*___ to the soup. Then put in some ___*salt*___.
         (pea)   (salt)

1. Do you like to eat ___*fruit*___?
                       (fruit)

2. Oranges, grapefruits, and lemons are ___*fruits*___ that
                                         (fruit)
   have a lot of Vitamin C.

3. When children eat a lot of ___*candy*___, they sometimes
                               (candy)
   get sick.

4. Let's go shopping. There is no ___*food*___ in the house.
                                    (food)

5. Milk and eggs are ___*foods*___ that contain cholesterol.
                      (food)

6. She's going to make ___*rice*___ and
                        (rice)
   ___*beans*___ for dinner.
      (bean)

10.4 | Describing Quantities of Count and Noncount Nouns

Examples	Explanation
She ate three **apples** today. He ate four **eggs** this week.	We can put a number before a count noun.
I ate two **slices of bread**. Please buy a **jar of olive oil**. She drank three **glasses of milk**.	We cannot put a number before a noncount noun. We use a unit of measure, which we can count.

Ways we see noncount nouns:

By Container	By Portion	By Measurement¹	By Shape or Whole Piece	Other
a bottle of water a carton of milk a jar of pickles a bag of flour a can of soda (pop)² a bowl of soup a cup of coffee a glass of milk	a slice (piece) of bread a piece of meat a piece of cake a piece (sheet) of paper a slice of pizza a piece of candy a strip of bacon	a spoonful of sugar a scoop of ice cream a quart of oil a pound of meat a gallon of gasoline	a loaf of bread an ear of corn a piece of fruit a head of lettuce a candy bar a roll of film a tube of toothpaste a bar of soap	a piece of mail a piece of furniture a piece of advice a piece of information a work of art

EXERCISE 4 Fill in the blanks with a logical quantity for each of these noncount nouns.

EXAMPLES   She bought ___*one pound of*___ coffee.

She drank ___*two cups of*___ coffee.

Answers will vary.

1. She ate _____ meat.

2. She bought _____ meat.

3. She bought _____ bread.

4. She ate _____ bread.

¹For a list of conversions from the American system of measurement to the metric system, see Appendix G.
²Some Americans say "soda"; others say "pop."

Expansion

Grammar Bring in a ball (such as a soccer ball). Have students sit in a circle or have groups sit in a circle. Say: *The person who has the ball throws the ball to someone else and says a unit of measure such as* a piece. *The person who catches it must say the unit of measure plus a noncount noun that can be used with it. For example,* a piece of cake. *Then that person throws the ball to someone and calls out another unit of measure, and so on.*

10.4 | Describing Quantities of Count and Noncount Nouns

1. Have students cover up grammar chart **10.4.** Say: *We can use numbers with count nouns, but we can't use numbers with noncount nouns. With noncount nouns, we use units of measure, such as a bottle, a glass, a can, etc.*

2. Write the following categories across the board in chart form: *container*
portion
measurement
shape or whole piece
other
Then write a list of ten phrases on one side of the board:
a bag of flour
a pound of meat
a work of art
a slice of pizza
a carton of milk
a piece of meat
a quart of oil
a piece of information
a roll of film
an ear of corn.
Say: *Try to guess where these nouns and units of measure go.* Have volunteers fill in the chart on the board with the ten phrases.

3. Have students look at grammar chart **10.4.** Say: *Now compare your work with the chart.* Go over any errors. Review the example sentences and the units of measure in the chart.

EXERCISE 4

1. Have students read the direction line. Ask: *What do we write on the blanks?* (a logical quantity/unit of measure) Go over the examples in the book.

2. Have students complete the exercise individually. Go over the answers with the class.

3. If necessary, review grammar chart **10.4** on page 313.

10.5 | A Lot Of, Much, Many

1. Have students go back to the reading on pages 308–309. Say: *Many, a lot of, and* much *mean a large number of something. Scan quickly through the article. Circle* a lot of, much, *and* many *and the nouns that follow. Ask: What kind of nouns follow* a lot of? *(count and noncount)* Much? *(noncount)* Many? *(count)*

2. Have students look at grammar chart **10.5**. Say: *Use* many *for count nouns and* a lot of *for count and noncount nouns. Use* much *in negative sentences and questions with noncount nouns. Go over the examples.*

3. Direct students to the Language Notes. Explain that when the noun is omitted, use *a lot*, not *a lot of*.

EXERCISE 5

1. Have students read the direction line. Remind them that sometimes more than one answer is possible. Go over the examples in the book.

2. Have students complete Exercise 5 individually. Go over the answers with the class.

3. If necessary, review grammar chart **10.5** on page 314.

---

5. She bought _____ rice.

6. She ate _____ rice.

7. She bought _____ sugar.

8. She put _____ sugar in her coffee.

9. She ate _____ soup.

10. She ate _____ corn.

11. She bought _____ gas for her car.

12. She put _____ motor oil into her car's engine.

13. She used _____ paper to do her homework.

14. She took _____ film on her vacation.

10.5 | A Lot Of, Much, Many

Use *many* for count nouns. Use *much* for noncount nouns. Use *a lot of* for both count and noncount nouns.

	Count (plural)	Noncount
Affirmative	He baked **many** cookies. He baked **a lot of** cookies.	He baked **a lot of** bread.
Negative	He didn't bake **many** cookies. He didn't bake **a lot of** cookies.	He didn't bake **much** bread. He didn't bake **a lot of** bread.
Question	Did he bake **many** cookies? Did he bake **a lot of** cookies? **How many** cookies did he bake?	Did he bake **much** bread? Did he bake **a lot of** bread? **How much** bread did he bake?

Language Notes:
1. *Much* is rarely used in affirmative statements. Use *a lot of* in affirmative statements.
2. When the noun is omitted (in the following case, *cookies*), use *a lot*, not *a lot of*.
   He baked a lot of cookies, but he didn't eat **a lot.**

EXERCISE **5** Fill in the blanks with *much, many,* or *a lot of.* In some cases, more than one answer is possible.

EXAMPLES She doesn't eat ____*much*____ pasta.

_____*Many*_____ American supermarkets are open 24 hours a day.

_____*A lot of*_____ sugar is not good for you.

1. In the summer in the U.S., there's _____ a lot of _____ corn.
2. Children usually drink _____ a lot of _____ milk.
3. _____ Many _____ American people have an unhealthy diet.
4. I drink coffee only about once a week. I don't drink _____ much _____ coffee.
5. There are _____ many or a lot of _____ places that sell fast food.
6. It's important to drink _____ a lot of _____ water.
7. How _____ many _____ glasses of water did you drink today?
8. How _____ much _____ fruit did you eat today?
9. How _____ much _____ cholesterol is there in one egg?
10. It isn't good to eat _____ a lot of or much _____ candy.

10.6 | A Few, A Little

	Examples	Explanation
Count	I bought **a few** bananas. She ate **a few** cookies. She drank **a few cups** of tea.	Use *a few* with count nouns or with quantities that describe noncount nouns (*cup, bowl, piece*, etc.).
Noncount	He ate **a little** meat. He drank **a little** tea.	Use *a little* with noncount nouns.

EXERCISE 6   Fill in the blanks with *a few* or *a little*.

EXAMPLES   He has _____ a few _____ good friends.
He has _____ a little _____ time to help you.

1. Every day we study _____ a little _____ grammar.
2. We do _____ a few _____ exercises in class.
3. The teacher gives _____ a little _____ homework every day.
4. We do _____ a few _____ pages in the book each day.
5. _____ A few _____ students always get an A on the tests.
6. It's important to eat _____ a little _____ fruit every day.
7. It's important to eat _____ a few _____ pieces of fruit every day.

10.6 | A Few, A Little

Have students look at grammar chart **10.6**. Say: A few *and* a little *mean small quantities. We use* a few *with count nouns and* a little *with noncount nouns.* Go over the examples.

EXERCISE 6

1. Have students read the direction line. Go over the examples in the book.
2. Have students complete Exercise 6 individually. Go over the answers with the class.
3. If necessary, review grammar chart **10.6** on page 315.

Expansion

Exercise 5 Have students write about the food they bought or ate over the last week (e.g., *On Monday, I ate two slices of pizza. I also drank a can of soda and a 1/2 gallon of milk . . .*).

10.7 | Some, Any, and A/An

1. Have students look at grammar chart **10.7** on page 316. Say: *We are going to look at the use of* some, any, *and* a/an *in affirmative and negative sentences and in questions.* Point out the top of the chart. Read through the categories (singular count, plural count, and noncount).
2. Say: *For affirmative sentences, we use* a/an *with singular nouns,* some *with plural nouns, and* some *with noncount nouns.* Go over all of the sentences.
3. Say: *In the negative, we use* a/an *with singular nouns,* any *after negative verbs with plural nouns, and* any *after negative verbs with noncount nouns.* Go over all of the sentences. Explain that if they use an affirmative verb, they can use *no* before a plural noun and a noncount noun.
4. Say: *Finally, for questions you can use* some *or* any *with plural and noncount nouns. With singular nouns we use* a/an. Go over the sentences.

EXERCISE 7

1. Have students read the direction line. Ask: *When do we use* an*? (*An* is used before a vowel sound.) Go over the example in the book.
2. Have students complete Exercise 7 individually. Go over the answers with the class.
3. If necessary, review grammar chart **10.7** on page 316.

---

8. I use _____*a little*_____ milk in my coffee.
9. I receive _____*a little*_____ mail every day.
10. I receive _____*a few*_____ letters every day.

10.7 | *Some, Any,* and *A/An*

	Singular Count	Plural Count	Noncount
Affirmative	I ate **a** peach. I ate **an** apple.	I ate **some** peaches. I ate **some** apples.	I ate **some** bread.
Question	Do you want **a** sandwich?	Do you want **any fries?** Do you need **some** napkins?	Do you want **any** salt? Do you need **some** ketchup?
Negative	I don't need **a** fork.	There aren't **any** potatoes in the soup. There are **no** potatoes in the soup.	There isn't **any** salt in the soup. There is **no** salt in the soup.

Language Notes:
1. We can use *any* or *some* for questions with plural or noncount nouns.
2. Use *any* after a negative verb. Use *no* after an affirmative verb.
   Wrong: I didn't eat *no* cherries.

EXERCISE **7**   Fill in the blanks with *a, an, some,* or *any.* In some cases, more than one answer is possible.

EXAMPLE   I ate ____*an*____ apple.

1. I ate ____*some*____ corn.
2. I didn't buy ____*any*____ potatoes.
3. Did you eat ___*some or any*___ watermelon?
4. I don't have ____*any*____ sugar.
5. There are ____*some*____ apples in the refrigerator.
6. There aren't ____*any*____ oranges in the refrigerator.
7. Do you want ____*an*____ orange?
8. Do you want ___*some or any*___ cherries?
9. I ate ____*a*____ banana.
10. I didn't eat ____*any*____ strawberries.

EXERCISE **8** Make a statement about people in this class with the words given and an expression of quantity. Practice count nouns.

EXAMPLES Vietnamese student(s)
There are a few Vietnamese students in this class.

Cuban student(s)
There's one Cuban student in this class.

Answers will vary.
1. Polish student(s)
2. Spanish-speaking student(s)
3. American(s)
4. child(ren)
5. woman/women

6. man/men
7. teacher(s)
8. American citizen(s)
9. senior citizen(s)
10. teenager(s)

EXERCISE **9** Fill in the blanks with an appropriate expression of quantity. In some cases, more than one answer is possible. Practice noncount nouns.

EXAMPLE Eggs have _a lot of_ cholesterol.

1. You shouldn't eat so much red meat because meat has _a lot of_ fat.
2. Only animal products contain cholesterol. There is _no_ cholesterol in fruit.
3. Diet colas use a sugar substitute. They don't have _any_ sugar.
4. There is _some/a little_ sugar in a cracker, but not much.
5. Plain popcorn is healthy, but buttered popcorn has _a lot of_ fat.
6. Coffee has caffeine. Tea has _some_ caffeine too, but not as much as coffee.
7. She doesn't drink _a lot of_ tea. She only drinks tea occasionally.
8. I usually put _some/a little_ butter on a slice of bread.
9. I'm going to put some sugar in my coffee. Do you want _any/a little/ some_ sugar in your coffee?
10. My sister is a vegetarian. She doesn't eat _any_ meat at all. She doesn't eat _much/a lot of_ fish or chicken either.

1. Have students read the direction line. Go over the examples. Ask: *How do we say: no Cuban students in the class?* (*There aren't any Cuban students in the class* or *There are no Cuban students in the class.*)
2. Have students answer the questions individually. Quickly go over the answers as a class.
3. If necessary, review grammar chart **10.7** on page 316.

🕐 To save class time, have students do half of the exercise in class and complete the other half in writing for homework. Or if students do not need speaking practice, the entire exercise may be skipped or done in writing.

EXERCISE 9

1. Have students read the direction line. Remind them that more than one answer may be possible. Say: *For example, sometimes* much *and* a lot of *can be used for the same noun.* Go over the example. Ask: *What are some other expressions of quantity?* (*much, many, a little, a few,* etc.)
2. Have students answer the questions individually. Then have students compare answers in pairs. Circulate to give help as needed.
3. If necessary, review grammar charts **10.4** on page 313, **10.5** on page 314, **10.6** on page 315, and **10.7** on page 316.

🕐 To save class time, have students do half of the exercise in class and complete the other half for homework. Or assign the entire exercise for homework.

Expansion

Exercise 9 Have students discuss their countries' food and diet in groups. If possible, put students together from different countries. Have groups report interesting information to the class.

EXERCISE 10

1. Have students read the direction line. Say: *Remember,* much *is used with questions and with the negative for noncount nouns.* Go over the examples in the book. Model the examples with volunteers.
2. Have students complete Exercise 10 in pairs. Have students take turns asking and answering questions. Circulate to observe pair work. Give help as needed.
3. If necessary, review grammar chart **10.5** on page 314.

EXERCISE 11

1. Have students read the direction line. Ask: *What kind of questions are we asking?* (yes/no questions) *Make sure to answer with a complete answer.* Go over the examples in the book. Model the examples with volunteers.
2. Have students complete Exercise 11 in pairs. Have them take turns asking and answering questions. Circulate to observe pair work. Give help as needed.
3. If necessary, review grammar charts **10.5** on page 314, **10.6** on page 315, and **10.7** on page 316.

🕐 To save class time, have students do half of the exercise in class and complete the other half in writing for homework, answering the question themselves. Or if students do not need speaking practice, the entire exercise may be skipped or done in writing.

EXERCISE 12

🎧 *CD 2, Track 14*

1. Have students read the direction line. Go over the example.
2. Explain that this is a conversation between a husband and a wife. Point out the photo of the husband and wife. Have students complete Exercise 12 individually.
3. Check answers as a class. Then have students practice the conversations in pairs.
4. If necessary, review grammar charts **10.5** on page 314, **10.6** on page 315, and **10.7** on page 316.

🕐 To save class time, have students do half of the exercise in class and complete the other half for homework. Or assign the entire exercise for homework.

EXERCISE 🔟 ABOUT YOU Ask a question with *much* and the words given. Use *eat* or *drink.* Another student will answer. Practice noncount nouns.

EXAMPLES
candy
A: Do you eat much candy?
B: No. I don't eat any candy.

fruit
A: Do you eat much fruit?
B: Yes. I eat a lot of fruit.

Eat
1. rice   *Do you eat much rice?*
2. fish   *Do you eat much fish?*
3. chicken   *Do you eat much chicken?*
4. pork   *Do you eat much pork?*
5. bread   *Do you eat much bread?*
6. cheese   *Do you eat much cheese?*

Drink
7. apple juice   *Do you drink much apple juice?*
8. lemonade   *Do you drink much lemonade?*
9. milk   *Do you drink much milk?*
10. tea   *Do you drink much tea?*
11. coffee   *Do you drink much coffee?*
12. soda or pop   *Do you drink much soda or pop?*

EXERCISE 🔢 ABOUT YOU Ask a question with "Do you have . . ." and the words given. Another student will answer. Practice both count and noncount nouns.

EXAMPLES
American friends
A: Do you have any American friends?
B: Yes. I have a lot of American friends.

free time
A: Do you have any free time?
B: No. I don't have any free time.

Answers will vary.
1. money with you now
2. credit cards
3. bread at home
4. bananas at home
5. orange juice in your refrigerator
6. plants in your apartment
7. family pictures in your wallet
8. time to relax

EXERCISE 🔢 This is a conversation between a husband (H) and wife (W). Choose the correct word or words to fill in the blanks.

H: Where were you today? I called you from work
   _____*many*_____ times, but there was no answer.
   (examples: much, many)

W: I went to the supermarket today. I
   bought _____*a few*_____ things.
   (1 a little, a few)

H: What did you buy?

318   Lesson 10

Expansion

Exercises 10 and 11 Create two rings of students. Have half of the students stand in an outer ring around the classroom. Have the other half stand in an inner ring, facing the outer ring. Instruct students to ask and answer the questions from Exercise 10 or 11. Call out *"turn"* every minute or so. Students in the inner ring should move one space clockwise. Students now ask and answer with their new partners. Have students ask questions in random order. Make sure students look at each other when they're speaking.

Exercise 12 Variation

To provide practice with listening skills, have students close their books and listen to the audio. Repeat the audio as needed. Ask comprehension questions, such as: *Where did the husband call from?* (work) *How many times did he call?* (many times) *Did the wife answer the phone?* (no) Then have students open their books and complete Exercise 12.

W: There was a special on coffee, so I bought ___*a lot of*___
(2 *a lot of, much*)

coffee. I didn't buy ___*any*___ fruit because the prices
(3 *any, no*)

were very high.

H: How ___*much*___ money did you spend?
(4 *much, many*)

W: I spent ___*a lot of*___ money because of the coffee. I
(5 *much, a lot of*)

bought ten 1-pound bags.

H: It took you a long time.

W: Yes. The store was very crowded. There were ___*many*___
(6 *much, many*)

people in the store. And there was ___*a lot of*___ traffic at
(7 *a lot of, much*)

that hour, so it took me ___*a lot of*___ time to drive home.
(8 *a lot of, much*)

H: There's not ___*much*___ time to cook.
(9 *much, many*)

W: Maybe you can cook today and let me rest?

H: Uh . . . I don't have ___*much*___ experience. You do it
(10 *much, no*)

better. You have ___*a lot of*___ experience.
(11 *a lot of, much*)

W: Yes. I have ___*a lot*___ because I do it all the time!
(12 *a lot of, a lot*)

EXERCISE **13**

This is a conversation between a waitress (W) and a customer (C).
Fill in the blanks with an appropriate quantity word. (In some
cases, more than one answer is possible.)

W: Would you like ___*any (or some)*___ coffee, sir?
(*example*)

C: Yes, and please bring me ___*some/a little*___ cream too. I don't
(1)

need ___*any*___ sugar. And I'd like a
(2)

___*glass*___ of orange juice, too.
(3)

A few minutes later:

W: Are you ready to order, sir?

C: Yes. I'd like the scrambled eggs with three ___*strips/slices*___
(4)

of bacon. And some pancakes, too.

Count and Noncount Nouns; Quantity Words **319**

1. Have students read the direction
line. Go over the example. Remind
students that more than one answer
may be possible.
2. Explain that this is a conversation
at a restaurant between a waitress
and a customer. Direct students'
attention to the picture of the
waitress and customer. Have
students complete Exercise 13
individually.
3. Check answers as a class. Then
have students practice the
conversations in pairs.
4. If necessary, review grammar charts
10.5 on page 314, **10.6** on page 315,
and **10.7** on page 316.

To save class time, have
students do half of the exercise
in class and complete the other half for
homework. Or assign the entire
exercise for homework.

Expansion

Exercise 12 Have students role-play all or part of the conversation in front of the class.

Exercise 13 Variation

To provide practice with listening skills, have students close their books and listen to the
audio. Repeat the audio as needed. Ask comprehension questions, such as: *What does the
customer want to drink?* (coffee with cream and orange juice) *What kind of eggs does the
customer want?* (scrambled) *Does the customer want pancakes?* (yes) Then have students
open their books and complete Exercise 13.

Eat Less, Live Longer (Reading)

1. Have students look at the photo. Ask: *What is this child doing?* (watching TV and eating junk food) *Is he overweight?* (yes) *What might we call someone who watches a lot of TV and doesn't get a lot of exercise?* (a couch potato)
2. Have students look at the title of the reading. Ask: *What is the reading about? How do you know?* Have students use the title and photo to make predictions about the reading.
3. Preteach any vocabulary words students may not know, such as *overweight* and *consume*.

BEFORE YOU READ

1. Have students discuss the questions in pairs.
2. Ask for a few volunteers to share their answers with the class.

To save class time, skip "Before You Read" or have students prepare answers for homework ahead of time.

—Breakfast Menu—

Eggs
scrambled..............$2.50
sunny side up..........$2.00
hardboiled.............$1.00
Waffles.................$3.50
French Toast............$3.25
Pancakes
plain...................$3.50
strawberry.............$4.50
blueberry..............$4.50
Side Orders
bacon...................$1.50
sausage................$2.00
home fries.............$1.50

W: Do you want ___any/some___ syrup with your pancakes?
        (5)

C: Yes. What kind do you have?

W: We have ___many/a lot of___ different kinds: strawberry, cherry,
        (6)
blueberry, maple . . .

C: I'll have the strawberry syrup. And bring me ___some/a little/a lot of___
                                                        (7)
butter too.

After the customer is finished eating:

W: Would you like ___any/some___ dessert?
                        (8)

C: Yes. I'd like a ___piece of/slice of___ cherry pie. And put
                        (9)
___some/a little/a lot of___ ice cream on the pie. And I'd like
          (10)
___some/a little___ more coffee, please.
        (11)

After the customer eats dessert:

W: Would you like anything else?

C: Just the check. I don't have ___any/much/a lot of___ cash with me.
                                        (12)
Can I pay by credit card?

W: Of course.

EAT LESS, LIVE LONGER

Before You Read

1. Do you think the American diet is healthy?
2. Do you see a lot of overweight Americans?

Expansion

Exercise 13 Have students create similar conversations. Then have volunteers role-play their conversations in front of the class.

Culture Note

About 127 million adults in the U.S. are overweight, 60 million are obese, and 9 million are severely obese. Currently, 64.5% of U.S. adults are overweight and 30.5% are obese. Obesity is the second leading cause of preventable death in the U.S.

Read the follwing article. Pay special attention to *too much, too many*, and *a lot of*.

About 65 percent of Americans are overweight. The typical American consumes **too many** calories and **too much** fat and doesn't get enough exercise. Many American children are overweight too. Children spend **too much** time in front of the TV and not enough time getting exercise. Eighty percent of commercials during children's programs are for food products. In four hours of Saturday morning cartoons, there are over 200 ads for junk food.

Twenty-five percent of American pets are overweight too. Like their owners, they eat **too much** and don't get enough exercise.

There is evidence that eating fewer calories can help us live longer. Doctors studied the people on the Japanese island of Okinawa, who eat 40 percent less than the typical American. The Okinawan diet is low in calories and salt. Also Okinawans eat **a lot of** fruit, vegetables, and fish and drink **a lot of** green tea and water. Okinawa has **a lot of** people over the age of 100.

How can we live longer and healthier lives? The answer is simple: Eat less and exercise more.

10.8 | *A Lot Of* vs. *Too Much/Too Many*

Examples	Explanation
It is good to eat **a lot of** fruit. In Okinawa, there are **a lot of** people over the age of 100. I don't eat **a lot** in the morning.	*A lot (of)* shows a large quantity. It is a neutral term.
You shouldn't eat a lot of ice cream because it has **too many** calories. If you drink **too much** coffee, you won't sleep tonight.	*Too much* and *too many* show that a quantity is excessive and causes a problem. Use *too many* with count nouns. Use *too much* with noncount nouns.
If you eat **too much,** you will gain weight.	Use *too much* after verbs.

 EXERCISE Circle the correct words to fill in this conversation between a mother (M) and her 12-year-old son (S).

M: I'm worried about you. You spend too (*much/ many*) hours in front
(example)

of the TV. And you eat too (*much/many*) junk food and don't get
(1)

enough exercise. You're getting fat.

S: Mom. I know I watch (*a lot of/a lot*) TV, but I learn (*a lot/a lot of*)
(2)   *(3)*

from TV.

Reading Variation

To practice listening skills, have students first listen to the audio alone. Ask a few comprehension questions. Repeat the audio if necessary. Then have students open their books and read along as they listen to the audio.

Reading Glossary

consume: to eat and drink
overweight: heavier than the normal or permitted weight

Exercise 14 Variation

To provide practice with listening skills, have students close their books and listen to the audio. Repeat the audio as needed. Ask comprehension questions, such as: *Why is the mother worried about her son?* (She thinks he watches too much TV, eats too much junk food, and doesn't get enough exercise.) *What's the new rule?* (The son can't watch TV until he finishes his homework.) Then have students open their books and complete Exercise 14.

Reading CD 2, Track 16

1. Have students read the text silently. Tell them to pay special attention to *too much, too many,* and *a lot of.* Then play the audio and have students read along silently.
2. Check students' comprehension. Ask questions such as: *What percentage of Americans are overweight?* (65 percent) *Why are so many Americans overweight?* (They consume too much and exercise too little.) *What does the Okinawa diet consist of?* (fruit, fish, water, and green tea)

To save class time, have students do the reading for homework ahead of time.

10.8 | *A Lot Of* vs. *Too Much/Too Many*

1. Have students cover up grammar chart **10.8.** Then have them turn to the reading on page 321. Say: *Find too many, too much, and a lot of. Pay attention to how they're used. Does the usage feel negative or neutral?*
2. Tell students to look at grammar chart **10.8.** Say: A lot of *is used to describe a large quantity. It is a neutral term. But* too much *and* too many *show that something is excessive. We use* too much *with noncount nouns and* too many *with count nouns. Go over all the example sentences. Point out that* too much *is also used after verbs.*

EXERCISE 14

 CD 2, Track 17

1. Have students read the direction line. Go over the example.
2. Explain that this is a conversation between a mother and her 12-year-old son. Have students complete Exercise 14 individually.
3. Then have students practice the conversations in pairs.
4. If necessary, review grammar chart **10.8** on page 321.

M: No, you don't. Sometimes you have (*a lot of*/*too much*) homework,
(4)

but you turn on the TV as soon as you get home from school.
I'm going to make a rule: No TV until you finish your homework.

S: Oh, Mom. You have too (*much*/*many*) rules.
(5)

M: That's what parents are for: to guide their kids to make the right

decisions. There are (*a lot of*/*too many*) things to do besides watching
(6)

TV. Why don't you go outside and play? When I was your age, we
played outside.

S: "*When I was your age.*" Not again. You always say that.

M: Well, it's true. We had (*too much*/*a lot of*) fun outside, playing with
(7)

friends. I didn't have (*a lot of*/*too much*) toys when I was your age.
(8)

And I certainly didn't have video games or computer games. Also we

helped our parents (*a lot*/*too much*) after school. We cut the grass
(9)

and washed the dishes.

S: My friend Josh cuts the grass, throws out the garbage, and cleans the

basement once a month. His mom pays him (*too much*/*a lot of*)
(10)

money for doing it. Maybe if you pay me, I'll do it.

M: Not again. "*Josh does it. Josh has it. Why can't I?*" You always say
that. You're not Josh, and I'm not Josh's mother. I'm not going to pay
you for things you should do.

S: OK. Just tell me what to do, and I'll do it.

M: There are (*a lot of*/*too much*) leaves on the front lawn. Why don't
(11)

you start by putting them in garbage bags? And you can walk

Sparky. He's getting fat, too. He eats (*too much*/*too many*) and
(12)

sleeps all day. Both of you need more exercise.

Expansion

Exercise 14 Have students create their own dialogues in pairs. Say: *Use Exercise 14 as a model.* Then have volunteers role-play their conversations in front of the class.

EXERCISE **15** Fill in the blanks with *much* or *many*, and complete each statement.

EXAMPLE   If I drink too ___*much*___ coffee, ___*I won't be able to sleep tonight.*___

Answers will vary.   1. If the teacher gives too _____ homework, _____

_____

2. If I take too _____ classes, _____

_____

3. If I eat too _____ candy, _____

_____

4. If I'm absent too _____ days, _____

_____

5. Too _____ cholesterol _____

_____

10.9 | *Too Much/Too Many* vs. *Too*

Examples	Explanation
I don't eat ice cream because it's **too** fattening. He should lose weight. He's getting **too** fat.	Use *too* with adjectives and adverbs.
I don't eat ice cream because it has **too many** calories and **too much** fat.	Use *too much* and *too many* before nouns. Use *too many* with count nouns. Use *too much* with noncount nouns.

EXERCISE **16** Fill in the blanks with *too, too much,* or *too many.*

Situation A. Some students are complaining about the school cafeteria. They are giving reasons why they don't want to eat there.

EXAMPLE   It's ___*too*___ noisy.

1. The food is _____*too*_____ greasy.
2. There are _____*too many*_____ students. I can't find a place to sit.
3. The lines are _____*too*_____ long.
4. The food is _____*too*_____ expensive.
5. There's _____*too much*_____ noise.

1. Have students read the direction line. Say: *What tense do we use in the main clause after an if clause?* (the future) Go over the example in the book. Have a volunteer model the example.
2. Have students complete the exercise individually. Then have students compare answers in pairs. Circulate to observe pair work. Give help as needed.
3. If necessary, review grammar chart **10.8** on pages 321.

To save class time, have students do half of the exercise in class and complete the other half for homework. Or assign the entire exercise for homework.

10.9 | *Too Much/Too Many* vs. *Too*

1. Have students look at grammar chart **10.9**. Say: *We use* too *with adjectives and adverbs.* Too much *and* too many *are used with nouns.* Too much *is used with noncount nouns, and* too many *is used with count nouns.*
2. Go over the examples and explanations in the grammar chart.

EXERCISE 16

1. Say: *There are two situations in this exercise. Situation A is about students who are complaining about the cafeteria. Situation B is about students who are complaining about their class and their school.* Have students read the direction line. Ask: *What do we write in the blanks?* (too, too much, or *too many*) Go over the example.
2. Have students complete the exercise individually. Go over the answers as a class.
3. If necessary, review grammar chart **10.9** on page 323.

EXERCISE 17

1. Say: *Now it's your turn to complain!* Have students read the direction line. Go over the example. Model the exercise for the students with your own complaints.
2. Have students complete the exercise individually. Then have students compare answers in pairs.
3. If necessary, review grammar chart **10.9** on page 323.

EXERCISE 18

1. Have students read the direction line. Say: *Remember, we use* too, too much, *and* too many *if there is a problem or something is excessive. We use* a lot of *when we want to show a large quantity.* Go over the example. Model the exercise for the students with your own complaints.
2. Have students complete the exercise individually. Then have students compare answers in pairs.
3. If necessary, review grammar charts **10.8** on page 321 and **10.9** on page 323.

To save class time, have students do half of the exercise in class and complete the other half for homework. Or assign the entire exercise for homework.

Situation B. Some students are complaining about their class and school.

1. The classroom is _____*too*_____ small.
2. There are _____*too many*_____ students in one class.
3. We have to write _____*too many*_____ compositions.
4. The teacher gives _____*too much*_____ homework.
5. There are _____*too many*_____ tests.

EXERCISE **17** ABOUT YOU Write a few sentences to complain about something: your apartment, your roommate, this city, this college, etc. Use *too, too much,* or *too many* in your sentences.

EXAMPLE My roommate spends too much time in the bathroom in the morning. He's too messy.[3]

_____Answers will vary._____

EXERCISE **18** Fill in the blanks with *too, too much,* or *too many* if a problem is presented. Use *a lot of* if no problem is presented.

EXAMPLE Most people can't afford to buy a Mercedes because it costs _____*too much*_____ money.

1. There are _____*a lot of*_____ noncount nouns in English.
2. "Rice" is a noncount noun because the parts are _____*too*_____ small to count.
3. If this class is _____*too*_____ hard for you, you should go to a lower level.
4. Good students spend _____*a lot of*_____ time doing their homework.
5. If you spend _____*too much*_____ time watching TV, you won't have time for your homework.
6. It takes _____*a lot of*_____ time to learn English, but you can do it.
7. Oranges have _____*a lot of*_____ vitamin C.
8. If you are on a diet, don't eat potato chips. They have _____*too many*_____ calories and _____*too much*_____ fat.
9. Babies drink _____*a lot of*_____ milk.
10. If you drink _____*too much*_____ coffee, you won't sleep.

[3]A *messy* person does not put his or her things in order.

Expansion

Exercise 17 Have pairs of students create a dialogue out of one or both of the lists of complaints. Then ask volunteers to role-play their dialogues in front of the class.

Exercise 17 Have students write a letter of complaint to someone, such as a local government representative, based on the sentences they wrote in Exercise 17.

EXERCISE 19 *Combination Exercise.* A doctor (D) and patient (P) are talking. Fill in the blanks with an appropriate quantity word or unit of measurement to complete this conversation. (In some cases, more than one answer is possible.)

D: I'm looking at your lab results and I see that your cholesterol level is very high. Also your blood pressure is _____*too*_____

(example)

high. Do you use _____*a lot of/any*_____ salt on your food?

(1)

P: Yes, Doctor. I love salt. I eat _____*a lot of*_____ potato chips and

(2)

popcorn.

D: That's not good. You're overweight, too. You need to lose 50 pounds. What do you usually eat?

P: For breakfast I usually grab _____*a cup of/some*_____ coffee and a

(3)

doughnut. I don't have _____*much/any*_____ time for lunch, so I

(4)

eat _*a few/some/a lot of/a bag of*_ potato chips and drink

(5)

_____*some/a cup of*_____ soda while I'm working. I'm so busy that I

(6)

have _____*no*_____ time to cook at all. So for dinner, I

(7)

usually stop at a fast-food place and get a burger and fries.

D: That's a terrible diet! How _____*much*_____ exercise do

(8)

you get?

P: I never exercise. I don't have _____*much/any*_____ time at all. I

(9)

own my own business and I have _____*too much*_____ work.

(10)

Sometimes I work 80 hours a week.

D: I'm going to give you an important _____*piece of*_____ advice.

(11)

You're going to have to change your lifestyle.

P: I'm _____*too*_____ old to change my habits.

(12)

1. Have students read the direction line. Remind students in some cases more than one answer is possible. Go over the example.
2. Explain that this is a conversation between a doctor and patient. Have students complete Exercise 19 individually.
3. Then have students practice the conversation in pairs.
4. If necessary, review grammar charts **10.4** on page 313, **10.5** on page 314, **10.6** on page 315, **10.7** on page 316, **10.8** on page 321, and **10.9** on page 323.

🕑 To save class time, have students do half of the exercise in class and complete the other half for homework. Or assign the entire exercise for homework.

Exercise 19 Variation

To provide practice with listening skills, have students close their books and listen to the audio. Repeat the audio as needed. Ask comprehension questions, such as: *How is the patient's cholesterol level?* (too high) *How is the patient's blood pressure?* (too high) *Does the patient eat a lot of salt?* (yes) Then have students open their books and complete Exercise 19.

Expansion

Exercise 19 Have volunteers role-play all or part of the conversation.

Summary of Lesson 10

Words that we use before count and noncount nouns Have students cover up the singular count, plural count, and noncount noun columns in the chart. Then go through each word, beginning with *the*, and ask if singular count nouns (such as *book*), plural count nouns (such as *books*), and noncount nouns (such as *tea*) can be used with the word. For an extra challenge, have students write a sentence using the word with a noun. If necessary, have students review: **Lesson 10.**

Editing Advice

Have students close their books. Write the example sentences without editing marks or corrections on the board. For example:

1. I want to give you an advice.

2. My mother gave me many advices.

3. He received three mails today.

Ask students to correct each sentence and provide a rule or explanation for each correction. This activity can be done individually, in pairs, or as a class. After students have corrected each sentence, tell them to turn to pages 326–327. Say: *Now compare your work with the Editing Advice in the book.*

D: You're only 45 years old. You're _____ too _____ young to die.
                                        (13)

And if you don't change your habits, you're going to have a heart attack. I'm going to give you a booklet about staying healthy. It has _____ some/a lot of _____ information that will teach you about diet
            (14)

and exercise. Please read it and come back in six months.

SUMMARY OF LESSON 10

Words that we use before count and noncount nouns:

Word	Count (Singular) Example: *book*	Count (Plural) Example: *books*	Noncount Example: *tea*
the	x	x	x
a	x		
one	x		
two, three, etc.		x	
some (affirmatives)		x	x
any (negatives and questions)		x	x
a lot of		x	x
much (negatives and questions)			x
many		x	
a little			x
a few		x	

EDITING ADVICE

1. Don't put *a* or *an* before a noncount noun.
                    some
   I want to give you an advice.

2. Noncount nouns are always singular.
                    a lot of
   My mother gave me many advices.
                    pieces of
   He received three mails today.

---

3. Don't use a double negative.

   any
   He doesn't have ~~no~~ time.   OR   ~~He has no time.~~

4. Don't use *much* with an affirmative statement.

   UNCOMMON: There was much rain yesterday.
   COMMON: There was a lot of rain yesterday.

5. Use *a* or *an*, not *any*, with a singular count noun.

   a
   Do you have ~~any~~ computer?

6. Don't use *a* or *an* before a plural noun.

   She has a~~ ~~blue eyes.

7. Use the plural form for plural count nouns.

   s
   He has a lot of friend.
   ^

8. Omit *of* after *a lot* when the noun is omitted.

   In my country, I have a lot of friends, but in the U.S. I don't have
   a lot of.

9. Use *of* with a unit of measure.

   of
   I ate three pieces bread.
   ^

10. Don't use *of* after *many, much, a few,* or *a little* if a noun follows
    directly.

    She has many ~~of~~ friends.
    He put a little ~~of~~ milk in his coffee.

11. Only use *too much/too many* if there is a problem.

    a lot of
    He has a good job. He earns ~~too~~ ~~much~~ money.

12. Don't use *too much* before an adjective or adverb.

    I don't want to go outside today. It's too ~~much~~ hot.

13. Don't confuse *too* and *to*.

    too
    If you eat ~~to~~ much candy, you'll get sick.

Lesson 10 Test/Review

For additional practice, review, and assessment materials, see Assessment CD-ROM with *ExamView Pro, More Grammar Practice* Workbook 1, Interactive CD-ROM, and Web site http://elt.thomson.com/gic

PART 1

1. Part 1 may be used in addition to the Assessment CD-ROM with *ExamView Pro* as an in-class test to assess student performance. Have students read the direction line. Ask: *Does every sentence have a mistake?* (no) Go over the examples with the class.
2. Have students complete the assignment individually. Collect for assessment.
3. If necessary, have students review: **Lesson 10.**

LESSON 10 TEST/REVIEW

PART **1**   Find the mistakes with the underlined words, and correct them. Not every sentence has a mistake. If the sentence is correct, write *C*.

EXAMPLES   My dog doesn't get enough exercise. He's <u>too much</u> fat.

You can be happy if you have <u>a few</u> good friends.   *C*

1. He doesn't have <u>no</u> money with him at all. *(any)*
2. He's a lucky man. He has <u>too many</u> friends. *(a lot of/many)*
3. There are a lot of tall buildings in a big city. There aren't <u>a lot of</u> in a small town. *(a lot)*
4. I don't have <u>much</u> time to help you.   *C*
5. A 14-year-old person is <u>too much</u> young to get a driver's license.
6. <u>A few</u> students in this class are from Pakistan.   *C*
7. I don't have <u>some</u> time to help you. *(any/much)*
8. I don't have <u>any</u> car. I use public transportation. *(a)*
9. Did we have <u>many</u> snow last winter? *(a lot of/much)*
10. <u>Many</u> people would like to have <u>a lot of</u> money in order to travel.   *C*
11. He doesn't have <u>any</u> time to study at all.   *C*
12. I'd like to help you, but I have <u>too many</u> things to do this week. Maybe I can help you next week.   *C*
13. She drinks <u>two cups of coffee</u> every morning.   *C*
14. I drink <u>four milks</u> a day. *(glasses of milk)*
15. He bought five <u>pounds sugar</u>. *(of)*
16. How <u>much</u> bananas did you buy? *(many)*
17. <u>How much</u> money did you spend?   *C*
18. This building doesn't have <u>a</u> basement.   *C*
19. I have <u>much</u> time to read because I'm on vacation now. *(a lot of)*
20. She gave me <u>a good advice</u>. *(some)*
21. The piano is <u>too much</u> heavy. I can't move it. *(too)*
22. I have <u>a lot of CDs</u>, probably over 200.   *C*

Lesson Review

To use Part 1 as a review, assign it as homework or use it as an in-class activity to be completed individually or in pairs. Check answers and review errors as a class. Reteach grammar points that students haven't mastered. Then student learning may be assessed using a test generated from the Assessment CD-ROM with *ExamView Pro.*

---

23. I don't have <u>much experience</u> with cars. *c*

24. I can't help you now. I'm <u>t̶o̶</u> busy.
      too

25. There are <u>many of̶</u> books in the library.
      many

26. I have <u>a little time</u>, so I can help you. *c*

PART **2**   Fill in the blanks with an appropriate measurement of quantity.

EXAMPLE   a <u>*cup*</u> of coffee

Answers will vary.

1. a _____ of soda
2. a _____ of sugar
3. a _____ of milk
4. a _____ of furniture
5. a _____ of mail

6. a _____ of advice
7. a _____ of bread
8. a _____ of paper
9. a _____ of meat
10. a _____ of soup

PART **3**   Read the following composition. Choose the correct quantity word or indefinite article.

I had <u>*some*</u> problems when I first came to the U.S.
    (example: some, any, a little)

First, I didn't have <u>*much*</u> money.
    (1 much, a, some)

<u>*A few*</u> friends of mine lent me <u>*some*</u>
(2 A few, A little, A few of)   *(3 some, a, any)*

money, but I didn't feel good about borrowing it.

Second, I couldn't find <u>*an*</u> apartment. I went to
    (4 a, an, no)

see <u>*some*</u> apartments, but I couldn't afford
    (5 some, a little, an)

<u>*any*</u> of them. For <u>*a few*</u>
(6 an, any, none)   *(7 a little, a few of, a few)*

months, I had to live with my uncle's family, but the situation wasn't good.

Third, I started to study English, but soon found

<u>*a*</u> job and didn't have <u>*much*</u>
(8 a, any, some)   *(9 no, much, a few)*

time to study. As a result, I was failing my course.

However, little by little my life started to improve, and I don't need

<u>*much*</u> help from my friends and relative anymore.
(10 no, some, much)

Count and Noncount Nouns; Quantity Words   **329**

PART 2

1. Part 2 may also be used in addition to the Assessment CD-ROM with *ExamView Pro* as an in-class test to assess student performance. Have students read the direction line. Go over the example with the class.
2. Have students complete the exercise individually. Collect for assessment.
3. If necessary, have students review:
   10.4 Describing Quantities of Count and Noncount Nouns (p. 313).

PART 3

1. Part 3 may also be used in addition to the Assessment CD-ROM with *ExamView Pro* as an in-class test to assess student performance. Have students read the direction line. Go over the example with the class.
2. Have students complete the exercise individually. Collect for assessment.
3. If necessary, have students review:
   10.5 *A Lot Of, Much, Many* (p. 314)
   10.6 *A Few, A Little* (p. 315)
   10.7 *Some, Any*, and *A/An* (p. 316)
   10.8 *A Lot Of* vs. *Too Much/Too Many* (p. 321).

Lesson Review

To use Parts 2 and 3 as a review, assign them as homework or use them as in-class activities to be completed individually or in pairs. Check answers and review errors as a class. Reteach grammar points that students haven't mastered. Then student learning may be assessed using a test generated from the Assessment CD-ROM with *ExamView Pro*.

Lesson **10**   **329**

Expansion Activities

These expansion activities provide opportunities for students to interact with one another and further develop their speaking and writing skills. Encourage students to use grammar from this lesson whenever possible.

🕐 To save class time, assign parts of the activities as homework. Then use class time for interaction and communication. If students do not need additional speaking practice, some of the activities may be assigned as writing activities for homework, or skipped altogether.

CLASSROOM ACTIVITIES

1. Have students work individually to fill out the chart. Then put students in pairs to compare charts. If possible, have students from different countries work together. Then have students compare charts in groups. Ask: *Who is the healthiest person in your group?* Have groups report to the class.

2. Have students work individually to complete the chart. Point out the pictures of the submarine sandwich, tortilla chip, and pretzels. Then have students compare charts in groups. Ask: *What foods are the most popular?* Have groups report to the class.

EXPANSION ACTIVITIES

Classroom Activities

1. Make a list of unhealthy things that you eat. Make a list of things that you need to eat for a healthy diet.

Unhealthy things I eat	Things I should eat

2. These are some popular foods in the U.S. Put a check (✓) in the column that describes your experience of this food. Then find a partner and compare your list to your partners list.

Food	I Like	I Don't Like	I Never Tried
pizza		✓	
hot dogs			
hamburgers			
tacos			
submarine sandwiches			
breakfast cereal			
peanut butter			
cheesecake			
tortilla chips			
potato chips			
popcorn			
chocolate chip			
cookies			
fried chicken			
pretzels			

Expansion

Classroom Activities For Activity 2, have students make a chart with five to ten food items commonly eaten in their native countries. Then have students exchange charts with a partner. Have the pairs fill out each others' charts. Have students discuss interesting food items with the class.

3. Cross out the phrase that doesn't fit and fill in the blanks to make a true statement about the U.S. or another country. Find a partner and compare your answers.

EXAMPLE   People in _____Argentina_____ eat/don't eat
_____a lot of_____ meat.

a. People in _____ eat/don't eat
_____ natural foods.

b. People in _____ drink/don't drink
_____ tea.

c. People in _____ shop/don't shop for food every day.

d. People in _____ eat/don't eat in a movie theater.

e. People in _____ drink/don't drink
_____ bottled water.

Talk About it

1. Look at the dialogue that takes place in a restaurant on pages 319–320. Do you think this man is eating a healthy breakfast? Why or why not?

2. Americans often eat some of these foods for breakfast: cereal and milk, toast and butter or jelly, orange juice, eggs, bacon, coffee. Describe a typical breakfast for you.

3. Most American stores sell products in containers: bags, jars, cans, and so forth. How do stores in other countries sell products?

4. Do stores in other countries give customers bags for their groceries, or do customers have to bring their own bags to the store?

5. Some things are usually free in an American restaurant: salt, pepper, sugar, cream or milk for coffee, mustard, ketchup, napkins, water, ice, coffee refills, and sometimes bread. Are these things free in a restaurant in other countries?

6. The following saying is about food. Discuss the meaning. Do you have a similar saying in your native language?

You are what you eat.

Outside Activities

1. Bring to class a package of a food or drink you enjoy. Read the label for "Nutrition Facts." Look at calories, grams of fat, cholesterol, sodium, protein, vitamins, and minerals. Do you think this is a nutritious food? Why or why not?

2. Bring a favorite recipe to class. Explain how to prepare this recipe.

Count and Noncount Nouns; Quantity Words   **331**

3. Have students work individually to make true statements. Then have students compare answers in pairs.

TALK ABOUT IT

Have students discuss each point in pairs, in groups, or as a class.

OUTSIDE ACTIVITIES

1. Have students bring a packaged food item or drink to class. If possible, have extra packaged food on hand in case students forget theirs. Have students discuss their food in groups. Then do a quick survey. Which of the foods that the students brought in is the least healthy?

2. Have students bring in a favorite recipe. If possible, have extra recipes on hand in case students forget theirs. Have students explain how to prepare the recipe in groups. Then have them discuss if the recipes are healthy or not.

Expansion

Talk About it Have students make presentations about food, eating habits, and shopping customs in their countries. Encourage students to make posters, create skits, or even prepare food.

Outside Activities For activity 2, have students prepare the dish to be eaten in class. Ask volunteers to explain how to prepare their dishes to the class.

WRITE ABOUT IT

Have students read the direction line. Brainstorm other information to include. Have students complete the assignment individually. Collect for assessment and/or have students present their paragraphs to a group.

INTERNET ACTIVITIES

1. Say: *You are going to find an article on nutrition on the Internet.* Have students note any interesting information on nutrition from the article. Then have them compare the information against their own diets. Ask a few volunteers to share their information with the class.

2. Brainstorm with students names of foods they like to eat. Check for correct spelling. As an extra challenge, have students find, print out, and bring pictures of the foods to go along with their recipes.

Describe shopping for food in the U.S. or in another country. You may include information about the following:

- packaging
- open market vs. stores
- self-service vs. service from salespeople
- shopping carts
- fixed prices vs. negotiable prices
- freshness of food

1. At a search engine, type in "nutrition." Find an interesting article. How does your diet compare?

2. Use the Internet to find a recipe for something you like to eat. Bring the recipe to class.

Additional Activities at http://elt.thomson.com/gic

Internet Activities Variation

Remind students that if they don't have Internet access, they can use Internet facilities at a public library or they can use traditional research methods to find out information including looking at encyclopedias, magazines, books, journals, and newspapers.

Lesson | 11

LESSON

11

GRAMMAR
Adjectives
Noun Modifiers
Adverbs

CONTEXT: Great Women
Helen Keller
Grandma Moses

Helen Keller (1882–1968)

Lesson Overview

GRAMMAR

Ask: *What did we study in Lesson 10?* (count and noncount nouns, quantity words) *What are we going to study in this lesson?* (adjectives, noun modifiers, and adverbs) *What is an example of an adjective? An adverb?* Have students give examples. Write them on the board.

CONTEXT

1. Activate students' prior knowledge. Ask: *Who is Helen Keller? Who is Grandma Moses?*
2. Have students share their knowledge and personal experiences. Ask students to name some great women from their countries.

Photo

1. Direct students' attention to the photo. Ask: *When do you think this photo of Helen Keller was taken?* (when she was a young woman) *What is Helen Keller doing in this photo?* (reading something in Braille) *What is Braille?* (a writing system made up of raised dots) *Have you ever seen anything written in Braille? Who uses Braille?* (people with vision impairments)
2. Ask: *Do you know anyone that reads Braille? What other aids do people with vision impairments use?* (audio books, canes, seeing eye dogs)

To save class time, have students do the Test/Review at the end of the lesson, or administer a lesson test generated from the Assessment CD-ROM with *ExamView® Pro*. Skip sections of the lesson that students have already mastered. You may also assign some sections for self-study for extra credit.

Expansion

Theme The topic for this lesson can be enhanced with the following ideas:

1. A sample of something in Braille
2. A book by Helen Keller; a book about Helen Keller with photos
3. A book on Grandma Moses; prints of Grandma Moses's paintings

Helen Keller (Reading)

1. Have students look at the photo. Say: *Helen Keller is the young girl. The woman was her teacher, Anne Sullivan. What are they doing?* (talking with their fingers)
2. Have students look at the title of the reading. Ask: *What is the reading about?* Have students use the title and photo to make predictions about the reading.
3. Preteach any vocabulary words students may not know, such as *remarkable, wild, patient, extensive,* and *tireless.*

BEFORE YOU READ

1. Have students discuss the questions in pairs.
2. Ask for a few volunteers to share their answers with the class.

🕐 To save class time, skip "Before You Read" or have students prepare answers for homework ahead of time.

Reading 🎧 *CD 2, Track 19*

1. Have students read the text silently. Tell them to pay special attention to adjectives and adverbs. Then play the audio and have students read along silently.
2. Check students' comprehension. Ask questions such as: *Was Helen Keller deaf and blind at birth?* (No; she became deaf and blind after an illness at 19 months.) *What happened when she couldn't understand anything?* (She became frustrated and angry.) *Who taught Helen to communicate?* (Anne Sullivan) *How old was Helen when she graduated from college?* (24)

🕐 To save class time, have students do the reading for homework ahead of time.

HELEN KELLER

 Before You Read

1. Do you know of any special schools for handicapped people?
2. What kind of facilities or services does this school have for handicapped people?

Helen Keller
and Anne Sullivan

🎧 Read the following article. Pay special attention to adjectives and adverbs.

Did You Know?

In Washington, D.C., there is a special college for deaf students—Gallaudet University.

Do you know of anyone with a disability who did remarkable things? Helen Keller was a truly **remarkable** woman.

Helen Keller was a **healthy** baby. But when she was 19 months old, she had a **sudden** fever. The fever disappeared, but she became **blind** and **deaf**. Because she couldn't hear, it was difficult for her to learn to speak. As she grew, she was **angry** and **frustrated** because she couldn't understand or communicate with people. She became **wild**, throwing things and kicking and biting.

When Helen was seven years old, a teacher, Anne Sullivan, came to live with Helen's family. First, Anne taught Helen how to talk with her fingers. Helen was **excited** when she realized that things had names. Then Anne taught Helen to read by the Braille system. Helen learned these skills **quickly**. However, learning to speak was harder. Anne continued to teach Helen **patiently**. Finally, when Helen was ten years old, she could speak **clearly** enough for people to understand her.

Helen was very **intelligent**. She went to an institute for the blind, where she did very **well** in her studies. Then she went to college,[1] where she graduated with honors when she was 24 years old. Helen traveled **extensively** with Anne. She worked **tirelessly**, traveling all over America, Europe, and Asia to raise money to build schools for **blind** people. Her **main** message was that **handicapped** people are like everybody else. They want to live life **fully** and **naturally**. Helen wanted all people to be treated **equally**.

While she was in college, Helen wrote her first of many books, *The Story of My Life*, in 1903.

[1] In the U.S., the words *college* and *university* usually have the same meaning.

Reading Variation

To practice listening skills, have students first listen to the audio alone. Ask a few comprehension questions. Repeat the audio if necessary. Then have students open their books and read along as they listen to the audio.

Reading Glossary

extensive: great in amount or area, considerable
patient: having or showing patience, calm, or being undisturbed
remarkable: worthy of attention, noticeable
tireless: dedicated
wild: unruly, uncontrolled

11.1 | Adjectives and Adverbs

Examples	Explanation
Helen was a **healthy** baby. She seemed **intelligent.** She became **blind.** Anne Sullivan was a **wonderful** teacher.	Adjectives describe nouns. We can use adjectives before nouns or after the verbs *be, become, look, seem,* and other sense-perception verbs.
Anne taught Helen **patiently.** Helen learned **quickly.** People want to live life **fully.**	Adverbs of manner tell how or in what way we do things. We form most adverbs of manner by putting *-ly* at the end of an adjective. Adverbs of manner usually follow the verb phrase.

EXERCISE **1** · Decide if the underlined word is an adjective (*adj.*) or adverb (*adv.*).

EXAMPLES   Helen was a <u>healthy</u> baby. *adj.*

Ꮤe should respect all people <u>equally</u>. *adv.*

1. When Helen was <u>angry</u>, she threw things. *adj.*
2. She seemed <u>wild</u>. *adj.*
3. She was <u>blind</u> and <u>deaf</u>. *adj.*
4. She learned to speak <u>clearly</u>. *adv.*
5. She had a <u>good</u> teacher. *adj.*
6. Anne was a <u>patient</u> woman. *adj.*
7. Helen learned <u>quickly</u>. *adv.*
8. Helen wanted to live life <u>fully</u>. *adv.*
9. She was a <u>remarkable</u> woman. *adj.*

11.1 | Adjectives and Adverbs

1. Have students cover up grammar chart **11.1.** Write the sentences from the grammar chart on the board in random order. Underline the adverb or adjective. For example, write:

   Helen learned <u>quickly</u>.
   She became <u>blind</u>.
   Helen was a <u>healthy</u> baby.

   Tell students: *Adjectives describe nouns. We can use adjectives before nouns or after the verbs* be, become, look, seem, *and other sense-perception verbs.* Then say: *Adverbs of manner tell how or in what way we do things. They usually follow the verb phrase.* Ask students which words are adjectives and which words are adverbs. Tell them to pay attention to the verbs they follow.

2. Have students look at grammar chart **11.1.** Say: *Now compare your work with the chart.*

3. Quickly go over the examples and explanations in the chart.

EXERCISE 1

1. Have students read the direction line. Say: *The abbreviation for adjective is* adj. *The abbreviation for adverb is* adv. Go over the examples in the book.

2. Have students complete Exercise 1 individually. Check the answers as a class.

3. If necessary, review grammar chart **11.1** on page 335.

11.2 | Adjectives

1. Have students cover up grammar chart **11.2.** Activate prior knowledge. Say: *I'm going to read you some statements about adjectives, and you're going to tell me if they are true or false.* Read these statements:
Adjectives describe verbs. (false)
Adjectives are always singular. (true)
Some words that end in -ed are adjectives, for example, married. (true)
We can never put two adjectives before a noun. (false)

2. Then have students look at grammar chart **11.2.** Say: *Let's look at these examples and see if we were wrong or right.* Go over the examples and explanations.

3. Point out that after an adjective, we can substitute a singular noun with *one* and a plural noun with *ones.*

4. Explain that you can only use an article before an adjective if the adjective is in front of a noun.

EXERCISE 2

1. Have students read the direction line. Ask: *What are we going to write in the blanks?* (an adjective and sometimes an article—*a* or *an*) Go over the examples in the book.

2. Have students complete Exercise 2 individually. Go over the answers as a class.

3. If necessary, review grammar chart **11.2** on page 336.

11.2 | Adjectives

Examples	Explanation
Anne was a **patient** teacher. Helen was an **intelligent** person.	Adjectives describe nouns.
Anne was a **good** friend. I have many **good** friends.	Adjectives are always singular. *Wrong: goods friends*
Helen felt **frustrated** when she couldn't communicate. She was **excited** when she learned her first word. **Handicapped** people are like everybody else.	Some *-ed* words are adjectives: *married, divorced, excited, frustrated, handicapped, worried, finished, tired, crowded.*
Helen was a **normal, healthy** baby. Anne was a **patient, intelligent** teacher.	Sometimes we put two adjectives before a noun. We can separate the two adjectives with a comma.
Some people have an easy childhood. Helen had a hard **one.** Do you like serious stories or funny **ones?**	After an adjective, we can substitute a singular noun with *one* and a plural noun with *ones.*
Anne was **a kind teacher.** Anne was kind.	Only use an article before an adjective if a noun follows. *Wrong: Anne was a kind.*

EXERCISE **2**   Fill in the blanks with an appropriate adjective. (Change *a* to *an* if the adjective begins with a vowel sound.)

EXAMPLES   When Helen couldn't communicate, she became _____ *wild* _____.

Helen was a *n interesting* _____ person.

1. Helen was a _____ *normal* _____ baby.

2. Before Helen learned to communicate, she felt very _____ *frustrated* _____.

3. She had a _____ *full* _____ life.

4. She wanted _____ *fair* _____ treatment for blind people.

5. Helen had a _____ *patient* _____ teacher.

6. Helen was a very _____ *intelligent* _____ woman.

7. The story about Helen Keller was _____ *interesting* _____.

8. _____ *Blind* _____ people can read with the Braille method.

Expansion

Exercise 2 Have students write a few sentences about a remarkable person from their countries. Ask them to use adjectives. Have students compare their writing in pairs. Ask volunteers to share their information with the class.

EXERCISE **3** Fill in the blanks with an appropriate adjective. (Change *a* to *an* if the adjective begins with a vowel sound.)

EXAMPLES   This is a _____*big*_____ class.

This is a _*n interesting*_____ class.

1. This classroom is ____*Answers will vary.*____

2. The classrooms at this school are _____

3. English is a _____ language.

4. This book is very _____

5. We sometimes have _____ tests.

6. We read a _____ story about Helen Keller.

7. Did you learn any _____ words in the story?

EXERCISE **4** ABOUT YOU Ask a question of preference with the words given. Follow the example. Use *one* or *ones* to substitute for the noun. Another student will answer.

EXAMPLES   an easy exercise / hard

A: Do you prefer an easy exercise or a hard one?
B: I prefer a hard one.

funny movies / serious

A: Do you prefer funny movies or serious ones?
B: I prefer funny ones.

1. a big city / small
   Do you prefer a big city or a small one?
2. an old house / new
   Do you prefer an old house or a new one?
3. a cold climate / warm
   Do you prefer a cold climate or a warm one?
4. a small car / big
   Do you prefer a small car or a big one?
5. a soft mattress / hard
   Do you prefer a soft mattress or a hard one?
6. green grapes / red
   Do you prefer green grapes or red ones?
7. red apples / yellow
   Do you prefer red apples or yellow ones?
8. strict teachers / easy
   Do you prefer strict teachers or easy ones?
9. noisy children / quiet
   Do you prefer noisy children or quiet ones?
10. used textbooks / new
    Do you prefer used textbooks or new ones?

Adjectives; Noun Modifiers; Adverbs   **337**

1. Tell students that this exercise is about their class. Have students read the direction line. Ask: *What are we going to write in the blanks?* (an adjective and sometimes an article—*a* or *an*) Go over the examples in the book.
2. Have students complete Exercise 3 individually. Have students compare answers in pairs. Circulate to observe pair work. Give help as needed.
3. If necessary, review grammar chart **11.2** on page 336.

🕐 To save class time, have students do half of the exercise in class and complete the other half for homework. Or assign the entire exercise for homework.

1. Say: *You're going to learn what things your partner prefers.* Have students read the direction line. Go over the examples in the book. Have volunteers model the examples.
2. Have students complete the exercise in pairs. Circulate to observe pair work. Give help as needed.
3. If necessary, review grammar chart **11.2** on page 336.

🕐 To save class time, have students do half of the exercise in class and complete the other half in writing for homework, answering the questions themselves. Or if students do not need speaking practice, the entire exercise may be skipped or done in writing.

Expansion

Exercise 4 Have students write four more questions to ask their partners. Then do a quick survey of the class to find out what students prefer.

11.3 | Noun Modifiers

1. Have students look at grammar chart **11.3**. Say: *We can use a noun to describe another noun.* Point out that when two nouns come together, the second noun is more general. The first noun describes the second noun.

2. Explain that when two nouns come together, the first noun is always singular. Go over the examples in the chart.

EXERCISE 5

1. Have students read the direction line. Ask: *Which goes first: the general noun or the specific noun?* (the specific noun) Go over the example in the book.

2. Have students complete Exercise 5 individually. Point out the picture of the wedding ring. Go over the answers with the class.

3. If necessary, review grammar chart **11.3** on page 338.

11.3 | Noun Modifiers

Examples	Explanation
Helen learned to communicate using **sign** language. She wrote her **life** story.	We can use a noun to describe another noun.
a. Helen had a **college education.** b. Did she go to a **state college?**	When two nouns come together, the second noun is more general than the first. In sentence (a), *college* is a specific kind of education. In sentence (b), *college* is general and *state* is specific.
Helen lost her **eyesight** when she was a baby. When Helen was a ten-year-**old** child, she could finally speak. Helen learned **sign** language.	When two nouns come together, the first is always singular. *Eyesight* is sight of the eyes. A *ten-year-old child* is a child who is ten years old. *Sign language* is language that uses hand signs.

EXERCISE 5 Fill in the blanks by putting the two nouns in the correct order.

EXAMPLE People need a _____winter coat_____ in cold climates.
(coat/winter)

1. You have an important _____phone call_____.
(phone/call)

2. Do you own a _____cell phone_____?
(phone/cell)

3. We use a _____paint brush_____ to paint the walls.
(brush/paint)

4. If you want to drive, you need a _____driver's license_____.
(driver's/license)

5. Do you like to learn about _____U.S. history_____?
(history/U.S.)

6. A married person usually wears a _____wedding ring_____ on his or her left hand.
(wedding/ring)

7. Please put your garbage in the _____garbage can_____.
(can/garbage)

8. The college is closed during _____winter vacation_____.
(vacation/winter)

9. There's a good _____TV program_____ at 7 p.m.
(program/TV)

10. I'm taking a _____math course_____ this semester.
    (course/math)

11. We like to visit the _____art museum_____ on Saturdays.
    (museum/art)

12. Does your father have a _____college education_____ ?
    (college/education)

EXERCISE 6   Fill in the blanks. Make sure that the noun modifier is singular.

EXAMPLE   A store that sells groceries is a _____grocery store_____ .

1. A store that sells books is a _____book store._____

2. A store that has departments is a _____department store._____

3. A department that sells shoes is a _____shoe store._____

4. Language that communicates with signs is _____sign language._____

5. Glasses for eyes are _____eye glasses._____

6. A pot for flowers is a _____flower pot._____

7. A garden of roses is a _____rose garden._____

8. A bill of five dollars is a _____five dollar bill._____

9. A child who is six years old is a _____six-year-old child._____

10. A vacation of two weeks is a _____two week vacation._____

11. A brush for teeth is a _____tooth brush._____

12. A man who is 6 feet tall is a _____6-foot-tall man._____

Adjectives; Noun Modifiers; Adverbs   **339**

1. Have students read the direction line. Say: *Remember, when nouns are combined together, the first noun is singular.* Go over the example in the book.

2. Have students complete Exercise 6 individually. Have students compare answers in pairs. Circulate to observe pair work.

3. If necessary, review grammar chart **11.3** on page 338.

🕐   To save class time, have students do half of the exercise in class and complete the other half for homework. Or assign the entire exercise for homework.

11.4 | Comparing Adverbs of Manner and Adjectives

1. Have students cover up grammar chart **11.4**. Write the following two columns side by side on the board (underline the adjectives and adverbs):

   ADJECTIVES
   Anne was a patient teacher.
   Helen was a quick learner.

   This is a fast car.
   We had a hard test.

   Helen was a good student.

   ADVERBS
   She taught patiently.
   She learned quickly.

   He drives fast.
   I studied hard.

   She did well in school.

   Say: *Study the adjectives and adverbs. What's different about them? What's the same?* Write students' ideas on the board.

2. Have students look at grammar chart **11.4**. Say: *Now compare your work with the chart.* Point out that adverbs of manner tell *how* we do something, while adjectives describe nouns. Go over any errors. Review the example sentences in the chart.

3. Direct students' attention to the bottom section of the chart. Point out the position of the adverb in the example sentences. Explain that an adverb comes before the verb or after the verb phrase. An adverb cannot come between the verb and the object. Point out that you can use *very* before an adverb of manner.

EXERCISE 7

1. Say: *This is a comprehension exercise based on the reading about Helen Keller.* Have students read the direction line. Go over the example in the book.

2. Have students complete Exercise 7 individually. Go over the answers with the class.

3. If necessary, review grammar chart **11.4** on page 340.

11.4 Comparing Adverbs of Manner and Adjectives

An **adverb of manner** tells *how* we do something. It describes the verb (action) of the sentence. An **adjective** describes a noun.

Adjectives	Adverbs	Explanation
Anne was a **patient** teacher. Helen was a **quick** learner. She had a **clear** voice. She had a **full** life.	She taught **patiently**. She learned **quickly**. She spoke **clearly**. She lived life **fully**.	We form most adverbs of manner by putting -ly at the end of an adjective.
This is a **fast** car. I have a **late** class. We had a **hard** test. I have an **early** appointment.	He drives **fast**. I arrived **late**. I studied **hard**. I need to wake up **early**.	Some adjectives and adverbs have the same form.
Helen was a **good** student.	She did **well** in school.	The adverb *well* is completely different from the adjective form *good*.

Adverbs and Word Order	
Helen learned sign language **quickly**. Helen **quickly** learned sign language.	An adverb of manner usually follows the verb phrase. Or it can come before the verb. It cannot come between the verb and the object. *Wrong:* Helen learned *quickly* sign language.
Helen learned **very** quickly. She did **very** well in college.	You can use *very* before an adverb of manner.

EXERCISE 7 Check (✓) if the sentence is true or false.

	True	False
1. Helen lost her hearing slowly.		✓
2. Anne taught Helen patiently.	✓	
3. Helen learned quickly.	✓	
4. Helen never learned to speak clearly.		✓
5. Helen didn't do well in college.		✓
6. Helen wanted deaf people to be treated differently from hearing people.		✓

Expansion

Exercise 7 Have students underline adjectives and circle adverbs in the sentences in Exercise 7.

11.5 | Spelling of -ly Adverbs

Adjective Ending	Examples	Adverb Ending	Adverb
y	easy lucky happy	Change y to i and add -ly.	eas**ily** luck**ily** happ**ily**
consonant + le	simple double comfortable	Drop the -e and add -ly.	simp**ly** doub**ly** comfortab**ly**
e	nice free brave	Just add -ly.	nice**ly** free**ly** brave**ly**

Language Note: There is one exception for the last rule: *true—truly*

EXERCISE 8   Write the adverb form of each adjective. Use correct spelling.

1. bad _____ *badly* _____
2. good _____ *well* _____
3. lazy _____ *lazily* _____
4. true _____ *truly* _____
5. nice _____ *nicely* _____
6. responsible _____ *responsibly* _____
7. polite _____ *politely* _____
8. fast _____ *fast* _____
9. constant _____ *constantly* _____
10. terrible _____ *terribly* _____

EXERCISE 9   Fill in the blanks with the adverb form of the underlined adjective.

EXAMPLE   He's a <u>careful</u> driver. He drives *carefully* _____.

1. She has a <u>beautiful</u> voice. She sings _____ *beautifully* _____.
2. You are a <u>responsible</u> person. You always act _____ *responsibly* _____.
3. You have a <u>neat</u> handwriting. You write _____ *neatly* _____.
4. I'm not a <u>good</u> swimmer. I don't swim _____ *well* _____.
5. He is a <u>cheerful</u> person. He always smiles _____ *cheerfully* _____.
6. He is <u>fluent</u> in French. He speaks French _____ *fluently* _____.
7. You have a <u>polite</u> manner. You always talk to people _____ *politely* _____.
8. Nurses are <u>hard</u> workers. They work _____ *hard* _____.
9. She looks <u>sad</u>. She said goodbye _____ *sadly* _____.
10. You are a <u>patient</u> teacher. You explain the grammar _____ *patiently* _____.
11. My answers are <u>correct</u>. I filled in all the blanks _____ *correctly* _____.

Expansion

Exercise 8 Bring in a ball (such as a soccer ball). Have students sit in a circle or have groups sit in a circle. Say: *The person who has the ball throws the ball to someone else and calls out an adjective or an adverb, such as* nice. *The person who catches it must say the adverb or adjective form, for example,* nicely. *Then that person throws the ball to someone and calls out another adjective or adverb, and so on.* If students find it difficult to think of adjectives or adverbs to call out, write a list of adjectives on the board for reference.

11.5 | Spelling of -ly Adverbs

1. Have students cover up grammar chart **11.5** in their books. Copy the lists of adjectives and adverbs from grammar chart **11.5** on the board. Make sure you separate the three sets of adjectives and adverbs. For example:
   easy easily
   lucky luckily
   happy happily

   simple simply
   double doubly
   comfortable comfortably

   nice nicely
   free freely
   brave bravely

2. Say: *There are three rules for spelling* -ly *adverbs. Can you guess what they are?* If students have difficulty, give them hints.

3. Have students look at grammar chart **11.5**. Say: *Compare our rules with the rules in the book.* Review the rules in the grammar chart. Make sure to point out that the spelling of *truly* is an exception to the last rule.

EXERCISE 8

1. Have students read the direction line. Have a volunteer do #1.
2. Have students complete Exercise 8 individually. Go over the answers with the class.
3. If necessary, review grammar chart **11.5** on page 341.

EXERCISE 9

1. Have students read the direction line. Ask: *What do we write on the blanks?* (the adverb form of the underlined adjective) Go over the example.
2. Have students complete the exercise individually. Then have students compare answers in pairs. Circulate to give help as needed.
3. If necessary, review grammar chart **11.5** on page 341.

⏱ To save class time, have students do half of the exercise in class and complete the other half for homework. Or assign the entire exercise for homework.

EXERCISE 10

1. Have students read the direction line. Say: *Write a sentence that's true for you. Use adverbs of manner to tell how you do these things.* Go over the example in the book. Say: *Don't forget to change pronouns.* Have a volunteer model #1.

2. Have students complete Exercise 10 individually. Then have students compare answers with a partner. Circulate to observe pair work. Give help as needed.

3. If necessary, review grammar chart **11.5** on page 341.

🕐 To save class time, have students do half of the exercise in class and complete the other half in writing for homework. Or if students do not need speaking practice, the entire exercise may be skipped or done in writing.

EXERCISE 11

1. Say: *Now we're going to learn a little more about Helen Keller's teacher.* Have students read the direction line. Go over the examples in the book.

2. Have students complete Exercise 11 individually. Then have students compare answers in pairs. Circulate to observe pair work. Give help as needed.

3. If necessary, review grammar charts: **11.1** on page 335, **11.2** on page 336, **11.3** on page 338, **11.4** on page 340, and **11.5** on page 341.

🕐 To save class time, have students do half of the exercise in class and complete the other half for homework. Or assign the entire exercise for homework.

EXERCISE **10**   Tell how you do these things.

EXAMPLE   write
I write a composition carefully and slowly.

Answers will vary.
1. speak English
2. speak your native language
3. dance
4. walk
5. study
6. do your homework

7. drive
8. sing
9. type
10. work
11. dress for class
12. dress for a party

EXERCISE **11**   Read the story of Helen Keller's teacher, Anne Sullivan. Find the mistakes with adjectives, adverbs, and noun modifiers in the underlined words. Correct them. Not every sentence has a mistake. If the sentence is correct, write C.

When Helen was a <u>small</u> child, she was a <u>blind</u> and <u>deaf</u>. She behaved <u>wild</u>.
       C (example)   C (example)   C (1)   wildly (2)

When she was a seven-<u>years</u>-old child, her parents found a <u>wonderful</u>
                    (3)   C (4)

teacher to work with her. The teacher's name was Anne Sullivan.

Anne was from a <u>poorly</u> immigrant family. She had a <u>terrible</u> life.
                 (5)   C (6)

When she was a <u>child-small</u>, she had a disease that left her almost blind.
               small child (7)

When she was eight <u>years</u> old, her mother died. A few years later, her
                    C (8)

father abandoned the family, and Anne went to live in an orphanage.

When she was fourteen years old, she could not see <u>clear</u> and she could
                                                    clearly (9)

not read. But she got the opportunity to go to a school for the blind. So at

the age of 14, she started <u>school-elementary</u>. She was a <u>student very bright</u>
                            elementary school (10)   very bright student (11)

and graduated from high school as the <u>top</u> student.
                                       C (12)

Expansion

Exercise 10 Have students make questions from the items in Exercise 10. Have students take turns asking and answering questions. Say: *Answer the questions with an adverb. For example:* Do you speak English? Yes. I speak English well. *Or:* How do you speak English? I speak English well.

She heard about a job to teach a blind girl,
$\overset{C}{\underset{(13)}{}}$

Helen Keller. Anne went to live with Helen's

family. Anne worked *patiently* patient with Helen, showing
$\underset{(14)}{}$

her that things had names. Within one month,

Helen learned signs language . After that, Helen
$\underset{(15)}{}$

learned quickly and wanted to study in school.
$\overset{C}{\underset{(16)}{}}$

Anne attended *college classes* ~~classes college~~ with Helen,
$\underset{(17)}{}$

spelling out the lectures and reading to her after

class. Helen graduated from college with honors.

Anne got *married* ~~marry~~ in 1905, when Helen was 23. But it wasn't a happy
$\underset{(18)}{}$ $\overset{C}{\underset{(19)}{}}$

Did You Know?

Aristotle said, "The sign of a great teacher is that the accomplishments of his students exceed his own."

marriage, and Anne separated from her husband. She continued to help

Helen for the rest of her life. But her *eye sight* ~~sight eyes~~ became worse and she
$\underset{(20)}{}$

became completely blind. She died in 1936. Helen lived until 1968.

EXERCISE 12

Use the adjective in parentheses or change it to an adverb to fill in the blanks.

I have two friends who are complete opposites. My friend Paula

complains _____ *constantly* _____ about everything. I always tell her
(example: constant)

that she is a _____ *healthy* _____ person and that is the most important
(1 healthy)

thing in life. But she is never _____ *happy* _____ . She says that
(2 happy)

 CD 2, Track 20

1. Have students read the direction line. Say: *You must decide whether to use an adjective or an adverb.* Go over the example.
2. Have students complete Exercise 12 individually. Point out the picture of the wheelchair on page 344. Then check answers as a class.
3. If necessary, review grammar chart **11.4** on page 340.

To save class time, have students do half of the exercise in class and complete the other half for homework. Or assign the entire exercise for homework.

Exercise 12 Variation

To provide practice with listening skills, have students close their books and listen to the audio. Repeat the audio as needed. Ask comprehension questions, such as: *Are the two friends similar?* (No. They are complete opposites.) *What does Paula constantly do?* (complain about everything) *Is Paula happy?* (no) Then have students open their books and complete Exercise 12.

everyone is _____impolite_____. When she drives, she behaves
            (3 impolite)

_____rudely_____ to other drivers. She says they're all
       (4 rude)

_____crazy_____, but I think Paula is the crazy one. She doesn't
       (5 crazy)

make changes _____easily_____. She had to move two months
             (6 easy)

ago and she hates her _____new_____ apartment. I think it's a
                      (7 new)

_____nice_____ apartment, but she finds something wrong with
       (8 nice)

everything.

I have another friend, Karla. Karla is handicapped, in a wheelchair,

but she has a _____positive_____ attitude about life. She's also an
              (9 positive)

_____active_____ person. She swims _____well_____.
       (10 active)   (11 good)

She's always learning new things. She's studying French and can speak

it _____fluently_____ now. She learns _____quickly_____
   (12 fluent)   (13 quick)

and is _____curious_____ about everything. She goes to museums
       (14 curious)

_____frequently_____ and knows a lot about art. She is a good role
       (15 frequent)

model for her friends.

Expansion

Exercise 12 Have students write about two of their friends. Tell students to use the composition in Exercise 12 as a model. Then have students exchange their writing with a partner.

Before You Read

1. Do you know of any old people who have a healthy, good life?
2. Who is the oldest member of your family? Is he or she in good health?

The Old Oaken Bucket in Winter by Grandma Moses

Read the following article. Pay special attention to *very* and *too*.

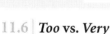

They say you can't teach an old dog new tricks. But is this really true? Anna Mary Moses proved that even elderly people can start a new career or take up a new hobby.

Anna Mary Moses was born in 1860. She had a **very** hard life working as a farmer's wife in New York state. She was always interested in art, but she was **too** busy working on the farm and raising her five children to paint. In her 70s, she became **too** weak to do hard farm work. She liked to do embroidery, but as she became older, she couldn't because of arthritis. It was easier for her to hold a paintbrush than a needle, so she started to paint. She painted pictures of farm life. A New York City art collector saw her paintings in a drugstore window and bought them. Today, some of her paintings are in major art museums.

When she was 92, she wrote her autobiography. At the age of 100, she illustrated a book. She was still painting when she died at age 101. Better known as "Grandma Moses," she created 1,600 pictures.

11.6 | *Too* vs. *Very*

Examples	Explanation
Grandma Moses was **very** old when she wrote her autobiography. Her paintings became **very** popular.	*Very* shows a large degree. It doesn't indicate any problems.
She was **too** busy working on the farm to paint. She became **too** weak to do farm work.	*Too* shows that there is a problem. We often use an infinitive after *too*.

Reading Variation

To practice listening skills, have students first listen to the audio alone. Ask a few comprehension questions. Repeat the audio if necessary. Then have students open their books and read along as they listen to the audio.

Reading Glossary

elderly: old, aged
embroidery: fine needlework

Grandma Moses (1860–1961) (Reading)

1. Have students look at the photo. Ask: *What do you think of this painting?*
2. Have students look at the title of the reading. Ask: *What is the reading about?* Have students use the title and photo to make predictions.
3. Preteach any vocabulary words students may not know, such as *elderly* and *embroidery*. For *embroidery*, direct students to the picture on page 345.

BEFORE YOU READ

1. Have students discuss the questions in pairs.
2. Ask for a few volunteers to share their answers with the class.

To save class time, skip "Before You Read" or have students prepare answers for homework ahead of time.

Reading 🎧 CD 2, Track 21

1. Have students first read the text silently. Tell them to pay special attention to *very* and *too*. Then play the audio and have students read along silently.
2. Check students' comprehension. Ask questions such as: *What does* You can't teach an old dog new tricks *mean?* (It's hard for older people to learn something new.) *What did Grandma Moses do before she became a painter?* (She was a farmer's wife.) *Why didn't she start painting earlier?* (She was too busy.) *What kind of pictures did she paint?* (pictures of farm life) *Are her paintings well known?* (Yes. Some hang in major art museums.)

To save class time, have students do the reading for homework ahead of time.

11.6 | *Too* vs. *Very*

1. Have students read through the first half of the second paragraph of the reading on page 345 again. Ask them to pay special attention to the use of *too* and *very*. Ask: *Which shows that there's a problem:* too *or* very? (*too*)
2. Have students look at grammar chart **11.6**. Read through the examples and explanations. Point out that we often use an infinitive after *too*.

EXERCISE 13

1. Have students read the direction line. Go over the examples.
2. Have students complete Exercise 13 individually. Point out the picture of the turtle. Go over the answers as a class.
3. If necessary, review grammar chart **11.6** on page 345.

11.7 | *Too* and *Enough*

1. Have students cover up grammar chart **11.7** on page 346. Write the following sentences from the grammar chart on the board:
   In her 70s, Grandma Moses was too weak to do farm work.
   When she was younger, she worked too hard to have time for painting.

   She was talented enough to get the attention of an art collector.
   She painted skillfully enough to get her pictures in art museums.

   When she was younger, she didn't have enough time to paint.
2. Say: *Look at the first two sentences. What do you notice about adjectives and adverbs and too?* (*Too* is used before adjectives and adverbs.) To help students, write on the board: *too* + _____
3. Then say: *Look at the next sentences. What do you notice about adjectives and adverbs and enough?* (*Enough* is used after adjectives and adverbs.)
4. Say: *Now what do you notice about the use of* enough *in the last sentence? What does it come before in the sentence?* (*Enough* is used before nouns.)
5. Have students look at grammar chart **11.7.** Go over the examples and explanations.

EXERCISE **13**   Fill in the blanks with *very* or *too*.

EXAMPLES   Basketball players are ___*very*___ tall.

I'm ___*too*___ short to touch the ceiling.

1. In December, it's ___*too*___ cold to go swimming outside.
2. June is usually a ___*very*___ nice month.
3. Some elderly people are in ___*very*___ good health.
4. Some elderly people are ___*too*___ sick to take care of themselves.
5. It's ___*very*___ important to know English.
6. This textbook is ___*too*___ long to finish in three weeks.
7. The president has a ___*very*___ important job.
8. The president is ___*too*___ busy to answer all his letters.
9. Some Americans speak English ___*too*___ fast for me. I can't understand them.
10. I can speak my own language ___*very*___ well.
11. When you buy a used car, you should inspect it ___*very*___ carefully.
12. A turtle moves ___*very*___ slowly.
13. If you drive ___*too*___ slowly on the highway, you might get a ticket.

11.7 | *Too* and *Enough*

	Examples	Explanation
Too + Adjective/Adverb	In her 70s, Grandma Moses was **too weak** to do farm work. When she was younger, she worked **too hard** to have time for painting.	Use *too* **before** adjectives and adverbs. Be careful: Don't use *too much* before adjectives and adverbs. *Wrong:* She worked *too much* hard.
Adjective/Adverb + *Enough*	She was **talented enough** to get the attention of an art collector. She painted **skillfully enough** to get her pictures in art museums.	Use *enough* **after** adjectives and adverbs.
Enough + Noun	When she was younger, she didn't have **enough time** to paint.	Use *enough* **before** nouns.

EXERCISE **14** Fill in the blanks with *too* or *enough* plus the word in parentheses ( ).

EXAMPLES Your son is four years old. He's _____*too young*_____ to go to first grade.
(young)

My sister is 18 years old. She's _____*old enough*_____ to get a driver's
(old)
license.

1. I can't read Shakespeare in English. It's _____*too hard*_____ for me.
(hard)

2. My brother is 21 years old. He's _____*old enough*_____ to get married.
(old)

3. My grandfather is 90 years old and in bad health. My family takes
care of him. He's _____*too sick*_____ to take care of himself.
(sick)

4. I saved $5,000. I want to buy a used car. I think I have _____*enough*
_____*money*_____.
(money)

5. I'd like to get a good job, but I don't have _____*enough experience*_____.
(experience)

6. She wants to move that piano, but she can't do it alone. She's not
_____*strong enough*_____.
(strong)

7. The piano is _____*too heavy*_____ for one person to move.
(heavy)

8. I sit at my desk all day, and I don't get _____*enough exercise*_____.
(exercise)

EXERCISE **15** *Combination Exercise.* Find the mistakes with the underlined
words and correct them. Not all underlined words have a mistake.

We just read a story about Grandma Moses. We learned that you are
never too much old to learn something new. I always thought I was
    (example)
                    C
too old to learn another language, but now that I'm in the U.S. I have no
    (1)
                                                        quickly
choice. Most of the students in class are young and learn very quick.
                                                        (2)
                    C
But I am 58 years old, and I'm not a fast learner at my age. I don't catch
                    (3)

---

1. Have students read the direction line. Go over the examples. Ask: *In the first example, is the boy going to go to first grade?* (No, he's too young.) *In the second example, can she get a driver's license?* (Yes, she's old enough.)
2. Have students complete Exercise 14 individually. Then have students compare work in pairs. Circulate to observe pair work. Give help as needed.
3. If necessary, review grammar chart **11.7** on page 346.

EXERCISE 15

🎧 *CD 2, Track 22*

1. Have students read the direction line. Ask: *Does every underlined word have a mistake?* (no) Go over the example in the book.
2. Have students complete Exercise 15 individually. Then check answers as a class.
3. If necessary, review grammar charts **11.1** on page 335, **11.2** on page 336, **11.3** on page 338, **11.4** on page 340, **11.5** on page 341, **11.6** on page 345, and **11.7** on page 346.

🕐 To save class time, have students do half of the exercise in class and complete the other half for homework. Or assign the entire exercise for homework.

Exercise 15 Variation

To provide practice with listening skills, have students close their books and listen to the audio. Repeat the audio as needed. Ask comprehension questions, such as: *What did this person learn from the story about Grandma Moses?* (that you're never too old to learn something new) *Where is this person now?* (in the U.S.) *Is this person the same age as the other students in the class?* (no) Then have students open their books and complete Exercise 15.

on as quickly as my younger classmates. However, most of them have a

job so they don't have enough time *C* to study. Some of them have small
(4)

children, so they are very busily *busy* and don't always have enough energy *C*
(5)   (6)

to do their homework. I'm not working and my children are enough old *old enough*
(7)

to take care of themselves. In fact, they're in college also. So I have

enough time *C* to do all my homework. My kids are proudly *proud* of me for going
(8)   (9)

to college at my age. My teacher always tells me I'm doing too well *very* in her
(10)

class. After learning English, I'm planning to get a degree in history. I am

too *very* interested in this subject. It was my favorite subject when I was in high
(11)

school. When I finish my degree, I'll be in my 60s. It will probably be

too late *C* for me to find a job in this field, but I don't care. I just have a very
(12)   (13)

great love of this subject. My kids think it will be too much hard for me
(14)

because history books are hardly *hard* to read. But I am too *very* motivated, so I know
(15)   (16)

I can do it. Besides, if Grandma Moses could learn to paint in her 70s and
write a book when she was 92, I can certainly study history at my age.

Grandma Moses is a very well *good* role model. Who says you can't teach an
(17)

old dog news *new* tricks?
(18)

SUMMARY OF LESSON 11

1. Adjectives and Adverbs:

ADJECTIVES	ADVERBS
She has a **beautiful** voice.	She sings **beautifully**.
She is **careful**.	She drives **carefully**.
She has a **late** class.	She arrived **late**.
She is a **good** driver.	She drives **well**.

2. Adjective Modifiers and Noun Modifiers:

ADJECTIVE MODIFIER	NOUN MODIFIER
a clean window	a store window
a new store	a shoe store
warm coats	winter coats
a new license	a driver's license

3. *Very/Too/Enough:*

He's **very** healthy.
He's **too** young to retire. He's only 55.
He's old **enough** to understand life.
He has **enough** money to take a vacation.

EDITING ADVICE

1. Don't make adjectives plural.

   Those are ~~importants~~ ideas.

2. Put the specific noun before the general noun.

   He is a ~~driver~~ truck. *(truck driver)*

3. Some adjectives end in *-ed*. Don't omit the *-ed*.

   I'm finish_ with my project. *(ed)*

4. If the adjective ends in *-ed*, don't forget to include the verb *be*.

   He_ married. *(is)*

5. A noun modifier is always singular.

   She is a letters carrier.

Summary of Lesson 11

1. **Adjectives and Adverbs** Have students cover up the Summary on page 349. On the board, write:
   beautiful
   careful
   late
   good
   Say: *Write eight sentences with these words. Use each word as an adjective and as an adverb.*
   Then have students compare their sentences with the ones in the Summary.
   If necessary, have students review:
   11.1 Adjectives and Adverbs (p. 335).

2. **Adjective Modifiers and Noun Modifiers** Have students cover up the Summary on page 349. Create an exercise on the board. Write:
   clean
   driver's
   new
   winter
   warm
   shoe
   store
   new
   Then write the following in two columns:

   Adjective modifier
   a _____ window
   a _____ store
   a _____ coats
   a _____ license

   Noun modifier
   a _____ window
   a _____ store
   a _____ coats
   a _____ license

   Say: *Fill in the blanks with the appropriate word.* Then have students compare their work with the Summary.
   If necessary, have students review:
   11.2 Adjectives (p. 336)
   11.3 Noun Modifiers (p. 338).

3. *Very/Too/Enough* Have students cover up the Summary on page 349. Create an exercise on the board. Write:
   He's _____ healthy.
   He's _____ young to retire. He's only 55.
   He's old _____ to understand life.
   He has _____ money to take a vacation.

Say: *Complete these sentences with very, too, or enough.*
Then have students compare their work with the Summary.
If necessary, have students review:
11.6 *Too* vs. *Very* (p. 345)
11.7 *Too* and *Enough* (p. 346).

Editing Advice

Have students close their books. Write the example sentences without editing marks or corrections on the board. For example:

1. Those are importants ideas.

2. He is a driver truck.

Ask students to correct each sentence and provide a rule or explanation for each correction. This activity can be done individually, in pairs, or as a class. After students have corrected each sentence, tell them to turn to pages 349–350. Say: *Now compare your work with the Editing Advice in the book.*

6. Put the adjective before the noun.
   very important
   He had a meeting very important.

7. Don't use an article before an adjective if there is no noun.

   Your house is a beautiful.

8. Use *one(s)* after an adjective to substitute for a noun.
   one
   He wanted a big wedding, and she wanted a small.

9. Don't confuse *too* and *very. Too* indicates a problem.
   very
   My father is too healthy.

10. Don't confuse *too much* and *too. Too much* is followed by a noun. *Too* is followed by an adjective or adverb.

    It's too much hot today. Let's stay inside.

11. Put *enough* after the adjective.
    old
    He's enough old to drive.

12. Don't use *very* before a verb. *Very* is used only with adjectives and adverbs.

    He very likes the U.S. very much.

13. Put the adverb at the end of the verb phrase.
    late
    He late came home.
    slowly
    He opened slowly the door.

14. Use an adverb to describe a verb. Use an adjective to describe a noun.
    ly
    He drives careful.

    That man is very nicely.
    well
    You speak English very good.

PART 1 Find the mistakes with the underlined words and correct them. Not every sentence has a mistake. If the sentence is correct, write C.

EXAMPLES She is very <u>carefully</u> about money.

She drives very <u>carefully</u>. C

1. I took my <u>olds</u> shoes to a <u>shoes</u> repair shop.
2. It's <u>too much</u> cold outside. Let's stay inside today.
3. Basketball players are <u>too</u> tall. *very*
4. The <u>very rich</u> woman bought <u>an expensive birthday present</u> for her <u>beautiful daughter</u>. C
5. She is only 16 years old. She's <u>too young</u> to get married. C
6. I found a <u>wonderful job</u>. I'm <u>too</u> happy. *very*
7. My father is only 50 years old. He is <u>too much</u> young to retire.
8. He speaks English very <u>good</u>. *well*
9. You came home late last night. I was very <u>worry</u> about you. *worried*
10. He worked <u>very hard</u> last night. C
11. He counted the money <u>very carefully</u>. C
12. My sister is <u>marry</u>. *married*
13. I prefer a <u>small car</u>. My wife prefers a <u>large</u>. *one*
14. He won a prize. He seems very <u>happily</u>. *happy*
15. I <u>very</u> like my new apartment.
16. Those sisters are very <u>differents</u> from each other.
17. This class is <u>a</u> big.

PART 2 Find the mistakes in word order and correct them. Not every sentence has a mistake. If the sentence is correct, write C.

EXAMPLES He writes very carefully his compositions.

He has enough time to do his homework. C

1. I got my license driver's last year.
2. My brother is only 15 years old. He's not enough old to drive.
3. He early ate breakfast.

Lesson 11 Test/Review

For additional practice, review, and assessment materials, see Assessment CD-ROM with *ExamView Pro*, *More Grammar Practice* Workbook 1, Interactive CD-ROM, and Web site http://elt.thomson.com/gic

PART 1

1. Part 1 may be used in addition to the Assessment CD-ROM with *ExamView Pro* as an in-class test to assess student performance. Have students read the direction line. Ask: *Does every sentence have a mistake?* (no) Go over the examples with the class.
2. Have students complete the assignment individually. Collect for assessment.
3. If necessary, have students review: **Lesson 11.**

PART 2

1. Part 2 may also be used as an in-class test to assess student performance, in addition to the Assessment CD-ROM with *ExamView Pro*. Have students read the direction line. Go over the examples with the class.
2. Have students complete the exercise individually. Collect for assessment.
3. If necessary, have students review:
   11.1 Adjectives and Adverbs (p. 335).

Lesson Review

To use Parts 1 and 2 as a review, assign them as homework or use them as in-class activities to be completed individually or in pairs. Check answers and review errors as a class. Reteach grammar points that students haven't mastered. Then student learning may be assessed using a test generated from the Assessment CD-ROM with *ExamView Pro*.

1. Part 3 may also be used as an in-class test to assess student performance, in addition to the Assessment CD-ROM with *ExamView Pro*. Have students read the direction line. Go over the example with the class.

2. Have students complete the exercise individually. Collect for assessment.

3. If necessary, have students review:

    11.4 Comparing Adverbs of Manner and Adjectives (p. 340).

---

4. She opened (slowly) the door.

5. She speaks English very fluently. *C*

6. They are too young to retire. *C*

7. He bought a car (very expensive).

PART **3**   Fill in the blanks with the correct form, adjective or adverb, of the word in parentheses ( ).

EXAMPLE   Sue is a ___*patient*___ person. Don does everything ___*impatiently*___.
                    (patient)   (impatient)

1. Sue has ___*neat*___ handwriting. Don writes ___*sloppily*___. I can't
               (neat)   (sloppy)
   even read what he wrote.

2. She likes to drive ___*carefully*___. He likes to drive ___*fast*___.
                       (careful)   (fast)

3. She speaks English ___*fluently*___. He has a ___*hard*___ time with
                        (fluent)   (hard)
   English.

4. She learns languages ___*easily*___. Learning a new
                          (easy)
   language is ___*difficult*___ for Don.
                   (difficult)

5. She types ___*accurately*___. He makes a lot of mistakes.
                (accurate)
   He needs someone to check his work ___*carefully*___.
                                       (careful)

6. She has a very ___*soft*___ voice. He speaks ___*loudly*___.
                   (soft)   (loud)

7. She sings ___*beautifully*___. He sings like a ___*sick*___ chicken.
               (beautiful)   (sick)

8. She is always very ___*responsible*___. He sometimes
                        (responsible)
   behaves ___*childishly*___.
                (childish)

9. She saves her money ___*carefully*___. He buys things
                      (careful)
   he doesn't need. He spends his money ___*foolishly*___.
                                 (foolish)

10. She exercises ___*regularly*___. He's very ___*lazy*___
                  (regular)   (lazy)
   about exercising.

352   Lesson **11**

Lesson Review

To use Part 3 as a review, assign it as homework or use it as an in-class activity to be completed individually or in pairs. Check answers and review errors as a class. Reteach grammar points that students haven't mastered. Then student learning may be assessed using a test generated from the Assessment CD-ROM with *ExamView Pro*.

---

1. Circle the words that best describe your actions. Find a partner and compare your personality to your partner's personality. How many characteristics do you have in common?

a. I usually spend my money	carefully	foolishly
b. I do my homework	willingly	unwillingly
c. I write compositions	carefully	carelessly
d. I usually walk	slowly	quickly
e. I write	neatly	sloppily
f. I like to drive	fast	slowly
g. I write my language	well	poorly
h. Before a test, I study	hard	a little
i. I exercise	regularly	infrequently
j. I play tennis	well	poorly
k. I like to live	dangerously	carefully
l. I make important decisions	quickly	slowly and methodically
m. I learn languages	easily	with difficulty
n. I learn math	easily	with difficulty
o. I make judgments	logically	intuitively

2. Game: "In the manner of"

Teacher: Write these adverbs on separate pieces of paper or on index cards: gladly, suddenly, slowly, comfortably, simply, steadily, foolishly, efficiently, accurately, quietly, surprisingly, excitedly, promptly, fearlessly, fearfully, indecisively, carefully, carelessly, neatly, smoothly, repeatedly. Make sure the students know the meaning of each of these adverbs. Ask one student to leave the room. The other students pick one adverb. When the student returns to the room, he/she asks individuals to do something by giving imperatives. The others do this task in the manner of the adverb that was chosen. The student tries to guess the adverb.

EXAMPLE   Edgar, write your name on the blackboard.
Sofia, take off one shoe.
Maria, open the door.
Nora, give me your book.

3. Name something.

EXAMPLE   Name some things you do well.
I speak my native language well.
I swim well.

a. Name some things you do well.
b. Name some things you don't do well.

Adjectives; Noun Modifiers; Adverbs   **353**

Expansion Activities

These expansion activities provide opportunities for students to interact with one another and further develop their speaking and writing skills. Encourage students to use grammar from this lesson whenever possible.

🕐 To save class time, assign parts of the activities as homework. Then use class time for interaction and communication. If students do not need additional speaking practice, some of the activities may be assigned as writing activities for homework, or skipped altogether.

CLASSROOM ACTIVITIES

1. Have students work individually to complete the personality survey. Check that students know the meaning of all the adverbs. Then put students in pairs to compare. If possible, have students from different countries work together.

2. For an easier version of the game, have all of the students behave according to only one adverb. The student who leaves the room only has to find one adverb that describes the way his or her classmates are behaving.

3. Have students work in pairs. Partners take turns naming things. One partner says: *Name some things you do well.* The other partner names three to five things he or she does well. Have volunteers tell the class what their partners can do.

Expansion

Classroom Activities For activity 1, do a quick survey of the class. Write the results for each item on the board. How do the students rate the "personality" of the class?

TALK ABOUT IT

Have students discuss each point in pairs, in groups, or as a class.

WRITE ABOUT IT

1. If students have difficulty thinking of anyone to write about, brainstorm famous people who have accomplished things in spite of a disability or age.
2. Say: *You can write about anyone whom you admire—the person can be famous or just someone you know.*

OUTSIDE ACTIVITY

Ask students to watch the movie at home and then be prepared to talk about the movie in class.

INTERNET ACTIVITIES

1. Survey the class to see how many students know who the people on the list are and what they're famous for.
   Erik Weihenmayer—the first blind climber to scale Mount Everest
   Sherman Bull—the oldest (64) climber to scale Mount Everest
   Enrique Oliu—a blind baseball radio commentator
   Lance Armstrong—the American cyclist who won the Tour de France six times and is also a cancer survivor
2. Ask students if anyone knows the American Sign Language alphabet. Ask students to research it on the Internet and to be prepared to spell their names for the class.
3. Ask students to look for some of Grandma Moses's paintings on the Internet. Have volunteers describe their favorite paintings.

Talk
About it

c. Name some things you do quickly.
d. Name some things you do slowly.
e. Name something you learned to do easily.

1. In a small group or with the entire class, discuss the situation of older people in your native culture. Who takes care of them when they are too old or too sick to take care of themselves? How does your family take care of its older members?

2. In a small group or with the entire class, discuss the situation of handicapped people in the U.S. or in another country. Are there special schools? Are there special facilities, such as parking, public washrooms, elevators?

3. Discuss the meaning of this quote by Grandma Moses:

"What a strange thing is memory, and hope. One looks backward, the other forward; one is of today, the other of tomorrow. Memory is history recorded in our brain. Memory is a painter. It paints pictures of the past and of the day."

Write
About it

1. Write about a famous person you know about who accomplished something in spite of a handicap or age.

2. Write about a man or woman whom you admire very much. You may write about a famous person or any person you know (family member, teacher, doctor, etc).

Outside
Activity

Rent the movie *The Miracle Worker*. It's the story of Helen Keller and Anne Sullivan.

Internet
Activities

1. Use the Internet to find information about the following people. Who are they and what extraordinary things did they do?

- Erik Weihenmayer
- Sherman Bull
- Enrique Oliu
- Lance Armstrong

2. Use the Internet to find the American Sign Language finger alphabet. Try to make the letters with your hand.

3. Use the Internet to find some paintings by Grandma Moses.

 Additional Activities at http://elt.thomson.com/gic

354   Lesson 11

Expansion

Talk About it Have students make presentations about food, eating habits, and shopping customs in their countries. Encourage students to make posters, create skits, or even prepare food.

Write About it Variation

Have students exchange first drafts with a partner. Ask students to help their partners edit their drafts. Refer students to the Editing Advice on pages 349–350.

Internet Activities Variation

Remind students that if they don't have Internet access, they can use Internet facilities at a public library or they can use traditional research methods to find out information including looking at encyclopedias, magazines, books, journals, and newspapers.

LESSON

12

GRAMMAR
Comparatives
Superlatives

CONTEXT: U.S. Geography
U.S. Geography
A Tale of Two Cities

The Sears Tower, Chicago

The Empire State Building, New York

The Space Needle, Seattle

355

Lesson | 12

Lesson Overview

GRAMMAR

1. Ask: *What did we study in Lesson 11?* (adjectives, adverbs, and noun modifiers)
2. Ask: *What are we going to study in this lesson?* (comparatives and superlatives) *What are some examples of comparatives and superlatives?* Have students give examples. Write them on the board.

CONTEXT

1. Activate students' prior knowledge. Ask: *Does anyone know a lot about U.S. geography? How many states can you name? What are some famous cities?*
2. Have students share their knowledge and personal experiences. Ask students to talk about places they've visited around the world.

Photos

1. Direct students' attention to the photos. Ask: *Has anyone been to these cities? Do you recognize these buildings? Has anyone been to these buildings?*
2. *What famous places or buildings are in your country? Why are they famous?*

🕑 To save class time, have students do the Test/Review at the end of the lesson, or administer a lesson test generated from the Assessment CD-ROM with *ExamView® Pro*. Skip sections of the lesson that students have already mastered. You may also assign some sections for self-study for extra credit.

Expansion

Theme The topic for this lesson can be enhanced with the following ideas:

1. Pictures, postcards, and books about different states
2. A large colorful map of the U.S.
3. A yearbook with class superlatives (funniest student, best-looking student, etc.)

Culture Notes

The Sears Tower Built in 1973, it was the tallest building in the world until 1998. It is 1,450 feet tall, covers two city blocks, and has more than 4 million square feet of office and commercial space. It is still one of the tallest buildings in the world.

The Empire State Building Construction on the Empire State Building began in 1930. The building took only one year and 45 days to build. It is 1,250 feet tall and is currently the tallest building in New York City.

The Space Needle The Space Needle was built in 1962. It is 605 feet tall and has a revolving restaurant at the top. Every year, more than one million people visit the Space Needle. It is the biggest tourist attraction in the Northwest.

U.S. Geography (Reading)

1. Have students look at the map. Ask: *Where have you been in the U.S.? What parts of the U.S. would you like to visit?*
2. Have students look at the title of the reading. Ask: *What is the reading about?* Have students use title and map to make predictions about the reading.
3. Preteach any vocabulary words your students may not know, such as *population* and *minority*.

BEFORE YOU READ

1. Have students discuss the questions in pairs.
2. Ask for a few volunteers to share their answers with the class.

🕐 To save class time, skip "Before You Read" or have students prepare answers for homework ahead of time.

Reading 🎧 *CD 2, Track 23*

1. Have students first read the text silently. Tell them to pay special attention to comparatives and superlatives. Then play the audio and have students read along silently.
2. Check students' comprehension. Ask questions such as: *Which city has the most people?* (New York) *Are there more Hispanics in the U.S. than African Americans?* (yes—since 2003) *Is Alaska bigger than California?* (yes)

🕐 To save class time, have students do the reading for homework ahead of time.

DID YOU KNOW?

California's state motto is *Eureka,* which is a Greek word meaning *I have found it.* It is believed that the motto refers to the discovery of gold during the California Gold Rush.

U.S. GEOGRAPHY

 Before You **Read**

1. What is the tallest building in this city?
2. In your opinion, what is the most interesting city? Why is it interesting?
3. What cities or regions have the best climate?

The United States of America

 Read the following information. Pay special attention to comparative and superlative forms.

1. In area, the United States is the third **largest** country in the world (after Russia and Canada). In population, the U.S. is the third **largest** country in the world (after China and India).
2. The **biggest** city in the U.S. in population is New York. It has about 8 million people.
3. The **tallest** building in the U.S. is the Sears Tower in Chicago (442 meters or 1,450 feet tall). But it is not the **tallest** building in the world. That building is in Kuala Lumpur (452 meters or 1,483 feet tall).
4. New York City has the **highest** cost of living. But the cost of living in Tokyo is much **higher** than in New York.
5. Hispanics are the **fastest** growing minority in the U.S. In 2003, Hispanics passed African Americans as the **largest** minority.
6. Rhode Island is the **smallest** state in area (1,145 square miles or 2,700 square kilometers).
7. Alaska is the **largest** state in area. Alaska is even **larger** than Colombia, South America.

Did You Know?
Before 1849, the population of California was very small. In 1849, gold was found in California and about 100,000 people rushed there to try to get rich.

356 Lesson **12**

Expansion

Reading Quiz students on their knowledge of some of the regions in the U.S. Ask: *Do you know which states form New England?* (CT, RI, MA, VT, NH, and ME) *Which states are considered the Northeast?* (New England plus NY, NJ, and PA) *Which states are considered the South?* (FL, GE, SC, NC, MD, WV, VA, KY, TN, AK, LA, MS, AL, OK, and TX) *The Midwest and the Great Plains?* (OH, MI, IN, WI, IL, MN, IA, MO, ND, SD, NE, and KS) *The Rocky Mountain States?* (MT, ID, WY, NV, UT, CO, AZ, and NM) *The Southwest?* (CO, NM, UT, AZ, NV, and CA) *The Pacific States* (CA, OR, and WA)

Reading Variation

To practice listening skills, have students first listen to the audio alone. Ask a few comprehension questions. Repeat the audio if necessary. Then have students open their books and read along as they listen to the audio.

Reading Glossary

minority: people of a different race, ethnic background, or religion from those of the majority of people in a nation
population: all of the people living in a specific area

Niagara Falls

8. The **least populated** state is Wyoming. It has **less** than half a million people.
9. California is the **most populated** state. It has about 34 million people. There are **more** people in California than in Peru.
10. Juneau, Alaska gets the **most** snow, about 101 inches per year.
11. Phoenix, Arizona, gets the **most** sunshine. Eight-five percent of the days are sunny.
12. Mount McKinley is the **highest** mountain in the U.S. (20,320 feet or 6,193 meters). It is in Alaska.
13. There are five great lakes in the U.S. The **biggest** is Lake Superior. The others are Lake Huron, Lake Michigan, Lake Erie, and Lake Ontario.
14. The **tallest** waterfall in the U.S. is in California. But Niagara Falls in New York and Ontario, Canada, is **more famous**. It is one of the **most popular** tourist attractions. Twelve million tourists a year visit Niagara Falls. It has the **greatest** volume of water.
15. The state that is the **farthest** north is Alaska. The state that is the **farthest** south is Hawaii.
16. The **most recent** state to join the U.S. is Hawaii. It joined in 1959.
17. The **oldest** state is Delaware. It became a state in 1787.

12.1 | Comparatives and Superlatives—An Overview

Examples	Explanation
New York City is the **biggest** city in the U.S. California is the **most populated** state in the U.S.	We use the superlative form to point out the number–one item in a group of three or more.
Los Angeles is **bigger** than Chicago. There are **more** people in California than in Peru.	We use the comparative form to compare two items.

EXERCISE **1** Circle the correct word to complete the statement.

EXAMPLE Chicago is *bigger* / *smaller* than Los Angeles.

1. The tallest building in the world *is* / *isn't* in the U.S.
2. The most populated state is *Alaska* / *California*.
3. The U.S. *is* / *isn't* the largest country in the world in area.
4. *Alaska* / *California* has the largest area.
5. The fastest growing minority is *Hispanics* / *African Americans*.

12.1 | Comparatives and Superlatives—An Overview

1. Have students cover up grammar chart **12.1.** Say: *We use the superlative to point out the number-one item in a group of three or more. We use the comparative to compare two items.* Then have students go back to the reading on pages 356 and 357. Say: *Underline five superlatives and five comparatives.* Ask volunteers to name the adjectives they underlined and circled, and ask them to explain how they identified them as comparative or superlative (e.g., *Third largest country in the world—there are more than three countries in the world.*).
2. Have students look at grammar chart **12.1.** Say: *Now compare your work with the chart.*
3. Quickly go over the examples and explanations in the chart.

EXERCISE 1

1. Have students read the direction line. Say: *These facts are based on the reading.* Go over the example in the book.
2. Have students complete Exercise 1 individually. Check the answers as a class.
3. If necessary, review grammar chart **12.1** on page 357.

12.2 | Comparative and Superlative Forms of Adjectives and Adverbs

1. Have students cover up grammar chart **12.2**. Write the following adjectives on the board:
   tall, fast
   easy, happy
   frequent, active
   important, difficult
   Ask: *What do you notice about each group of adjectives?* If students have difficulty, give them a hint: *Look at the syllables.*

2. Then have students look at grammar chart **12.2**. Say: *Let's look at how we form the comparative and superlative forms. For short adjectives, we usually add -er for the comparative form. For the superlative we add -est. For longer adjectives, we add* more *before the adjective to form the comparative and* the most *before the adjective to form the superlative.* Go over the examples and explanations for each kind of adjective. Explain that some two-syllable adjectives have two forms.

3. Point out that *-ly* adverbs use *more* and *most*. The last category of adjectives and adverbs is irregular; their forms must be memorized. Explain that except for *good/well* and *bad/badly*, the adjective and adverb are the same.

4. Direct students' attention to the Language Notes. Point out the exceptions. Say: *Even though* bored *and* tired *are short adjectives, we form the comparative by adding* more *and the superlative, by adding* the most. Point out the other two-syllable adjectives that have two forms.

12.2 | Comparative and Superlative Forms of Adjectives and Adverbs

	Simple	Comparative	Superlative
One-syllable adjectives and adverbs*	tall	taller	the tallest
	fast	faster	the fastest
Two-syllable adjectives that end in -y	easy	easier	the easiest
	happy	happier	the happiest
Other two-syllable adjectives	frequent	more frequent	the most frequent
	active	more active	the most active
Some two-syllable adjectives have two forms.**	simple	simpler	the simplest
		more simple	the most simple
	common	commoner	the commonest
		more common	the most common
Adjectives with three or more syllables	important	more important	the most important
	difficult	more difficult	the most difficult
-ly adverbs	quickly	more quickly	the most quickly
	brightly	more brightly	the most brightly
Irregular adjectives and adverbs	good/well	better	the best
	bad/badly	worse	the worst
	far	farther	the farthest
	little	less	the least
	a lot	more	the most

Language Notes:
1. *Exceptions to one-syllable adjectives:

bored	more bored	the most bored
tired	more tired	the most tired

2. **Other two-syllable adjectives that have two forms:
   handsome, quiet, gentle, narrow, cleaver, friendly, angry, polite, stupid

Spelling Rules for Short Adjectives and Adverbs			
Rule	Simple	Comparative	Superlative
Add -er and -est to short adjectives and adverbs.	tall fast	taller faster	tallest fastest
For adjectives that end in e, add -r and -st.	nice late	nicer later	nicest latest
For adjectives that end in y, change y to i and add -er and -est.	easy happy	easier happier	easiest happiest
For words ending in consonant-vowel-consonant, double the final consonant, then add -er and -est. Exception: Do not double final w. new—newer—newest	big sad	bigger sadder	biggest saddest

EXERCISE 2   Give the comparative and superlative forms of the word.

EXAMPLES   fat   _fatter_   _the fattest_

important   _more important_   _the most important_

1. interesting   _more interesting_   _the most interesting_
2. young   _younger_   _the youngest_
3. beautiful   _more beautiful_   _the most beautiful_
4. good   _better_   _best_
5. common   _commoner/more common_   _the commonest/ the most common_
6. thin   _thinner_   _the thinnest_
7. carefully   _more carefully_   _the most carefully_
8. pretty   _prettier_   _the prettiest_
9. bad   _worse_   _the worst_
10. famous   _more famous_   _the most famous_
11. lucky   _luckier_   _the luckiest_
12. simple   _simpler/more simple_   _the simplest/ the most simple_
13. high   _higher_   _the highest_
14. delicious   _more delicious_   _the most delicious_
15. far   _farther_   _the farthest_
16. foolishly   _more foolishly_   _the most foolishly_

12.2 | Comparative and Superlative Forms of Adjectives and Adverbs (*cont.*)

5. Direct students' attention to the rules for spelling short adjectives and adverbs. Have students cover up the rule side of the chart. Say: *Study these adjectives and adverbs and their superlative and comparative forms. Can you guess the rules?*

6. Have volunteers write the rules on the board. Then have students look at the grammar chart on page 359. Say: *Now compare your work with the chart.* Go over the examples and rules.

EXERCISE 2

1. Have students read the direction line. Ask: *What are we going to write in the blanks?* (the comparative and superlative forms of the adjectives) Go over the examples in the book.

2. Have students complete Exercise 2 individually. Go over the answers as a class.

3. If necessary, review grammar chart **12.2** on page 358.

Expansion

Exercise 2 Have a spelling bee. Make a list of 40 or so adjectives and adverbs. Divide the class into Team A and Team B. Give one team member from Team A an adjective or adverb and tell him or her to spell the comparative or superlative form on the board. Do the same with Team B. Then give Team B an adjective or adverb and ask one member to spell the comparative or superlative form, and so on. Make sure team members take turns.

12.3 | Superlative Adjectives

1. Have students look at grammar chart **12.3**. Say: *When you use the superlative, use the before it. It's wrong to say:* New York is biggest city in the U.S. Also, point out that a prepositional phrase is usually at the end of a superlative sentence. Go over the examples. Have students circle the prepositional phrases in each sentence in the grammar chart.

2. Explain that we often use *one of* before a superlative. Say: One of the most popular tourist attractions *means that there are others that are just or almost as popular.* Go over the examples.

EXERCISE 3

1. Have students read the direction line. Ask: *What are we going to write in the blanks?* (the superlative of the adjective and *the*) Go over the example in the book.

2. Have students complete Exercise 3 individually. Have students compare answers in pairs. Circulate to observe pair work. Give help as needed.

3. If necessary, review grammar chart **12.3** on page 360.

12.3 | Superlative Adjectives

Examples	Explanation
New York is **the biggest** city in the U.S. California is **the most populated** state in the U.S. China has **the largest** population in the world.	We use the superlative form to point out the number-one item of a group of three or more. Use *the* before a superlative form. We often put a prepositional phrase at the end of a superlative sentence: in the world in my family in my class in my country
Niagara Falls is **one of the most popular** tourist attractions in the U.S. The Sears Tower is **one of the tallest** buildings in the world.	We often put "one of the" before a superlative form. Then we use a plural noun.

EXERCISE 3 Fill in the blanks with the superlative form of the word in parentheses ( ). Include *the* before the superlative form.

EXAMPLE   Alaska is _____the largest_____ state in area.
                                    (large)

1. _____The biggest_____ lake in the U.S. is Lake Superior.
            (big)

2. _____The longest_____ river in the U.S. is the Missouri.
            (long)

3. _____The highest_____ mountain in the U.S. is Mount McKinley.
            (high)

4. Johnson is one of _____the commonest/ the most common_____ last names in the U.S.
                                    (common)

5. Niagara Falls is one of _____the most popular_____ tourist attractions.
                                    (popular)

6. San Francisco is one of _____the most expensive_____ cities in the U.S.
                                    (expensive)

7. San Francisco is one of _____the most beautiful_____ American cities.
                                    (beautiful)

8. Harvard is one of _____the best_____ universities in the U.S.
                        (good)

9. The Sears Tower is _____the tallest_____ building in the U.S.
                            (tall)

10. Crime is one of _____the worst_____ problems in the U.S.
                        (bad)

11. Boston is one of _____the oldest_____ cities in the U.S.
                        (old)

Expansion

Exercise 3 Have students write facts about their countries (*e.g., La Paz, Bolivia is the highest capital city in the world. The Andes is the longest mountain range in the world.*). If possible, have students from the same country work in pairs or groups.

EXERCISE 4   ABOUT YOU   Talk about the number-one person in your family for each of these adjectives.

EXAMPLES   interesting
My aunt Rosa is the most interesting person in my family.

tall
The tallest person in my family is my brother Carlos.

Answers will vary.

1. intelligent
2. kind
3. handsome/beautiful
4. stubborn
5. lazy
6. tall

7. serious
8. nervous
9. strong
10. funny
11. responsible
12. neat

EXERCISE 5   Write a superlative sentence, giving your opinion about each of the following items. (You may use "one of the . . ." plus a plural noun.)

EXAMPLE   big problem today
The biggest problem in the U.S. today is crime.

OR

One of the biggest problems in my country today is the economy.

1. exciting sport

Answers will vary.

2. bad war

3. bad tragedy in the world or in the U.S.

4. important invention of the last 100 years

5. interesting city in the world

6. big problem in the U.S. today

7. bad job

Comparatives; Superlatives   **361**

EXERCISE 4

1. Say: *You're going to write about your family now.* Have students read the direction line. Go over the examples in the book. Have volunteers model the examples.
2. Have students complete the exercise individually. Point out the picture of a strong person. Then have students compare work in pairs.
3. If necessary, review grammar charts **12.2** on pages 358–359 and **12.3** on page 360.

To save class time, have students do half of the exercise in class and complete the other half in writing for homework. Or if students do not need speaking practice, the entire exercise may be skipped or done in writing.

EXERCISE 5

1. Have students read the direction line. Say: *When you use* one of the . . . *don't forget to use a plural noun.* Go over the examples in the book. Have volunteers model the examples.
2. Have students complete Exercise 5 individually. Then have students compare answers in pairs or groups.
3. If necessary, review grammar charts **12.2** on pages 358–359 and **12.3** on page 360.

To save class time, have students do half of the exercise in class and complete the other half for homework. Or assign the entire exercise for homework.

Expansion

Exercise 5   Do a survey of the class and have a discussion about the items in Exercise 5.

12.4 | Word Order with Superlatives

1. Direct students' attention to chart **12.4.** Tell students to look at the first example. Ask: *Where does the superlative adjective belong?* (before the noun)

2. Have students look at the second example. Ask: *What verb is connecting the subject noun to the superlative + noun?* (be) *How many ways can we write this sentence?* (two) Write a scrambled sentence on the board: *the tallest mountain/in the world Mount Everest is* Ask students to unscramble the sentence in two ways.

3. Have students look at the next example. Ask: *Where are the superlative adverbs in these two sentences?* (after the verb)

4. Have students look at the fourth row. Ask: *Is the most in these sentences an adjective or an adverb?* (an adverb) *Where are the adverbs in these two examples?* (after the verb) Say: The most, the least, the best, *and* the worst *come after a verb.* Then have students look at the last row. Ask: *Are the* most *and the* least *adjectives or adverbs in these sentences?* (adjectives) *Where are they located in the sentence?* (before the noun)

5. Review all the examples and explanations with the class.

EXERCISE 6

1. Have students read the direction line. Say: *In this exercise, we are putting the superlative after the verb. Are the superlatives in these sentences adjectives or adverbs?* (adverbs) Be sure students understand they are to make statements about the members of their family. Go over the examples in the book. Have students model them.

2. Have students complete Exercise 6 individually. Have students compare answers in pairs. Circulate to observe pair work.

3. If necessary, review grammar chart **12.4** on page 362.

---

8. good job

_____

9. hard teacher at this school

_____

10. popular movie star

_____

12.4 | Word Order with Superlatives

Examples	Explanation
What is **the biggest** lake? California is **the most populated** state.	A superlative adjective comes **before** a noun.
The Sears Tower is **the tallest building** in the U.S. OR **The tallest building** in the U.S. is the Sears Tower.	When the verb *be* connects a noun to a superlative adjective + noun, there are two possible word orders.
The Hispanic population **is growing** *the most* **quickly** in the U.S. The population of India **is increasing** *the most* **rapidly** in the world.	We put superlative adverbs **after** the verb (phrase).
It **rains** *the most* in Hawaii. It **snows** *the most* in Alaska.	We put *the most, the least, the best, the worst* **after** a verb.
Phoenix gets *the most* sunshine. Alaska has *the least* sunshine in the winter.	We put *the most, the least, the best, the worst* **before** a noun.

EXERCISE 6 Name the person in your family who is the superlative in each of the following activities. (Put the superlative form after the verb phrase.)

EXAMPLES cook well
My mother cooks the best in the family.

eat a lot
My brother eats the most in my family.

Answers will vary.
1. talk a lot
2. drive well
3. walk fast
4. speak English well
5. stay up late
6. get up early
7. speak softly
8. eat a lot

EXERCISE **7** ABOUT YOU Name the person in your family who is the superlative in each of the following activities. (Put the superlative form before the noun.)

EXAMPLE watch a lot of TV
My brother watches the most TV. He watches TV four hours a day.

Answers will vary.
1. spend a lot of money
2. get a lot of mail
3. drink a lot of coffee
4. spend a lot of time in the bathroom
5. spend a lot of time on the telephone
6. have a bad temper
7. use a lot of makeup

A TALE OF TWO CITIES[1]

Before You Read
1. Compare this city to another city.
2. Do you have any friends or relatives in American cities? Do you visit them?

San Francisco

Chicago

[1]These statistics are from 2001.

Comparatives; Superlatives   **363**

Reading Variation

To practice listening skills, have students first listen to the audio alone. Ask a few comprehension questions. Repeat the audio if necessary. Then have students open their books and read along as they listen to the audio.

EXERCISE 7

1. Have students read the direction line. Say: *In this exercise, we are putting the superlative before the noun. Are the superlatives in these sentences adjectives or adverbs?* (adjectives) Go over the example in the book. Say: *Whenever possible, give additional information.* Have a volunteer model the example.
2. Have students complete Exercise 7 individually. Then have students compare answers in pairs. Circulate to observe pair work. Give help as needed.
3. If necessary, review grammar chart **12.4** on page 362.

To save class time, have students do half of the exercise in class and complete the other half in writing for homework. Or if students do not need speaking practice, the entire exercise may be skipped or done in writing.

A Tale of Two Cities (Reading)

1. Have students look at the photos. Ask: *If the names of the cities weren't on these photos, would you know which cities they are? How? Has anyone been to one or both of these cities? Do you think they're very different from each other? Which one do you like the most?*
2. Have students look at the title of the reading. Ask: *What is the reading about?* Have students use the title and photos to make predictions about the reading. Ask: *Which city do you think has more people? Which city do you think is more expensive to live in? Which do you think is more polluted? More dangerous?*
3. Preteach any vocabulary words your students may not know, such as *ozone* and *climate*.

BEFORE YOU READ

1. Have students discuss the questions in pairs.
2. Ask for a few volunteers to share their answers with the class.

To save class time, skip "Before You Read" or have students prepare answers for homework ahead of time.

Lesson **12**   **363**

Reading CD 2, Track 24

1. Have students first read the chart and the text silently. Tell them to pay special attention to comparative forms. Then play the audio and have students read along silently.

2. Check students' comprehension. Ask questions such as: *Which city has more people?* (Chicago) *Which city is more expensive?* (San Francisco) *Which city is more polluted?* (Chicago) *Which city is more dangerous?* (Chicago)

🕐 To save class time, have students do the reading for homework ahead of time.

Look at the following chart. Then read the sentences that follow. Pay special attention to comparative forms.

	San Francisco	Chicago
Population	777,000	2,900,000
Cost of home*	$604,000	$260,000
Unemployment	2.5%	4%
Cost of living (100 = national average)	208	96
Average family income	$40,561	$30,707
High school graduates	78% of population	66% of population
Average temperature in July	59 degrees	75 degrees
Average temperature in January	51 degrees	22 degrees
Rainfall (inches annually)	20	37
Number of clear days (no clouds) per year	162	94
Air pollution (amount of ozone in air; US average = 100)	42	79
Crime (per 100,000 people)	7,595	9,454

*Cost of home is based on 2,000 square feet in 2001.

- Chicago has a **larger** population **than** San Francisco.
- A house in San Francisco is **more expensive than** a house in Chicago.
- Unemployment in Chicago is **higher than** in San Francisco.
- The average family income is **more** in San Francisco **than** in Chicago, but San Francisco has a **higher** cost of living.
- San Francisco has **more** high school graduates **than** Chicago.
- San Francisco has a **better** climate **than** Chicago. Chicago gets **more** rain **than** San Francisco. San Francisco is **sunnier than** Chicago.
- Chicago is **warmer** in the summer.
- Chicago is **colder** in the winter.
- Chicago has **more** air pollution **than** San Francisco.
- Chicago has **more** crime.

364 Lesson **12**

Reading Glossary

climate: the type of weather that a place or region has

ozone: a poisonous gas found in parts of the earth's upper atmosphere, which is a form of oxygen

12.5 | Comparisons

Examples	Explanation
Chicago has a **larger** population **than** San Francisco. San Francisco is **more expensive than** Chicago.	We use the comparative form to compare two items. We use *than* before the second item of comparison.
Chicago is **colder than** San Francisco in the winter, but it is **warmer** in the summer.	Omit *than* if the second item of comparison is not included.
The cost of living in San Francisco is **much higher than** in Chicago. Unemployment is **a little higher** in Chicago.	*Much* or *a little* can come before a comparative form.
Formal: You know more about American cities than **I do.** Informal: You know more about American cities than **me.** Formal: I can speak English better than **he can.** Informal: I can speak English better than **him.**	When a pronoun follows *than*, the correct form is the subject pronoun (*he, she, I, etc.*) Usually an auxiliary verb follows (*is, do, did, can, etc.*). Informally, many Americans use the object pronoun (*him, her, me, etc.*) after *than*. An auxiliary verb does not follow.

EXERCISE **8**   Circle the correct words to complete the statement.

EXAMPLE   Chicago has (more) / less crime than San Francisco.

1. Chicago has a (larger) / smaller population than San Francisco.

2. Chicago is a safer / (more dangerous) place to live than San Francisco.

3. Houses in Chicago are more expensive / (less expensive) than houses in San Francisco.

4. Winter in Chicago is better / (worse) than winter in San Francisco.

5. Chicago has (more) / less rain than San Francisco.

12.5 | Comparisons

1. Have students look at grammar chart **12.5** on page 365. Go over the examples. Explain that the comparison is used to compare two items. Point out that *than* is used before the second item of comparison.

2. Say: *If there is no comparison with a second item, omit* than. Write the example from the chart on the board.

3. Say: Much *and* a little *can be used in front of a comparative.* Go over the examples in the chart.

4. Explain that there are two ways to make comparisons when pronouns are used after *than*: a formal way and an informal way. Say: *In the formal way, you use an auxiliary verb after the subject pronoun. In the informal way, you use an object pronoun and no verb.* Go over the examples.

EXERCISE 8

1. Have students read the direction line. Say: *This exercise is based on the facts from the reading.* Go over the example.

2. Have students complete Exercise 8 individually. Go over the answers with the class.

3. If necessary, review grammar chart **12.5** on page 365.

Grammar Variation

Have students go back to the reading on pages 363–364. Ask: *Is* than *always used?* (no) *When is it used?* (when there are two items being compared in the sentence) *When is it not used?* (when only one item is mentioned in the sentence) Then go over the examples and explanations in grammar chart **12.5.**

1. Say: *Now you're going to make comparisons.* Have students read the direction line. Say: *You can make a comparison with yourself or with two other people.* Go over the examples. Have volunteers model the examples.

2. If necessary, review the meanings of the adjectives. Have students complete the exercise individually. Then have students compare answers in pairs. Circulate to give help as needed.

3. If necessary, review grammar chart **12.5** on page 365.

EXERCISE 10

1. Have students read the direction line. Have volunteers model the examples. If necessary, review the meanings of the adjectives.

2. Have students complete Exercise 10 individually. Point out that students should start their statements with *In my opinion.* Then have students practice telling each other their opinions in pairs. Circulate to observe pair work. Give help as needed.

3. If necessary, review grammar chart **12.5** on page 365.

🕐 To save class time, have students do half of the exercise in class and complete the other half in writing for homework. Or if students do not need speaking practice, the entire exercise may be skipped or done in writing.

EXERCISE 11

1. Have students read the direction line. Say: *You can make comparisons with any city you know.* Go over the examples in the book. Have volunteers model the examples.

2. Have students complete Exercise 11 individually. Then have students compare answers in pairs. Circulate to observe pair work. Give help as needed.

3. If necessary, review grammar chart **12.5** on page 365.

🕐 To save class time, have students do half of the exercise in class and complete the other half in writing for homework. Or if students do not need speaking practice, the entire exercise may be skipped or done in writing.

EXERCISE 9   ABOUT YOU Compare yourself to another person, or compare two people you know using these adjectives.

EXAMPLES   tall
My father is taller than I am. (OR than me.)

talkative
My mother is more talkative than my father.

Answers will vary.
1. tall	5. thin	9. successful
2. educated	6. quiet	10. strong
3. friendly	7. stubborn	11. nervous
4. lazy	8. patient	12. polite

EXERCISE 10   Compare men and women. Give your own opinion. Talk in general terms. Discuss your answers.

EXAMPLE   intelligent
In my opinion, women are more intelligent than men.
OR
In my opinion, men are more intelligent than women.

Answers will vary.
1. polite	7. talkative
2. strong	8. patient
3. tall	9. romantic
4. intelligent	10. sensitive
5. kind	11. logical
6. friendly	12. responsible

EXERCISE 11   Compare this city to another city you know.

EXAMPLES   big
Tokyo is bigger than Boston.

crowded
Tokyo is more crowded than Boston.

Answers will vary.
1. crowded	4. noisy	7. cold in winter
2. modern	5. beautiful	8. dirty
3. big	6. interesting	9. sunny

366 Lesson **12**

Expansion

Exercise 10 Do a survey. What does the class think of women and men? Does anyone think they're the same? Write the results on the board.

Exercise 11 If possible, have students from the same country or region (South America, for example) compare towns and cities.

12.6 | Word Order with Comparisons

Examples	Explanation
Houses in San Francisco **are more expensive** than houses in Chicago. I want to move to a **warmer climate.**	Put comparative adjectives **after** the verb *be* or before a noun.
The Hispanic population **is growing more quickly** than the African American population.	We put comparative adverbs **after** the verb (phrase).
It **rains more** in Chicago. It **snows more** in Chicago.	We put *more, less, better, worse* **after** a verb.
San Francisco has **more sunshine** than Chicago. San Francisco has **less pollution.**	We put *more, less, fewer, better, worse* **before** a noun.

EXERCISE 12 Compare men and women. Give your own opinion. Talk in general terms. Discuss your answers.

EXAMPLES work hard
In my opinion, women work harder than men.

talk a lot
In my opinion, women talk more than men.

Answers will vary.
1. run fast
2. gossip a lot
3. take care of children well
4. worry a lot
5. drive foolishly
6. work hard
7. drive fast
8. spend a lot on clothes
9. think fast
10. live long
11. get old fast
12. make decisions quickly

EXERCISE 13 Compare this city to another city you know. Use *better, worse,* or *more.*

EXAMPLES factories
Chicago has more factories than Ponce.

public transportation
Moscow has better public transportation than Chicago.

Answers will vary.
1. traffic
2. climate
3. rain
4. crime
5. pollution
6. job opportunities
7. factories
8. tall buildings
9. people
10. sunshine
11. snow
12. homeless people

Comparatives; Superlatives **367**

Expansion

Exercise 12 Do a survey. What does the class think of women and men? Does anyone think they're the same? Write the results on the board.

Exercise 13 If possible, have students from the same country or region (South America, for example) compare towns and cities.

12.6 | Word Order with Comparisons

1. Have students cover up grammar chart **12.6.** Make a matching exercise on the board:
   1. Houses in San Francisco are more expensive than houses in Chicago.
   2. I want to move to a warmer climate.
   3. The Hispanic population is growing more quickly than the African American population.
   4. It rains more in Chicago.
   5. San Francisco has more sunshine than Chicago.
   a. Put *more, less, better,* and *worse* after a verb.
   b. Put comparative adjectives after the verb *be.*
   c. Put *more, less, fewer, better,* and *worse* before a noun.
   d. Put comparative adjectives before a noun.
   e. Put comparative adverbs after the verb.
   Have volunteers match the examples with the explanations on the board.
2. Have students compare their work with grammar chart **12.6.** Go over the examples and explanations.

EXERCISE 12

1. Say: *We're going to be comparing men and women again.* Have students read the direction line. Point out that their statements should begin with *In my opinion.* Go over the examples. Have volunteers model the examples.
2. Have students complete Exercise 12 individually. Then have them discuss their opinions in pairs. Circulate to observe pair work. Give help as needed.
3. If necessary, review grammar chart **12.6** on page 367.

EXERCISE 13

1. Have students read the direction line. Go over the examples in the book. Have volunteers model the examples.
2. Have students complete Exercise 13 individually. Then have students compare answers in pairs. Circulate to observe pair work. Give help as needed.
3. If necessary, review grammar chart **12.6** on page 367.

EXERCISE 14

1. Have students read the direction line. Say: *Look at the words you're going to make comparisons with: are they adverbs or adjectives?* Go over the examples. Ask: *In the first example, is the comparison with an adverb or adjective?* (adjective) Point out that students should give reasons for their opinions. Have a volunteer model the example.

2. Have students complete Exercise 14 individually. Then have students compare work in pairs. Circulate to observe pair work. Give help as needed.

3. If necessary, review grammar chart **12.6** on page 367.

To save class time, have students do half of the exercise in class and complete the other half for homework. Or assign the entire exercise for homework.

EXERCISE **14**   Make comparisons with the following words. Give your opinion and reasons. You may work with a partner or in a small group.

EXAMPLE   men / women—have an easy life
In my opinion, men have an easier life than women. Women have to work two jobs—in the office and at home.

Answers will vary.

1. men / women—have responsibilities

2. men / women—live long

3. American women / women in my native culture—have an easy life

4. American couples / couples in my native culture—have children

5. married men / single men—are responsible

6. American teenagers / teenagers in my native culture—have freedom

7. American teenagers / teenagers in my native culture—have responsibilities

8. American children / children in my native culture—have toys

9. American children / children in my native culture—have a good education

10. American teachers / teachers in my native culture—have high salaries

11. American teachers / teachers in my native culture—get respect

Expansion

Exercise 14 Have students discuss their opinions in groups. If possible, put students from different countries in groups.

EXERCISE **15** Fill in the blanks with the comparative or superlative form of the word in parentheses ( ). Include *than* or *the* where necessary.

EXAMPLES   August is usually ___*hotter than*___ May in Chicago.
(hot)

January is usually ___*the coldest*___ month of the year in Chicago.
(cold)

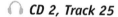

Seattle Space Needle

1. Los Angeles is ___*warmer than*___ San Francisco.
(warm)

2. Seattle is ___*the biggest*___ city in Washington.
(big)

3. The state of Hawaii is ___*the farthest*___ south in the U.S.
(far)

4. Mexico City is ___*more crowded than*___ New York.
(crowded)

5. New York is ___*more crowded than*___ Los Angeles.
(crowded)

6. Mexico City is one of ___*the most crowded*___ cities in the world.
(crowded)

7. New York is a crowded city, but Tokyo is ___*more crowded*___.
(crowded)

8. San Francisco is one of ___*the most beautiful*___ cities in the U.S.
(beautiful)

9. ___*The tallest*___ building in the world is not in the U.S.
(tall)

10. The population of India is growing ___*more rapidly than*___
(rapidly)
the population of the U.S.

EXERCISE **16** Two students in Seattle are talking. Fill in the blanks with appropriate words to make comparatives and superlatives.

A: I'm planning to visit Chicago.

B: You're going to love it. It's a beautiful city. In fact, it's one of ___*the most beautiful*___ cities in the U.S.
(example)

A: It's the second largest city, isn't it?

B: Not anymore. Los Angeles is now ___*larger than*___ Chicago.
(1)

A: What should I see while I'm there?

B: You can visit the Sears Tower. It's ___*the tallest*___ building in
(2)
the U.S. It has 110 stories. On a clear day, you can see many miles.

A: Did you go to the top when you were there?

Comparatives; Superlatives   **369**

EXERCISE 15

1. Say: *In this exercise, you must decide if you're going to use a superlative or a comparative.* Have students read the direction line. Go over the examples in the book.
2. Have students complete Exercise 15 individually. Then have them compare answers in pairs. Circulate to observe pair work. Give help as needed.
3. If necessary, review grammar charts **12.1** on page 357, **12.2** on pages 358–359, and **12.3** on page 360.

To save class time, have students do half of the exercise in class and complete the other half for homework. Or assign the entire exercise for homework.

EXERCISE 16

🎧 *CD 2, Track 25*

1. Have students read the direction line. Explain that this is a conversation between two students Go over the example in the book.
2. Have students complete Exercise 16 individually. Then check answers as a class.
3. If necessary, review grammar charts **12.1** on page 357, **12.2** on pages 358–359, **12.3** on page 360, **12.4** on page 362, **12.5** on page 365, and **12.6** on page 367.

To save class time, have students do half of the exercise in class and complete the other half for homework. Or assign the entire exercise for homework.

Expansion

Exercise 15 Have students work in pairs to write similar statements about cities in other parts of the world. For more of a challenge, have students from different countries and regions work together.

Exercise 16 Variation

To provide practice with listening skills, have students close their books and listen to the audio. Repeat the audio as needed. Ask comprehension questions, such as: *What's person A planning to do?* (visit Chicago) *Does person B think Chicago is a beautiful city?* (yes) *What's the second largest city in the U.S.?* (Los Angeles) Then have students open their books and complete Exercise 16.

B: When I was there, the weather was bad. It was raining. I hope you
have _____better_____ weather than I had. When are you going?
(3)

A: In August.

B: Ugh! August is the _____hottest_____ month of the year. It's
(4)
often 90 degrees or more. If you get hot, you can always go to the
beach and cool off.

A: Is Chicago near an ocean?

B: Of course not. It's near Lake Michigan.

A: Is it big like Lake Washington?

B: It's much _____bigger_____ than Lake Washington. In fact, it's
(5)
one of the _____biggest_____ lakes in the U.S.
(6)

A: Is Chicago very rainy?

B: Not in the summer. It's sunny. In fact, it's much
_____sunnier/drier_____ than Seattle.
(7)

A: What do you suggest that I see?

B: You should see the famous architecture downtown. The
_____best_____ architects in the U.S. built buildings in
(8)
Chicago.

A: Do I need to take taxis everywhere or does Chicago have a good
public transportation system?

B: Taxis are so expensive! They're much _____more expensive_____ than
(9)

the buses and trains. You should use the public
transportation. But remember there's a lot of crime
in Chicago, so it's not safe to travel alone at night. It's
_____safer_____ in the daytime.
(10)

A: Does Chicago have _____more_____ crime
(11)
than Seattle?

B: Yes. But if you're careful, you'll be OK. I'm sure
you'll enjoy it. It's an interesting place because it
has people from all over the world. In fact, I
think it's one of the _____most interesting_____
(12)
cities in the U.S.

Lake Michigan

Expansion

Exercise 16 Have students practice this conversation or create a similar conversation
about two other cities in pairs. Then have volunteers role-play all or part of the
conversation in front of the class.

SUMMARY OF LESSON 12

1. Comparison of Adjectives

   SHORT ADJECTIVES
   Chicago is a **big** city.
   Chicago is **bigger than** Boston.
   New York is **the biggest** city in the U.S.

   LONG ADJECTIVES
   Houston is a **populated** city.
   Chicago is **more populated than** Houston.
   New York is **the most populated** city in the U.S.

2. Comparison of Adverbs

   SHORT ADVERBS
   She drives **fast.**
   She drives **faster than** her husband.
   Her son drives **the fastest** in the family.

   -LY ADVERBS
   You speak English **fluently.**
   You speak English **more fluently than** your brother.
   Your sister speaks English **the most fluently** in your family.

3. Word Order

   VERB (PHRASE) + COMPARATIVE ADVERB
   She **speaks English more fluently** than her husband.
   She **talks more** than her husband.

   COMPARATIVE WORD + NOUN
   She has **more experience** than her husband.
   She has a **better accent** than her sister.

EDITING ADVICE

1. Don't use a comparison word when there is no comparison.

   California is a bigger state.

2. Don't use *more* and *-er* together.

   My new car is more better than my old one.

3. Use *than* before the second item in a comparison.

   than
   He is younger that his wife.

Summary of Lesson 12

1. **Comparison of Adjectives**
   Have students cover up the Summary on page 371. Say: *Write three sentences with* big *and three sentences with* populated. *Write a sentence with* big *as a simple adjective, as a comparative, and as a superlative. Do the same with* populated. Then have students compare their sentences with the ones in the Summary.
   If necessary, have students review:
   12.2 Comparative and Superlative Forms of Adjectives and Adverbs (pp. 358–359)
   12.3 Superlative Adjectives (p. 360)
   12.5 Comparisons (p. 365).

2. **Comparison of Adverbs** Have students cover up the Summary on page 371. Say: *Write three sentences with* fast *and three sentences with* fluently. *Write a sentence with* fast *as a simple adverb, as a comparative, and as a superlative. Do the same with* fluently. Then have students compare their sentences with the ones in the Summary.
   If necessary, have students review:
   12.2 Comparative and Superlative Forms of Adjectives and Adverbs (pp. 358–359)
   12.5 Comparisons (p. 365).

3. **Word Order** Have students cover up the Summary on page 371. Scramble the four example sentences in the book, and write them on the board. Have students unscramble the sentences and compare them with the ones in the summary. Then have students compare their sentences with the ones in the Summary. If necessary, have students review:
   12.6 Word Order with Comparisons (p. 367).

Editing Advice

Have students close their books. Write the example sentence without editing marks or corrections on the board. For example: *California is a bigger state.* Ask students to correct each sentence and provide a rule or explanation for each correction. Then have them compare their work with the Editing advice on pages 371–372.

Lesson 12 Test/Review

For additional practice, review, and assessment materials, see Assessment CD-ROM with *ExamView Pro, More Grammar Practice* Workbook 1, Interactive CD-ROM, and Web site http://elt.thomson.com/gic

PART 1

1. Part 1 may be used in addition to the Assessment CD-ROM with *ExamView Pro* as an in-class test to assess student performance. Have students read the direction line. Ask: *Does every sentence have a mistake?* (no) Go over the examples with the class.
2. Have students complete the assignment individually. Collect for assessment.
3. If necessary, have students review: **Lesson 12.**

4. Use *the* before a superlative form.

  the
  China has ⌄ biggest population in the world.

5. Use a plural noun after the phrase "one of the."

  s
  Jim is one of the tallest boy ⌄ in the class.

6. Use the correct word order.

  ~~drives faster~~
  She ~~faster drives~~ than her husband.

  more
  I have ⌄ responsibilities ~~more~~ than you.

  country
  The U.S. is the country most powerful ⌄ in the world.

7. Don't use *the* with a possessive form.

  My ~~the~~ best friend lives in London.

8. Use correct spelling.

  happier
  She is ~~happyer~~ than her friend. .

LESSON 12 TEST/REVIEW

PART 1 Find the mistakes with the underlined words and correct them. Not every sentence has a mistake. If the sentence is correct, write *C*.

EXAMPLES
  than
  I am taller ⌄ my father.
  I am tall, but my brother is taller. *C*

1. Paul is one of the youngest student ⌄ in this class.
   s

2. She is ~~more~~ older than her husband.

3. I'm the ~~most tall~~ person in my family.
   tallest

4. My father is more educated ⌄ my mother.
   than

5. She is the most intelligent person in her family. *C*

6. New York City is ⌄ biggest city in the U.S.
   the

Lesson Review

To use Part 1 as a review, assign it as homework or use it as an in-class activity to be completed individually or in pairs. Check answers and review errors as a class. Reteach grammar points that students haven't mastered. Then student learning may be assessed using a test generated from the Assessment CD-ROM with *ExamView Pro.*

7. My sister's <u>the oldest</u> son got married last month.

8. Houston is a very <u>big</u> city.   *C*

9. He is <u>much older</u> than his wife.   *C*

10. New York is <u>bi^gger</u> than Los Angeles.

11. I speak English <u>more better than</u> I did a year ago.

12. Book One is <u>eas^{ier}yer</u> than Book Two.

PART **2**   Find the mistakes with word order and correct them. Not every sentence has a mistake. If the sentence is correct, write *C*.

EXAMPLES   You more know about the U.S. than I do.
Soccer is more interesting than football for me.   *C*

1. I have problems more than you.
2. I earlier woke up than you.
3. Paris is the city most beautiful in the world.
4. She speaks English more fluently than her brother.   *C*
5. You faster type than I do.
6. My father is the most intelligent person in the family.   *C*
7. Your car is expensive more than my car.
8. You sing more beautifully than I do.   *C*
9. I travel more than my friend does.   *C*
10. You have more money than I do.   *C*

PART **3**   Fill in the blanks with the comparative or the superlative of the word in parentheses ( ). Add *the* or *than* if necessary.

EXAMPLES   New York is ____*bigger than*____ Chicago.
                                   (big)

New York is ____*the biggest*____ city in the U.S.
                                   (big)

1. Mount Everest is ____*the highest*____ mountain in the world.
                                   (high)

2. A D grade is ____*worse than*____ a C grade.
                                   (bad)

Comparatives; Superlatives   **373**

Lesson Review

To use Parts 2 and 3 as a review, assign them as homework or use them as in-class activities to be completed individually or in pairs. Check answers and review errors as a class. Reteach grammar points that students haven't mastered. Then student learning may be assessed using a test generated from the Assessment CD-ROM with *ExamView Pro*.

PART 2

1. Part 2 may also be used in addition to the Assessment CD-ROM with *ExamView Pro* as an in-class test to assess student performance. Have students read the direction line. Go over the examples with the class.
2. Have students complete the exercise individually. Collect for assessment.
3. If necessary, have students review:
   12.4 Word Order with Superlatives (p. 362)
   12.6 Word Order with Comparisons (p. 367).

PART 3

1. Part 3 may also be used in addition to the Assessment CD-ROM with *ExamView Pro* as an in-class test to assess student performance. Have students read the direction line. Go over the examples with the class.
2. Have students complete the exercise individually. Collect for assessment.
3. If necessary, have students review:
   12.2 Comparative and Superlative Forms of Adjectives and Adverbs (pp. 358–359)
   12.3 Superlative Adjectives (p. 360)
   12.5 Comparisons (p. 365).

Expansion Activities

These expansion activities provide opportunities for students to interact with one another and further develop their speaking and writing skills. Encourage students to use grammar from this lesson whenever possible.

🕐 To save class time, assign parts of the activities as homework. Then use class time for interaction and communication. If students do not need additional speaking practice, some of the activities may be assigned as writing activities for homework, or skipped altogether.

CLASSROOM ACTIVITIES

1. Have students work individually to complete the information. Then put students in groups to compare.

---

3. Johnson is one of _____*the most common/ the commonest*_____ last names in the U.S.
   (common)

4. Tokyo is _____*more populated than*_____ Miami.
   (populated)

5. June 21 is _____*the longest*_____ day of the year.
   (long)

6. The teacher speaks English _____*better than*_____ I do.
   (well)

7. Lake Superior is _____*the largest*_____ lake in the U.S.
   (large)

8. Children learn a foreign language _____*more quickly than*_____ adults.
   (quickly)

9. Do you think that Japanese cars are _____*better than*_____ American cars?
   (good)

10. A dog is _____*friendlier/more friendly than*_____ a cat.
    (friendly)

11. Women drive _____*more carefully than*_____ men.
    (carefully)

12. Who is _____*the best*_____ student in this class?
    (good)

13. The teacher speaks English _____*more fluently than*_____ I do.
    (fluently)

14. A dog is intelligent, but a monkey is _____*more intelligent*_____.
    (intelligent)

EXPANSION ACTIVITIES

Classroom Activities

1. Form a small group of three to five students. Fill in the blanks to give information about yourself. Compare your list with the lists of other members of your group to make superlative statements.

   EXAMPLE   Susana has the most relatives in this city.

   a. Number of relatives I have in this city _____

   b. My height _____

   c. Number of letters in my last name _____

   d. Number of children I have _____

   e. Number of sisters and brothers I have _____

   f. Age of my car _____

Expansion

Classroom Activities For activity 1, do a quick survey to find the class superlatives (e.g., *Sara is the funniest girl in the class. Ahmed is the tallest guy in the class.*).

g. Number of hours I watch TV per week _____

h. Number of hours I exercise per week _____

i. Money I spent today _____

j. Distance I travel to come to this school _____

k. Cups of coffee I drank today _____

l. Number of miles I usually drive or walk per day _____

m. Number of movies I usually see per year _____

2. Work with a partner from the same native culture, if possible. Compare American men and men from your native culture. Compare American women and women from your native culture. Report some of your ideas to the class.

3. The manager of a company is interviewing two people for the same job: a younger woman (24 years old) and an older woman (55 years old). He can't decide which one to hire. Find a partner. One person (the manager) will make a statement. The partner will say, "Yes, but . . ." and follow with another statement.

EXAMPLES   A: Older people are wiser.
            B: Yes, but younger people are quicker.
            A: Older people have more experience.
            B: Yes, but younger people are more flexible.

4. Find a partner. Choose one of the following pairs and decide which of the two is better. Write five reasons why it is better. One person will make a statement saying that one is better than the other. The other person will follow with, "Yes, but . . ." and give another point of view.

EXAMPLE   A: I think dogs are better pets than cats. They are more loyal.
           B: Yes, but dogs need more attention.

* cats and dogs
* big cities and small towns
* travel by train and travel by plane
* houses and condos
* spring and fall
* voice mail and answering machines

Write About it

1. Choose one of the topics below to write a comparison:

a. Compare your present car with your last car.
b. Compare two cities you know well.

Comparatives; Superlatives   **375**

CLASSROOM ACTIVITIES (*cont.*)

2. Model some possible comparisons: *In the U.S., women work more outside the home. In the U.S., women have less children.*

3. Have volunteers tell the class some of the arguments they made for hiring the younger or the older woman. Take a class vote. Who should get hired?

4. After students have discussion in pairs, ask volunteers to tell the class some of their arguments. Then take a class vote to see what things are the most popular.

WRITE ABOUT IT

1. Students can write about one of the topics in the book, or they can write a comparison about another topic that interests them.

Expansion

Classroom Activities For activity 2, after students discuss men and women in pairs, have a class discussion to compare different cultures.

LESSON **12**   **375**

2. Brainstorm some ideas with the class. Write the ideas on the board. Students can complete the writing task individually or they can work in pairs.

OUTSIDE ACTIVITY

Have students prepare the questions in writing in class. Ask students if there are additional topics they would be interested in asking about.

INTERNET ACTIVITIES

1. Brainstorm ways to search for sites that compare cities. Ask students to print out the information they find on the Internet and to bring it in to class.
2. Have students prepare a brochure for their city with the information they find on the Internet.

---

c. Compare American women and women in your native culture.
d. Compare American men and men in your native culture.
e. Compare soccer and football.
f. Compare your life in the U.S. and your life in your native country.
g. Compare a place where you lived before with the place where you live now.

2. Write about the biggest problem in the world (or in your native country, or in the U.S.) today. Why is this a problem? How can we solve the problem?

Interview a native speaker of English. Get his or her opinion about the superlative of each of the following items. Share your findings with the class.

EXAMPLE   good car
            What do you think is the best car?

a. good car
b. beautiful actress
c. good president in the last 25 years
d. beautiful city in the U.S.
e. good university in the U.S.
f. popular movie at this time
g. terrible tragedy in American history
h. big problem in the U.S. today
i. popular singer in the U.S.
j. best athlete
h. handsome actor

1. Using the Internet, find a site that compares cities. Compare any two American cities that interest you.
2. Using the Internet, find out about the city where you live. Find out:

* the name of the mayor
* the population
* the annual rainfall
* the coldest month
* interesting places to visit

Additional Activities at http://elt.thomson.com/gic

376 Lesson **12**

Outside Activity Variation

As an alternative, you may invite a guest to your classroom (e.g., an administrator, a librarian, or a service worker at your school) and have students do a class interview. Students should prepare their interview questions ahead of time.

Expansion

Outside Activity Ask students to make a poster of the interview. Hang the posters up in class and let students circulate to look at them.

Internet Activities Variation

Remind students that if they don't have Internet access, they can use Internet facilities at a public library or they can use traditional research methods to find out information including looking at encyclopedias, magazines, books, journals, and newspapers.

GRAMMAR

Auxiliary Verbs with *Too* and *Either*
Auxiliary Verbs in Tag Questions

CONTEXT: Dating and Marriage

Dating and Marriage
Saturday with Meg and Don

377

Lesson | 13

Lesson Overview

GRAMMAR

1. Ask: *What did we study in Lesson 12?* (comparatives and superlatives)
2. *What are we going to study in this lesson?* (auxiliary verbs with *too* and *either*; auxiliary verbs in tag questions) *What are auxiliary verbs?* Have students give examples. Write them on the board.

CONTEXT

1. Ask: *How many people here are married? Is being married difficult? Why or why not?*
2. Have students share their knowledge and personal experiences.

Photo

Direct students' attention to the photo. Ask: *What's happening in this photo?* (This couple just got married and is probably driving from the ceremony to the reception.)

🕐 To save class time, have students do the Test/Review at the end of the lesson, or administer a lesson test generated from the Assessment CD-ROM with *ExamView® Pro*. Skip sections of the lesson that students have already mastered. You may also assign some sections for self-study for extra credit.

Expansion

Theme Ask students to talk about the differences between dating and marriage. Have students discuss the benefits and drawbacks of both dating and marriage. Is one better than the other?

Dating and Marriage (Reading)

1. Have students look at the photo. Ask: *Are these people married or are they dating? Why do you think so?*
2. Have students look at the title of the reading. Ask: *What is the reading about?* Have students use the title and photos to make predictions about the reading.
3. Preteach any vocabulary words your students may not know, such as *lifestyle* and *lonely*. Use the pictures on page 379 to teach *carry-out dinners* and *fast-food restaurants*.

BEFORE YOU READ

1. Have students discuss the questions in pairs.
2. Ask for a few volunteers to share their answers with the class.

 To save class time, skip "Before You Read" or have students prepare answers for homework ahead of time.

Reading ⌒ *CD 2, Track 26*

1. Have students first read the text silently. Tell them to pay special attention to auxiliary verbs and *too* and *either*. Then play the audio and have students read along silently.
2. Check students' comprehension. Ask questions such as: *How long after they met did Meg and Don decide to get married?* (one year) *When did they discover they had differences?* (when they started to plan the wedding) *What are some ways they have resolved differences?* (Once a month, they do something with friends; when Don goes on a fishing trip, Meg goes out with her friend.)

 To save class time, have students do the reading for homework ahead of time.

DATING AND MARRIAGE

Before You **Read**

1. How is dating different from marriage?
2. Do American married couples spend more or less time together than couples in your native culture?

🎧 Read the following article. Pay special attention to auxiliary verbs and *too* and *either*.

Most married couples want to spend time together, but the busy American lifestyle often doesn't allow it. Meg and Don are a typical American couple.

Before Meg and Don met, they were both lonely. Meg didn't want to be alone, and Don **didn't either.** They both wanted to get married. Meg believed that marriage would mean a lot of togetherness, and Don **did too.** When they were dating, they spent all their free time together. They discovered they had a lot in common. A year after they met, they decided to get married. As they planned their wedding, they discovered their first differences in making plans for their wedding: Meg wanted a big wedding, but Don **didn't.** Meg wanted an outdoor wedding, but Don **didn't.** They solved their differences by having a big indoor wedding.

Reading Variation

To practice listening skills, have students first listen to the audio alone. Ask a few comprehension questions. Repeat the audio if necessary. Then have students open their books and read along as they listen to the audio.

Reading Glossary

lifestyle: the manner in which one lives
lonely: alone and feeling sad

As a married couple, they are now facing the realities of busy schedules and different interests. Don works hard, and Meg **does too.** They often have to work overtime. Don likes to cook, and Meg **does too,** but they rarely have time to do it. They often bring home carry-out dinners or eat in fast-food restaurants. On weekends, Don likes to go fishing, but Meg **doesn't.** So Don takes fishing trips with his friends, and Meg stays home. Meg likes to go to movies, but Don **doesn't.** He prefers to stay home and watch TV when he comes home from work. Both of them are planning to take college courses soon, which will give them even less time together.

So how do they solve these differences and stay close as a married couple? Once a month, they invite friends over on weekends to have dinner and watch a movie or a football game on TV. When Don goes on a fishing trip, Meg gets together with her best friend and they go to a movie. That way, Don enjoys himself, and Meg **does too.**

Even though the realities of marriage are different from the romance of dating, Meg and Don are finding ways to adjust to married life.

Auxiliary Verbs with *Too* and *Either*; Auxiliary Verbs in Tag Questions   **379**

13.1 | Auxiliary Verbs with *Too* and *Either*

1. Have students cover up grammar chart **13.1**. Write on the board:
be
do, does, did
modals (can, could, will, etc.)
Say: *These verbs are all auxiliary verbs.* Have students go back to the reading on pages 378–379. Say: *Go back to the reading and study how these auxiliary verbs are used with* too *and* either. Ask volunteers to give you some examples from the reading (*Meg wanted to get married, and Don did, too. Meg works hard, and Don does, too.*). Elicit the answer. Explain that auxiliary verbs with *too* and *either* are used to show similarity. Ask: *Why do we use auxiliaries with* too *in these sentences?* (to avoid repeating the same verb phrase)

2. Have students look at grammar chart **13.1**. Say: *Now let's look at the chart.* Go over the examples and explanations in the chart. Point out that *too* is used with affirmative statements and *either* is used with negative statements. Explain that in informal speech we often say *me too* and *me neither*. They're both expressions of agreement. Point out that Americans substitute *do, does, did* for *have*, but the British use *have*.

EXERCISE 1

1. Have students read the direction line. Go over the example in the book. Ask: *What tense are the main verb and the auxiliary verb in?* (present)

2. Have students complete Exercise 1 individually. Check the answers as a class.

3. If necessary, review grammar chart **13.1** on page 380.

EXERCISE 2

1. Have students read the direction line. Go over the example in the book. Ask: *What tense are the main verb and the auxiliary verb in?* (present)

2. Have students complete Exercise 2 individually. Remind students that they need to use the same tense as the main verb. Go over the answers as a class.

3. If necessary, review grammar chart **13.1** on page 380.

13.1 | Auxiliary Verbs with *Too* and *Either*

The auxiliary verbs are *do, does, did,* the modals, and *be*. We use auxiliary verbs with *too* and *either* to show similarity and avoid repetition of the same verb phrase.

Examples	Explanation
Don is busy, and Meg **is too.** Don likes to cook, and Meg **does too.** Don was lonely, and Meg **was too.** Don lived alone, and Meg **did too.**	For affirmative statements, use the auxiliary verb + *too*.
Don doesn't have much free time, and Meg **doesn't either.** Don can't see his friends very often, and Meg **can't either.**	For negative statements, use the auxiliary verb + *either*.
Don: I like to cook. *Meg:* **Me too.** *Don:* I don't have much time. *Meg:* **Me neither.**	In informal speech, we often say *me too* and *me neither*.
American: Meg has a hard job, and Don **does too.** **British:** Meg has a hard job, and Don **has too.**	When *have* is the main verb, Americans usually use *do, does, did* as a substitute. The British often use *have*.

EXERCISE 1 Fill in the blanks with an auxiliary verb + *too* to show what Meg and Don have in common. Make sure you use the same tense as the main verb.

EXAMPLE Don likes to cook, and Meg ___does too___.

1. Don has a hard job, and Meg ___does too___.
2. Don is a hard worker, and Meg ___is too___.
3. Don will take some college courses next semester, and Meg ___will too___.
4. Don was lonely before, and Meg ___was too___.
5. Don worked last Saturday, and Meg ___did too___.

EXERCISE 2 Fill in the blanks with an auxiliary verb + *either* to show what Meg and Don have in common. Make sure you use the same tense as the main verb.

EXAMPLE Don doesn't like fast food, and Meg ___doesn't either___.

1. Don didn't finish college, and Meg ___didn't either___.
2. Don isn't interested in baseball, and Meg ___isn't either___.

Expansion

Exercise 2 Have students write about themselves and their spouses or boyfriend/girlfriend. Alternatively, have them write about their parents or another couple they know.

3. Don doesn't have much free time, and Meg _____doesn't either_____.

4. Don can't find time to cook, and Meg _____can't either_____.

5. Don doesn't have any brothers or sisters, and Meg
_____doesn't either_____.

13.2 | Auxiliary Verbs with Opposite Statements

We can use auxiliary verbs with *but* to show contrast and avoid repetition of the same verb phrase.

Examples	Explanation
Don likes to go fishing, **but** Meg **doesn't**. Don is happy watching TV, **but** Meg **isn't**. Don doesn't like to go to movies, **but** Meg **does**. Don didn't want to have a big wedding, **but** Meg **did**.	We can use *but* to connect opposite statements. We often put a comma before *but*.
Meg: I want a big wedding. *Don*: I **don't**.	In conversation, we don't need *but* when one person says the opposite of another.

EXERCISE 3 Fill in the blanks with an auxiliary verb to show what Meg and Don don't have in common.

EXAMPLE Don likes to go fishing, but Meg _____doesn't_____.

1. Meg likes to go to movies, but Don _____doesn't_____.

2. Meg doesn't like to watch football on TV, but Don
_____does_____.

3. Meg reads when she has free time, but Don _____doesn't_____.

4. Don wanted to have a small wedding, but Meg _____didn't_____.

5. Meg is interested in politics, but Don _____isn't_____.

6. Meg isn't interested in cars, but Don _____is_____.

7. Meg can play the piano, but Don _____can't_____.

EXERCISE 4 Fill in the blanks to compare the U.S. and another country you know. Use *and . . . too* or *and . . . either* for similarities between the U.S. and the other country. Use *but* for differences. Use an auxiliary verb in all cases.

EXAMPLE The U.S. is a big country, _____and Russia is too._____
OR
The U.S. is a big country, _____but Cuba isn't._____

Auxiliary Verbs with *Too* and *Either*; Auxiliary Verbs in Tag Questions   **381**

Expansion

Exercise 3 Have students write about themselves and their spouses or boyfriend/girlfriend. Alternatively, have them write about their parents or another couple they know.

13.2 | Auxiliary Verbs with Opposite Statements

1. Have students go back to the reading on pages 378–379. Say: *Find a sentence where Meg and Don don't agree (Meg wanted a big wedding, but Don didn't.). What word shows they have an opposite opinion? (but)*

2. Then have students look at grammar chart **13.2**. Say: *We can use auxiliary verbs with* but *to show contrast.* Go over the examples and explanations. Point out the position of the comma.

3. Explain that in conversation, we don't usually use *but* when one person says the opposite of another person. Ask students to go through the reading and underline all the statements with *but* and an auxiliary verb.

EXERCISE 3

1. Have students read the direction line. Say: *Don't forget to put the auxiliary verb in the same tense as the main verb.* Go over the example in the book.

2. Have students complete Exercise 3 individually. Have students compare answers in pairs. Circulate to observe pair work. Give help as needed.

3. If necessary, review grammar chart **13.2** on page 381.

EXERCISE 4

1. Say: *Now you're going to compare countries.* Have students read the direction line. Go over the examples in the book. Have volunteers model the examples.

2. Have students complete the exercise individually. Then have students compare work in pairs. Circulate to observe pair work. Give help as needed.

3. If necessary, review grammar charts **13.1** on page 380 and **13.2** on page 381.

To save class time, have students do half of the exercise in class and complete the other half for homework. Or assign the entire exercise for homework.

EXERCISE 5

1. Have students read the direction line. Go over the example in the book. Have volunteers model #1.
2. Have students complete the chart individually. Then have them exchange books and write statements about themselves and their partners.
3. If necessary, review grammar charts **13.1** on page 380 and **13.2** on page 381.

🕐 If students do not need speaking practice, this exercise may be skipped.

---

1. The U.S. has more than 290 million people, __Answers will vary.__
2. The U.S. is in North America, _____
3. The U.S. has a president, _____
4. The U.S. doesn't have a socialist government, _____
5. The U.S. fought in World War II, _____
6. The U.S. was a colony of England, _____
7. Americans like football, _____
8. Americans don't celebrate Labor Day in May, _____
9. American public schools are closed on December 25, _____

_____

10. The U.S. has a presidential election every four years, _____

_____

EXERCISE **5** ABOUT YOU Check (✓) *yes* or *no* to tell what is true for you. Exchange your book with another student. Make statements about you and the other student.

EXAMPLE I don't speak Spanish, but Luis does.

Answers will vary.

	Yes	No
1. I speak Spanish.		✓
2. I'm interested in football.		
3. I'm interested in soccer.		
4. I have a car.		
5. I use the Internet.		
6. I can drive.		
7. I plan to move to another city.		
8. I'm going to buy a computer this year.		
9. I would like to live in a small American town.		
10. I exercise every day.		
11. I'm studying math this semester.		
12. I studied English when I was in elementary school.		
13. I finished high school.		
14. I'm a vegetarian.		
15. I have a cell phone.		

382 Lesson **13**

Expansion

Exercise 4 Have students write about towns and cities in their countries or regions. If possible have students from the same country or region work together.

Exercise 5 For an extra challenge, have students ask and answer questions (*Do you speak Spanish? Yes, I do.*) instead of exchanging books. Then have students make statements about themselves and their partners.

EXERCISE **6** Fill in the blanks in the conversation below. Use an auxiliary verb and *too* or *either* when necessary.

A: I'm moving on Saturday. Maybe you and your brother can help me. Are you working on Saturday?

B: My brother is working on Saturday, but I __*'m not*_____.
   (example)

   I can help you.

A: I need a van. Do you have one?

B: I don't have one, but my brother _____*does*_____. I'll ask him
   (1)

   if we can use it. By the way, why are you moving?

A: There are a couple of reasons. I got married recently. I like the

   apartment, but my wife _____*doesn't*_____. She says it's too
   (2)

   small for two people.

B: How many rooms does your new apartment have?

A: The old apartment has two bedrooms, and the new one

   _____*does too*_____. But the rooms are much bigger in the new
   (3)

   one, and there are more closets. Also, we'd like to live near the lake.

B: I _____*would too*_____, but apartments there are very expensive.
   (4)

A: We found a nice apartment that isn't so expensive. Also, I'd like to
   own a dog, but my present landlord doesn't permit pets.

B: Mine doesn't _____*either*_____. What kind of dog do you plan
   (5)

   to get?

A: I like big watchdogs. Maybe a German shepherd or a doberman. I

   don't like small dogs, but my wife _____*does*_____.
   (6)

B: I don't like small dogs either. They just make a lot of noise.

A: So now you know my reasons for moving. Can I count on you for
   Saturday?

B: Of course you can.

Auxiliary Verbs with *Too* and *Either*; Auxiliary Verbs in Tag Questions   **383**

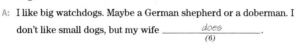

EXERCISE 6

🎧 *CD 2, Track 27*

1. Have students read the direction line. Go over the example in the book. Point out the pictures of the van and the dogs (German shepherd and poodle).
2. Have students complete Exercise 6 individually. Then check answers as a class.
3. If necessary, review grammar charts **13.1** on page 380 and **13.2** on page 381.

🕐 To save class time, have students do half of the exercise in class and complete the other half for homework. Or assign the entire exercise for homework.

Exercise 6 Variation

To provide practice with listening skills, have students close their books and listen to the audio. Repeat the audio as needed. Ask comprehension questions, such as: *What is person A doing on Saturday?* (moving) *What is person B's brother doing on Saturday?* (working) *Can person B help move person A?* (yes) Then have students open their books and complete Exercise 6.

Expansion

Exercise 6 Have students practice the conversation in pairs. Then ask volunteers to act out the conversation for the class.

13.3 | Tag Questions

1. Have students cover up grammar chart **13.3.** Ask students questions using tags (e.g., *It's cold outside, isn't it? This is a big room, isn't it?*). Ask: *Does anyone know what those little questions I'm putting on the end are called?* (tag questions) Say: *We use tag questions to ask if a statement is correct or if a listener agrees with you.*
2. Have students look at grammar chart **13.3** on page 384. Go over the examples and explanations. Point out that the verb in the tag question is in the same tense as the main verb.

Saturday with Meg and Don (Reading)

1. Have students look at the photo. Ask: *Do Meg and Don look different than they did in the first photos? If so, in what ways? What might they be talking about?*
2. Have students look at the title of the reading. Ask: *What is the reading about?* Have students make predictions.
3. Preteach any vocabulary words your students may not know.

BEFORE YOU READ

1. Have students discuss the questions in pairs.
2. Ask for a few volunteers to share their answers with the class.

To save class time, skip "Before You Read" or have students prepare answers for homework.

Reading 🎧 *CD 2, Track 28*

1. Have students first read the chart and the text silently. Tell them to pay special attention to tag questions. Then play the audio and have students read along silently.
2. Check students' comprehension. Ask questions such as: *Why doesn't Don want to go to the movies?* (He's tired.) *What kind of activities do they do on the weekends?* (They usually do chores such as cleaning and shopping. They don't do anything fun.) *Is Meg happy?* (Yes, but she wants to spend more "quality time" with Don.)

To save class time, have students do the reading for homework ahead of time.

13.3 | Tag Questions

Examples	Explanation
Married life is hard, **isn't it?** You don't like to go fishing, **do you?** Meg and Don work hard, **don't they?** Americans don't have much free time, **do they?**	A tag question is a short question that we put at the end of a statement. Use a tag question to ask if your statement is correct of if the listener agrees with you. The tag question uses an auxiliary verb in the same tense as the main verb.

SATURDAY WITH MEG AND DON

Before You Read
1. When families talk about "quality time," what do you think they mean?
2. What do you like to do with your free time?

 Read the following conversation between Meg (M) and Don (D). Pay special attention to tag questions.

M: Would you like to go out to a movie tonight?
D: Not really.
M: Before we got married, you always wanted to go to movies, **didn't you?**
D: I suppose so. But I'm tired now. I'd rather stay home and watch TV or rent a movie.
M: You're always tired, **aren't you?**
D: Well, actually, yes. I work hard all week, and now I just want to relax.

Reading Variation

To practice listening skills, have students first listen to the audio alone. Ask a few comprehension questions. Repeat the audio if necessary. Then have students open their books and read along as they listen to the audio.

M: When we got married, we planned to spend a lot of time together, **didn't we?**

D: I know. But married life is hard. Besides, we spend a lot of time together on weekends, **don't we?**

M: Yes, we do. We go shopping, we do the laundry, we visit your parents, we cut the grass, we clean the house. But we don't have any fun together anymore, **do we?**

D: Fishing is fun for me. Next weekend I'm going fishing with my buddies. But you don't like fishing, **do you?**

M: Not really.

D: Before we got married, you said you'd try fishing with me, **didn't you?**

M: Yes, I did. But I was just trying to please you then. I realize I like to eat fish, but I don't like to catch them.

D: Well, somebody has to catch them if you want to eat them.

M: But we never eat them because we don't have time to cook. Now that it's Saturday, we're both too tired to cook. What are we going to do for dinner tonight?

D: We can get some carry-out from that new Chinese place nearby, **can't we?**

M: I suppose so.

D: You're not happy, **are you?**

M: That's not true! I love you, but I just want to spend more "quality time" with you.

D: I have an idea. Let's invite some friends over next weekend, and we can make our special fish recipe for them. That will be fun, **won't it?**

M: That's a great idea.

Auxiliary Verbs with *Too* and *Either*; Auxiliary Verbs in Tag Questions   **385**

Lesson **13**   **385**

13.4 | Auxiliary Verbs in Tag Questions

1. Have students cover up grammar chart **13.4**. Tell students to go back to the reading on pages 384–385. Say: *Underline negative tag questions and circle affirmative tag questions.* Ask: *How do you form the tag question after an affirmative statement?* (auxiliary verb + *not* + subject pronoun) *How do you form the tag question after a negative statement?* (auxiliary verb + subject pronoun) Point out that a comma separates the statement and tag question.

2. Write the following sentences from the grammar chart on the board: *There isn't a lot of free time, is there?*
This is a typical marriage, isn't it?
These are normal problems, aren't they?
Say: *Study these sentences. What does each sentence begin with? How is each tag question formed?* Elicit the answers: *If the sentence begins with* there is *or* there are, *what do we use in the tag?* (*there*) *If the sentence begins with* this *or* that, *what do we use in the tag?* (*it*) *If the sentence begins with* these *or* those, *what do we use in the tag?* (*they*)

3. Have students look at grammar chart **13.4**. Go through the examples and explanations. On the board, review how to make contractions in negative tag questions.

4. Explain that *Am I not?* is very formal. For more informal occasions, use *Aren't I?*

EXERCISE 7

1. Have students read the direction line. Go over the example in the book. Ask: *If the main clause is affirmative, what tense will the tag question be in?* (negative)

2. Have students complete Exercise 7 individually. Go over the answers as a class.

3. If necessary, review grammar chart **13.4** on page 386.

13.4 | Auxiliary Verbs in Tag Questions

Affirmative Statements	Negative Tag Questions	Explanation
Don likes fishing,	**doesn't** he?	An affirmative statement has a negative tag question. Make a contraction with the auxiliary verb + *not* and then use a subject pronoun.
You're always tired,	**aren't** you?	
We can eat out,	**can't** we?	
We planned to spend time together,	**didn't** we?	
Meg is unhappy,	**isn't** she?	

Negative Statements	Affirmative Tag Questions	Explanation
You aren't happy,	**are you?**	A negative statement has an affirmative tag question. Use the auxiliary verb + a subject pronoun.
You don't like fishing,	**do you?**	
We never have fun together anymore,	**do we?**	

Using Tag Questions

Examples	Explanation
There isn't a lot of free time, **is there?** There are a lot of things to do, **aren't there?**	If the sentence begins with *there is* or *there are*, use *there* in the tag.
This is a typical marriage, **isn't it?** That will be fun, **won't it?**	If the sentence begins with *this* or *that*, use *it* in the tag.
These are normal problems, **aren't they?** Those romantic days are over, **aren't they?**	If the sentence begins with *these* or *those*, use *they* in the tag.
Informal: I'm right, **aren't I?** Formal: I'm right, **am I not?**	*Am I not?* is a very formal tag. Informally, we usually say *aren't I?*

EXERCISE 7   Add a tag question. All the statements are affirmative and have an auxiliary verb.

EXAMPLE   This class is large, ___*isn't it?*___

1. You're a foreign student, ___*aren't you?*___
2. You can understand English, ___*can't you?*___
3. We'll have a test soon, ___*won't we?*___
4. We should study, ___*shouldn't we?*___
5. There's a library at this school, ___*isn't there?*___
6. You'd like to improve your English, ___*wouldn't you?*___

386   Lesson 13

Exercise 7 Variation

First have students underline the verb or modal in the main clause that will be substituted in the tag (*You'd like to improve your English*), then have students write the tags.

7. This is an easy lesson, _isn't it?_

8. I'm asking too many questions, _aren't I?_

EXERCISE **8**   Add a tag question. All the statements are negative and have an auxiliary verb.

EXAMPLE   You can't speak Italian, _can you?_

1. You aren't an American citizen, _are you?_

2. The teacher can't speak your language, _can she?_

3. We shouldn't talk in the library, _should we?_

4. You weren't absent yesterday, _were you?_

5. There aren't any Japanese students in this class, _are there?_

6. This exercise isn't hard, _is it?_

EXERCISE **9**   Add a tag question. All the statements are affirmative. Substitute the main verb with an auxiliary verb in the tag question.

EXAMPLE   You have the textbook, _don't you?_

1. English has a lot of irregular verbs, _doesn't it?_

2. You want to speak English well, _don't you?_

3. You understood the explanation, _didn't you?_

4. You have a cell phone, _don't you?_

5. They bought a laptop last week, _didn't they?_

6. We had a test last week, _didn't we?_

Auxiliary Verbs with *Too* and *Either*; Auxiliary Verbs in Tag Questions   **387**

1. Have students read the direction line. Go over the example in the book. Ask: *If the main clause is negative, what tense will the tag question be in?* (affirmative)

2. Have students complete Exercise 8 individually. Then have students compare answers in pairs. Circulate to observe pair work. Give help as needed.

3. If necessary, review grammar chart **13.4** on page 386.

1. Have students read the direction line. Ask: *If the main verb is not a modal or the verb* be, *what auxiliary verb do we use in the tag?* (the verb *did*) Go over the example.

2. Have students complete Exercise 9 individually. Then have students compare answers in pairs. Circulate to give help as needed.

3. If necessary, review grammar chart **13.4** on page 386.

To save class time, have students do half of the exercise in class and complete the other half for homework. Or assign the entire exercise for homework.

EXERCISE 10

1. Have students read the direction line. Go over the example. Remind students that the statements are negative. Ask: *If the main verb is negative, what will the auxiliary verb be?* (affirmative)
2. Have students complete Exercise 10 individually. Then have students compare answers in pairs. Circulate to observe pair work. Give help as needed.
3. If necessary, review grammar chart **13.4** on page 386.

🕐 To save class time, have students do half of the exercise in class and complete the other half for homework. Or assign the entire exercise for homework.

EXERCISE 11

🎧 *CD 2, Track 29*

1. Have students read the direction line. Say: *Remember, the auxiliary verb should be in the same tense as the main verb and if the main verb is negative, the auxiliary verb should be affirmative.* Explain that this is a conversation between two acquaintances, Bob and Sam, and that Sam can't remember where he met Bob. Go over the example in the book.
2. Have students complete Exercise 11 individually. Check answers as a class.
3. If necessary, review grammar chart **13.4** on page 386.

🕐 To save class time, have students do half of the exercise in class and complete the other half for homework. Or assign the entire exercise for homework.

EXERCISE **10**   Add a tag question. All the statements are negative.

EXAMPLE   We don't have class on Saturday, _____ *do we?* _____

1. The teacher doesn't pronounce your name correctly, _____ *does she?* _____
2. Your brother didn't take the last test, _____ *did he?* _____
3. You didn't bring your dictionary today, _____ *did we?* _____
4. We don't always have homework, _____ *do you?* _____
5. I don't have your phone number, _____ *do I?* _____
6. Your mother doesn't speak English, _____ *does she?* _____

EXERCISE **11**   This is a conversation between two acquaintances,[1] Bob (B) and Sam (S). Sam can't remember where he met Bob. Fill in the blanks with a tag question.

🎧

B: Hi, Sam.

S: Uh, hi. . . .

B: You don't remember me, _____ *do you?* _____
    (example)

S: You look familiar, but I can't remember your name. We were in the same chemistry class last semester, _____ *weren't we?* _____
    (1)

B: No.

S: Then we probably met in math class, _____ *didn't we?* _____
    (2)

B: Wrong again. I'm Meg Wilson's brother.

S: Now I remember you. Meg introduced us at a party last summer, _____ *didn't she?* _____ . And your name
    (3)
    is Bob, _____ *isn't it?* _____
    (4)

B: That's right.

S: How are you, Bob? You graduated last year, _____ *didn't you?* _____
    (5)

[1]An *acquaintance* is a person you don't know well.

Exercise 11 Variation

To provide practice with listening skills, have students close their books and listen to the audio. Repeat the audio as needed. Ask comprehension questions, such as: *Does Sam remember Bob's name?* (no) *Does he remember Bob's face?* (yes) *Did they meet in math class?* (no) Then have students open their books and complete Exercise 11.

B: Yes. And I've got a good job now.

S: You majored in computers, ___*didn't you?*___
   (6)

B: Yes. But I decided to go into real estate.

S: And how's your sister Meg? I never see her anymore. She moved back
   to California, ___*didn't she?*___
   (7)

B: No. She's still here. But she's married now, and she's very busy.

S: Who did she marry?

B: Don Tripton. You met him, ___*didn't you?*___
   (8)

S: Yes, I think so. Say hello to Meg when you see her. It was great
   seeing you again, Bob.

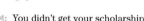 EXERCISE 12 A mother (M) is talking to her daughter (D). Fill in the blanks with
a tag question.

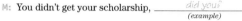

M: You didn't get your scholarship, ___*did you?*___
   (example)

D: How do you know?

M: Well, you look very disappointed. You can apply again next year,
   ___*can't you*___?
   (1)

D: Yes. But what will I do this year?

M: There are government loans, ___*aren't there*___?
   (2)

D: Yes.

M: And you don't have to pay them back until you graduate,
   ___*do you*___?
   (3)

D: No.

M: And your professors will give you letters of recommendation,
   ___*won't they*___?
   (4)

D: I'm sure they will.

M: So don't worry. Just try to get a loan, and you can apply again next
   year for a scholarship.

Auxiliary Verbs with *Too* and *Either*; Auxiliary Verbs in Tag Questions   **389**

EXERCISE 12

 CD 2, Track 30

1. Have students read the direction
   line. Explain that in this
   conversation, a mother is talking to
   her daughter. Go over the example.
2. Have students complete Exercise 12
   individually. Then check answers as
   a class.
3. If necessary, review grammar chart
   13.4 on page 386.

🕐 To save class time, have
   students do half of the exercise
in class and complete the other half for
homework. Or assign the entire
exercise for homework.

Expansion

Exercise 11 Have students practice the conversation in pairs. Ask volunteers to role-play all
or part of the conversation in front of the class.

Exercise 12 Variation

To provide practice with listening skills, have students close their books and listen to the
audio. Repeat the audio as needed. Ask comprehension questions, such as: *Did the daughter
get her scholarship?* (no) *How did the mother know?* (The daughter looks very disappointed.)
When can the daughter apply for the scholarship again? (next year) Then have students open
their books and complete Exercise 12.

Expansion

Exercise 12 Have students practice the conversation in pairs. Ask volunteers to role-play all
or part of the conversation in front of the class.

13.5 | Answering a Tag Question

1. Have students cover up the explanations side of grammar chart **13.5** on page 390. Say: *Study the tag questions and the short answers. Do you see any patterns?* Have students try to figure out the patterns.

2. Have students look at grammar chart **13.5** on page 390. Have them look at the explanations. Go over all the examples. Explain that answering *no* or *yes* to tag questions can get a little confusing even for native speakers. Often a second sentence is needed to clarify a response.

EXERCISE 13

1. Have students read the direction line. Say: *First complete the short answers on the left side. Then work with a partner to decide the meaning of the short answer.* Go over the example.

2. Have students complete Exercise 13. Go over answers with the class. Then have students take turns asking and answering the questions.

3. If necessary, review grammar chart **13.5** on page 390.

13.5 | Answering a Tag Question

Statement with Tag Question	Short Answer	Explanation
Meg and Don are married now, **aren't they?**	**Yes,** they are.	When we use a negative tag, we expect the answer to be *yes*.
They work hard, **don't they?**	**Yes,** they do.	
They don't have much free time, **do they?**	**No,** they don't.	When we use an affirmative tag, we expect the answer to be *no*.
Meg doesn't like to go fishing, **does she?**	**No,** she doesn't.	
Don: You aren't happy, **are you?**	*Meg:* **Yes,** I am. I love you.	Answering *yes* to an affirmative tag shows disagreement.
Meg: You like to go to movies, **don't you?**	*Don:* **No,** I don't. I like to watch movies at home on TV.	Answering *no* to a negative tag shows disagreement.

EXERCISE 13 Complete the answer in the left column. Then check the meaning of the answer in the right column. (You may work with a partner.)

A: You don't have a car, do you? B: Yes, ___I do.___	✓ Person B has a car. Person B doesn't have a car.
A: You aren't married, are you? B: No, I ___'m not.___	Person B is married. ✓ Person B isn't married.
A: You don't like this city, do you? B: No, ___I don't.___	Person B likes this city. ✓ Person B doesn't like this city.
A: The U.S. is the best country in the world, isn't it? B: No, ___it isn't.___	Person B agrees with the statement. ✓ Person B doesn't agree with the statement.
A: You don't speak Russian, do you? B: No, ___I don't.___	Person B speaks Russian. ✓ Person B doesn't speak Russian.
A: You can drive, can't you? B: No, ___I can't.___	Person B can drive. ✓ Person B can't drive.
A: You don't have a watch, do you? B: Yes, ___I do.___	✓ Person B has a watch. Person B doesn't have a watch.
A: You work on Saturday, don't you? B: Yes, ___I do.___	✓ Person B works on Saturday. Person B doesn't work on Saturday.

Expansion

Exercise 13 Have students clarify their answers with another sentence. For example: *You don't have a car, do you? Yes, I do. I have a minivan.*

EXERCISE 14   Read a statement to another student and add a tag question. The other student will tell you if this information is correct or not.

EXAMPLES   You speak Polish, _don't you?_
No, I don't. I speak Ukrainian.

You aren't from Poland, _are you?_
No, I'm not. I'm from Ukraine.

You came to the U.S. two years ago, _didn't you?_
Yes, I did.

1. You're married, _aren't you?_
2. You have children, _don't you?_
3. You didn't study English in elementary school, _did you?_
4. You have a car, _don't you?_
5. You don't live alone, _do you?_
6. You'll take another English course next semester, _won't you?_
7. You won't graduate this year, _will you?_
8. You took the last test, _didn't you?_
9. You have to work on Saturday, _don't you?_
10. The teacher doesn't speak your language, _does she?_
11. You can type, _can't you?_
12. This class isn't too hard for you, _is it?_
13. There was a test last Friday, _wasn't there?_
14. You don't speak German, _do you?_
15. I'm asking you a lot of personal questions, _aren't I?_

EXERCISE 15   Fill in the blanks with a tag question and an answer that tells if the information is true or not.

A: You come from Russia, _don't you?_
(example)

B: _No, I don't_. I come from Ukraine.
_(1)_

A: They speak Polish in Ukraine, _don't they?_
_(2)_

B: _No, they don't_. They speak Ukrainian and Russian.
_(3)_

Auxiliary Verbs with _Too_ and _Either_; Auxiliary Verbs in Tag Questions   **391**

EXERCISE 14

1. Have students read the direction line. Say: _If your answer is negative, then add the correct information._ Go over the examples. Have students model the examples.
2. Have students complete the tag questions individually. Then have students ask and answer questions in pairs. Circulate to observe pair work. Give help as needed.
3. If necessary, review grammar chart **13.5** on page 390.

🕐   To save class time, have students do half of the exercise in class and complete the other half in writing for homework, answering the question themselves. Or if students do not need speaking practice, the entire exercise may be skipped or done in writing.

EXERCISE 15

🎧 **CD 2, Track 31**

1. Say: _In this conversation, you will be writing tag questions and giving short answers._ Have students read the direction line. Go over the example in the book.
2. Have students complete Exercise 15 individually. Then check answers as a class.
3. If necessary, review grammar chart **13.5** on page 390.

🕐   To save class time, have students do half of the exercise in class and complete the other half for homework. Or assign the entire exercise for homework.

Expansion

Exercise 14 Have students create five more statements with tag questions to ask their partners. Then have students take turns asking and answering their new questions.

Exercise 15 Variation

To provide practice with listening skills, have students close their books and listen to the audio. Repeat the audio as needed. Ask comprehension questions, such as: _Where does person B come from?_ (Ukraine) _Do people speak Polish in Ukraine?_ (No, they speak Ukrainian and Russian.) _Is Ukraine part of Russia?_ (no) Then have students open their books and complete Exercise 15.

1. Say: *This conversation is between Meg, the woman from the reading, and her best friend, Lydia.* Have students read the direction line. Go over the example in the book.
2. Have students complete Exercise 16 individually. Then check answers as a class.
3. If necessary, review grammar chart **13.5** on page 390.

🕐 To save class time, have students do half of the exercise in class and complete the other half for homework. Or assign the entire exercise for homework.

A: Ukraine isn't part of Russia, _____is it?_____
      (4)

B: _____No, it isn't_____. Ukraine and Russia are different. They were
      (5)

both part of the former Soviet Union.

A: You come from a big city, _____don't you?_____
      (6)

B: _____Yes, I do_____. I come from Kiev. It's the capital of Ukraine.
      (7)

It's very big.

A: Your parents aren't here, _____are they?_____
      (8)

B: _____Yes, they are_____. We came together two years ago. I live with
      (9)

my parents.

A: You studied English in your country, _____didn't you?_____
      (10)

B: _____No, I didn't_____. I only studied Russian and German. I never
      (11)

studied English there.

A: You're not going to go back to live in your country,

_____are you?_____
      (12)

B: _____No, I'm not_____. I'm an immigrant here. I plan to become an
      (13)

American citizen.

EXERCISE 16 This is a conversation between Meg (M) and her best friend, Lydia (L). Fill in the blanks with tag questions and answers.

🎧

M: Hello?
L: Hi, Meg. This is Lydia.
M: Oh, hi, Lydia.
L: Can you talk? I hear the TV in the background. Don's home,

_____isn't he?_____
      (example)

M: _____Yes_____, he _____is_____. He's watching
      (1)   (2)

TV, as usual.

Expansion

Exercise 15 Have students practice the conversation in pairs. Then ask volunteers to act out the conversation for the class.

Exercise 16 Variation

To provide practice with listening skills, have students close their books and listen to the audio. Repeat the audio as needed. Ask comprehension questions, such as: *Where's Don?* (at home) *What's he doing?* (watching TV) *Who is Peter?* (Lydia's new boyfriend) Then have students open their books and complete Exercise 16.

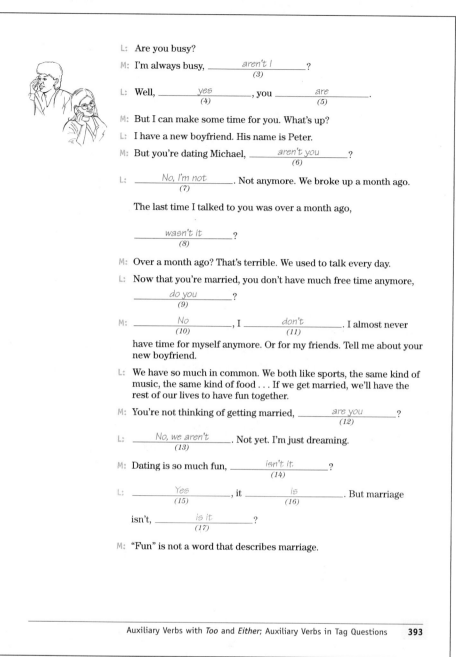

L: Are you busy?

M: I'm always busy, ___aren't I___ (3) ?

L: Well, ___yes___ (4), you ___are___ (5).

M: But I can make some time for you. What's up?

L: I have a new boyfriend. His name is Peter.

M: But you're dating Michael, ___aren't you___ (6) ?

L: ___No, I'm not___ (7). Not anymore. We broke up a month ago.

The last time I talked to you was over a month ago,

___wasn't it___ (8) ?

M: Over a month ago? That's terrible. We used to talk every day.

L: Now that you're married, you don't have much free time anymore,

___do you___ (9) ?

M: ___No___ (10), I ___don't___ (11). I almost never have time for myself anymore. Or for my friends. Tell me about your new boyfriend.

L: We have so much in common. We both like sports, the same kind of music, the same kind of food . . . If we get married, we'll have the rest of our lives to have fun together.

M: You're not thinking of getting married, ___are you___ (12) ?

L: ___No, we aren't___ (13). Not yet. I'm just dreaming.

M: Dating is so much fun, ___isn't it___ (14) ?

L: ___Yes___ (15), it ___is___ (16). But marriage

isn't, ___is it___ (17) ?

M: "Fun" is not a word that describes marriage.

Expansion

Exercise 16 Have students practice the conversation in pairs. Then ask volunteers to act out the conversation for the class.

Summary of Lesson 13

1. **Use auxiliary verbs to avoid repetition of the same verb phrase.** Have students cover the chart in the Summary on page 394. On the board, create an exercise from the summary chart. Have students fill in the blanks.

*Affirmative + **too***
Meg has a job, and Don _____.
Meg is busy, and Don _____.

*Negative + **either***
Meg doesn't work on Saturdays, and Don _____.
Meg can't find free time, and Don _____.

Negative
Meg finished college, but Don _____

Don likes fishing, but Meg _____

Affirmative
Don doesn't like movies, but Meg _____

Don didn't want a big wedding, but Meg _____.

Then have students compare their answers with the Summary on page 394. If necessary, have students review:

13.1 Auxiliary Verbs with *Too* and *Either* (p. 380)
13.2 Auxiliary Verbs with Opposite Statements (p. 381).

L: But you had a lot of fun with Don before you got married, _____*didn't you*_____ ?
    (18)

M: _____*Yes*_____ , we _____*did*_____ . But things
    (19)   (20)
changed after the wedding. Now all we do together is laundry, shopping, and cleaning.

L: That doesn't sound very interesting. But there are good things about being married, _____*aren't there*_____ ?
                                                    (21)

M: Of course. Don's my best friend. We help each other with all our problems.

L: Before you got married, I was your best friend, _____*wasn't I*_____? But now I almost never see you.
    (22)

M: You're right, Lydia. I'll try harder to call you more often.

SUMMARY OF LESSON 13

1. Use auxiliary verbs to avoid repetition of the same verb phrase.

Affirmative	and	Shortened Affirmative + *Too*
Meg has a job,	and	Don does too.
Meg is busy,	and	Don is too.

Negative	and	Shortened Negative + *Either*
Meg doesn't work on Saturdays,	and	Don doesn't either.
Meg can't find free time,	and	Don can't either.

Affirmative	but	Shortened Negative
Meg finished college,	but	Don didn't.
Don likes fishing,	but	Meg doesn't.

Negative	but	Shortened Affirmative
Don doesn't like movies,	but	Meg does.
Don didn't want a big wedding,	but	Meg did.

394 Lesson **13**

2. Use auxiliary verbs in tag questions

Affirmative	Negative Tag
You're busy now,	aren't you?
We have a hard life,	don't we?
There are a lot of things to do,	aren't there?

Negative	Affirmative Tag
You don't like fishing,	do you?
I can't go fishing alone,	can I?
We never have time together,	do we?

EDITING ADVICE

1. Don't omit the auxiliary from a shortened sentence with *too* or *either*.

    My brother has a new house, and I ~~do~~ too.

    John didn't take the test, and I ~~didn't~~ either.

2. Don't confuse *too* and *either*.

    Jack doesn't speak French, and his wife doesn't ~~too~~ *either*.

3. If half your sentence is negative and half is affirmative, the connecting word is *but*, not *and*.

    He doesn't speak French, and ~~but~~ his wife does.

4. Be careful to answer a tag question correctly.

    New York isn't the capital of the U.S., is it? ~~Yes~~ *No*, it isn't.

5. Use a pronoun (or *there*) in the tag question.

    That's your hat, isn't ~~that~~ *it*?

    There's some milk in the refrigerator, isn't ~~it~~ *there*?

6. Be careful to use the correct auxiliary verb and the correct tense.

    Her sister didn't go to the party, ~~does~~ *did* she?

    She won't go back to her country, ~~does~~ *will* she?

2. **Use auxiliary verbs in tag questions.** Have students cover the chart in the Summary on page 395. On the board, create an exercise from the Summary chart. Have students fill in the blanks.

Negative Tag
You're busy now, _____?
We have a hard life, _____?
There are a lot of things to do, _____?

Affirmative Tag
You don't like fishing, _____?
I can't go fishing alone, _____?
We never have time together, _____?

Then have students compare their answers with the Summary on page 395. If necessary, have students review:
13.3 Tag Questions (p. 384)
13.4 Auxiliary Verbs in Tag Questions (p. 386)
13.5 Answering a Tag Question (p. 390).

Editing Advice

Have students close their books. Write the example sentences without editing marks or corrections on the board. For example:

1. My brother has a new house, and I too.

2. John didn't take the test, and I either.

Ask students to correct each sentence and provide a rule or explanation for each correction. This activity can be done individually, in pairs, or as a class. After students have corrected each sentence, tell them to turn to page 395. Say: *Now compare your work with the Editing Advice in the book.*

Lesson 13 Test/Review

For additional practice, review, and assessment materials, see Assessment CD-ROM with *ExamView Pro, More Grammar Practice* Workbook 1, Interactive CD-ROM, and Web site http://elt.thomson.com/gic

PART 1

1. Part 1 may be used in addition to the Assessment CD-ROM with *ExamView Pro* as an in-class test to assess student performance. Have students read the direction line. Ask: *Does every sentence have a mistake?* (no) Go over the examples with the class.
2. Have students complete the assignment individually. Collect for assessment.
3. If necessary, have students review: **Lesson 13.**

PART 2

1. Part 2 may be used in addition to the Assessment CD-ROM with *ExamView Pro* as an in-class test to assess student performance. Have students read the direction line. Point out that this is a conversation between two students who are meeting for the first time. Go over the examples with the class. Say: *Remember, not every sentence needs* too *or* either.
2. Have students complete the exercise individually. Collect for assessment.
3. If necessary, have students review:
   13.1 Auxiliary Verbs with *Too* and *Either* (p. 380)
   13.2 Auxiliary Verbs with Opposite Statements (p. 381).

LESSON 13 TEST/REVIEW

PART **1** Find the mistakes with the underlined words and correct them. Not every sentence has a mistake. If the sentence is correct, write *C.*

EXAMPLES Today is Friday, isn't ~~today~~? *it*

My friend doesn't like soccer, and I don't either. *C*

1. My mother speaks English well, ~~and~~ my father doesn't. *but*
2. My mother speaks English well, and my brother does too. *C*
3. The vice president doesn't live in the White House, does he? ~~Yes~~, he doesn't. *No*
4. A soccer team has 11 players, and a football team too. *does*
5. Bob doesn't have a car, and Mary doesn't too. *either*
6. You're not an American citizen, do you? *are*
7. You didn't finish your dinner, do you? *did*
8. There will be a test next week, won't there? *C*
9. Your father can't come to the U.S., can he? *C*
10. This is the last question, isn't this? *it*

PART **2** This is a conversation between two students who meet for the first time. Fill in the blanks with an auxiliary verb to complete this conversation. Use *either* or *too* when necessary.

C: Hi. My name is Carlos. I'm a new student.

E: I _____*am too*_____. My name is Elena.
   (example)

C: I come from Mexico.

E: Oh, really? I _____*do too*_____. I come from a small town in the northern part of Mexico.
   (1)

C: I come from Mexico City. I love big cities.

E: I _____*don't*_____. I prefer small towns.
   (2)

C: How do you like living here in Los Angeles?

E: I don't like it much, but my sister _____*does*_____. She has a
   (3)

   good job, but I _____*don't*_____. I miss my job back home.
   (4)

396 Lesson **13**

Lesson Review

To use Parts 1 and 2 as a review, assign them as homework or use them as in-class activities to be completed individually or in pairs. Check answers and review errors as a class. Reteach grammar points that students haven't mastered. Then student learning may be assessed using a test generated from the Assessment CD-ROM with *ExamView Pro.*

C: I love it here, and my family ___does too___ . The climate is
     (5)
   similar to the climate of Mexico City.

E: What about the air quality? Mexico City doesn't have clean air, and Los
   Angeles ___doesn't either___ , so you probably feel right at home.
                 (6)

C: Ha! You're right about the air quality, but there are many nice things
   about Los Angeles. Do you want to get a cup of coffee and continue
   this conversation? I don't have any more classes today.

E: I ___don't either___ , but I have to go home now. I enjoyed our talk.
        (7)

C: I ___did too___ . Maybe we can continue it some other time.
        (8)
   Well, see you in class tomorrow.

PART 3   In this conversation, a new student is trying to find out
         information about the school and class. Add a tag question.

A: There's a parking lot at the school, ___isn't there?___
                                            (example)

B: Yes. It's east of the building.

A: The teacher's American, ___isn't she?___
                               (1)

B: Yes, she is.

A: She doesn't give hard tests, ___does she?___
                                    (2)

B: Not too easy, not too hard.

A: We'll have a day off for Christmas, ___won't we?___
                                           (3)

B: We'll have a whole week off.

A: We have to write compositions, ___don't we?___
                                      (4)

B: A few.

A: And we can't use a dictionary when we write a composition,
   ___can we?___
       (5)

B: Who told you that? Of course we can. You're very nervous about
   school, ___aren't you?___
               (6)

A: Yes, I am. It isn't easy to learn a new language, ___is it?___
                                                         (7)

B: No.

PART 3

1. Part 3 may be used in addition
   to the Assessment CD-ROM with
   ExamView Pro as an in-class test to
   assess student performance. Have
   students read the direction line. Go
   over the example with the class.

2. Have students complete the
   exercise individually. Collect for
   assessment.

3. If necessary, have students review:
   13.3 Tag Questions (p. 384)
   13.4 Auxiliary Verbs in Tag
       Questions (p. 386)
   13.5 Answering a Tag Question
       (p. 390).

Lesson Review

To use Part 3 as a review, assign it as homework or use it as an in-class activity to be
completed individually or in pairs. Check answers and review errors as a class. Reteach
grammar points that students haven't mastered. Then student learning may be assessed using
a test generated from the Assessment CD-ROM with *ExamView Pro*.

Expansion Activities

These expansion activities provide opportunities for students to interact with one another and further develop their speaking and writing skills. Encourage students to use grammar from this Lesson whenever possible.

🕐 To save class time, assign parts of the activities as homework. Then use class time for interaction and communication. If students do not need additional speaking practice, some of the activities may be assigned as writing activities for homework, or skipped altogether.

CLASSROOM ACTIVITIES

1. Have students work individually to complete the information. Then put students in pairs to take turns asking and answering questions.

A: And I should ask questions about things I want to know,
_____shouldn't I?_____
(8)

B: Yes, of course. You don't have any more questions,
_____do you?_____
(9)

A: No.

B: Well, I'll see you in the next class. Bye.

EXPANSION ACTIVITIES

Classroom
Activities

1. Complete each statement. Then find a partner and compare yourself to your partner by using an auxiliary verb.

EXAMPLES
A: I speak _____Chinese_____.
B: I do too. OR I don't.

A: I don't speak _____Spanish_____.
B: I don't either. OR I do.

a. I speak _____.
b. I don't speak _____.
c. I can _____.
d. I have _____.
e. I don't have _____.
f. I'm _____.
g. I usually drink _____ every day.
h. I'm going to _____ next week.
i. I come from _____.
j. I'm wearing _____ today.
k. I bought _____ last week.
l. I went _____ last week.
m. I don't like _____.
n. I brought _____ to the U.S.
o. I don't like to eat _____.
p. I can't _____ very well.
q. I should _____ more.

Expansion

Classroom Activities For activity 1, have students compare answers in groups. Then have groups report interesting results to the class.

2. Find a partner. Tell your partner some things that you think you know about him or her and about his or her native culture or country. Your partner will tell you if you are right or wrong.

   EXAMPLES   The capital of your country is New Delhi, isn't it?
   Hindus don't eat beef, do they?
   You're studying engineering, aren't you?

3. Work with a partner to match Column A with Column B.
   (Alternate activity: Teacher, copy this page. Cut the copied page along the lines. Give half the class statements from Column A and half the class tag questions from Column B. The students walk around the room to match the statement to the tag question.)

Column A	Column B
Washington is the capital of the U.S.,	is it?
Los Angeles isn't the biggest city,	isn't there?
Puerto Ricans are American citizens,	don't they?
Americans have freedom of speech,	does it?
There's an election every four years,	are you?
Americans fought in World War II,	wasn't she?
There will be a presidential election in 2012,	isn't it?
The president lives in the White House,	doesn't he?
George Washington was the first American president,	won't there?
You're not an American citizen,	did she?
Amelia Earhart didn't come back from her last flight,	aren't they?
Florida doesn't have cold winters,	wasn't he?
Helen Keller was a great woman,	didn't they?

4. The teacher will read each statement. If the statement is true for you, stand up. Students will take turns making statements about two people.

   EXAMPLE   Teacher: Stand up if you drank coffee this morning.

   Student: I drank coffee this morning, and Tom did too.
   Mario didn't drink coffee this morning, and
   Sofia didn't either.
   I drank coffee this morning, but Lisa didn't.

   Stand up if you . . .
   • have more than five sisters and brothers
   • walked to class today
   • will buy a house in the next two years

2. Tell students to find a partner they don't know very well. Have volunteers tell the class something new they learned about their partners.

3. Have students work in pairs to complete the matching activity, or give each student a clause and have them circulate to find the matching clause.

4. Model the activity. Have a student call out the first statement. Then stand up and make a statement as if the statement were true for you.

Expansion

Classroom Activities For activity 3, have students ask a partner the completed tag question. The partner answers the tag question. Then switch roles. For example:

A: *Washington is the capital of the U.S., isn't it?*
B: *Yes, it is.*
B: *Los Angeles isn't the biggest city, is it?*
A: *No, it isn't. New York is the biggest city.*

CLASSROOM ACTIVITIES (*cont.*)

5. Have students work with a partner to write six to ten questions on what they think they know about the U.S. and Americans. Respond to the questions in front of the class.

6. Have students discuss in groups what they feel makes a strong marriage. Then have groups report to the class. If students have trouble, suggest they think about what makes a weak marriage and what would be needed to make the marriage strong.

WRITE ABOUT IT

1. Students can choose any of the topics in the book, or they can write a comparison about another topic that interests them.

2. Put students in pairs that do not know each other very well. Have them talk for a few minutes to get to know their similarities and differences. Then have volunteers talk about things they found out about their partners that surprised them.

INTERNET ACTIVITY

Have students discuss any interesting advice they found on Web sites in groups. Then have groups report to the class.

- are wearing running shoes
- have a photo of a family member in your pocket or bag
- want to review this lesson
- went to a movie last week
- can't swim
- plan to buy a car soon
- are tired now
- aren't married
- ate pizza today
- speak Polish
- don't like this game
- can understand American TV
- didn't take the last test

5. Tell the teacher what you think you know about the U.S. or Americans. You may work with a partner. The teacher will tell you if you're right or wrong.

   EXAMPLES Most Americans don't speak a foreign language, do they?
   Alaska is the largest state, isn't it?

6. Discuss what makes a strong marriage.

Write About it

1. Choose two sports, religions, countries, people, or stores and write sentences comparing them.

   EXAMPLE   my mother and my father
   My father speaks English well, but my mother doesn't.
   My father isn't an American citizen, and my mother isn't either.
   My father was born in 1938, and my mother was too.

2. Find a partner. Write a list of some things you have in common and some differences you have.

   EXAMPLES *Alex plays the violin, and I do too.*
   Alex is majoring in chemistry, but I'm not.
   Alex doesn't have a computer, and I don't either.

   _____
   _____
   _____

Internet Activity

Find a Web site that gives marriage, dating, or relationship advice. Bring an article to class and discuss the advice.

Additional Activities at http://elt.thomson.com/gic

Internet Activity Variation

Remind students that if they don't have Internet access, they can use Internet facilities at a public library or they can use traditional research methods to find out information including looking at encyclopedias, magazines, books, journals, and newspapers.

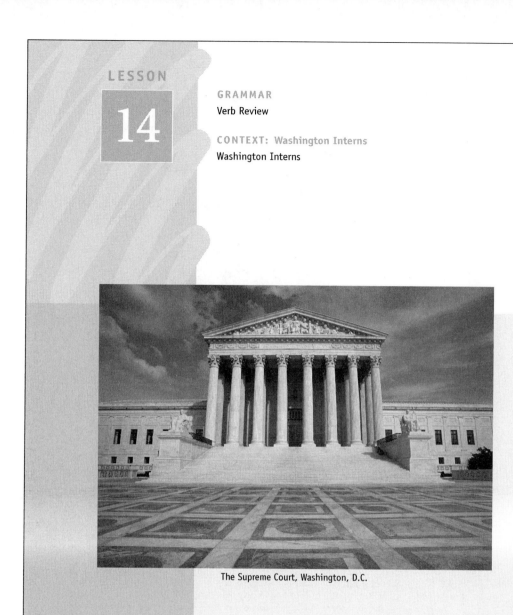

LESSON

14

GRAMMAR
Verb Review

CONTEXT: Washington Interns
Washington Interns

The Supreme Court, Washington, D.C.

401

Lesson | 14

Lesson Overview

GRAMMAR

1. Ask: *What did we study in Lesson 13?* (auxiliary verbs with *too* and *either*; auxiliary verbs in tag questions)
2. *What are we going to study in this lesson?* (all the verb tenses) *Do you remember all the tenses we've learned?* Have students give examples. Write them on the board.

CONTEXT

1. Ask: *How many people here have ever worked as an intern? Where?*
2. Have students share their knowledge and personal experiences.

Photo

Direct students' attention to the photo. Ask: *Where is the Supreme Court?* (in Washington, D.C.) *Have you ever been there?*

🕐 To save class time, have students do the Test/Review at the end of the lesson, or administer a lesson test generated from the Assessment CD-ROM with *ExamView®️ Pro.* Skip sections of the lesson that students have already mastered. You may also assign some sections for self-study for extra credit.

Expansion

Theme The topic for this lesson can be enhanced with the following ideas:

1. Advertisements seeking Washington interns
2. Articles about being an intern

Theme Ask students to talk about government internships in their countries. Does this type of work exist in their countries? Are they paid or voluntary positions?

Culture Note

There are three branches of the U.S. government: the executive (the president), the legislative (the congress), and the judicial (the Supreme Court). The first Supreme Court was assembled in 1790. The principal role of the Supreme Court is to act as the final authority on the U.S. Constitution. U.S. justices are appointed for life. There have only been 16 chief justices in American history. Compare that with more than 40 U.S. presidents!

Washington Interns (Reading)

1. Have students look at the photo. Ask: *What kind of person does this young woman seem like?* (confident, determined, ambitious, etc.)
2. Have students look at the title of the reading. Ask: *What is the reading about?* Have students use the title and photo to make predictions about the reading.
3. Preteach any vocabulary words your students may not know, such as *gain* and *manage*.

BEFORE YOU READ

1. Have students discuss the questions in pairs.
2. Ask for a few volunteers to share their answers with the class.

🕐 To save class time, skip "Before You Read" or have students prepare answers for homework ahead of time.

Reading 🎧 *CD 2, Track 33*

1. Have students first read the text silently. Tell them to pay special attention to verb tenses. Then play the audio and have students read along silently.
2. Check students' comprehension. Ask questions such as: *Do interns get paid?* (no) *Why is it a good idea that Lena interns at the Supreme Court?* (She's going to law school next year.) *How did she feel at first?* (lost and lonely) *What else is she doing?* (taking classes at Georgetown University) *Who does she share an apartment with?* (Nicole, an intern at the Department of Education) *What is something she doesn't like about her job?* (wearing formal clothes) *How did she pay for her work clothes?* (She used her parents' credit card.)

🕐 To save class time, have students do the reading for homework ahead of time.

WASHINGTON INTERNS

 Before You Read

1. How can a college student get work experience?
2. What do most college students do during their summer break?

🎧 Read the information and letter that follows it. Pay special attention to verb tenses.

Some college students **want** to find interesting work and **gain** valuable experience in the summer. One way **is** to work as an intern in Washington, D.C. Interns **don't get** paid; the reward **comes** from the experience and knowledge they **gain**. Interns **learn** about the U.S. government and politics.

Lena Rosen **decided** to work in Washington last summer as an intern. Here **is** a letter she **wrote** to her parents.

Dear Mom and Dad,

I **can't** believe it! I'**m working** at the Supreme Court. I'**m gaining** so much experience here. When I **go** to law school next year, I **will have** a much greater understanding of American law. And when I **apply** for a job, this internship **will look** really good on my résumé.

At first, I **felt** a little lost and lonely because I **didn't know** anyone. But that soon **changed.** Through my classes and job, I **meet** new and interesting people every day.

Reading Variation

To practice listening skills, have students first listen to the audio alone. Ask a few comprehension questions. Repeat the audio if necessary. Then have students open their books and read along as they listen to the audio.

Reading Glossary

gain: to obtain, acquire
manage: to run something, be in charge of something

Besides my work, **I'm taking** classes at Georgetown University. My professors are great! **I'm learning** so much. My knowledge about American law **is increasing** rapidly.

I have an interesting roommate, too. She**'s** from California. Her name **is** Nicole. She**'s working** at the Department of Education. She**'s planning** to become a teacher. We **have** a small but comfortable apartment. We **have to shop** and **make** our own meals. So besides learning about the Supreme Court, **I'm learning** how to cook. **I'm becoming** much more responsible. **Are** you surprised?

Whenever Nicole and I **have** free time, we **go** to see the interesting places in Washington. But we rarely **have** free time because of our jobs and our classes. We **might go** to the art museum this weekend if we have enough time.

There **is** one thing I **don't like:** I **have to wear** formal clothes every day. I **can't wear** blue jeans at my job. We **must look** very professional for our jobs. I **didn't have** the right kind of clothes when I **arrived,** so I **went** shopping and **spent** about $500 on new clothes. I **hope** you **don't mind.** I **put** the charges on your credit card. As you know, **I'm not making** any money here. But **don't worry. I'm not going to spend** any more money.

When I **get** home, **I'll tell** you much more about my experience this summer. I **know** I **should write** more often, but I just **don't have** the time.

Love,
Lena

**FAQs (Frequently Asked Questions)
About Washington Internships:**

* How **does** a student **get** an internship?
  Students **should contact** their senators or representatives to apply for an internship.

* What kind of work **do** interns **do?**
  They **work** in research, **help** plan events, **manage** databases, and **write** for newsletters.

* Where **do** they **live?**
  They **live** in on-campus apartments at Georgetown University.

* **Do** they **have to take** classes?
  Yes, they **do.** And they **must participate** in other activities.

* How busy **is** their schedule?
  It **is** *very* busy. Interns **learn** about education, politics, and government.

* **Will** they **receive** college credit for the internship?
  Yes. They **will receive** six hours of college credit.

Verb Review   **403**

14.1 | Verb Tenses

1. Have students cover up grammar chart **14.1**. Write on the board:
   simple present tense
   present continuous tense
   future tense
   simple past tense
   be
   modals
   Say: *Find two examples for each in the reading.* Have volunteers write example sentences under each category on the board.

2. Have students look at grammar chart **14.1**. Go over the examples and explanations in the chart.

14.1 | Verb Tenses

Simple Present Tense

Examples	Uses
Washington **is** the capital of the U.S. Some students **want** summer jobs. Washington interns **take** classes at Georgetown University.	• Facts
American students **have** vacation in the summer. Many American students **wear** blue jeans to class.	• Customs and habits
They **take** classes every day. When they **have** free time, they **go** to interesting places.	• Regular activities
I **have** a great roommate now. I **like** my job now.	• With nonaction verbs
When I **get** home, I'll show you my pictures.	• In a future time clause
If you **become** an intern in Washington, you will get valuable experience.	• In a future *if* clause
My roommate **is** from California. My roommate **comes** from San Diego.	• With place of origin

Present Continuous Tense

Examples	Explanation
Lena **is writing** a letter to her parents now.	• Actions that are happening now
Lena **is learning** how to cook. She **isn't making** any money this summer.	• Actions that are happening in a present time period

Future Tense

Examples	Explanation
They **are going to return** to college in the fall. Nicole **is going to become** a teacher.	• Plans for the future (use *be going to*)
I **will** never **forget** this experience. This experience **is going to help** me in my future.	• Predictions (use *will* or *be going to*)
I'll **write** more later.	• Promises (use *will*)

404 Lesson 14

Simple Past Tense

Examples	Explanation
I **went** shopping because I **needed** clothes. I **spent** $500 on clothes. I **used** your credit card.	▫ Actions that happened at a specific time in the past

Be

Examples	Explanation
Washington **is** the capital of the U.S.	▫ To classify or define the subject
Washington **is** interesting.	▫ To describe the subject
The Supreme Court **is** in Washington.	▫ To tell the location of the subject
Nicole **is** from San Diego.	▫ With a place of origin
She **was born** in California.	▫ With *born*
There **are** many government buildings in Washington.	▫ With *there*

Modals

Examples	Explanation
Lena **can** wear jeans to class. Lena **can** study at night.	▫ Permission ▫ Ability
She **should** write to her parents more often. If you want more information about internships, you **should** write to your senator.	▫ Advisability
She **must** look professional in her job. Interns **must** participate in activities.	▫ Necessity
They **might** go to the art museum this weekend. Lena **may** visit Nicole in California next year.	▫ Possibility

Language Notes:

1. An infinitive doesn't show tense.
   I **want to go** to Washington.
   She **wants to go** to Washington.
   They **wanted to go** to Washington.
2. The verb after a modal is always the base form.
   She **should study.**
   Wrong: She should to study.
   Wrong: She should studying.

Verb Review   **405**

3. Direct students to the Language Notes. Point out that infinitives don't show tense and that verbs after modals are always the base form.

1. Have students read the direction line. Go over the example in the book. Say: *This exercise is based on the reading on pages 402–403. Check your work after you complete the exercise.*
2. Have students complete Exercise 1 individually. Then have students check their answers against the reading on pages 402–403.
3. As students check their answers, circulate around the room to see if there are any common trouble spots. Review those points with the whole class.

EXERCISE **1** Fill in the blanks with the correct tense or form of the verb in parentheses ( ).

I can't _____*believe*_____ it! I _____*'m working*_____ at
      (example: believe)   *(1 work)*

the Supreme Court now. I _____*'m gaining*_____ so much experience
                     (2 gain)

here. When I _____*go*_____ to law school next year, I
            (3 go)

_____*will have*_____ a much greater understanding of American law.
    (4 have)

And when I _____*apply*_____ for a job, this internship
          (5 apply)

_____*will look*_____ really good on my résumé.
    (6 look)

At first, I _____*felt*_____ a little lost and lonely because I
           (7 feel)

_____*didn't know*_____ anyone. But that soon _____*changed*_____.
  (8 not/know)   *(9 change)*

Through my classes and job, I _____*meet*_____ new and
                     (10 meet)

interesting people every day.

Besides my work, I _____*take/am taking*_____ classes at Georgetown
              (11 take)

University. My professors _____*are*_____ great! I
                   (12 be)

_____*'m learning*_____ so much. My knowledge about American law
    (13 learn)

_____*is increasing*_____ rapidly.
    (14 increase)

I _____*have*_____ an interesting roommate, too. She
      (15 have)

_____*is*_____ from California. Her name is Nicole. She
    (16 be)

_____*works*_____ at the Department of Education. She's planning
    (17 work)

to _____*to become*_____ a teacher. We _____*have*_____ a small
    (18 become)   *(19 have)*

but comfortable apartment. We have to _____*shop*_____ and
                     (20 shop)

_____*make*_____ our own meals. So besides learning about the
    (21 make)

Supreme Court, I _____ 'm learning _____ how to cook. I
(22 learn)

_____ am becoming _____ much more responsible. Are you surprised?
(23 become)

Whenever Nicole and I _____ have _____ free time, we
(24 have)

_____ go _____ to see the interesting places in Washington. But
(25 go)

we rarely _____ have _____ free time because of our jobs and our
(26 have)

classes. We might _____ go _____ to the art museum this
(27 go)

weekend if we _____ have _____ enough time.
(28 have)

There is one thing I don't like: I have to wear formal clothes every day.

I can't _____ wear _____ blue jeans at my job. We must
(29 wear)

_____ look _____ very professional for our jobs.
(30 look)

I _____ didn't have _____ the right kind of clothes when I
(31 not/have)

_____ arrived _____, so I _____ went _____ shopping and
(32 arrive)   (33 go)

_____ spent _____ about $500 on new clothes. I hope you
(34 spend)

_____ don't mind _____. I _____ put _____ the charges on your
(35 not/mind)   (36 put)

credit card. As you know, I'm not making any money here. But don't

worry. I _____ 'm not spending _____ any more money.
(37 not/spend)

When I _____ get _____ home, I _____ 'll tell _____ you
(38 get)   (39 tell)

much more about my experience this summer. I know I should

_____ write _____ more often, but I just don't have the time.
(40 write)

Love,
Lena

_____

Verb Review   **407**

Exercise 1 Variation

Have students exchange books with a partner to check their work.

14.2 | Statements and Questions

1. Have students close their books and work in pairs to write statements and questions using the tenses and verbs in the chart. For the simple present tense, write the following on the board:

   simple present tense (live/wear)
   Say: *Write the following for the simple present tense:*
   1. an affirmative statement
   2. a negative statement
   3. a question
   4. a short answer
   5. a wh- question
   6. a negative question
   7. a subject question
   Tell students to write seven sentences with the -s form and seven sentences with the base form. Say: *Use the verbs in parentheses.* Ask a volunteer to give an example of an -s form and a base form in a sentence. Circulate to observe pair work. Give help as needed.

2. For the present continuous tense, write on the board:
   present continuous tense (plan/take)
   Tell students to use one of the verbs in parentheses to write the seven sentence types using *is,* and the other verb to write another seven sentences using *are.*

3. For the future tense, write on the board:
   future tense (go/buy)
   Tell students to use one of the verbs in parentheses to write the seven sentence types using *will,* and the other verb to write another seven sentences using *be going to.*

4. For the simple past tense, write on the board:
   simple past tense (use/buy)
   Tell students to write the seven sentence types using *use* (regular verb), and another seven sentences using *buy* (irregular verb).

14.2 | Statements and Questions

Simple Present Tense

-s Form	Base Form
Lena **lives** with a roommate.	Interns **wear** formal clothes.
She **doesn't live** alone.	They **don't wear** jeans.
Does she **live** in a dorm?	**Do** they **wear** formal clothes to class?
No, she **doesn't.**	No, they **don't.**
Where **does** she **live?**	What **do** they **wear** to class?
Why **doesn't** she **live** in a dorm?	Why **don't** they **wear** jeans to work?
Who **lives** in a dorm?	How many students **wear** jeans?

Present Continuous Tense

Nicole **is planning** to become a teacher.	They **are taking** classes.
Lena **isn't planning** to become a teacher.	They **aren't taking** music classes.
Is she **planning** to teach in California?	**Are** they **taking** classes at Georgetown?
No, she **isn't.**	Yes, they **are.**
Where **is** she **planning** to teach?	What kind of classes **are** they **taking?**
Why **isn't** she **planning** to teach in California?	How many students **are taking** classes?
Who **is planning** to teach in California?	

Future Tense

Will	Be Going To
They **will go** home at the end of the summer.	Lena **is going to buy** books.
They **won't go** on vacation.	She **isn't going to buy** more clothes.
Will they **go** back to college?	**Is** she **going to buy** a computer?
Yes, they **will.**	No, she **isn't.**
When **will** they **go** back to college?	What **is** she **going to buy?**
Why **won't** they **go** on vacation?	Why **isn't** she **going to buy** a computer?
Who **will go** back to college?	Who **is going to buy** a computer?

Simple Past Tense

Regular Verb	Irregular Verb
She **used** her parents' credit card.	She **bought** new clothes.
She **didn't use** cash.	She **didn't buy** jeans.
Did she **use** their card a lot?	**Did** she **buy** formal clothes?
No, she **didn't.**	Yes, she **did.**
Why **did** she **use** their card?	Why **did** she **buy** formal clothes?
Why **didn't** she **use** cash?	Why **didn't** she **buy** jeans?
Who **used** the card?	Who **bought** formal clothes?

408 Lesson **14**

Be	
Present	**Past**
They **are** in Washington.	Lena **was** lost at first.
They **aren't** at college.	She **wasn't** happy.
Are they at Georgetown?	**Was** she alone?
Yes, they **are.**	Yes, she **was.**
Why **are** they in Washington?	Why **was** she alone?
Why **aren't** they at college?	Why **wasn't** she happy?
Who **is** at college?	Who **was** alone?

Modals	
Can	**Should**
She **can** wear jeans to class.	She **should** study every day.
She **can't** wear jeans to work.	She **shouldn't** go to parties every day.
Can she wear jeans at college?	**Should** she study about American government?
Yes, she **can.**	Yes, she **should.**
What **can** she wear?	What else **should** she study?
Why **can't** she wear jeans to work?	Who **should** study?
Who **can** wear jeans?	

EXERCISE 2 Fill in the blanks with the negative form of the underlined verb.

EXAMPLE   Lena <u>is</u> in Washington this summer. She ___*isn't*___ at home.

1. She's <u>getting</u> experience. She ___*isn't getting*___ money for her work.

2. She <u>bought</u> new clothes. She ___*didn't buy*___ jeans.

3. She <u>writes</u> a lot for her classes. She _____ ___*doesn't write*___ a lot of letters.

4. She'll <u>finish</u> college next year. She ___*won't finish*___ _____ college this summer.

5. She's <u>going to return</u> to college in the fall. She _____ ___*isn't going to return*___ to Washington next summer.

6. She <u>can wear</u> jeans to class. She ___*can't wear*___ _____ jeans to work.

7. She <u>must look</u> professional at work. She ___*must not look*___ _____ informal at work.

Verb Review   **409**

5. For the verb *be*, have students write the seven sentence types using the simple present form of *be*, and another seven sentences using the simple past form of *be*.

6. For the modals, write on the board: *modals (can/should)* Tell students to write the seven sentence types using *can*, and another seven sentences using *should*.

7. Then have students look at grammar chart **14.2** on pages 408–409. Say: *Check your work against the chart.* Go over the examples and explanations. Find out where students had difficulty and provide a more thorough review of that grammar point.

EXERCISE 2

1. Have students read the direction line. Tell students that this exercise is about Lena. Go over the example in the book.

2. Have students complete Exercise 2 individually. Then have students check answers in pairs. Circulate to observe pair work. Give help as needed.

3. As students check their answers in pairs, circulate around the room to see if there are any common trouble spots. Review those points with the whole class.

EXERCISE 3

1. Have students read the direction line. Go over the examples in the book. Ask: *What kind of questions do we write here?* (yes/no questions)
2. Have students complete Exercise 3 individually. Then have students check answers in pairs. Circulate to observe pair work. Give help as needed.
3. As students check their answers in pairs, circulate around the room to see if there are any common trouble spots. Review those points with the whole class.

🕐 To save class time, have students do half of the exercise in class and complete the other half for homework. Or assign the entire exercise for homework.

EXERCISE 4

1. Have students read the direction line. Point out that they are writing *wh-* questions. Go over the example in the book.
2. Have students complete Exercise 4 individually. Then have students check answers in pairs. Circulate to observe pair work. Give help as needed.
3. As students check their answers in pairs, circulate around the room to see if there are any common trouble spots. Review those points with the whole class.

🕐 To save class time, have students do half of the exercise in class and complete the other half for homework. Or assign the entire exercise for homework.

EXERCISE **3**   Fill in the blanks with a question about interns.

EXAMPLES   *Do interns get money for their work?*
No, they don't. They get experience, not money.

Will the internship end in September?
No, it won't. The internship will end in August.

1. *Do interns have to take classes?*
Yes, they do. They have to take classes.
2. *Do they live in dorms?*
No, they don't live in dorms. They live in apartments.
3. *Are they busy?*
Yes, they are. They are very busy with classes, work, and activities.
4. *Will they receive six hours of college credit?*
Yes, they will. They will receive six hours of college credit.
5. *Can she wear jeans to work?*
No, she can't. She can't wear jeans to work.
6. *Is she learning how to cook?*
Yes, she is. She's learning how to cook.
7. *Did she know anyone when she arrived in Washington?*
No, she didn't. She didn't know anyone when she arrived in Washington.
8. *Does she work in the Supreme Court?*
Yes, she does. She works in the Supreme Court.
9. *Did she buy some new clothes?*
Yes, she did. She bought some new clothes.

EXERCISE **4**   Write a question with the *wh-* word given. Use the same tense. (An answer is not necessary.)

EXAMPLE   Lena is calling her mother. Why *is she calling her mother?*

1. Lena will go home soon. When *will she go home?*

2. Her mother doesn't remember the roommate's name. Why *doesn't her mother remember the roommate's name?*

3. Lena can't go home for a weekend. Why *can't Lena go home for a weekend?*

Expansion

Exercise 3 Have students practice asking and answering questions from Exercise 3 in pairs.

4. Lena doesn't have much money. How much money _does Lena have?_

5. Lena is learning a lot this summer. What _is she learning?_

6. She doesn't have time to write letters. Why _doesn't she have time to write letters?_

7. Lena went to Virginia last weekend. Who(m) _did she go_ _____ with?

8. Nicole comes from a different state. Where _does she come_ _____ from?

9. Lena didn't cook before this summer. Why _does she cook now?_

10. Someone went to Virginia. Who _went to Virginia?_

11. The internship will help Lena in the future. How _will the internship help Lena?_

12. She is working in a government department. In which department _is she working?_

13. Lena felt lonely at first. Why _did she feel lonely?_

14. She can't wear jeans to work. Why _can't she wear jeans to work?_

15. She must take classes. How many classes _must she take?_

16. She is going to get college credits for her internship. How many credits _is she going to get?_

17. Lena should call her parents more often. How often _should she call them?_

Expansion

Exercise 4 Have students practice asking and answering questions from Exercise 4 in pairs.

CD 2, Track 34

1. Have students read the direction line. Explain that this is a phone conversation between Lena and her mother. Lena is calling from Washington. Go over the example in the book.

2. Have students complete Exercise 5 individually. Then have students check answers in small groups.

3. As students check their answers, circulate around the room to see if there are any common trouble spots. Review those points with the whole class.

To save class time, have students do half of the exercise in class and complete the other half for homework. Or assign the entire exercise for homework.

EXERCISE **5** Lena (L) is talking to her mother (M) on the phone. She is calling from Washington. Fill in the blanks with the correct form of the words in parentheses ( ).

M: Hello?

L: Hi, Mom. This is Lena.

M: Hi, Lena. I ___am___ happy to ___hear___ your voice.
   (example: be)   (1 hear)

   You ___never write___.
       (2 never/write)

L: I'm sorry, Mom. I ___don't have___ much time.
                     (3 not/have)

M: Why ___don't you have___ time?
       (4 you/not/have)

L: I have to work, go to classes, and participate in activities all day.

   Last weekend we ___went___ to Virginia.
                    (5 go)

M: Who ___drove___?
       (6 drive)

L: No one. We ___went___ by metro. Public transportation
               (7 go)

   is really good here.

M: ___Are you getting___ enough to eat this summer? Who
       (8 you/get)

   ___cooks___ for you?
      (9 cook)

L: I ___'m learning___ to ___cook___ this summer.
       (10 learn)   (11 cook)

   ___Are you___ surprised?
      (12 be/you)

M: Yes, I am. When you were home, you never ___cooked___.
                                             (13 cook)

   You ___hated___ it.
       (14 hate)

L: Not anymore. Nicole and I often ___cook___, and we
                                    (15 cook)

   ___invite___ our friends for dinner on the weekends.
      (16 invite)

M: Who ___'s___ Nicole?
       (17 be)

Exercise 5 Variation

To provide practice with listening skills, have students close their books and listen to the audio. Repeat the audio as needed. Ask comprehension questions, such as: *Why is Lena's mother happy?* (because Lena called) *Does Lena write often?* (no) *Why doesn't Lena have time?* (She has to work, go to classes, and participate in activities all day.) Then have students open their books and complete Exercise 5.

L: I _____ told you _____ in my last letter. She's my roommate.
        (18 tell)

_____ Don't you remember _____?
      (19 you/not/remember)

M: Yes, of course. Now I ____ remember ____. How ____ old is she ____?
          (20 remember)

L: She's the same age as I am—19. She ____ comes ____ from
                 (21 come)

California.

M: How ____ is your job ____? ____ Do you like ____ it?
    (22 be/your job)   (23 you/like)

L: It's great! I ____ am learning ____ so much this summer.
        (24 learn)

M: _____ Will this internship help _____ you in the future?
    (25 this internship/help)

L: Yes, it will. It will be great on my résumé.

M: ____ Do you have ____ enough money?
   (26 you/have)

L: No, I don't. I _____ spent _____ most of the money you
       (27 spend)

_____ gave _____ me when I got here.
   (28 give)

M: You _____ can use _____ my credit card. But don't spend money
     (29 can/use)

on foolish things.

L: I won't.

M: I _____ miss _____ you. _____ Can you come _____ home for a
   (30 miss)   (31 can/you/come)

weekend? We _____ 'll pay _____ for your ticket.
     (32 pay)

L: I can't, Mom. We _____ have _____ activities on weekends, too.
    (33 have)

M: _____ Will you call _____ again next week?
   (34 you/call)

L: If I _____ have _____ time, I _____ 'll call _____.
   (35 have)   (36 call)

But I _____ have _____ so little free time.
   (37 have)

M: I'm sure you have enough time for a ten-minute phone call to your
mother.

Expansion

Exercise 5 Have students practice the conversation in pairs. Then ask volunteers to act out the conversation for the class.

Editing Advice

Have students close their books. Write the example sentences without editing marks or corrections on the board. For example:

1. *Where does work your brother?*
    Why you can't find a job?
    How old your brother is?

Ask students to correct each sentence and provide a rule or explanation for each correction. This activity can be done individually, in pairs, or as a class. After students have corrected each sentence, tell them to turn to pages 414–415. Say: *Now compare your work with the Editing Advice in the book.*

L: You're right. I _____'ll call_____ you again next week. Give my
       (38 call)
   love to Dad.
M: I will.

EDITING ADVICE

1. Use the correct word order for questions.
                        your brother work?
   Where does work ~~your brother~~?
       can't you
   Why ~~you can't~~ find a job?
            is your brother
   How old ~~your brother is~~?

2. Do not forget to use *do* or *does* or *did* in a question.
            does your father live
   Where ~~lives your father~~?
       did   *give*
   When the teacher gave a test?

3. Do not use *be* with a simple present-tense or past-tense verb.

   I ~~am~~ eat breakfast every morning.
                saw
   Yesterday, he ~~was see~~ a good movie.

4. Use the base form after *do*, *does*, and *did*.
                go
   I didn't ~~went~~ to the party.
            buy
   Did you ~~bought~~ a new car?

5. For the simple present tense, use the *-s* form when the subject is *he*, *she*, *it*, or a singular noun. Use the base form in all other cases.
                      s
   Lisa never drink coffee in the morning.

   My friends usually visits me on Saturday.

6. Use the correct past form for irregular verbs.
      left
   We leaved the party early.
      fell
   He felt down on the ice.

7. Use the base form after *to*.
                drive
   I wanted to ~~drove~~ to New York.

   He likes to eats popcorn.

---

8. Use the base form after a modal.

  study
  She should studies more.

  We must to drive under 55 miles per hour.

  I can't helping you now.

9. Connect two verbs with *to* (unless one is a modal).

  to
  I forgot ^ do the homework.

  to
  She needs ^ find a job.

10. Do not use the present continuous tense with nonaction verbs.

  I am knowing the answer now.

  s
  He is hearing the noise in the next room.

11. Do not use *be* before a simple future verb.

  The doctor will be see you at 3:15.

12. Use the correct form of *be*.

  were
  They was late to the meeting.

  are
  You is always on time.

13. Use the correct negative form.

  don't
  They not know the answer.

  don't
  You doesn't need a pen.

14. Do not forget to include a form of *be* in a present continuous sentence.

  is
  She ^ washing the dishes now.

  am
  I ^ studying now.

15. Do not use the future tense in a time clause or an *if* clause. Use the simple present tense.

  When I will graduate, I will get a job.

  are
  You will fail the course if you will be absent more than five times.

16. Do not use the *-ing* form for the simple present tense.

  I drinking coffee every morning.

Lesson 14 Test/Review

For additional practice, review, and assessment materials, see Assessment CD-ROM with *ExamView Pro*, *More Grammar Practice* Workbook 1, Interactive CD-ROM, and Web site http://elt.thomson.com/gic

PART 1

1. Part 1 may be used in addition to the Assessment CD-ROM with *ExamView Pro* as an in-class test to assess student performance. Have students read the direction line. Ask: *Does every sentence have a mistake?* (no) Go over the example with the class.
2. Have students complete the exercise individually. Collect for assessment.
3. If necessary, have students review: **Lesson 14.**

LESSON 14 TEST/REVIEW

PART **1**   Find the mistakes with the underlined words and correct them. Not every sentence has a mistake. If the sentence is correct, write *C*.

EXAMPLES   She <u>writing</u> a letter now.   *is*

I <u>felt</u> sick yesterday.   *C*

1. We <u>taking</u> a test now.   *are*
2. Interns <u>doesn't</u> make money.   *don't*
3. Lena <u>spended</u> a lot of money on clothes.   *spent*
4. How <u>a student can</u> get an internship?   *can*
5. Where <u>live student interns</u>?   *do student interns live*
6. Lena <u>live</u> in an apartment.   *s*
7. She <u>can to cook</u>.
8. She <u>might needing</u> new clothes.
9. She <u>don't like</u> to wear formal clothes.   *doesn't*
10. When I <u>will get</u> home, I <u>will show</u> you my pictures.
11. Lena <u>was bought</u> some new clothes for her job.
12. Where <u>did she went</u> last weekend?   *go*
13. I <u>will be never forget</u> my new friends.
14. I <u>am not knowing</u> all the other interns.   *don't know*
15. Does Lena <u>has</u> a car?   *have*
16. She <u>wanted to went</u> to a party last weekend.   *go*
17. She <u>should studying</u> now.   *be*
18. She <u>needs take</u> many courses.   *to*
19. They <u>was</u> in Virginia last week.   *were*
20. Lena <u>liking</u> her job.   *likes*

Lesson Review

To use Part 1 as a review, assign it as homework or use it as an in-class activity to be completed individually or in pairs. Check answers and review errors as a class. Reteach grammar points that students haven't mastered. Then student learning may be assessed using a test generated from the Assessment CD-ROM with *ExamView Pro*.

PART **2** Fill in the blanks with the correct tense or form of the words in parentheses ( ).

I _____*come*_____ from India. I ____*decided to move*____ to the
(example: come)   (1 decide/move)

U.S. ten months ago. It was difficult _____*to leave*_____ my friends
(2 leave)

and family, but I ____*wanted to come*____ to the U.S. and have more
(3 want/come)

opportunities.

    When I _____*lived*_____ in India, I was a draftsman. When I
(4 live)

_____*came*_____ to the U.S. in July, I _____*didn't find*_____
(5 come)   (6 not/find)

a job at first because my English wasn't good enough. Last September,

I _____*found*_____ a job in a laundromat. I don't like my job at all.
(7 find)

I ____*wanted to find*____ a better job soon. I know I _____*'ll get*_____
(8 want/find)   (9 get)

a better job when I _____*speak*_____ English better. I
(10 speak)

_____*am saving*_____ my money now. When I _____*have*_____
(11 save)   (12 have)

enough money, I ____*'ll begin to take*____ engineering courses at the
(13 begin/take)

university. My parents _____*will be*_____ proud of me when I
(14 be)

_____*graduate*_____.
(15 graduate)

    Right now, I _____*'m taking*_____ ESL courses at a college near my
(16 take)

house. I _____*studied*_____ English in India, but it was different
(17 study)

from American English. When I listen to Americans at my job or on TV, I

____*can't understand*____ a lot of things they say. Sometimes when I
(18 can/not/understand)

_____*speak*_____ with Americans at my job, they ____*don't understand*____
(19 speak)   (20 not/understand)

me. They sometimes _____*laugh*_____ at my pronunciation. They
(21 laugh)

aren't bad people, but they ____*don't understand*____ that it is hard
(22 not/understand)

_____*to learn*_____ another language and live in another country.
(23 learn)

I usually _____*stay*_____ by myself at work. I _____*know*_____
(24 stay)   (25 know)

I ____*should practice*____ more, but I'm very shy.
(26 should/practice)

Verb Review   **417**

PART 2

1. Part 2 may also be used in addition to the Assessment CD-ROM with *ExamView Pro* as an in-class test to assess student performance. Have students read the direction line. Go over the example with the class.
2. Have students complete the exercise individually. Collect for assessment.
3. If necessary, have students review: **Lesson 14.**

Lesson Review

To use Part 2 as a review, assign it as homework or use it as an in-class activity to be completed individually or in pairs. Check answers and review errors as a class. Reteach grammar points that students haven't mastered. Then student learning may be assessed using a test generated from the Assessment CD-ROM with *ExamView Pro.*

1. Part 3 may also be used in addition to the Assessment CD-ROM with *ExamView Pro* as an in-class test to assess student performance. Have students read the direction line. Ask: *Which form of the underlined words do you write?* (the negative) Go over the example with the class.
2. Have students complete the exercise individually. Collect for assessment.
3. If necessary, have students review: **Lesson 14.**

1. Part 4 may also be used in addition to the Assessment CD-ROM with *ExamView Pro* as an in-class test to assess student performance. Have students read the direction line. Ask: *What do you write on the line?* (a *yes/no* question and a short answer) Go over the example with the class.
2. Have students complete the exercise individually. Collect for assessment.
3. If necessary, have students review: **Lesson 14.**

When I _____was_____ in India, I _____lived_____
     (27 be)   (28 live)
in a big house with my parents, sisters and brothers, and grandparents.

Now I _____have_____ a small apartment and live alone.
    (29 have)

Sometimes I _____am_____ lonely. I would like
      (30 be)

_____to get_____ married someday, but first I want
 (31 get)

_____to earn_____ some money and _____save_____
 (32 earn)   (33 save)

for my future.

PART 3 Write the negative form of the underlined words.

EXAMPLE He <u>moved</u> to the U.S. He _____didn't move_____ to England.

1. He <u>studied</u> English in India. He _____didn't study_____ German.
2. He <u>wants to work</u> as an engineer. He _____doesn't want to work_____ in a laundromat.
3. He <u>is going to study</u> engineering. He _____isn't going to study_____ art.
4. He <u>is taking</u> courses at a community college now. He _____isn't taking_____ _____ courses at a university.
5. He's <u>saving</u> his money to get married. He _____isn't saving_____ his money to go back to his country.
6. His coworkers <u>know</u> that he is a foreigner. They _____don't know_____ _____ how difficult his life is.
7. He <u>should</u> practice English with Americans. He _____shouldn't_____ _____ be shy.
8. He <u>can understand</u> some TV programs. He _____can't understand_____ _____ all TV programs.

PART 4 Read each statement. Then write a *yes/no* question about the words in parentheses ( ). Write a short answer.

EXAMPLE He <u>studied</u> English in India. (American English)
    Did he study American English? No, he didn't.

1. He'll <u>study</u> engineering. (accounting)
    Will he study accounting? No, he won't.

Lesson Review

To use Parts 3 and 4 as a review, assign them as homework or use them as in-class activities to be completed individually or in pairs. Check answers and review errors as a class. Reteach grammar points that students haven't mastered. Then student learning may be assessed using a test generated from the Assessment CD-ROM with *ExamView Pro*.

2. Americans <u>don't understand</u> him. (Indians)

   Do Indians understand him? Yes, they do.

3. He's <u>studying</u> American English now. (American history)

   Is he studying American history? No, he isn't.

4. He <u>lives</u> in a small apartment. (with his family)

   Does he live with his family? No, he doesn't.

5. He <u>can understand</u> British English. (American English)

   Can he understand American English? No, he can't.

6. It is hard <u>to learn</u> another language. (live in another country)

   Is it hard to live in another country? Yes, it is.

7. He <u>wants to get</u> married. (next year)

   Does he want to get married next year? No, he doesn't

8. He <u>lived</u> with his parents in India. (with his grandparents)

   Did he live with his grandparents in India? Yes, he did.

PART 5   Read each statement. Then write a *wh-* question with the words in parentheses ( ). (An answer is not necessary.)

EXAMPLE   He <u>left</u> India. (why)

   Why did he leave India?

1. He <u>is saving</u> his money. (why)

   Why is he saving his money?

2. He <u>is going to get</u> married. (When)

   When is he going to get married?

3. Some people <u>laugh</u> at him. (who)

   Who laughs at him?

4. He <u>is</u> lonely. (why)

   Why is he lonely?

5. His parents <u>aren't</u> in the U.S. (why)

   Why aren't his parents in the U.S?

6. He <u>didn't find</u> a job at first. (why)

   Why didn't he find a job at first?

7. He <u>will graduate</u> from the university. (when)

   When will he graduate from the university?

1. Part 5 may also be used in addition to the Assessment CD-ROM with *ExamView Pro* as an in-class test to assess student performance. Have students read the direction line.
   Ask: *What do you write on the line?* (a *wh-* question) *Do you write an answer?* (no) Go over the example with the class.

2. Have students complete the exercise individually. Collect for assessment.

3. If necessary, have students review: **Lesson 14.**

Lesson Review

To use Part 5 as a review, assign it as homework or use it as an in-class activity to be completed individually or in pairs. Check answers and review errors as a class. Reteach grammar points that students haven't mastered. Then student learning may be assessed using a test generated from the Assessment CD-ROM with *ExamView Pro*.

Expansion Activities

These expansion activities provide opportunities for students to interact with one another and further develop their speaking and writing skills. Encourage students to use grammar from this lesson whenever possible.

🕐 To save class time, assign parts of the activities as homework. Then use class time for interaction and communication. If students do not need additional speaking practice, some of the activities may be assigned as writing activities for homework, or skipped altogether.

CLASSROOM ACTIVITIES

1. Have students interview each other in the class. If everyone or nearly everyone in your class is from the same country, have them interview people from outside the class. Then put students in pairs to take turns asking and answering questions. Have students write out the questions before the interview.

---

8. He <u>came</u> to the U.S. alone. (why)

Why did he come to the U.S. alone?

9. His coworkers <u>don't understand</u> his accent. (why)

Why don't his coworkers understand his accent?

10. He <u>lived</u> in a big house. (when)

When did he live in a big house?

EXPANSION ACTIVITIES

1. Interview a student from another country. Use the words below to ask and answer questions. Practice the simple present, the present continuous, the future, and the simple past tenses.

EXAMPLES   you / from Asia
A: Are you from Asia?
B: Yes, I am. OR No, I'm not.

where / you / from
A: Where are you from?
B: I'm from Pakistan.

a. when / you / leave your country

b. how / you / come to the U.S.

c. you / come / to the U.S. alone

d. where / you / born

e. what language(s) / you speak

f. you / return to your country next year

g. you / have a job now

h. you / have a job in your country

i. how many brothers and sisters / you/ have

j. your country / big

k. your country / have a lot of petroleum

l. you / live in an apartment in your hometown

m. you / study English in your country

n. what / you / study this semester

o. what / you / study next semester

p. you / like this class

q. the teacher / speak your language

r. this class / hard for you

s. who / your teacher last semester

t. who / your teacher next semester

2. Write sentences in each category, if you can. Write one for the simple present, one for the present continuous, one for the future, and one for the simple past tense.

	Simple Present	Present Continuous	Future	Simple Past
Job	I work in a factory.	I'm looking for a new job.	Next week I'm going to have an interview.	In my country, I was a taxi driver.
School				
Family				
Weather				
Apartment				
Job				

2. Have students fill out the charts individually. Then put students in pairs to compare charts.

OUTSIDE ACTIVITY

Have students read the direction line. Explain that the words in parentheses are for follow-up questions after a *yes/no* question. Ask students to make a poster of their interview with the native speaker. If possible, have students include a picture of the person interviewed. Have students discuss with the class the questions they were asked by the native speaker.

INTERNET ACTIVITY

Have students discuss any interesting information they found on Web sites in groups. Then have groups report to the class.

Outside Activity

Use the words below to interview a native speaker of English at this school. Practice the simple present, the present continuous, the future, and the simple past tenses. Report something interesting to the class about this student.

EXAMPLE   you have a car (what kind)
    A: Do you have a car?
    B: Yes, I do.
    A: What kind of car do you have?
    B: I have a Honda.

1. you / study another language now (what language)
2. you / live alone (who . . . with)
3. your family / live in this city
4. you / like this city (why / why not)
5. you / go to high school in this city (where)
6. what / your major
7. you / graduate soon (when)
8. what / you do / after / you / graduate
9. you / like to travel (when . . . your last vacation) (where . . . go)
10. you / own a computer (what kind) (when . . . buy it)
11. you / eat in a restaurant / last week (where)
12. you / buy something new / in the near future (what)
13. you / do something interesting / last weekend (what . . . do)
14. you / plan to do something interesting / next weekend (what . . . do)

Invite the native speaker to interview you. Write down the questions that he or she asks you.

Internet Activity

Using a search engine, look up "Washington internship" on the Internet. Find out what some students say about their experience as an intern.

Additional Activities at http://elt.thomson.com/gic

Outside Activity Variation

As an alternative, you may invite a guest to your classroom (e.g., an administrator, a librarian, or a service worker at your school) and have students do a class interview. Students should prepare their interview questions ahead of time.

Appendices

The Verb *GET*

Get has many meanings. Here is a list of the most common ones:		
• get something = receive		
I got a letter from my father.		
• get + (to) place = arrive		
I got home at six. What time do you get to school?		
• get + object + infinitive = persuade		
She got him to wash the dishes.		
• get + past participle = become		
get acquainted	get worried	get hurt
get engaged	get lost	get bored
get married	get accustomed to	get confused
get divorced	get used to	get scared
get tired	get dressed	
They got married in 1989.		
• get + adjective = become		
get hungry	get sleepy	
get rich	get dark	
get nervous	get angry	
get well	get old	
get upset	get fat	
It gets dark at 6:30.		
• get an illness = catch		
While she was traveling, she got malaria.		
• get a joke or an idea = understand		
Everybody except Tom laughed at the joke. He didn't get it.		
The boss explained the project to us, but I didn't get it.		

Continued

- get ahead = advance

  He works very hard because he wants to get ahead in his job.

- get along (well) (with someone) = have a good relationship

  She doesn't get along with her mother-in-law.

  Do you and your roommate get along well?

- get around to something = find the time to do something

  I wanted to write my brother a letter yesterday, but I didn't get around to it.

- get away = escape

  The police chased the thief, but he got away.

- get away with something = escape punishment

  He cheated on his taxes and got away with it.

- get back = return

  He got back from his vacation last Saturday.

- get back at someone = get revenge

  My brother wants to get back at me for stealing his girlfriend.

- get back to someone = communicate with someone at a later time

  The boss can't talk to you today. Can she get back to you tomorrow?

- get by = have just enough but nothing more

  On her salary, she's just getting by. She can't afford a car or a vacation.

- get in trouble = be caught and punished for doing something wrong

  They got in trouble for cheating on the test.

- get in(to) = enter a car

  She got in the car and drove away quickly.

- get out (of) = leave a car

  When the taxi arrived at the theater, everyone got out.

- get on = seat yourself on a bicycle, motorcycle, horse

  She got on the motorcycle and left.

- get on = enter a train, bus, airplane

  She got on the bus and took a seat in the back.

- get off = leave a bicycle, motorcycle, horse, train, bus, airplane

  They will get off the train at the next stop.

- get out of something = escape responsibility

  My boss wants me to help him on Saturday, but I'm going to try to get out of it.

- get over something = recover from an illness or disappointment

  She has the flu this weak. I hope she gets over it soon.

- get rid of someone or something = free oneself of someone or something undesirable

  My apartment has roaches, and I can't get rid of them.

Continued

- get through (to someone) = communicate, often by telephone
    She tried to explain the harm of eating fast food to her son, but she couldn't get
        through to him.
    I tried to call my mother many times, but her line was busy. I couldn't get through.

- get through (with something) = finish
    I can meet you after I get through with my homework.

- get together = meet with another person
    I'd like to see you again. When can we get together?

- get up = arise from bed
    He woke up at 6 o'clock, but he didn't get up until 6:30.

APPENDIX B

MAKE and *DO*

Some expressions use *make.* Others use *do.*

Make	Do
make a date/an appointment	do (the) homework
make a plan	do an exercise
make a decision	do the dishes
make a telephone call	do the cleaning, laundry, ironing, washing, etc.
make a reservation	do the shopping
make a meal (breakfast, lunch, dinner)	do one's best
make a mistake	do a favor
make an effort	do the right/wrong thing
make an improvement	do a job
make a promise	do business
make money	What do you do for a living? (asks about a job)
make noise	How do you do? (said when you meet someone for the first time)
make the bed	

Question Formation

1. Statements and Related Questions with a Main Verb.

Wh- Word	Do/Does/Did (n't)	Subject	Verb	Complement
When	does	She she	watches watch	TV. TV?
Where	do	My parents your parents	live live?	in Peru.
Who(m)	does	Your sister she	likes like?	someone.
Why	did	They they	left leave	early. early?
How many books	did	She she	found find?	some books.
What kind of car	did	He he	bought buy?	a car.
Why	didn't	She she	didn't go go	home. home?
Why	doesn't	He he	doesn't like like	tomatoes. tomatoes?

Subject	Verb (base form or -s form or past form)	Complement
Someone Who	has has	my book. my book?
Someone Who	needs needs	help. help?
Someone Who	took took	my pen. my pen?
One teacher Which teacher	speaks speaks	Spanish. Spanish?
Some men Which men	have have	a car. a car?
Some boys How many boys	saw saw	the movie. the movie?
Something What	happened. happened?	

2. Statements and Related Questions with the Verb *Be*.

Wh- Word	*Be*	Subject	*Be*	Complement
Where	is	She she?	is	in California.
Why	were	They they	were	hungry. hungry?
Why	isn't	He he	isn't	tired. tired?
When	was	He he	was	born in England. born?
		One student Who Which student	was was was	late. late? late?
		Some kids How many kids Which kids	were were were	afraid. afraid? afraid?

3. Statements and Related Questions with an Auxiliary (Aux) Verb and a Main Verb.

Wh- Word	Aux	Subject	Aux	Main Verb	Complement
Where	is	She she	is	running. running?	
When	will	They they	will	go go	on a vacation. on a vacation?
What	should	He he	should	do do?	something.
How many pills	can	You you	can	take take?	a pill.
Why	can't	You you	can't	drive drive	a car. a car?
		Someone Who	should should	answer answer	the question. the question?

Alphabetical List of Irregular Past Forms

Base Form	Past Form	Base Form	Past Form
arise	arose	forget	forgot
awake	awoke	forgive	forgave
be	was/were	freeze	froze
bear	bore	get	got
beat	beat	give	gave
become	became	go	went
begin	began	grind	ground
bend	bent	grow	grew
bet	bet	hang	hung[1]
bind	bound	have	had
bite	bit	hear	heard
bleed	bled	hide	hid
blow	blew	hit	hit
break	broke	hold	held
breed	bred	hurt	hurt
bring	brought	keep	kept
broadcast	broadcast	kneel	knelt (or kneeled)
build	built	know	knew
burst	burst	lay	laid
buy	bought	lead	led
cast	cast	leave	left
catch	caught	lend	lent
choose	chose	let	let
cling	clung	lie	lay
come	came	light	lit (or lighted)
cost	cost	lose	lost
creep	crept	make	made
cut	cut	mean	meant
deal	dealt	meet	met
dig	dug	mistake	mistook
do	did	pay	paid
draw	drew	put	put
drink	drank	quit	quit
drive	drove	read	read
eat	ate	ride	rode
fall	fell	ring	rang
feed	fed	rise	rose
feel	felt	run	ran
fight	fought	say	said
find	found	see	saw
fit	fit	seek	sought
flee	fled	sell	sold
fly	flew	send	sent

Continued

[1]*Hanged* is used as the past form to refer to punishment by death. *Hung* is used in other situations. She *hung* the picture on the wall.

Base Form	Past Form	Base Form	Past Form
forbid	forbade	set	set
shake	shook	stink	stank
shed	shed	strike	struck
shine	shone (or shined)	strive	strove
shoot	shot	swear	swore
shrink	shrank	sweep	swept
shut	shut	swim	swam
sing	sang	swing	swung
sink	sank	take	took
sit	sat	teach	taught
sleep	slept	tear	tore
slide	slid	tell	told
slit	slit	think	thought
speak	spoke	throw	threw
speed	sped	understand	understood
spend	spent	upset	upset
spin	spun	wake	woke
spit	spit	wear	wore
split	split	weave	wove
spread	spread	weep	wept
spring	sprang	win	won
stand	stood	wind	wound
steal	stole	withdraw	withdrew
stick	stuck	wring	wrung
sting	stung	write	wrote

APPENDIX E

Meanings of Modals and Related Words

- Ability, Possibility

  Can you drive a truck?

  You **can** get a ticket for speeding.

- Necessity, Obligation

  A driver **must** have a license (legal obligation)

  I **have** *to* buy a new car. (personal obligation)

- Permission

  You **can** park at a meter.

  You **can't** park at a bus stop.

- Possibility

  I **may** buy a new car soon.

  I **might** buy a Japanese car.

- Advice

  You **should** buy a new car. Your old car is in terrible condition.

- Permission Request

    May I borrow your car?

    Can I have the keys, please?

    Could I have the keys, please?

- Polite Request

    Would you teach me to drive?

    Could you show me your new car?

- Want

    What **would** you *like* to eat?

    I'd like a turkey sandwich.

APPENDIX F

Capitalization Rules

- The first word in a sentence: **My** friends are helpful.

- The word "I": My sister and **I** took a trip together.

- Names of people: **Julia Roberts**; **George Washington**

- Titles preceding names of people: **Doctor** (**Dr.**) **Smith**; **President Lincoln**; **Queen Elizabeth**; **Mr. Rogers**; **Mrs. Carter**

- Geographic names: the **United States**; **Lake Superior**; **California**; the **Rocky Mountains**; the **Mississippi River**

    NOTE: The word "the" in a geographic name is not capitalized.

- Street names: **Pennsylvania Avenue** (**Ave.**); **Wall Street** (**St.**); **Abbey Road** (**Rd.**)

- Names of organizations, companies, colleges, buildings, stores, hotels: the **Republican Party**; **Heinle Thomson**; **Dartmouth College**; the **University of Wisconsin**; the **White House**; **Bloomingdale's**; the **Hilton Hotel**

- Nationalities and ethnic groups: **Mexicans**; **Canadians**; **Spaniards**; **Americans**; **Jews**; **Kurds**; **Eskimos**

- Languages: **English**; **Spanish**; **Polish**; **Vietnamese**; **Russian**

- Months: **January**; **February**

- Days: **Sunday**; **Monday**

- Holidays: **Christmas**; **Independence Day**

- Important words in a title: **Grammar in Context**; **The Old Man and the Sea**; **Romeo and Juliet**; **The Sound of Music**

    NOTE: Capitalize "the" as the first word of a title.

Metric Conversion Chart

Length				
When You Know	**Symbol**	**Multiply by**	**To Find**	**Symbol**
inches	in	2.54	centimeters	cm
feet	ft	30.5	centimeters	cm
feet	ft	0.3	meters	m
yards	yd	0.91	meters	m
miles	mi	1.6	kilometers	km
Metric:				
centimeters	cm	0.39	inches	in
centimeters	cm	0.03	feet	ft
meter	m	3.28	feet	ft
meters	m	1.09	yards	yd
kilometers	km	0.62	miles	mi
Note:				
1 foot = 12 inches				
1 yard = 3 feet or 36 inches				

Area				
When You Know	**Symbol**	**Multiply by**	**To Find**	**Symbol**
square inches	in^2	6.5	square centimeters	cm^2
square feet	ft^2	0.09	square meters	m^2
square yards	yd^2	0.8	square meters	m^2
square miles	mi^2	2.6	square kilometers	km^2
Metric:				
square centimeters	cm^2	0.16	square inches	in^2
square meters	m^2	10.76	square feet	ft^2
square meters	m^2	1.2	square yards	yd^2
square kilometers	km^2	0.39	square miles	mi^2

Continued

Weight (Mass)

When You Know	Symbol	Multiply by	To Find	Symbol
ounces	oz	28.35	grams	g
pounds	lb	0.45	kilograms	kg
Metric:				
grams	g	0.04	ounces	oz
kilograms	kg	2.2	pounds	lb
Note:				
16 ounces = 1 pound				

Volume

When You Know	Symbol	Multiply by	To Find	Symbol
fluid ounces	fl oz	30.0	milliliters	mL
pints	pt	0.47	liters	L
quarts	qt	0.95	liters	L
gallons	gal	3.8	liters	L
Metric:				
milliliters	mL	0.03	fluid ounces	fl oz
liters	L	2.11	pints	pt
liters	L	1.05	quarts	qt
liters	L	0.26	gallons	gal

Temperature

When You Know	Symbol	Do this	To Find	Symbol
degrees Fahrenheit	°F	Subtract 32, then multiply by $5/9$	degrees Celsius	°C
Metric:				
degrees Celsius	°C	Multiply by $9/5$, then add 32	degrees Fahrenheit	°F

Sample temperatures	
Fahrenheit	**Celsius**
0	– 18
10	– 12
20	– 7
30	– 1
40	4
50	10
60	16
70	21
80	27
90	32
100	38

APPENDIX H

Prepositions of Time

- **in** the morning: He takes a shower *in* the morning.
- **in** the afternoon: He takes a shower *in* the afternoon.
- **in** the evening: He takes a shower *in* the evening.
- **at** night: He takes a shower *at* night.
- **in** the summer, fall, winter, spring: He takes classes *in* the summer.
- **on** that/this day: October 10 is my birthday. I became a citizen *on* that day.
- **on** the weekend: He studies *on* the weekend.
- **on** a specific day: His birthday is *on* March 5.
- **in** a month: His birthday is *in* March.
- **in** a year: He was born *in* 1978.
- **in** a century: People didn't use cars *in* the 19th century.
- **on** a day: I don't have class *on* Monday.
- **at** a specific time: My class begins *at* 12:30.
- **from** a time **to** another time: My class is *from* 12:30 *to* 3:30.
- **in** a number of hours, days, weeks, months, years: She will graduate *in* three weeks. (This means "after" three weeks.)

- **for** a number of hours, days, weeks, months, years: She was in Mexico *for* three weeks. (This means during the period of three weeks.)

- **by** a time: Please finish your test *by* 6 o'clock. (This means "no later than" 6 o'clock.)

- **until** a time: I lived with my parents *until* I came to the U.S. (This means "all the time before.")

- **during** the movie, class, meeting: He slept *during* the meeting.

- **about/around** 6 o'clock: The movie will begin *about* 6 o'clock. People will arrive *around* 5:45.

- **in** the past/future: *In* the past, she never exercised.

- **at** present: *At* present, the days are getting longer.

- **in** the beginning/end: *In* the beginning, she didn't understand the teacher at all.

- **at** the beginning/end of something: The semester beings *at* the beginning of September. My birthday is *at* the end of June.

- **before/after** a time: You should finish the job *before* Friday. The library will be closed *after* 6:00.

- **before/after** an action takes place: Turn off the lights *before* you leave. Wash the dishes *after* you finish dinner.

APPENDIX I

Glossary of Grammatical Terms

- **Adjective** An adjective gives a description of a noun.

    It's a *tall* tree.   He's an *old* man.   My neighbors are *nice*.

- **Adverb** An adverb describes the action of a sentence or an adjective or another adverb.

    She speaks English *fluently*.   I drive *carefully*.
    She speaks English *extremely* well.   She is *very* intelligent.

- **Adverb of Frequency** An adverb of frequency tells how often the action happens.

    I *never* drink coffee.   They *usually* take the bus.

- **Affirmative** means *yes*.

- **Apostrophe '** We use the apostrophe for possession and contractions.

    My *sister's* friend is beautiful.   Today *isn't* Sunday.

- **Article** The definite article is *the*. The indefinite articles are *a* and *an*.

    I have *a* cat.   I ate *an* apple.   *The* president was in
                                                New York last weekend.

- **Auxiliary Verb** Some verbs have two parts: an auxiliary verb and a main verb.

  He *can't* study.　　We *will* return.

- **Base Form** The base form, sometimes called the "simple" form, of the verb has no tense. It has no ending (*-s* or *-ed*): *be, go, eat, take, write.*

  I didn't *go* out.　　He doesn't *know* the answer.

  You shouldn't *talk* loudly.

- **Capital Letter** A B C D E F G . . .

- **Clause** A clause is a group of words that has a subject and a verb. Some sentences have only one clause.

  She speaks Spanish.

  Some sentences have **a main clause** and a **dependent clause.**

MAIN CLAUSE	DEPENDENT CLAUSE (**reason clause**)
She found a good job	because she has computer skills.
MAIN CLAUSE	DEPENDENT CLAUSE (**time clause**)
She'll turn off the light	before she goes to bed.
MAIN CLAUSE	DEPENDENT CLAUSE (*if* **clause**)
I'll take you to the doctor	if you don't have your car on Saturday.

- **Colon** :

- **Comma** ,

- **Comparative Form** A comparative form of an adjective or adverb is used to compare two things.

  My house is *bigger* than your house.

  Her husband drives *faster* than she does.

- **Complement** The complement of the sentence is the information after the verb. It completes the verb phrase.

  He works *hard.*　　I slept *for five hours.*　　They are *late.*

- **Consonant** The following letters are consonants: *b, c, d, f, g, h, j, k, l, m, n, p, q, r, s, t, v, w, x, y, z.*

  NOTE: *y* is sometimes considered a vowel, as in the world *syllable.*

- **Contraction** A contraction is made up of two words put together with an apostrophe.

  He's my brother.　*You're* late.　　They *won't* talk to me.

  (*He's* = *he is*)　(*You're* = *you are*)　(*won't* = *will not*)

- **Count Noun** Count nouns are nouns that we can count. They have a singular and a plural form.

  1 pen — 3 pens　　1 table — 4 tables

- **Dependent Clause** See **Clause.**

- **Direct Object** A direct object is a noun (phrase) or pronoun that receives the action of the verb.

    We saw *the movie*.   You have *a nice car*.   I love *you*.

- **Exclamation Mark !**

- **Frequency words** Frequency words are *always, usually, often, sometimes, rarely, seldom, never*.

    I *never* drink coffee.   We *always* do our homework.

- **Hyphen** –

- **Imperative** An imperative sentence gives a command or instructions. An imperative sentence omits the word *you*.

    Come here.   *Don't be* late.   Please *sit* down.

- **Infinitive** An infinitive is *to* + base form.

    I want *to leave*.   You need *to be* here on time.

- **Linking Verb** A linking verb is a verb that links the subject to the noun or adjective after it. Linking verbs include *be, seem, feel, smell, sound, look, appear, taste*.

    She *is* a doctor.   She *seems* very intelligent.   She *looks* tired.

- **Modal** The modal verbs are *can, could, shall, should, will, would, may, might, must*.

    They *should* leave.   I *must* go.

- **Negative** means no.

- **Nonaction Verb** A nonaction verb has no action. We do not use a continuous tense (*be* + verb *-ing*) with a nonaction verb. The nonaction verbs are: *believe, cost, care, have, hear, know, like, love, matter, mean, need, own, prefer, remember, see, seem, think, understand, want*.

    She *has* a laptop.   We *love* our mother.

- **Noncount Noun** A noncount noun is a noun that we don't count. It has no plural form.

    She drank some *water*.   He prepared some *rice*.

    Do you need any *money*?

- **Noun** A noun is a person (*brother*), a place (*kitchen*) or a thing (*table*). Nouns can be either count (*1 table, 2 tables*) or noncount (*money, water*).

    My *brother* lives in California.   My *sisters* live in New York.

    I get *mail* from them.

- **Noun Modifier** A noun modifier makes a noun more specific.

    fire department   *Independence* Day   *can* opener

- **Noun Phrase** A noun phrase is a group of words that form the subject or object of the sentence.

    A very nice woman helped me at registration.

    I bought *a big box of candy*.

- **Object** The object of the sentence follows the verb. It receives the action of the verb.

  He bought *a car.*   I saw *a movie.*   I met *your brother.*

- **Object Pronoun** Use object pronouns (*me, you, him, her, it, us, them*) after the verb or preposition.

  He likes *her.*   I saw the movie. Let's talk about *it.*

- **Parentheses ( )**

- **Paragraph** A paragraph is a group of sentences about one topic.

- **Participle, Present** The present participle is verb + *-ing.*

  She is *sleeping.*   They were *laughing.*

- **Period .**

- **Phrase** A group of words that go together.

  Last month my sister came to visit.

  There is a strange car *in front of my house.*

- **Plural** Plural means more than one. A plural noun usually ends with *-s.*

  She has beautiful *eyes.*

- **Possessive Form** Possessive forms show ownership or relationship.

  Mary's coat is in the closet.   *My* brother lives in Miami.

- **Preposition** A preposition is a short connecting word: *about, above, across, after, around, as, at, away, back, before, behind, below, by, down, for, from, in, into, like, of, off, on, out, over, to, under, up with.*

  The book is *on* the table.

- **Pronoun** A pronoun takes the place of a noun.

  I have a new car. I bought *it* last week.

  John likes Mary, but *she* doesn't like *him.*

- **Punctuation** Period . Comma , Colon : Semicolon ; Question Mark ? Exclamation Mark !

- **Question Mark ?**

- **Quotation Marks " "**

- **Regular Verb** A regular verb forms its past tense with *-ed.*

  He *worked* yesterday.   I *laughed* at the joke.

- **s Form** A present tense verb that ends in *-s* or *-es.*

  He *lives* in New York.   She *watches* TV a lot.

- **Sense-Perception Verb** A sense-perception verb has no action. It describes a sense.

  She *feels* fine.   The coffee *smells* fresh.   The milk *tastes* sour.

- **Sentence** A sentence is a group of words that contains a subject[1] and a verb (at least) and gives a complete thought.

  SENTENCE: She came home.

  NOT A SENTENCE: When she came home

- **Simple Form of Verb** The simple form of the verb, also called the base form, has no tense; it never has an -*s*, -*ed*, or -*ing* ending.

  Did you *see* the movie?   I couldn't *find* your phone number.

- **Singular** Singular means one.

  She ate a *sandwich*.   I have one *television*.

- **Subject** The subject of the sentence tells who or what the sentence is about.

  My sister got married last April. *The wedding* was beautiful.

- **Subject Pronouns** Use subject pronouns (*I, you, he, she, it, we, you, they*) before a verb.

  They speak Japanese.   *We* speak Spanish.

- **Superlative Form** A superlative form of an adjective or adverb shows the number one item in a group of three or more.

  January is the *coldest* month of the year.

  My brother speaks English the *best* in my family.

- **Syllable** A syllable is a part of a word that has only one vowel sound. (Some words have only one syllable.)

  change (one syllable)   after (af·ter = 2 syllables)

  look (one syllable)   responsible (re·spon·si·ble = 4 syllables)

- **Tag Question** A tag question is a short question at the end of a sentence. It is used in conversation.

  You speak Spanish, *don't you?*   He's not happy, *is he?*

- **Tense** A verb has tense. Tense shows when the action of the sentence happened.

  SIMPLE PRESENT: She usually *works* hard.

  FUTURE: She *will work* tomorrow.

  PRESENT CONTINUOUS: She *is working* now.

  SIMPLE PAST: She *worked* yesterday.

- **Verb** A verb is the action of the sentence.

  He *runs* fast.   I *speak* English.

  Some verbs have no action. They are linking verbs. They connect the subject to the rest of the sentence.

  He *is* tall.   She *looks* beautiful.   You *seem* tired.

- **Vowel** The following letters are vowels: *a, e, i, o, u. Y* is sometimes considered a vowel (for example, in the word *syllable*).

[1] In an imperative sentence, the subject *you* is omitted: *Sit down. Come here.*

Verbs and Adjectives Followed by a Preposition

(be) accustomed to	forgive someone for	(be) proud of
(be) afraid of	(be) glad about	recover from
agree with	(be) good at	(be) related to
(be) angry about	(be) happy about	rely on/upon
(be) angry at/with	hear about	(be) responsible for
approve of	hear of	(be) sad about
argue about	hope for	(be) satisfied with
(be) ashamed of	(be) incapable of	(be) scared of
(be) aware of	insist on/upon	(be) sick of
believe in	(be) interested in	(be) sorry about
(be) bored with/by	(be) involved in	(be) sorry for
(be) capable of	(be) jealous of	speak about
care about/for	(be) known for	speak to/with
(be) compared to	(be) lazy about	succeed in
complain about	listen to	(be) sure of/about
(be) concerned about	look at	(be) surprised at
concentrate on	look for	take care of
consist of	look forward to	talk about
count on	(be) mad about	talk to/with
deal with	(be) mad at	thank someone for
decide on	(be) made from/of	(be) thankful to someone for
depend on/upon	(be) married to	think about/of
dream about/of	object to	(be) tired of
(be) engaged to	participate in	(be) upset about
(be) excited about	plan on	(be) upset with
(be) familiar with	pray to	(be) used to
(be) famous for	pray for	wait for
feel like	(be) prepared for	warn about
(be) fond of	prohibit from	(be) worried about
forget about	protect someone from	worry about

The United States of America: Major Cities

AL	Alabama	IN	Indiana	NE	Nebraska	SC	South Carolina
AK	Alaska	IA	Iowa	NV	Nevada	SD	South Dakota
AZ	Arizona	KS	Kansas	NH	New Hampshire	TN	Tennessee
AR	Arkansas	KY	Kentucky	NJ	New Jersey	TX	Texas
CA	California	LA	Louisiana	NM	New Mexico	UT	Utah
CO	Colorado	ME	Maine	NY	New York	VT	Vermont
CT	Connecticut	MD	Maryland	NC	North Carolina	VA	Virginia
DE	Delaware	MA	Massachusetts	ND	North Dakota	WA	Washington
FL	Florida	MI	Michigan	OH	Ohio	WV	West Virginia
GA	Georgia	MN	Minnesota	OK	Oklahoma	WI	Wisconsin
HI	Hawaii	MS	Mississippi	OR	Oregon	WY	Wyoming
ID	Idaho	MO	Missouri	PA	Pennsylvania	DC*	District of
IL	Illinois	MT	Montana	RI	Rhode Island		Columbia

*The District of Columbia is not a state. Washington D.C. is the capital of the United States.
 Note: Washington D.C. and Washigton state are not the same.

Index